Praise for *Night of Stone* by Catherine Merridale

"*Night of Stone* is a revelation . . . Merridale succeeds in making the oft-told tale of Russian brutality to Russians both fresh and unbelievably horrific. Reading Merridale will bring one as close as it may be possible to come to a vicarious understanding of what such losses mean. Even readers familiar with the history of twentieth-century Russia will be stunned by Merridale's careful accounting of the killing that took place. . . . Even more impressive than her accounting is her literary skill. Her book is a tour de force."

—*The Washington Post*

"A wrenchingly poignant examination of how the Russian people have coped with a century of tragedy and loss. [Merridale] does not ignore statistics, but folds them seamlessly into her mesmerizing narrative. The author proceeds through the century in riveting and occasionally nauseating detail. Written with consummate skill and enormous compassion."

—*Kirkus Reviews* (starred review)

"A wide-ranging discursive exploration of the culture of death in Russia, of the world of widows and orphans, of silence, of tears, of loss so great no one could cry. The story is complex, its message disturbing, its images haunting. It's unpleasant, but important."

—*St. Louis Post-Dispatch*

"Merridale's account of how ordinary Russians coped with violent death on a scale few of us can even imagine is an epic and moving history."

—Misha Glenny, *The Observer*
(Best Books of the Year choice)

"Were Merridale not such a fine writer the stories she is telling here might well be unendurable. The worst she has to tell she delivers calmly, without fuss, with a sensibility that blends reason and emotion in a way you associate more with literature or music than with the writing of history. Much of what she writes here is startling. The best historical and political writing is often the sort that brings no comfort. Merridale's searching sensibility, her refusal to be satisfied with easy answers will likely please neither the left nor the right. This book is an example of moral and emotional bravery. Merridale has contemplated the worst without invective. That she has done so while maintaining her steady, pained, questioning and restless voice pays honor to the dead and sets an example for everyone left pondering their fates."

—Salon.com

"A sensitive and highly original investigation of the effect on the Russian mind today of its long accumulated experiences of suffering and death. Illuminating reading." —Robert Conquest, author of *The Great Terror*

"Beautifully and simply written [*Night of Stone*] is full of extraordinarily vivid glimpses of the past. . . . The author's acceptance, and admiration, of the survival techniques and endurance of her interlocutors are among the reasons why this enthralling book so successfully sheds light on what she rightly calls 'a beautiful but tortured culture.'"

—*The Times* (London)

"An elegiac biography of a country during its most tragic—let us hope—century. *Night of Stone* is a remarkable book, written in elegant, flowing prose that weaves exhaustive research with extensive interviews from the field."

—*The Raleigh News & Observer*

"You don't have to be morbid—or a Russian scholar—to respond to this extraordinary and important book . . . *Night of Stone* is an admirable attempt to bridge the gulf in perception which still divides Russia and the West. Ms. Merridale is never condescending towards those she meets, and she listens not just to their words. She knows that in Russia, if you really want to understand, you have to listen to the silences."

—*The Economist*

PENGUIN BOOKS

NIGHT OF STONE

Catherine Merridale is a Reader in History at the University of Bristol and the author of two books on Russia. She has degrees from Cambridge and Birmingham Universities. She lives near Bristol, England.

NIGHT OF STONE

Death and Memory in Twentieth-Century Russia

CATHERINE MERRIDALE

PENGUIN BOOKS

PENGUIN BOOKS
Published by the Penguin Group
Penguin Putnam Inc., 375 Hudson Street, New York, New York 10014, U.S.A.
Penguin Books Ltd, 80 Strand, London WC2R 0RL, England
Penguin Books Australia Ltd, 250 Camberwell Road, Camberwell, Victoria 3124, Australia
Penguin Books Canada Ltd, 10 Alcorn Avenue, Toronto, Ontario, Canada M4V 3B2
Penguin Books India (P) Ltd, 11 Community Centre,
Panchsheel Park, New Delhi-110 017, India
Penguin Books (N.Z.) Ltd, Cnr Rosedale and Airborne Roads, Albany, Auckland, New Zealand
Penguin Books (South Africa) (Pty) Ltd, 24 Sturdee Avenue,
Rosebank, Johannesburg 2196, South Africa

Penguin Books Ltd, Registered Offices: Harmondsworth, Middlesex, England

First published in Great Britain by Granta Books 2000
First published in the United States of America by Viking Penguin,
a member of Penguin Putnam Inc. 2001
Published in Penguin Books 2002

1 3 5 7 9 10 8 6 4 2

Grateful acknowledgment is made for permission to reprint excerpts
from the following copyrighted works:
Selections from *Poems of Akhmatova* selected, translated, and introduced by
Stanley Kunitz with Max Hayward (Mariner Books/Houghton Mifflin Co.) © 1973 by
Stanley Kunitz and Max Hayward. Reprinted by permission of Darhansoff &
Verrill Literary Agency on behalf of Stanley Kunitz.
Translations of "Conversations with a Neighbor" by Olga Bergholts, "The Scythians" by
Aleksandr Blok, "Remember Alyosha" by Konstantin Simonov, and "Babi Yar" by Yevgeny
Yevtushenko from *Twentieth-Century Russian Poetry* selected by Yevgeny Yevtushenko.
Copyright © 1993 by Doubleday, a division of Bantam Doubleday Dell Publishing Group,
Inc. Used by permission of Doubleday, a division of Random House, Inc.
"The Collective Mind: Trauma and Shell-Shock in Twentieth-Century Russia" by
Catherine Merridale, *Journal of Contemporary History*, vol. 35, no. 1, 2000.
Reprinted by permission of Sage Publications Ltd., London.

THE LIBRARY OF CONGRESS HAS CATALOGED THE AMERICAN HARDCOVER EDITION AS FOLLOWS:
Merridale, Catherine, 1959–
Night of stone : death and memory in twentieth-century Russia / Catherine Merridale.
p. cm.
Includes bibliographical references and index.
ISBN 0-670-89474-5 (hc.)
ISBN 014 20.0063 9 (pbk.)
1. Funeral rites and ceremonies—Russia (Federation)—History—20th century.
2. Death—Social aspects—Russia (Federation)—History—20th century.
3. Death—Psychological aspects—Russia (Federation)—History—20th century.
4. Russia (Federation)—Religious life and customs—History—20th century. I. Title.
GT3256.2.A2 M47 2001
393'.0947—dc21 00-043357

Printed in the United States of America
Set in Adobe Garamond / Designed by Carla Bolte

ACKNOWLEDGMENTS

I could not have written this book without the encouragement of the many people in Russia and Ukraine—survivors of catastrophe, soldiers, policemen, doctors, social workers, priests, nuns, funeral directors, and political campaigners—who answered my questions, corrected my misapprehensions, and generously concerned themselves with my progress. No words from me can do full justice to their courage or their warmth.

I also owe an incalculable debt to my research assistant and friend, the ethnographer Elena Stroganova. Everything that I have written bears testimony to the quality of her work. She accompanied me on almost all the journeys that I made, patiently negotiating bureaucracy, making friends wherever she turned, and developing a bracing commentary on the economic situation in the provinces. Her companionship made this whole project easier, and also a great deal less bleak.

Many other friends and colleagues in the former Soviet Union offered advice, encouragement, and ideas. In particular, I should like to thank Sergei Panarin, always resourceful, and a supporter of the project from the beginning, and also Oksana Bocharova, Valery Mikhailovski, Andrei Popov, Vladimir Shkol'nikov, Aleksei Smirnov, Ol'ga Vasil'chenko and Ol'ga Zubets. I am also indebted to the staff of the All-Russian Center for the Study of Public Opinion, and especially to Aleksei Levinson, for their assistance with some of the interviews. Among the others who helped me to meet war veterans and other survivors were Il'ya Altman and his staff at the Holocaust Center in Moscow, Vadim Ionovich Feldman in Kiev, officials of the Russian Society of Veterans, and the staff of the Solnechnyi rehabilitation center in Zelenograd. Members of the Memorial Association could not have been more generous, and I am especially indebted to Valeriya Ottovna Dunayeva in Moscow and to Veniamin Viktorovich Iofe and Irina Reznikova in St. Petersburg.

My research in Russia was formally sponsored by the Russian Academy of Sciences, and I would like to thank its personnel, and especially Vladimir Davydov and Lyudmila Kolodnikova, for their help. I am also grateful to the staff of the many archives and libraries where I was fortunate to work. Their conditions are not always ideal, and the pressures on them are considerable. It was all the more impressive, in the circumstances, that they could offer such a range of expertise, bibliographic advice, and technical help. This book owes much to their collective skill.

The project could not been completed without generous financial support and extended research leave. The latter was made possible by the Cambridge office of Common

Security Forum, whose sponsors during my fellowship from 1996 to 1998 were the John D. and Catherine T. MacArthur Foundation. Common Security Forum funded two years of uncomplicated sabbatical from Bristol, as well as providing superb conditions for research. I am also grateful, personally, to Emma Rothschild, its codirector, who has encouraged me since I began to discuss this project. Few people have shown more faith in it for longer. I was also fortunate to be offered a Fellowship of Robinson College during my time in Cambridge. I am grateful to the Warden and Fellows for their stimulating company and for providing me with a home between my journeys to Russia.

The remainder of my research costs—a considerable sum—were met through a generous grant from the Economic and Social Research Council and by the British Academy through its exchange with the Russian Academy of Sciences. I am grateful to each of these organizations for their support, their good-humored efficiency, and the imagination they showed in taking a risk on an unusual piece of interdisciplinary work.

The process of writing was made much easier by my friends and colleagues in England. It would be hard to imagine this book without them. My greatest debt as a writer is to the people who read every draft and whose creativity is woven into every finished chapter. Peter Robinson, my literary agent, understood what I was trying to do from the outset, and patiently cajoled me into achieving it over two difficult years. He also found two remarkable publishers to bring the project into print. Neil Belton, my editor at Granta, drew out the best from the shakiest of early drafts, encouraged me to experiment, and worked through the final manuscript with extraordinary skill and self-restraint. I have benefited from his expertise, as a writer and historian as well as an editor, at every stage. In the United States, Wendy Wolf, my editor at Viking, lent her magnificent support to a manuscript she had not seen, commented brilliantly on the final draft when it appeared, and guided the manuscript through the editorial process with humor and determination.

Three other people—Ira Katznelson, Steve Smith, and Derek Summerfield—also read and commented on the entire manuscript. Each is a master in his own field, and each has had a great deal to teach me, but I am grateful, above all, for conversations, for helping me to see what I had written, for intellectual companionship, and for brilliant criticism. Tim Cole, Ian Collins, Jill Glover, David Good, Clare Macourt, Nicola Miller, Catherine Roth, and Linda Saunders all read and commented on parts of the book at crucial moments, and I am also grateful to Joanna Bourke, Alain Blum, Dori Laub, Margaret Mitchell, Arieh Shalev, Judith Shapiro, Jonathan Steinberg, and Deborah Thom. Jay Winter helped me to think about mourning back in 1993 and has continued to encourage me to talk and write about it ever since. I am also grateful to the Harry Frank Guggenheim Foundation for invitations to speak and listen at a series of workshops on death, trauma, and violence between 1995 and 1997. For kindly tolerating my absences, physical and spiritual, over the years, and for welcoming me back from my extended journeys, I also thank my colleagues and students at the University of Bristol.

A book like this usually bears a dedication, and lately it has become almost routine for this to be addressed to Stalin's victims. I find the presumption awkward, no less in my case than in any other. But I have no choice. If I began this book to find a meaning for the dead, I end it in their debt.

CONTENTS

Nothing is left but dusty flowers.
the tinkling thurible, and tracks
that lead to nowhere. Night of stone
whose bright enormous star
stares me straight in the eyes,
promising death, ah, soon!

—"Requiem," Anna Akhmatova

AGAINST THE DARKNESS: AN INTRODUCTION

The town of Medvezhegorsk exists because of the railway. If you go north from St. Petersburg you will reach it in about twelve hours. The line runs roughly northeast, detouring from time to time around lakes and marshes. At the first breath of autumn, which comes in mid-September, the wetlands are briefly host to thousands of clamoring geese and wild swans on their way south for the winter. But the woods are almost silent. The only major town on the route is Petrozavodsk, the provincial capital, which stands on the western shore of Lake Onega. If you travel in daylight you will glimpse the lake, as big as an inland sea, shining like cold metal beyond the endless stands of pine and larch. Medvezhegorsk itself lies on its northern tip, and in summer grandmothers and little children crowd along the shore, basking, under cotten hats, in the precious northern sunshine. Some say the water has healing properties. Others point to the rusting hulks that pierce the shallows and mutter about chemicals and the rape of Russia's wilderness. Medvezhegorsk is not beautiful.

The town attracts few visitors. Most continue north. Farther up the line, after another lake, lies the White Sea, an attractive tourist destination for people with an interest in ancient monasteries or modern prisons. If you stay on the train beyond that—by which time, if you have come from the southern terminus in St. Petersburg, you will have been traveling for two days—you will reach the port city of Murmansk, once a thriving naval center, marooned now, like so many other arctic towns, by the collapse of Russia's economy. You are unlikely to meet many foreigners on this route. Instead, you will have the pleasure of passing your time with people from the region, most of whom make the journey as a matter of routine.

Russians are surely among the most accomplished long-haul rail travelers in the world. Their preparations are formidable. If you join them, you will be treated, at irregular hours of the day and night, to hard-boiled eggs, pickled cucumber, sausage, lukewarm vodka, and sweet black tea. It will begin to become apparent that the windows of most old Soviet railways cars do not open. But the conversation will always be lively. On this route, it is likely to be dominated by prices, wages, the iniquities of Moscow, and the impending scarcity of heating fuel. Almost always, at least one of your companions will mention Brezhnev or even Stalin, and a discussion will begin about the merits of communism.

We made the journey in 1997, at the end of October. The winter had set in early that year, and even St. Petersburg had its first covering of snow. Outside the city, and especially as we traveled north, the snow had taken over the landscape completely, leveling the gentle contours of the forest floor and turning the black pines a brilliant white. We had left the city at midnight, and now, as the late sun rose, we were already in another world. Lake Onega lay becalmed, a dead sea of rose and gray blue. "It's like a fairy story, isn't it?" whispered one of my neighbors. The remark would have been banal in any other setting. But the woman who had said it, a pediatrician in her thirties, was trying to control fresh tears. It is hard to find things to say when you are on your way to a mass grave, the burial place of murdered grandparents whom you never knew. There are no social conventions to cover unmourned loss. "They brought them here in their shirts, you know," she continued. "It must have been so cold. They would have been frightened, wouldn't they?" The man from Murmansk who had been sharing our compartment slipped on his plastic flip-flops and disappeared into the corridor. His mind was full of an engineering project, and he had heard enough of our unseemly talk. When it comes to death, Russians can be unexpectedly prim.

We stayed in the only hotel for miles, a crumbling, freezing, Soviet-style block on the edge of Medvezhegorsk. When everyone had gathered, there were about eighty of us. Our destination was a pine forest near Sandormokh, a Karelian village—the name sounds alien even in Russian—about three-quarters of an hour by bus from the town. On 26 October 1937, exactly sixty years before, the first group of condemned prisoners had arrived here. They had traveled south through the night from the infamous White Sea prison at Solovki. The man in charge was Mikhail Rodionovich Matveyev, a secret police officer with a quota to fulfill by the end of the week. He used trucks, not the train, and he transported his prisoners at night so that the citizens of Medvezhegorsk would not be provoked to wonder—none was likely to talk—about the unaccustomed traffic. His first batch included both men and women, some of whom had left young children behind in the camp. The prisoners were chained together in pairs, and they were indeed cold, as well as frightened, for they had been forced to leave their boots and warm clothes behind. It was a security measure, they were told. There had been an incident, and a guard had been slightly injured. There would be no more problems of that kind now. That night, and for several nights to come, the clearing echoed to the sounds of picks, spades, and gunfire. By 4 November, eleven hundred men and women had been murdered there.

Unusually, the site would not be used for killing again. Its telltale pits and hummocks were deliberately camouflaged, in the 1950s, by a plantation of young pines. The locals knew what had happened, but they forgot about it, outside their dreams, as soon as they could. Before long, no one really knew which part of the forest was haunted. There were graves everywhere, people told me, the woods were full of bodies. There were Finnish soldiers and Russians partisans, civil war graves, and the lost cemeteries of older settlers, religious communities, peasant homesteaders, deserters. Although they did not like to discuss it, most people thought that the secret grave, the Stalinist one, was a mile or two in another direction. Then, in the summer of 1997, an archaeologist and two historians from St. Petersburg found the real site. They took the local mayor to see it. He was horrified. As a boy, he said, he had gone mushrooming there, oblivious to the history under his feet. The grave was younger than his own father, but the truth of it came as a genuine shock. Surprise and guilt were great motivators. In provincial Russia in 1997, nothing else, short of a miracle, could have produced a paved access road for our buses in less than three weeks.

The grave at Sandormokh is not the first of its kind to be rediscovered. Since the late 1980s, amateur historians and archaeologists have located dozens like it across the former Soviet Union. Every time, there are decisions to be taken. These are not ancient sites. The bones they contain belong to the fathers and grandfathers of living people, many of whom have spent their whole lives in the hope that one day they will be able to hold the earth of their parent's grave. Most will die without knowing precisely where their parents' bodies are. The only way to be sure whose bones a site contains is to find police documents from the time of the killing. The records exist, but they are among the hardest to prise out of the archives of the former KGB. Those who have seen them are reluctant to talk about the details. "We cannot show them to the families," a human-rights campaigner told me. "Because if they could read about the killing, they would also have to know what happened to the prisoners before they were shot. Let them think their parents were only killed." The police have lists and maps, but in spite of glasnost, it is still the archaeologists who are exposing the truth about Stalinism.

Even the simple question of numbers raises problems. Historians and demographers have been arguing about the overall scale of Stalin's atrocities, and about Soviet losses in the two world wars, for decades. The debate is crucial, if macabre. But it is hard enough to establish exactly how many people lie buried in a single site. Some relatives do not wish the earth to be disturbed. They ask that the dead be left in peace, the only dignity remaining to them. Others, eager to catalog each outrage, prefer to dig the sites and count the bones. Afterward, they promise, the skeletons can at least be given the funeral they were denied half a century before.

In a country where lies are routine, this mania for material evidence, for exact numbers, is easy to understand. But even counting is not straightforward. The bodies, a twisted mass in death, have rotted now, and the skeletons are impossible to separate. It is inadvisable to rely on a skull count because most of the skulls were damaged, if they were not shattered, by the executioners' bullets, and the delicate bones crumble easily. Broken skulls were also especially vulnerable to the dogs and rats that plundered the shallow graves. If you want to count the victims now, you need to bring along several large boxes. (People use the ones that farmers keep for harvesting potatoes in the autumn.) Into these, you sort the bones: skulls in one, ribs in another, and limbs, if you can identify them, into two or three more. When you have finished, you count the femurs and divide by two. In most cases, the figure will run into thousands.

The people who found the bones at Sandormokh decided, in the end, to let them lie. Exceptionally, after all, they already had a list that named each of the victims. The grave was documented in this way because Matveyev himself was eventually convicted and shot. His crime, in the surreal world of Stalin's terror, was defined as an excess of zeal. At his trial in 1939, excerpts from the transcript of which have been published, he confessed to the killings and described the procedure he had followed in unusual detail.[1] He had been asked to liquidate a number of prisoners from Solovki, which he had done. At the same time, and with equal efficiency, he had arranged for the murder of others from the prisons and transit camps around the city then called Leningrad. He did not question his instructions, and he showed no curiosity about the alleged guilt of the poets, writers, and musicians in his charge. Some were accused of organizing national resistance centers. Among these were the most prominent political figures from Ukraine and what is now Belarus, as well as leaders of the Tartar and Gypsy peoples. Many of the rest were intellectuals, including several bishops, an envoy from Rome sent by the pope to establish the truth about

Stalin's crimes, and the inventor, mystic, and priest Pavel Florenskii, a man often described as Russia's answer to Leonardo.

Once they had decided to leave the bones in peace, the people who had found the grave were faced with the problem of commemoration. Here again, they were not working without precedent. Most of them were volunteers from the Memorial Association, an organization that has devoted ten years to the exposure of Stalin's crimes and the commemoration of his victims. But diplomacy is always needed. Part of the problem—and it is not unusual—was that the bones in the forest were not all Russian and Orthodox. Orthodox believers would like to see a church on every martyrs' grave. But some of these skeletons, inseparable forever, belonged to Catholics, Lutherans, Jews, or Muslims. There are plans for several chapels on the site. On the day it was dedicated, there were already two large crosses there, side by side. One of the builders told me that even these had not been uncontroversial. Fortunately, the argument about which was taller, the Catholic or the Orthodox, had been settled in the nick of time by a surveyor working in the presence of witnesses from each side.

The opening ceremony had been planned to the last detail.[2] There was to be a welcoming speech, and representatives of the main victims' associations joined political and church leaders beside the site entrance to gather for photographers. Many local victims' groups had subscribed to wreaths for the occasion, and these were proudly compared as we waited. A man from the Urals, four or five days' ride away by train, now asked to be photographed beside his solemn tribute. It was an oval four feet high, woven from artificial evergreens and white ribbon, and set with white and purple plastic lilies. We could not decide, as we admired it, whether the red plastic roses that others had chosen might not have been more tasteful. The wreaths must have cost as much as these pensioners could ever afford, hundreds of thousands of inflation-battered rubles apiece. This is a society that values inviolability and permanence. Plastic flowers cost twice as much as living ones.

If you are accustomed to Soviet-style, open-air meetings, you will be used to standing around and watching people whose hearts and minds are entirely disengaged from the performance they are about to give. It was common knowledge, in the Soviet era, that the measure of a good public gathering was the quality of the sandwiches and vodka that followed it. There was something of this in the air that morning, something dishonest, or impatient, at least, about the large men in suits and furs as they prepared to give their megaphone public speeches. The church authorities were there, and the town council, provincial politicians, and even representatives of the Duma in Moscow. There were human-rights activists, media intellectuals, and representatives from the national governments of newly independent Ukraine and Belarus. Whatever they had expected, they were about to be surprised.

Just as the first speaker was preparing his text, a woman in a black woolen shawl began to wail and wring her hands in the snow a few yards from the tribune. As she threw herself onto the frozen ground, another joined her, and then more. The sound they were making was the unearthly poetry of lament. A hundred years ago, this wailing would have accompanied every death and continued for days. Funerals were neither solemn nor silent. What we were hearing was not a revived tradition. Karelia is remote, and there are women there who have never learned to behave like discreet Soviet mourners beside a family grave. They wept for their lost husbands; they described the lifelong search that was about to end, the bitter years through which they longed to find the grave that soon they hoped to share. The city men coughed uneasily and looked around for security. Eventually someone began to move the women away, and the crowd closed over the places they had claimed.

Some of the speeches from that day were printed later, and the texts are no doubt sitting in someone's file in Moscow. It was, of course, essential that the graves' existence should be recognized and publicly deplored by representatives of the state. Since the mid-1990s, contrition about the past has been at a premium in Russia. The public repudiation of Stalin's atrocities is less straightforward than it was a decade ago. The high tide of repentance has turned, and there are plenty of people who regret that Stalin's communism is dead. The politicians who made the effort to come up north that day were taking a risk, identifying themselves with a specific cause, not reaping easy votes.

For all their principles, however, even these speakers could not capture, with their public words, the spirit of the occasion we were witnessing. For one thing, their speeches were addressed to the present and to the future. But the principal mourners were entirely focused upon the past. While the politicians talked of action, and pledged their efforts to secure a more honorable society, the families who had traveled from Moscow, St. Petersburg, and beyond were quietly, oddly, passionately celebrating. For them, the search was over. October 27 would become an anniversary in their lives. Many of them wept. But their tears, like their embraces and their prayers, were overwhelmingly actuated by relief.

What was most incongruous about the public ceremonial that day, however, was the way that it coexisted with the intense privacy of the family mourning. Though any grief is a personal affair, the losses borne by Stalin's victims are exceptionally private, even secret. For fifty years, until the fall of communism, families had kept bereavement of this kind to themselves. Some hid their pain from everyone, including their own children, for fear of the damage it might cause. It was dangerous, after all, to mourn the passing of an enemy of the people—and compromising even to be related to one. The scale of the murders, which are still euphemistically referred to as "repressions," was officially denied. It was easy, therefore, for individual victims to regard themselves as uniquely cursed.

Even in the 1980s, when stories about the past were being printed in every national paper as part of Gorbachev's policy of openness, a population that had learned to hide its shame did not entirely believe the night was over. One of the women who transcribed the tapes of interviews used in this book, a Russian originally from Siberia, told me that she had cried as she worked. She was amazed to find that other families had stories to match her own. Instead of feeling ashamed, she said, she would begin to find out more about her tight-lipped parents, her runaway grandmother, and the grandfather, a Siberian shaman, who had disappeared in the 1930s. People with stories like this did not forget. They did not necessarily cease to grieve. But whatever pain they felt was largely hidden. The end of the story, for most of the relatives at Sandormokh, was like the culmination of a secret dialogue.

When the crowds had left, I wandered around the grave site with my camera, trying to make sense of the private rituals that had been taking place while the politicians talked. I had seen places like it before. The secret police often concealed mass graves by planting trees over them. In a landscape of untended woods and scrub, only the oddly regular pattern of the young pines would have suggested a plantation rather than some remnant of the wilderness. Since the graves have been exposed, however, the woods have been reclaimed. Today they are like encyclopedias of funeral practice, reflecting every belief about death that has survived in modern Russia. Tokens of silent grief adorn the trees. They lie scattered among the symbolic markers that act as surrogates for gravestones. The people have invented their own symbols of remembrance. The results are makeshift and sometimes absurd, but in the silence of the KGB's memorial forest, they are haunting and timeless.

The mourners of Medvezhegorsk brought most of their tokens with them. The only thing that the organizers of the event provided on the day was a random arrangement of wooden posts, each one surmounted by a pitched roof. The people who designed these were careful not to add a crosspiece for fear of offending atheists and other non-Christian mourners. No one suggested that these posts marked real graves (they were not even precisely located over the original trench), but people seem to need a plot of earth. Their adoption of it can be lavishly creative. By the end of that freezing day, every post had been decorated, usually with flowers and a candle. Nearly all of them displayed a photograph. The woods were full of images of the young and middle-aged; civil war heroes in uniform, smooth-faced women in fine linen, young party men whose idealism remains undimmed though all they ever valued lies in ruins. Some people had pinned photocopies of trial transcripts or penal sentences to the posts, others used copies of the official notes they had received informing them, after fifty years, that their father, mother, or husband had been murdered. Though the ice will destroy them in a single season, many of these were carefully wrapped in plastic bags or tape. Since it has always been traditional in Russia to share food with the dead, too, the woods were strewn with cakes, bread, and apples. Some of the memorial posts had hard candies tied to them, one or two now sheltered pots of jam. There is little regularity to this kind of commemoration. It is not merely that the occasion itself is unique. All funerary ritual in modern Russia is a mixture of personal invention, modern expediency, revived religion, superstition, and the flotsam and jetsam of other kinds of practice—everything, in fact, from the pre-Christian to the rationalistic Soviet and the New Age. Before 1917, Russian ways of death were among the most extravagant and lively in Europe. Two revolutions—the Soviet, achieved over almost two decades from 1917, and the anti-Soviet (it is harder to give this one an ideological tag), the one that began in the late 1980s and is still in progress—have left their mark on private as well as public ritual, and there is little that has not been altered, superficially at least, even the meaning of the dead.

The first indicators of change, including anticlericalism and a growing interest in science, were already apparent before czarism collapsed in 1917. Industrial and urban development have challenged traditional religious beliefs throughout the world, and czarist Russia, in its last decades, was already in the throes of its own kind of transformation. But a whirlwind began after the Bolsheviks took power. Their revolution promised a new world, and the promise was fulfilled, not just through their own deliberate acts, but also because the empire was in crisis, its economy in ruins, its people at the limits of their patience. As this exasperation gathered into civil war, the Bolsheviks' first priority was to defend their revolution, to remain in power. The old order, and many of its values and beliefs, would be shattered almost entirely in the process.

The church was one of the first targets of the Bolsheviks' campaign. Their antipathy to it derived in part from the fact that some church leaders actively opposed them, using their influence to foment counterrevolution. But not all priests engaged in politics; the Bolsheviks' attack upon religion was also part of an idealistic scheme to replace the world of gods and saints with one based on rationality, to build utopia on earth. For those who wanted to create new Soviet people, the church, with its teaching and its ritual, was a relic of the past, a barrier to be broken down to clear the way for a better and more scientific life.

The fight against religion came in waves, with periods of respite in between, and sometimes there was little effort made to find replacements for it. Nonetheless, within a few years of its victory, Soviet power had wrenched apart the web of ritual, if not necessarily the beliefs, surrounding death. The churches were closed and the cemeteries turned into parks and sports grounds. Priests were arrested, believers intimidated, religious services banned or disrupted. New educational campaigns were launched to teach children the virtues of atheism; there were posters and street parades, even new ceremonies; and all of them were aimed at propagating the idea of a rationalist godlessness.

The Communist Party monitored the impact of its work. Its researchers collected data about fading belief, about the rise in party membership, the decline of religious observance, and the choices people made about their baptisms, their weddings, and their funerals. Whether the statistics reflected permanent changes in private belief, rather than a desire to give the "right" answer, to register a protest, or perhaps to score some point in a family argument (religion divided households as well as leadership and people), is still unclear. The church came back from its limbo when Gorbachev declared his policies of openness and restructuring in the late 1980s, and now there are millions of people who claim—with just as little possibility of proof—that they never abandoned their beliefs, even if they could not practice them openly, through all the years of censorship.

When I first began to think about Russians and death, it was this aspect, the disruption and reinvention of ritual, that interested me most. I had been intrigued by the idea that a modern revolution could try to create an entirely new kind of person. As I began to collect material about the Bolsheviks' first efforts, about the League of the Militant Godless and the Society for the Dissemination of Scientific Cremation, the history I thought I was writing was a study of ideology, propaganda, and mentalities. Death, or rather the rituals and beliefs that surrounded it, played the part of a test case. I could measure the impact of Bolshevik power by looking at the ways that people chose to bury and grieve for one another. Rites of death, after all, are notoriously resistant to change.

It did not take long, as I leafed through flimsy carbons in the Communist Party archive, to find the Bolsheviks purblind and even cruel. Their idealism, the revolutionary fervor that had driven their quest for power, would become forced, coercive. Their campaign against ritual degenerated into vandalism. Their resentment of the church—however bloated an anachronism it may have become—was often crude and hysterical. The atheism that they sought to establish was inconsistent, heavily disputed, bleak. Within a decade of seizing power they had even created a substitute cult of the dead for themselves. Lenin's preserved corpse was installed at the heart of their new capital, and Red Square, the parade ground of Soviet power, became a grave.

But the story of scientific atheism was only one of the threads in an exceptionally rich weave. Russia's culture of death was—and remains—extraordinarily vivid. This vitality is an important fact in itself—its story, on its own, would have made an interesting subject for this book. Death is not a matter that most people—parents, children, friends—in Russia take lightly, they are not inured to it, or no more so than any other group of people; and among the things they value still, despite their turbulent history, are the music at a funeral, the earth in which a burial takes place, commemoration, anniversaries, and mourning. The point is worth making because Russia's story of death has been obscured so often. Rather than thinking of the ritual and the grief, most histories of Soviet Russia write of death from the point of view of politics or demography. They talk of it in terms of mass catastrophe—the wars and repressions, the famines—and they talk of repeated violence, of a tradition that makes Russia unique, its history exceptional.

The idea of continuity, and especially of repeated violence, has been a theme for historians of Russia for generations. The United States ambassador to the Soviet Union in the late 1940s, Walter Bedell Smith, wrote a preface to a new translation of the travel journals of the Marquis de Custine, who had visited Russia a century earlier, in 1839, which typifies it. "I could have taken many pages from his [Custine's] journal," Bedell Smith wrote, "and, after substituting present-day names and dates for those of a century ago, have sent them to the State Department as my own official reports." Bedell Smith, in other words, was happy to think of applying Custine's description of the nineteenth-century autocracy—"absolute monarchy moderated by murder"—to the post-war Stalinist state. He saw no need to make amendments.[3] In 1999, newspaper reports of Putin's war in Chechnya made very similar points. The Russian bear was on the prowl again.[4] The killing of Chechen civilians was described as the latest outrage in a long—and largely undifferentiated—tradition of barbarism.

The scale of the violence in Russia's modern history, and of its suffering and loss, has been so great that it is indeed tempting to assume that this is a society that has been distorted by some fault, some freak of custom, culture, or geography. But this is lazy thinking, sheer evasiveness. It is far harder, after all, to imagine another kind of truth, which is that the people who lived and died in Russia and the Soviet Union in the twentieth century were no less prone to suffer and to mourn than we might be, and that their history of violence did not grow from some national eccentricity, like a taste for eating chunks of salted lard, but from particular combinations of events and circumstances. This truth is disconcerting, too, because it carries awkward implications: that Russia's suffering was always caused, and therefore might have been preventable; that it was not unique; and that no outside observer can afford the luxury of self-congratulation, to assume that their society is guaranteed to be immune to violence on this scale forever. The Russian people had and still do have their own ideas about the meaning of the deaths, their own responses to the violence—not all of them equivalents of mine—but although they have a distinct culture and a specific history, they are not members of a different humanity.

More than 50 million Soviet lives were lost, between 1914 and 1953, to violence, famine, and epidemic disease. Half of these deaths were the result of the Great Patriotic War alone. The people died defending bombed-out cities; they died in burning villages; they starved in besieged Leningrad, or on the river boats of refugees. Some were killed by their own side. Almost no family was unaffected, some by war, some by hunger, exile, or epidemic, some by continuing political repression—the arrests and the shootings did not stop—some by the accumulated exhaustion of successive losses and emergencies. In some places there are bodies waiting to be buried still. For many, too, the war was the greatest of what had been a series of personal upheavals, often including bereavements, the first of which, in any family's history, might have begun in 1914, with the outbreak of the czar's last war; in 1904, when Russia went to war with Japan; or earlier, in 1891, for instance, when millions of peasants starved in one of czarist Russia's greatest famines.

Our understanding of all this was clouded for years by the Soviet government's response, which was to suppress most information and to deny loss. Few disasters were openly discussed in the Soviet Union itself while Stalin was alive. Although there was a devastating famine in 1932 to 1933, for instance, affecting tens of millions of people, and accounting for at least 5 million lives, the words "famine" and "hunger" were banned from press reports within the Soviet empire in the 1930s. The postwar famine of 1946, when tens of thousands starved, was scarcely reported at all. Thereafter, until the collapse of communism, the extent of the Soviet tragedy was always understated in Russia. Statistics relating to demographic loss were doctored or kept hidden. An entire census, in fact, was locked away in 1937, and the officials who knew its secrets were arrested and shot. The first duty of history, in these circumstances, was justifiably to reestablish the figures, to set a framework within which other issues could be judged. But statistics are only ever part of a story like this. The argument about them, in fact, used to provide some easy cover in which to hide from the human reality that they described.

Another escape from human reality, and another reason why the impact of these deaths remains obscure, was grand politics, ideology. The problem was acute during the Cold War. Counting the bodies was often a way of making other kinds of arguments about the relative merits of the Soviet system and its Western rival. The Soviet government itself used statistics about longevity and public health as indicators of the superiority of communism as a way of life. It was a cynical policy, grim, manipulative, an aspect of the regime's larger disregard for individual life and truth. But Cold War critics of the Kremlin also took the bait. They, too, fixed on the numbers, frequently inflating them, as if the story of human loss and suffering were not bleak enough, as if it needed to be made still darker so that, by contrast, democratic capitalism might appear more bright.

The shadow of this line of argument will fall across this book however I can write it. There is no way of considering these mass deaths—and especially of looking carefully at their impact on specific people, on the relatives, the neighbors, and the heirs—that does not carry an ideological charge. All I can say is that I did not start from a position of ideological attack—the Cold War, after all, is over—but that my motive was and is the need to understand a mental world. The questions I have asked, often in conversation with survivors of repression, war, and hunger, could not have been put twenty years ago. The collapse of Soviet secrecy and state control has been a precondition for my work. But it is also because of that political upheaval that the questions I have had to put, the ones that address the human histories I encountered and not one lost, once all-consuming battle, do not begin or end with formal ideology.

This, then, is not another great black book. There will be much in the stories that I have to tell that will show successive czarist, Soviet, and post-Soviet societies at their darkest—death, after all, is usually grim. But it does no favors to the hopes and idealism of Russia's visionaries, or to the pride and courage of its citizens, to ignore their history of loss for fear of what it is that we might learn, to leave its writing to those who seek to simplify it for some other purpose. Russia's story still bears directly on the preoccupations of the contemporary world. But the high politics of communism and postcommunism should not be discussed without reference to the people and their memories, to human pain and endurance, brutality, trauma, mercy, bitterness, and grief.

While I started with an idea about revolutionary culture, then, I have ended up with an investigation into mass mortality and survival. This is a book about revolutionary change—the changes wrought by successive revolutions, the most recent of which, as I have said, continues. But it is also a history of the mentalities, the culture and the sense of self, that shaped the way a people mourned, sustained, and understood successive millions of deaths. The story is partly based on interviews, and that means that the book is also full of voices. Revolutionary ideology, and above all, revolutionary collectivism, was certainly an influence on these voices, but so were economic change, war, peace, and the impact of mass communication, and so, in different ways, were the experiences of being a parent, a widow, the processes of aging.

Anyone who has collected spoken testimonies will know how they confound even the most meticulously planned research. You arrive with clear-cut questions, neatly typed; you leave with narratives, dialogues, evasions, long digressions, laughter, more phone numbers, photographs, and tears. But the anarchy is even greater if your subject happens to be death. No one knows what it really is, for a start, including you, the interviewer, and few are willing to focus on it for long. In this case, too, the sheer weight of the losses, colored though they may be by stories of escape, by courage and generosity, by flashes of humor, even by the surreal, is such that any listener is likely to be burdened, to view the easy questions that they brought with near contempt. Nonetheless, since this is an introduction, I will at least outline the questions that I started with; although these were to change, and although, in my desire to capture the unpredictable, the personal, the bits that do not fit, the randomness of individual mentalities as well as the patterns that make social history, I did not ask people to keep to them and them alone.

The idea of cultural continuity, the idea that human life, in Russian history, was usually cheap, was one of these starting points. To question it, I have looked at the last decades of the czarist empire, at the government's policies toward mortality, especially among the poor, and at famine, suicide, and state repression. I have also looked at funerals, and at the treatment of the different social classes of corpse. I have tried to identify the particular social habits that might have made violence easier to condone, and I have looked at the ways that children saw it, since they were often among the first to die or be bereaved, and since they, too, as adults, would often be participants in violence for themselves.

Stories of death and memories of violence were traced to the present in discussion with three generations of survivors, with the people who care for them, and with the people who used to care for the dying in the past—doctors who served at the front in the 1940s, for instance; psychologists who worked with political prisoners; priests, nuns, and nurses; Communist Party agitators. In search of the continuing history of death ritual, I have looked through the archives of municipal authorities and funeral trusts, the papers of church organizations, agitational pamphlets, and memoirs. I have also talked to grave diggers, funeral directors, yet more priests, and to the men and women who lead the hunt for unclaimed bones.

Because the issue of cultural continuity and change is complicated enough without adding the dimension of multicultural comparison, I have tried to keep to the history of Russian mentalities, although the story of an imperial people—and especially of a continuous land empire—cannot be confined within such limits all the time. In general, the focus on Russia has meant looking at the ways of death in a society whose ideas were dominated, until the 1917 revolution, by the Orthodox Church (or by opposition to it), whose world was shaped by a powerful tradition of sin and judgment, redemption, damnation, and immortality. I have given little space to the minorities and sects, and have not really discussed the evolution of belief and doubt among non-Russian communities, including influential ones such as the Muslims, Jews, and Lutherans. Where I have traveled beyond Russia, literally as well as intellectually, it has been to look at other Eastern Slavs, and notably the peoples of Ukraine and Belarus, neither of which could separate its fate, or much of its culture, from Russia's in the nineteenth or the twentieth centuries.

Thinking about brutality and trauma has been harder, and not merely because the subjects are so grim. The theory of brutalization, which can be approached from the disciplines of psychiatry and social psychology as well as through historical research, cannot be challenged unless specific instances are studied for themselves. You cannot say with any certainty that people acted from unique and historically specific motives at any point unless you look at the cases for yourself. If you do not do this, a general dismissal of the detail, a cry of despair, is all that you will manage. Most of the people who talked to me limited themselves to that, declaring that Russians are violent by nature, that their attitude is genetic, that it is a legacy of the Tartars, a curse of their inhuman climate. Self-deprecating racism like this is commonplace in Moscow, but elements of the same idea creep into foreigners' accounts as well. I set out to unwrap the bundle of assumptions—I hope that I have challenged some of them—but the process was not pleasant, and some of the evidence will not be easy stuff to read.

The obvious staring point for understanding modern cultures of violence, especially in an autocracy, must be the state. The value that a government places on individual life will influence mortality itself—through public health schemes, for instance, to take the blandest example, or by the way it chooses to wage war—and it will also shape the way that people mourn death in their public ceremonies. The state may also condone some kinds of crime—in Russia it sometimes instigated them—and by its secrecy create a world in which there is no possibility of protest.

These things can be investigated using documents; they can be illustrated dispassionately with diagrams and tables. A more delicate issue, however, concerns the values of the citizens themselves. The state may write of demographic loss, its leaders learn to sleep in spite of their collusion in a campaign that went wrong, or, worse, some exercise in deliberate repression, but the people have to deal with vivid death, with fear, bereavement, poverty, anger, vengeance, memory. Their mental world must be explored before it is assumed that death, in a society, is taken lightly, seen as normal. I have used archives and memoir accounts again to help me think about these issues, and I have also listened to hundreds of personal narratives. I have talked to the professionals who care for the allegedly brutalized, too, and to Russian philosophers who think about death, as well as to the people who fought, killed, and dreamed about the killing for themselves.

The other side of brutalization is trauma. Western accounts of stress and violence, and above all, of genocide, now commonly accept the idea that people who witness and survive atrocity will bear the psychological scars for years (whether or not they suffer physical ones as well). It is sometimes also stated that trauma can be passed from parents to their children. Some of the best writing on these topics—and certainly the most moving—has been written in response to the Holocaust, the Nazi death camps, and it explores the issues of mental scarring, memory, testimony, and generational change. When I began to think about the price that Soviet Russia paid, in human terms, in the twentieth century, it was this literature—memoirs and personal essays as well as academic research—that I read first.

The Holocaust, however, was unique, and while the meditations of its heirs and survivors will influence our thinking about violence and loss for many years to come, each country's story should suggest interpretations of its own. I have tried to see what this might mean in Russia's case. The demographic catastrophes there had a range of causes—wars, famines, acts of political violence—and each had a different kind of impact. The whole process was prolonged through several generations, extending for more than fifty years. The roles of perpetrator and victim were frequently confused, too, so that the ethical issues, the questions of good and evil, were not reliably clearcut. Even memory has not been consistent, for the meanings of many deaths have changed over time, especially as communism collapsed, and there are conflicts still about what constitutes a hero, what kinds of sacrifice deserve reward, and what kinds of killing cannot be condoned.

The idea of psychological damage—mental distress, trauma (a central theme of Holocaust writing)—is something that most Russians reject. Even psychologists and doctors have their doubts, and for many of the older ones, the ones who trained while Stalin was alive, the concept itself is entirely strange. They cannot picture it, this trauma, and they do not understand its privileged place in the Western understanding of violence and its consequences. I have tried to explore why this might be. Part of the answer is that even the idea of mental illness remains largely taboo in Russia. But it is also possible that this particular diagnosis and its treatment are so alien to the Russian way of thinking about life, death, and individual need that notions of psychological trauma are genuinely irrelevant to Russian minds, as foreign as the imported machinery that seizes up and fails in a Siberian winter.

The hypothesis is not an easy one to test. It is possible to create the answers that you want to hear. Words can mislead, their associations, in different languages, are not equivalent, and even silence is ambiguous. Some Western psychoanalysts, for instance, associate it with trauma, calling it denial; but in the Soviet Union it was a conscious strategy, and its purpose was often political. Many careers depended on an individual's ability to keep her secrets to herself.

The first Russian psychiatrist who ever discussed the subject with me, a senior doctor in a Moscow hospital, was living proof of this. I asked her about the prevalence of trauma and posttraumatic stress among her patients. Her response was immediate. This was a hospital for Alzheimer's patients, she insisted; the people were all elderly, and if they had sustained injuries in the past the majority were physical ones, including wartime broken bones and head injuries. Brain damage, physical damage, she could understand (many psychiatrists of her generation learned a great deal about it in the postwar years), but she did not recognize the diagnosis posttraumatic stress.

The doctor was so adamant and so offended that I decided to rescue the conversation by asking her for an opinion about the nature of another psychiatric problem, schizophrenia. At this point her Soviet composure broke and she buried her face in her hands. She was on the brink of tears. Glancing nervously at her astonished colleague, she told me that she had herself been born in a Stalinist prison camp. She did not usually talk of it, had never told a stranger. Now she described how the experience had shaped parts of her life. She also conceded that many of the inmates of the hospital had suffered in the same way. A few days later, she found a few who were willing to talk to me. They were depressed, they told me; frightened, haunted, lonely. If I had pressed them, or led them in a certain way, I could have made them tell me stories that I could then have classified as evidence of posttraumatic stress. In almost every case, however, and certainly in the doctor's, each lifetime's habit of silence could as easily have been attributed to state violence—the threat of arrest or demotion—as it could to psychological denial. Their stories can be told in several ways. The causes of their mental illness, too, were not, as the doctor rightly insisted, necessarily directly linked to trauma from the remote past.

Few survivors willingly relate their lives as tales of suffering (this choice is one they share with the survivors of catastrophe elsewhere). In fact, they do not readily describe the darkest episodes at all, and if they do agree to speak of them, they often use a stilted, abstract, disembodied vocabulary. Some do this out of guilt—many have awkward pasts, regardless of the real origins of the blame—but others, in this most politicized society, have used silence all their lives because it was their only practical option. They have also learned to tell their stories in ways that comfort rather than distress them. The same themes appear almost every time. Russians are strong, they will tell you, the people are honest, mother was a heroine, my own life has been miraculously charmed. If you listen respectfully to this and drink your tea—better still, if you eat the cakes and admire the family photographs—your host will be satisfied, and you will have seen how yet another person has dealt with facts that talking, of this kind at least, can never alter.

If you want to find out more—and there is almost always more—you will have to take a decision about responsibility. It is not difficult to provoke or shock some people into revisiting the past. Sometimes it is enough to show them a photograph. Often a simple question of detail—the color of a jacket, the smell of a wheat field, the last expression on the face of a dying child—will burn directly to the story's core. But I remain uncertain whether mere visitors have a right to violate these people's privacy. The testimony of witnesses is crucial. Atrocities are readily denied by those who helped to perpetrate them, and also by those who passively condoned whatever violence was done. The story of Russia's past has been denied for long enough. Secrecy was part of the system that made the massive losses possible, even including many wartime deaths. Atrocities that go unexamined may remain easier to repeat. But testifying, for survivors, civilians, those who suffered, has to be a matter of personal choice. Whether they call their memories traumatic, painful, or merely ugly—the Russian word "not beautiful"—some people still choose, fifty years later, to keep them to themselves.

Trauma is, anyway, only one of the many costs of violence and death. The people I met in Russia certainly have other words to describe the price that they have paid. The more sensitive readily acknowledge that some people have suffered for a lifetime because of what they witnessed. Emotional damage has been compounded, however, in nearly every case, by sustained material hardship, some of which was a direct result of bereavement, dispossession, or exile. Many people seemed to regard psychological suffering as a luxury, superfluous to their world of hunger, cold, and basic physical insecurity. The last years of Soviet power brought little enough in the way of affluence to the unskilled, the people whom circumstance condemned to lives in the provincial towns. But the post-Soviet world, if anything, has been even harder. Economic reform has not made many Russians rich. The elderly—which most of the survivors are—face hardship on a scale that other developed countries seldom witness.

Most people talked about survival. The whole society, as they rightly pointed out, did not collapse. They found ways of their own of dealing with their losses—human and material—and they are proud, up to a point, of their endurance. They see this, too, as something Russian, and in many ways they are correct. The Soviet Union was isolated, so the solutions that its people developed were entirely generated from within a single set of cultures. More radically, however, because so much of the grief that people suffered was kept secret, and because the public exercise of religion was curtailed, many of the answers that the people evolved from the 1920s onward were personal and unique. The anarchy of Sandormokh's grave decorations is a visible manifestation of this long isolation. The history of funerary culture was not the only thing that Soviet policy interrupted. While some kinds of death—the heroes' deaths—were honored and commemorated, the collective discussion of many less acceptable forms of loss was muted for most of the twentieth century. The silence was sometimes a source of suffering (some people wanted very much to talk and grieve collectively). It left some murders unavenged. Even the people who prefer not to discuss the past resent the way that state atrocities, accidents, and even natural disasters passed unremarked for decades. But silence, on the part of the mourners, does not have to imply weakness.

I discussed all this with one of the organizers at Sandormokh as we walked, arm in arm, away from the crowd that afternoon. Valeriya Ottovna is an impressive woman. In her late sixties, she manages most of the social provision offered by the Moscow branch of the Memorial Association. She listens to the complaints of elderly survivors every day. Most of the time, she says, the problems that they bring are simple and economic. Some cannot pay their rent, others have no money for food. When I visited her at the office in December, I found her distributing rubber boots to a crowd of eager pensioners. The pairs were torn apart and passed around. There was an ugly crush to get the right size; the task was hopeless and the scrum undignified. Valeriya Ottovna dealt with all of it. She is generous but tough. At Sandormokh, however, she cried for hours. "These people are the lucky ones," she said, gesturing toward the mourners with their photographs and candles. "I have been looking all my life, and I still do not know where my mother is buried. They took her away. She was a schoolteacher. Tell me, what could she have done?"

Despair like this is not to be comforted. The heart of this book, in the end, is absence and loss. Silence, and not answer, lies at its core. Valeriya Ottovna was not asking for pity, and she did not want me to chatter about her misery. Words would have been too easy. So, too, although the people's need is evident, would a glib offer of material aid. There are some kinds of writing about distress that build toward a kind of self-affirming condescension. The terrible things that happen elsewhere, it is implied if not stated, demand from the more fortunate our charity and aid. Maybe we have advice to offer, maybe we have goods, but either can be given cheaply, without another thought. A small gift solves the problem—our problem, our discomfort and unease—in a moment.

This kind of satisfaction is not available to us if we really contemplate death. There are always diversions—tomb architecture, peasant naïveté, mafia funerals, the absurdities of the epitaph. But if we remain at the center of the issue, if we stare at the object—death—without blinking, there is nothing to see. Our answers are no better than any others, inventions designed to lend substance—dignity, beauty, a shared meaning—to a reality that is beyond our grasp. I asked Valeriya Ottovna what she wanted—from me, from my writing, from anyone that I might reach or know. Her answer was characteristic of the woman. The previous night, after all, she had put a stop to a slightly tipsy group discussion about Lenin's corpse by reminding us all that to take revenge is to sacrifice something of one's integrity. "Tell them we want their compassion," she said to me. "Ask them to try to understand."

The snow will have fallen on the graves at Sandormokh for four more winters now. The wooden markers will have begun to rot. The chapel will have been adopted by the village, and most of the people who use it will not think about its original purpose. The bones will lie undisturbed. Few of the people who made the journey that October will ever manage to repeat it. But everyone who was there has become a witness. The task is not easy, and I suspect that it will never end. It is a burden, certainly, and a responsibility. It is also a privilege.

The people who told their stories for this book did more than offer me the keys to a beautiful but tortured culture. Almost all had seen darkness of a kind that I hope never to encounter. Their responses to it were not necessarily grim. But they were personal, individual, unmediated, vital. It is difficult, I know, to do them justice. Even the simple act of translating the words—of bringing them into another social setting, with all its different associations—involves changing them, depriving them of context, losing their cadence. But as the last survivors age and die, their stories—only fragments of a history, perhaps, and endlessly refracted in the shifting light of ideology and social change—cannot be left to blur and fade. They are a vivid testimony, and they show that there are many ways of thinking about death, that custom and belief can be suppressed and nonetheless survive, and that, as Valeriya Ottovna would certainly insist, there are many unexpected things to try to understand.

1

ANOTHER LIGHT

"We are the people without tears," Anna Akhmatova wrote in 1922. "Straighter than you, more proud."[1] Generations of Russians have described their courage in the same way, as something that is shared, unique to their culture, a virtue born of suffering and nurtured by some deep, collective inspiration. Some writers have imagined its source in the landscape, the forests, the steppe, the snow, the boundless northern sky. Others have connected it with the earth, with clay or loam, "the Russian soil on which I was born."[2] For many it has been hardship itself that forges spiritual toughness. But almost every reference to the mysterious quality of Russianness, to the Slav soul, locates it within the mass, among the simplest people, a spark of the consuming Russian flame within each person's heart. "Darya Vlasyevna," wrote Ol'ga Berggol'ts in 1941, addressing an imaginary neighbor, an ordinary woman, in the depths of the hardest winter of the Leningrad blockade. "The whole land will be renewed by your strength. The name of this strength of yours is 'Russia.' Like Russia, stand and take heart!"[3]

The idea of a mystic Russian nationhood has flourished through centuries of violent history—through wars, invasions, famines, and natural disasters. Soviet Russia's isolation helped reinforce it in the twentieth century, into a time when other societies were beginning to talk of global culture. To an outsider, the idea of a spiritual nation may seem absurd and even pernicious. The territory of Russia, after all, is home to many different ethnic groups. The Russian population itself is a hybrid shaped by trade, conquest, migration, and intermarriage across the largest continental landmass on earth. It makes no difference. The idea of a mystical toughness persists in many people's minds, and the Russian soul itself is often described, even now, as a genetic characteristic, like fair skin. Its quality, the literature agrees, is paradoxical, contradictory. Foreigners have been raising liberal eyebrows at Russian chauvinism for centuries, but a paradox must always have another side, and here it is the stoicism and the poetry, the real evidence of endurance, the exceptional familiarity with death. "Russia is a sphinx," wrote Alexander Blok in 1918. "Exulting, grieving, and sweating blood."[4]

Blok's powerful image suggests some kind of continuity—his poem invokes the Scythians, the ancient warriors of the southern steppe—but the elements that formed the Russian people's attitudes to suffering and death have not been constant over time. Even to go back to the years of his childhood in the late nineteenth century is to revisit a society that was on the brink of dissolution. It is a strange, almost unrecognizable world. Most educated Russians of that time would have had no problem in identifying its main characteristics. Religion—Orthodox Christianity—was one, and autocracy, the absolute rule of the czar, another. In both cases, these pillars of the old world helped to support a sense of unity, of collectivity (the Russian word is the untranslatable *sobornost'*, which is linked to ideas of the Trinity, of the One that subsumes the many). Nineteenth-century peasants referred to themselves as "the Orthodox" as readily as they called themselves Russians, laborers, or residents of a specific region, and before the revolution, Orthodoxy was the official faith of about 94 percent of all ethnic Russians. The czar ruled by divine right, and the distance that separated him from God was scarcely wider than the gulf that divided ordinary people from their monarch.

A century later, when Soviet communism collapsed, millions of Russian people strove to recover something of this world. They were looking for a lost unity, for certainty and an imagined honor. They turned to the Orthodox Church again in their tens of thousands, and some even talked of reconstructing czarism. They resurrected the discredited symbols of autocracy—the eagle, the tricolor flag, some of the patriotic saints, the ones who slay their demons from the backs of prancing horses—and they flocked to the churches. The yearning for an end to conflict, for an indelible identity, for a reunion with imagined versions of the past, was overwhelming. It was as if the thread of history could be cut, and two of the broken ends, the prerevolutionary fin de siècle and the postcommunist renaissance, spliced and bound across a century of Soviet socialism.

It was a vanished world, however, that filled the people's dreams as they stood amid the darkness with their lighted candles, watching the congregation bow in unison, lost amid the richness of the chant. Like any other refuge from the present, the prerevolutionary Russia that its great-grandchildren imagined was a fantasy. The nineteenth century was neither a golden age of national unity nor merely the soil from which, despite the revolution and its aim of reinventing culture, the story of the twentieth century, of Soviet Russia, would emerge. It was a time of rapid change, of anxiety, and of multiple, conflicting, possibilities. Its future was not sealed.

There is no living memory of that time. Even the written sources that we have are thin—memoirs and letters, government statistics, the careful notes of antiquarians and ethnographers, occasional travelers' tales. The preoccupations that inspired these writings were not usually our own, and it is easy to miss the themes that run between the lines, the things that were so obvious to people at the time that they did not even leave a visible trace. Death was yet to be the colony of medicine that it would become, the processes of mourning and of burial played real parts in a soul's passage to the other world, and the fires of hell were still alight. We can salvage some relics from this world, but it takes a real effort to imagine its whole landscape, the way that people thought about themselves, the mentalities, the assumptions, values, and taboos. Even the idea of a self, in fact, of an individual with rights of choice and private feelings, might well have puzzled many people from that other generation.

The written sources offer a series of separate images. Handbooks from the late nineteenth century, for instance, describe the official Orthodox view of life and death in literal detail. They give a picture of heaven and hell; they tell us what believers thought would happen to their souls; and they remind their modern readers about sin, about blasphemy, and about the role of sacraments and prayer. To understand what they meant, however, we have to go beyond the text, to imagine a world in which the religious mind was neither exceptional nor eccentric, and where the church's principal worries were less about shrinking congregations than about the persistence of the things it saw as heresies, mistakes, and superstitions. There were passive believers everywhere, and many who doubted aspects of the catechism they had learned, but for most Russians of the late nineteenth century, belief was so deeply embedded that it had become a reflex, independent of formal dogma, a set of metaphors and images that described the processes of dying, death, and afterlife as if there were no other reasonable cosmology.

Because these metaphors are not my own, I have to start, like a recent convert, with a basic primer. One of the clearest is the Monk Mitrofan's comprehensive *Life After Death: How the Dying Live, and How We Too Shall Live through Death*, published in St. Petersburg in 1897.[5] As Mitrofan explains, Russian Orthodoxy is a religion that has always based itself on hope. The festival that forms its core was, and remains, not Christmas, but Easter. It is Christ in Majesty, the resurrected Lord, who presides at the great ceremonies, and not a broken figure on a cross, or even the fragile infant Jesus. The conquest of death remains eternal, and human souls, as fragments of the godhead, will share in it if they escape damnation. Hell is the only alternative to salvation and eternal life in heaven. The Orthodox do not imagine a purgatory any more than they can countenance the idea of different kinds of truth, different shades of meaning, or bargaining along the path that leads to spiritual revelation. Their liturgy is beautiful, but it is calculatedly mysterious, inaccessible, designed to be accepted without question.

Death, in this scheme, is not the end of life but a transition, almost a rebirth. "With the saints let the soul of thy servant go in peace, O Christ," runs the Orthodox prayer for the dead, "where there is neither pain nor sorrow nor lamentation but life eternal."[6] Those comforting words echo beside the other aspect of the faith, which is its sense of awe. Death and judgment have not been domesticated in this religion, and though the faithful know that death is the threshold to eternal life, even they may doubt that it is peaceful. The prospect of the soul's journey—for death is often explained as the beginning of a voyage, of a journey undertaken by boat, or by a sledge drawn by three wild horses—is a dreadful one, a reckoning and a test.

Mitrofan was careful to set out the stages of this odyssey, describing them with geographical literalness and giving them a schedule in real time. The soul remains on earth, his book explains, for three days and nights, and in that time it visits the places where it spent most of its mortal hours. It is not alone, for its guardian angel accompanies it, but the companionship is not necessarily consoling. The angel is not simply benign, a good fairy by another name. Its task is to reveal to the astonished soul the true meaning of its lifetime's deeds and choices, however terrible they may now appear. The prayers that the mourners offer for the soul's peace at this time ought to be earnest, for very few can contemplate this kind of truth, unmediated, without fear. The Orthodox funeral service, as another authority explains, is "not a ritual, but spiritual sustenance for the living human soul which has departed from the mortal body, a spiritual act which affirms the immortality of the soul in Christ and a manifestation of the people's solicitude for the soul at the moment when it enters another realm."[7]

Three days after the person's death, on the day that had been used for the funeral for more than a century by Mitrofan's time, the soul ascends to heaven to meet its God. What follows, in the textbook version, is more revelation; a six-day glimpse of heaven and a longer view of hell. By the time Mitrofan wrote he was already having to counteract a certain amount of skepticism about damnation, a feeling that the skewers and the pitchforks in the demons' hands might well be allegorical ones. So his description here resounds with notes of ancient terror. The Orthodox believer does not contemplate the afterlife with blissful calm, and the most fearful event of all awaits each mortal just forty days after his death. This is the moment of individual judgment, when everything the soul has learned on its journey becomes real, when it begins to face the consequences of actions that it might have chosen to forget, and when it faces the genuine prospect of torment stretching onward to the end of time.

There are some consolations, and even the old books will list them all. The faithful, of course, like saints and martyrs, will be saved. For the rest, every judgment that is passed while the world is still in being will be provisional. The final judgment, the universal reckoning, when the dead will rise up in their flesh, will be the only unalterable one. Even in the depths of hell, therefore, the wretched souls of sinners can begin the process of their own redemption. The saints and martyrs can pray for them, but so can living human beings, which is why it is the duty of the living to pray for the dead, to observe the regular festivals that remember them, and also to follow the fates of individual souls, gathering not just for the funeral itself but also for the commemorative prayers that take place on the ninth and fortieth days after a death and each year on its anniversary.

The demarcation between formal doctrine and custom wears very thin at this point, even in Mitrofan's book. The soul of an Orthodox may not belong to the world, but it certainly returns to earth, damned or saved, and it retains a material relationship with the soil, and especially with its own grave. Some say the souls come back on specific days, including the night of Easter Sunday; *radunitsa* (the second Tuesday after Easter); Trinity Sunday; and All Souls. Others will add that the soul takes material form when it makes these visits (it is essential that a body should be buried whole, and that it should not be cremated, for this will violate the process of material resurrection), that it washes, eats, and drinks, and that its family and friends can talk to it, send messages with it to others who are longer dead, or simply use its presence as an opportunity for prayer. In the nineteenth century, returning souls walked in the footsteps of far older spirits, among the demons that inhabited woods, marshes, and streams, for instance, or in the company of ghosts. Mitrofan drew the line at ghosts—there were no demons lurking in the birchwoods near his church—but those who read his book might well have believed several things at once, as people often do, professing canonical faith at the funeral in the church after they had put their kopecks in the coffin back in the hut to pay the ferryman his fare.

Religious belief was so much a part of life that many of the documents assume it, preferring to focus on the difficulties of raising funds, fighting immortality, or reconciling local feuds.[8] By contrast, the philosophy and pretensions of the other pillar of nineteenth-century Russian culture, the autocracy, are disproportionately represented in the printed texts, in newspapers, official documents, and memoirs. It may be difficult, now, to imagine that the power of a czar was divinely ordained, especially when you reflect upon the human personalities involved, but this is an instance when the sources help, especially those that deal with death and funerals. The notion of a god-given hierarchy was one that the czar's ministers were eager to reinforce, especially in the anxious months of transition that followed any monarch's death. They made their message crystal-clear. The czar was not an ordinary mortal, or even a mundane king; the nation was united through blood and the sacred Russian soil, but also in its grief, and God would protect the next czar as he assumed the heavy burden of autocracy on behalf of his stricken people.

The last czar to die before the revolution was Alexander III. The accounts of the nation's grief, and of the ritual that the court thought fitting for an autocrat, offer a political view of nineteenth-century Russia, a view that supplements the spirituality of Mitrofan and his fellow monks. Here the emphasis is upon power, on inequality, deference, and the mystery of a sovereign who dies but still remains to watch over his people. The church's role is little more than that of a tragic chorus. It is the body of the czar itself, the incarnation of mystical nationhood and divine rule, that holds the center of the stage.

Alexander III died at 2:15 in the afternoon on 20 October 1894. He had been staying at the royal palace in Livadiya, in the Crimea, where doctors had been attending him for weeks, struggling to mitigate the effects of the kidney disease that would kill him at the relatively young age—for a czar—of forty-nine. St. Petersburg heard of his death five hours later, when a black-bordered announcement was posted on the walls of the public library on Nevsky Prospekt. The massive bells in every church across the capital began to toll, and the sound continued through the night, a solemn, unrelenting beat. People crushed toward the library to catch a glimpse of the official notice, and within minutes a line had also formed outside the Kazan' Cathedral, where the first ceremony of requiem, sung by the choir of the Mariinsky Theater, was to be held.[9] All the cathedrals were packed that night, as somber figures, some weeping, bowed their heads in a haze of incense and candle smoke. The whole city, the entire country, went into mourning, donning the regulation black clothes, ordering commemorative wreaths, and canceling its theater and concerts in favor of church services and prayer. Full public mourning continued for three months.

The czar's body itself became the focus of the nation's attention. The Orthodox preoccupation with matter, the bond that unites the soul with mortal flesh, accorded an almost sacred importance to human tissue, bone, hair, and muscle.[10] Perhaps because of that, or perhaps because the fact of death had to be made as clear as possible at a time of political succession, the details of the czar's last illness were published almost immediately, along with the autopsy report, on the front pages of the best newspapers. Readers of the *St. Petersburg Gazette* were treated to a description of each of Alexander III's vital organs over their breakfast on 29 October, and the curious who read on were spared neither fatty deposits nor stomach gas.

The autocrat was embalmed (somewhat unsuccessfully; each of these procedures would later be followed by the Bolsheviks in the cases of Lenin and Stalin), and his body was laid out for a long series of social engagements. His journey from Livadiya, on the shoulders of his guardsmen and then on swags of velvet in the carriage of a special train, would take two weeks. The cortege paused for last visits to provincial towns such as Simferopol', Kharkov, Kursk, Orel, and Tula, and paid an extended visit to Moscow, where a requiem was sung in the Cathedral of the Archangel Michael. By the time he reached St. Petersburg, the czar was visibly rotting.[11]

The description of physical illness and death (though not of decomposition; this remained a secret) was customary, and its purpose was not to portray the czar as an ordinary human being. Nicholas II, who proclaimed his own intention of ruling by the grace of God (and without reference to anyone else) two days after his father's death, described the late ruler as "the Lord [*gosudar'*]," who had passed on "to the Infinite" but whose concern for "His native soil, which He loved with all the strength of His Russian soul" would continue to protect the nation.[12] The new czar, a weaker and less confident man than his father, at least shared with him a commitment to the institution of divinely ordained autocracy. "The truth is absolute," wrote his mentor, Konstantin Pobedonostsev, "and only the absolute may be the foundation of human life. Things not absolute are unstable."[13] The czar was not bound by politics. Instead, he was a semidivine ruler, and his connection with the people, they were supposed to believe, was mystical, spiritual, and beyond challenge.

Among the thousands who could read a newspaper like the *St. Petersburg Gazette*, a serious broadsheet that made no concession to gossip or to what it would have seen as the more vulgar tastes, the preservation of the autocracy was as much a matter of instinct, loyalty, and habit as it was an article of religious faith. Many of the paper's wealthy urban readership were as interested in the civic competition over wreaths and commemorative silverware as they were in the mysteries of Russian nationhood. Large metal wreaths entwined with jeweled flowers were especially fashionable in 1894, and their cost and weight were listed in the better newspapers, together with the names of some of the more generous subscribers. The czar's death was an opportunity for business, especially if yours was selling the mourning dress that would be worn for a whole year, each detail of which, compulsory at court, was carefully prescribed.[14] Advertisements for tailors and cloth merchants appeared overnight in the press, while shop windows in every town had pictures of the late czar on display by the morning of 21 October, each one of which was carefully draped with black crape.

By the morning of Alexander III's entombment, 1 November, the whole of St. Petersburg seemed to have taken to the streets. The monarchy was not the only institution whose status was about to be affirmed. The procession that followed the coffin from the Nikolaevskii station to the Peter Paul Cathedral contained nearly two hundred individual sections, each with its designated place. The palace guard came first, of course; but it was followed by standard-bearers carrying the insignia of each of the empire's major cities, of its towns, its political institutions, its official classes (peasants, traders, merchants), and of its foreign allies. Even the voluntary associations were there, each in rank order. There were representatives of the Russian Music Society, the Russian Association of Gardeners, the Numerological Society, the Association of Enthusiasts for Old Manuscripts, the Historical Association—dozens of individual groups, each with its charter, each carrying a banner, marching slowly between the black-draped buildings, keeping to a schedule agreed by the court, confirming, without even thinking much about it, that the empire was a place of hierarchy, Orthodoxy, and autocratic power. The crowd that watched them had been waiting since the previous night, camping out along the route, grateful that the weather stayed unseasonably mild. "Nothing like it has ever been seen in the capital," agreed the papers the next day.

While the procession marched and the bells tolled, however, there were others in the capital, a minority, who regarded the whole ceremony, like the autocracy itself, as a charade, an insult to human decency, an anachronism to be uprooted and destroyed. These were the revolutionaries whose writings were assiduously censored by officials in the Third Department of the Czarist Interior Ministry, whose movements were regularly followed and logged, whose thoughts, however serious or trivial, have become important in retrospect because their heirs, a generation later, would take control of the empire in the name of all its people. But there were other kinds of beliefs, too, and many of these were never written down, or not, at least, by those who actually held them.

Very little can be said about the way that the majority of Russia's people mourned its czar. The newspapers did not ignore them entirely, but they made no effort to collect their comments or record their ceremonies of farewell. Nearly 80 percent of the people in the Russian empire were classed as peasants, which meant that in the 1890s their numbers exceeded 96 million. They had almost no political influence under czarism, however, and the Bolsheviks, after 1917, would also come to regard them as backward, dark, and potentially treacherous. They left few records for themselves—it was unusual for peasants to write at all before the 1920s—and so the evidence that we have comes almost entirely from outside their ranks. Nonetheless, their views, their beliefs, and their mentalities formed the bedrock of the Russian popular view of death, and when it came to revolutionary change, to the introduction of new ideas, new rituals, and scientific values, the peasants' faith would prove the most resilient. Parts of it would survive, in fact—some fragments, splinters reassembled in a different context—to shape the universe of death for their great-grandchildren a century later.

The peasants' religious universe was difficult to challenge from outside because it did not depend on priests, on formal structures, or on written texts. For this reason, too, many writers of the nineteenth century, discovering village culture for the first time, saw peasant beliefs as timeless, primal, and characteristically Russian. The idea that the nation's spirit burned most brightly in the common people was an attractive one for the kinds of romantics who found technological and social change confusing. People of that cast of mind collected peasant sayings as if they held the keys to a secret world, a disappearing wisdom that literate men and women, deprived of daily contact with the earth, could only enviously glimpse.

The yearning for peasant wisdom was not merely a matter of nostalgia, and the Victorian idea of folklore does not capture it either. Writers like Tolstoy looked to the peasants as the source of all that was purest and most admirable in Russian spirituality; they wanted to renew their failing world by searching for its true, authentic soul. One of the themes that this brought up, inevitably, was death. As usual, the corruption and complexity of the city were contrasted with the simplicity of the village. Intellectuals might suffer "a severance, a spiritual wound" in the face of bereavement, and their own deaths might be agonizing, baffling, a philosophical burden, but the common man, the Russian *muzhik*, confronted death directly. Like a drop of water, Tolstoy wrote in 1869, their lives "simply overflowed and vanished."[15]

Tolstoy would use the theme of peasant simplicity, counterposing it to a futile rationalism, in many of his later writings. It was a peasant, for instance, who helped the tormented Levin, one of the most sympathetic characters in the novel *Anna Karenina*, first published in 1877, to find a way out of his suicidal despair. The peasants' secret was to live rightly, in a godly way, "to live for your soul and remember God."[16] The philosophy was typically simple, and offered casually, but it produced in the sophisticated intellectual "the effect of an electric spark." Life and death, expressed that plainly, suddenly became tolerable again for Levin, and, by implication, for Tolstoy. "The peasants took death calmly," agreed Aleksandr Solzhenitsyn. "They did not bluster, fight back, or boast that they would never die. Far from postponing the final reckoning, they got ready, little by little, and in good time decided who was to get the mare and the foal, who the homespun coat and who the boots, then they passed on peaceably, as if simply moving to another cottage."[17]

The folklorists of the nineteenth century discovered that the peasant simplicity for which they yearned could coexist with peasant poetry, with the weird rhythm of lament, for instance, or the charm of fable and epic legend. The 1870s and 1880s were the founding years of Russian ethnography.[18] Society was changing rapidly everywhere, and there were growing anxieties about loss, about the dilution of authentic Russian values and ideas. Some wealthy scholars began to make expeditions to the deep country as soon as the roads became passable each year. Others sent their servants or recruited local agents. One of these, Prince Tenishev, had teams of lowlier correspondents—priests, doctors, and the occasional local clerk—reporting to him from across the provinces. His papers, which are stacked in hundreds of dark blue files and occupy an entire archive in St. Petersburg, reflect all aspects of religious life, from weddings and well-cursings to funerals and ghosts. Other enthusiasts for the old culture, such as E. V. Barsov, originally trained as priests, and collected folktales and poetry in their spare time. Barsov himself spent long summer afternoons in 1867 in a hut in the northern district of Petrozavodsk, scribbling down the laments that were dictated by the peasant poet Irina Andreyevna Fedosova.[19] He published them in Moscow to wide acclaim in 1872.[20]

The problem with all this anxious collecting, and even with the sermons of Tolstoy and his followers, was that, like any other writing of its time, it concentrated on selected aspects of the whole. The ethnographers were mainly interested in practice and custom. They had no way of writing adequately of mentality. Most of their work described rustic virtue, poetry, quaintness, and, at the very worst, mere fecklessness or greed. The impulse of most folklorists was conservative in the literal sense; they wanted to preserve something that they had learned to value.

Reformers of the same period, by contrast, would find little to praise in the peasants' world. Maxim Gorky, for instance, who toured Russia in the early twentieth century, wrote less admiringly of village life. "By nature the peasant is not stupid and knows it well," he declared in 1922. "He has composed a multitude of wistful songs and rough, cruel stories, created thousands of proverbs embodying the experience of his difficult life." Gorky also cited a folklorist of his own: "A historian of Russian culture, characterising the peasantry, said of it: a host of superstitions, and no ideas whatsoever. This judgement is backed up by all the Russian folklore."[21] Alexander Pasternak, the architect, agreed. He found that a single summer spent in Safontyevo, a village about forty miles from Moscow, was acquaintance enough with "the decayed Russian peasantry in all its ugly destitution." Pasternak could discern no secret wisdom within the "smoky, soot-encrusted huts . . . awash with wet muck that no-one bothered to clear away." On the contrary, "the villagers' passive submissiveness, their total indifference to filth and poverty, seemed to me a denial of their humanity."[22]

The peasants' lives, then, could exasperate a visitor as readily as they could evoke nostalgia. To make matters more complicated still, there was not one peasant mentality but thousands, for the distances between settlements, and the varied climates, landscapes, and histories of Russia's different regions, favored the evolution of separate stories, different styles of speech, and even different views of violence, punishment, death, and afterlife. These are the things that it is easy to forget under the mesmerizing influence of certain kinds of Russian poetry, the qualifications and alternatives that lie in wait for anyone who visits the peasants' world in search of the origins of an imagined Russian nationhood, a Russian soul. Variety is also the strongest evidence against that bleaker view of continuity, the one that seeks to blame the terrible bloodshed of Russia's twentieth century upon some cultural flaw, some legacy of barbarism. A more imaginative view of this lost world would turn the question around, and weigh the value that a rural people placed on ritual, on faith, on common languages of grief. It would ask what price these men and women, bound by custom and geography, reliant as they were on family and soil, were about to pay for the upheavals of the twentieth century. To acquire the authority to answer this, or any other question about Russia's peasant culture at this time, however, you have to make a journey of your own.

There was no easy way to travel in rural Russia, even in the last years of the czarist empire. There were some railways, many of them single tracks, the most important of which connected the two capitals, St. Petersburg and Moscow. By the end of the nineteenth century, there were also lines running south to the Black Sea and the Caucasus; western Siberia was reached in the 1890s; and from 1904, if you were prepared to take the ferry across Lake Baikal, you could travel all the way to the Pacific Coast, to Vladivostok. Nonetheless, the villages were mostly inaccessible by rail. If you were looking for typical households and ordinary peasant life, the only option would have been to leave the train at a provincial halt, perhaps no more than a drafty platform, and to wait for a horse and cart to take you further.

When Mikhail Bulgakov, recently qualified as a doctor, made his own journey to the village of Nikol'skoe in 1916, it took his driver twenty-four hours to cover the thirty-two miles that separated the local station from his lodgings. The country roads were buried deep in mud, the landscape sodden, featureless, and bleak. The two men arrived at the village soaked to the skin and "ossified with cold." "Who would believe you can freeze as easily in the middle of a grey, miserable September as in the depth of winter," Bulgakov muttered as the driver heaved his dripping suitcase down to him from the cart. "Ah well, it seems you can. And as you die a slow death there's nothing to look at except the same endless monotony. On the right the bare undulating fields and on the left a stunted copse, flanked by five or six grey dilapidated shacks. Not a living soul in them, it seems, and not a sound to be heard."[23]

The emptiness of the Russian landscape could evoke panic in a person used to city streets and buildings, gas lamps, crowded shops, and human noise. Darkness, damp, and aching cold are mentioned by almost every visitor. It was usually wise to pack your city clothes away and adopt the peasant's sheepskin coat, felt boots, and fur-lined cap. Mere cloth, even the finest wool, was seldom proof against the knifing wind, while snow, and later, mud, were knee-deep in the lanes. Heavily dressed like that, and deterred by the weather and the roads from getting about for most of the year, even the most determined traveler began to feel a little trapped, a prisoner in the huge expanse of steppe, under the open sky. Maxim Gorky was one who believed that the landscape played a role in limiting human imagination. "The boundless plains on which the wooden, thatch-roofed villages crowd together," he wrote, had "the poisonous peculiarity of emptying a man, of sucking dry his desires. . . . The peasant has only to go out past the bounds of the village and look back at the emptiness around him to feel that this emptiness is creeping into his very soul. Nowhere around can one see the results of creative labour . . . Round about lie endless plains and in the centre of them, insignificant tiny man abandoned on this dull earth for penal labour."[24]

"Penal labour" was a fair description of peasant life in Gorky's time and for years after his death. By the turn of the century, however, one major reform had already changed the peasants' legal status, and in many ways it had transformed their prospects and their dreams. Until 1861, the peasants of the Russian empire had been serfs, the property of their landlords or the state, disposable like cattle. The act of emancipation, which granted them their freedom, represented a major shift in official thinking—and a major gamble, for the czar's ministers feared revolution—and it also changed the serfs' sense of themselves forever. Their economic prospects, however, were hardly improved, since they were obliged to pay for the land they farmed at a price calculated to indemnify their former owners for the loss of human property. In practice, redemption, as it was called, remained beyond their economic grasp. They were indebted, impoverished, condemned to unremitting labor, and they remained tied to the land.

This land was important because it played an almost sacred role in peasant life. The Russian peasants were not, as Gorky claimed, "empty . . . sucked dry," and nor were they "indifferent" to their poverty, but the preoccupations that inspired them were distinct from those of city-bred outsiders. Such visitors might doubt it, contemplating undrained marsh, deep clay, and sour pinewood, but any land that a person tilled was believed to belong to him by God-given right. To put it more accurately, the land belonged to the community, the *mir,* of which most peasants were members, for individual ownership was almost unknown. The peasants' world, in fact, followed a logic of its own, using some words that outsiders from the cities might recognize, but having different values, different aims, and investing concepts like truth, equality, and justice with distinct meanings to suit local needs.[25]

The basic unit in any village was not the individual, but the household, and the social order, as well as any person's sense of his or her place within it, depended on this collectivity. Beyond the household, it was the mir that allocated land, the mir that granted permission for any individual to travel in search of factory work, and the mir, often, that made local decisions about security and justice. The larger hierarchy of Russian society was mirrored in this subordination to the group. It was a system that protected the weak, at least to some extent; conservative, but not merely—as some reformers saw it—retrogressive and corrupting.

There was also an ambivalence within the patriarchy that ruled in peasant households. Women are usually subordinate members of peasant societies, but the prerevolutionary Russian case was an extreme. While the men addressed the other males in the *mir* as "brother," the women scarcely enjoyed basic human rights. Wife beating was considered normal, "completely legal and natural," although the same wife was regarded as an equal when it came to "ploughing, planting, raking and gathering the hay and grain." "A hen is not a bird and a woman is not a person," was the peasant quip.[26] But patriarchy alone does not entirely capture the women's status, for it was women who largely took control when someone died; they who keened and sang, creating poetry of a kind; and they who had the job of passing family tradition through the generations to their daughters.

These were the general features of the peasants' world, but the type of farming, the distribution of work, and many other details of the local culture varied according to the climate, the location, and the soil. Villages in the Black Earth to the south, favored with one of the best arable soils in Europe, centered around grain growing—principally wheat—and supported dense, and even overpopulated human settlements. Grain was the main crop everywhere, accounting for about 90 percent of cultivated land, but outside the Black Earth there were more varied crop rotations, more potatoes and rye, less wheat, smaller profits, harder winters, greater distances to walk. In some places, the ones along the railway lines or close enough to some large town to benefit from trade, there was money to be made from cabbages, from making curd cheese and sour cream, transporting apples and cucumbers to the markets.[27] Other villages had long traditions of apprenticeship, by which their sons trudged miles to Petersburg, Ivanovo, or Podol'sk, whichever town it was that offered men from their region work as pattern-cutters, toolmakers, builders, coopers, brickmakers, or railwaymen. Such opportunities might challenge entrenched ideas, as well as breaking up the traditional family. Peasant society was far from static by the 1890s.

Despite the changes, however, peasant religion was one thing that an outsider might hope to find unaltered and secure. Churches and bell towers remained the most distinctive landmarks in the open country. There were some places where you had to walk for miles, for a day, to find one, let alone to find the priest; the population was growing so fast that some settlements were too recent, and some landlords were too poor, to fund another public building.[28] Elsewhere, groups of dissenting peasants, including Old Believers and the members of millenarian and other sects, had set up chapels of their own, following beliefs that explicitly rejected much of the religious practice of the larger community.[29] Nonetheless, there were few places where the skyline was not broken, eventually, among the poplars and the larch, by the familiar wooden churches, their domes a pattern of interlocking shingles, jigsaws of weathered pine that reflected the light like the scales of brown carp. Some villages even had solid brick churches, and some had their own bronze bells—expensive, heavy, the gift of a wealthy local family.

To step inside one of these buildings, even a relatively poor one, was to enter a different world. Its messages were painted on the walls, remembered in the enigmatic gaze of the holy icons, reflected in the gleam of metal, in bronze or brass if not always the city's gold. Wood, sometimes extravagantly carved, was used to mark out sacred space, and embroidered linen draped the most important icons, the crosses, and the altar. For a population used to mud, damp wool, and straw, the polished metal and the candlelight would have been sublime enough, even without the icons, the frescoes, the singing, and the Old Slavonic prayers. Viewed by a peasant in the nineteenth century, before the persecution that would make it part of counterculture, the Orthodox Church was a corrupt institution, a hierarchy shot with intrigue, a constant drain on everyone's finances, and an irritating source of prohibitions, but it was also the custodian of transcendence, its ceremonies offering glimpses of eternity through clouds of incense and the unaccompanied bass voices of the priest and choir.

That, at least, was half the truth. Religion was a part of daily life in the villages—the reflex to cross oneself was almost as natural as sneezing[30]—but the church, as an institution with a formal dogma, was not. While Mitrofan was writing his comforting words for literate believers in the capital, peasants were surviving in a universe that was neither benign nor cheerful. Evil was real; sin was everywhere—natural disasters were the proof of it—and the poor Orthodox, which meant the peasants, had no choice but to look out for themselves. They did so with a ruthless practicality.

The most important influences on the peasant economy, the things that made the difference between a good year and a famine, were beyond the people's control and impossible to predict. Of these, the most decisive was the weather.[31] A drought could ruin entire crops, reducing fertile soil to dust. But almost anything could make a difference—ill health among the cattle, flooding in a store, late frosts or summer hail. It was because their lives were so precarious and so easily cursed that the peasants' faith centered on the earth, on fate, and on their own communtiy. Their beliefs were not magical or superstitious, or not as far as the peasants themselves were concerned. They were a matter of piety, for almost everyone believed in God, and they were founded on self-evident commonsense, providing insurance against disaster. They were also the only means available of predicting the outcome of a sowing or a harvest, both of which were, naturally, in God's hands.

The formal teachings of the church had little to say about these things. Village priests might understand the problems—for they were usually peasants like their flock, and lived by farming the land and by extracting fees, often in kind, for any services that they performed—but the ideas that their prayerbooks offered ran against the grain of family preoccupations like childbearing, animal health, and the daily battle against supernatural misfortune, the so-called unclean force, whose work included vampirism. To make matters worse, many priests were too identified with the people, too frequently seen in the tavern or the market, too busy with the endless needs of their own large families.[32]

Semyen Kanatchikov, who grew up in Moscow province in the 1890s, recalled the visits to his school of a "broad-shouldered, long-haired priest from a neighbouring village." This luminary gave his class after lunch on Fridays, on his way home from a nearby open-air market. "A bit tight, speaking inarticulately, he would ask us to say the prayers and make us read the Gospels in Church Slavonic and translate them into Russian," Kanatchikov remembered. The message was given emphasis by regular thrashings.[33] But this, in educational terms, was progress. Earlier generations had learned nothing more than a basic catechism. As one scholar remarks, "the most difficult doctrines of Christianity, such as the Trinity, remained unassimilated."[34]

Peasant religion, then, included elements that formal doctrine did not mention, including rituals for predicting and evading death, as well as a whole gallery of local patron saints, spirits, and demons. It took its universe more literally than its more urbane, conventional equivalent in the towns, and it based itself more firmly in the community. Families included dead as well as living members. The village did not forget the so-called good dead, the ancestors or fathers, and later burials united their children with them through the soil.[35] Although that soil was consecrated by the church, enclosed within the cemetery, it was no less important, in its own right, than the prayers the priest might say. To be buried in alien soil was a great misfortune, and anyone who had to leave the village would assume that his body would be brought home after his death. Some exiles kept cups of their native earth to sprinkle on their graves, and it was a common practice for returning soldiers to bring earth from the battlefield home to offer to bereaved families. It might be kept for years, covered with a cloth beside the icon, until the widow or the mother died herself, when it was mingled with the earth of her own grave.

Graves themselves, which were marked by a wooden cross, or possibly by a wooden stake topped by a roofed shelter, like a tiny pigeon coop, to shelter the returning soul, were important places, social space. You could sit beside them and talk—the people believed their conversations were two-way—you could send messages for relatives who had long been dead, and if you were pious you could ask a soul to pray for you in the "other light," where prayer might have more effect. These conversations could take place at any time, but certain days were special. These included Shrove Tuesday (*maslenitsa*), when the first pancake would customarily be offered to the dead; three or four "ancestors' Saturdays" in Lent; the second Tuesday after Easter; and the Thursday of the seventh week after Easter (*rusal'naya*), when a funeral service was also held for anyone who had not been given a proper burial. On each of these occasions, the cemeteries filled with people, graves were tidied, and the conversation centered on the family—the living and the dead. Grave visiting and shared memories also followed individual deaths. *Pominki*, or ceremonies of remembrance, were held on the ninth and fortieth days after anyone had died, keeping in mind the church's timetable—the soul's first perilous visit to acquaint itself with hell and later on the day of judgment that would follow.

There were very few exceptions to the rule that the "good" dead should be buried in consecrated soil. One was inspired by peasant logic. Some people feared that the priest was actually an informer. The strange words that he uttered by their graves, or wrote, in the guise of prayers, and placed inside their coffins, were thought by some to be mere lists of sins for God to read. One way of avoiding betrayal of this kind was to get your friends to agree to bury you in the woods before the priest arrived. Another was to slip a bribe—vodka or cash—inside your coffin. Alternatively, a dying person might change his name with his last breath. The angels, after all, used lists that gave the Christian names of every sinner in their care. A freshly renamed person would be as innocent in the eyes of God as a new baby.[36]

Ideas derived from everyday life featured in every part of peasant ritual. Food and drink were especially important. Funerals were followed by a communal meal; the priest was paid, in part, in vodka; and food was always shared at the *pominki*. Funeral meals were held in the dead person's house, but other graveside ceremonies easily turned into picnics. The dead were not ethereal; they needed real food, not flowers; and their relatives shared eggs (a symbol of rebirth), honey (to make eternal life more sweet), yeast cake, and even vodka with them. The cost of this communal eating was not small. Entertaining the relatives, the carpenters, the gravediggers, and the priest, in particular, accounted for a good proportion of a funeral's total expense, and since priests also customarily demanded a cash payment in advance before performing ceremonies such as funerals and requiems, a succession of deaths could easily land an entire community in debt.[37] Fortunately, however, the financial burden, like the grieving itself, was spread throughout the extended family, and sometimes among all the members of the mir.

The church and its teaching, then, were integrated into a stronger, family-based religion. No hut was without its icons and its lamp; the priest might visit when there was a special prayer to read, but the souls of the dead were never far away, and the cemetery had properties that formal dogma never really sanctioned. It also had some uses that the church officially condemned. On summer afternoons the animals would sometimes stray across its wall to graze among the crosses and the mounds, and sometimes, when there was a festival to run, the enclosed space provided shelter for the traders with their vodka, beer, and pies.[38]

Ethnographers in Russia have sometimes called the peasants' faith an example of *dvoeverie*, "dual belief," explaining that it combined elements of Christianity with vestiges of paganism. This explanation misses out the dynamism of the peasants' faith, the way it adapted as circumstances altered, even in the slow-moving world of the farm. It was traditional, for instance, for a prayer to be placed between a corpse's hands before burial, beseeching God or Saint Peter to be merciful. By the end of the nineteenth century, this document had already begun to be known as the corpse's "papers," and in the twentieth it would be replaced, in some instances, by a real passport. Schoolboys who died in their teens were sometimes buried with their examination certificates, and sometimes with their strange, expensive books.[39] These new objects joined the traditional ones that people kept to place beside their bodies; plaits of a woman's hair from the time of her marriage, for instance, or small sharp stones, whose purpose was supposed to be to remind a person of his sins as he walked painfully to judgment.[40]

Among the greatest dangers with a death, the peasants knew, was the risk that other people would succumb at the same time. A large number of customs developed to avoid this possibility, including prescriptions about the size of the coffin (small, so that no others could be fitted in beside the corpse), and instructions to close a corpse's eyes so that it could not glance at someone else and call them on to follow it. The most terrifying element of all, however, was the so-called unclean force. Exactly what it was could not be said—it was unwise even to pronounce its name—but it was never far away, and at a time of crisis, such as a death, its influence was especially to be feared.

Any negligence might bring destruction. When someone died, her body was washed on a board in the hut, and the soap and water quickly disposed of in a neglected corner outside.[41] The hut was also swept. Nikolai Mikhailovich Borodin, who grew up in the Don region of Ukraine in the 1900s, remembered when his great-grandfather died. "The floor of the cottage was immediately brushed and the dust buried in the yard," he wrote. "My grand-uncle told me that this was necessary to prevent the corpse from coming back in the night from its grave. This explanation terrified me and on discovering a corner which was not well brushed I cleaned it energetically, carefully catching all the dust and burying it outside."[42] It was also to prevent haunting that a body might be carried to the church through an open window, or even through a specially cut hole in the thatch, rather than through the door of its old home. The idea was to confuse the dead person's spirit, making it more difficult for the ghost to find its own way back.

The charms and rituals were innumerable, varying slightly between regions, always based on a practical view of what a soul might need and what it might do wrong. Another place that was swept with particular care, for instance, was the bathhouse, the wooden hut with a charcoal stove that was regularly filled with steam and used as a kind of communal sauna. The dead were believed to steam themselves before the great festivals, including Easter, and in anticipation of this the bathhouse was prepared and vacated for them for the entire night. The locals kept away, for it was said that evil would befall anyone who was careless enough to witness their return, to hear their shouts and songs or glimpse their orgiastic bathing.[43] The bathhouse was a favorite haunt of the unclean force, in fact, and so were marshes, ravines, and unfrequented forests.

When it came to the imagination of the soul, its journey, and of heaven and hell, the priorities of the village blended with the wisdom of the icons. Everyone referred routinely to the afterlife as "the other light" (*tot svet*). The words were as casually uttered as a mundane geographical direction. Heaven was usually described as a green meadow dotted with small houses. A more material paradise, invented in the nineteenth century, included a church, but it was built of pies; its roof was made of pancakes; and its floor was paved with solid Russian gingerbread.[44] Hell was usually hot, and following the imagery of the frescoes and the icons, it was fiery. The final judgment was always an occasion for terror. An eighteenth-century icon of it, now displayed in St. Petersburg's Kazan' Cathedral, shows God, surrounded by the angels, with a balance in his hand. The saints stand meekly on one side and the sinners—a majority, as ever—wait anxiously on the other. A massive serpent curls menacingly toward them as they cluster in their scale; and demons—black, horned, and hairy—are skewering their comrades as they tumble downward from the clouds. Ingenious peasants added further touches. It was believed, for instance, that a woman who had aborted a child would be forced, in hell, to eat raw flesh and chew upon an infant's bones.[45]

In the midst of all this drama was the soul, a fragile, timorous thing, always described as pale, a doll-like copy of a person, perhaps, as delicate as a newborn child. Some people imagined it with wings, flying out of the body with the last breath.[46] Icons representing martyrdom often showed the soul as a younger, miniature version of the dying saint whose body it was leaving. A common representation of the Assumption shows the soul of the Virgin as an infant in the protective arms of her son, a reversal of the classic icon of the Virgin and Child. Souls were the distinguishing essence of a human being. Animals did not have them, though an exception was sometimes made for bears.[47] The possession of a soul was evidence of the human share in godhead, but it may have seemed a doubtful privilege. No laments or traditional peasant songs describe the journey toward judgment as a pleasure, and the outcome always seems to be foredoomed. A traditional religious verse, a song learned by children and sung at funerals and by the graves, describes the soul's last cry:

"Farewell, pale corpse,
Pale corpse of many sins.
While you will lie in the damp earth
They are calling me to judgement
Calling me to judgement before God."
. . . And the soul arrived at the eastern sunrise
Where heaven is and all its courts,
And in them sit the souls of the blessed,
"But for me, soul, there will be no room."[48]

Death was so common in the villages, and also so visible, its victims often young and in the prime of life, that there were never many people around, including children, who had not witnessed it. Even people who had never touched a real corpse would certainly have played at death. The celebrations at Christmas often included a mock funeral, and while a healthy young adult usually took the part of "corpse," a real body was sometimes used as the focus of vaudeville lamentation and general laughter.[49] Funerary rituals still featured at some weddings; the women might lament the symbolic "death" of the bride as she left her own family for that of her husband.[50] Children played funerals as readily as they played house, and little girls assisted the old women in the laying-out of corpses. Girls were also made to learn and practice the improvisation of laments. The latter was a skill that featured in discussions about marriage. A young woman who could not lament (and there would be no time to practice if her talents were really needed) was regarded as deficient in the same way as was one who could not spin or cook.

Laments were poetry, keening music, ethereally repetitive, and rigidly formulaic. Certain words would always recur. Grief was always bitter, for instance; a dead son was always brave and handsome; and widows were always destined for inconsolable solitude and hard work.[51] The main theme threaded its way recurrently through improvised lines describing the dead person's life from cradle to grave—the lament was also an obituary—and detailing his or her position in an extended family. Lamenting might begin as soon as someone died. It was loud, it was eerie, it was not harmonious, and the church officially disapproved,[52] but usually the only tranquil moments in the process of a death and burial were the ones led by the priest.

It was through the words of these laments, as well as through the children's songs and folktales, that the peasants shaped their views of death itself. The church tried to suggest that death was a friend, but custom always feared and shunned it. The least unpleasant images described it as a woman, an angel in the form of a human skeleton, hooded and cloaked, who came down from heaven on God's instructions to claim her victims. Shooting stars were thought to be the angel blazing down in search of prey.[53] Death was also a bird, usually a falcon, though it might take the dark form of a creature accustomed to a life of secrecy in marshes, woods, and distant hills.[54] To the women as they sang it was the sunset, the extinction of stars, snow falling on a fire, the destruction of a tree by frost, the breaking of a great stone by water.[55] In another set of images, it was a carriage drawn by birds or horses, sometimes it was a boat, and always it was carrying the soul away to judgment. "My days of happiness are over," goes a traditional song (the recording I have is sung by primary school children), "I am confused and lost. I can say farewell for all eternity to the joys of earth."[56]

These rituals tell us something about peasant life, about its values, and about the way that ordinary Russians understood the fact of death. It was a universe that change, violent change, was about to shatter. First the Great War—imperial Russia's war with Germany—then revolution, and finally a bitter civil war would break apart the peasants' isolated world, destroy some of its sacred spaces, and defy its gods. The impact of all this, especially at a time of profound grief, cannot be understood without a sense of what it was the people had to lose. It is too easy to assume that "they" somehow endured it all because they had become so hard. But the violence of the early twentieth century was also influenced by peasant values. Peasants were the foot soldiers of every twentieth-century war; they carried the village with them, for a time at least, when they moved to the cities; their rivalries and feuds intensified the cruelty of Stalin's revolution from above. Their culture contained many different resources. It is too easy to write as if the Gulag were created in a rural tavern. But the question has been raised so often that it has to be explored. "Where does this wolf-tribe come from?" asked Aleksandr Solzhenitsyn in the 1970s. "Does it really stem from our own roots? Our own blood? It is our own."[57]

Mortality in nineteenth-century Russia was generally very high, and peasant households witnessed more deaths, including infant deaths, than any others.[58] The bodies of the "good" dead were not removed at once, and someone in the village would have to wash and dress them, lay them out, and help the family to carry them first to church and later to their grave. As members of a relatively static and communal world, too, the dead did not readily vanish from memory. All this does not describe a casual approach to death—it was an enemy, after all—nor does it suggest that customarily life was cheap. A death, in fact, might offer neighbors a chance to explore their solidarity.

Solidarity, however, implies that there are people whom the group excludes. Even the most basic rituals were eloquent about outsiders. Peasant life was not a gentle affair of sunlit gatherings and fireside tales. Among the problems that beset the countryside, poverty and ignorance combined with a basic resistance to change—especially if it came from reformers, from the city—creating an enclosed world, suspicious, often deliberately blind. The peasants distinguished, in all their calculations, between "ours" and the rest, the aliens who were seldom given a collective name, so terrible was the mere thought of bringing down their anger.

The moral codes involved were cruel. Peasants treated deviants within their own ranks like carriers of plague; their very presence threatened ruin. Summary justice, or *samosud*, within the villages was reminiscent of medieval Europe at its most bloodthirsty. Women suspected of witchcraft, for instance, might be burned alive in their own huts, and thieves, especially horse thieves, were liable to be tortured until they died, their spines systematically broken, their bodies beaten, branded, or butchered.[59] The segregation of "us" and "others" also continued through and after death. Prejudice excluded those who had died a "bad" death—those who had not died baptized and shriven, criminals, suicides, and individuals suspected of bringing bad luck—from the community forever.[60] Suicides—there were not many of them in the Russian village—were not supposed to be buried in the cemetery. Their crime would bring a curse upon the village, they were the devil's servants—some said he rode them, like a horse, at night—and their damnation was not to be relieved by prayer.[61]

Nineteenth-century Russia was haunted, too, by vampires. They might be known by their work—the Russian ones did not suck blood, preferring to bring crop failure, cattle plague, and other routine kinds of misfortune—or by the condition of their bodies when they were exhumed. The remedies were brutal. Corpses might still, even in the twentieth century, be buried with their heads or limbs hacked off, to prevent them from walking, or with their hands and feet bound tightly together or broken.[62] Some were buried with thorns under their tongues; others, with aspen stakes rammed into their mouths or hearts. They were also thrown into rivers and marshes, pitched into ravines, or dug up, in times of famine or illness, to be systematically mutilated, or simply to be reburied at a safe distance from the village and its church.[63]

Mutilation, of the dead and of the living miscreant as he died, was a punishment that would persist into the afterlife and hell. The Orthodox believed, and the peasants usually understood, that a soul who could not hear the prayers of the faithful, and who was not buried in sacred earth, would have no rescue from damnation. It was also important for a body to be buried whole, for while mortal flesh corrupted on earth, it was the same body, eventually, that would finally clothe the soul on the day of universal resurrection.[64] This belief was so powerful that saints who bodies had been damaged (many were mummified, but they became very brittle) were sometimes given prosthetic limbs, new hands and feet. It was not unknown, for the same reason, for murderers to gouge out their lifeless victims' eyes, or smash their faces, so that they could not testify, thereafter, to the crime or against its perpetrator.[65] This literal response to religious teaching was taken by Maxim Gorky, in the cruel years of the civl war, to explain the peasants' taste for gruesome methods of execution, including disemboweling. The peasants had learned some of the arts of torture, he argued, from medieval tales of martyrdom.[66]

Exemplary violence, the kind that writes its messages on the bodies of its victims, was inscribed for eternity upon the corpses of petty criminals, suspected horse thieves, freaks, deviants, and the mentally ill. An account from Penza province written in 1899 recounts the fate of "the hermaphrodite Vassili-Vassa." The child, who was thought to be a little girl, had gradually developed male sexual organs as she matured. "As she grew strong," the report explained, "her parents beat her every day." For a while, she was a village spectacle, barely tolerated, and whispered comments followed her wherever she walked. In the end, however, the whole village encouraged her to take her own life. She was seventeen. She was buried in a lonely pit, and no prayers were said for her, because the people feared that she would bring bad luck—the unclean force—into their healthy lives.[67]

These stories form a kind of scaffolding—Paul Thompson, in his defense of oral history, has called it a "lop-sided, empty frame"[68]—but because we cannot talk to the survivors, there are details at the heart of peasant identity that never can be known. The problem is that an illiterate society was never adequately understood by the outsiders who described it. The grieving for a child, for instance, can still be read in contradictory ways. Ethnographers report that children were buried under thresholds, that there was no requiem said for them, and that the mothers were supposed to cross themselves and mutter, "The

Lord giveth, the Lord taketh away."[69] "You have to see that Russia was—and to some extent still is—an old-style demographic regime," a sociologist in Moscow explained when I asked him about this. "That means that child mortality is not important, and in fact, mortality as a whole is high. It's not important because there are always lots of children. Just like Africa."[70]

All that is easy enough to say, but it does not explain why mothers who had lost a child were warned not to weep too much, for fear of harming its escaping soul, for fear of making it grieve for them, and even for fear that an evil spirit, the *nalet* (which also preyed on widows), would swoop down suddenly and snatch away their own lives. They were not supposed to lay the child's body out, either, as their tears would certainly distress it, and possibly bind its soul to earth forever.[71] The evidence of ritual points both ways, and so we talk of high-mortality regimes, or of the relative unimportance, economically, of a child.[72] That leaves us ignorant, however, about grief.

Poor and anxious women will often complain, to affluent outsiders, about the burden of bringing up their children. They may insist that there are too many, and some may give them up, or one of them, to ease the hunger of the rest. Small children do not offer much, while they are small, to the working of a rural economy (and nor do the old, if they have ceased to be the objects of respect, which is why some peasants bargained with the priest to bury them quickly and cheaply, especially if they died at harvest time).[73] These general remarks are true, but neither demography, nor ritual, nor even economics, can tell us much about the irrational attachment of a mother to this particular child, the first, the youngest, the luckiest, the weakest, the one, of all of them, that she had hoped to save.[74] The account from Penza, too, says nothing about the private despair of the sexually ambivalent Vassa's parents as they glumly speculated about their daughter and their curse. The parents or other relatives of a suicide commonly begged and bargained to secure a place for the body in a consecrated grave.[75] The culture contained blueprints for uncommon cruelty, certainly, especially when people were afraid or when they felt they had been cheated and had no redress, but there were other resources in it, too. The future would depend, in part, on the material prospects, on fear or security, repression or civil peace.

"What could be more universal than death?" asked the anthropologists Richard Huntington and Peter Metcalf. "Yet what an incredible variety of responses it provokes. . . . The diversity of cultural reaction is a measure of the universal impact of death. But it is not a random reaction; always it is meaningful and expressive."[76] Russian funerary culture was certainly both of these.

The peasants' way of death was not the only one in czarist Russia, but it was the most widespread. Its meaning was ambiguous, but the importance of its rituals was not. Peasant languages of grief captured the interdependency of life and death, community and place, in a preindustrial, prerevolutionary world.

The peasants' culture would have changed in any event. There is evidence that it was already doing so by the end of the nineteenth century, and the process would have continued, even had there been no revolution. Urbanization, mass literacy, travel, television, leisure, and tourism all eat away at preindustrial worlds, wherever they are. But the pace and manner of the change are crucial, and the timing, the bargaining and communication between generations, and the option that the people have to keep this part for now, and this, perhaps, forever. It was one of the most painful aspects of the revolution and of the dislocation that went with it: the deliberate destruction of a familiar mental universe, a set of beliefs and practices, and even of the sacred places where the people went, whatever they believed, whenever they were in trouble or someone that they loved had died. "Life ceased to look to death for its perspective," wrote Lucien Febvre of an earlier social dislocation.[77] But death still left the family to mourn—even if they did not know how to construct the laments of the past—the survivors to explain their own good fortune, and the witnesses to deal with their disturbing dreams.

2

A CULTURE OF DEATH

No one is sure exactly how it works, but most people agree that there is some kind of connection between Russia's culture and its history of high mortality. Average male life expectancy at birth in Russia, in the mid-1990s, was about fifty-eight. In the early 1990s, indeed, Russia was one of the few developed countries in the world where life expectancy—for men and women, though women do not generally die as young—was actually falling.[1] Experts talked of a health crisis, the dimensions of which, measured in terms of a decrease in life expectancy, in the single year 1992–93, of 3 years for men and 1.8 for women, meant that more civilian Russians were dying prematurely—or earlier than might have been predicted in a country where death rates were already high—than were being lost, on all sides, as a result of the war in Chechnya. It is hard to give a precise figure, but health experts suggest that the crisis was responsible, from 1989 through 1994, for a total of 1.3 million so-called excess deaths, by which they mean deaths that would, under better or "normal" circumstances, have been prevented.[2] The most acute phase in a period between 1992 and 1994 lasted for about eighteen months, and the trend has since been reversed, but the picture is still grim, especially when it is viewed comparatively. In Western Europe, men can expect to live, on average, until they are at least seventy-three, and even in the countries of the former Warsaw Pact the average is about sixty-three.[3]

There has never been a time, since the statistics were collected, when demographers have not observed this gap between Russia and the rest of Europe. At the end of the nineteenth century, average life expectancy in Russia was about thirty-two, compared with forty-seven in France.[4] Mortality rates, measured in terms of the crude death rate (the number of deaths per thousand of the population) can illustrate the same fact differently. Across the world, in the late nineteenth and early twentieth centuries, the pattern of mortality reflected the difficulty of overcoming disease before the advent of modern drugs and effective schemes for public health. By way of comparison, today's crude death rates vary from just under 9 per thousand in the United States to between 18 and 21 per thousand in the most desperate parts of the developing world.[5] Even the most prosperous parts of Europe had not achieved these rates by the time of the First World War. But mortality was generally falling. In France, for instance, the crude death rate dropped from 22.4 per thousand in the four years from 1876 to 1880 to an average of 19.2 per thousand between 1906 and 1910.[6] Russia itself could boast of an improvement in its death rates in these years, from 38 per thousand in the early 1870s to 28 per thousand between 1900 and 1913.[7] But these were still the highest rates in Europe.

A range of explanations has been adduced for Russia's poor record. Contemporary accounts, such as that offered by the mathematician Vladimir Shkol'nikov, are cautious, constructed by age cohort, examining the exact incidence, for example, of violent death among young men, the relative probability that someone who survives his heart disease will later die of cancer, the epidemiological comparisons with the United States and France. The principal conclusions are sobering. Russia's most recent health crisis was the result of long- and short-term trends. Among the former are the personal habits that form a culture—patterns of diet, alcohol consumption, smoking—and social problems such as poor health care and inadequate housing. Among the latter, in the early 1990s, was a dramatic increase in violent deaths, including suicides. Rising crime, personal insecurity, fears for the future, and sheer poverty conspired, through one of Russia's great historical turning points, to create a situation in which the absolute size of its population actually declined.

Although there is no shortage of statistics, and although the information available to present-day demographers is comprehensive, the exact causes of the most recent crisis remain unclear. The mortality of past decades, let alone the nineteenth century, is an even more elusive subject. The Russian demographers of the late nineteenth and early twentieth centuries did not have access to full or accurate information. Even the diseases from which their populations died were sometimes defined in terms that were dubiously exotic or vague. The local registers of deaths, which are incomplete and cover only parts of the empire (the whole of Siberia, for instance, was excluded), were compiled on the basis of the crudest of reports.[8] The parish priest—whose knowledge of medicine was often rudimentary, and whose faith in the will of God left little space for science—was often the only person on the spot to fill out any forms that might exist. Among the explanations for a death most favored by these gentlemen were convulsions and old age. Some of the other diseases on their lists sound like the mythic plagues. Several different colors of typhus, for instance, with or without spots; darkness of the soul; and fevers, undifferentiated, are among the headings that regularly recur.[9] A demographer who watched me struggling, dictionary in hand, in the archive one afternoon began to laugh. "Just because English people don't die from it," he said, "you can't necessarily say that it doesn't exist."

His comment was, of course, a joke, but in fact it is more serious than it sounds. For the other feature of Russian patterns of mortality, and one that has also been discernible since the nineteenth century, appears to have a national or ethnic bias. The pioneering Russian demographer A. N. Novosel'skii noticed the problem in 1916. By every indicator, he discovered, the Orthodox Russian population within the czarist empire fared less well than comparable groups with other ethnic or religious backgrounds, and especially the Catholics, Lutherans, and Jews.[10] Orthodox Russians lived less long, their children died in greater numbers and at earlier ages, and they, as adults, were more likely to perish by violence or untimely disease. The reasons that Novosel'skii gave for this were speculative and fragmentary, and that is how later explanations have remained. Perhaps the Jews had an inborn immunity to tuberculosis, Novosel'skii hypothesized, the result of generations of enforced urban living.[11] Perhaps the Lutherans did not indulge in binge drinking. Vladimir Shkol'nikov suggests that maybe some dietary habit of the Orthodox, some practice relating to the care of mothers or children, left infants weaker. But like everyone else, he cannot give a final answer. There is a fine line between demographic reality, cultural generalization, and racism, and he is careful not to cross it.[12]

The conclusions of demography tend principally to be based on long cycles—the prospects for individual health throughout an entire lifetime; through two or more generations; the echo of one episode of high mortality on birth and death rates at a lag of twenty, thirty, forty years; and then another generation.[13] But it is important to distinguish between the demographer's underlying trends and the historian's cultural continuities. It is easy to despair in the face of Russia's history of death, of its record of violence—that of the state and that of the people—and to assign the explanation to some quirk of Russian identity: the cheapening of human life, the climate, the culture, the way that it has always been.[14] Post-Soviet Russians do it readily, muttering about the so-called Asiatic tradition or the legacy of the Tartar yoke. Russia's backwardness also gets invoked. Here, it is stated, is a country permanently doomed to limp behind the West, forever losing patience with the slowest and most lumpen of its citizenry, a place where a medieval fatalism still lurks, with all its attendant cruelty.

These theories suit the winter evenings, but as history they are hardly adequate. They overlook what is specific about each different moment, the changing cultural patterns that followed two revolutions, the different roles played over time by ignorance, retribution, or fear. They also fail to take account of the brief intervals of improvement, the innovations and reforms that allowed liberals and utopians alike to dream, with reason, that their world was on the brink of transformation. The demographic history of twentieth-century Russia has not been one of unrelieved disaster.

Demography—and social science in general—was still a novelty in Russia in the late nineteenth century. Its pioneers were trying to understand society, but they were also committed to improving it. A tiny minority within the czarist empire, the graduates of its nine universities, they drew their comparisons with Western Europe in order to learn from it, to provide a setting for reform, and because they believed that Russia was not unique, but part of a European system of social and economic development. Mortality in the empire was high, they believed, because, as Novosel'skii put it, Russia was "an agricultural country, backward in terms of culture, sanitation and economic development."[15] But these were things that could be overcome. The basic approach was liberal; the solutions a matter of education, investment, industrial regulation, and carbolic soap.

It was in that spirit that reformers drew attention to the desperate issue of housing—rural and urban—the lack of clean water, and the widespread ignorance of basic sanitary precautions. It was only later that a revolutionary government would declare these things to be peripheral to the main problem, symptoms rather than causes. As Lenin and his colleagues realized, the social crisis of late czarism, compounded as it was by politics, would ultimately demand a political solution. The reformers were powerless, as Bolshevik health officials would later point out, in the face of the gaping inequality of incomes. They could not even allude to the inequity of a structure that left the majority of the empire's people without a voice in any part of the political process.[16] To have done that, in a society where censorship was pervasive, would have been to court not disapproval, but arrest.

The imperial Russian government of the late nineteenth century, as an autocratic monarchy, had ample opportunity to address the issues of public health, mortality and violence from above. Successive ministries would include varying numbers of reformers; the problem was neither lack of information nor absence of alternatives. A thoughtful conservative, after all, could have looked at Bismarck's Berlin to see reforms that improved public health, strengthened the monarchy, and simultaneously spiked the guns of critics on the left. Russia took a different path. The autocracy was characterized by an arrogant conservatism—smug, aloof, and simpleminded. The church, a major institutional player, was even less enlightened, condemning what it called the "fever of reform," and shunning public works as if they were a distraction from man's sacred purpose. "The pious Russian," wrote Konstantin Pobedonostsev, the procurator of the Holy Synod and an adviser to both of Russia's last two czars, "will think twice before opening his purse in support of formal educational and philanthropic institutions." Happy, instead, was "the man in whom burns a spark of love for the spiritual life . . . He will truly enlighten with a light in the place of darkness, he will revive the dead and raise the fallen . . . and redeem a multitude of sins."[17]

It is not enough, however, to leave the story there, with a histrionic flourish of justifiable despair. For imperial Russia was divided against itself. Away from the imperial court, and especially among the small class of liberal professionals, a genuine commitment to change—even if it were only the alleviation of personal suffering in one town, one district—was beginning to alter the cultural landscape. The fate of these liberals is known—their failure, the way that the revolution would swallow them utterly, with its demand that change should be immediate and total—but memory, or hindsight, should not deprive them of their place. For just as Soviet medicine, in the 1960s and 1970s, would slowly and unspectacularly improve the lives of a later generation, only to see its work reversed, temporarily, two decades later, so the efforts of czarist doctors, administrators, and teachers were beginning to create a different understanding of life and death in the years before the First World War.

The reforms that would begin this process were introduced in the wake of the emancipation of the serfs in 1861. They were not glamorous, but the *zemstvos*, or local assemblies, that were set up after 1864, would take responsibility for some of the most pressing local issues, including rural development, public health, and education.[18] Individual zemstvos set their own agendas from the 1860s, which meant that some did relatively little, while others—such as the Poltava zemstvo, which was among the first to develop a full-scale network of local medicine—took on wide responsibilities. Funding was a problem, especially in view of the range of tasks that the reforming zemstvos tackled, and the zemstvos' position was always compromised by their narrow social base. The principal objects of their concern, the peasants, had no constitutional power to elect or influence them. They were also suspected by conservatives within the imperial government, many of whom still nurtured fears that too much information, even if it concerned the incidence of measles, might feed the spark of insurrection.[19]

The zemstvos were not revolutionary. Their existence, in fact, coincided with a period of division and regrouping within the revolutionary movement, a time during which, unless you believed in terror, it was beginning to seem that radical and insurrectionary tactics would not work. "Going to the people," the dream of peasant mobilization that had enthralled a generation of radical students in the 1870s, had turned out to be a thankless mission. Young activists, inspired by fantasies of the peasant soul and its instinctive socialism, had set out for the provinces to ignite the embers of primitive revolt.[20] Many were handed unceremoniously to the local police. The peasantry may have been cheated of their patrimony, of the land, by the terms of the emancipation act, but they did not look to earnest young men and women in black coats and spectacles for their answers. They did not trust the doctors, either. It is all the more impressive, in fact, that in a society where all authority was suspect, the modest but ambitious work of these men, and of the other reforming zemstvo officials who supported them, should have made so great an impact.

A growing awareness of the causes and prevention of disease was also apparent in the work of local and municipal authorities. They worked in an atmosphere of suspicion and resistance, and opposition could arise in unexpected places. Cost was always an issue. "The burial of dead bodies in cemeteries in the major population centers represents a serious financial burden for the public authorities," concluded an Interior Ministry report in 1905. Nonetheless, concern about the condition of cemeteries, and measures to ensure the prompt burial of infected corpses, were helping to reduce the impact of typhus and other diseases by 1914.[21]

Better health came at a price, however. For the poor of Moscow and St. Petersburg, the new regulations spelled the end of the traditional intimacy of mourning. Health reform, like urbanization and increasing literacy, would ultimately work against the traditional understanding and commemoration of death. In cases of infectious disease, for instance, the use of open coffins was banned, and for everyone who could not afford a grave plot on the grounds of some popular church, the new provisions meant a long journey to cemeteries that were now located an hour or more from the city center. Twenty thousand corpses a year were being transported by rail from the working-class districts of St. Petersburg to these suburban sites by 1905. The poor were being kept at bay in death if not in life. A single line in the regulations stipulated that no coffin was to be carried past the Winter Palace.[22]

The task the liberals faced would have been daunting in any political context. The cultural pessimists are not wrong to identify long-term problems in Russia. Epidemic disease was rife, its prevention and treatment widely misunderstood. Prayer, not lye or sulfur, was the people's first resort when illness struck, their reflex influenced more directly by the Book of Revelation than by medicine. Other aspects of Russian life were equally deadly. Alcohol, principally vodka, was a major killer, although not really because of the absolute quantities that the people drank. What did the damage was the custom that concentrated the whole business into occasional violent binges. The figures for total alcohol consumption in prerevolutionary Russia were actually lower than those for comparable European countries, including Germany, France, and even Belgium. But when the alcohol that was consumed was almost always vodka, rather than the weaker wine or beer; when each tumbler, as Alexander Herzen noted in the mid-nineteenth century, was "emptied at a gulp"; and when most of the drinking took place on a few specific days—at weddings, wakes, and funerals, for instance, as well as at the scheduled festivals of the church—its impact was devastating. The sight of a drunk lying dead in the snow was not unusual in Russian cities, and drink-related violence was a regular scourge of rural as well as urban life. Overall, the death rate from alcohol in the Russian empire at the end of the old regime was four to five times higher than in Western Europe.[23]

Rural Russia was also especially vulnerable to natural disasters. Emancipation had not left the peasants free to leave the village. Most of them still belonged within the mir, and their collective burden of debt tied them to the soil and to a primitive and unimprovable system; wooden tools, medieval crop rotations, a tolerance—for they had no option—of exhausted, poor, or undrained land. The commune made decisions on everyone's behalf, and it also redistributed the land among its members according—theoretically—to need. It was Europe before enclosure, a three-field strip-farming system, and in many places it had to operate in the most severe climatic conditions. To make matters worse, the most productive regions of the Russian empire were also the most densely populated; according to the census of 1897, there were 150 people per square mile in Ukraine.[24] By the beginning of the twentieth century, the number of people in the czarist empire was increasing each year by 1.6 million, placing an ever-greater stress on agricultural production.[25] A bad harvest, a drop in the price of grain, soil erosion, a plague among the cattle—all these could mean the difference between survival and destitution.

The villages of the Black Earth, the grain-growing belt to the south, in Ukraine and along the Volga, were perpetually liable to crop failure. Grain that was sown in September might freeze in a dry winter if there was too little snow to cover it, hard frosts often held on into May, and drought could bake the soil by mid-July to shrivel the harvest of a promising spring. The peasants were accustomed to hunger; famine seemed to visit on a three- or four-year cycle. In 1891, however, a blistering summer reduced thousands of square miles of crowded farmland in southern Russia to desolation. Upward of 30 million peasants starved.[26] Those who could still walk turned up at railway stations and in provincial towns, begging for food, for money, for work. "Everyone prayed," wrote an official from Orlov district. "In the end, they could only save the children . . . Only robbers and money-lenders had enough to eat."[27] Famine was followed in 1892 by typhus and then cholera, which spread, in a few months, from Astrakhan on the Caspian Sea to the hungry villages of the steppe.[28] The precise number of deaths from famine and disease remains unknown (a little under half a million people are thought to have died of cholera[29]), but Novosel'skii's aggregate figures suggested that a terrible price had been paid. He estimated that Russia's crude death rate, in 1892, had risen to 41 per thousand.[30] Typically, the court and ministries did little to help. Even the officials whose job it was to collect mortality statistics sometimes affected detachment from the crisis, passing questions to each other about what they described as an anomalous decline in population.[31] Material relief, from official sources, was slow to arrive, and usually took the form of repayable loans. The victims of the famine relied, in the end, upon the charity of Russia's small but outraged middle class.[32]

Hunger and typhus were the scourges of the countryside; but in the towns there were other diseases, too, and violence, including suicide (although this was still rare), was more prevalent as a cause of death than in the villages. Economic growth was beginning to change the way the people worked, lived, and died. Some industries, and especially textiles, continued to base themselves near centers of rural population, and drew upon the entire village, including women and children, for their workforce. By 1914, however, two massive investment booms, in the 1890s and again on the eve of the First World War, had also transformed the skylines and factory districts of cities like St. Petersburg, Moscow, Odessa, and Baku. The populations of these cities swelled, more than doubling between 1897 and 1914, as the young men came—on foot, by rail, on the backs of tradesmen's carts—from their provincial homes, unskilled, often hungry, unprepared. They would live in crowded barracks, grateful for a bed, working ten- or twelve-hour shifts, testing their place in the new world, sometimes learning revolution.

They came, for the most part, on their own. The ones who were married were unlikely to bring their wives, so that a work contract that had started as a temporary experiment (or a desperate last throw) could easily stretch into years of separation. The population census of 1897 showed, for example, that while 52.9 percent of male workers living in Moscow were married, only 3.8 percent were heads of households living with their wives.[33] The regulation of industry proceeded slowly, though an eleven-and-a-half-hour day was imposed in 1896 after the St. Petersburg textile workers' strike.[34] Industrial accidents and diseases were common, and home life could be as deadly as any work—the factory districts were ill supplied with clean water, and for the most part they were dark, overcrowded, and choked with fumes.[35]

For all these reasons, it was the young men who were dying in disproportionate numbers in the new industrial centers. Tuberculosis was a major cause of this, and also typhus, which accounted for a quarter of the deaths of men in their twenties in St. Petersburg, the capital, in the years before 1914.[36] Detailed statistics from different precincts of the major cities would underline the link between urban poverty and death. The connection was not something that the demographers were able to make public, but their raw data were clear enough. While death rates in the prosperous quarters of cities like Moscow, St. Petersburg, and Kiev were well below the national average, neighboring slum areas suffered from exceptionally high mortality rates. In 1870 the death rate in the best district of St. Petersburg was lower than 17 per thousand, while in parts of the city's working-class Narva district, it was nearly three times as high—in excess, in fact, of 50 per thousand.[37]

The deaths of young men in the cities were striking because in the villages it was the women, the most-abused, poorest-nourished, and often the hardest-working members of the patriarchal peasant household, who were dying in their twenties.[38] The most appalling statistics, however, related to children. Basic preventive medicine, including prenatal care and immunization programs, has reduced levels of infant mortality everywhere in the world in the last fifty years. In sub-Saharan Africa, for instance, the rate of mortality among children in their first year of life is currently about 103 per thousand. In Afghanistan, which in 1996 was the worst country in the world in which to be born, it was 165 per thousand.[39] But these rates do not look excessively high when compared to those in the developed nations of Europe at the end of the nineteenth century. The comparable figure for Germany, for example, was 163 per thousand, and for Britain, 111.

When all the qualifications have been considered, however, czarist Russia remains in a class by itself. The counting of infant deaths was not an exact science. Many babies were born and died before either fact could be recorded. Cases of infanticide were also more common in the Russian countryside than in comparable parts of Europe, and although the courts were usually lenient with the mothers who faced trial, many more escaped detection altogether.[40] The official figures for infant mortality are almost certainly underestimates. Even so, they give an overall rate in Russia from 1911 to 1913 of 273 per thousand. It is likely that the true rate exceeded 300 per thousand.[41] In some places, and infamously in children's homes in the big cities, the rate was almost twice as high. A baby born in some parts of industrial Moscow in the first decade of the twentieth century, in other words, was more likely than not to die before its first birthday.[42]

It is against this background that the efforts and successes of zemstvo medicine must be assessed. It is easy to say that provision was inadequate. The number of doctors in Russia roughly doubled between 1870 and 1910, from twelve thousand to twenty-five thousand, but in a population that was rapidly increasing, and whose size, in 1897, was already more than 125 million, there was no room for complacency. Isolation put a strain on the doctors, too. The despair that many of them suffered—graduates from St. Petersburg, from Kiev, the students of internationally reputed specialists—as they settled and grew melancholy in their adopted provinces, became the stuff of literature. "Today I received last week's newspapers," writes Bulgakov's fictional Dr. Polyakov in his diary. "Alone every evening. I light the lamp and sit down. Perpetual blizzards . . . I'm sick of it." Polyakov, who has gone to a remote town to forget a woman who abandoned him, becomes addicted to the morphine in his own dispensary; the darkness becomes intolerable, and eventually he shoots himself.[43]

Bulgakov's own medical career also began and ended in the countryside. He survived in his bleak village for less than two years before returning to Kiev. Anton Chekhov, too, found a better home for his talents in literature than medicine. For each of these, however, there were hundreds of provincial doctors who somehow kept their practices alive, and several of them, including E. Ya. Zalenskii, would later publish diaries about their work.[44] Like any doctor's diary, these rely on the reader's collusion, the sharing of confidences, the glimpses that, as readers—literate people, of whom there were precious few in rural Russia—we can catch of one man's encounters with the quaint, the colorful, the eternally unregenerate peasant. We can follow Zalenskii into a mildewed hut, anxious, as ever, as he wonders how he will talk to the family, a little squeamish as he observes the lice, the smell. When our eyes are accustomed to the darkness, we can watch him as he bends over the old man on his filthy sheet, sharing his professional rage in the face of superstition, his frustration as, once again, the wife prefers a prayer or sorcery to his learning and his pills. The icon in the corner protects no one, the herbs and the grease were never part of the university's pharmacopoeia. It is the kind of material that another writer might have used principally to entertain. In Russia, however, and in Zalenskii's hands, it is clear that the culture that underlies the stories is one of service.

The science that czarist doctors practiced was social medicine, the fight against disease as it affected entire communities. "Russian physicians adopted a distinctive social position," writes one of their historians, "an overriding interest in public health and welfare . . . Working primarily in the public sector, their daily tasks affected the general welfare, and their concerns centered on public needs."[45] Unfortunately, it was precisely this relationship with local government, with the state, that compromised them in the eyes of peasant patients. State-funded doctors were all too easily identified with the hated "authorities," the "powers" (*vlasti*), whose ranks included tax inspectors and the police. The Orthodox Church, at the local level, did little to encourage a more cooperative attitude, suspicious as it was of formal reason, and doubtful of the morality of interfering with the will of God. "The doctor is neither brother, nor lord [*barin*], nor priest," wrote Zalenskii. "And so he is alien to the peasants." Hospitals, too, were the objects of fear. "Praise to Christ, and keep me from the hospital," was a common prayer, muttered by peasants as they waited for the doctor's visit. The village gossip held that "they don't give you any medicine there. They just cut, cut—they can take away your arm or your leg . . . It would be better to die in one piece." There were even rumors that hospitals were processing plants for human fat.[46]

The disease that focused these prejudices most sharply was cholera. In June 1892 rumors of an outbreak brought panic to the small town of Khvalinsk, in Saratov province. People began to repeat the stories they had heard from further down the river, anxious that the police were preparing to imprison them, convinced that local doctors were in league with a group of foreigners and that they had accepted money to destroy the "pitiable Orthodox." "They have already made the coffins for us," ran the story. "They have dug our grave, they have bought quicklime, and they have got hooks ready to drag us there." Visitors to the area brought rumors of quarantine ships on the Volga, crewed by corpses; of the coffins piled up in the cholera barracks in Saratov; and of the twitching bodies that had nonetheless been certified as dead.[47]

The town found its scapegoat in the person of the most senior local doctor, A. M. Molchanov. On the eve of the fatal day, this man had spent several hours discussing the cholera riots in Saratov with colleagues from the local public health services. The discussion was interrupted when he was handed an anonymous note warning him to leave the town at once or face a public lynching. Instead of fleeing, however, Molchanov and his colleagues requested protection from the local militia—instructing them to keep their weapons well concealed—and issued a leaflet to explain the treatment of cholera. They promised, optimistically, that no one would be kept in the hospital against his wishes. It was a brave move, but a rumor that the town's water supply had turned red brought thousands of angry men and women into the streets that evening. The town of Khvalinsk was calling for Molchanov's blood.

Molchanov's last mistake was to address the crowd himself. A local priest, Father Karmanov, remonstrated with his "Orthodox brothers," but to no avail. "We're not going to die," they shouted. "He is!" Molchanov was beaten unconscious to the ground. He recovered for long enough to plead for his life. According to a report that appeared in the next issue of *The Physician,* the mob then "butchered him beyond recognition . . . tossed him aside, and left to menace others . . . Ruffians jeered the corpse and peasant women spat in its face."[48] No one had the courage to collect the body. "Even the next day the dead Molchanov was not left in peace," recorded Zalenskii. "Some people threw stones at his corpse, while others spat or swore at it."[49]

Cholera was a disease that few in Russia understood, and it had the power, because of its terrible effects, to release the savagery of a whole town with unique force. The murder of Molchanov shocked the medical profession, but obstructive responses to the epidemic were not uncommon. In one area, the people protected themselves by marching around the village in a procession headed by icons, banging drums and shouting, "Death! Get out!" In places where there was any to be had after the famine, they drank pepper vodka and ate bitter herbs, and everywhere the pious went to their priests in search of cures and medical advice.[50]

Zalenskii cannot have been the only doctor to find, in the early twentieth century, that greasy scraps of paper, scrawled with prayers or charms, were thought by some to be the most effective means of keeping death at bay.[51] It could take all his powers of persuasion to prise these from their owners' feverish grasp. "In the name of the Father, the Son, and the Holy Ghost," one of the miracle-working incantations began. Zalenskii took the paper to the door of the hut where an old man lay dying and held it to the light to read the rest. It was a garbled mix of peasant religion, magic, and misogyny:

> Unexpectedly the sea parted and from it emerged twelve virgins with wild, unkempt hair and among them were Diofa and Chudeif and three evangelists Luke, Mark and John the Divine came up to greet them. They asked them what virgins are you. We are the children of Tsar Irlug. And where are you going. To the world of men to the people of God. To break the bones of Fomin Vasilii's weary body but when we see or hear this text we will flee from Vasilii the servant of God. The evangelists seized the girls and beat them within an inch of their lives. Amen.[52]

As Zalenski observed elsewhere in his diary, many of the poorest peasants could only be persuaded to take effective measures against epidemic disease, including the disinfection of clothing and the prompt burial of corpses, when they were "afraid of punishment."[53]

In spite of the people's mistrust, however, zemstvo medicine made significant changes to the treatment and popular understanding of disease. Anton Chekhov, who abandoned his books for several months to help with the cholera epidemic in Moscow province, declared in August 1892 that "they performed miracles in Nizhnii that would force even Tolstoy to respect medicine and the contributions of cultured people to public life."[54] The anxious Bulgakov was surprised by the respect he had earned after fifteen months in the village, exhausted by his growing practice, working eleven hours a day. In the wake of a later epidemic of cholera, even Zalenskii observed, tentatively, that among younger people a respect for the new medicine was supplanting the old ways. "They are visiting the old women [*baby*] less often these days," he wrote in 1908.[55] There was a long way to go. The grip of suspicion in the countryside was still strong. But the dislocation and panic of war and revolution, the desperate clutching at the past, after 1917, in the face of terror—all this was the reversing of a process, and not, in simple terms, a case of continuity.

Fifteen years after the devastating famine of 1891–92, at the end of the summer of 1906, the harvest in southern Russian failed again. The streets of provincial towns such as Khvalinsk, Saratov, Penza, and Nizhnii Novgorod filled again with hungry beggars; railway stations attracted ragged crowds; the dusty squares drew mothers with their swollen children, orphans, and refugees, all waiting hopelessly for rescue, their gums bleeding from scurvy, their faces disfigured by open sores. In the Crimea, which was the worst-affected region of all, the hunger was harder to bear through that first winter because of a shortage of firewood. The Tartars, it was rumored, were selling their daughters in the local markets to pay for grain and fuel.[56] Among the fertile hills of the Crimean peninsula, around the whole north shore of the Black Sea, and along the Volga almost as far north as Moscow itself, people were dying.

This time, the voluntary agencies, including the Red Cross, were on the scene more quickly, and the local zemstvos also took a hand in organizing famine relief with such resources as they had. Far away in St. Petersburg, an organization clumsily called the "central committee for providing medical and food aid to the population that is suffering from harvest failure" began to meet under the auspices of the Ministry of the Interior.[57] It was a step in the direction of organized famine relief, an advance on 1891, but most of the czar's officials stayed in their comfortable offices, coordinating paper, and the sums involved, when it came to real money, bags of flour, or milk and sausage for the children, were pitifully small. As ever, too, the local relief societies were informed that any money they might receive was to be treated as a loan. "It takes just five kopecks a day to feed a child," the volunteers lamented in reply. (There are a hundred kopecks in a ruble. When the harvest was good, a village priest could expect a fee of three rubles for conducting a funeral service.)

In May 1907 the paper *Birzhevye vedomosti,* St. Petersburg's equivalent of the *Wall Street Journal,* published an extract from a doctor's notes after her visit to a public kitchen in the Simbirsk district, on the Volga. The doctor was shown around by a woman health official from the local zemstvo. Her guide began by telling her the facts, explaining that between forty and fifty children were fed at the kitchen every day, not usually on meat, but on hot soup, kasha, or tea with sugar. The money to provide all this was running out, and so were the stocks of donated flour from Moscow. Feeding the adults was almost impossible. If the mothers came at all, the zemstvo worker said, they would try to take the food away, to keep it for their children, failing to help themselves. "There have been so many deaths!" she sighed as they walked through to her own small room. "So many flies everywhere! It's hard here, especially when you look at the children. The little ones don't even cry anymore. They only moan, and they moan sorrowfully, but almost without making a sound at all. Their voices have become so weak, so quiet."

As she left the village, almost weeping herself, the doctor looked around at the ruined huts, the dust, and at the silent, apathetic orphan, the last survivor of a family of ten, whom she had decided to take with her. "It was quiet," she wrote. "And all around were new graves, new crosses, without inscriptions, abandoned, wordless, silent."[58] Her notes, and the appeals of other visitors from the capital, helped stir the liberal consciences of donors in the north, but this was still a famine that claimed thousands of peasants' lives.

The suffering in the villages was a far cry from the splendor of the court, or even from the gratifying plots and counterplots that St. Petersburg's political elite was hatching as it prepared for the forthcoming elections to the state Duma that spring. The gap between rich and poor in prerevolutionary society was so wide, and the physical distances between the capital and the stricken countryside so great, that the peasants in their fly-blown huts might well have thought themselves abandoned by all help. The czar, to his poor subjects, was an abstraction, a man but not a human presence, too exalted to be involved with the real business of their daily lives. This was a view that Nicholas II, Russia's last czar, appeared wholeheartedly to share. Although there was increasing pressure, from the liberal and reforming middle class, for the state to take more notice of the poor, the czar himself remained aloof from his people, preferring the idea of a spiritual communion with the nation to the earthy business of real government.

His reign began with a catastrophe that demonstrated this aloofness in full public view. In 1896 the accession of the new Tsar was marked by massive public celebrations. As the holiday began, a huge crowd gathered on Khodynka field, on the edge of Moscow, eager to take part, and drawn, perhaps, by stories of free food and commemorative souvenirs. But the site had not been adequately prepared, and there was some word that the supply of decorated mugs and sausage was about to run out. The crowd pushed, surged, and panicked. Fourteen hundred people were crushed to death, and another six hundred were injured. The czar, however, continued with his public engagements, beginning with a ball at the French ambassador's that evening.[59] Nicholas's response to the disaster at Khodynka outraged the Russian public, and other events in the next ten years would ensure that it was not forgiven.

Mere negligence, however, was not the autocracy's only failing when it came to the preservation of human life. Many of the deliberate policies of the Russian ruling class seemed calculated to encourage unnecessary death. It was not an abstract "system" that disdained to preserve lives, but policymakers within a government blindly wedded to the perpetuation of a certain type of autocratic monarchy, a certain status for the empire, and time-honored rules for social conduct. Nicholas II's government went to war twice, in 1904 and again in 1914. In each instance, Russia's involvement was unnecessary, in that it was fighting not to defend itself against aggression but rather to assert its position within an international system. On both occasions, an outmoded honor code among the officers, a pig-headed refusal to retreat, would cost its armies dear. "Among the mass of officers," wrote the army priest O. G. Shavel'skii, "there prevailed the view that the military art was courage, daring, and a readiness to die bravely, and the rest was not really important."[60]

The same mentality—a casual approach to the deaths of ordinary men and women—was evident in the government's response to increasing civil unrest. In 1905 and again in 1912, Russian troops would fire on civilians, killing hundreds, shocking and then depressing a population that was growing weary of the excuses its czar and ministers would always offer. The violence left little room for peaceful, liberal compromise. "There has never been so much tension," a secret police reporter wrote after the massacre of strikers at the Lena goldfields in 1912. "People can be heard speaking of the government in the most unbridled tones . . . It is a long time since even the extreme Left has spoken in such a way."[61]

The Russo-Japanese war, which began in February 1904, was ostensibly fought for territory in Korea and Manchuria. Typically, the Russian government regarded it enthusiastically as a solution to domestic problems. It was to be a patriotic spectacle, a distraction from the siren whispers of the revolutionaries, the "short, victorious war" that Interior Minister Vyacheslav von Plehve sought so eagerly. Plehve's gamble soon proved to be disastrous. The war was expensive, placing more burdens on a discontented people. Among its costs, by the summer of 1905, was the loss of almost the entire Baltic fleet, which was sunk by the Japanese at Port Arthur with scarcely any damage to their own vessels. Newsreel pictures of the war brought every detail to the attention of a horrified civilian population in the larger Russian cities, belying the complacent statements of the War Ministry. Russian propaganda described the Japanese as "knock-kneed, weaklings . . . a puny kind of monkey, invariably dubbed 'Japs' or 'macaques,'" but public opinion was not fooled.[62] The whole empire felt the weight of military disgrace. Individual families also suffered as the first news of Russian casualties began to filter back. By the summer of 1904, there were riots at recruitment stations and angry demonstrations along six thousand miles of railway line as the trains carried troops away to the eastern front.[63]

Plehve himself would not live to see the consequences of his policy. He was assassinated by socialist revolutionaries in July 1904.[64] His successors failed to quell the protests of hungry workers, anxious conscripts, radical trade unionists, liberals, intellectuals, and constitutionalists. As the news of successive defeats reached the capital, a group of industrial workers, led by a priest, Father Gapon, planned to take a peaceful protest to the gates of the Winter Palace. Gapon himself, who worked in collusion with members of the secret police, attempted to cancel the march in early January when it began to look as if there would be a confrontation with the state. The idea was to contain the workers' radicalism, not to inflame it. Unfortunately, the autocrat on the other side of the barricades was a man to whom the idea of appeasement was entirely alien.

The march took place on 9 January 1905. Its organizers still hoped to keep it peaceful, advising the participants to carry icons and crosses, checking their ranks to make sure there were no troublemakers, encouraging a mood of humble petition among men and women whose concerns included hunger, poverty, and the exhaustion of a relentless northern winter. It was all useless. The famous Bloody Sunday culminated in the snow on Palace Square. Mounted detachments of the army fired on the ranks of hymn-singing marchers as they assembled opposite the Winter Palace, and others spurred their horses into the panic-stricken crowd, cutting their faces and arms with sabers, trampling the fallen in a thunder of hooves. Even the marchers who were heading for the Winter Palace, on Trinity Bridge and along the streets that led to the Neva from the working-class Vyborg Side, came under fire as groups of soldiers were ordered to head them off by any means. No one knows how many people died. The estimates vary from two hundred to five thousand.[65] Whatever the figure, however, the callousness of the slaughter horrified the whole nation.

The government had prepared for its own violence by warning the hospitals, the previous evening, to expect casualties. The carnage still overwhelmed the city's medical services. The bodies of the dead and wounded were taken wherever there was space to treat them. Many were carried by strangers, lost to their families, so that the frightened relatives, anxious about a missing brother or child, would have to tramp from hospital to hospital, begging the weary clerks to check their records once more, desperately resisting the fear that the answer really lay in the morgue. The next day, and the next, hospitals posted lists of names, but these were always incomplete.[66]

The government's cynicism is still chilling. As if the order to fire were not evidence enough of its callous attitude toward civilian lives, its actions after the massacre included a deliberate policy of concealment. A partial statement by the police, giving details of some of the casualties, was wrung from the authorities in the weeks after 9 January, but no one ever proposed to tell the truth. On the night of 11 January, the bodies of protesters were secretly collected from each of the city's hospital mortuaries and transported by rail, under heavy guard, to a clandestine burial site in the Preobrazhenskoe cemetery.[67] The pain of loss, for each bereaved family, would be compounded now by permanent uncertainty. These bodies had no funeral, there were to be no conversations by their unmarked grave, no eggs or vodka, no prayers or scattered soil. The single mass grave was a long way from the city center, two hours, on average, on slow suburban trains. That meant, as the authorities had hoped, that it would not be used as a public platform, but it was also too remote to be included in the regular visits that even urban mourners still made according to the habits of their childhood.

Bloody Sunday was the catalyst for strikes, protests, and disturbances across the Russian empire. The revolution of 1905, an uprising that began without formal organization, would force even Nicholas II to grant a limited series of concessions, including the famous (and grudging) constitution of October. Russia was to have a parliament, the Duma, although its powers were limited, and the country would see elections at last. There was also to be a reform of agriculture, including an end to rural debt. But the concessions were accompanied by threats. The wider goals of the urban revolution—the wage demands, the attempted creation of trade-union democracy, the requests for better conditions of life—these were not met. The constitution was to be the autocracy's final word. From 1906 a new prime minister, Petr Stolypin, would begin to restore the government's writ with a gruesome series of reprisals. The prime minister was so enthusiastic about hanging that the rope became known as "Stolypin's necktie."

Stolypin began to implement a series of reforms, notably a cautious privatization of agriculture, the liberation of the most enterprising peasants from the stultifying grip of the commune, from superstition, want, and the straitjacket of the three-field system. The plan was to allow some peasants to consolidate their holdings and farm as yeomen entrepreneurs. Stolypin believed that reforms like this, accompanied by constitutional reform and economic growth, could transform the Russian political landscape in decades. But the scheme needed time—it would never have that before 1914—and it called for civil peace. Stolypin's response to revolutionary violence was driven by paternalistic rage, but the provocation, as he saw it, was real. Frustrated by the limited achievements of 1905, and encouraged by the success of their assassination campaigns, sections of the revolutionary movement continued to take action even after the constitution had been granted. Between October 1905 and September 1906, 3,611 czarist officials were killed or wounded. Detachments of the main revolutionary parties not only indulged in high-profile political murder; they also organized bank robberies and other forms of "expropriation" (as they called it) in order to fund their work. "The violence so notable in the Tsarist empire was not an exclusively Russian phenomenon," writes one of its historians, citing examples from Europe, India, and the United States, "but nowhere was it more widespread than in Tsarist Russia."[68]

"Terror," however, was a word that the government chose to interpret broadly. Local military courts were permitted to hand out death sentences for a range of offenses, including revolutionary violence, revenge killings, murder, looting, sedition, and sabotage. When state security was involved, the courts could be replaced by local commissions, or even by a single man at a desk with a pistol at his elbow. Public hanging was no longer the norm, but capital punishment, in the Russian empire, would become little more in these years than civic instruction by other means.[69] The law provided that people under twenty-one or over seventy years of age should not be executed, but in other respects it was ruthless. Women who were pregnant at the time of sentence, for instance, were allowed to live for just forty days after they had given birth.[70] The church, meanwhile, continued to advocate a pious devotion to God and czar. Its leading members had no problem with the death penalty. If anything bothered them, in fact, other than the ravages of progress, rationalism, and the Antichrist, it was the ending, at a time of moral crisis, of public execution as an educational spectacle.[71]

It is largely on the basis of episodes like the Stolypin reaction that czarist Russia has come to be regarded among historians as an extreme example of repressive statehood, a government that deserves its reputation for cruelty and summary justice. There were many reformers within Russia at the time who would have agreed, and by the early twentieth century they had collected impressive amounts of evidence in support of their case. The young M. N. Gernet, a statistician and sociologist, produced a map that graphically made the point. The capitals of the world were shaded in darkening shades of gray, and stylized nooses, guillotines, and pistols specified the methods of execution used by the different governments. Among the regimes for which the statistics were known, the Russian empire held the record. According to Gernet's figures, 1,340 people faced execution there in 1908. Since he did not know how many of the 505 people condemned to death in British India in 1906 had actually died, he listed the United States next in his table, but it was a poor second. In the relevant year only 116 of its citizens had been executed.[72]

Gernet's work, however, was in part a deliberate polemic against capital punishment, and despite his careful footnotes, there were things that he chose to overlook. The most important was the fact that the autocracy's record on capital punishment was not consistently the worst in Europe.[73] The violence by which Russia's political culture has often been identified was actually, in general terms, most closely associated with the major turning points in the country's history. The years 1850 to 1862, for example, before and immediately after the emancipation of the serfs, saw a marked increase in the number of hangings in Russia. The excesses of 1906 to 1910 followed the abortive 1905 revolution. Russia's history of violence, like its record on education or public health, was not an unrelieved tale of darkness. To say this, however, is not to exonerate the regime of Nicholas II. The fact that there were always choices—the czars, after all, were among the best-educated men in Europe, and had access, if they wished it, to excellent political advice—puts the fact of their deliberate selection of the most damaging policies into the coldest light.

Violence by the state affected the whole society. It evoked extreme responses from the discontented and even from reformers. The spectacle of official brutality was a propaganda bonus to the advocates of terror, and it confirmed the worst predictions of activists in the revolutionary movement. But insurrection was only one of several possible responses. More common was a mood of numb despair. The revolutionaries at least believed that there might, one day, be progress. Others were less sanguine. In 1913, on the eve of the First World War, the jurist N. S. Tagantsev wrote a passionate essay on the effects of judicial murder. He had not been an enemy of change, he explained; he had welcomed Russia's twentieth century as a new beginning, bright, as he saw it, with the potential for dispelling the ignorance, barbarity, and lawlessness that had darkened the past. On the other hand, as he wrote, "It is painful to know that the dawn of our new order takes its colours from streaks of blood."[74]

His principal argument was that violence on the part of the state set a grim example to society as a whole. Death, of itself, was less of a problem than the spectacle of cold-blooded retributive killing. What he went on to write might have served as a more general commentary on death in Russia then and later:

> Catastrophic mortality is not unusual in the life of a nation: it is inescapable as a curse of nature; it is unavoidable, or believed to be unavoidable, as an evil within the state. Earthquakes, floods, all kinds of other elemental disasters can cause, and often do cause, the deaths of thousands, and even tens of thousands, of people. They also chill the human soul; and they bring, without discrimination, suffering, mutilation, and death . . . And any contemporary war, even a mere battle waged with modern weapons of human destruction . . . will destroy the health or lives of many thousands, people who die in the name of patriotic service . . . And then there are the victims of the new Moloch—of hard economic conditions, of misery. There are thousands and tens of thousands of these; children, youths and adults dying of hunger, of the lack of healthy air . . . That is why I repeat: the horror is not the number of condemned, the number of artificial deaths, for itself alone, but also the consequences that these sentences are having for our national life.[75]

The consequences that Tagantsev had in mind included the spectacle of czarist Russia's death row, where "hundreds, and more than hundreds" daily awaited execution, the contempt for human dignity that it represented, and the fatalistic attitude that ordinary people now showed in the face of unconstrained state violence. But the death penalty's impact in Russia was not exclusively abstract or moral. As a lawyer and an abolitionist, Tagantsev would also have known of the spate of deaths among Russian children between 1908 and 1914. The problem was that playground games of "death penalty," inspired by the prevailing culture, sometimes went out of control. In one case, a girl of five accidentally strangled her three-year-old brother after condemning him to death in a mock trial in their nursery. In others, school bullies would stage larger-scale "courts" (sometimes they called them "military courts") and condemn fellow pupils to "death." If the children panicked, or the bully went too far, the "sentence" was carried out all too realistically before the eyes of terrified onlookers.[76]

"Death penalty" was not the only game schoolchildren played. The years after 1905 also saw an epidemic of teenage suicide. The Ministry of Education had kept files on this from the 1890s, but the numbers involved were generally insignificant. Only seventeen children took their own lives in 1899, for instance. By 1908, however, when forty-one St. Petersburg schoolchildren committed suicide in a single month, even the newspapers were beginning to talk of an epidemic. The peak years were 1907 to 1911, but the problem haunted the schools until 1914. In general, the church's view prevailed that suicide was a sign of sinful weakness. Teenagers who shot or hanged themselves lacked "Christian principles," or suffered from "abnormalities."[77] "Only an awareness of our responsibility before God for our deeds on earth and also a consciousness of the need for each of us to carry his cross without complaint," said *Sovremennoe obozreniye* (*Contemporary Review*), could save the young from self-destruction. Suicide, which had become "a fashion" was evidence, to another paper, of "a light-minded, indifferent attitude to life and death, and a weakening or even absence of healthy life energy."[78]

It is the ministry's own collection of suicide notes and schoolteachers' reports that suggests a different kind of answer. There is a Latin vocabulary book in one of these, for instance, each page of which, at first, is neatly scored to make two columns for carefully written Russian words (*lyublyu, dumayu*) and their Latin equivalents (*amo, cogito*). The back pages, however, are blotted and scrappy, and there are doodles of gallows, skulls, and crosses. The last entry in the vocabulary section is written in an elaborate gothic script. "What is life?" it asks. "What is the Ideal?"[79] The teachers who prepared a report on the boy after his death were at a loss to find a simple cause for his despair. "What meaning can life have," concluded another final note, this time the work of a girl in her early teens, "when alien, rough people can take it from you at any moment?"[80]

The epidemic was later attributed, by the experts, to the so-called Werther effect, a recognized pattern of emulation that creates clusters of suicides around a number of high-profile cases.[81] Even at the time, however, the liberals who took this more informed view agreed that the malaise was evidence of a wider crisis. The harsh regime in Russian schools, which so terrified some youngsters that, by their own admission, they preferred death to the prospect of examination failure, was part of it, and so was the violent culture of corporal punishment, playground fights, and dueling.[82] Individual suicide notes also mention the usual preoccupations of teenagers—unrequited love, a sense of personal worthlessness, unfulfilled longing for adventure. But confrontational politics were pervasive. The gang wars in some schools reflected national political feuds, with groups who called themselves the "Black Hundreds" (after the extreme right-wing thugs of the time) attacking others known as "Reds." Students who refused to join in at all were boycotted and bullied, while the opposing sides not only fought but refused to meet each other in any context at the school or out of it.[83]

It was through playground dramas like this that relatively privileged children (at least they were at school) were able to vent their anxieties about the greater violence of the adult world. Maxim Gorky had no hesitation in blaming the institutional and state violence of czarism for the brutality that would later darken the revolution. "The conditions in which the Russian people lived in the past," he wrote in 1917, "could foster in them neither respect for the individual, nor awareness of the citizen's rights, nor a feeling of justice—these were conditions of absolute lawlessness, of the oppression of the individual, of the most shameless lies and bestial cruelty."[84]

High politics, the insensitivity of the court, was not the only possible source of this "bestial cruelty." The continuation of practices like public flogging in the countryside can hardly have encouraged a conciliatory attitude among the people. Economic conditions, too, generated despair, insecurity, and violence. The rage that drove a group of peasants to burn their landlord's house or property—the fires were called "red cockerels" in the countryside—was as much a product of economic and social uncertainty as of political exclusion. The poverty that was part of rural life was made bitter by frustrated hope, by debt, and by the unexpected challenges and anxieties that an economy in the throes of industrial and urban development inevitably provoked. The same pressures operated in the towns—conflicts between established populations and newcomers, suspicion about wage deals, fears of conspiracy and betrayal.

By far the ugliest manifestation of these tensions was the pogrom. The word itself is common to the Russian and Yiddish languages, and its root meaning is "devastation." The many cholera riots of the nineteenth century, the most extreme of which involved the murder of Molchanov, were described as pogroms against the medical profession, evoking images of an angry mob, irrational violence, and the victimization of scapegoats. The most frequent targets for provincial ignorance, chauvinism, and brutality, however, were permanent, identifiable outsiders, and in the areas where they had been permitted to settle, that usually meant the Jews. Anti-Semitism had a long history in the Russian empire, but the pogroms of the late nineteenth and early twentieth centuries were not simply the enactments of ancient racial hatreds. At other times, Jews and Russians, or Jews and Ukrainians, Poles and Belorussians, could live together without incident, and there were parts of the empire where entire urban cultures relied on the interaction between the majority—Ukrainians, for instance—and large minorities, including Jews, but also comprising others—Armenians, Germans, Poles, or Greeks, many of them identified by trade and culture rather than by race. Pogroms had specific causes, but they also testified to the criminal negligence, and the complicity, of individual officials in the hierarchies of church and state.

It was no accident, then, that the worst attacks of the late czarist era all happened in the years 1903 to 1906, the time of greatest unrest, of Russia's humiliating Japanese war, of debt and shortage, and also of the 1905 revolution. All that was needed in any case was a pretext, and the anti-Semitic yellow press was always ready with a story. One of the cruelest pogroms of the period, the 1903 Easter massacre in Kishinev, was sparked by the discovery, in the nearby town of Dubossary, of the murdered body of fourteen-year-old Mikhail Rybachenko.[85] The boy had disappeared almost a week earlier after attending church with his parents. Subsequent investigation proved that he had been stabbed by one of his uncles, but this did not prevent a rumor from circulating, encouraged by local anti-Semitic newspapers, that he had been the victim of ritual murder by Jews. His stab wounds were explained by the tale that Jews needed human blood to make their Passover matzos. The gossip became more fantastic—he had been found with puncture marks on his body, they said, his blood had been mysteriously drained, his mouth and eyes had been stitched closed.

The scandal coincided with the Easter holiday, which gave the people time to discuss it, and brought crowds of peasants and traders into the town of Kishinev for the customary street market. The violence that followed was the work of these visiting peasants, together with the local market roughs who drank themselves to a fury on the first evening and then ran riot. They began by destroying property—smashing windows, setting fire to houses and market stalls—but eventually they took to hunting human beings, chasing Jewish men and women through the streets, ignoring their victims' pleas as well as the terrified screams of the onlookers. Several dozen men and women were beaten to death.

Blind rage and drink were among the causes of the Kishinev massacre, but the story did not begin on the provincial town's commercial streets, and it did not end there. The reactionary pamphleteers who had provoked the incident were never punished, and the regional authorities continued to ignore or tolerate their work. The czar himself did not condemn anti-Semitism. His scribbled notes on documents from the time suggest that, like many of his advisers, he held the Jews themselves to be responsible. His officials could have acted sooner. They could, for instance, have denied in public that it was the czar who had personally ordered the killing of Jews, for they knew of the rumor, just as they later knew that Jews had been accused of selling arms to Russia's enemies, the Japanese. There is no need to credit the many conspiracy theories that continue to surround the pogroms of 1903 to 1906; the fact that the authorities refused to issue their brief statements and to make a few arrests is explanation enough.

The legacies of violence like this were difficult to evade. Pogroms would continue after 1917; they were among the most appalling manifestations of Russian insecurity, economic frustration, chauvinism, and rage. Other forms of cruelty, many of them traceable to village feuds and jealousies, also resurfaced in the civil war. It is true that the misery of the First World War helped to shape the early years of Lenin's revolution in its turn, as did the panic associated with the collapse of almost every social institution after 1917. It is unwise to draw too many lines between the old world and the new. But the lessons that some people had learned would not be easy to forget. Habits that had been acquired in the last years of czarism, the anger that had been fomenting through five long decades of reaction, would not evaporate, even in the heat of revolution. Skills that had been acquired in one police force could be applied by others; soldiers who had faced the whips and sabers of the Cossacks would not forget their efficacy.

There would be many tragic ironies. One centered on the cemetery where the bodies of the victims of Bloody Sunday lay in their common grave. In 1929 the Bolshevik government organized a reburial ceremony at the site, bringing uniformed cadets, too young to remember the massacre, to stand in handsome ranks beside the pit. The skeletons were exhumed and placed in coffins, each of them draped with the red flag of revolutionary martyrdom.[86] As the guns saluted, however, and the invited mourners doffed their hats, there were others, not present, who grieved for deaths that were more recent. From 1918 onward, the Preobrazhenskoe cemetery, now renamed and bright with banners, had been adopted by the Bolshevik secret police as a suitable site for the burial of counterrevolutionaries, terrorists, bourgeois, and anyone else unfortunate enough to get in their way.[87] These burials, too, were secret, and the number of the dead, and even their names, remain to be discovered.

Tagantsev, the jurist, was another who must have wondered how much had really changed. He was in his eighties when he came out of retirement, a frail old man, to plead again for mitigation in a case of capital punishment. It was 1921, and the Bolsheviks had just arrested his son. The younger Tagantsev was a professor of geology, a respected figure in St. Petersburg's scientific establishment. The charges of conspiracy against him were obscure. It was not clear, either, why he, and the small group of men who would die with him, had been selected for exemplary justice. The bitterest years of civil war were coming to an end, the accused did not have an obvious connection with counterrevolution. Nonetheless, and despite his father's protestations, the younger Tagantsev was shot in August 1921.[88] Among the people who shared his fate was Nikolai Gumilev, the poet and former husband of Anna Akhmatova, a woman destined to survive the Stalin years with sharp, unblinking fortitude. "Why is this age worse than earlier ages?" she had asked in 1919. "Death is already chalking the doors with crosses, and calling the ravens, and the ravens are flying in."[89]

3

THE PALACE OF FREEDOM

The world of Bolshevism has become a foreign country. Even in Russia the revolutionary program seems absurd these days. The Bolsheviks stirring slogans have lost their magic, and their ideology, whose goals included social justice, freedom from want, the end of class and international conflict, and the perfection of human society on earth, looks like a naive—perhaps a cursed—dream. At best, the Bolshevik Revolution is now interpreted as an experiment that went wrong. Among the people who are blamed for it are Marx and Engels, as well as an elite of revolutionaries whose ideas—as today's Russians insist—were shaped in European exile, through long hikes in the Alps, and not in the factories and prisons of the czarist empire. The implication is clear. Bolshevik government was something imposed from outside, something for which "they," not "we" must be responsible. It was not organic, Russian, but a "regime"; the work, perhaps, of foreigners, outsiders, fanatics, the collective forces of someone else's mad idea of history.

This reinterpretation of the past, in the former Soviet Union, is not a shift of emphasis, the discovery of a different line of debate, but a complete reversal of the previous dogma. Its thoroughness and speed, the overnight revocation of an entire world view, was a surprise to almost every witness at the time. It should not have been. This, after all, is what a revolution means, what it can do, before the eyes of living witnesses and even in an age of film and sound recording, to language and communication, to ideas, and, above all, to memory. Behind the rapid change, however, unexamined habits of thought have persisted, sheltered by enduring social networks for mutual support and protection, and so have many patterns of belief about morality, about ritual, death and afterlife.

It was the same in 1917. The Bolshevik Revolution was never only Marxist, and although it overturned the old world in a few brief months, some habits and beliefs survived, shaping aspects of Soviet culture well into the twentieth century. The revolution was supported, initially at least, by many people whose only practical ambition was to remove the autocracy. The next steps were not always clear, let alone agreed on. While millions believed that they were about to create an entirely new kind of life, a different social order, some changes were given more priority than others, and some were largely ignored.

Religion was contentious. Some wanted to see it swept away, while others regarded it as irrelevant to the immediate political struggle. Attitudes to death itself went largely unexamined by the majority, although a few enthusiasts produced ideas for conquering it, for reimagining the afterlife, for rationalizing burial, for anthems, slogans, and new forms of funerary architecture. The revolutionary movement could be surprisingly traditional in its approach to death, in fact, drawing heavily on the familiar idea of martyrdom. Revolutionary funeral rites, so crucial to the men and women who took part in them, were influenced by the bourgeois fashions of the day as much as by the iconography of European socialism. Like every other aspect of popular culture at the time, they were also marked by the collective experience of the First World War, by images of suffering that could not be made beautiful except by reference to a better future, to heroism and sacrifice. The treatment of death was an aspect of Bolshevik culture that owed as much to the Russian soil on which it had developed as it did to scientific Marxist ideology.

This reality was deliberately obscured, at the time, by Bolshevism's own internationalist rhetoric. The Russian Revolution was always supposed to be a symbol, a moral fable, the example to the international proletariat, an absolute that marked the beginning of an irreversible world historical epoch. The Polish Marxist Rosa Luxemburg, a leading radical in the socialist movement of her adopted Germany, was one of the first, initially, to applaud the revolution on these grounds. As she wrote from a Berlin prison cell in 1918, "The October uprising was not only the actual salvation of the Russian Revolution; it was also the salvation of the honour of international socialism."[1]

For years thereafter, the Soviet Union's own historians worked upon the myth. A weave of peasant wars and urban riots, national liberation movements, crazy millenial dreams, and well-informed campaigns—socialist, feminist, anticlerical, trade unionist, democratic—was simplified and repackaged to become the heroic struggle of the proletariat and poor peasants under the leadership and guidance of the Communist Party of the Soviet Union, Bolsheviks. The result was memorable history. It was also universal property, not just a Russian tale. Everyone could know who the principal characters were, what they wanted, and what happened.

Most of the major actors and events have a standard place in the drama—predictable, two-dimensional—like pantomime characters, perhaps, or the archetypal figures in a classical play. Lenin is the most familiar. As I write, it might still be possible, if you hurry, to visit him in his tomb. These days you will not be vetted by the soldiers at the door, as I was, brusquely jostled until you stand up straight, take your hands out of your pockets, smarten up your tie. It is still not quite acceptable to laugh. The urge may well be there, but so are tears, and so is a certain kind of embarrassment, for here he is, in the electric candlelight, preserved, exposed, and dumb, a little man, balding, ginger, bearded. He has been kept, a cold anachronism.

Unless a very great deal has changed, an old lady in the line beside you will be crying, for he remains her hero. He had such energy, she says, such eyes, and he was devoted to his party and its cause, unsparing in the service of the revolution. The old films bear this out. Even a silent one will show his passion as he speaks. He is in a public hall, a theater, and the crowd is rapt. He talks without notes, his upper body always in motion, his eyes never still, grasping the podium, stabbing the air with an index finger, making fists, his confidence magnificent. The film is black and white, but you know that the banner that hangs triumphantly behind him is, as ever, red; and the cyrillic letters on it form the slogan of the hour: PROLETARIANS OF ALL COUNTRIES, UNITE!

The simple story created by his followers is not hard to tell. The oppressiveness of czarism is already in place, the liberals are failing, and in 1914 the empire lurches into war. Its fate is sealed, for this is an imperialist war, a folly of capitalism; and Russia is not ready to compete—its industry is undeveloped, its infrastructure creaking. The only people who really understand this are the Marxists, and especially Lenin's faction, because they see that Russia's weakness is an opportunity. The revolution they will make will inspire the proletariat across the globe. The workers of the other European nations will seize their chance, the war will drive them to it, and capitalism will fall in Germany, in France, Britain, Italy. There will be revolutions in America—for the crisis will spread to other industrial powers; capitalism is global and already interdependent—and then the colonies will rise up, India, Africa, the oppressed, exploited people of China. The Russian Revolution was never meant, in 1917, to be confined to Russia. As Lenin said in 1917, when he argued for the peace with Germany that would begin the revolutionary process, "to secure an armistice now would mean to win the whole world."[2]

The focus of the drama is St. Petersburg, now renamed Petrograd in deference to the country's Slavic, anti-German mood, and the heroes—beside the Party—are the proletariat, the Petrograd working class. Their revolutionary consciousness has grown since 1905, though Bloody Sunday remains a vivid and inspiring memory. The years of reaction, of Russia's limited parliamentary experiment, brought nothing they could value. They were excluded from the suffrage, continually exploited, banned from associating in their workplace and local soviets (the Russian word means "council"—the original soviets were elected by direct suffrage, a show of hands), controlled and harassed by police and Black Hundreds. The Lena goldfields massacre of 1912 is another turning point, its martyrs added to the numbers of the cause, but until the war of 1914 there seems little immediate hope for change.

The war, however, whose dismal progress soon destroys the remnants of the workers' tolerant patriotism, provides a catalyst for insurrection within the capital and across the country. It takes three years, but by February 1917, the poor of Petrograd are prepared to mount a spontaneous attack upon the czar, on complacency, oppression, hunger, the disastrous record of defeat. There are no leaders—the revolution's future heroes are all in prison, in exile, abroad, or in Siberia—but the collective mood of anger and despair is inspiration enough. Just as they had done in 1905, the Petrograd workers take to the streets—it is International Women's Day—and this time the troops do not obey their orders to keep the peace. Some days of fighting follow, the revolution is not bloodless, but the cause of czarism is lost. Even the Imperial Guards eventually defect, spelling an end to Nicholas II's fantasy of counterrevolution. Ten days after the first shots, on 2 March, the czar, who is still away from home pretending to command the armed forces, will sit alone in his private railway car to compose and sign the document that spells his abdication.[3]

Petrograd is now in chaos. There is no obvious leadership. Almost by default, the last members of the former duma, the fourth duma, elected on the narrowest of suffrages in 1912, have met and will agree to take control on a temporary basis. The provisional government's first leader, from the duma days, is

Prince Lvov, but from July he is succeeded by the charismatic left-winger, thirty-six-year-old Alexander Kerensky. This man enjoys the people's confidence. He is handsome; he smiles and works to please the city crowds, and for a short time the provisional government's reputation rallies. But he cannot regard himself as a permanent leader (whatever dreams in that direction he may have), for the idea is still that the constituent assembly elections must be held and that a legitimate government will then be formed, the one that will lead Russia on to victory and peace.

Meanwhile, however, the workers have remade their soviets, including one, the most powerful, which represents the proletarians and soldiers of the capital, the Petrograd Soviet, although they do not think of it—because it is their own—as part of the official state. It is Lenin who will change all this, as always simplifying, going for the point that he regards as central. "The basic question of every revolution," he writes in *Pravda,* his party's newly legalized newspaper, in April 1917, "is that of state power . . . The highly remarkable feature of our revolution is that it has brought about a dual power . . . Alongside the Provisional Government, the government of the bourgeoisie, another government has arisen, so far weak and incipient, but undoubtedly a government that actually exists and is growing—the Soviets of Workers' and Soldiers' Deputies."[4]

From April 1917, the future leader's line is clear and never wavers (in this, he differs from his lesser followers, several of whom, and notably the renegades, Grigorii Zinoviev and Lev Kamenev, occasionally favor compromise). The only slogan for the Bolsheviks, and the one that distinguishes them from every other revolutionary party, including the other Marxist faction, the Mensheviks, is "All Power to the Soviets." The provisional government, in Lenin's view, will always be "oligarchic, bourgeois, and not a people's government." It cannot provide "peace, bread, or full freedom."[5] In opposing it, the Bolsheviks are simultaneously standing out against the war, and this, too, is deliberate. The war, after all, is "a predatory, imperialist war," and no socialist should support its continuation. "Revolutionary defencism," the position adopted by other Marxist groups, is unworkable. Capitalism itself must be overthrown, in Russia and then in Europe, for while it survives "it is impossible to end the war by a truly democratic peace, a peace not imposed by violence."[6]

Lenin's apparent betrayal of revolutionary Russia's national interests is unpopular at first, for there remains a widespread hope that the provisional government will succeed where the autocracy failed. For a few months, until some time in June, a free Russia enjoys the illusion of boundless possibility. But history cannot be cheated. Defeat attends Brusilov's army in Galicia, while transport chaos, food shortages, strikes, and riots take hold across the country. There is even an abortive insurrection in the capital in July, which has the unfortunate effect of landing several leading revolutionaries in jail and forcing Lenin into exile. But though the July Days provoke a brief reaction, and draw the people closer to the government for a while, the discontent is not assuaged. Members of the main revolutionary parties begin to talk of seizing power, of government by a socialist coalition, uniting the Mensheviks, who, like Lenin, are basically Marxists; the Socialist Revolutionaries, heirs of the populist, pro-peasant parties of the 1870s; and—if it were possible—the cooperative wing of Lenin's Bolsheviks, including men like Kamenev. Their talk begins to focus on a specific date—October 1917—because this is when the Second Congress of Soviets is due to meet.

What happens next was made for propaganda. Kerensky has panicked in the face of growing proletarian unrest, and the measures he is taking are increasingly repressive. There is censorship, the revolutionary press is harassed, and there are rumors that a coup is being planned. In fact, Kerensky has appealed, in September, to General Lavr Kornilov, the conservative "with a lion's heart and a sheep's brain," to advance his troops into the region of the capital. The idea was to threaten, not attack. Kornilov, however, decides to seize the moment and begins an open mutiny. The democratic revolution is in danger. Kerensky has to choose. What he does is to appeal directly to the Petrograd Soviet. He also frees the revolutionary leaders, and it is they who lead the crowds that meet Kornilov's troops and talk them into standing down. Fraternal persuasion is backed up by arms. The Soviet forms a Military Revolutionary Committee to defend the city, and this will not disband. Petrograd is out of danger, the revolution is safe, red banners flutter in the autumn breeze above the stranded carriages of Kornilov's men, and Trotsky, as one of the masterminds of the Military Revolutionary Committee, has seen the nucleus of an insurrectionary force.

Lenin himself is still in hiding, but in September he begins the campaign that will bring his men to power. He bombards the Central Committee of his party with letters. "It is clear that all power must pass to the Soviets," he writes. "It should be equally indisputable for every Bolshevik that proletarian revolutionary power (or Bolshevik power—which is now one and the same thing) is assured of the utmost sympathy and unreserved support of all the working and exploited people all over the world in general, in the belligerent countries in general, and among the Russian peasants especially."[7] The party's task is insurrection, and its goal is proletarian dictatorship, or Bolshevik dictatorship, for, as he says, the two—in the official Soviet version—are really the same thing. Rosa Luxemburg did not dissent. "The Bolshevik tendency performs the historic service of having proclaimed from the very beginning, and having followed with iron consistency, those tactics which alone could save democracy and drive the revolution ahead," she commented. As she saw it, too, the "true dialectic of revolutions" was Lenin's own: "Not through a majority to revolutionary tactics, but through revolutionary tactics to a majority."[8]

The Bolsheviks took power on the night of 24 October 1917. Lenin's proclamation was issued at ten o'clock the following morning. "The Provisional Government has been deposed," he announced. "State power has passed into the hands of the organ of the Petrograd Soviet of Workers' and Soldiers' Deputies—the Revolutionary Military Committee, which leads the Petrograd proletariat and the garrison. The cause for which the people have fought, namely, the immediate offer of a democratic peace, the abolition of landed proprietorship, workers' control over production, and the establishment of Soviet power—this cause has been secured."[9] The most glorious chapter of the official tale hereby comes to an end.

Even a Bolshevik would have realized that a good deal of the detail here was missing. That morning, 25 October, as Lenin's proclamation rolled off the party's press, the Winter Palace was still in government hands. There was also the awkward matter of the Congress of Soviets, and petulant speeches, rifts, and declarations—from the defeated socialist majority, from Mensheviks like Martov, Dan, and others, all of whom had somehow lost their nerve—vowing not to cooperate with the usurpers. More seriously, the Russian empire as a whole had yet to hear about the new regime. The identification of revolutionary interests with Bolshevism was something that the months ahead would test.

Among the immediate problems was the untimely convocation of the constituent assembly, the body that had been elected after the coup, by universal suffrage, to decide on Russia's democratic future. The country had waited months for the elections, which had been deferred by Kerensky throughout that troubled summer, but great hope had been placed in the outcome, a hope for reconciliation and government by consent. When the votes were counted, in late November, the Bolsheviks did not command a majority. "A republic of Soviets is a higher form of democracy than the usual bourgeois republic with a Constituent Assembly," declared Lenin. "There is not, nor can there be, even a formal correspondence between the will of the mass of the electors and the composition of the elected Constituent Assembly."[10] "It took the October

Revolution to expose the fact that Lenin and Trotski were political literalists," writes Lenin's biographer, Robert Service.[11] They meant to rule alone. Russia's first—and for seventy years its only—universally elected body met once, on 18 January 1918; selected a Socialist Revolutionary, Chernov, to lead it; and was dispersed, the following day, by Bolshevik militia.

This was the sticking point for Rosa Luxemburg. What she wrote of Lenin's strategy, the consequences of which she would not live to see (she was murdered by Prussian troops in the wake of a failed revolutionary putsch in Berlin), would be prophetic. "Freedom for only the supporters . . . of one party," she said, "is no freedom at all. Freedom is always and exclusively freedom for the one who thinks differently . . . Without general elections, without unrestricted freedom of the press and assembly, without a free struggle of opinions, life dies out in every public institution, becomes a mere semblance of life, in which only the bureaucracy remains the active element." Her premonition of Soviet Russia's political future was uncanny. In a system of one-party rule, she wrote from her cell, "only a dozen outstanding heads do all the leading, and an elite of the working class is invited from time to time to meetings where they applaud the speeches of the leaders and approve proposed resolutions unanimously . . . a dictatorship, to be sure, not however of the proletariat but only of a handful of politicians."[12]

Luxemburg's critique is famous, and it cuts to the heart of the most important political questions of Leninism. What it does not do, however, is to range outside the world of politics, state politics, and even then the story is defined, obviously, in Marxist terms. This Marxist framework, at its crudest, was one that could be moved, imposed on the histories of other countries; it gave a formula that could be applied to explain, as it would have to do, the failure of the European revolutions of 1918 to 1919, the first to follow Russia's international example.[13] The element of class struggle was idealized, made uniform, as if the classes fitted neatly in their frames, as if, indeed, they existed, as classes, at all. Society, as a player, was reduced to a scheme, a pattern of blocks or a formless mass.

The classic story of Lenin's revolution became, therefore, a story of state power, the struggle to acquire it, to consolidate and use it. As Antonio Gramsci, a different kind of Marxist, would add from a prison of his own, "in Russia, the state was everything. Civil society was primordial and gelatinous."[14] It is a line that Marxists and post-Marxists have continued to repeat. The dissident intellectual Boris Kagarlitsky offered the view, in 1989, that "in Russia, the ruling strata are always trying to impose some kind of western-style development, while the population is always resisting it, either actively or passively."[15] But there is more to life than politics, and even gelatinous societies must use a language, share a culture. State and society interact. The state that grew in Soviet Russia became monstrous, but even that was not a process that remained apart from life, from the people. They did not vote for repression; they did not ask, in simple terms, for the grotesque extremes of Stalinism. But to say only that Lenin's dictatorship was imposed, to look no further than a late-night coup, ignoring the deeper processes of the revolution, the atmosphere of hope, of radicalism, of fear, exasperation, and emergency, is too simple.

The Bolshevik Revolution belongs to the prehistory of this dictatorship. For a brief moment, perhaps until the beginning of 1918, by which time the seriousness of the crisis that would turn to civil war was already inescapable, there was a mood of optimism among the mass of the revolutionary rank and file, the legacy of years through which the hopes and schemes of every kind of radical had still been largely innocent of power. The differences dividing them were untried in a state setting, whatever private feuds they had already run, and it was possible to dream that the overthrow of the twin enemies—autocracy and capitalism—would anyway dissolve the bitterness that still oppressed the mass.

Despite the pluralism within the revolutionary movement, there was still a general sense that history was being made and that it had a single, irreversible trajectory. It was in terms of that—of the collective future of the cause on earth—that revolutionaries and radicals in Russia would make sense of the deaths of their comrades in these years. The metaphors that they used—of suffering, sacrifice, and collective salvation—certainly fitted the established language of the revolution, but they derived from older sources, too. It was still a time of experiment, in other words, a time when death and the memories that it helped create were open to a range of interpretations, and also a time—for the people had little leisure to spend on reinventing this uneconomic, unpolitical aspect of culture—when death was left to manage by itself. It would be several years before the rank and file of revolutionaries would see how controversial even the dead could be.

Nikolai Ernestovich Bauman was killed in one of the riots that broke out in Moscow in the wake of the promulgation of Nicholas II's manifesto in October 1905. He would become a revolutionary hero.[16] Unlike the victims of Bloody Sunday ten months earlier, he was buried with full revolutionary honors, and his funeral was a spectacle that closed the city's central streets for hours. It was a sight that Alexander Pasternak, who was a student in the city at the time, would never forget. He watched the procession from the front steps of the Moscow Art School. "Row upon monotonous row of ten or more," he wrote; the mourners passed, "steady, silent, subdued, hour after hour, they filled the broad Myasnitskaya down to Lyubyanskaya Square. The silence of that moving mass was most menacing; it was so heavy you wanted to scream, till it was broken by voices singing the requiescat, or the valedictory hymn of the time, 'You fell as victims in the fight . . .' Then silence fell once more. The rhythmical ranks paced on below. Rank upon rank upon rank, hour after hour after hour."[17]

Bauman's was a "red" funeral, a revolutionary ritual in a time of censorship. The mourners, marching in the first chill of the Russian autumn, came from the city's factories, from the cramped lanes of the Presnya and the suburbs to the north and east, beyond the Kremlin; they were printworkers, metalworkers, employees from the giant textile mills and the newly founded chemical plants. There were students, too, and members of the revolutionary intelligentsia, Mensheviks, mostly, since they were the strongest Marxist group in Moscow at the time, but also nonaligned, nonparty radicals, united for the moment by a shared desire for change. Within the lines of marchers there were knots of friends, and people who had come from the same plant or district, but the crowds at these mass gatherings did not know one another, and the dreams that motivated them, though momentarily focused on a single act of mourning, were varied and even incompatible.

Radicalism of this kind was not created from above. It was born in the factories, the mills; it was discussed after hours; it fed on utopian dreams, some of them Marxist, but others drawn from Tolstoy, from the half-remembered teachings of old peasant sects, from millenarian readings of the Bible, or from the popular new genre of science fiction.[18] It is true that revolutionary activists gave formal instruction to selected workers, gathering them in secret study circles to pore together over the forbidden texts, and many people met and read their Marx this way.[19] But even willing students were not empty vessels waiting to be filled. They formed their own impressions of the city, of the good community, and even of the liberating possibilities of technology; and they also had their own ideas about the paths to freedom. Some never got much further than imagining the day they would go home, back to the village, although the real village might have faded into fantasy. Others certainly believed in struggle, and in a future forged through collective suffering, and it was they who understood the deaths of comrades, however sad, as sacrifice that brought the dawn of freedom closer. Behind that theme, however, among the mourners in a single crowd, united, now, by opposition to a universal enemy, autocracy, there stretched a range of possible ideas, of political programs, half-baked or calculated—radical, revolutionary, populist, Marxist, or none of these.

The circumstances of their meeting as a crowd were still unusual—a revolution, the abortive one of 1905, that made demonstrations on this scale, for a brief interlude, acceptable—but the ritual of red funerals had been evolving for decades. The emotion they evoked needed no propaganda to encourage it. The significance of someone's life, so often, was only clear in retrospect, when they were dead; the crowds collected to express their shock and sense of loss. But the gatherings' political use was not ignored. Public meetings were controlled in czarist Russia—and routine demonstrations of revolutionary solidarity would have been unthinkable—but funerals were harder to restrict. An elite of full-time revolutionaries already understood that mourning was an opportunity. As the crowds marched past the government buildings, the palaces, the grandest shops, red banners were unfurled. The people carried large processional wreaths of palms and lilies, three feet or more across. The wreaths were bound with ribbons bearing messages of solidarity, radical slogans, and greetings from the workers to the dead.

This kind of ritual began in the 1870s. The funeral of the writer Nekrasov, in 1877, was marked by radical speeches at the graveside. In 1891 Shelgunov's funeral at St. Petersburg's Volkovo cemetery included an organized demonstration by seven hundred men and women, "the first appearance," according to its leader, M. I. Brusnev, "of the Russian working class in the arena of political struggle." The banners that the mourners carried, collected from the organizers or prepared at meetings on the previous day, were addressed, in nearly every case, "to the indicator of the path of freedom and brotherhood from the St. Petersburg workers."[20]

Big public funerals were not exclusive to the revolutionary left. The funeral of Tchaikovsky, on 23 October 1893, was one of the social highlights of that year in St. Petersburg. The crowds turned out, for politics was not the only thing that moved the mass of people to grief. Tchaikovsky's funeral was also the first occasion, appropriately enough, on which a full orchestra formed part of the processional cortege, an innovation that the Bolsheviks would soon wholeheartedly embrace.[21] Eventually, in fact, they would adopt much of the pomp and ritual that had been reserved for wealthy members of the middle class. From 1917, for instance, the deaths of important revolutionaries would be announced with black-bordered statements in the press, and their laying-out and burial would be attended by giant wreaths, expensive candles, honor guards, and imported flowers.

The prerevolutionary bourgeois funeral that provided all these precedents was basically religious (not always Orthodox), its ritual derived from the familiar symbols: the spiritual journey, the prayers for salvation and for peace, shared food—whole grains and honey, eggs, incongruously simple in a wealthy urban setting—the sacred earth, the grave. This last was getting more elaborate as the Russian middle class grew richer; more people could afford the marble and the bronze, more businessmen invested in a vault, wrought iron railings fenced the plots, and cemeteries began to look like cities of the dead. Noble graves had once been marked by simple level slabs (the rest were marked only with a temporary wooden cross or stake), but now the wealthy wanted columns, urns, reliefs in colored stone, and sometimes lines of verse or prose, though epitaphs remained exceptional.[22]

The bourgeois funeral was usually draped in sumptuous quantities of white. The hearse, which was drawn by pairs of horses, was a white carriage, and the coffin on the back was hidden behind swags of white brocade. Inside, the corpse was usually dressed in white, and even if a business suit had replaced the traditional linen, the coffin would be lined with white, and white would be the dominant color of the flowers in the wreaths around it. The priests, often four, five, or more of them, and deacons and lectors, too, wore white, and though the mourners, by this time, increasingly wore black or gray, they stood apart, behind the ranks of priests, like relics from another world. The color was traditional, its origins unknown, but it had come to symbolize the "other light," transfiguration. Red funerals, by contrast, defined themselves in earthly terms. Their color was the blood of martyrs spilled on real stone.

This point was made in every gesture. The coffin at a red funeral was draped in red cloth, the corpse was often dressed in it, and the mourners, in whatever clothes they had, would carry red banners, red flowers, and wreaths with scarlet ribbons. The coffin seldom traveled on a hearse. It was carried on the shoulders of strong comrades, and there were no priests. Finding a site for the grave might be a problem—the church controlled most city-center cemeteries until 1918—but wherever it was, however simply marked, it could become a place of pilgrimage. The custom of leaving flowers, or a single flower, on the graves of public heroes predates the Bolshevik Revolution, as does the use of graves as tribunes for the affirmation of the cause.

Not everyone, in this formative period, regarded the red ritual as adequate.

For the bereaved families themselves, if they were present, there were often conflicts to resolve. The red funeral, with its solemn speeches and tight-lipped revolutionary formality, was no place for traditional lamentation. It was an embarrassment; the death of a red martyr, originally from some village, might bring the grandmother to town, an awkward representative of the old world. It was not uncommon for black-clad women, breaking away from the solemn ranks, to prostrate themselves across the coffins, shrieking their weird lines. The men who had come with speeches would have to move them away, sometimes lifting them physically from the earth. Other families simply claimed their body, removing it from the morgue, taking it away for burial at home, or for a religious ceremony with traditional prayers. Red martyrs' coffins were often marked, under the drape, with Orthodox crosses.[23] But a red funeral remained an honor and it offered lasting solidarity to the bereaved. In Sevastopol, where more than forty thousand people took to the streets to bury the victims of another riot in October 1905, the marchers were heard whispering approvingly that "it would not be so terrible to die in the cause of freedom if you knew they would bury you with so much respect."[24]

The acquiescence of the families—and of lapsed believers, occasional believers, and fellow travelers—in secular ceremonial must raise the question of belief more generally. Death has always been a litmus test for atheism. There are even writers who assert that it was the fact of death that originally made religion a necessity.[25] Russia's revolutionary movement, before 1917, included thousands of men and women who were not atheists, and many more who saw the fight against religion as a lower priority than other kinds of political struggle. Nonetheless, widespread belief had serious implications for the revolutionary parties, including divided loyalties (believers recognized an authority higher than the Party), persistent superstitions, and attachments to the past as it was represented by the ancestors, the dead, the so-called fathers, who remained, unreconciled and critical, within the spiritual community. Religion was also a distraction from the task of socialist construction, a hangover from the bourgeois past.

Even mourning, if it hindered someone's work and drew him out of the community, could come to be seen as self-indulgence. This last idea was repeated by the marching crowds at successive red funerals, for one of their favorite anthems, "Do Not Weep," precisely forbade mourning: "Do not weep over the bodies of fighters," it begins, "who fell with their weapons in their hands; do not sing mourning poetry for them." The dead do not need songs, or even tears, it continues, for they demand a better gift. "Step without fear over the bodies of the dead," the song goes on, "And carry their banner forward."[26] Death, in these lines, is final, and even a comrade's body, as a body, requires no special reverence. It is the cause that matters, and the cause, not human souls, is the only thing that will not die.

Lenin himself, in public life and in his philosophical writing, was intolerant of all religious habits; viciously anticlerical, but also hostile to millenarian and idealist thinkers in the ranks of his own party. "The philosophy of Marxism is materialism," he wrote in 1908 in refutation of Bogdanov, a former colleague whose writing had taken a spiritual turn. "The Marxist doctrine is omnipotent because it is true . . . The enemies of democracy have always . . . advocated various forms of philosophical idealism, which always, in one way or another, amounts to the defence or support of religion."[27] With a dogmatism typical of him, Lenin thus rejected any attempt to look for a spiritual meaning in socialism to try to invest the comradeship of human beings with any but an economic and political significance.[28] Bogdanov was ejected from the Bolshevik faction.

The louder Lenin himself protested, naturally, the stronger has been the temptation, among historians, to identify the religious tone and metaphor in his thought and writing. The same fate has befallen Stalin, whose speeches often hinted at his early education in a religious seminary, and whose dogmatism, like Lenin's, was in itself an echo of the Orthodox religious message, the word of the one true church, the heir of new Byzantium, from which all schism and deviation was heresy. Their atheism was a kind of protest—the argument goes—the reflex that inspired it was basically religious.[29] It is an interesting speculation, but whatever the origins of their ideology, the inner world of these men's hearts is absolutely closed. The private, for them, was unimportant.[30]

There are no statements of their personal grief, one of the keys to selfhood in the matters of love and death, because they would not have considered it to be a matter worthy of record. What counted for them was politics, state power. They identified themselves entirely with the cause. The first chairman of the Cheka, the Bolshevik secret police, Feliks Dzerzhinskii, expressed the idea bleakly in his prerevolutionary prison diary. "Life is such that it rules out sentiment," he wrote, "and woe to the man who lacks the strength to overcome his feelings."[31] Dedication like this was extreme, but the general idea, the definition of a person's life in terms of collective goals, was not unusual. The notion of the self as an individual ego, of private as opposed to public grief, was a novelty in Russia at this time, a luxury for the better-off, the literate, and the ones with space to sit apart.[32] Village culture was collective, factory culture no less so, and revolutionaries had been dedicating their lives to the cause since the 1840s.

There is no answer, then, to the question of Lenin's personal response to the execution of his brother, Alexander, for his part in a plot to assassinate Alexander III in 1887.[33] Vladimir Il'ich was seventeen at the time, an industrious student (he presented himself for a written examination on the day of his brother's execution). One of his biographers speculates that the future leader's introspectiveness may have been heightened by the loss, as it may also have been by the death of his father the previous year.[34] Lenin did not go to Alexander's funeral, though his mother did, and the strain on her is said to have turned her hair white in the space of a few weeks. By all accounts, however, it was Vladimir's sister Ol'ga's death, from typhus, that hit him hardest, largely because the two had been so close, a year apart in age, the middle children in a family of six.[35] When he made his triumphant return to Petrograd from Geneva in April 1917, stepping down from the famous sealed train, one of his first acts was to visit the graves of his mother and this favorite sister in the Volkovo cemetery.[36] But there are few other genuine records of his emotional life.

Stalin was a little more forthcoming—once. His first wife, Ekaterina Svanidze, also died of typhus, and at her funeral he would mutter that she was "a creature who could soften my heart of stone."[37] His response to the suicide of Nadezhda Alliluyeva, his second wife, remains uncertain. Some say he was angry, that he felt betrayed. Others describe him as suffering from depression.[38] It is all a matter of rumor and guesswork. There is no real testimony.

The private feelings of two ruthless men may not matter, in the end, because their actions were not constrained by sentiment; but the shared emotion of the crowd, a social phenomenon, remains important. There are two issues. One is the relationship between Leninism and its followers, the question of how much the Bolsheviks could draw on preexisting patterns of belief; how much they had to change, impose; how far the revolution in mentalities, as well as politics, was ever revolution from below. The other issue is the supposition of indifference or casualness in relation to death, the precondition for brutality. This aspect was the one that frightened Pasternak—the alien crowd instilled in him a sense of menace. Other writers, too, could watch a funeral procession and find it sinister. The conservative historian, Yurii Vladimirovich Got'e, who worked in Moscow, observed the funeral of the anarchist Petr Kropotkin in February 1921. "The crowd was rather impressive," he noted, a little grudgingly, adding that "on the radio and in reports it will probably assume greater proportions . . . Anarchist groups with black flags occupied a very prominent place," he continued. "Dull, simian, uncivilised, barbarian faces."[39]

Elsewhere the same Got'e talked about the revolutionaries as "gorillas," contrasting them with the faithful mourners at the ceremony he attended in the Church of the Great Ascension. "Revolution from below," in such an image, acquires a dark meaning, as if the crowd itself were callous, capable of stepping, grim-faced, across the bodies of its dead. In fact, the evidence points the other way. Neither atheism nor materialism, among red mourners in these early years, would signify indifference, an instrumental view of death. As the autocracy had shown, moreover, religious piety does not of itself stop people from behaving cruelly, from undervaluing the lives of other human beings. Either way, a good deal of popular religion survived, even in the folds of the red flag, and even many radicals retained a vivid, sometimes literal, sense of afterlife.

Got'e was right, from his perspective as a believer, to regret the fact that revolutionary men—though not, as frequently, the women—often proclaimed themselves to be atheists, the formal disciplines of belief abandoned as they joined the factory, talked to comrades, learned the rules of science, read their Marx, their Darwin, their Jules Verne.[40] Village boys who came to the city retained their habits of religious faith at first. Many would cross themselves without thinking, especially as they passed a church, especially if they went home; and some revered the icons on the factory wall, accepting, for a while, the comfort of the priest.[41] There were some factories where religious instruction was organized after hours, and many had their own chapels.[42] The Synod approved the practice of beginning and ending the working day with prayers, and some employers joined their men, bareheaded at the front, like headteachers at assembly.[43]

Although some vestiges of religion could persist, even in revolutionary hearts, the pressure to find other worlds of belief, parallel ones or complete alternatives, was almost irresistible. There were not many churches in the poorest areas. The industrial district of Orekhovo-Zuevo, for instance, an overgrown village just outside Moscow, had only one church for its forty thousand inhabitants at the turn of the century.[44] There were not many women, either, or not many of the churchgoing kind, the village women who kept the icon lamps alight. The rhythms of industry, too, were only tenuously linked to the agricultural cycle. It was easy to forget the religious calendar in the heat and darkness of the foundry. Semyen Kanatchikov remembered his early drift into atheism, inspired by a young worker called Savinov. As Savinov insisted, "not even a priest" could have conceived a hell more terrible than the furnaces beside which both men worked.[45] The image of the factory as a place of suffering would feature in the workers' poetry of the time, with "chains of iron," "scorching furnaces," and the hammers that beat nails into their flesh.[46]

A widespread anticlericalism also helped to keep the people out of church. Workers, like many of their peasant cousins, complained that priests were grasping, that they were in the pockets of the masters, and that they did not understand ordinary peoples' lives. State power in Russia was closely identified with the church, so revolutionaries commonly rejected both. Even the religious were turning against the Orthodox hierarchy by the 1890s. The strongest challenge from that direction came from a movement called the Brethren (*Bratsy*) or Teetotallers (*Trezvenniki*), which started in St. Petersburg in the 1890s, basing itself on decent, simple faith, a direct link with God, the rejection of mystery, indulgence, and the alcohol that seemed to flow so freely on saints' days.[47] As one metalworker put it in 1894, "a religious man does not like priests."[48] The movement was not always prim. Workers who had sung religious songs in their childhood were just as eager, in the 1890s, to learn the anticlerical "tale of a priest," whose words, they said, were too obscene to repeat in public.[49]

The most important spur to atheism, however, was probably the power of science. In that respect, there was a link, in terms of inspiration, between the radicalism of unbelief and Marxism, with its faith in progress and its "science" of dialectical materialism. Kanatchikov, for instance, remembered his conversion from religion in terms of his friend Savinov's demonstration of "scientific" creation. The atheist worker suggested that anyone who was skeptical of Darwinian theory, who insisted on adhering to the church and Genesis, should collect some earth in a box. "You'll see that without fail worms or little insects will begin to appear," he continued. "And in the course of four, five, or maybe even ten thousand years, man himself will emerge." Kanatchikov was so impressed with this idea that he used it later when he became a propagandist, calling it "one of the most convincing arguments in my debates."[50]

Atheism, then, was common currency among the radical left. Before the Bolsheviks came to power, however, it was not an ideological requirement. Red funerals were secular, not atheist. The mourners and the victims might belong to any religion or to none. In Ekaterinoslav there was a mass demonstration, also in October 1905, to bury the Jewish victims of a pogrom, another manifestation of the hatred that the revolution and its failure had unleashed.[51] On this occasion, and on many others, the ritual, the speeches, and the songs were drawn from a wide range of sources. Music from another revolution was one inspiration. The *Marseillaise* was sung (when the police allowed it) and so were popular verses dating from Russia's last patriotic war, the war against Napoleon of 1812. Military images, of struggle and embattled honor, were safe despite the censor, and the most popular red funeral anthem, as Pasternak recalled, became "You Fell as Victims." The original words to this were guarded:

You fell as victims in the fatal fight
*Of unselfish love for the people [*narod*]*
You gave up all that you could for them,
For their honour, their life and their freedom!

But later verses, some of which were added in the 1890s, were more overtly revolutionary:

The despot feasts in his princely hall,
Drowning the warning in wine,
But on the wall the fearsome writing
Has long spelled its fatal message!

The time is at hand—and the people awake,
Colossal and powerful and free!
Farewell, then, brothers, with honour you walked
Your valiant path, thankfully![52]

The words are typical not only for their spirit of sacrifice but also because they draw on a recognizably biblical image, the writing on the Babylonian emperor's palace wall. A great deal of the revolutionary poetry of the time, and not only the hymns to the fallen, made use of similar religious themes. The radical workers of 1905 and 1917, after all, whatever their professed beliefs, were heirs to a religious culture. Religious imagery saturated their language. Even their favorite expletives usually referred to God or to the saints in one form or another. Beyond the words and unexplored allusions, too, there was a larger metaphorical understanding of life. As Mark D. Steinberg puts it in an article on belief among the working-class elite, "They typically viewed human existences as a mythic journey through suffering toward deliverance from affliction, evil and even death. Images of martyrdom, crucifixion, transfiguration and resurrection remained part of their creative vocabulary as did narrative attention to suffering, evil, and salvation."[53]

As Steinberg rightly adds, the use of religious imagery like this was not in fact a proof of Christian faith. Belief, even among the select ranks of literate workers, was informal, and people did not examine their assumptions very often. The afterlife survived, and the poetry of the time refers to conversations with the dead, but it was possible to believe in these ideas without accepting other parts of Orthodox cosmology. Revolutionary writing abounds with images of immortality. The dead come back to talk to the living; they visit dreamers in their sleep. One radical writer, a contributor to the workers' paper *Rabochaya zhizn'* [*Working Life*], in January 1918, described, for instance, how he "saw" a victim of Bloody Sunday. His vision was the man as he lay dying, and the words the martyr uttered, as the czarist bayonet was withdrawn, were: "Lord, forgive him, for he knows not what he does."[54]

A democratic vision such as that contrasts with the world of spiritualism itself, which also flourished in the troubled atmosphere of Russia's fin de siècle. Modern spiritualism originated in the United States in the 1840s, but it found fertile soil in Russia, and was fashionable among members of the elite in the big cities, including the writer Vladimir Dal' and the chemist Dmitrii Mendeleev, a man better known today for his creation of the periodic table.[55] Spiritualists were more than usually fascinated by death. At a personal level, they were urged to keep it firmly in their sights, to "feed their hungry souls," so that their own deaths would transpire "with the least pain (not in the physical sense) and with the least terror."[56] Naturally, too, it was the crossing over into death, into a real—and densely populated—world of afterlife, that freed the spirits of the dead to speak.

Their messages were published, after 1907, in a paper called *Ottuda* [*From the Other Side*]. Its regular section "Fraternal Tips from the Mediums" was full of advice, like an agony column, and also featured warnings and predictions. Because they carried the authority of another world, the messages involved were not negotiable. Spiritualism was generally inimical to democracy, and the spirit mediums were particularly receptive to messages that predicted its destruction. One medium called Nebo announced in 1907, for instance, that a war would come in 1910 between Russia and France. This conflict would spread to the whole world, and its outcome would be the destruction of every democratic government. "Pray only to God and to St. Nikola," another medium commanded (such advice was typical), this time in answer to a request—it was not published—for supernatural assistance in locating a lost girl.[57]

The movement never had a mass following, but it influenced the thinking and the language of more people than the narrow circle of its own confirmed disciples. The same was true of the most exotic of the many other Russian groups that were preoccupied with death. Like spiritualism, this one drew heavily upon the Orthodox religion. The man who elaborated it, Nikolai Fyedorovich Fyedorov (1828/9?–1903), was a devout believer. He was also, however, a man obsessed with the possibilities of the collective human mind. His philosophy has been summarized in the statement that "Man's purpose is to achieve universal collective material salvation on earth."[58] Fyedorov believed that human beings should abandon their urge to procreate, as the sexual act was a distraction, and concentrate instead upon their prime moral duty, which was to resurrect the dead.

To do this, a collective and conscious unity of purpose was essential. The work involved a literal reanimation of matter, the reassembly, from the cosmic dust, of every particle that had ever constituted the living molecules of a human body. The descendants of these individuals would be the first to find them. "Without doubt," Fyedorov wrote, "the science of small molecular movements, perceived only by the sensitive hearing of sons . . . will search out . . . the molecules that went to form the matter that gave them life. The waters that brought forth from the womb of the earth the dust of the dead, will make themselves obedient to the universal will of the sons and daughters of men."[59]

The search for these dispersed molecules could never be confined to one small planet. Space travel was essential, for cosmic dust was scattered through the universe. Fortunately, Fyedorov was optimistic about that, believing that mankind would soon develop viable spacecraft, and arguing, too, that the universe would then provide expansive possibilities for colonization by the millions of reanimated dead. "The resurrection of all mankind," he explained, "will result in a complete victory over space and time." Conquering the universe would be the victory over space, while "the transition from death to life, the simultaneous coexistence of all ages of time (generations), the coexistence of their succession, is a triumph over time." The idea was a gift to the scientific spirit of the age. Fyedorov himself linked the immortality project with related problems such as genetic engineering and the prolongation (to infinity) of individual human lives. The theory sounds bizarre, perhaps, but so does universal resurrection, a central tenet of the faith of millions, and so, for that matter, may human brotherhood, "to each according to his needs," to audiences unaccustomed to utopian dreams.

The Bolsheviks and radicals who took up Fyedorov's cosmic theories discarded the redundant figure of God. For them, it would be man himself who symbolized transcendence. Lenin's views on theories of this kind, following the dispute with Bogdanov, were infamous, so "god-building," as it was known, the idea of substituting man for God within a divine, eternal framework was never part of official ideology. Former god-builders, including the commissar for enlightenment, Lunacharskii, were given influential posts in government, however, and some of the ideas would filter out, entering debates about the prospects for a perfect society—its likely conquest of old age, for instance, of disease, and even, through the ultimate triumph of science, of death itself. The eventual conquest of death was widely anticipated within the Party and outside it. It was an irony, in view of Lenin's hostility to it all, but these ideas, in fact, would inspire Leonid Krasin, a member of the Immortalization Commission, when the moment came to deal with the leader's corpse. Letters from the masses, sacks of them, would follow the same lines—preserve the mortal body using science, and one day science, too, will resurrect it.[60]

Exotic tales of immortality in the material sense would never dominate the thinking of the Leninist elite. Other types of immortality, however, were not only possible but vitally important. The revolutions of 1917 cost hundreds of lives, and solemn crowds gathered on the streets to mourn them. At least in the capital cities, in Petrograd and Moscow, where everyone believed that Russia's history was being broken and recast, the meaning of such deaths could not be other than portentous. It was an opportunity no politician could ignore, a chance to claim the bodies for the cause and turn their blood into a sacrifice, a secular communion.

The context influenced every choice that revolutionary mourners made. By 1917 the press had spent three years finding the words to grieve for Russia's fallen; religious and political leaders had tried to find a meaning for the slaughter at the front, and most had settled on the same image of oblation, the patriotism of Russian men, their simple faith, their great gift to the nation. Languages of martyrdom were part of everyone's vocabulary. The search for meaning, for pathos, even for kitsch, had become part of life. To have neglected it, to have left the revolutionary martyrs as mere dead, would have seemed strange indeed, an innovation that the Bolsheviks would not have thought to make. By picking up the idiom of the time, however, they also took on some of its religious associations. More neutrally, it could be added that they also drew on their own traditions, forged through suffering of a different kind, and on the deep resources of their people's culture, heavy with the ancient poetry of requiem.

One of the first and grandest public ceremonies after the collapse of czarism in February 1917 was the funeral for its revolutionary dead. The accepted total of these, the official "Victims of February," was 1,382, of whom 869 were soldiers who had joined the mutiny and 237 were workers.[61] Only a minority of these—180—would end up in the red-draped coffins that were carried along Nevsky Prospekt on a wet and murky afternoon that March. The rest were claimed and buried by their families. The attractions of a red funeral, after all, must soon have tarnished as delay piled on delay, and the spectacle of a political wrangle, with arguments about the route, the site, and the ceremonial, can hardly have comforted the bereaved. The debate involved the Soviet, since it was deemed to be the custodian of these revolutionary dead; the city's leading radical intellectuals; and the provisional government, which conceded that a civil ceremony should take place but took no formal part in organizing it.

The burial site, it was agreed at once, would have to be important, eloquent, a place of pilgrimage within the city center. There was no question of adopting an existing cemetery. The obvious place was thought to be the square beside the Winter Palace—expansive, elegant, a focus for the city's life, a place of martyrdom already, and possibly the most magnificent public space in Russia. It was Maxim Gorky, the writer, who saved Palace Square, arguing that it was a priceless architectural treasure. The alternative, which would become—at least that year—the revolution's most prestigious cemetery, was Mars Field, a short walk away from the palace in the other direction.[62]

The postponed funeral took place at last on 23 March. It was an occasion for reflection, an afternoon of mourning for the city as a whole, marked by long silences within the crowd. They turned out in their thousands, walking miles from distant suburbs, always orderly, the workers in their grubby padded jackets beside bourgeois in their furs, soldiers and nurses in uniform, children muffled in warm coats, hats, and scarves against the biting northern wind. The procession stretched the length of Nevsky Prospekt, out beyond the station, several miles, and in its ranks were revolutionaries of every kind, sympathizers, radicals, not only proletarians and certainly not only Bolsheviks. YOU GAVE THE PEOPLE HAPPINESS, said one of the placards that they carried. ETERNAL MEMORY TO YOU, ETERNAL PEACE! They sang the *Marseillaise* (at last without the interference of police) and the full version of "You Fell as Victims," but the funeral was not meant as an exclusively political affair. When the coffins were finally uncovered and lined up beside the grave, a number would turn out, again, to be inlaid with Orthodox crosses.

For the would-be leaders of the proletariat, however, a ceremony like this could not go by without interpretation. Because Lenin was still in Switzerland, the most senior member of the Bolshevik faction in Petrograd at the time was Lev Kamenev. "Do not weep over the bodies of the fallen," his paper, *Pravda,* insisted on the day of the funeral. It published a full text of the anthem on its front page. Inside, Aleksandra Kollontai had written a piece entreating mourners "not to linger" in their grief—the call to action, rejecting sentiment. The true monument to the fallen, she went on, would not be tears or slabs of stone, but "a new, democratic Russia."[63] Kamenev's style drew more directly on religion. "In chains of iron Russia lay at the feet of her oppressors," he wrote on 25 March. "She asked for peace, and they gave her a river of blood, bitterness and corpses." The sacrifice could not be made in vain. "We will build the palace of freedom," he promised, "on the bones of the fighters of February. We will carry their banner on to liberty. We will not compromise."[64]

The Bolshevik paper *Pravda* now appropriated a long line of martyrs for its cause, not only those of February. As Kamenev explained, there had been few opportunities in the past to commemorate them, which meant, conveniently, that they could be named as if they stood behind the living leaders of the Bolshevik faction. The list he printed included Lenin's brother, Alexander, as well as scores of other revolutionaries, including the victims of Bloody Sunday, almost none of whom, in fact, had ever been a Bolshevik at all.[65] It was a style that would become familiar, creating a geneology for the new state, establishing it, as Russian custom might demand, on human bones. Spontaneous emotion—the genuine grief and awe that brought the crowds out in those days of fear, guilt, and anxiety—was soon to be defined and channeled, and a ritual of organized revolutionary mourning, state ceremonial, could now begin to emerge.

October's martyrs were the 238 victims of ten days of street fighting in Moscow. The site that was chosen for their burial was the Kremlin wall. Like Palace Square, it was a secular location that symbolized the Russian state, and choosing it meant placing these new bodies at the heart of a new kind of power. Every factory in the city was closed for the occasion. The crowds were there, just as they had been in Petrograd in February, and their grief was not something that the leaders had to fake. At the same time, however, October's ceremony was the first of a new type. The organizers had arranged for tickets to be issued; delegates from the regions attended as an ordered mass; the press were there; and speakers, from the infant government, focused on socialism, the international proletariat, and the tasks before the world. Banners fluttering form the Kremlin towers carried the slogans, too: LONG LIVE THE REPUBLIC OF WORKERS AND PEASANTS. CREATE AN HONORABLE AND DEMOCRATIC PEACE. FRATERNITY AMONG THE WORKERS OF THE WORLD. John Reed, the American journalist, was in the procession. He wrote that he heard women uttering "inhuman shrieks"—lamenting, falling on the earth—but the sound was drowned out by the megaphones and massed bands.[66]

The red martyrs of 1917 continued to be honored in the years to come. At first, the ceremonies were spontaneous. In January 1918, for instance, the first anniversary of 1905 to fall after the revolution turned into a day of silence. No one wanted pomp and marching. The factories stayed closed, the streets were empty, and the people did whatever grieving they might choose to do at home. In later years there would be compensation, however; new holidays in honor of new kinds of saint.[67] The revolutionary pantheon was built and filled almost at once.

There was, however, something missing. The contrast with Western Europe makes its absence clear, although you would not find it now if you only read the Soviet revolutionary press. At the time, of course, it would have been so much a part of everyone's imagination that no one would have thought of making it an issue. It was not so much the backdrop to both revolutions as the very heart of the despair that gave them life. It shaped the way even the revolutionaries saw their world, colored their view of death, brought millions of their future subjects into contact with violence and fear for three long years before they came to power and brought it to an end. It claimed not tens, but millions of lives. Because it was not commemorated after 1917, however, it vanished from the Bolshevik foundation myth. Few stories illustrate the power of social memory more clearly. There is no Soviet national monument to the First World War.[68]

The czarist empire would not, left to itself, have failed to make the slaughter a part of its historical mythology. Like every other European power, it welcomed the war in the first months because it seemed to rally the whole nation, turning people's attention away from strikes and shortages and directing it instead at enemies everyone could hate. Right-wing intellectuals who had feared that Russia's spiritual vitality was decreasing celebrated, too, and virtually every major writer offered his or her support through patriotic columns in the daily press. Even the suicide rate went down.[69] The men went off "to die for Christ and for Holy Russia," and the church bells rang in celebration of a sacred cause.[70] The church, in fact, would take immediate responsibility for most of the war dead. Army chaplains (not all of them Orthodox—there were Catholic priests, rabbis, and mullahs at the front as well) had the job of writing many of the letters to bereaved families, and priests were always called upon to bless the mass graves that everyone supposed might one day be made formal, permanent, and marked with stone. Photographs show priests in the middle of this act of blessing, standing fully robed beside large mounds of earth, higher than a man, each one banked up with turf or bracken and surmounted by a single wooden cross.

No one who saw the front could ever have idealized it. Russia's troops, professional and conscript, confronted their opponents in desperate conditions. They were not necessarily ill-equipped, or not at first, but they could not match the Prussian troops they faced. Where soldiers in the West fought for years across a single strip of Flanders and Picardy, the armies of the East would move, fighting through the Polish and Galician plains and marshes, skirting the Carpathians, and wading in the endless mud along the Danube. The casualties on all sides were heavy, but the Russians, characteristically, lost more than anyone else. Within a year the government department that collected the names of the dead was overwhelmed. Their precise numbers will never be known. It is estimated, however, that between 1.6 million and 2 million men died as a result of the fighting between 1914 and 1917, though as the authors of one study explain, "this excludes many soldiers who were sent back from the front wounded or sick, but whose lives were shortened."[71] This figure can be compared with that for the British Empire as a whole, which lost approximately 767,000 men between 1914 and 1918; France, which lost 1,383,000; and Germany, which suffered very heavily in its war on two fronts, losing a total of about 1,686,000 men. The United States, which entered the war late and never sustained casualties on home territory, lost 81,000 men.

Back in Russia's cities, the patriotic press did more than just encourage civilian readers to work harder. It also began the process that in other countries would create what the historian Goerge Mosse called "the myth of the war experience."[72] An article in *Olonetskaya nedelya,* a local paper for the northern provinces, was typical. Printed in the first weeks of the war, its piece entitled "How Our Soldiers Die" by "A Serving Officer" combined religion, patriotism, death, and wartime kitsch. The author was visiting the scene of a recent battle, he wrote, when he came upon "an example of our profoundly Christian way of death." He happened to see a "poor soldier boy [*soldatik*]" lying wounded, "apparently beyond all hope." The young man nonetheless called out, "and I, despite the fact that I was in a great hurry, stopped, handed my horse to my attendant, and approached the dying man." What the soldier wanted, the officer discovered, was a cross to hold in his last moments. "It was hard, but I obtained one from somewhere," he continued, "and placed it in his hands. His chest was shattered by a shell fragment and his bandages were soaked with blood . . . But seeing his cross, he began to shake, took the chain in his left hand and the cross in his right and began to pray . . . After a few words his voice began to grow weaker . . . When I took his hand I found there was no pulse already. But still he clutched his cross, and his eyes remained fixed upon the crucifixion. I crossed myself and could not hold back my own tears as I left this hero."[73]

This sort of thing would have made excellent (or rather, typical) propaganda for an image of "our brave boys." There were echoes of it (without the crosses and the prayers) in the sentimental literature of death and mourning in the civil war of 1918–1921, and even stronger reverberations of the same kinds of theme during the Great Patriotic War of 1941–1945.[74] But the image of the First World War was not developed, for propaganda purposes, in Bolshevik Russia after 1917. Postwar Soviet treatments of the Great War diverged sharply from those in Western Europe. There was no blossoming of antiwar poetry after 1917, for instance, no Owen or Sassoon to challenge patriotic images of sacrifice. That is to say, there were war poets in Russia, and some did write of mutilating horror, others of piety and the nation, but their work did not become part of the Soviet literary canon. In several cases it could later be adapted, without explanation, and used in later conflicts.[75]

A similar fate befell postwar Soviet art. In Europe, experimental genres—dada and surrealism, anarchic celebrations of the unconscious—fluorished in the ruins after 1918, a challenge to the old elite, a question mark to keep beside enduring dreams of human rationality and progress. These forms were never prominent in Soviet official art (though the surreal—unspecified and unexamined—was a prime feature in the people's private memories of war). On the contrary, as if to negate the evidence before everyone's eyes, the idea that society was perfectible, and that human beings, freed from oppression, were fundamentally rational and good, would form the core of socialist realist art and literature until the time of Nikita Khrushchev.

Because the war did not become a central part of the Soviet master narrative, the foundation myth of the new state, its legacy was confusing. Everyone had their memories, millions were living with the permanent consequences—

an amputated limb, lost sight, tuberculosis, shrapnel wounds. But private memories are difficult to place without a public framework, especially in conditions of continuing social chaos. It was not just that there was no physical, architectural commemoration, or even that there was so little public history. The collective story of the war was lost in years of mass migration and civil war. Landmarks and even fields were destroyed, and houses, streets, factories, churches, shops—all kinds of public space. Families, too, were broken into fragments, sometimes by emigration, sometimes by desperation, death, or hunger. What all this meant was that there was no simple story of the war, "our war," but millions upon millions of them, each one so painful that its narrator must have felt that his or her suffering was unique.

In the months that separated the two revolutions the Petrograd Soviet was bombarded with letters testifying to this disorientation, loss and pain. Tens of thousands wanted help in finding their missing relatives—"at least tell me they are dead, so that I can pray for them"—while others pleaded for their sons and husbands to come home. "They have taken them all," one woman wrote, now hoping that a democratic government would make amends. "There will be a food crisis and a famine," wrote another. "Please release them for agricultural work and save us all from famine."[76] In other times, such stories might one day have formed a part of postwar state mythology, the people's suffering, but Soviet Russia would have other raw material for that.

The Treaty of Brest-Litovsk, in March 1918, would end Soviet Russia's part in capitalist Europe's war. The terms were hardly glorious for Russia, including as they did the loss of Poland, Ukraine, and the Baltic provinces, between them accounting for more than a third of the former empire's industry, its richest agricultural land, and 62 million of its citizens. Defeat alone, however, was not the reason for the Soviet government's reticence about the war in future years. Germany made propaganda capital, after all, out of the fabled "stab in the back" by left-wing mutineers in 1918, and the myth of brave fighters sustained it in the darkest years of humiliation and hardship. For Soviet Russia, however, the war was prehistory, a catalyst for the inevitable, as tragic and as wasteful as autocracy would always be. Immediately after it ended, too, there would be millions of more important bodies—red heroes of the civil war—for the new state to honor.

No censorship was needed here. It was merely a case of neglect. A certain amount of research into the war—historical research, investigations of its health and economic costs, and studies of strategy and generalship—was carried out in the 1920s, but the subject did not feature prominently in official stories of the new regime.[77] Even the mounds of earth began to crumble, lost among the marshes to the West, and if they are unearthed today, it can be hard to say for certain, unless there are some shreds of uniform, buttons, badges, bullets, or gold teeth, whether they are soldiers from the First World War, the civil war, the Patriotic War, or partisans, deserters, even Germans. In 1997 and 1998, I asked five groups of adults and about twenty individuals to name the three most deadly wars in Russia's twentieth-century history. Almost no one even mentioned the war of 1914. To some, indeed, my mentioning it came as a surprise—"Oh, that!" The contrast with my own society, which remains so deeply fascinated by its own lost generation, trenches, mud, and shell shock, could hardly be more stark.

4

TRANSFORMING FIRE

The Bolsheviks came to power in a country already in chaos. Government and civil order had been crumbling in every province. Almost the whole of southern Russia was in open revolt by the late summer of 1917. In other places the peasants had seized land or other property, there were outbreaks of banditry, and, again increasingly from July, pogroms against Jews. The army, too, was falling apart. In some parts of the armed forces, discipline had entirely collapsed, and desertion was becoming common. Soldiers who had seen no pay for weeks were running riot, and there were reports of mutinies, murdered officers, and the violent looting of frontline villages.[1] In the cities the number of strikes increased as autumn approached, and there were plans, by September, for a prolonged general strike in support of Soviet, as opposed to parliamentary government. "We certainly did not understand the dictatorship of the proletariat as a dictatorship of the Bolshevik Party," Eduard Dune, a worker at the Provodnik plant near Moscow, later wrote. "We were looking for allies, for other parties willing to go with us along the path of building soviet power . . . Yet we were beginning to tire of words."[2]

The old world was dissolving. Like many radical workers, Dune believed the time had come for the people to seize the initiative. "The workers thought that the conditions for a proletarian dictatorship had matured," he remembered, "that there was no time to wait, that danger loomed."[3] For those who did not share this view, civilization itself appeared to be on the brink of collapse. "We are only fit to be manure for peoples of higher culture," Yurii Vladimirovich Got'e wrote in his diary that July. "There is no army, no money, and no-one wants to work. Complete anarchy reigns in the towns and villages. The railroads are in ruins; the harvest is bad in a significant part of Russia. The foreign war has been lost, the internal war is intensifying. Life this winter is going to be a nightmare."[4]

Even the pessimistic Got'e could not have predicted the darkness that would follow. The First World War had introduced millions of conscripts to modern, industrial, warfare, with its machine-gun fire, its trenches, endless noise, and mud. The civil war would show what an entire people could do—and what they could endure—when their society fell apart, when their hopes, their livelihoods, and their very survival were threatened. The years immediately following the revolution were among the most terrible, the most deadly, the most vicious and macabre in modern Soviet history. Between 9 million and 14 million people died; starving, cold, racked with disease, or tortured and killed in bitter fighting. Survivors would witness more cruelty, and suffer more personal hardship, than most people remembered from entire lifetimes under czarism.

A little more than half of the deaths were a direct result of the war and of the epidemics that accompanied it before the end of 1920.[5] The rest came in the wake of the famine that gripped the grain-producing regions of the south in 1921–1922.[6] "The people died like autumn flies," recalled one survivor. "If it had been possible they would have eaten the lice that crowded over them, but the lice were stronger and ate the people, infecting them with typhus. Death reached the exhausted at work, at home, in the streets, doorways, platforms of railway stations and public lavatories. The lice survived their hosts, and, being hungry, moved over the stiff corpses for a long time."[7] People ate earth, grass, and carrion. Some ate human flesh. The struggle to rebuild the state through six years of war and revolution eventually consumed the whole society.

Even the new leaders of Soviet Russia would later admit to doubts. "The spring and summer of 1918 were unusually hard," Trotsky wrote. "At times it seemed as if everything were slipping and crumbling, as if there were nothing to hold on to, nothing to lean upon. One wondered if a country so despairing, so economically exhausted, so devastated, had enough sap left in it to support a new regime and preserve its independence. There was no food. There was no army. The railways were completely disorganized. The machinery of state was just beginning to take shape. Conspiracies were being hatched everywhere."[8] For those who had the means to do so—mostly the better-off—one option was emigration. It has been estimated that between 2 million and 3 million people left the former Russian empire between 1917 and 1920.[9]

The news of the Bolshevik coup spread remarkably fast. Got'e, in Moscow, heard about it within twenty-four hours. Like almost everyone else, however, he was unsure, at first, what it might mean. "The bolshevik action has begun in Petrograd and Moscow with the proclaiming of the transfer of power to the Soviets of Workers' Deputies," he wrote on 26 October. "There is no precise news from Petrograd, all kinds of rumours are circulating, but which of them correspond to the truth and which don't, you can't tell."[10] Dune and his comrades at the Provodnik factory heard a different version of the same events. "On Saturday 26 October news came that shooting had started in Moscow," he wrote, "and that the officer cadets had attacked the Soviet. It was said that in Piter [Petrograd] the situation was the same, and that the Moscow-Petrograd railway was not operating." A further bulletin from Moscow described the growing chaos there. "Armed cadets were marching through the centre," Dune was told, "the trams were not working, the workers' militias were ready but were staying at their workplaces for the simple reason that they had no weapons."[11]

Fighting began almost at once in several cities of the Russian empire. Workers' militias, bands of volunteers, confronted government troops, and there were pitched battles outside public buildings and railway stations. The transfer of power was contested, but the fighting, at this stage, was usually sporadic and disorganized, a far cry from the series of concerted campaigns that would follow in the summer of 1918. For most people, the main problems that first winter were hunger and cold. "No hour passes without a soviet," someone scrawled on the side of a building in Moscow in January 1918. "No day without a decree. But there is no bread as yet."[12]

The economy, in fact, was on the verge of complete collapse. There was no heating fuel in the cities in the winters of 1918, 1919, and 1920 (the people ripped up floorboards, tore down wooden roofing, burned anything they could find to keep from freezing), and there was almost no food. The citizens of Petrograd, the men and women who had made a revolution for bread, were nearly starving in the winter of 1919; in Moscow, which became the capital in 1918, few outside the Kremlin fared much better.[13] It was in these conditions, too, that an exhausted and weakened population faced a succession of epidemics—influenza ("the Spanish disease") in 1918–1920, cholera in 1920–1921, and successive attacks of typhus. The crude death rate in Petrograd shot up from 23.4 per thousand in 1917 (itself a year of war and revolution) to 70.5 per thousand in 1919.[14] "Moscow is not only scattering," Got'e wrote in December 1918. "It is dying off."[15]

It would be the great cities of the north—Moscow and Petrograd in particular—that suffered most in these early years. The populations of the two capitals alone fell by almost two-thirds between 1917 and 1920.[16] But the countryside fared little better. The villages were subjected to grain requisitions by all sides, the organized seizure of produce, sometimes involving the flogging or execution of suspected hoarders. In three years of unremitting hardship, and at a time when they had been expecting justice and freedom at last, rural communities in their turn lashed out at scapegoats: the government, White generals, former landlords, and minorities within their own ranks—outsiders, settlers of different ethnic origin, and Jews. The number of pogroms rose in 1918 and reached a peak in 1919, the darkest year of the civil war. As many as 200,000 people are thought to have been killed as a result—mainly in the western parts of the former empire—between 1917 and 1920. The perpetrators included groups of peasants and the soldiers of every side—nationalists, Whites and partisans, and sometimes also Reds.[17]

Crises of every kind disrupted established patterns of life. While agriculture was devastated by war and banditry, the factories almost ceased to function. By 1920 industrial output had fallen to about a fifth of prewar levels.[18] Survival, for the urban population, was now a matter of barter. "In order to eat it was necessary to resort, daily and without interruption, to the black market," wrote Victor Serge. "The Communists did it like everyone else."[19] Workers who had depended on their wages were forced to make suitable goods to exchange. The result, as Serge observed in Petrograd, was that the factories were "dead." "The workers spend their time making penknives out of bits of machinery," he wrote, "or shoe-soles out of conveyor-belts, to barter them on the underground market . . . Fortunately the town residences of the late bourgeoisie contained quite a lot in the way of carpets, tapestries, linen, and plate. From the leather upholstery of sofas one could make passable shoes; from the tapestries, clothing."[20] Serge himself kept out of the cold by wrapping himself in "a fur-lined riding jacket, which, cleared of its fleas," made him look "wonderful."[21]

Transport, too, was in chaos. The railways had been both overused and neglected during the First World War, and the system was on the brink of collapse before the civil war began. From 1918, there would be more pressure, including requisitions, interruptions, and widespread sabotage. But these were also years of massive population movement; the railways and the major waterways would have to carry millions of refugees.[22] At any station there would be groups of women struggling with unnumbered shapeless bags, ragged children, deserters, and hollow-eyed workers fleeing starvation and the city. Anxious strangers also huddled in the crowds, identifiable by their better luggage, their smoother hands, the sharp words spoken to their children as they stared. For though the wealthiest found safer routes to China and to France, the railways still carried thousands of the bourgeoisie, en route to lives they could not even picture, their lifetime's savings now reduced to wads of useless cash or any stones and bits of gold that they could sew into the linings of their coats.[23]

Whatever their class or purpose, travelers were always vulnerable. They were hungry, exhausted, often cold, crowded together in airless carriages or on the decks of river boats. They were always among the first to fall ill, and they were also the least likely to recover. According to a report of 1919, large numbers of the refugees who reached Moscow were dying at the railway stations, or at most within twenty-four hours of their arrival.[24] They also helped to spread the diseases that they carried. Even the smaller towns on the refugee routes would see increases in their mortality rates in these years of such a size that the number of births no longer kept pace with deaths.[25] The crisis had begun to attract government attention before Lenin's coup. In September 1917, doctors who agreed to work with cholera victims were excused from military service. But the gesture was inadequate. The doctors began to die themselves, and nothing eased the people's basic hunger. As officials in Saratov pointed out in 1919, it was futile for the state to issue decrees on quarantine and sanitation when there was not even bread to eat.[26]

The diseases that followed hunger and exhaustion caused the most deaths in these years, but the fighting, too, was murderous. There was not one but many civil wars. History has privileged the story of Red versus White, revolutionaries against monarchists and conservatives, but there were other challenges to the Bolsheviks, too, as well as other wars, some of which had little to do with Moscow. Separate White armies advanced on the capital from Siberia and from the Urals, from the Don in the south, and from the forests and marshes that lay to the north of Petrograd. But another army, based in Samara, and reinforced by a detachment of Czech and Slovak former prisoners of war, was raised by the defeated Socialist Revolutionaries, the majority party in the former constituent assembly, when they declared themselves to be the true socialist government of the new Russia in the spring of 1918. Multiparty soviets in a string of cities outside Petrograd similarly condemned the Bolshevik coup. Partisans—often known as greens—defended everything from peasant rights to newborn nationalisms. The war also included an international dimension, as British, French, Polish, and Japanese troops invaded from Murmansk, Arkhangel'sk, Odessa, and the Far East. The combatants were not always ethnic Russians. There were fierce national wars in the Caucasus, for example, between historic enemies such as the Azeris and Armenians. In some places, especially outside the borders of Russia itself, the fighting would continue until 1923.[27]

Each of these wars was primitive; "primeval," in the words of one living witness.[28] Throughout the bleakest, most anarchic years, survival was the only goal. No part of the empire was spared. Every district, however, believed their war to be unique. Perhaps the isolation of each region, the mistrust that people had of rumor, preserved some sense of hope. It would have been impossible to comprehend, after all, that every provincial town might have its piles of mutilated bodies, their hands and feet cut off, their eyes gouged out; that rows of corpses, their entire flesh burned black, charred, blistered, and swollen, were now a common sight in countless villages across the steppe.[29] Anyone who was able to do so wrote desperately to Moscow. "Do you know what is happening in the countryside?" a former comrade asked Lenin's friend and aide Vladimir Bonch-Bruevich in 1918.[30] "Where is our honour," wrote a former Bolshevik, despairing at the slaughter around him. "Where is our love of freedom?"[31]

Red Guards like Eduard Dune made sense of the catastrophe in terms of political reaction. "Events unfolded not according to some calculated system of peace, world labor, and world revolution, but along the path of world counter-revolution," he wrote. "In April 1918 the Red Army numbered only 106,000 volunteers,[32] but by autumn 299 regiments had been formed from among draftees . . . Enemies appeared on all sides, preventing the center from receiving food supplies, raw materials, and fuel for its dying industries . . . One could not remain a passive observer when the fate of Soviet power hung not here in the rear but wherever our troops were sent."[33] Got'e regarded the struggle as more anarchic, another outbreak of primitivism on the part of the "gorillas." Either way, organized fighting was only part of the struggle. There was no real civilian life during the civil war. Everything could become a part of someone's military campaign, from coal production to trade, the fight against deserters to the battle for grain.

All sides—Reds, Whites, Greens, anarchists (Blacks), and nationalists—used terror, including the mass slaughter of civilians, as part of their political and military strategy. In the confusion of the fighting, the killing appeared arbitrary to the horrified witnesses, but in fact it was neither irrational nor blind. As far as the Reds were concerned, for instance, terror was used to establish discipline in the army, to break the resistance of potentially hostile civilian groups, and to destroy the substantial opposition—beginning with that of the anarchists and Socialist Revolutionaries—that still existed in the first three years of Bolshevik rule. From the summer of 1918, when the infamous Red Terror was launched, mass killing was used as a propaganda tool. The attempt on Lenin's life in August 1918 provided a pretext for further excess.[34] "All Soviets are to arrest right Socialist-revolutionaries, representatives of the haute bourgeoisie and former officers and to hold them as hostages," read an announcement on the front page of *Petrogradskaya pravda* on 5 September. "If they attempt to resist or to hide, they are to be shot summarily without discussion."[35]

The Bolshevik organization responsible for much of this brutality, the Extraordinary Commission, or Cheka, had been set up in December 1917 under the leadership of Feliks Dzerzhinskii. From small beginnings—a few dozen men—it expanded rapidly, involving itself in issues as diverse as economic speculation, the repression of religion, and antibourgeois class war. By the summer of 1918, when the Terror began, it was already infamous. "The machine of the Red Terror works incessantly," wrote the sociologist Pitirim Sorokin. "Every day and every night, in Petrograd, Moscow, and all over the country the mountain of dead grows higher . . . In a few years the soil along the Irinovskaia and Finlandskaia railroads, behind Okhta and in the yards of the Chekha should be very fertile. Ten thousand men and women have fertilised that soil with their bodies . . . Every night we hear the rifle fire of execution, and often some of us hear from the ditches, where the bodies are flung, faint groans and cries of those who did not die at once under the guns. People living near those places begin to move away. They cannot sleep."[36]

The shooting took place everywhere, in provinces and villages as well as in the cities. "For the least attempt of any kind by partisan counter-revolutionary forces to overthrow Soviet power," ran a decree by the military-revolutionary committee in Orenburg that November, "all officers, aristocrats, and white guards in the hands of Soviet power in Orenburg are to be shot, regardless of their personal opinions. For every murdered red guard . . . ten members of the Orenburg bourgeoisie will be shot."[37] The Whites were no less systematic. Nikolai Borodin remembered the appalling resignation of a group of Red prisoners of war, one in five of whom, on this occasion, was shot in front of a crowd of civilian onlookers. "When their turn came each condemned man quickly undressed, as soldiers do," he wrote, "and having put their folded clothes aside walked in their worn-out dirty underwear to their last resting place, trying not to step into the cold rain-pools with their bare feet. At the edge of the grave some of them were whispering, and no-one knew whether it was their last oath or their last prayer. Some crossed themselves with the orthodox cross, then all quickly disappeared into the grave."[38]

The victims usually dug their own mass graves. Borodin, who was hardly more than a child at the time, remembered the soil, its color and claggy wetness. "After the first layer of soil there was bright yellow clay," he wrote. "A heap of it rested on the other side of the grave. It was sticky and heavy after the rain, and here and there there was a trickle of yellow water running down into the grave." The shambles was typical, routine in terms of civil war brutality. Human life was so unimportant that it hardly mattered whether the victims had died at once or not. "The grave was covered with the clay," Borodin remembered, "and the next day the arms and legs of the executed could be seen and some of them waved feebly."[39] Victims of the terror in Moscow, according to Got'e, were "dumped" in the Kalitnikovskoe cemetery in 1918 and 1919.[40] Other bodies were left at night in heaps outside the gates of local hospitals.[41] Those who were publicly hanged might be left for days, others lay in the streets where they had been shot. "We live in a terrible time," declared one White colonel, "when a man is becoming an animal. These unbridled hooligans understand only one law: an eye for an eye, a tooth for a tooth. But I would propose two eyes for one, and all teeth for one."[42]

Whole populations had become legitimate military targets. An entire social group could stand as surrogate in acts of savage vengeance for the revolution, for czarism, and for any excess of the civil war itself. In Makiivka, in the Don region, White troops under Kaledin attacked representatives of the proletariat early in the war by gouging out the eyes of civilian mineworkers, slitting their throats, and throwing some others to their deaths down open shafts. White troops also reenacted the public corporal punishment of the darkest prerevolutionary days, flogging peasants to death in a gesture of revenge for the revolution and land seizures.[43]

These floggings helped to remind the peasants of the things they had to lose if the extreme right prevailed. They did not, for the most part, welcome Bolshevik rule, but the return of the landlords, which would have meant the loss of recently acquired land and freedom, was usually seen as the greater evil. At the same time, however, the peasants' view of "us" and "them," "ours" and the rest, mistrusted all outsiders, while the Bolsheviks, in their determination to establish order, spent little time acquainting themselves with the complexities of village life. Pitirim Sorokin described what happened in one region, Tambov, after the Antonov rebellion against Bolshevik power in 1920. "Once or twice a peasant turned on a Communist and murdered him," he wrote. "In retaliation the Communist agents mutilated peasants before shooting them, cutting off the ears, hands, legs and pudendas of their victims, gouging out their eyes, or violating their wives and daughters in their sight. The peasants caught some of the agents unawares and mutilated them in similar fashion. Some they killed by binding their legs to the tops of two bent trees, letting the trees slowly straighten. Others they tied to the tails of horses and dragged to death."[44] It was also this region that the young Red hero Tukhachevsky decided to "cleanse with poison gas" in 1921. "The cloud of poison gas shall be spread completely over the whole forest," he ordered, "exterminating everything concealed in it."[45]

Terror could also be turned inward against the troops or civilians of one's own side. Trotsky did not hesitate to use it to create his fighting force. "The communists were explaining, exhorting, and offering example," he wrote, "but agitation alone could not radically change the attitude of the troops."[46] He knew, in fact, that it was not cowardice that paralyzed his men, but exhaustion. Many of them had been fighting continuously for three years by 1917. Some—the veterans of the Russo-Japanese war—had been in uniform for even longer. What they wanted from the revolution, their revolution, was peace, and a chance to go home, to begin the work—farm work, mostly—that would guarantee their basic economic survival.[47] "We have already served our dear land enough," one of them wrote in 1917, "and we have exhausted our energies and shed our blood. We have lost the years of our youth."[48] "Many were troubled less by a fear for their own skin than by the disorder of the rear," added the loyal Dune. "Many lost heart from the widespread confusion."[49]

Exhortation would not motivate these weary, famished men. Instead, the death penalty, whose abolition within the army had been one of the February revolution's first achievements, was reinstated at the front. "I give warning that if any unit retreats without orders," ran Trotsky's official declaration of 1918, "the first to be shot down will be the [political] commissary of the unit, and next the commander . . . This I solemnly promise in the name of the entire Red Army."[50] Soldiers who had called the death penalty a "barbarian measure" a few months earlier, and who had signed petitions against its use in wartime, describing it as "a danger to a democratic state" would now have to choose between a bullet from their own side or another twenty months in uniform.[51]

There was no trace of remorse or hesitation in Trotsky's writing. "To a gangrenous wound," he said, "a red-hot iron was applied."[52]

Trotsky's taste for discipline—which he would later seek to apply with equal severity to civilian industrial workers—contributed to a general mood of disillusionment outside the party. Some of the Bolsheviks' most ardent supporters of 1917 were also beginning to question the new order. "Most provincial comrades regard anyone who opens his mouth as counter-revolutionary," complained a former activist from Vladimir province in 1918. Others thought that violence was counterproductive, that it drove potential Communists away. Rank and filers were also afraid of ghosts. They admitted to avoiding the fresh graves, haunted by the specters of their own impulsive cruelty.[53] One world was shattered, another had turned sour. There was little refuge left for faith.

The principal alternative to revolutionary idealism, and the most obvious source of general solace, religion, was also under heavy attack. "During the firing intervals," Borodin wrote, recalling what would have been a typical scene, "I once or twice saw an unknown priest praying at the graves with groups of people, 'for the peaceful rest of our perished brethren, the names of whom only Thou, O Lord, knoweth.' But then the priest disappeared and it was said that he had been denounced to the Reds for his sympathies with the Whites, and he was shot dead."[54] Priests, like bourgeois, could be considered guilty under any circumstances. As Dzerzhinskii put it in 1920, "Communism and religion are mutually exclusive." He added, more ominously, that "only the Cheka is capable of destroying religion."[55] The civil war, and, to an even greater extent, the 1921 famine, provided the Bolsheviks with a series of excuses to close churches, arrest their priests, and seize their property.[56] Whatever doubts about religion some people may have had, and even if they utterly rejected it, such acts destroyed a large part of their universe. It would be a serious loss when other forms of consolation were so scarce.

The collapse of hope, of faith, of physical security and apparently, too, of respect for life was noticed by every writer at the time. Many wondered what its long-term implications would be. Their fears had begun, in fact, before the civil war, and even before the Bolsheviks came to power. "Human life has become cheap, very cheap, too cheap," wrote a contributor to *Rabochaya zhizn'* in 1917. His concern focused on the First World War. "For a fourth year human blood is being spilled," he wrote, "for a fourth year mankind gives up to the Moloch of war its finest achievement—its priceless gift—its life . . . Man has lost the best aspects of his nature, love and compassion." The consequences he foresaw were terrible. If the war were prolonged, he believed, "if the younger generation, children, are reared in an abominable atmosphere of violence and bloodshed, then the older generation will not be succeeded by new defenders of the best ideals of mankind but by human beasts, capable of realising only the basest forms of existence."[57]

Within two years the world that had disturbed this writer would be gone, dissolved in a slaughter that even he could hardly have imagined. The violence of the civil war was so sickening, so relentless, that few could have survived it without changing in some way. The experts—doctors and psychiatrists—who advised Lenin's government did not evade the issue. "A number of years of slaughter in war cannot have failed to affect the mass," explained one doctor. He was discussing the new phenomenon—unknown even in the famine year of 1891—of cannibalism among the starving. "They have become accustomed to bloodshed," he continued, "their respect for life—both that of others and their own—has been subjectively lowered."[58] Petr Gannushkin, the psychiatrist, went further, telling Lenin in 1922 that roughly half of Russia's population was suffering from some form of mental illness. "It is not normal," he is reported as saying, "for sons to kill their fathers and fathers their sons." In his opinion, the damage would be compounded over the years as these "abnormal" sons produced children of their own.[59]

The historians who write about the civil war have tended to agree. There is a general consensus that it "brutalized" the population, that it "coarsened" public life, and that it actively promoted a political culture of callous violence and disregard for life. Stalinism, runs the argument, was built on these foundations.[60] Many of the officials who carried out the killings of those later years had learned their methods at the front. Lenin's beleaguered government relied on the unscrupulous, on former criminals, and even, some have claimed, on psychopaths.[61] The most cruel individuals were promoted because their skills were needed, and they in turn promoted others like them. The trauma and the violence, it is said, would shape the Soviet future as much as any ideology, as much as economic pressures or the conflict over tactics.

Several separate theories lie buried in this general scheme. They are not equally easy to verify. Civil war rhetoric and practice certainly left a lasting impression on public life. It is also true that as a whole society was marked by the brutality. All kinds of violence, including murder and banditry, became more common; the population grew accustomed to news of bloodshed, and groups of soldiers picked over the bodies of their victims in the field, chatting as they pulled out the gold teeth.[62] Anything that involved social interchange, including the language itself, became coarser, more familiar, and brusque.[63] But when it comes to individuals, the idea of brutalization is crude, limp, too broad, and even inhumane. Callousness and brutalization, as general theories of behavior, are easily applied, perhaps, to documentary and statistical evidence, but they are harder to sustain in the face of individual testimony. Some people acted brutally, others did not, and the longer-term effects on individuals varied.

The questions that this raises are disturbing. It may be easier to imagine that the civil war's excesses were perpetrated and sustained by human animals than to face a truth more simple and mundane. The people acted out of fear, under orders, from ideological zeal, in ghastly mimicry of their own enemies, in panic, anger, and cold revenge. They would remember later that their hunger often made them numb, but it did not transform them into members of some other species, and their acts were not always hysterical or blind.[64] There was also the question of recovery. Some people did continue to suffer, unable to escape from the atrocities in their minds. Most of these were not brutalized, not eager to continue with the violence, but ill, traumatized. Despite Gannushkin's fears, however, they were a minority. Most survivors did not lose their sanity that way, and most were able to remake their lives. What they wanted, in the 1920s, was usually peace, domesticity, an office job. The new world would bring compensating satisfactions. Even the most extreme events, in other words, were eventually assimilated, albeit partially, in edited form, distorted by intrusive pieces of official narrative, into the catalog of lived, continuous human experience.

"*The Bolsheviks* had won," writes Robert Service, "and felt that their ideas had helped them to this end . . . Dictatorship and terror appealed to them as means of solving problems."[65] The generalization, applied, at least, to the elite, is remarkably apt. Civil war images, military jargon, and terse, martial-style decrees would feature prominently in their political style for decades. The notion of a state embattled, "encircled," remembered from the days of British, French, and Japanese invasion, could be invoked at any time to justify a siege atmosphere, the repression of opposition, and public vigilance.[66] Local needs and wishes were easily overlooked in a system geared to centralized decision making. Problems and misunderstandings generated in the regions were ignored, neglected, or addressed by summary and capricious directives.[67] And terror, once begun, was hard to extirpate. The Cheka was restructured, formally dissolved, and replaced by the OGPU (the Unified Central Political Administration) in 1923. But even new recruits to this would call themselves

"Chekists," and the goals and techniques of its predecessor were not forgotten. Dzerzhinskii remained in charge until his death in 1926.

The argument that certain types of politician flourished and grew powerful during the civil war is also largely true. Lenin's immediate entourage consisted mainly of the men that he had come to know in European exile—Kamenev and Zinoviev, for instance, each of whom held several responsible posts throughout the civil war—together with the most experienced of the "Russian" faction, the men and women who had managed to remain inside the empire, in exile or at liberty, until 1917. But these were not enough to form and staff a government. The Party expanded and evolved in the civil war years, and the new members, in many cases, had an intellectual style that differed from that of the founder members and Old Bolsheviks, more direct administrative ambitions, and fewer scruples.

Lenin's "European" comrades, like many of the Party's founding members, and certainly its intellectual elite, were not as coarse—and often not as practical—as the generation that would be promoted after 1918. Kamenev, for instance, would never favor terror. In January 1918 he and Dzerzhinskii, an unlikely pair, were asked to draw up a code of practice for the Cheka. Predictably, they disagreed. "My comments have been just a touch radical," the bookish Kamenev wrote to Lenin. In fact, he had proposed a Soviet version of habeas corpus, by which no individual should be held for more than three days without charge. The draft proposal is still in the archive. The word "days" has been crossed out in Dzerzhinskii's hand, and the word "months" is substituted.[68] Kamenev did not give up. Later in 1918 he would protest about specific excesses. There were more than a thousand arrests a month taking place in Moscow at the time, but in this instance, Lenin personally investigated and overturned the charges.[69]

Men like Kamenev were a wasting asset in the Party elite, however. Dzerzhinskii himself was also a revolutionary of long standing, but it was the crisis after November 1917 that developed his peculiar range of talents. Others were encouraged to adopt a brusque political style in the emergency, or found that the crude administrative manner that they favored, intolerable in other circumstances, was not only acceptable during the war but positively advantageous. Stalin was one of these, a talented but surly comrade who had joined the party in the Caucasus in 1904 and seemed to take a particular interest in administration and nationalities policy. His coarseness and vindictive style were easy enough to overlook in the brutal years of war, and anyway his skills as an organizer were in desperately short supply. It was only later, in the years of peace, that the price of his preeminence began to worry even Lenin. Trotsky was a maverick, too. His reputation rested on his role as tactical director of the October coup, but it was his leadership of the Red Army that really secured his place, till 1924, as Lenin's second in command.

It was the party in the provinces, however, beyond the privileged Kremlin circle, that really altered in the years of civil war. Thousands of the older generation left it, sometimes to avoid the Red Army draft, more often out of disillusionment. What they had wanted, soviet democracy, was lost, and in its place came single-party rule and terroristic government by decree. The people who replaced them at least could live with both. "Command-administrative methods" were not alien to them; many made their reputations first as soldiers, and then through military-style campaigns for labor discipline, grain requisition, or economic reconstruction. Karl Bauman, the Latvian left-winger who chaired the Communist Party in Moscow in 1929, was one of these; Lazar Kaganovich, the great survivor among Stalin's entourage, and a man whose reputation was made during his repressive rule in civil war Nizhnii Novgorod, another.

These new men and women were certain of their righteousness. Opposition, they believed, was doomed. The relics of the former world had no place in the new. Terror was inescapable because it served the cause. No one would have admitted to enjoying it. Members of the Cheka, as Dzerzhinskii famously decreed, should have "cool heads, warm hearts and clean hands." Yudif Borisovna Severnaya, the daughter of a civil war Chekist, now in her nineties, remembered her father as exactly this ideal of the incorruptible public servant. Boris Severnyi was in charge of the Cheka in the Black Sea port of Odessa. The city, as she recalled, was in constant turmoil. "There were Gaidamaki, Petlyurovtsy, Germans, White Guards—the whole time fighting from hand to hand," she said, remembering the different armies that had fought over Ukraine. "And there was [French] intervention. Father was always the head of underground counter-espionage. His main role was always intelligence." No questions or prompting could deflect her from this view. "There were masses of enemies of Soviet power," she would answer, "masses of bandits, we had to have some order. Banditry is terrifying." Severnyi was still dealing with the "terrifying" disorder outside when his daughter, a privileged member of the new elite, began her first piano lessons.[70]

Some aspects of the work of men like Severnyi were actually made easier by the general crisis. "What is going on; is anything at all going on?" Got'e asked in his diary on 18 July. In fact, the former czar, Nicholas II, and his entire family had just been murdered. The killing, which took place on 16 July, was ordered from the capital, although it was a local Bolshevik group in the town of Ekaterinburg that organized and carried it out.[71] But the shots in the basement of the Ipatiev house went almost unnoticed in the general turmoil. Ekaterinburg itself was in danger of falling to the Whites. Elsewhere, there were equally pressing issues to occupy the late czar's former subjects. Got'e mentioned the killing almost in passing (and after a long paragraph about his own plans to leave for Kharkov) several weeks later.[72] More direct censorship, an emerging culture of secrecy, was relatively easy to implement in a world that was already fractured and starved of news.

Beyond censorship, however, a new mentality was forming. A public language, a new way of describing the world in ideologized terms, was beginning to develop. The dilution of words that this involved was arguably more effective than direct censorship, and it certainly acted more insidiously upon mourning, grief and memory. The "people are bewitched by grand illusions," wrote Pitirim Sorokin. "All around, ferocity and slaughter reign supreme, but they do not desist repeating that the brotherhood of man is being realised . . . All around, morality crumbles away, license, sadism and cruelty are everywhere—the masses call it a moral regeneration."[73] The critics, the people who did not join the parades or wave the banners, had little to focus on beyond their own subsistence. "We went out to mow early in the morning," wrote Got'e from his country house on 15 July 1918. "The newspapers did not come at all . . ." "I wrote nothing yesterday," he added on 19 July, "because we worked all day."[74] The world of "Sovdepiya," as he called the new government, echoing its own use of acronyms, remained remote—dissociated—from his Moscow study and his country estate.

The new morality was far more interested in the future of the revolution than in the individual lives or deaths of citizens. Violence itself was often imagined as a necessary and purifying aspect of the revolutionary process. Poetry and art reflected this, and so did the changing pattern of everyday speech. "Explode / Chop apart / The old world!" began a poem of the time. "Be / Merciless! / Strangle / The bony body of destiny!"[75] Even ordinary work was lurid. "The evil Moloch drinks workers' blood," ran a poem about a factory. "You are meat for my vampire's meal, it cries. Lunch and breakfast for the machine."[76] Everyone started using the words and slogans of the army. By the end of the civil war, the newspapers were announcing "fronts" for everything from the grain harvest to personal hygiene, "campaigns" were launched against lateness or alcoholism; and there were "vanguards" in every factory and down every mine.[77] Public discourse also became less respectful, as the barrack-room and student habit of addressing everyone in familiar forms ("Comrade" was usually accompanied by "*ty*," the Russian equivalent of the familiar, singular, "you") was adopted as a general rule.

Rhetorical violence was complemented by a heightened public emotionality. Even routine political speeches appealed to the pathos of the revolution, the extreme crisis of the war, and the glorious victory ahead.[78] Bereavement in particular was a popular theme of the sentimental poetry that found its way into the press. But it was unreal, kitsch, contained. At the height of the typhus epidemic, for instance, when thousands were dying in the streets, on trains, and in squalid basement rooms, *Rabochaya zhizn'* printed a succession of hospital poems, all set in silent wards and shrouded in clean linen.[79] Radical religious sentiment often added to the general mood of poignancy. Young mothers kept up prayerful vigils by their dying children's beds, and everyone went to the cemetery to reflect. "On the earth—fires, but in heaven—stars," began a contribution, "At the Cemetery." "In my soul is darkness, and I look for you in vain. Your friends and sisters sleep beside you."[80] It was all a fantasy. Sleep, by 1918, was not the obvious image for real cemeteries. Most people, in fact, avoided them. Mourners were afraid of pestilence, appalled by the heaps of corpses, the stink, the flies. And no one could avoid the hungry dogs that loitered in the melting snow.

In public, then, the civil war was understood in echoes of brutality, violence, and unrealistic sentimentalism. But the private responses of individual survivors cannot be inferred from published sources. Many had terrible memories to assimilate, and many had been involved in atrocities that would be difficult to forget. The ideologized culture that was being built around them did not, for the most part, translate into their real lives. It was a long way from the "commanding heights" to the reality of deserted factories, starving workers, and plundered tool stores. Even the cabbage harvest was now the subject of heroic effort and proletarian self-sacrifice. The language began to lose its most effective words, deafened by euphemism and hyperbole. Because there were few adequate words in which to share it, pain became dumb. As a secret, it remains, for the historian, difficult to track. Nonetheless, it is clear that the tragedy that each survivor faced, as the civil war drew to a close, was not so much brutalization as inexorable loss; the loss of community, of family, of many of their hopes; the loss of material security, and, insensibly at first, the loss of the means to share their searing images of the past. "You become an accomplice even though you are an adversary," wrote a former Bolshevik, "because you are unable to express disapproval even if you are ready to pay with your life."[81]

Two kinds of response were common among survivors of the civil war. The most extreme was trauma. Virtually everyone had haunting memories. A substantial minority was disabled by them. Large numbers of these suffered from nightmares, unexplained phobias, and the psychosomatic illnesses associated with their years of strain and fear, but the most serious casualties—an estimated 1.5 million among First World War veterans alone—were too ill to work, or even to return to family life.[82] Most other people, the survivors who rebuilt their lives in the new world, developed ways of coping with a dual reality. In public they were Soviet citizens. In private, they somehow kept on living with their own quite separate histories.

Official memoirs of the fighting were, of course, collected, but the published propaganda—triumphant, emotional, and dripping with that saccharine pathos—did not describe reality for many people. Even a Red Guard like Dune, whose memoirs contain almost no reference to his own feelings, gave way to anxiety and doubt as he contemplated the destruction of industry and the exhaustion of his fellow workers. The idea of proletarian victory no longer convinced him. After all, Lenin himself was saying, by 1922, that the Russian proletariat had disappeared. Dune was left to wonder how to understand "a regime that rested upon a myth," the regime for which he had fought so hard. "Was it," he asked, "that . . . we had given birth to a classless, starving collection of people, with silent factories and mills?"[83]

Others had never even started to believe the Leninist master narrative of class-based revolution and world brotherhood. Some found alternative structures, fitting their memories into religious patterns, or using epic images from folklore, music, and lament. Some began to live with a sense of uniqueness, later developing into guilt, believing themselves to be exceptions, even freaks. Inconvenient facts had quietly to be suppressed. "We used to play civil war when we were kids," the daughter of an Old Bolshevik explained. "Reds versus Whites." The rest had gone, the inconvenient and ugly realities—the ethnic conflict, the complex partisan engagements, the misery and disease. "The girls," she added, "always had to be the Whites."[84]

Revolutionary Russia had no special facilities for patients who suffered from psychological trauma. The worst affected were kept in ordinary hospitals, albeit sometimes in separate mental wards. Nikolai Borodin, who worked in one of these in the early 1920s, remembered that "almost everyone called it the madhouse." Working there was unpleasant. Many of the patients received little treatment other than physical restraint. "I could not truthfully call the patients nice and kind," he continued. "Some were interesting, but all of them were pathetic. The majority of them were insane because their minds were not strong enough to resist the things they saw during the Civil War and the Great Famine."[85] Letters to Semashko, the commissar for public health, took Borodin's distaste a step further by referring to the behavior of some trauma patients as "scandalous" and "disordered."[86] An official in Moscow complained that they were "indisciplined," "forgetful," and "evasive"; "they do not take responsibility for their own behavior . . . and create a very unpleasant atmosphere for others."[87]

Prejudice of this kind was typical of the population as a whole, and even of some members of the medical profession, but within the Russian psychiatric establishment the idea of trauma—though not the word itself—was widely recognized. The phenomenon that British doctors called shell shock (known in Russian by various terms—contusion, for symptoms thought to be linked to physical damage to the brain or nerves; and neurasthenia, that general catch-all of the late nineteenth century, for less specific nervous problems) had been identified during the Russo-Turkish war of 1877–1888, and was studied by several specialists throughout the Russo-Japanese war of 1904–1905. Russian psychiatrists had stayed in touch with colleagues in Britain and France after 1914, and exchanged information at a series of international conferences during the First World War.[88] A substantial core of doubters remained, skeptical of any theory that condoned apparent cowardice or lack of religious faith, but in that respect, too, psychiatry within the Russian empire was not exceptional.[89]

There was no time to think of trauma during the civil war. A committee, known by its clumsy acronym Vserokompom, was set up in 1919 to coordinate provision for war veterans, but until 1921 it did little more than "draw the attention of the broad worker and peasant mass, and equally of the party and economic organs" to the problem of invalids.[90] In 1923, however, after a long institutional struggle, a group of military psychiatrists persuaded it to fund a single experimental hospital for trauma patients near Yalta, in the Crimea. The moving spirit was the shell shock expert Professor S. A. Preobrazhenskii, who had written and lectured extensively on the problem to audiences in Petrograd before the revolution. The director of the new hospital was another trauma specialist, A. V. Livanov, from Moscow. The neuropsychological center was given a military title, Red Star.

On paper, then, the Soviet Union was taking a pioneering initiative, inspired, in part, by Germany, where shell-shocked patients were being put to productive use in industry after brief periods of rehabilitation.[91] Preobrazhenskii in particular would work to create an understanding of trauma among Soviet health officials, and he encouraged them to take a very broad view. He estimated, for example, that the psychological casualties of recent wars outnumbered those with physical illnesses four to one. Psychological illnesses, he added, were often complicated (and masked) by other problems, including malnutrition and tuberculosis. The most sensitive understanding of the causes of trauma would be needed to effect a cure, while generous material support, including adequate food and restful conditions, would also have to be provided. Red Star, initially, proposed to offer all of these.

The reality, however, was bleak. A chilling paper in the clinic's early records called for a "normalization of living conditions" in it, and later documents cataloged its troubles; the shortages of food, clothing, and boots; the unavailability of medicine. Resources were scarce in every area of Soviet life in the early 1920s, and Red Star's patients did not attract much sympathy. They were no easier to like than the invalids in Borodin's madhouse. Many were alcoholics, some were addicted to morphine. More than a quarter also suffered from syphilis.[92] Hard-pressed officials outside the hospital saw little point in spending time and money on its work, especially when there were lines of more conventional invalids still waiting for their operations, their pensions and their drugs. Back in the capital, a representative of the Moscow Soviet proposed that traumatized veterans should be exiled to colonies in the far north. Failing that, he suggested, the best way to deal with them was to put them to productive work, anything they could manage, and to make sure they did it by standing over them "with a loaded Mauser in your hand."[93] It was this kind of view that prevailed by 1927. Red Star was quietly closed.

Beyond the clinic, however, trauma would remain an issue. It gave rise to special concern, in fact, within the Communist Part itself. Party members were particularly prone to exhaustion, depression, and anxiety. "Neurasthenia," which included languor, lack of motivation, depression, and psychosomatic symptoms, was among the most common diagnoses among them—as frequent as tuberculosis—in the mid-1920s.[94] Residents of the Kremlin usually received the best treatment available, even if it meant a trip to Germany.[95] But the majority received no such understanding or help. Suicide rates, especially among the young, rose sharply as the emergency of war receded. Once again, there seemed to be a gap between the grandiloquent, unattainable public world—the official world—and the private reality of scarcity, depression, and overwork. Young Communists despaired, turning their frustration against themselves with all the energy of their ideals. The revolution had not worked out as they had dreamed. No amount of self-sacrifice seemed to be adequate. The mythic cause of the masses, of history, and the world proletariat demanded more than they could give.[96]

Experts linked the prevalence of neurosis to social causes.[97] The imperialist and civil wars, the famine, material uncertainty, and even price inflation were all investigated in an attempt to isolate the most important.[98] Advocates of social medicine believed that suicide should be preventable, and in the 1920s they attempted to develop a scientific formula for controlling it. Questionnaires were issued to the police, and to the doctors who attended suicides, from as early as 1920.[99] The victims were to be described by category—social background, age, gender, occupation, whether left- or right-handed. Even their suicide notes were analyzed.[100] This kind of sympathy, however, was increasingly out of step with the new times. The objective study of suicide ended in the late 1920s, to be replaced by a new Soviet dogma. In December 1925, the Communist Party's ideological spokesman, E. M. Yaroslavskii, told a Party meeting in the city that had recently been renamed Leningrad that suicides were "weak-willed, weak of character" and lacking in faith in "the power and strength of the Party."[101] A Russian historian of the issue recently added that suicide, by the late 1920s, appeared to some to be "a witness to the free right of an individual to choose his own fate. And that did not suit Soviet power at all."[102]

As it turned out, anything that focused on the individual was likely to attract official criticism in Soviet Russia by the end of the 1920s. The ideas of Freud were an early casualty. At first, some Communists had regarded psychoanalysis as a tool that might be used to transform vanguard representatives of the human species into Nietzschean supermen. Trotsky took a close interest in it, as did his friend, the Bolshevik Adol'f Ioffe.[103] One witness recalled that "in the 1920s it was not just not dangerous to be involved in psychoanalysis. It was prestigious."[104] The "International Solidarity" experimental children's home, whose aim was to rear babies and children along Freudian principles, counted among its elite inmates in 1921 the six-month-old Vasilii Stalin, son of the famous Iosif Vissarionovich.[105] But psychoanalysis was slow, expensive and potentially subversive. The Bolsheviks wanted quicker results, and they did not want unscripted conversations to take place between doctors and their patients. Individualism was dangerous, counterproductive, and bourgeois.

The engineers of human souls turned their attention from analysis to reeducation, from the individual to the mass. As psychiatrist A. B. Zalkind told a meeting in 1929, "in the USSR as nowhere else, enormous attention is drawn to the study of human personality . . . The toiling masses, the mass human personality, growing swiftly and creatively, expanding the boundaries of their aspirations, have come to power, to culture, to construction. These masses, ignored by bourgeois science, must be studied anew both in the sense of identifying their genuine characteristics and in the sense of identifying methods of educational influence on them."[106] Lenin's friend Nikolai Bukharin put it more earthily: "If we consider the individual personality in its development," he remarked in 1924, "we see that it is in essence like a little sausage skin stuffed with the influences of the environment."[107]

The Bolsheviks would study to fill these "little sausage skins" with carefully chosen meat. There would be public demonstrations, slogans, marches; free time was occupied with socially productive work. The private sphere would shrink. A person who could or would not swallow this—whether neurotic, neurasthenic, obsessed, or phobic—would come to be regarded as weak rather than ill or injured. Depression, now seen as antisocial, became a source of shame.[108] Many people hid their symptoms, repressed their anxieties and carried on as best they could. For those whose illness was too severe for concealment, drugs and electroconvulsive therapy were among the continuing options. Anyone lucky enough to escape these therapies would find that hypnosis, not talk, had become the treatment of choice. As one psychiatrist put it, "you went to the great man, the leader, you sat down and closed your eyes and he put you right." It was an approach that fit better with emerging Soviet culture.[109]

Mental illness was exceptional, however. Most people dealt with memory in other ways. They also adapted to the new collectivism. It would be years before the full, triumphant Soviet mentality took shape, the one that celebrated victory in 1945. But some of its dimensions were already becoming clear, emerging from the chaos of the civil war and from the shattered fragments of the old regime. Hard work became the commonest and most effective means of recreating a person's sense of self, asserting his or her social value, and silencing intrusive ghosts and questions. Among the most emphatic answers that people gave when I asked them how they coped with painful memories in the decade after the revolution was simply, "We had too much else to think about." The solution worked, at least in part, because it was so perfectly tailored to the socialist collective ethos.

At the same time, the brashness of collectivism was deflated, in private, by irony. "Long Live the Soviet of Workers and Peasants!" ran a party slogan. "Long Live Fresh Air!" someone quipped beside it.[110] "It is enough to see an article headed 'More attention to agriculture!' or 'Face to the Red Fleet!'" wrote a literary critic in the early 1920s, "to know that there is no point in reading it."[111] Reality was also bent to shape by means of Russia's favorite sedative, vodka. Alcoholism and drunkenness remained widespread, despite the exhortations of the state and the episodic shortages that followed prohibition.[112] Others resorted to narcotic drugs. Opiates had been available in almost every field hospital during the First World War, and they were still in common use into the 1920s.[113]

Outside the cities, too, the old world survived. Religion was almost certainly the most important source of comfort for believers in the villages, and even when religion was attacked, the traditional languages of mourning—especially those of the earth and of lament—provided a framework for memory in country districts at least until the outbreak of the Great Patriotic War.[114] An ethnographer who visited a group of villages on the shores of the White Sea in the 1930s found women whose memories were almost all framed in pre-Soviet language. Their recollections were full of references to traditional preoccupations such as the recovery of the body, reverent burial, and the bitterness of living alone. Premonitions, ghosts, and supernatural vengeance were also crucial, making sense of images whose power might otherwise have endured, formless and oppressive.

One woman described how she and her neighbors spent a night in hiding after soldiers came to their village. The darkness echoed with shots, but none of the frightened refugees knew what was happening back home. It was already light when the men arrived, carrying the dying son of a neighbor to the hideout, slung across the back of a horse. As she helped to bury the boy, however, the woman who told the story suddenly knew that her own son was also dead. Grief overcame her, and she cried inconsolably, though none of the witnesses could understand why. She insisted on returning to the village at once. It turned out that her son had helped to repulse a band of Whites. "The Communists came out of the village to meet us, carrying a flag," she remembered. But their gratitude and sympathy meant nothing to her. The boy had died, and "a mother is still a mother."[115]

Another woman remembered how she had been summoned to identify a body. It had been found in a shallow grave near the road. The authorities who were holding it asked her to describe the clothes her son had been wearing when he was last seen. Only then did they allow her to see the corpse. White troops had cut off the boy's hands and feet, and he had been dead for several days. "But I knew, I recognised, how could I not recognise . . . my own."[116] Like many other women, she found people to help her to transport and then bury the body. And while the record of the interview says nothing about priests (the omission may have been the ethnographer's own—religion was not a fashionable research topic in 1930), it does reproduce some of the words of her lament. The researcher wrote down several of these, the more elaborate of which might have been taken straight from Barsov's ethnographic collections of the 1870s. This mother's, however, was simpler:

O, I carried you,
O, I bore you,
In vain to the pale light,
But I taught you kindly . . .
So evil people have killed you,
With weapons they came and attacked,
So that you have left your little mother.
Who will work beside your mother now?
And who will take her place?[117]

The ethnographer who collected this material was surprised by the apparent calmness of the women as they talked; their interest in seemingly irrelevant issues such as the price of tea, their pride in their embroidery, their pleasure in gossip. When they did talk about bereavement, the stories often came suddenly, directly following some remark about the state of the crops. They were usually reluctant to discuss the violence at all. None wept. They seemed, the ethnographer noted, to be ashamed of their tears.[118] Her conclusion was that the trivial details of life had swallowed her respondents' grief, reducing their memories of the war to "heroic tales of the ideal."

Between the lines of her reports, however, which were collected over several summers, there are some other hints about the women's lives. They were canny. They did not want to bare their souls to a stranger from the city, and anyway they could not know, at first, exactly what it was that the well-spoken young woman from Moscow really wanted. They told their stories, trial and error leading them toward the version that would satisfy her. It is also unlikely that she, as a good Soviet citizen, would have encouraged them to dwell on the most uncomfortable parts of their experience.[119] Her own prudishness may have helped to mute the women's recollections. They may even have wanted to spare her the worst—as they might spare a child—by keeping the most shocking images to themselves. But what this indicates is their resilience. They did not need to talk, but nor did they avoid it. The trivia that interested them—and disappointed the ethnographer, who noted sadly that there had been relatively few deaths in the region—were actually, too, the stuff of real life. It should have been a cause for celebration, ten years after the slaughter, that the price of tea and the shape of a new dress were interesting subjects.

The old words and keening rhythms had been forgotten in other parts of Russia, and families and communities had been shattered. Despite all this, there were still some clear reminders of the truth. Some were written in the landscape. "It is enough to travel a few versts out of Kursk in order to feel the breath of the civil war," wrote an observer called Yakovlev in March 1923. "Trees across a huge area have been hacked and damaged. You often see abandoned houses, with their windows broken and their roofs in ruins. Glass itself is rare in any dwelling. The only thing that distinguishes the schools is that they are in an even worse state. If a building has no doors or windows, it means it's a school." The hope of social improvement, education, bequeathed by nineteenth-century zemstvos, was hardly even a memory after the catastrophe. Religion, however, was beginning to rally everywhere. As Yakovlev added, the only houses that had been kept up, and the only ones with glass, belonged to priests.[120]

The crisis had made all religions more important. As soon as the fighting ended, as soon as there was a breathing space and a little extra time, the people flocked back to the churches to thank their gods and patron saints. "In the spiritual life of Russia," Sorokin wrote, "a great revival awoke. While other buildings were left to decay, the churches were repaired." In 1921 the Orthodox Easter coincided with the socialist May Day festival. "The Communist Party demonstration was attended by only a few thousand," he continued. "But a religious procession, held on the following day, was attended by about 300,000 people. The procession was so big and impressive that the Communists themselves were obliged to take off their hats in respect."[121] Got'e agreed. "Easter has vanquished the First of May," he wrote in his diary that evening.[122] But this, for Bolshevism, was intolerable. The civil war broke up the state and destroyed all but the shadow of the czarist polity. The time had come to burn its icons, and in their place, perhaps, to shape a new mentality, if not exactly a religion, of their own creation.

5

COMMON AND UNCOMMON GRAVES

At any other time, the directive about the thirteenth-century saint might have caused offense, consternation, or even ironic laughter. But these days nothing is shocking, and very little is ever funny. The Justice Department of the Northern Region had announced that mummified corpses are a threat to Soviet power.[1] But there are many others at this moment, and most of them are still alive. The directive bristles, too, with contradictions, hidden catches. The Ministry itself, the Justice Ministry, has called for the exercise of tact, but tact has hardly been its own priority in recent months. Do not upset religious believers, it orders. That would be easier if hundreds were not being shot in the yard of the Big House and out near Smolny every night; it would be easier if they would stop arresting priests and monks, stop driving nuns into the streets. The task itself is tactless. There is no delicate way of marching into a monastery and seizing its most sacred treasure, and if you open a coffin you are bound to disturb the dead. Even the medical part, the scientific examination of the corpse, is an obscenity. And then there are the real fears. Perhaps it is true that the bodies of the saints have supernatural powers. Perhaps there will be a curse. The city soviet files the document and takes no further action for almost two years.

It is 1919. March. Petrograd is locked in ice. To the west is the sea, the Gulf of Finland, frozen. To the east stretch six thousand miles of forest and steppe, still buried deep in snow. Petrograd itself is a city of ice. Its palaces are festooned with it, dripping with thousands of icy stalactites. Elegant details of their architecture are lost in ice; sills, ledges and architraves distorted by ice. Snowdrifts entirely conceal grand marble steps, the sweep of an entrance, stone lions, balustrades. Ice gardens, frozen palms and lilies, have grown across the casement windows and the glazed doors that lead to wrought-iron balconies, blunting the winter light, obscuring the view of the new world from any window that still has glass. Many do not. Many do not even have window frames, for the wood burns well, and it is easier to rip out a frame this size than to hack through parquet floors or hardwood paneling. The people have learned this, just as they have learned to patch their coats with old curtains, just as they have learned to trade silver watches for salt, as they have learned to keep their mouths shut. Thousands have left. These days there are no crowds on Nevsky Prospekt, there is no casual sociability.

It helps, perhaps, that the city is no longer the capital. Directives can be shelved more readily, priorities adjusted. It has already been a year since the Bolsheviks removed their headquarters to Moscow. They left Grigorii Zinoviev in charge, as arrogant a politician as ever graced a disused ballroom, but they took large numbers of their staff with them. The offices of five thousand clerks, superintendents, secretaries, copyists, inspectors, and postboys are empty. The proud buildings are half abandoned, the largest halls and galleries blind and dark. But in the smaller rooms, down corridors, clustering together like bees in a winter hive, the lowlier breeds—municipal officials, the men and women who see to street lighting and drains—have begun their work of colonization. Officials of the old regime work side by side with the deputies of the new, earnest clerks and threadbare accountants beside former welders—the promoted beneficiaries of proletarian Soviet democracy. They struggle to find a common language. But it is easier to concentrate on that, to pass empty notes in the new Soviet jargon, than it is to think about the work that must be done.

It is the vanguard of the godless, the zealots of the ideological front, that has initiated the policy on saints. Even in the depths of the civil war, they understand that it is religion that is the greatest single challenge to Bolshevism as an ideology, the strongest buttress of the old world, the Trojan horse, as they would say, of reaction, monarchism, and passivity. In their despair the people have been praying; they have no other hope. In some places the Communists themselves are filing into church; the crisis has made everyone more superstitious.[2] The rumors of miracles are everywhere; the people believe in icons, prodigies, sacred signs. Even an academic like Got'e is half convinced. "A miracle occurred today," he wrote in May 1918. "The Nikol'skie gates were draped in red, and so was the icon, which had been wrecked already in the October days. Suddenly the red drapery began to fall away and exposed the icon; the fabric unfolded as if some kind of acid had been poured on it. A crowd gathered . . . there was a public prayer, and then firing in the air to disperse the crowd."[3]

Icons can be burned, and eventually many will be, but the saints are more resilient. The danger is that they will act as inspiration for some popular revolt. Direct assault is not an option. There have been incidents—excesses, as the bureaucrats will call them, involving angry crowds and torches, crowbars, pickaxes—and these have been a public relations disaster. Cool heads in Moscow resolve, for now, that the best way of dealing with the issue is through the application of science. The bodies of the saints, as everyone knows, are not supposed to rot. They smell sweet, they weep real tears, they watch over the faithful; their power is holy, and to touch them is to be blessed, healed, protected. The men in the Justice Ministry decide to bring the coffins into the rational light, to open them, unwrap the bones, and strip them of their magic.

The Bolsheviks will later claim that the campaign against the mummified corpses originated among the mass, and they will use the mass as scapegoats whenever the policy backfires.[4] The authorities, officially, are interested only in fact, in decency, and in maintaining order. But there must be consistency. Over in Moscow, the body of Saint Sergius of Radonezh, the holy founder of the Trinity Monastery, has just been exposed, prodded, and publicly scrutinized (Kolchak's White armies were about to advance from Omsk and Perm, and in the south Tsaritsyn was still under heavy attack). The second capital cannot be left behind. Its most famous relic is Prince Alexander Nevsky. Eventually his coffin will have to be opened just like all the rest. A second letter from the Justice Department reminds the soviet that it must comply. "The cult of dead bodies and of these dolls must end," it decrees. There must be "an end to the various contradictory, dark and negative rumors" that are circulating with regard to these "so-called relics . . . We are acting on the initiative of the conscious revolutionary mass."[5]

The policy will yield mixed results. A ceremony of exposure—the opening of a coffin—in Moscow, Tver', and later, too, in Petrograd—always attracts large crowds. It is a diversion from the grim routine of life, a spectacle. Most people are fascinated, curious, and many half believe that something strange will happen, divine vengeance or a revelation. The lines collect in the streets, exhausted people swathed in coats and scarves, uncertain what to feel. But the dust and bone that they will see will not kill their belief. "I took a close look at the uncovered skeleton of St Sergius," Got'e wrote in April 1919. "They have left it as it was upon exhumation . . . They say the examining doctors confirmed that the skeleton has lain for five hundred years and that the yellow hair that was discovered was grey, but yellowed by time. Thus our priests, using their wits and leaving the relics uncovered, correctly wish to show: look, we do not conceal what was and what is—and in doing so, of course, they only strengthen religious feeling."[6]

The civil war, however, is generally a time of frozen inanition. Most people are too numb and too preoccupied to give the campaign much attention. "There is neither religious nor historical feeling in me," Got'e added. "The one and the other have been destroyed by what is going on."[7] This mood will last until the peace, until the spring of 1921. In March that year the emergency begins to recede; the colors begin to seep back into city streets; the people, to return. The Bolshevik government announces a relaxation in the rules governing private trade, the New Economic Policy. It legalizes the deals and barter that have been going on in secret for three years. The shops fill once again with bread, and there are market stalls selling moth-eaten furnishings, silver tankards, rabbits, chickens, icon lamps. Traders visit from the villages with cucumbers, sacks of buckwheat, butter, meat, and tallow candles. In the big cities, at least, it is almost possible to breath again, to plan, to hope. This optimism will gather pace for several years, until 1927 or 1928. Thereafter, the government will create another kind of crisis, a crisis based on panic, and this will be the precondition, from 1929, for Stalin's decision to collectivize the peasants and race toward industrial growth, to catch up and overtake the rest of Europe and America.

The economic revival of the early 1920s will be slow, but what is instant is a general sense of liberation, of deliverance. Perhaps the world has not been shattered for all time. The people grope for half-forgotten words and prayers, unwrap civilian clothes. Private trade is not the only habit they will rediscover. "There is a church outside my window," Trotsky wrote from Moscow in April 1922. "Out of every ten people who pass (counting everyone, even children), at least seven, if not eight, cross themselves as they walk by it. And that includes large numbers of Red Army soldiers and many young people."[8] The same Red Army men are also leaving Moscow, going home, back to the villages. As they arrive they will drop their shabby rucksacks, kiss their children, mutter a curse or two about the state of the land, and bow to cross themselves before the icon in the hut.[9] "The goat of revolution," said Got'e's friends, "will break its horns on the church wall."[10] The Bolsheviks had won the war, but the church was set to spread its blessing like a cloud across their peace.

The steps that revolutionaries will take in answer to this challenge will be fateful, and not only for the church, with all its rituals and wealth. Death will be central to the flush of innovation. A faction in the Bolshevik Party will set out to break the grip of the past, to exorcise the ghosts of precedent and counterrevolution, and even to supplant traditional languages of mourning, especially where these face backward into time, remember, brood on the realities of loss. The new culture will focus on the future, on the material task, each person's duty to a socialist society. The emphasis that different kinds of revolutionary will choose a place on each of these aspects will vary. Some people—the ones whose interest is power—disdain to think of new mentalities, while others think and write of little else. The policies will be inconsistent. They will also be more successful when it comes to demolition—the exposure of saints, for instance, or the dynamiting of a church—than in the sphere of reconstruction, the making of new worlds, new images, new rituals of memory and grief. But inconsistent as they are, and often unsuccessful, in their own terms, the antireligious campaigns will ultimately affect every Soviet citizen, will color their attitudes to death, and change the framework of their memories forever.

The rationalists often had the best intentions, but in the end the policies were cruel. In other circumstances, perhaps, a secular funeral ritual would have superseded elaborate religious ceremonies almost by default. Religion had not been universally popular among the Russian people, and there were other pressures on tradition at this time—such as the changing social patterns associated with industry and with cities—that worked to drive the old world out of mind. If these processes had continued steadily, more or less organically, the old ways might have been forgotten as unobtrusively as they had been in the industrialized countries of Western Europe. As it was, the Soviet campaign against tradition in the 1920s and 1930s would be enacted amidst massive upheaval and distress. Millions died, and tens of millions mourned.

A crisis of this kind—or rather, a succession of crises—would usually have pushed those who survived it back to the familiar world of unexplored but comforting belief, back to the structure and the words that religion always offered, back to the compensations of a promised afterlife. A decade later, during the Great Patriotic War, even Stalin would recognize the value of religion for these reasons. This time, however, the rituals and the sanctuaries would be undermined—damaged and fragmented, rather than destroyed—and nothing adequate would take their place.

Most of the pain that Stalinism would cause would be assuaged by more or less traditional means; the prayers went on, the glasses of vodka continued to be poured, and people still believed, in an unfocused way, in peace and afterlife, if not in hell.[11] These continuities might lead us to suppose, looking back at the events with hindsight, that little changed. At the time, however, each change was conspicuous, even shocking, and it was not clear to anyone that later generations would declare that this was a resilient funerary culture. The absences, the improvisations, the enforced shortcuts and makeshifts might just as easily have been deplored as the beginning of the end, as the first of a series of losses that signified the collapse of a whole world. The basic decencies that people had learned, from childhood, to expect, were not observed as they might wish. For those who preferred secular rites, the new collective ceremonies also remained unsatisfying. If they thought about death, their own or that of anyone they loved, millions of Soviet citizens would find the turbulent years of Stalinism dark and comfortless, uncanny, haunted, bleak.

The Soviet funeral industry got off to a bad start. Pitirim Sorokin was one of several diarists to write about it with disgust. "To die in Russia in these times is easy," he commented, "but to be buried is very difficult."[12] It was a reflection prompted after he had spent four days "standing hours in line, interviewing dozens of officials" in order to secure permission to bury the daughter of one of his friends.[13] "It seems that it is even inconvenient to die nowadays," Got'e wrote in November 1918. "The gravediggers will not bury more than seven bodies a day, and will not bury earlier than 1 P.M." At the recent burial of another acquaintance, he continued, "the grave had not been dug deep enough and the coffin had to be raised to the ground again; they lost the cross, which had been prepared beforehand, and they were rude and disgruntled—a typical manifestation of the Russian Revolution."[14] By 1922 things were even worse. "The funeral of M. M. Ryndin lasted six days," he wrote, "since we got permission to bury him . . . only two days after the death." The burial order, for a prestigious place in Moscow's Novodevich'e cemetery, was finally secured in exchange for "a pair of galoshes from Glavrezina [the state rubber monopoly]." The meticulous historian added a note about rising costs. "Ninochka's funeral in November 1919 cost 30,000," he wrote; "Uncle Edward's funeral in December 1921 was 5,000,000; M. M.'s funeral in March 1922 was 33,000,000. Bread cost 60,000 a pound."[15]

The truth was that the local soviets were overwhelmed. The officials could not cope. The rules were always changing. There were new rubber stamps, of course; but there was no paper; there was certainly no tea; and the range of bureaucratic responsibility expanded by the day as the new government took over urban services that once had been the province of a thousand private companies. War Communism, the operating principle of the civil war, provided for the nationalization of almost everything, and that included the funeral industry. On 7 December 1918 the Bolsheviks announced that it was to be a soviet monopoly. The decree itself was characteristically optimistic, normative. Henceforth, it stated, "distinctions of rank, whether they apply to the place of burial or to the style of the funeral, are to be annihilated."[16] The gravediggers, as public employees, were to be given production quotas—to protect them from exploitation—theoretically the limit was two full-sized graves per day per person, or four smaller ones, designed for children.[17] The price of coffins was to be fixed, and the coffin makers were issued with a list of specifications—three sizes, one style.[18] There were even provisions for the mass production of wreaths and colored paper.[19]

One problem was that death and dying were difficult things to manage on a central basis. There were bottlenecks, bureaucratic oversights, piles of coffins in a yard in Volokolamsk and none at all in Moscow. Bribery, as Got'e discovered, became a routine part of burial arrangements. But bribery and bottlenecks were features of the Soviet commercial world; they would define it for another seventy years. What happened between 1918 and 1921 was exceptional, and it was really the result of high mortality. By 1918 unburied corpses were piling up—literally—at the cemetery gates of every large city. Inspectors scribbled horrified reports and issued questionnaires: How many corpses do you have awaiting burial, how long have they been waiting, what condition are they in, the responsible official is to sign this document and forward it at once.[20] When they had time they toured the cemeteries. The reports they wrote were blunt and shocked. These men, whose views on decency were formed in gentler times, could not contain their worries for the new society.

A group of officials from the Petrograd Soviet visited the suburban cemetery in which the victims of Bloody Sunday had been buried in 1905. When they made their tour, in the third week of February 1920, they found 241 unburied corpses there. "Some of them are in coffins, and some of these have been partly crushed, so that the corpses are exposed . . . None of the corpses looks very fresh, but rather as if they have been lying in hospital mortuaries for a long time." Documents indicated that some of the bodies at the cemetery that day had been waiting for burial since 20 January. A shed in which others were stacked, without coffins, was in such poor condition that dogs had strayed inside to gnaw on some of the decaying limbs.

The inspectors estimated that at least twenty-five gravediggers would be needed to deal with the existing piles of corpses, let alone to keep pace with the thirty to forty new ones that would continue to arrive each day. When they made their visit, however, there were only seven men working at the site, and several of these had been absent for long periods because of illness. The local people knew exactly what was happening. A good many of them had brought the bodies of their dead along to the cemetery gates themselves, pulling them on sledges, because it was so hard to get a carter to drive them. They had haggled with the gravediggers, pleaded, wept, then watched, aghast, as the door to the cemetery shed was opened. Workers at a nearby factory had not complained, but the inspectors nonetheless noted reports of "disorders" at the cemetery itself.[21]

The situation was no easier in Moscow. An engineer who reported on the cemeteries there in April 1919 found it impossible to track the bodies of typhus victims from the local hospitals where they had died to their places of burial. The bodies were simply shipped out, without documents, without coffins, often without clothes, and buried in common pits, some of which were not even inside the territory of a cemetery. Members of the public could not always be certain that a relative had even died, and inquirers would never know where he or she was. "These conditions," the engineer noted, "are giving rise to accusations and dissatisfaction."[22] Some people finally began to bury their relatives themselves, digging graves wherever there was space.[23]

Most people preferred to think of other things, and everyone was struggling to survive, but sometimes the crisis at the cemeteries leaked back into the residential streets. In 1918 there was almost a riot in a district of central Moscow. Someone in a local hospital had made the mistake of piling thirty-two bodies into an ordinary passenger wagon, with windows, instead of the usual closed mortuary car. The tram clattered across the city, drawing shocked remarks, but when it stopped at a busy station, three hundred to four hundred people collected to stare. What they could see through the smeared glass were heaps of bodies dressed in rags, in their underclothes, or completely naked, some of them in a "terrible and disordered state."[24] The people jostled, shoved, and craned their necks, they called their friends, and the crowd began to lose its temper. "Let's see how Soviet power treats us," someone shouted. Sixty recruits from the nearby Red Army barracks were summoned, but it took them twenty minutes to break through the mob. A doctor who witnessed the incident confirmed that it had made an "appalling impression."[25]

The funeral departments of the Soviets were willing to try almost anything to end this situation. Their squeamishness about the use of common graves was quickly overcome. Finding the people to dig them, however, was more difficult. In Moscow, they tried using convicts to do the work, but the experiment was abandoned when most of these escaped.[26] It was also difficult to dig large graves in the winter, when the ground was frozen solid and buried deep in snow.[27] Some cemeteries suspended all burials for the month of January. Back in the mortuaries, as a result, the piles of bodies grew ever higher, "one on top of the other, on the floor and on every shelf, so that you cannot document or count them."[28] Several inspectors noted the strong smell pervading the area around the city-center hospitals.[29] There were also fears for groundwater.[30]

It was not surprising that harassed committees should have begun to consider the cheap, hygienic, and potentially labor-saving device of cremation. Moscow's consultant expert was frank about his proposal. "I can foresee," engineer Gashinskii wrote at the end of his enquiry in April 1919, "that cremation, as an innovation, could arouse protest among relatives or friends of the deceased, as a result of religious and other prejudices." Such difficulties would not arise, however, in the case of people who died without the knowledge of "their parents or kin."[31] With that difficulty out of the way, Moscow's crematorium, "or several crematoria," could be designed with one paramount goal, the rapid disposal of bodies. Decorative extras could wait. Getting the oven to a high enough temperature was the only real problem. Gashinskii's trial experiment with the body of a horse had not been encouraging, but he was certain that when his installation went into mass, as opposed to individual, production, the problems he had encountered—incomplete combustion and excessive quantities of ash—would be overcome. Indeed, he was so confident about his incinerator that he suggested it might also be used for the disposal of rubbish. Suitable forms of refuse, he added, would in turn make excellent fuel.[32]

The religious problems that Gashinskii had in mind were not trivial. The Orthodox Church forbade cremation. The whole materialist structure of its teaching about decay and resurrection, about the intimate connections that linked a soul forever to its flesh, relied on burial. More primitive beliefs about the earth were also hard to overlook. A body should return to soil, and not to fire; the mourners needed their grave. The cost-cutting and hygienic proposals to build a crematorium in St. Petersburg that had been considered in the 1890s had foundered for these reasons. The idea was regarded widely with revulsion. By 1919, however, the need for quick disposal was acute. A necessity, moreover, now opened agitational vistas of a most attractive kind. The church would have no power, and its ceremonies no relevance, in a new, industrialized, and scientific world of flame and ash.

The innovators faced innumerable obstacles. The minutes of their meetings record many words, and many hours of earnest planning, but almost no real progress from month to month and year to year. There was no obvious site in Moscow. Efficiency-inspired plans to build the crematorium beside one of the major civilian hospitals were abandoned when they almost caused a public riot. Red Army soldiers unhelpfully opposed the plan to locate it next to their military hospital.[33] The crematorium subcommittee of the Moscow Soviet promptly formed a working party to consider the "psychological aspects" of its new scheme. Gashinskii himself was sacked in December 1919, exactly a year after he had taken on the job. His successors took years to overcome the other technical problems, which included difficulties with the control of furnace temperature.[34] Moscow's crematorium finally opened in 1927, in grounds requisitioned from the Don monastery.

Petrograd's experts were more successful, at least in the short term. They were also more sensitive to the aesthetic and moral sensibilities of their public. They even held an open design competition for the crematorium complex. The entries, submitted in the autumn of 1919 (Yudenich's White army had almost reached the city's suburbs, and still there was no bread or sausage), ranged from the bizarre to the architecturally implausible. They all included elements of revolutionary kitsch, and many were inspired by the religious sentiment so evident in other forms of workers' art at the time. Engineer A. G. Dzhorogov's was among those to receive a commendation (none was built). "Let it be done grandly, artistically," he wrote of the cremation process. "Anything heavy, anything crude, anything which reminds one of burning" was ruled out of his plan. Instead, he wrote, "Let the building be a high one, so that it reaches nearer to heaven." His tower was inspired by Jacob's ladder, connecting heaven and earth, and the proposed entrance to his garden of rest was adorned with the words "Come unto me all that travail, and I will refresh you."[35] Petrograd's Standing Commission for the Building of the First State Crematorium and Morgue eventually ignored it all. Its own stationery featured a crow, curling smoke, and a human skull.

Serious planning continued throughout 1919 and 1920. As in Moscow, the choice of site was a major obstacle. The commission felt that the location should be central, accessible, and, ideally, at the heart of a region where mortality was especially high. In March 1919 it settled on a plot of land next to the Alexander Nevsky monastery. It was near a large canal, as well as the main arterial route through the city center, and it was only a few minutes away from Petrograd's largest railway station.[36] But the objections started at once. The Petrograd Soviet had other plans for the site, which it had scheduled for conversion into a public park. Its members also worried about the ash, dust, and smoke that the installation would generate in a densely populated district.[37] A rival engineer pointed out that the obvious route along which the hundreds of corpses to be cremated would be brought each day, mostly in horse-drawn carts, was Nevsky Prospekt, arguably still the finest street in Europe. "It will be known," he warned, "as the street of death." The solution, in his view, was to treat the new facility as if it were a factory, and isolate it in some suitably neglected suburb.[38]

While the planners squabbled, however, an experiment was under way that would make Petrograd the first city in Russia to operate a crematorium for its unclaimed dead. Engineers using convict labor were in the process of converting a bathhouse on Vasil'evskii Island into the world's first wood-burning crematorium.[39] The conversion of the building did not go smoothly, and there were endless technical difficulties with the furnace. But the main problem was a shortage of skilled labor. Everyone knew that the melting snow each spring could bring another epidemic. The yellow water trickled over thawing corpses—crows, horses, dogs, old men, and drunks—piles of garbage warmed and steamed, the maggots hatched, the creaking pipes and sewers leaked. The spring of 1919 had taught the Soviet its lesson, but as winter approached that year, the furnace—a prototype designed to burn at least six hundred infected corpses a month—was still far from ready. They drafted in more convicts; they found some army engineers with experience of boiler making and stoking. By the end of December, with four months, at best, to go before the death rates would begin to rise, they were even giving out bottles of cognac to the men to make them finish faster.[40] The scheme was still nine months at least behind completion.

The Petrograd crematorium finally opened for business in December 1920. It was not a success. A shortage of fuel made its oven inefficient, so that its average rate of productivity remained below 120 bodies a month. But the real problem was the roof, which was wooden. In February 1921 the bathhouse-crematorium overheated and burned down.[41] Fewer than 400 bodies had been burned. That such a fate should have befallen Petrograd's innovative engineering marvel was hardly something the commission wished to publicize. But other, darker shadows hovered round the operation. The bodies that were turned so inefficiently, and after so much labor, to charred bone and ashes were not those of willing volunteers. A single ceremonial service, complete with uniformed attendants and a handsome coffin, was held for propaganda purposes, but later photographs of the oven in operation show corpses for incineration lying naked on a slab. Petrograd's commissioners were experimenting with the efficient disposal of outcasts, refugees, and the carriers of plague. The same technique was later used, in Moscow, to dispose of the bodies that the secret police delivered to the crematorium at night, in batches, to be incinerated at once, "without waiting their turn."

Cremation, then, was not the answer to the problem of the dead, or not on any realistic scale. That left the new regime to ponder on the cemeteries. It nationalized them, of course, along with burials and the coffin industry, in December 1918.[42] But the fact remained that many were directly attached to churches and monasteries. The rest usually had chapels within their grounds. These facts alone were inconvenient, but so were all the monuments, statuary, and ornaments that called the past—and a different hierarchy of power—so readily to mind. From 1920 the Soviets in several cities began to discuss proposals to turn old cemeteries into parks. They said they wanted to remove the damaged and depressing stones, to level the sites, to landscape them, and to encourage the development of healthy proletarian leisure.

The new use of space brought benefits to some. An extension to the Dinamo factory in Moscow was built on the consecrated ground of the cemetery that formerly belonged to the Simonov monastery. Many of the stones were taken for the new building, and the remaining space was used to build apartment blocks for the expanding workforce.[43] Less attractively, the enclosure around the Spaso-Andronnikov monastery was used, for a time, as a camp for political prisoners. Still in Moscow, cemeteries attached to the Alekseyev and Danilov monasteries became workers' clubs and parks, while the Pokrovskoe cemetery was razed and leveled for a soccer field in 1924.[44]

The policy of obliteration worked. People who played soccer on the haunted ground would soon forget its origin. Migrant workers and new residents from distant villages would have no memory of the old landscape, no sense of desecration. Very few city dwellers were even aware of the fact that their apartment blocks were built on bones. Meanwhile, the Bolsheviks would take possession of selected artists, poets, and musicians from the past. These dead, the ideologically favored dead, were taken out of their original context—or rather, the stones that marked their graves were moved, for generally speaking the bones themselves stayed in the earth. Their monuments were moved to special memorial enclosures, corraled within Potemkin cities of the dead, facades without their contents.[45] Within a year or two, the heroes had become the property of the Soviet era, lined up in new rank order. Glinka became a Soviet composer. Church choirs no longer sang within earshot of the bones of poets and musicians from the czarist court. Soviet power annexed to itself the most useful moments of Russia's past, even to the point of changing the appearance of familiar landmarks, and left the rest to be forgotten.

The monuments that were not considered important were liable to be moved, defaced, or broken up for builders' scrap. Not all the damage was the government's fault. The "disordered state" of many graveyards was beyond the control of busy clerks; there was no one to stop the grazing and the chicken keeping; the marble and the bronze were pilfered; and drunks slept well among the leaning stones.[46] By the 1930s, however, the effects of this neglect provided the Finance Commissariat with its chance to seize and recycle anything that was still worth stealing.[47] Local soviets drew up lists of their graveyard assets, reckoning their value in tons of stone and negotiable metal. Gravestones, especially any that were made of fine marble, were removed for building projects. The older stations of the famous Moscow metro still contain large quantities of tombstone marble (most of the marble for the statues on the platforms of the Revolution Square station came from the cemetery of the Don monastery). Iron, bronze, and granite were also taken, sometimes directly for industrial use and sometimes for resale. In 1931 a secret estimate concluded that the closure of old cemeteries would yield more than forty thousand tons of usable metal for the national industrialization drive. The Finance Commissariat supervised a good deal of this activity, but its dual purpose—which included the removal of uncomfortable reminders of the immediate religious past—was unmistakable.

By the standards that had been established in the 1920s, the removal of cemetery valuables was so mild a violation that it attracted little comment. The 1920s and 1930s were decades of demolition. Church buildings were prime targets. They were turned into grain stores, cowsheds, arsenals; their roofs were stripped; their stones recycled; and the most annoying were blown up. Church bells were lifted from brick towers and melted down. Icons were ripped from their frames. The gold and silver disappeared into the budget deficit, while the painted wooden boards, blackened by a century of soot, and polished by the kisses of the faithful, were thrown unceremoniously aside. Some were burned or used for target practice, others were nailed together to make boxes for potatoes. "They made feeding troughs out of them," a believer remembered. "You'd lean over the trough, and jump back startled . . . Either Christ or the Blessed Virgin was staring at you from the feeding trough—their stern faces and big eyes—it gave you the shivers."[48]

The precedent that first made these excesses possible (though they were always in the cards, the pretext was a matter of mere chance) was the budget crisis and the famine of 1921–1922. Up to that point, even Lenin had been inconsistent. His ideology insisted that all religions must be doomed, and the churches, as institutions, broken. Superstition of any kind, like sentiment, appalled him. Unlike the mass of rank and filers, however, and many of his own propagandists, he was not interested in the creation of a new kind of human being, the shaping of a new mentality. He described the idea as "like playing with dolls—a pastime of well-bred ladies and not politically serious."[49] He was also aware of the propaganda dangers of an antireligious campaign. The Bolsheviks struck a succession of political deals with willing members of the Orthodox hierarchy, and they would find them very useful in the darkest years of Patriotic War.

There were moments, however, when Lenin's hatred of the church, and especially of its power, could overcome his sense of statecraft. The scales were tipped at the end of 1921 when his government was desperate for gold. It needed the church's wealth. Negotiations were opened with De Beers to sell the diamonds. The famine of 1921–1922 was a convenient excuse. "All our information suggests that we will not succeed if we try this at a later stage," Lenin wrote that spring. "No event other than a desperate famine could provide us with such a mood among the broad peasant mass, a mood which will ensure us either their sympathy or, at least, will neutralise them to the extent that victory in the struggle to seize church valuables will lie entirely and unconditionally with our side."[50]

The campaign began seriously in March 1922. Senior church leaders, including Petrograd's Patriarch, Vinyamin, were ambivalent, watchful, but not implacably opposed to the idea.[51] The humanitarian impulse, as Lenin rightly guessed, was not entirely dead. Resistance came from the localities. The most infamous case began in the small town of Shuya, near Ivanovo-Voznesensk. The rumor that the church's gold was to be seized arrived there in advance of the Red Guards. A crowd collected to defend the precious treasure, arming itself with cudgels, pitchforks, knives, and pilfered firearms. Fighting broke out when the Red Guards arrived, and by evening there were several dead and a dozen seriously wounded. Lenin's response—which was so venomous that even the Communist Party concealed it until 1990—was set out in a letter to Moscow. "I have reached the firm conclusion," he wrote, "that we must now undertake a decisive and merciless battle against the clergy. We must suppress their opposition with so much cruelty that they will not forget it for several decades. The more . . . clergy . . . which we succeed in shooting for this reason, the better."[52]

The Cheka was happy to oblige. The figures are uncertain, but it has been calculated that 2,691 priests, 1,962 monks and 3,447 nuns disappeared in one way or another in 1922 to 1923. Some convents and monasteries—notably the popular monastery of Saint John of Kronstadt—were closed. Leading churchmen, Petrograd's Vinyamin among them, were tried and executed. Believers could hope only for a miracle. Almost anything would do. Members of the latest generation of monks at the Don monastery still tell the story of the Red Army officer who took a potshot at an icon in the cemetery, only to be killed—it was the hand of God—by his own bullet as it ricocheted off the icon's granite mount.[53]

The battle over church property was vicious, but it was a rule that force was seldom used against religious ritual while a funeral was actually in progress. Enthusiastic members of the Young Communists League, the Komsomol, might break up Easter parades and heckle the old ladies as they went to church, but they were generally more circumspect about the dying. There were exceptions, when young thugs in leather heaved the priest away from someone's bedside, but these were rare enough to be reported in an outraged tone.[54] Although the ideologues wrote screeds about the need for atheist, Communist, and rationalist funerals, the Party leadership did not encourage provocation. It was another piece of hypocrisy, a cruel inconsistency. While churches were being closed, the Party continued to defend the freedom of individual conscience. Satan discovered what this meant when he paid the visit to Moscow which is the subject of Mikhail Bulgakov's literary fantasy *The Master and Margarita.* "Oh yes," he is assured by a local resident. "We are both atheists. But we can discuss it with perfect freedom."[55]

For anyone who had a real funeral to organize, the options, from 1921, were confusing. The funeral industry was reprivatized, in accordance with the New Economic Policy, in 1921. But the law prescribed that subsidies would be available for approved municipal and nonreligious rites. Large numbers of people seem to have preferred to pay. They rushed to take advantage of an opportunity for ceremonial nostalgia. Even if they could not have a priest, and even if they were not certain of the words of all the prayers, they craved the incense and the candles, white drapery, and traditional chant.[56] They also wanted personal attention. "There were so many hairdressing establishments and funeral homes in the town of N.," wrote the satirists Il'f and Petrov in 1928, "that the inhabitants seemed to have been born merely in order to shave, get their hair cut, freshen up their heads with toilet water and then die."[57]

"Citizens' funerals are still a rarity," *Bezbozhnik u stanka* [*The Workbench Atheist*] complained in 1923. Deliberate attempts to change all this through persuasion were generally unsuccessful. The Society for the Dissemination of the Idea of Cremation in the Russian Federation (ORRIK, founded in 1927) did not have many followers outside the capital.[58] The older generation never really gave up its allegiance to religious ceremonial.[59] What happened was that changes in the 1930s would rob them of the option. Another campaign of church closure began in 1928, and it would continue through the terrible years of famine and collectivization. The worst year for believers was probably 1938, when the number of working churches in Leningrad alone was cut from thirty-three (already a fraction of the prerevolutionary total) to five.[60] One estimate, although likely to be on the low side, suggests that there were only just over a hundred churches holding regular services in all of Russia that year.[61] In 1942 (after several had been reopened to make way for prayer at the beginning of the Great Patriotic War), there were only seventeen, as opposed to the prerevolutionary figure of six hundred, in Moscow.[62] "I think this is the first time in my life that I have not gone to the morning service," a resident of Leningrad, Lyubov Shaporina, wrote at Easter in 1939. "There's nowhere to go. There are just three churches left in the city, and all are completely packed,[63] there's no Easter procession, and you won't even hear the words 'Christ is risen' spoken on the streets. And I'm simply exhausted."[64]

Private funeral parlors also disappeared, along with any other kinds of private enterprise, as part of Stalin's campaign of industrialization after 1929. The business of disposal passed entirely to the ZAGS, the registries of births, marriages, and deaths, and to the funeral departments of the local soviets—state-run monopolies, like those of 1918, whose task it was to manage the procurement of coffins and wreaths and to allocate burial sites in what were now mainly municipal cemeteries. There was no choice but numb acceptance. In the towns, where burial was a bureaucratic business, the mourners had to do what they were told. They stood at yet another little window and awaited their instructions. Sign here, pay this sum, no smoking, shouting, or spitting on the ground.[65] In country districts, the old customs took longer to fade, and even though the younger generation was beginning to turn away from prayer, there were still Communists who kept their icons somewhere near.[66] Where religious funerals had been the norm in the early 1920s, however, by the outbreak of the Great Patriotic War, the full Orthodox ritual was rare. There were still prayers, but they were muttered by the women, and the mourners who gathered at the wake, shaking their heads in surprise at the idea of "burial without a priest," raised glasses to a soul whose shape and habits—and indeed whose very existence—many now had come to doubt.[67]

The sacred spaces that remained were visited in semisecret. No one knows how many visitors there were. The official figures on religious belief say nothing of the half-believers, the ones who seldom, if ever, went to church or to confession, the ones who never risked admitting to whatever of their faith still haunted them. But people did go to the cemeteries. They needed the calm, the company of the ancestors, some kind of temporary peace. More rigorous believers also sought to counteract the blasphemies, to perform whatever sacraments they could in duty to their God. Even disused cemeteries were visited, prayed in, and decorated with palm fronds. The ones that functioned often served as surrogates for a vanished church.[68] People laid flowers, eggs, and fragments of bread at the cemetery wall if they found the gates were locked. If they could, they continued the practice of regular visits, the sharing of food, and even the conversations with the dead that had been so important to their parents in the past. Saturday had always been the traditional day for this activity, but Soviet citizens tended to do their visiting on Sundays, or any day on which, when a ten-day week was introduced, they had time to rest.[69] The basic ideas behind their rituals—and even the expression "ancestors' Saturdays"—did not change. Nothing had emerged from all the theory that answered the mourners' needs as beautifully.

It might have been possible to have designed a workable atheist ritual for the masses—the Party certainly worked hard enough to do so for its leaders—but as it was the Soviet innovations dulled the spirit. Their focus was a person's work, their contribution to the revolution, and their sense of Party loyalty—their *partiinost'*—if they had one. Death became as drab as life, at least for ordinary people, as unimportant as their democratic voice and their individuality. "I went to Kuzma Sergeevich's funeral," Shaporina wrote in her diary in February 1939. "If he could have been present, sensitive and impressionable as he was, he would have been shocked." Her disapproval was partly the result of religious despair, but the behavior of the gravediggers did not help. "The band struck up a funeral march," she wrote. "They grabbed the ropes, pulled the boards out from under the coffin and started to lower it, but suddenly it slipped and tumbled into the grave upright, and the lid flew open . . . Then the loud cursing of the gravediggers again, as the band launched into a spirited performance of the Internationale. The sounds of clods of earth hitting against the coffin. The apologies and excuses of the drunken gravedigger."[70]

The atheist approach to death, reduced to its most basic, was simple. "Comrades," wrote Central Committee member M. S. Ol'minskii in July 1924, "I am a long-time supporter of the funeral ritual which the Party advocates. I think that all survivals of religious practice (coffins, funerals, the leave-taking from the corpse or cremation and all that) are nonsense. It is more pleasant for me to think that my body will be used more rationally. It should be sent to a factory without any ritual, and in the factory the fat should be used for technical purposes and the rest for fertilizer. I beg the Central Committee most seriously on this matter."[71] At the time the propagandists who were writing on the subject would have applauded him. The necessity of death and decomposition, the theory of universal entropy, was a theme to which their earnest little pamphlets endlessly returned. Only an amoeba, explained one writer, is immortal. The rest of us must die. It is the price of individuality, of evolution. The only thing that we can call immortal is our labor.[72] Heaven, too, was no place for a Bolshevik. "Whether it is joyful or boring will depend on your personal taste," wrote the propagandist Rozhitsyn in 1923. "But there is no doubt that the picture of heavenly bliss can only please the sort of person who does not like working or thinking. To be in heavenly peace is something that only a lazy person would want for his body."[73]

Ol'minskii died in 1933. The Central Committee ignored his rationalist will. Members of the elite did not have any choice about the manner of their funerals. They could not rot in peace, and funerals for them were state occasions. The dead man's body was laid out in the appropriate bolshevik fashion, surrounded by expensive flowers and palm fronds, in the Central Executive Commissions' building (the future GUM department store) on Red Square. It was then cremated in Moscow's new crematorium, and the ashes were buried in the Kremlin wall.[74]

The truth was that Bolshevism could not afford to dispense with the eternal afterlife of memory. Heaven could be destroyed, but not the home of revolutionary heroes, the Communist Valhalla. A new calendar of saints and holy days was also introduced. And ultimately, with the most grotesque of ironies, a new and incorruptible relic was created, a miracle for the scientific age: the mummified corpse of the leader, Lenin, himself.

A good deal of the new ritual, including the language and much of the ceremonial detail, continued patterns that had been established before the revolution, in the days of underground resistance and red funerals. Whenever a leading Bolshevik died, the streets were decked with banners, red and black; the newspapers came out with black borders, and they printed doggerel verse about the hero's courage, his dedication, his tenderness to children and pitiless oppression of the revolution's enemies. Red funeral ceremonies would be arranged, including large processions, red banners printed with emotive slogans, and military orchestras (there were often several of these, together with a choir, at public funerals, even in 1918[75]). There would often be long graveside speeches of revenge. The funerals of the Bolshevik officials Volodarskii and Uritskii, both of whom were killed in Petrograd in the summer of 1918, and both of whom were buried near 1917's "Victims of February" on Mars Field, were typical of the genre. MAY THE EARTH BE AS FEATHERS FOR YOU TO SLEEP read the slogan on one banner at Volodarskii's funeral, while others announced that WE WILL DIE, BUT WE WILL NOT SURRENDER.[76]

Red funerals would also be arranged for less important people, the ones whose deaths were poignant, and whose lives could serve as revolutionary parables. No opportunity for pathos was ignored if a young woman died in uniform, for instance, especially if she could be buried with due ceremony and blank verse. "Yesterday we buried Mariya Yakovlevna Bogdanova," announced *Petrogradskaya pravda* on 10 October 1918. She was a Communist, a Bolshevik, and only twenty years old. "She died at her post," the paper continued, "at the front in Saratov, at the front against our most fearsome enemy, the greatest enemy of the working class and the ally of all counter-revolutionaries, the enemy of hunger." The young woman was pregnant, too, so that "she not only gave up her young life but also that of her child, the child that she carried beneath her heart." The funeral was arranged at Petrograd's Mitrofanov cemetery, the body having been brought home by colleagues from the organization for which Mariya Yakovlevna had worked, and it featured two choirs, an orchestra, and an artillery salute.[77]

The railway journey and the flowers, the banners, orchestras and choirs cost money. Column inches in the press, the censored, state-run press, were virtually free, but the paper itself was not, and the time a funeral might take out of a politician's day was precious, too. The rites were valuable enough to set considerations of that kind aside. The same priority operated when it came to the creation of a revolutionary calendar. In April 1918, on the anniversary of the state funeral for the "Victims of February," *Pravda* attempted to establish a proletarian equivalent of the traditional saint's day. "Today is the . . . day we remember the people who gave their lives for the liberation of the exploited classes," it explained. "Today we remember that they are no longer with us, but that their spirit, the spirit of revolutionaries and fighters, is with us."[78] Less than a fortnight later, it was the turn of the victims of the Lena goldfields massacre of 1912. The headline was three inches high. TODAY IS THE SIXTH ANNIVERSARY OF THE SHOOTING OF THE LENA WORKERS! it read. "They fell as victims in the struggle for the workers' cause . . . Their blood was shed for the proletariat of all Russia. And the proletariat of the new socialist Russia will always hallow [*svyatochit'*] the memory of the Lena fighters."[79]

Memorials of stone and bronze were also commissioned; the work of architects and sculptors studied and assessed. In the summer of 1918, around the time the British forces landed in Murmansk, Zinoviev commissioned a memorial to be built at the Schlisselburg Fortress outside Petrograd, a former czarist prison. Five large granite tombs were created, together with a tall red granite monument topped with a shield (a cross had been ruled out at the planning stage). A large area of derelict land had to be leveled and fenced before the site was completed. The project fell behind schedule, and at one point the fortress itself was almost lost amid the fighting. More men were drafted in, however, because the site was due to open with a public ceremony on 22 January 1919, the anniversary of Bloody Sunday. In the end, the total cost of the memorial itself was 18,681 rubles, almost double the amount originally allocated for it.[80]

Zinoviev opened his grand site on schedule. It was bitterly cold that January morning, overcast, and a sharp wind drove tiny particles of ice into the faces of the crowd. The official guests, however, would have to stand and shiver in their places throughout the leader's speech, a characteristic masterpiece of bombastic repetition that lasted for an hour and a half. The revolution, he announced, was proud to honor its debt to the fallen. "It is easy to be a revolutionary now," he explained. "The worst that awaits us is only death, only shooting." For the prisoners of Schlisselburg, locked up for life, the price of resistance had been "a living death" and oblivion. As people say, Zinoviev continued, "the darker the night, the brighter the stars." A little of the luster from the thirty-two political prisoners who were known to have perished in the fortress under Alexander III and Nicholas II reflected on the Bolsheviks at last. More crucially, a government that was in power, and that was using power to devastating effect, crushing the resistance and the spirit of the millions who opposed it, revived and burnished its most precious propaganda asset: the sense that it was still an underground, still David to the counter revolution's evil Goliath, still righteous, moral, and innocent of calculation.

Like many people of his background, Yurii Vladimirovich Got'e read the reports of ceremonies like this with a conservative intellectual's distaste. "Yesterday the rulers celebrated the Lena massacre," he wrote in April 1918. A year later, on the anniversary of Bloody Sunday, he was even more impatient. "We are celebrating St. Gapon's Day and that of others of that ilk slain with him or without him, it's all the same. Everything is closed in Moscow, which makes no difference, since everything is closed on the other days as well."[81]

The note of cynicism here was justified—more justified, probably, than even Got'e could have known. No one outside the Kremlin quite appreciated the full extent of the inequality that already existed in Russia between the Bolshevik leaders and the so-called mass. No one could have guessed—a hungry and exhausted imagination does not run to such extremes of fantasy—how many of the tears were forced, how eagerly the men in military caps and polished leather boots were thinking of the banquet that awaited them, the wine, the talk, the political intrigue. When the crowds had all gone home, the leaders gathered for the customary meal. Attendance was not optional, for the political knives were always ready for an absentee, for anyone who did not cultivate his contacts.

Whoever had the job of organizing the reception, the ceremonial, or the meal could play the host, earn compliments, and bend the leader's ear. For all these reasons, Lev Kamenev, who was still under a cloud after his public denunciation of the October 1917 coup, was delighted to be given the job of organizing the funeral dinner for Ya. M. Sverdlov, the first of a succession of Party secretaries, who died in 1919. He used the dinner to mend his relations with Lenin. Kamenev and his wife, Ol'ga Davydovna (Trotsky's sister), went to great lengths, importing scarce, forgotten, and expensive delicacies from Europe.[82] Not for the last time in Soviet history, a Kremlin table groaned under its weight of food. The country's leaders huddled greedily near. The atmosphere of complicity was heightened because everyone knew that outside, beyond the Kremlin wall, across from the Manege and out toward the jumbled streets of the Arbat, the Russian proletariat was starving.

Lenin's death and funeral in January 1924 distilled and focused ten years of revolutionary emotion. A torrent of popular feeling—pain, loss, exhaustion, gratitude for deliverance, and fear for the present and the future—much of which had found no adequate outlet since 1914, gushed suddenly into life. Hundred of thousands of people wept. "In the pilgrimage to Lenin's coffin there was . . . curiosity," wrote a witness at the time, "but undoubtedly there was another impulse as well: to testify before the deceased to one's respect, love and gratitude towards him."[83] The death was also a political event. The funeral arrangements for Lenin were a vital stage in the struggle to identify his successor. The Kremlin hummed with intrigue, with contests over influence, spite, envy and political mistrust.

The people who were closest to Lenin had known that he was dying for over a year. From the time of his first stroke, the struggle to decide who should succeed him had been gathering pace. A cult of his personality designed to fill the gap his death would leave was also well developed by 1922. The stroke that killed him on 21 January 1924 was not, in other words, unexpected. A group of politicians had been talking about the funeral arrangements for months.[84] But no one could have predicted what would follow. It would have taken a particularly dark imagination to have foreseen that for half a year a group of the Soviet empire's most powerful men would have spent hours of their precious time monitoring the condition of a gently decomposing corpse.

The aftermath of Lenin's death included moments that were eerily reminiscent of the deaths of Russia's greatest czars. With medieval kings—and with Alexander I's general, Kutuzov—he would share the privilege of burial without his heart. Like any czar, he was subjected to an autopsy, much of which was carried out in the presence of some of his former comrades. The results were not released immediately—they had to be checked for political implications—but after a short pause they were printed, like those of the postmortem on Alexander III, almost in full. At the same time, the corpse's brain, heart, and the part of his neck that had been injured when Fanny Kaplan fired at him in 1918, were removed for research purposes.[85] These organs became totem objects. The Institute for the Study of Lenin's Brain was still in business when Mikhail Gorbachev embarked on the policy of glasnost' in 1987.[86]

The body was still cooling as the first committee, which included Lenin's friend Vladimir Bonch-Bruevich, met hastily to supervise its journey from the country house in Gorki, where the leader had died, to Moscow's Paveletsky Station. Other well-connected men, including Molotov, Dzerzhinskii, Enukidze, and Krasin, joined Bonch-Bruevich to discuss the funeral.[87] They had to plan the ceremony itself—arranging invitations and schedules, choosing music, buying wreaths—but they also had to supervise the propaganda that went with it. Leaflets were dropped from aeroplanes, posters appeared on public walls across the empire, meetings were ordered in the factories, and the newspapers indulged in a feast of pathos. Some of it was spontaneous. But Lenin's comrades also knew that the leader's death was an opportunity to build another patriotic myth—a myth, unlike some others, in which they more than half believed themselves.

The work of planning demanded a fine sense of ideological correctness. Every Communist in Moscow seemed to want to attend the funeral, and thousands requested permission to carry Lenin's coffin. The Funeral Commission delegated the task of issuing permits to the Moscow Communist Party.[88] A system of passes and tickets was instituted, and visiting hours were specified. Elaborate categories of viewing privileges—and the corruption that could circumvent them—sprang into force. But eventually the Hall of Columns, where the body lay in a bower of lilies, palm fronds, and red banners, was opened to the thousands who had been waiting patiently all night.

At least five hundred thousand people are thought to have flocked to the Hall of Columns between 23 and 26 January.[89] They lined up days and nights in temperatures that fell thirty degrees below freezing. When it is that cold, a person's breath turns instantly to ice, to silver dust, and there is a definite sound, a crackling, as the tiny spicules fall toward the ground. Even a man in thick felt boots is liable to frostbite if he stands outside for long. The Moscow Soviet did its best. Bonfires were lit along the route they designated for the line, and tea was sold in discreet stalls along Tverskoi Boulevard and near the Prague Hotel.

The line itself was orderly and mute. Each person had his or her memories; the man who had just died had changed their lives. They stood, they froze, they huddled, and every hour or so they shuffled further on, around another corner, a little closer to the end. It was a long, cold wait. But in the end each lucky person, each one who had managed to get to Moscow, had his chance. They were pushed forward, past the guards, through heavy doors, and into a magnificent room, another kind of light. It was dim inside, but there were hundreds of candles, and every surface glowed with the reflection of the scarlet banners. The air was heavy with the people's breath, with garlic, old tobacco, and damp sheepskin, but it also smelled of lilies, hundreds of them, heavy, sweet, and with the sharpness of the evergreens and palms that decked the catafalque. Lenin himself, at the center of it all, was both familiar and strange, paler, smaller, dressed in a tunic, his eyes closed, wordless and still. Hundreds of visitors were overwhelmed. A supply of stretchers was provided to remove the ones who fainted from the hall.[90]

The line and the funeral were landmarks in each person's life. Seventy-five years later, Yudif Borisovna Severnaya, whose father's work had brought him to live in Moscow from Odessa, could still remember how disappointed she had been because she had not been allowed to go. She was recovering from scarlet fever. Her parents made her stay at home—a privileged home—and allowed her nothing more than a glimpse of the bonfires from the balcony of their apartment on Tverskoi Boulevard. "I cried," she told me, "but they would not let me go and join in. Our family always preferred Trotsky, of course, because he was a soldier, and a man of culture, and so handsome. All the same, Lenin was a great man. Moscow did not sleep for five nights after he died."[91]

The funeral itself was scheduled for Sunday 27 January. Planning it was a nightmare for the anxious men of the commission. Every detail seemed to spark another argument. They even had difficulty deciding on the ceremonial music. Like many well-educated Europeans of their time (most had spent years in exile), they generally thought of the great set pieces: Mozart's *Requiem,* the funeral march from Beethoven's third symphony, parts of Verdi's *Requiem,* a little solemn Chopin. But the objections began at once. Lunacharskii, the commissar responsible for cultural matters, immediately vetoed the overtly religious choices. Beethoven he dismissed as "too boring for the masses." He approved the commission's choice of Wagner's *Death of the Gods* on the grounds that it was "fittingly grandiose," but there were others who thought it pompous. A composer from Petrograd offered a specially written piece for the occasion, but Krasin did not like it and it was dropped from the program. On 23 January, the funeral commission's fourth meeting approved a short extract from Wagner, the *Internationale,* the first part of Verdi's *Requiem,* and the funeral marches of Beethoven and Chopin. But later drafts of the same list deleted first Wagner and then Beethoven. Both were replaced in the final program by further repeats of the *Internationale.*[92]

Another problem was the question of the media, of permanent kinds of record. The possibility of a propaganda film for use at home and abroad was one of the main issues discussed by the first meeting of the funeral commission.[93] While the right cameras could preserve the moment, amplifying the Party's glory, too frank a picture might betray the cause. It was agreed that unofficial photographs of the lying in state, and especially of Lenin's face, were not to be permitted.[94] Soviet photographers would receive permits to record the ceremony itself on condition that nothing was published without prior approval from the commission.[95] Foreign cameras were not allowed at any point. Similarly, the doctors who attended the dying leader and carried out the autopsy were forbidden to talk to journalists. The commission itself would publish a "diary" of Lenin's last illness for mass circulation.[96] An official death mask was also prepared, as well as busts, official drawings, and a photographic exhibition for permanent display.[97] The Lenin Museum, which had been founded before the leader's death, made ready for a gallery of new exhibits.

This detailed planning and discussion were tiresome, but they were not fateful. It was a different story with the decision that Lenin's body should not be buried when the funeral was over. On 25 January a meeting agreed that the leader should be displayed for an indeterminate period within a makeshift crypt beside the Kremlin wall.[98] The idea was to allow more people—the millions from the provinces and faraway republics—to make the journeys they were planning and take their solemn leave. There was no time limit for the display, but few can have believed that the corpse would last forever. The architect A.V. Shchusev was commissioned to design a temporary viewing chamber.[99] They did not see it, but the Bolshevik leaders were painting themselves into a corner. Their refusal to accept the reality of death would ultimately leave them with two alternatives. Either they would have to embalm the body, which is what they did, or they themselves, and not a fatal hemorrhage, would be the agents who finally committed Lenin to the worms.

From 25 January the builders rushed to complete Shchusev's crypt—they had three days—while the commission met almost continually to direct the details of the funeral ceremony. No one could afford to make a mistake. An oversight in the ritual might betray their hidden, and fatal, incompetence. The responsibility of this burial, after all, was only the beginning of their collective responsibility for the future of the revolution itself. If some were shy of the challenge, however, others, Stalin among them, saw possibilities for themselves amid the chaos and the grief. In a move typical of him, Stalin is thought to have played a part in securing the strangest absence at the graveside that January. Trotsky, the most distinguished revolutionary after Lenin, did not attend the funeral, and he took no part in its planning. He had been unwell himself at the time of Lenin's last illness, and received the news of the leader's death on his way to a sanatorium in the Caucasus. Some say that he was tricked, and others that he was depressed. Either way, he did not come back to Moscow in time for the funeral. He missed a crucial opportunity to place himself at the head of the mourners and to reinforce his reputation as Lenin's closest aide and heir.[100]

It fell to the remaining revolutionary heroes—Kamenev, Zinoviev, Kalinin, and Stalin—to carry the coffin from the Hall of Columns to its temporary crypt and to make the speeches in Lenin's honor that everyone would remember. The funeral oration was read by Grigorii Evdokimov, reputedly the man with the loudest voice in Russia.[101] "We are burying Lenin," he told the freezing crowd. "The giant of thought, of will, of work has died." The cortege itself reflected the monstrous bureaucracy the dead man had created. The body was accompanied by representatives of workers' organizations and the Red Army, the Moscow garrison, the Central Committee of the Communist Party, the Central Control Commission, the Executive Committee of the Communist International, the Central Executive Committee, the diplomatic corps, trade union organizations, the Presidium of the Ninth Congress of Soviets, and representatives from party and state organs in the empire's republics, regions, and largest cities. Similar lists described the rank order of mourners following the coffin and the positions that each should take as it was laid in its tomb.[102]

The solemn moment of the leader's disposition was marked simultaneously by artillery fire and yet another stirring round of the *Internationale.* The echoes sounded for six thousand miles. They sang the *Marseillaise* by the Amur River. They stood till midnight in Kamchatka, in January dark and ice, and bared their heads in silence at the exact moment of the leader's interment in the distant capital.[103] Local meetings were often held by common graves that dated from the civil war.[104] A people that had suffered unimaginably for ten years would add another day of cold and darkness to its stock of memories. One hundred sixty-two of the soldiers who lined the route the coffin took in Moscow were later found to have suffered from frostbite.[105]

The corpse was in its tomb, but still it was not quite immortal. The issue of its fate would either be decided by the moulds that were already growing on its nose and fingers or it would have to be addressed by Bonch-Bruevich and his friends. They did not lack for advice. Letters and petitions streamed in from every city and province in the empire, most of them calling for the eternal commemoration of the greatest man in history. Not everyone wanted to see the leader embalmed. Some letters demanded that he be cremated, or even simply buried in the earth.[106] Some people just wanted a chance to get to Moscow before he disappeared. "We, the children of Rzhev village school . . . forty people in all, write to you to express our dearest wish to be allowed to visit the great grave of our dear Il'ich," ran a typical letter to Kalinin. "We beg and hope that our dearest dream will be realised."[107] But most wanted some form of monument to be created, a place where the people could commune with the dead leader and gather strength directly from his energy and matter.

The old idea of the cemetery, of communion with the dead as real presences, revived among the Party's rank and file. There was a welter of theorizing about immortality, too, about the possibility of reanimation, cosmic dust, all based on theories from that prerevolutionary dreamer, the pious, crazy, self-effacing Nikolai Fyedorov. Lenin's body should be kept, they said, until it could be reanimated, or at least until the final accomplishment of the world proletarian revolution.[108] It was a good idea, but it raised an obvious question. The leader would need to be preserved. The Funeral Commission was about to reinvent itself as the Immortalization Commission. Its meetings would stretch on for months.

The plan to embalm Lenin's body was opposed by some of the most influential people in Russia, including Lenin's widow, Nadezhda Krupskaya, and senior Bolsheviks such as Kamenev and Trotsky. But it became possible because of a series of coincidences. One, undoubtedly, was the enthusiasm of Leonid Krasin. Apart from Communism, his passions were technology and cosmism. He was fascinated by the scientific challenge of permanent embalming, and he was convinced of its potential benefits as a short cut to physical resurrection. "I am certain," he had told mourners at a funeral in 1921, "that the time will come when science will become all-powerful, and that it will be able to recreate a deceased organism. I am certain that the time will come when one will be able to use the elements of a person's life to recreate the physical person."[109] Lenin's death gave him a chance to explore the possibility with an almost limitless budget. He oversaw most of the engineering details of the project, and his energy carried doubters at several crucial moments. Others who advocated Lenin's mummification probably thought in terms of the appeal of a permanent monument to the dead leader, and even of the advertisement the body would make for Soviet technological excellence. Nina Tumarkin, in her history of the Lenin cult, also cites the interest at the time generated by the discovery of Tutankhamen's tomb and mummy in the Valley of the Kings.[110] There do not have to be precise reasons for a decision this bizarre. In the end, the scale was tipped by evidence that the body, still on display, had begun to rot.

Professor Abrikosov, the doctor in charge of Lenin's remains, had advised the commission immediately after the funeral that the corpse's fingers had suffered slight damage from the cold.[111] Its face, too, had grown some livid spots during the lying in state (the experts blamed the crowd, with its polluting breath). Dzerzhinskii, Bonch-Bruevich, Krasin, and others trouped up to the crypt a few days later to inspect the damage and decide upon a course of action. Nothing radical was agreed. For several weeks the commission hoped that refrigeration alone would keep the body fresh. When the Soviet refrigerator in which it was kept proved unreliable (the temperature varied too much to keep extremities like the nose in good condition), Krasin was allowed to import German equipment, the ultimate in engineering reliability.[112] But in early March there were alarming signs that the face was losing its tone, the nose deteriorating, the lips becoming blotched, and the eyes beginning to sink in their sockets.[113]

Though hoping that his fridge alone might do the trick, Krasin had been taking advice on embalming for some time. He now urged that a decision to preserve the body should be taken before it was too late. Two of the experts who would eventually carry out the work took a look at the corpse on 3 March and resolved to stay clear of Krasin's plan.[114] But the lure of an important job, of scientific innovation, eventually seduced them. Secretly at first, and then under the pressure of an official policy announcement, a team of doctors and scientists, many of whom had gained their experience with veterans of the First World War, began to experiment with embalming techniques. They tested their ideas on corpses; they worked at night; they kept up a twenty-four-hour vigil to ensure that Lenin should suffer no further deterioration. What they were doing had no precedent, and there was no guarantee that it would be possible. But on 26 July 1924 they announced that their work was complete.[115] The Immortalization Commission reconvened to gloat over its triumph.

Preserving the corpse meant building a mausoleum in which to display it. Shchusev's crypt was never intended to be anything more than a makeshift space. But the principles it embodied, primarily the importance of the cube as a perfect form and a symbol of the new order, were carried through into the wooden mausoleum that he built on Red Square in the summer of 1924. Other schemes had been considered. The usual national competition—a propaganda ruse to draw the people in—was held, eliciting proposals that included giant planetaria, globes, palaces, and temples to electric light. But Shchusev's scheme was practicable, and he could be relied on to understand the subtleties of the problem—including the political subtleties—without prompting. His grandiose wooden mausoleum, and the embalmed body within it, were opened to the world on 1 August 1924.[116] The building was replaced with a permanent granite structure six years later.[117] Lenin's body was evacuated from Moscow during the Great Patriotic War and kept for safekeeping, at enormous financial and logistical cost, in Tyumen' in Siberia.[118] But apart from that, and aside from periods of essential maintenance and repair, he could be viewed during the usual opening hours—and by special ticket, for the privileged, at other times—until the Communist empire finally collapsed.

Immortality, for Lenin, was not merely a matter of physical preservation. Even if his corpse had been allowed to rot, the thousands of Lenin monuments, Lenin buildings and streets, Lenin corners, and Lenin recruits to the Communist Party would have carried his memory into the next generation. The capital city of his revolution, Petrograd, changed its name to Leningrad in 1924. But it was in Red Square that the late leader's presence would be most visible for the rest of the twentieth century. Soviet power, which sought in so many ways to deny the power of death, turned the heart of its capital, the ceremonial core of its government, into a grave. The rebels who had forced open the coffins of the Orthodox saints now jealously preserved a relic of their own. They strenuously denied the continuity with religion, with the past. But the irony was inescapable. The empire was built upon the bones of a saint, and it had used its greatest mystery—technology—to ensure that the body would not corrupt. An iconoclastic revolution would celebrate all its most important festivals in the presence of a watchful father. Death had not been conquered. The Bolsheviks were trapped by it. Just as they would flinch from Ol'minskii's request to recycle his body for fat and fertilizer, they could not admit that life was crudely rational and finite. Or not, at least, for those whose memory they needed and revered. The rest, the millions, were not a problem. They might as well have been dust.

6

THE GREAT SILENCE

Like any modern government, the Stalinist leadership needed to know about the size and condition of its subject population, the extent of its human resources. It was not the project of counting itself that was unusual, but the method of processing the information. In 1937, exactly twenty years after the Russian Revolution, Stalin's government held an all-Union population census. It was not a discreet affair. The usual triumphant propaganda blanketed the press. Ten years after the launch of "our heroic fight for socialism" (the Party had adopted the first Five Year Plan for industrialization in December 1927) the census was calculated to provide evidence of "the great increase in our workers' standard of living."[1] "Only bourgeois and petty-bourgeois politicians fear statistics," explained *Pravda.* The Bolsheviks "never undervalued them," and Stalin's own "attitude towards statistical data is well-known."[2] The census was to be carried out, according to one of its organizers, "at a high political level, as a general Party and citizens' affair, with exceptional activism on the part of the broad mass of the population."[3]

There began the usual, now customary, trawl for volunteers. The Statistical Office needed hundreds of thousands of them. It appealed for 900,000 enumerators to collect the data, and for 130,000 instructors to supervise the enumerators. It took on thousands of extra staff in its regional offices to work on the reams of numbers. It prepared a pamphlet, "What Everyone Should Know About the Census," and distributed 2 million copies of it in twenty-nine languages. The public was swamped in a cascade of census publicity: newspaper articles about their leisure time and eating habits, wall newspaper and poster campaigns about the need for honesty, radio commentaries about the antics of the enumerators as they skied, trudged, shuffled, and marched around 40 million households in search of the statistical truth.[4]

The exercise of census taking has been described outside the Soviet Union as "a national ceremony and a symbol of the relation between citizen and government."[5] In that respect, too, Stalin's census of 1937 was no exception. The relationship between citizen and government, indeed, was exactly the thing that made it unique. For the results of all that counting and discussion were never published. Forty-eight hours after the census had been taken, before the purple ink on all the forms was really dry, an official with the task of analyzing the data wrote to his chief, Kraval, in Moscow: "The results of the census," he insisted, "judging by the preliminary data, render this material absolutely secret."[6] The men in the national Statistical Office had already reached the same conclusion.

The officials who worked on the data that spring would suffer from unusual kinds of stress. Their work, so complicated and so vast, a jigsaw of numbers, was rationed out to them in pieces. They could not discuss it; they could not ask about it; they dared not draw the necessary inferences. Security became an obsession. The archive contains a desperate letter from a clerk who absentmindedly left his briefcase on a suburban train. Like all the others, the ones who inadvertently shared their ration of pages with a colleague, who left an open ledger on a desk, he wrote in the shadow of exile to the labor camps.[7] All the officials who presided over the census at the national level were arrested, and some were later shot.

The story is as appalling as it is absurd. For the 1937 census was suppressed because it proved a truth that Stalin and his entourage already knew. Indeed, the evidence—stories of hunger and death; official requests for guidance; handwritten, sweat-stained pleas for help; last testaments and prayers—had poured across their desks for months in the winter of 1932, the anguished spring of 1933. What it described turned out to be the greatest famine in Soviet history, and one of the most devastating of the entire twentieth century. Exactly how many people died, from the effects of the famine itself or as a result of the campaign of collectivization that preceded it, is something that will never, probably, be known. For while it may be possible to count the adults, the people who had names and histories, and whose lives had made some impact on official records, the infants usually died before they were even given names. Demographers are still debating the disaster, and a range of mortality figures has been proposed. The most serious converge on a total between 5 million and 7 million.[8]

The catastrophe was without precedent. There are many ways in which the stories of starvation that people tell, from 1921 to 1922, from 1929 to 1933, and later from the postwar famine of 1946 to 1947, are similar. Survivors all recount their gradual loss of sensation, the numbness, even the loss of the feeling of hunger itself, the gradual descent into a twilight life, a waking death. All describe the desperate scavenging, the diet of lime leaves, bark, and carrion. There are always stories, too, of cannibalism, of infanticide, of human flesh disguised as rissoles or potted meat. But the epoch of collectivization, dekulakization, and the great famine—1929 to 1933—was the most intense and murderous of all. Whole villages simply disappeared. "We did not have enough books in which to enter these mass deaths," a local statistical office clerk, an employee of the ZAGS, the register of births and deaths, wrote to his supervisor in 1933. "Our priority was the burial of corpses."[9]

In some villages mortality was as high as 70 to 75 percent.[10] "It is not uncommon," ran a British Foreign Office report, "to find villages with a black flag flying at either end of the street, signifying that none of the population are left as a result of starvation and flight."[11] The starving "get swollen limbs and faces," explained another official witness. They "appear like some dreadful caricature of human beings, then gradually turn into living skeletons, and finally drop dead wherever they stand or go . . . Especially devastating is the mortality from hunger among children and elderly people . . . There are many cases of suicide, mostly by hanging, among the village population, and also many mental alienations."[12]

The people who escaped, the émigrés who found their way to western Europe in the wake of the German retreat from Ukraine and other western regions of the USSR after 1943, would remember the famine for the rest of their lives. Few of the historians among them could write of anything else.[13] Because the greatest mortality was in Ukraine, and because it coincided with renewed attacks upon the Ukrainian intelligentsia and church, upon the Ukrainian language, on local institutions of all kinds, Ukrainians regard it as an act of genocide. Since independence it has become a national symbol, the focus for dozens of oral history projects and documentary collections, for patriotic, anti-

Russian rage.[14] At the time, however, whatever people knew in Kiev, the truth about the deaths was kept out of the press.

In Russia itself, some parts of which saw equally appalling hunger, there is no real structure for remembrance even now. And in Kazakhstan, where city-based officials drew up plans, in 1929, for settled, fenced, and scientific agriculture, thereby condemning millions of traditional nomad herdsmen to starvation, there is hardly any memory to rouse. The survivors scattered, changing their identities.[15] The steppe is strangely empty, and the semidesert grassland bears no scars. Darya Khubova, who has collected oral testimonies of the famine in another region, the Kuban, has written that she found no evidence of collective memory there.[16]

The famine remained almost invisible, for the official purposes of the state and its citizens, throughout the Soviet era. Willed amnesia had become a habit. There were complaints about immediate problems, about bread lines, working hours, and public transport, but the larger issues, even the deaths of millions of people, were not openly broached. Rumors accumulated disconcertingly in each person's secret consciousness. But the things that people talked about in private remained separate; they did not usually translate into a public kind of knowledge, let alone a matter for dismay or protest. Some ignored them, some repressed them, and others resolved that they would never really know. Lev Razgon, the writer and historian, who was then living a privileged life in Moscow, still says that he was completely unaware, at the time, that there was a famine in the south.[17]

The statement is horrifying (there is no reason to doubt the truth of it) because the famine was so much a part of real life. If people really did not know of it, then their ignorance is a chilling witness to the cynicism of official censorship, but it is no more comforting to think that they repressed the images for themselves as a result of fear, indifference, or ideological tunnel vision. For though the deaths were usually denied, they were not really secret. The images that were suppressed were vivid, loud, insistent. Starvation itself is not a private matter. It certainly is not quiet. The people weep; they plead; they keen over their dead; their children scream and beg. You cannot hide a swollen body, either, or wasted limbs, infected sores. A human being who is dying from cholera suffers from violent and near-continuous diarrhea; he loses the lining of his guts and then he vomits wheylike, speckled spew until there is no fluid left in his exhausted tissues. The diseases of famine, like starvation, visibly consume a living body, noisily destroying the individual, the person, before they kill their biological host.

The starving also die in public. Many dropped dead in the streets, and there their corpses lay, for days, without cover, without mourners, blankly waiting for a stranger with the strength to move and bury them. It was true, despite all this, that families sometimes died at home, together, behind shutters and a silent door. But then their fly-blown bodies had to wait amid the ruins of their private world, and the intimacies of their stove, their beds, their childrens' toys, no longer secret, became clutter to be cleared or burned or looted by the living who discovered them. The famine was not heroic, it was not kitsch, but nor was it discreet.

Some people say they did not know what was happening because the passport system and a series of road blocks kept the visibly starving away from Moscow and the largest cities. But many hungry peasants tried to travel, and most of these found their way to the provincial railway stations. They died in their tens of thousands, and their bodies were buried by the local station masters wherever there was space to put them. The people did not always make it up the line, in other words, though rumors did, and so, occasionally, did letters. A journalist working for *Pravda* received one from his Jewish father in Ukraine in 1933. "This is to let you know that your mother is dead," it began. "She died from starvation and months of pain. I, too, am on the way . . . Your mother's last wish was that you, our only son, say kaddish for her . . . Would it be too much to hope for a letter from you, telling me that you have said kaddish for your mother—at least once—and that you will do the same for me? That would make it so much easier to die."[18] Some say they talked of famine whenever village life was mentioned in private conversations between friends.[19] The stories were not the kind that easily get ignored.

Today, however, after so many years, and after all the publicity of glasnost, the story of the rumors is hard to write. It is difficult to establish what it was that people knew, how much they ignored, how much they were forced to overlook or chose to condone. Historians who work with documents from the time find very little. The Soviet state did not encourage rumor. It even banned the word starvation from the press. It was "counter-revolutionary elements," they said, who were spreading the lie that "every death was the result of starvation." The motive of these enemies was to serve the interests of "certain anti-Soviet circles."[20] A hint like that was enough by then. The only other way to understand what people knew is by asking the survivors, but oral history is clouded, especially in this instance, by dense layers of guilt, repression, and later memory. "The famine does not interest me very much," a Russian survivor, now living in Kiev, said to me. He wanted to talk about Churchill and

Hitler, and he wanted to remember his father's horse, which they had later eaten.[21] The other memories that he still acknowledged were fragments, heavily overlaid with later fictions. All of them, too, were colored, as every older Soviet citizen's memories are, by the gathering shadow of the Great Patriotic War.

The result is a silence, and that is the sort of thing that historians, with their care for footnotes, seldom study. The excellent research that does exist on the famine has created two broad sets of images: the state, personified by Stalin, on the one hand, and the appalling landscape of starvation, with its hollow-eyed children and weeping women, on the other. Neither the documents nor the witnesses invite us to ask the other question, which is about the social context—itself a part, however passive and reluctant, of the mechanism that made it possible for so many to die in a modern industrial country, a country of mass literacy and communication. We have not asked how people thought about the deaths, how they lived with them, what shadow they cast upon the Soviet imagination at the time. And the reason why we have not asked is because the obliteration of memory, or at least its deep concealment, began immediately.

The other way to approach the issue, to understand the scale of the mental contortions that went on, is by stepping across the cultural gap and placing yourself, an English-speaking reader, in the position of a Soviet citizen of the 1930s. Consider again the 1937 census. Forget the things you already know about Stalinism and imagine, for a moment, the conversation that might, under normal circumstances, have taken place between a census enumerator and yourself, as a householder, on that January night in 1937, less than five years after this disaster. A man arrives at your door, bearing a sheaf of cheaply printed forms, and announces that he wishes to discuss a survey of the population, including the figures on its growth in the past decade. You know, or you have heard the rumors, that there has been starvation, mass mortality, a horror, people dying in the streets. You may be fascinated, or you may, because you had a letter once, a friend, a father, be grieving. And here is a representative of the state, a man who wants to talk about numbers, family size, standards of living. He is not the usual official, he is not even one of those who hides, on working days, behind a little window (with a shutter), taking requests (refusing most) between the hours of ten and two. He is a comrade, a volunteer, and he is alone.

The archives contain many letters from the enumerators themselves which describe what happened next. Some of them were bullied, kicked, and beaten. Some were robbed. Large numbers were subjected to abuse, and that included ill-tempered comments about politics and daily life (there had recently been more food shortages, the result of yet another harvest failure). The enumerators found that forms had been defaced. "Indecent remarks," they moaned, were printed by some people in the section that asked about religion. Uncooperative answers were also offered to the question about a person's citizenship ("anything but Soviet," someone wrote). But there is no report of criticism based on the recent deaths, no comment requesting clarification, no little supplement, as there would be on religion and on nationality, describing how to answer unsolicited questions. The enumerators, in their turn, did not demand to know what their research collectively disclosed.[22] Millions of people did not ask. It is a measure of the totality of this mental collusion—enforced by fear, but generally habitual—that people like me, who study the Soviet Union, and also most of the people who lived there, do not find it remarkable. The idea that some awkward questions might have been asked in 1937 merely seems naive.

It happened to "them," of course, not "us," to Ukrainians and Kazakhs (though also to tens of thousands of ethnic Russians in the grain-growing regions in the south), and there were always more immediate problems to consider, but the degree of self-censorship is still formidable. And though fear played its part—a decisive part, the people all agree—it was not the only factor at the time. Citizens and neighbors were not always too afraid to speak (their other questions and comments make this clear). The denial was part of a specific Soviet mentality—the product of a shattered culture, of broken communities, a civil war, of misplaced stoicism, the revolutionary mission, utopian hope, and the experience of repeated, massive suffering. It was also another feat of the new language. Euphemisms were found and slogans once again dissolved the traces of unspeakable catastrophe. The German agricultural attaché in Moscow, Otto Schiller, described part of the mechanism of denial when he reported home from the North Caucasus in 1933. "In some villages the population is almost extinct," he wrote. "I was told of many cases when sufferers, swollen from famine, implored help from the village soviets, only to be told that they should eat the bread which they had got hidden away, and that no famine at all existed."[23]

Within a generation or two, the memory of famine was blurred almost to oblivion. "It surprises me that there is not even a simple mention of the terrible tragedy of 1933 in any textbook," wrote Mikhail Alekseyev, the editor of *Moskva,* in 1988. "In our village only 150 out of 600 households remained . . . Many of my relatives and schoolfriends died in front of my eyes, many of them were buried in the ground where death from hunger had carried them off."[24] Denial like this, almost certainly, could have persisted indefinitely. "Judging by certain unrelated and contradictory data," wrote a Soviet historian in the 1970s, "the decline of the mortality rate slowed down somewhere in the period of reconstruction of the national economy. In various regions, the mortality rate declined at an uneven pace."[25] Schoolchildren swallowed this until the years of glasnost, and adults read the works of Party propagandists. "The collective farm system created hitherto unheard-of conditions for the flowering of socialist agriculture, for the cultured and prosperous life of the peasantry," explained the first secretary of the Communist Party of Ukraine, Petro Shelest', in 1970. "In the life of the Soviet land, in the construction of socialism, the years of the first Five Year Plan were heroic and victorious. They were, however, at the same time, difficult and complex. An especially difficult situation developed with food supply in 1933. But these difficulties, too, were overcome."[26]

The story of the great Soviet famine begins with the confrontation between Bolshevism and the peasantry; the mutual mistrust and misunderstanding; the Marxists' hatred of the village, the peasants' of the city. It has a pre-history in the famine of 1921–1922. The revolution was never made to benefit the countryside, though Lenin claimed that his party represented the poorest peasants. In return, the peasants, though they did not want the old world back (they seldom actively supported the Whites in the civil war), were wary of Bolshevism and often hostile to its agents. They did not like the note of obligation, the taxes, the house searches, and conscription. The grain requisitions of the civil war alienated millions from the new government. But the famine of the early 1920s would numb the spirit of resistance. It has been estimated (again, the numbers are uncertain) that about 5 million people died in those two years.

The fear of starvation had begun during the imperialist war, but by 1919 it had become a reality across the whole of southern Russia. A friend wrote to Got'e from Saratov in December 1919 with rumors of "two reliable instances of cannibalism" and a story that "university laboratory assistants were eating dogs and cats."[27] This food crisis was set to deepen. A bad harvest in 1920 was followed by an exceptionally dry spring in 1921.[28] That summer, the peasants began to sicken, then to die. It was the first great famine of the Soviet era. Even the civil war had not prepared the witnesses for all that they would see. As Sorokin, who traveled in the famine region, later wrote, "My nervous system, accustomed to many horrors in the years of Revolution, broke down completely before the spectacle of the actual starvation of millions in my ravaged country."[29] "Russia received the shock of famine broken not only in body, but in spirit," wrote the American relief worker, H. H. Fisher. "Distrust of the government and its agents, suspicion and hatred of neighbours, left the peasants confused and hopeless and less able to withstand the shock to which unfavourable natural conditions always exposed them. When in the summer of 1921 the signs of a greater famine became unmistakable, the peasants became panic-stricken, and fled the villages in their terror, or remained stolidly to wait for death."[30]

On this occasion, the Soviet government permitted foreign aid teams, and notably the American Relief Association (ARA), to operate within the famine zone. The idea had been controversial. Herbert Hoover, the future American president, had been pressing for a food campaign in the Soviet Union since 1919, when he brought the problem to the attention of the Allies at the Versailles peace conference, but the Soviet government did not allow the wagons to cross into the famine territory until 1921.[31] Bureaucratic delays and bottlenecks were always blamed, but the underlying reason, as the Americans knew, was the Soviet fear of spies, their visceral suspicion of the foreigner. The starving were fortunate this time (there would be no relief a decade later, for officially, that second time, there was no famine to relieve). By 1922 the ARA was feeding more than 8 million people a day.[32]

The scenes in villages across the Black Earth steppe would etch themselves on the Americans' memories. The famine was worst in the grain regions of the lower Volga around Saratov and Samara, in the provinces of Orenburg and Ufa, toward the Ural Mountains, and across an area to the north of these which took in the cities of Penza and Voronezh. Large parts of Ukraine, as well as the north Caucasus, were also affected. Fisher toured much of this countryside, and what he saw reduced him to near despair. "Men and women . . . exhumed dead animals," he wrote, "and hungrily devoured cats and dogs when they could be found."[33] When he visited the town of Ufa in late August, he saw about five hundred unburied bodies lying in the streets. Soviet doctors admitted that four-fifths of the corpses had died of hunger.[34] By this time, too, more than fifteen thousand people in Ufa province had already died of cholera. Other diseases, including typhus and dysentery, would account for thousands more. The Cheka privately estimated that one-fifth of the population in the region of Ufa had died of famine and its consequences by the end of 1921.[35]

"We entered the village of N. in the afternoon," Sorokin wrote. "This place was as though dead. Houses stood deserted and roofless, with gaps where windows and doors had been. The straw thatch of the houses had long since been torn away and eaten. There were no animals in the village, of course, no cattle, horses, sheep, goats, dogs, cats, or even crows. All had been eaten. Dead silence lay over the snow-covered roads until, with a creak, a sledge came in sight, a sledge drawn by two men and a woman and having on it a dead body."[36]

Reports of cannibalism now began to reach the cities. One version—for which there is a separate Russian word, *trupoyedstvo,* the eating of flesh from a corpse (as opposed to *lyudoyedstvo,* which is the killing and eating of living human beings)—might involve the butchery of dead neighbors, or of a person's own dead children, or else it might follow the robbery of a recent grave. "People spoke in the simplest manner about eating the foul impurities that passed for food," Fisher remembered. "And many would argue that the eating of human flesh was not a crime, since the living soul had departed, and the body remained only as food for worms in the ground."[37]

The other kind of cannibalism was more systematic, though rarer, and its victims were often homeless children, orphans, or friendless travelers. The stories persist even now. Adults from the famine regions will still remember—or perhaps still dream and fear—that they were lured along a side street once when they were children, and that a stranger offered them some sweets, a crust of bread. Some instinct, they will all continue, must have saved them, some extra sense of doubt or menace. They shudder. Other children died.

Such individual tales may well be fantasies, like urban myths, but the basic truth behind the fear is real. Indeed, officials in some of the worst-affected districts resorted to a ban on the sale of processed meats in the winter of 1921 in order to stop the trade in human flesh.[38] Grisly scenes were recorded by local medical inspectors and police. Nikolai Borodin's account of one such incident, though graphic, was not unusual. The police in his district of Ukraine had discovered a cellar under one of the peasants' cottages. Their suspicions were aroused by the fact that the man and woman who lived there had been selling rissoles in the local town. What they found when they opened the door, and what Borodin claims he saw as he stretched to see over the crush of official backs, were "barrels containing parts of children's bodies, sorted and salted, and scalped heads. In the centre of the cellar stood a butcher's block and there was a knife, an axe, and some rags on the floor. Behind me," he added, "someone vomited loudly."[39] He did not feel too well himself. He had bought and eaten one of the couple's rissoles the same day. Screams rang in his ears as he walked away. He looked back across the dusty square and saw the couple kneeling in a pool of their own blood while members of the crowd kicked them to death.

The Soviet public, ordinary citizens, was moved to genuine compassion by the famine, disgusted by the degradation and the suffering, concerned to offer help. Here might have been another chance for revolutionary pathos, an opportunity for charitable appeals. In fact, however, the leadership seems largely to have avoided these. Its attitude to private charity was severe. There was a precedent for this, an earlier echo of the new official tone, and it was set in 1891. At the time of czarism's last great famine, Lenin himself denounced the liberal impulse to collect money and give aid. "Psychologically," he declared, "this talk of feeding the starving is nothing but an expression of the saccharine sweet sentimentality so characteristic of our intelligentsia."[40] His view at the time was that most of the philanthropy merely buttressed the social order. The liberals were tinkering with details. He also rightly understood that charitable efforts would not solve the basic problems of indebtedness and rural overpopulation.

By 1921 the world had changed. Russia was a dictatorship of the proletariat and poor peasants. But small acts of personal giving were still "saccharine sweet." Everything was to be managed by the proper authorities. "The worker has known and still knows hunger," ran a leading article in *Kommunal'nyi rabotnik* in August 1921. "He needs no vivid, nerve-racking description of it." The paper gave none. "Personal gifts of money, personal items and spare food may, it is true, alleviate the peasants' need a little," it continued. "But these are not what the peasant expects from the worker, and they do not constitute the worker's real contribution." What the government really wanted, in the finest macroeconomic tradition, was an overall rise in labor productivity.[41]

The same detachment, so different from the propaganda of revolutionary martyrdom, was evident in most of the literature about the famine and its consequences. Readers of journals like *Kommunal'nyi rabotnik* learned that Russians were an enduring and stoical people, and that they would confront this enemy, as they had confronted counterrevolution, with hard work and rationality. Even cannibalism was described with scientific primness. A carefully written account intended for ordinary readers informed them that cannibalism in times of famine bore no resemblance to the blood-curdling rituals of primitive communities. Most of the perpetrators, indeed, would die soon after their first desperate meal of human flesh. They were unlikely to develop a taste for it. The practice could be compared to cannibalism among animals, the authors of the book explained, many species of which, "especially rabbits," devoured their own young when food was scarce.[42]

The peasants, unlike rabbits, begged and prayed. When the relief wagons arrived in the Urals at Easter in 1922, they broke down and wept. They "knelt in the shadows of the railway cars," wrote Fisher, "to thank God for their deliverance."[43] By this time, too, the government itself had taken effective steps to ease the crisis. The New Economic Policy, which was launched before the worst months of the famine began, in March 1921, was partially intended to alleviate the problems of the peasantry. It made little difference along the Volga and in Ufa that summer, but within three years the bulk of the Soviet Union's peasants—the ones who had, at least, survived—could feel the first touch of recovery. The burden of requisitions was removed, and they were able to trade at last, to keep whatever surplus they produced, to buy and rear a cow.

There were still difficult summers (in 1924, for instance, they beat the bounds with icons and prayers to stave off threatened hunger in many villages across the grain belt in the south.[44]), but the possibilities for security, if not prosperity, were improving. Survivors remember eating meat; there was cake at Easter, and vodka at New Year. No one could ever have called the agricultural sector rich, but the years from 1924 to 1928 were more than usually easy. "Our farm stock consisted of four cows and four horses," a woman from the Urals remembered in the 1990s. Her family was wealthy by the standards of the time. "We milled our own flour and we also baked our own bread," she added, although "we dressed very poorly; nothing was bought."[45] "I recall us keeping pigs and looking after the beehives," said another.[46] For those who prospered, even by these modest standards, the famine of 1921–1922 began to recede into the general memory of earlier hunger. Some people still confuse it with the hunger of 1917, of 1919, or 1924.

They do not make the same mistake with 1929. The campaign of mass collectivization changed every aspect of their lives. Its purpose was to turn the petty, inward-looking, and ideologically rebarbative Soviet peasants into models of enlightened socialism, to encourage them to abandon their household plots—the cow, the hens, the single filthy pig—and to combine in more efficient, large-scale collective farms. There would be favorable economies of scale, the fields would be larger, easier to till, mechanization (that great goal of scientific Bolshevism) would become possible, and there could be more rational divisions of agricultural labor. In fact, the farms could be transformed into the rural equivalent of factories, and ultimately they could be run in the interests of the entire society, according to the Five Year Plan, without recourse to all the head scratching and devious evasion that characterized relations between state and countryside in the 1920s. The peasants would also be easier to educate, and they might begin at last to forget the superstitious habits of their serf grandparents.

That was the Party's agitational version. Another way of looking at collectivization is to see it as an assault upon the peasantry. In the late 1920s the government was desperate to procure and export grain. It needed hard currency for its industrialization program. It also needed to provide basic food for its growing industrial cities. The story began to gain acceptance that "counterrevolutionaries" and "white guardists" among the peasants were deliberately hoarding grain in an effort to overturn the Five Year Plan and even to sabotage Soviet power itself. Collectivization, in its most coercive form, was an act of ill-concealed revenge for this stubbornness. It also included a series of aggressive moves designed to break the peasants' political will, to destroy the remnants of banditry and partisan separatism, and to blast from its foundations the enduring structure of a rival mental world.

The core of this policy was called the liquidation of the kulaks as a class. Officially, this was a policy directed against the rich, the so-called bourgeois peasantry. Kulaks were described as class enemies. They were set apart from the so-called poor and middle peasants (in practice these categories were sometimes arbitrary), and from the landless rural poor. The kulaks were also identified, in official discourse, as the most determined hoarders, the true saboteurs of socialist construction, spider-agents of the international bourgeoisie. Dekulakization, then, was thought to be two-edged. It was an attempt to create the same equality of access to wealth as was supposed by this stage to have been established in cities, and it was a move to rid the countryside of the last tenacious remnants of the counterrevolution. "We must deal with the kulak like we dealt with the bourgeoisie in 1918," declared one Party official. "The malicious kulak, actively opposing our construction, must be cast into Solovki [the infamous prison in the arctic White Sea]. In other cases resettle on the worst land."[47]

In practice, what the war against the kulaks really meant was that any peasant who offered resistance to collectivization (real or imagined), who fitted the largely invented category of "class enemy," or whose expulsion from the village was required, for whatever reason, to fill some arbitrary local quota of "dekulakised elements," would be driven from his house—complete with children, grandparents, and mother-in-law—and deprived of all his property: horses, cattle, sheepskin coats and blankets, cooking pots, citizenship documents, and civil rights. Approximately twenty thousand of them were executed on the spot. It was a comprehensive policy of ideologically driven purging, the social equivalent of 1990s ethnic cleansing. Among the groups affected were priests, active religious believers of all faiths, former landlords, bandits, partisans, criminals, and many other individuals whose presence in the new collective farms was deemed, by the OGPU or some other local agent of the state, to be politically undesirable.[48]

The policy began in the late autumn of 1929, but the hardest years were 1930 and 1931. There was a pause in the spring of 1930—the countryside was in chaos, there was armed resistance in some places, and Communists were being attacked and killed, even crucified—but it resumed again that summer and continued until the bulk of the Soviet Union's peasants had either joined collectives, lost their homes, or died. The estimates are crude again—the figures were not kept in any systematic way—but it is thought that about 5 million people were dekulakized (driven from their homes, locked in prisons, transported to the remotest parts of the taiga, shot, or starved to death). Of these, several hundred thousand died within two years. Some historians have put the total number of deaths at more than a million, some at twice that level.[49]

The basic policy of collectivization also involved violence. Few peasants seem to have welcomed the idea. It became a political campaign, and it was fought in the teeth of armed opposition.[50] "No force in the world," the leadership announced in January 1930, "no threats or howls from our opponents and the enemies of collectivisation . . . can now stop . . . this victorious advance."[51] Some people threw a rope across the beam and hanged themselves, some waited, grimly, for catastrophe, and others reached for pitchforks, whips, and pilfered civil war revolvers as the rough young agents—"they were just teenagers, really, kids, the worst," one woman told me—made their announcements. "My granny . . . could not understand the word *kolkhoz* [collective farm] at all," said another survivor. "Most of all she was afraid to die: it seemed to her that if everything was collective, then burials would be just the same."[52]

The people who carried out the policy included many who genuinely believed, at first, that they were bringing a new civilization to the villages. Factories in the industrial cities "adopted" collective farms and named them (hence the Ball-Bearing Collective Farm, the Hammer and Sickle Collective Farm, and the hundreds of Marx and Lenin collective farms all over the Soviet Union)[53] The idea was that there would be exchanges of expertise, of tools, volunteer workers, and even, maybe, food. Idealism of this kind was quickly crushed. Collectivization may not have begun, in everyone's minds, as a form of war against the peasants, but it soon acquired the characteristics of one. The people who enforced it—who drove the kulaks from their beds, coraled their scrawny beasts, and searched with iron rods beneath the floors of their abandoned huts for hidden grain—were trapped within the grip of orders.

Whatever ideas they may have had a first, whatever shady or utopian motives, they were soon locked in combat. As the crisis deepened, as individual volunteers, collectivization's front-line troops, began to comprehend the reality of life and death in the whirlwind of this second revolution, the Party itself began to fall apart. Some were appalled at the slaughter, obeying orders but sickened by their own responsibility.[54] Others feared—with justice—that their newly founded socialist civilization was about to shatter and collapse. The crisis of 1929–1932 was not merely an exercise in relentless state-directed economic voluntarism. It had an element of that, to be sure, especially at first. But what it turned into, for almost all the protagonists, was a desperate struggle for physical survival.

The easiest path to take, in these conditions, was the path of true belief. "Let the lot of them die," muttered the zealots. "But we will collectivise this region one hundred percent."[55] "We were deceived because we wanted to be deceived," wrote a former activist. "We believed so strongly in Communism that we were prepared to accept any crime if it was glossed over with the least little bit of Communist phraseology."[56] Even now, there are some people who remember the process in tidy, ideologized terms. "You only had to look at him," said a former neighbor of one deportee, "to see that he was a kulak from top to toe. You would only have to glance at him for a second to see that this person was not a Soviet type."[57]

When this kind of self-delusion palled, utopians could focus on their long-term vision. "We had to avert our eyes from the village," one former activist explained, "and contemplate the other parts of the picture."[58] But when that strategy also failed, there was no choice but to blame orders. The writer, Vasili Grossman, understood each version of the process. True belief, in his view, was a convenient mask behind which to hide. "The activist committee included all kinds," he wrote in his fictionalized account. "Those who believed the propaganda and who hated the parasites and were on the side of the poorest peasantry, and those who used the situation for their own advantage. But most of them were merely anxious to carry out orders from above. They would have killed their own fathers and mothers simply in order to carry out instructions."[59] One survivor, confirming this, recounted how his own family was dekulakized as if three brothers were actually a father and two sons. "No-one's going to check anyway," the village meeting agreed. "If we have to deal with each brother separately we won't be able to dekulakise them because we won't have any grounds . . . And it'll be our heads that'll roll for failure to carry out instructions."[60]

The collectivizers were also lured by personal gain. Thieves and bullies usually went unpunished. As Sheila Fitzpatrick remarks, "Reports of dekulakisers appropriating property for themselves are legion." She cites a case from the Perm region, where the people who turned a peasant called Timshin out into the street "ate up his honey on the spot and put his cigarettes into their pockets. Also they did not include a silver watch in the inventory and it was put into the pocket of the policeman, Igashev."[61] A famine survivor who told me his story in 1998 confirmed this pattern. "In our village lived people, there were people, who had never worked, drunks and that sort," he said. "They organised themselves into collectives, not *kolkhozy* [collective farms] but collectives, and kulakised [*kulachili,* sic]. They kulakised three people."[62] "They took everything for themselves," said another. "They saved themselves, and the people died."[63]

The people who were dekulakized were generally quite ordinary. Many were defined as kulaks simply because they had hired labor, thereby "exploiting" the landless poor. This designation was especially unfair. The peasants who needed extra help were often the weaker members of the village, the ones who could not get the harvest in without assistance—widows, the elderly, and disabled veterans of war.[64] Sometimes a moment's rage was enough to turn an ordinary peasant into a kulak, to cost them their entire world. "My aunt grabbed a pitchfork," remembered a woman from southern Russia, "and gestured with it, shouting, 'I won't let you near the horses!' She had two horses. And the next day they came and dekulakised her, took her things and sent her away to exile, and the children died."[65] Such vengeful actions sometimes alienated the whole community from the state and its representatives. It was not always true that poorer peasants smouldered with resentment of their neighbors.[66] Whatever anger it generated, however, the policy of expropriation was irresistible.

There are still survivors alive, seventy years later, to tell the story of the shock of dispossession. "First we were taken to some freezing cold barracks," recalls one of these. "I don't even know where they were. All I know is that we froze and starved a full ten days in those barracks . . . We lost Father and our eldest brother who was then twenty."[67] "They put us in a barracks," the daughter of other supposed kulaks told me. "The prisons were full. They had overfulfilled the plan in our area. So they put us in a barracks, all together. Just like that. On the bare floor."[68] Her family was relatively fortunate. Millions of other kulaks were driven further from their homes. "The terrible trouble with travelling in that cattle truck was that the timber walls let in the wind through all the chinks," one of these remembered. "The wind simply howled through the truck. You had no protection from it without warm clothing; and we were not allowed to take any with us; it was 'surplus to requirements . . .'"[69] Healthy adults could usually cope with the cold for a while, but the mortality rate among the infants was appalling. "A cossack woman gave birth on a deportation train," wrote Aleksandr Solzhenitsyn. "The baby, as was usual, died. Two soldiers threw the body out while the train was on the move."[70]

Those who survived journeys like this would often die once they arrived in the far north. They starved on the barren soil that they were given to work. Their children died of epidemics and neglect, not understanding why there was no milk, why father had disappeared, or where the endless railway journey had taken them. Cases where the local population attempted to help these "special exiles" by offering them food or shelter were common enough to attract official criticism. "Their bodies were covered with festering sores," wrote Solzhenitsyn, describing the transit community of former kulaks that was temporarily billeted in the town of Arkhangel'sk. "Spotted fever developed. People were dying. Strict orders were given to the people not to help the 'special resettlers' (as the deported peasants were now called). Dying peasants roamed the town, but no-one could take a single one of them into his home, feed him, or carry tea out to him."[71]

The winters of 1930 and 1931 were deadly for these exiles, but for those who remained behind on the collectives a new disaster would begin in the late summer of 1932. The harvest was poor that year, but the government continued to require its quota of grain and other agricultural products from the collectives, a quota that was set so high that many grain-producing areas were left almost without food. "During the last winter and spring," a committee of émigrés reported in 1933, "the population of these large agricultural regions [they principally meant Ukraine], almost completely deprived of its usual food, had to eat bark and grass, rats and dogs, which led to tremendous mortality, numerous cases of madness and cannibalism and a general state of exhaustion through lack of nourishment. Because the starving and the sick are not helped by anyone, the streets of villages and cities are strewn with corpses; entire villages are emptying as a result of death and mass exodus."[72]

"I was nine years old in 1933," recalled Marfa Pavlivna, a famine survivor from Vinnitsa province, in the 1990s. She spoke the language of the village, describing horror with a stark simplicity. "There were four of us children . . . They came to the door, there were strangers. They beat the floor with iron rods . . . and they tried to find where Dad had buried grain. They took our cow." The peasants on their collectives were still suspected of hoarding, and many households, like this one, were searched repeatedly for hidden stores. The hunger began after the last of the grain and butter had been taken, when the harvest for that year was gone. "We begged mother to feed us," Marfa Pavlivna continued. "We begged so hard. The youngest brother was crying, crying, and in the morning he died. My eldest brother, the one who was born in 1920, also died in the morning. They both lay there dead. Already three were lying there . . . Mother told the neighbours: already three of mine have died. And in two days, Father died. It was evening, Saturday. I slept so close to them, the dead . . . They came and took them, took them away from the village, to a pit."[73]

Hundreds of testimonies like this have recently been published in Ukraine. "The year of 1933 is like a terrible dream in my life," remembered Mariya Oksentiivna, who was born in 1914. She was part of a burial brigade in a village in Kiev province, a three-person team whose task it was to dig the collective pits. They buried twenty or thirty at a time, bringing the bodies to the burial trench on carts that were drawn at first by horses, and then, when the horses died, by human beings. She buried her own sister in such a trench, "and in the same grave were twenty-three bodies."[74] Other witnesses remembered similar scenes. One saw the corpse of a young woman propped up against a plank fence. The image haunts him still. "As we approached," he testified later, "we saw there was a child . . . who sucked the breast without realising there was no milk left. A sanitary truck, whose job it was to collect the dead bodies from the streets, pulled up as we watched. Two men jumped out of the truck, grabbed the body by the leg and dragged it up on top of the pile of bodies in the truck. Then they took the living child and threw it up with the dead bodies. My brother and I wept with pity for the child, but we realised that there was little that we or anyone else could do to help it, for we were all hungry."[75]

Tears and pity were luxuries in the starving villages. Many forgot how to weep, and many more had not the strength. Mariya Oksentiivna described what happened when a corpse was thrown into the pit and was not dead. "One of them," she said, "called out, 'Hey boys, don't bury me. I might manage to pull through.'" The burial team was unimpressed. "'We've got enough work without having to worry about you,' they said. That's what the famine did to people. Stalin reduced people to such a condition that they lost their reason, their conscience and their sense of mercy."[76] Crime of every kind increased in the famine regions. Its most extreme and characteristic form was murder, either as a preliminary to theft or as part of the growing scourge of cannibalism.[77] "The famine in the Soviet Ukraine of 1921 was undoubtedly a terrible one," wrote another witness, "but it appears like child's play in comparison to the present situation."[78]

Pity was in short supply among the activists and state officials, too. Teams of people, some from the cities, and some drawn from the peasantry itself, were entrusted with the job of enforcing the grain collections in the summer of 1932 and with protecting "socialist property" against the hungry villagers that autumn and winter.[79] The "property" in question was pathetic—scraps of gleaned corn, black potatoes, rotting cabbage. It made no difference. The penalty for theft included death by shooting. "Our great goal was the universal triumph of Communism," wrote the future critic of Stalinism, Lev Kopelev, as he tried to explain the activists' mentality of this time. "In the terrible spring of 1933 I saw people dying from hunger. I saw women and children with distended bellies, turning blue, still breathing but with vacant, lifeless eyes. And corpses—corpses in ragged sheepskin coats and cheap felt boots, corpses in peasant huts, in the melting snow of the old Vologda, under the bridges in Kharkov . . . I saw all this and did not go out of my mind or commit suicide . . . Nor did I lose my faith. As before, I believed because I wanted to believe."[80]

Faith like this was one of the things that made the famine happen as it did, that made it possible for millions to die, whole villages, whole families, while others ate their bread and soup and talked about production targets. But there were several other factors at work as well. The other side of active zeal was willed evasion. This was the rule, in fact, outside the famine regions. The newspapers were full of Soviet successes. All you had to do was to believe. The workers' standard of living was said to have improved, the peasants were being lifted out of their ancient darkness, children were healthier, the Soviet Union was an example to the world. Anyone who chose to question this would find they had no public voice. The only people whose protests might have influenced the policy itself, a handful of dissidents within the Party leadership, soon found that speaking out could cost them their careers, perhaps even their lives. Examples were made of them, the ritualized attacks were launched, the deadly accusations of treachery. The very act of opposition was becoming futile.[81]

Outside the ranks of the elite, as a result, there was a genuine confusion. The only printed material was the universal, publicly unchallenged propaganda. Triumphalist and bloodless, it acted like a filter, keeping out the truth.

The local Communist paper in one province of Ukraine, Vinnitsa, was a model of this euphemistic style. Thousands of children were starving in the region, and the first of many were starting to die, when the paper announced that "anyone who demobilises himself during the days of grain collection is helping counter-revolutionary sabotage." Those who knew the code would understand that this meant there was to be no softening of the Party line, no slackening in the face of a human plea. But the prose in which this chilling policy was stated was opaque, flat, and deadening. Three days later, the same paper declared that "the plan for grain collection in this region has been fulfilled by 100.1 percent."[82] A boring, empty statement like this was calculated to smother the truth about the real drama that was taking place. Less than two years before, during the first phase of collectivization, parts of Ukraine, including Vinnitsa, had been in a state of virtual civil war.[83] Now they were beaten and starving. But an outsider who picked up the paper that morning (or a foreigner who consulted it later in a library) might nod, yawn, quibble the fantastic figures, and turn the page in search of something else.

As far as the peasants themselves were concerned, there was almost no public opportunity to challenge official lies and distortions. Their own emaciated bodies were the most vivid evidence that they might have produced. But starving peasants were banned from traveling to the metropolis. Overt political opposition, though seriously attempted in the collectivization years, was not a possibility for them. Although some peasants took up arms again in the winter of 1932, desperate to resist the grain procurements, most men and women in the grip of famine did not have the physical strength to oppose a well-fed, well-armed, and numerous militia.[84] Many of their ringleaders had disappeared, moreover, during dekulakization, on to the backs of trucks or into shallow graves.

The secret police took an interest in any potential conspiracy, however small. The political control of public meetings and even social gatherings was judged, by a leadership in crisis, to be necessary to prevent the spread of justifiable dissension, the sharing of rumor, and the birth of an alternative politics. But it had other effects as well. The obvious places to meet and talk, the places where memories would have been fed and warmed, the churches and synagogues, came under deliberate attack.[85] "The religious life in Ukraine is at a total standstill," wrote a witness in September 1933. He added that "the people are more religious now than ever before," but faith and prayer were private things, enacted without priests. "Of course," he went on, "no religious wedding ceremonies, funerals, or christenings of babies, are performed nowadays."[86] It was the same story on the Volga, in the north Caucasus, and across the Black Earth belt. There was no chance to gather and conspire. But there was also little opportunity for consolation. The obvious framework for collective grieving, and later, for remembrance, was systematically wrecked.

The bodies themselves, and even their names, were also lost. Mass graves are hard to comprehend, the skeletons inside are jumbled, horrifying, anonymous. Local officials preferred to give rough estimates of the number of deaths, especially when they found an entire family lying dead and stinking in its hut. The men who counted the bodies in one region of the north Caucasus admitted that they had not recorded even half the likely total. In one specific case, where a whole family, including a woman and her three daughters, had died, they explained that they had entered only the father's death because the family name, Batsai, could not be rendered in the feminine plural.[87] The graves themselves were soon obliterated, often deliberately. One ex-kulak went back to find the camp where he and thirty-two thousand others, mainly families with children, had lived in ninety-seven crowded barracks. "There were outbreaks of measles and scarlet fever," he recalled, "but no medical care." Rations were tiny. The death rate, especially among the children, was very high, "with funerals all day." But when he visited the site in 1935, he found that the cemetery, "where endless crosses had stood, had now been levelled by the authorities."[88]

The memory of the dead was covered up in other ways as well. New settlers came to farm the land, old populations scattered. The Council of People's Commissars issued a decree in August 1933 that provided for the resettlement of what were described as the sparsely inhabited but fertile areas of Soviet territory. It was another euphemism, an oxymoron. As late as the 1920s, five years before, there had been no sparsely inhabited but fertile land to speak of in the grain-growing regions. They were the most densely settled places in the empire. By the end of 1933, however, 21,856 families, or 117,149 people, had been moved into Ukraine alone, mostly from the surrounding republics, including Belorussia and the western provinces of Russia itself.[89] The new settlers did not ask about the haunted land. They talked about their difficult lives, the trials of work and poverty, but not about the bones, the ghosts, the strange silences, a new life in a world where even the wild birds no longer sang.

It is a habit that they still keep up. The guilt that survivors express today, in interview, is usually about their identity as peasants, their decision to remain on the land. They know their lives would have been different if they had managed to join the great migration to the factories at the height of Stalin's industrialization drive. The demand for their labor at that time appeared to be insatiable. They also know that the person who is interviewing them is educated, and they are haunted by the thought that they, too, might once have found more glamorous and better-paid types of work. About 12 million people left the countryside for the cities between 1928 and 1932.[90] The process destroyed some patterns of remembering. It left the people who stayed, even the ones who did not starve, with an unfocused sense of loss. Whatever happened next, moreover, the memory of resettlement would be destroyed in 1941 under the tracks of German tanks.

"*A human being* survives," wrote Varlam Shalamov, "by his ability to forget."[91] It is possible, now, in Russia as well as in Ukraine, to find survivors of the Soviet Union's greatest peasant war and ask them for their stories. The new oral history collections restore a vivid, much-neglected image of the past. In some respects, however, the rediscovery of one kind of "real" story, a narrative of the physical facts, had obscured the other real theme, which is the process of accommodation, the means by which the people lived, for fifty years, and did not tell it all. Many of the collected accounts begin with phrases such as "I will never forget" and "I can still see" but in their search for facts the editors who published them have set aside the other words, the phrases and evasions that do not picture, actively forget. It was precisely this forgetting, however, that formed the universe for millions throughout the Stalin years. It was a necessary strategy even for the ones who now recall their early lives with such enthusiasm, talking so fluently (or so it seems, though my respondents seldom did) into the tape recorders as they whir.

The other type of memory is difficult to reproduce. It is foreign in its silences, private, remote from the public events that most historians write about, and there seems to be no place for it, post-glasnost, in a world that is still hungry for true life stories and grisly revelations. And yet it seems to me to be more typical at least of those who stayed and made their lives as Soviet citizens, the members of a new collective. The accounts I heard, more than a dozen from veterans of dekulakization, a dozen more from elderly people who survived the famine, were seldom neatly chronological. They did not keep to the point (the historian's point, that is). They were the fragments that were saved in private when there was no public framework for remembering. The narrators talked as if they were exceptions, and their memories, like their adult lives, were blighted by a need to justify themselves, as if their mere survival were a guilty scar.

An early conversation, which I found frustrating at the time, before I understood, may stand for others of its kind.[92] The woman who was talking was an eager volunteer. "Come and see me," she had said. "I was dekulakized. I am sure you will want to know about that." The problem was that in three hours (and then over a lengthy tea) she scarcely ever spoke of it. There were a few brief words about the first day in the barracks, the usual denial of wealth—"we fulfilled our quota, that is all"—and then more memories of her later life, the real life for which catastrophe prepared the way. The fact of her dekulakization had been a shameful secret for decades (it could have meant the loss of her career). It was a past that she had hidden, skillfully, for fifty years. Much of it was buried under later triumphs, and some of it was still disguised within the prejudice and superstition that are part, despite the Bolsheviks and their science, of every Soviet person's heritage.

She was seven years old when it happened. The men came to the house ("It was madness") and took her father away. She herself, the only daughter, and her mother and three brothers were herded into a barracks and abandoned without papers or money. What made her life so different (or so it seemed to her, though thousands more like her escaped by similar means) was the fact that her mother, trapped and despairing as the summer approached, and denied the freedom to travel for herself, had somehow managed to contact her own sister, the children's aunt. The other woman, Tanya, was married to a musician, "a real master." The couple had no children of their own. They came as soon as they could, threading their way along the Volga through desolate villages, avoiding the crowds of beggars and the starving children. They brought food and some old clothes for the mother to use for barter, but they also came with an offer. They would take one child.

The changes that they saw when they found their relatives would have shocked the couple from the town. The children were hungry, barefoot, and the little girl, Anna Timofeyevna, "was almost dead." She had rickets, and at seven was almost as tall as she would ever grow. Her uncle, so different from the "kulak" father who was never more than a shadow in his daughter's memory, made an immediate, indelible impression. "He was an artist," she said. "He was cultured; he knew everything. He understood straight away. He asked where it was written down that the children had to stay right there." She and her brothers watched the adults as they talked. Their mother was trying to persuade her relatives to take the oldest son, then eight years old, but Tanya had already seen the daughter. "He's already practically a man," she said, dismissing the eight-year-old. "I'll take Anna." "Mother gave me up," said Anna Timofeyevna. "She gave them all my documents and papers, everything. They took me. Uncle bailed me. There had to be security. We had been dekulakized, so I was on bail. Father had no rights, you see." His other children were all to die.

Anna Timofeyevna laughed. "They bathed me first," she said. "I remember the smell of the soap." The pace and tone of her narrative changed with the memory. The story shifted from the dark barracks to a tiny flat, sometimes a single room, and then to the circus. For two years, little Anna was too ill to work, but as soon as she was strong enough the musician who had taken the place of her father began to take her in hand. The discipline was relentless. "I did not know what he meant at first when he made me stand in the corner," she said. "I had never known anything like that." She laughed as she spoke, however (hardship of this kind, the hardship of another life, is part of almost all the former kulaks' stories), combining a note of pride with a memory of gratitude. "We were like orphans," she remembered of her family. Unlike her brothers, she was the one who was about to start a career. "My life was different," she said. "I was an artist. I always had to be creative. That was my anchor."

Acquiring an artist's skills is never an easy matter. "I had absolutely no childhood," she explained. "I would start with ordinary school in the mornings, and then I would go straight round to the circus in the afternoon. There was a short break for dinner, we always ate that together, and then I was back at my lessons, the circus school. In those days, you didn't just become a dancer or a musician. You had to do everything." She picked up the tunes quickly—her uncle made her a special accordion, scaled down to fit her short fingers and small hands—and she forced her wasted limbs to dance. Her uncle also made her change her name. "Not Bondarennikov, that was too long. No." Smiling, she threw her arms wide in a dramatic flourish and announced herself—her voice was as gritty as Piaf's—as if she were about to take the stage again. "Anna Timofeyevna Bondarenko." They set her up as a foil for her uncle's own musical performances. By the time she was thirteen, she had been sending money home to her mother for two years.

There are posters on the wall in her cramped sitting room to witness the life she then would lead—Bondarenko accompanying her uncle; Bondarenko playing and singing; Bondarenko with her husband, a musical double act. "We did a hundred and twenty-four concerts in one month," she said, remembering her contribution to the Soviet war effort. "Three or four concerts a day. I worked at the front until I was eight months pregnant. I have documents about that if you want to see them. I played till 4 August and I gave birth on 23 September." The baby would never be allowed to take up much of her time. She gave him to her mother to bring up. The stage, and the husband with whom she often shared it, was Anna Timofeyevna's life.

I am playing the tape back now—I have to get her words exactly right—and I am struck, as I was when we first spoke, by Anna Timofeyevna's priorities, so different from my own. The interview, for me about the kulaks, was something else for her. "Now he, of course," she said, some time after we started, "that man, the one by whom I had my son and who was already my husband, he was, uh, the only person in Moscow, in fact in the whole Soviet Union, the only professionally accredited artistic whistler. He was always the one. Whenever you heard whistling in a film, it was him." I hear her standing up, the scraping of a chair, and I know that she has crossed to a cupboard in the corner behind me. She produces a hefty black cassette recorder, fumbles with a tape. "Just a minute. He left nothing. I found this by going through some radio recordings that he made. I put it together myself from little fragments."

The Soviet cassette recorder was placed beside mine, the standard interviewer's Walkman Professional. "Is that working?" she asked. As I listen to my own tape again, I hear myself reassuring her and then I hear the dead man whistling. There is a piano accompaniment, then a full orchestra (the background to a frenzied piece by Khachaturian), and then, for the last number, an electric piano and synthesized drums. "It is going, isn't it?" she checks again. Ten minutes have passed and the tapes are still running. She pushes hers nearer to mine. As the last piece begins, a smoochy 1950s dance classic, she is crying. "Here, look at this," she whispers, keeping her voice down so as not to interrupt her husband, glancing anxiously from the tape to my face, checking again that everything is running to plan. She hands me a sheaf of photographs, then snatches them back again, pulling out the best. "That is Mother," she says, "and that is her sister, my aunt." The whistling stops, but the tapes record a lengthy silence. She has gone into the kitchen to find her handbag, a lipstick, and a handkerchief.

That husband was the center of her life, and those few minutes on my tape, the burst of whistling, were more important, and more moving, for my witness, than the story of her childhood and the farm. She also talked with pride about her war. "It was the biggest event in all our lives," she said. "The friendships we made then were always so strong." To some extent, they have redeemed the distant past, and certainly obscured it. "We played again on the fortieth anniversary of the victory," she said. "They say the most powerful memories are in the fingers. Mine seem to have remembered." There was another laugh, and then she played some Mozart, badly, smiling as she fingered stubborn keys.

You do not need to know the history of dekulakization to listen to the recording that I have of Efim, Anna Timofeyevna's husband, as he whistles. You can admire the technique (and the stamina, for he made eighty-five films), and you may even recognize the tunes. The story that goes with them, however, and the censorship, the silences, are harder to follow, and sometimes they are shocking. One thing that seems surprising in Anna Timofeyevna's story, for instance, is her lack of bitterness. The reason for it lies, in part, in her removal from it all, the remaking of her future in another city, and there must also be a role, no doubt, for various forms of memory repression and self-protection. But the other reason, and one that she shares with millions of her generation, is specific and historical. It is an aspect of the unique Soviet sense of self.

As soon as she was old enough, Anna Timofeyevna became a member of the Komsomol, the Young Communists League. She went on the parades, she wore the badges, she joined the class struggle on the winning side. In truth, as her uncle no doubt realized, she probably would not have been able to perform in public if she had not. Her stage career began at a time when the Communist Party's grip on public discourse of all kinds had become a stranglehold. But she did not make an effort to disbelieve. An optimist, a comrade, a keen member of any team, she built her world within the grander myth of socialist construction, dauntlessly adding whatever she could to the collective victory over fascism, and always working, working because work had been her path to life, working to contribute and belong. The collapse of Communism has freed her to talk of her origins, but she does not speak from an anger nurtured over six decades.

She mentioned the Komsomol as if in passing (twenty years ago, when the Communist Party was still in power, the emphasis would obviously have been different), but her membership of it drove her further from the village and from the family she had left. While she became a Soviet citizen, her mother remained in the limbo of shanty town Saratov. It was from the older woman, however, that Anna Timofeyevna would always hear the news of her family, and it is through her mother's words that their story continues.

The inspiration here predates the world of Bolshevism, the victory over

Germany, and all the euphemisms of the 1930s. Anna Timofeyevna's mother, born in a village in the grain country of Russia's central Black Earth region in the first three years of the twentieth century, was not a woman to see her life in terms of progress and class struggle. For her the universe was a place defined by good and evil, God and czar, heaven, hell, and ultimate judgment. There would be no Komsomol for her. The difference of a generation meant a lifetime of hardship rather than the blossoming of hope. Her daughter's voice is burdened, as she talks of the family, by her mother's shadow, recalling the conversations the two women must have had, the moments when the generations really met. "She was a tragic woman," Anna Timofeyevna explains. "Her fate touched everyone who stayed close to her. I was the only one who escaped."

It is destiny, then, that is used to explain the series of disasters that come next. It is a strange account to hear, a jarring echo of another kind of world. The family's story is set in the context, not of politics or of state violence, but of a primitive curse. The testimony must be heard with patience, for if you rip it open in a search for the familiar parts, for usable historical detail, you will lose a truth about this woman's life. In her account, the individual deaths take on a tragic form. Her own survival is miraculous; she is uniquely blessed.

The story raises questions, doubts. Perhaps there are confusions, self-deceit. As the events accumulate there are even moments—although the narrator was unaware of it—when the account begins, because of the shaping and the tone, to veer dangerously close to the boundary that separates a tragedy from farce. The repetition is too much. The subconscious mind rejects the darkness, especially as it is narrated at several removes, and in its weakness turns the unacceptable into comedy. The same kind of reflex, too, refuses to imagine numbers, cannot combine, in a single sentence, the image of repeated pain with an understanding that this person, too, this one who is talking, has witnessed it all, sustained the wounds, and shares the same humanity as oneself.

Anna Timofeyevna's father came back from his forced labor after only a year. He began to drink—there is no other description of him than that—and he died "within forty days." By then, at least one of his sons was already gone. When Tanya and the uncle left with Anna, their mother took the eldest son, the one who was "almost a man" and left her toddlers, a two- and a four-year-old, to fend for themselves while she bartered and foraged for food. "She left them with enough food for three days," Anna Timofeyevna explained, "but of course they ate it all straight away. They were hungry." When their mother did not return, the two boys set off to look for her. It was a time when the streets were full of lost children, *bezprizorniki,* the ones for whom no one cared, and another two small boys would not have attracted notice. They were still missing when their mother came back.

"They started looking everywhere, the hospitals, the morgues," their sister continued, relating the story as if she were talking about another life, "but no one had seen the boys. They would not have known their own surname. Eventually they found Valya. He said that they had eaten everything, and then the little one had started to cry. So he had said that they would go and find their mother. They walked the streets. Sometimes the people did feed them. But the little one—they never found him. We still don't know what happened to him. He would have been weak, he would have been easy to lead. They were together, though. Together. Perhaps he ended up in hospital. He wouldn't have known where he came from. Mother went everywhere. She always believed he was still alive. They did feed them, you know. So maybe he didn't die. His name was Zhenya. Zhenya."

Valya, the four-year-old in that story, would live to see his teens. He went to school in Saratov, and as the family began to reconstruct their lives, his prospects looked set to improve. They were building a new house. "It was 1940," Anna Timofeyevna said. "They hadn't got the roof on still. And one morning he just said: 'Mother, fetch a doctor. I am going to die.' Just like that. And he did. He was dead before that evening." In Anna Timofeyevna's account, that left their mother with Sasha, the eldest boy. "He fought in the Finnish war," his sister said, tapping the table with each phrase. "He fought in the Patriotic War; he went to the Supreme Soviet army school; he became an officer. He had two children. He was thirty-seven years old." It was 1959. Sasha was training some recruits. There was an accident. He was yelling at the soldier to run, to throw himself into a trench, and so he was the one who was still standing in the line of impact when the grenade exploded.

The way each story was told could leave no doubt about the ending. Even the mother's death—she tripped and fell into the path of a suburban electric train while on her way to church with Tanya—seems to have been shaped by inescapable doom. "One more step, just one, and she would have been safe," her daughter insists. The death of her own son, however, was something for which Anna Timofeyevna produced a range of interpretations. Vovka died within two months of his father. His grandmother's cursed destiny—the influence he absorbed as her adopted child—was always there. "Mother said it to me," Anna Timofeyevna whispered. "I am glad to love him—she knew I was not jealous—but he will share my fate. And he did. He had three heart attacks. He was forty-seven. She was a tragic woman." But questions produced another set of answers, the complicated relationships, the contradictory prejudices that make up any life. "No, I never told him about his origins," she said, rejecting my suggestion that he might have suffered on account of the trauma of his parents and adopted mother. "That was nothing to do with it. His heart. It was his private life; his wife refused him. No, she didn't leave him. She, er, she died. She died three years before him. She died of cancer. She was, you understand, she was a strange person. I had the impression that she was afraid to love. She was always calculating things. It seems to me—I think that she died, really—that she got cancer, because she was so malicious."

The Soviet Union has not been gone for long, and the Komsomol is still easier to understand—and arguably more attractive—than the fatalism, the superstition, and the prejudice that stand behind that judgment of a daughter-in-law. Shake the kaleidoscope again, however, just rearrange the fragments, and the traditional world from which the darkness springs becomes a place of festival. "The whole village turned out for my grandparents' wedding," Anna Timofeyevna relates, and her words evoke a procession of men and women in their best clothes, the embroidered shirts and sarafans, black and red on white, bright summer, and the scent and color of lupins and wild campion in every patch of garden. The only personal memory Anna Timofeyevna has of her village is about an Easter cake, the crumbs that she saved for her brothers, and a basket of vegetables that a neighbor offered to the hungry family as they waited for their uncle to arrive. Again, the memory is not painful, and the edges of it blur to please the listener.

To ask for more, however, is to touch the confusion and self-doubt that Communism's collapse has left behind among the people who worked to live within it. I asked Anna Timofeyevna about the family funerals. "Oh yes," she said. "We did everything. Of course. We gave all of them a send-off [*otpevali ikh vsekh*]. All of them. So what? Mother did it. She went to church. But in those days it wasn't on to talk about it—we were in the Komsomol, we—well, I—I had this attitude toward it . . . I wasn't exactly against it, but for myself I never—well, Easter, yes. She went to church. Great. But for me, you have to understand, I never told her off, I never asked her what she was doing. But, well, you have to do what you have to do." Anna Timofeyevna does not talk to priests to this day, though many in Russia have turned to the church where once the Communist Party served their purpose. "I take these herbs," she explained. "I have twenty-five different kinds. And when I need help, I can ring the man and he understands without having to see me."

For Anna Timofeyevna, these memories, these superstitions, fables, and silences, are among the most important constituents—for conversational purposes, at least—of an imaginative universe. In that sense, they are real, they are historical facts. "Mental representations," says Luisa Passerini in her classic study of the mentalities associated with Italian fascism, "are the other face of reality, which includes and is shaped by them."[93] Living memory is partial, and that is why it is so eloquent. In Russia, often, it has a quality of nightmare, the voice, occasionally, of solitary confinement, and hence that affinity with fate. Public silences about the famine were a kind of violence, another Stalinist atrocity, enforced by twisted calculations and pervasive fear. Activists who work with survivors like Anna Timofeyevna know that the task of overcoming their legacy is far from over yet. They warn us of oblivion's costs. "While humankind survives," one of them wrote in the 1980s, "it must preserve the memory of its forebearers [*sic*] to remain human and to avoid becoming . . . people without memory, whom it is easier to make slaves."[94]

Anna Timofeyevna is not a slave. In some respects—although the word does not come readily to mind on meeting her—she is a victim. Unlike her parents and her brothers, however, she has accommodated and survived the nightmare. She is not damaged, traumatized, embittered, or afraid. There is a case for saying that she is not only victim but collaborator, or rather that collaboration, enforced and passive, the best but also probably the only option, was part of certain kinds of victimhood. Her innocence, her negligence, her very eagerness to live all made her part of something that she did not choose or even actively imagine, a party to collective silence. There is no implication of culpability here. If anything, the necessity of collusion added to the burdens people carried, consciously or not. It was a strategy that millions, a majority, of Stalin's people had to use to get on with their lives.

Glasnost has not destroyed Anna Timofeyevna's Soviet mind, whatever layers it has added. For all her warmth, for all her fluency, she cannot tell the story that the textbooks give. "Come back," she said as I was leaving. "We can have an evening, and I will play you some more music." But I still do not know, and she will not remember, exactly what it was that she thought and understood when, as a child, she watched the men come storming to the door, and saw her mother hide her face, her father reaching for his jacket.

7

NIGHTS OF STONE

Varlam Shalamov spent the better part of twenty years in exile or in prison. The longest of his sentences, from 1937 to 1951, was served in Kolyma, the territory of the Soviet Union's arctic gold mines. His short stories about it describe a world that remains unimaginable. Kolyma is isolated beyond Siberia, north of Japan, the coldest place in the northern hemisphere. Its landscape is as deadening as it is alien, gray on gray, a world of permafrost, of buried rivers, ice-bound valleys, leaden coastlines, fog. Even where the snow has melted or scattered in the bitter wind, there is little color for most of the year, a few skeletons of larch, perhaps, dwarf cedar, stunted pines.

The ice and snow conceal a mountain range, but the other boundaries and reference points within the monochrome are artificial ones—watch towers, the pulleys and the steel ropes above the mines, the cruel outlines of barbed wire. Within the zone, as the prisoners called their world, there are also huts and woodpiles, darker gray, and once there were untidy bonfires, electric bulbs, the sullen glow of hand-rolled cigarettes. It all made little impact on the dark, the arctic cold.

A person, too, can easily disappear. If you go back to Kolyma now you will not find many. The valleys and the derelict mines are silent, and these days the barbed wire is rusting uselessly. But there are photographs that show how people used to fill this landscape, men and women in bundled rags, blurred figures against mist, haggard, filthy. The pictures were usually taken in daylight, so most of the time their subjects are the prisoners at work. It is the heaviest kind of labor. Men and women, even children, are digging, hacking at the rock and ice, breaking and leveling the beds for railway sleepers, hauling loads of precious dust, the gold, the lead, the tungsten, diamonds, and uranium.

This dust and rock would fascinate Shalamov. It played an unanticipated role. "In Kolyma," he wrote, "bodies are not given over to earth, but to stone." There were so many of them in the mountain near his own camp that it took a bulldozer to move the cover from their grave. Watching the scene from a distance, Shalamov thought at first that what he could see was a cascade of logs. It was only when he stood beside the pit that he recognized its secret. Years after the first mass deaths, Kolyma's graves "were filled to the brim with corpses." The ice and sterile rock preserved their flesh, their features, wounds, the marks of insect bites, the scars. The burial gangs had made the first mass graves in the mountain in 1938, "digging, exploding, deepening the enormous gray, hard, cold stone pits." It was an insult that the landscape would remember. "The bodies had not decayed," Shalamov wrote. "All of our loved ones who had died in Kolyma, all those who were shot, beaten to death, sucked dry by starvation, can still be recognised after tens of years."[1]

The faces on the corpses—Russian faces, Latvian, German, Polish, Ukrainian, Uzbek—are witnesses that Kolyma is not just endless rock and ice, convenient oblivion. Its graves, ten thousand miles at least from all of Europe's busy capitals, are part of Europe's story, as real a product of its culture as the palace at Versailles. The reminder is a necessary one, for the history of Soviet repression remains incomprehensible. Like all atrocities of its kind it is hard to face, repels research. But it also bears some added complications. The political murders of the Soviet era often (though by no means always) happened out of metropolitan Europe's sight. Before they died, their victims usually became as wretched and as undesirable as the meanest slaves, reproaching freedom, daily courtesy, accusing the comfortable world from which they came. Most seriously of all, for nearly fifty years their fates were threaded tightly round the gray warp of ideology. Their lives and deaths were weighed in the polemical balance of the Cold War.

The dismal history of Stalinism's basements, camps, and prisons could not be written inside Russia until Soviet power itself collapsed. Even in the West, however, in the countries where a history might have at least been attempted, the assessments that historians made would often bend under the weight of

Cold War politics. Opponents of the Soviet system, and of state socialism in general, exaggerated the crimes of the totalitarian state (as if they needed such exaggeration to be real).[2] Among the rest were some who argued, on occasion, that the excess and the bloodshed should be overlooked.[3] And everyone was blinkered by the universal lack of reliable evidence. The search for meaning, then, has hardly really started anywhere, although this is especially true for Stalinism's heirs. The bones are still there in their pits, and though some have been excavated, counted, photographed, and labeled, there are millions—millions of complete skeletons—left to find.

As ever, the exact tally of the victims, how many there are or have ever been, remains a matter for debate. The size of the Gulag population itself is still unknown, with estimates for the immediate prewar years (1937–1941) varying from about 2 million to more than 15 million (a figure at the lower end of this range is the more likely).[4] Some of the secret police's own statistics are now available, but even these appear to be incomplete.[5] Mass graves still wait to be unearthed in Ukraine, in Russia, and in Belarus as well as in Siberia, they date from any moment after 1937. The number of skeletons in the ones that have been opened still surprises the men and women who do the digging. The human-rights organization, Memorial, estimates that in one mass grave alone, at Bykovna in Ukraine, there may be as many as two hundred thousand bodies, and there are probably one hundred thousand in the pits at Butovo, near Moscow.[6]

Neo-Stalinists still insist that most of the bones belong to Soviet hostages of the German army, and that the killing was the work of foreign soldiers. In many cases, they are right—there are still unnumbered thousands of undiscovered wartime casualties in the earth—but not in all. Many of the graves predate the German invasion of 1941, some of the later ones contain the Soviet victims of Stalin's own police, and there are bullets among the skulls that never came from German guns. The Cold War is over, and the use of numbers as surrogates in the international confrontation between right and left is, mercifully, now irrelevant, but controversy inside Russia continues to obscure the story of Soviet political violence.

The numbers are important, for it matters that we know if it was one in ten or one in twenty of the Soviet Union's adult population who served time in the network of its camps and jails; it matters that we know that it was one in six of these, or one in seven, who never returned home. But numbers preserve a distance from the pain they represent. However terrible they may seem, they seldom focus human images, realities of survival, tricks, hopes, and stratagems, pilfered crusts, the gray weight of depression. Once we have brought ourselves to think of it at all, the greatest challenge of the Gulag, now as then, is to imagine the extent of it without losing sight of the singularity of human life, to defeat its promise of annihilation. "We learned—they taught us—that we were nothing," a survivor told me once. He clenched his fist. It was cold in his small room, but he was sweating. "You are nothing," he repeated. "You will die here. You are dust."

One way to crack the problem of this anonymity is to talk to the people who remember parents, partners, friends, and trusted mentors. Many of Stalin's victims were famous, internationally impressive figures, but it helps to get behind their reputations. "He was a wise man and a great Christian," Magdalena Alekseyevna explained of her grandfather, a respected member of the Orthodox religious hierarchy in 1920s Kiev, a friend of the writer Mikhail Bulgakov. But the way she actually remembered him, from the perspective of a five-year-old, was more personal. "We were always so happy when we could rush round after church to find him," she said. "He always had such warm hands, even in the coldest weather." The great man let his two grandchildren climb inside his enormous dark fur coat. He laughed when they played games with the sleeves. He always seemed to be smiling. His faith and humor did not fail him, rumor has it, even as he coughed himself to death in the arctic winter following his arrest.[7]

There is a tranquility about some of the remembered scenes. "I was his only child, his only daughter," Yudif Borisovna said of her long-dead father, the Chekist. "Of course he loved me really madly." All that was sixty years ago. She has made a strange kind of peace with the image. She knows that she did everything she could to find and rescue him after he disappeared. The twenty-year-old demanded answers, knocked on doors, stood patiently in lines, and even with her own arrest refused to let the matter lie. Others were haunted, distressed, guilty. "I knew which day it was they shot him because he came and told me," one survivor shuddered. "He was there. It did not feel at all good."

These stories help us to defy the anonymity of numbers, but their very individuality brings problems of its own. The same difficulties arise with the accounts of imprisonment and exile that the former convicts give. Every one of them had a prison number once, and most can still recite the terse and standardized configuration of their crime and sentence—Article 58,[8] counterrevolutionary agitation, ten years. But the stories that they tell—survivors' stories, accounts of deliverance and not of numbness and defeat—describe the individual speakers' special destiny—they often talk of fate—and maybe their good luck. There is seldom much sense of collectivity in the tales. "Tragedy is not deep and sharp if it can be shared with friends," Shalamov wrote.[9]

It was to find the traces of a more collective memory, a prison camp esprit de corps, that I chose to interview some of the survivors who agreed to talk to me in groups of four or five. As ever, the first occasion was the most revealing because of all the things that went wrong. There were five survivors in the group, and they gathered round a table in a Moscow office.[10] The only thing they had in common was arrest. Beside me sat Nadezhda Ivanovna. She described herself as a member of the third generation. "One of my grandfathers was shot in 1920," she explained, "and the second one, allegedly a bourgeois nationalist, was shot in 1929. My father was shot in 1937, and my mother was arrested in 1938. I was arrested in 1943 after the [German] occupation and I got fifteen years of hard labor under Article 54, Clause 1a." She served her time in Vorkuta, north of the Ural Mountains. Yudif Borisovna, who was arrested in 1937, did most of hers in Ivdel, a good eight hundred miles further south. Across the table were two former soldiers: Boris Leonidovich, a veteran of Stalingrad, of Kursk, and of Berlin, arrested in 1949; and Kiril Moiseyevich, a native of the Romanian province of Bessarabia, a Communist, whose most fervent hope, in his youth, had been to make a Soviet revolution.

The youngest member of the group was Kuz'ma Gavrilovich, who was arrested in 1941 in his home town of Kuibyshev. "It was when the government was evacuated there," he explained. "They arrested everyone, the guilty and the innocent, it didn't matter . . . Maybe you'd complained about the bread queues, maybe you'd said something, I've forgotten half of it . . . They only gave me five years . . . One of the other guys told me why they did that. 'They give you five years when you're not guilty of anything at all,' he told me, 'so as not to have to let you go. It's not the done thing to let people go in these parts.'" Kuz'ma Gavrilovich worked on the Baikal–Amur railway, beyond kilometer 57. In the winter of 1942 he and his comrades starved and froze. Their lice spread typhus through the camp. "There were about five hundred of us," he said. "In the space of six weeks three quarters of them died. I was not spared myself—I slipped into this delirium—but I suppose a younger body puts up more of a fight . . . I remained alive."

Each one of them described their exile differently. Each one believes, today, that they survived under a special star—Communist, religious, soldierly, youthfully optimistic, even a bit rakish (these are the recollections of a distant youth), plain lucky. "It's still like that," Yudif Borisovna insists. "There are about a thousand of us in my district and we are all different. Some of them are still crying even now, they suffer all the time, they sob, and others have got themselves under control, they have made some kind of life for themselves, done a bit more education. They've got on with things. It all depends on the individual, on the state of a person's mind."

I wanted to get the group to discuss and compare the things that they had seen. I wanted to bring the two extremes of Gulag history together, the numbers and the individual human beings. But that is precisely the thing that most of the survivors still find hardest. A fifty-year public silence has left them without the collective framework that is needed to contain debate, without the structures and points of reference that make discussion safe. I had hoped that talking as a group would prompt their common memories. But the level of debate, and even of exchange, was—from the strictly historical, factual point of view—disappointing. It was also a lesson in one of the mysteries of the Soviet prison camp mentality, at least as far as it is recollected, which is its terrifying isolation.

"It's useless doing it this way," Kuz'ma Gavrilovich told me later. "Everyone just wants to tell his own story." Nadezhda Ivanovna agreed. "You can get us in a room like that," she said, "but all you will get are monologues. We don't want to listen to each other. We only want to tell our own stories." I knew exactly what she meant. I had already heard a good many testimonies. Typically, with few exceptions, they were recited almost without pause, continuing for hours. Storytelling is still a strong feature of Russian culture; everyone knows how to hold the floor, and audiences are patient, eager to be entertained. But these were not the usual kitchen tales. In the most extreme cases, the speakers would talk in a kind of trance, oblivious to interruption, oblivious to passing real time. When this occurred, when the speaker disappeared into a fantasy about the past, there was no point in coughing, asking questions, looking at my watch. If I missed my dinner or the last train, the consolation was that these extended monologues were evidence in themselves, part of the complete picture that the words alone did not describe, part of the legacy of repression, silence, guilt, and lies.

Some monologues were used deliberately to fend off questions, talking out the time: "If you will only listen, I will tell you how it was." What followed was often generality, chunks of Solzhenitsyn, rumor, snatches from the Book of Revelation. But there was more to the long speeches than evasiveness. Even a quick, responsive woman like Yudif Borisovna presented large parts of her story in a fixed, prepackaged form. She kindly let me interview her twice—once on her own, in her small room, surrounded by her pictures, the second time as part of that group of her peers, of fellow native Russian speakers. On both occasions, there were several events that she described in exactly the same words and phrases. Even the timing that she used was the same, despite the fact that the second time around was not a formal interview but really a discussion. Elderly people repeat their stories in this way in other cultures, too, but seldom to the same extent. It makes a difference if you spent the best part of your life without the luxury of comparison or collective context, relating the story only to your closest friends, and sometimes even not to them, without refocusing the images. It also makes a difference if you never had the chance to acquire the knack, the discipline, of listening.

There are some similarities between these spoken monologues and the written testimonies that have been packed, raw, into collected volumes and published, since the 1980s, by survivors' organizations. These books announce that they are "real" histories, "how it really was," but this, too, is a symptom of the long silence. Usable history usually emerges from competing forms of collective memory, and it comes well after the individual's sense of shock, of personal exceptionalism, has been exposed and shared. It is a process that is based on negotiation, on cross-checks, and on documents. Fifty years of censorship have delayed all this in Russia, and the usual structures of civil society, the ones that work to build remembrance—ex-prisoners' associations, charities, educational trusts—have only just begun to form.

They are not emerging from a vacuum, however. The life of a former prisoner in a Soviet town or city was seldom one of isolation. The collective groups for remembering injustice and oppression did not exist, but others did, and there were powerful pressures on everyone to join them. The social incentives were obvious—acceptance, friendship, an enhanced sense of personal worth—but so were the material ones. Any member of the collectives that the state chose to encourage—the Party, the Komsomol, the all-important Society for Veterans of the Great Patriotic War, and even of the smaller, keener groups that celebrated the virtues of personal hygiene, abstinence from alcohol, cross-country running, rabbit breeding (for meat—this was not England), and international friendship—could expect better holidays, two-roomed apartments, easier promotion, and sometimes tins of ham. The temptation to accept what might be called a false collective memory was enormous. It was a privilege in the 1960s, after all, to have one's Party card restored.

To tell their stories now, therefore, survivors often have to cut their way through years of well-rehearsed, state-sanctioned fable. This is not always true. Some never accepted the euphemisms and propaganda, just as they refused (and still refuse) all consolation. Others, such as Magdalena Alekseyevna's father, who, like her grandfather, was a priest, had such strong beliefs of other kinds that they were never vulnerable to the seductive power of the Soviet collective. But others did not merely hide behind the banners. They grasped them with enthusiasm; they wanted to believe. These people have a fog of confusion to clear away, a web of lost identity, acceptance, grateful membership. In many cases, too, though this takes courage, there is a real faith to talk about, an ideology that did not always fail. "I was a Communist, yes of course," said Lev Razgon, "and I still am." His own arrest did not destroy his politics, and nor did the neglect—the passive murder—of Oksana, his diabetic wife.

"We always preferred Trotsky," Yidif Borisovna told me. "But we believed in the Party. We did not distinguish between Stalin and the Party." She, too, retains a wistful faith in Communism. She also tells a personal story of the leader. When she was fourteen, in the summer of 1929, the very eve of the campaign of mass collectivization, she went to Sochi, in the Crimea, on holiday with her father. They were in a sanatorium for members of the Central Committee. Everyone else had gone off to play volleyball, but Yudif had lost sight of them and was standing, looking confused, on the marble steps of what must have been a former palace. "My dress had got torn," she remembers. "Then he was there. I thought it was Budyennyi. There was a voice asking where I was going, and there he was. Right next to me. And I was in that state. He was dressed entirely in white—white suit, white boots, white cap, black mustache. We didn't know much about Stalin in 1929." The man she met on the steps would later have her father shot. But her memory of him—which is typical in its juxtaposition of her unworthiness (the torn dress) and his immaculate power—remains dazzled, as if the later cult of personality somehow shone backward. Later on that week, she would discover that he had put his Rolls-Royce at her disposal for a trip to Sukhumi.

Confusions about loyalty—not all of them as graphic as Yudif Borisovna's—help to explain why it is that some people still remain within the grip of memories that torment them. They were not happy in the past, but they cannot approve of the present, either. The economic problems that they have make all this worse.[11] The younger generation, the heirs of Stalinism, generally attack it now, but many of its former victims keep the faith. The explanations that they give for all the violence exonerate the revolution and its goals, its teleology and impatience, and focus on individual corruption, sadism, and weakness.

It is a bitter enough story, but the main alternative, for those who cannot look at larger kinds of explanation, is truly poisonous. It seems absurd, but some of Stalinism's survivors still work hard to demonstrate their innocence, and what they need is proof, not of the madness of the system as a whole, but of the error that was made in their one individual case. They prepare their files of documents before we meet, they point to articles of the law, they tap the pages with their fingers, check that they are understood.

Two things are striking here, and both are sad. The first is that so many people still believe in their own guilt, cannot accept the meaning of repressive politics, the propaganda messages of torture, show trials, and mass death. The second is that the victims are not alone in their belief. There are still millions of people, witnesses but not former prisoners, in Russia at least, if not elsewhere inside the former Soviet Union, who believe in the culpability of the people who were condemned. Survivors of the camps and prisons, even the ones who have their rehabilitation documents (the nearest that the state can ever bring itself to an apology), must constantly assert their innocence in the face of hostile skepticism.[12] One common view, largely derived from Christian teaching, and encouraged by the likes of Solzhenitsyn, still holds that suffering, for a Russian soul, is the crucible of redemption. For very many people, however, it is a mark of guilt.

"Archive No. 3 is the name of the office in the camp that records convict deaths," wrote Shalamov. "Its instructions read that a plywood tag must be attached to the left shin of every dead body. The tag records the prisoner's 'case number' . . . The practice strikes one as odd. Can there really be plans for exhumation? For immortality? For resurrection? . . . Theoretically speaking, all guests of the permafrost enjoy life eternal and are ready to return to us."[13] The problem is that they are not. Only the survivors can still speak, and most of them are old now, tired, and justifiably confused. In the end, too, they are survivors, they escaped. In view of the temptation that exists to look away, or even to deny the past, in view of the continued failure of history to explain what happened to the people with the greatest need to understand, it might be better if the owners of the tags could give their testimonies after all.

The use of state processes—arrest, interrogation, trials, imprisonment, exile, and murder—for political purposes in the Russian empire was neither uniquely Stalinist nor even uniquely Soviet. Siberian villages had been accustomed to the sight of prisoners and their accompanying guards for decades before the first railway track was laid across the taiga. The colony on the cold Pacific island of Sakhalin had been established for a generation by the time that Anton Chekhov paid his visit to it in 1890.[14] As the Bolsheviks continued to insist, Lenin's own brother had been among the thousands hanged, under the czars, for a political crime.

The revolution brought a momentary lull in state repression, but the hopes of revolutionary idealists would shrivel in the face of civil war. There was no space for opposition. Enemies seemed to surface in their millions. Arrests and summary executions became daily instruments of political security, and they continued to be used into the early 1920s. By then, the prison camp in the former Solovetskii monastery, universally known as Solovki, was full of priests, political polemicists, writers, nationalists, and other kinds of so-called former people.[15] The next stage, the use of Solovki, and then of other sites, as a corrective labor camp (as opposed to a prison where manual work was part of the regime) began in 1926.[16]

The Stalinist repressions, however, really date from 1929. The culture of arrest, denunciation, and terror was established on a mass basis. New kinds of thinking and new social patterns developed to accommodate it. Subcultures, bureaucratic rules, and social myths evolved to cope with fear. Methods were found to deal with the management of disappearing personnel, to live in the shadow of nightly arrests, the sound of gunfire. There was not one logic working in the terror, in other words, but many. Some people's contribution was no more than to ignore it all, just as millions of others (not always the same people) were also to ignore the famine. Others swallowed any propaganda they were offered, unreflectively, thereby turning a blind eye to their neighbors' fear. It was a closed system; there was no outside criticism, no alternative. Leonid Likhodeev, who grew up in the Ukrainian provincial town of Stalino, believed the account of politics that his teachers gave because it was confirmed by the newspaper that he read. As he understood it, class enemies (including starving kulaks) "risked their lives to spoil our optimism, our confidence in the bright future."[17]

The purpose of the terror—if anything as consistent as a purpose can be ascribed to what were really overlapping processes—was ultimately written in its very excess. The aspiration to citizenship, a democratic dream of 1917, was kicked to death; legality, pluralism, and political opposition were smothered; and the overarching needs of the state itself—for gold, for coal, for timber, and for weapons-grade uranium—were serviced by forced labor, by men and women working to a plan established and policed by their own prison service.[18] By the late 1930s, there were even career benefits, for the average local official, to be gained from fulfilling a high quota of arrests, and some tried to emphasize their Party loyalty by demanding that their norms be raised.[19] It was not exclusively a matter of state power. The deep-rooted tradition of personal denunciation, by which any individual could bring ruin to a neighbor, a former rival, or to an incomprehensible eccentric, was also encouraged, and it blossomed.[20]

Conflicts naturally arose between these different goals, and often they were not resolved. It does not make sense, for instance, knowingly to kill the prisoners that you are keeping for forced labor by starving and even randomly shooting them. The early Gulag administrators, especially E. P. Berzin, knew this. Referring to the mid-1930s, Shalamov spoke of "excellent nourishment, good clothing, four to six hours work in winter, ten in summer," the regime of a system that intended that its workers should survive. But from the summer of 1937 new men were found, such as the infamous Colonel Garanin, to run the labor camps. Summary execution and systematic neglect would become commonplace.[21] The result was an intensification, especially during the war, of the national shortage of manpower.[22] The preparations for war in the late 1930s were not exactly helped, either, by the rapid turnover of personnel in every tier of government. On average, each of the most senior positions in the provincial party and state apparatus would be vacated and refilled five or six times between 1937 and 1938.[23]

Stalinist terror on this massive scale was an innovation, whatever debts it owed to violent precedents in Russian history. The obvious contrast between the 1890s and the 1930s was one of numbers, but there were also differences in intention and in reach. Whatever ambitions toward political control the czarist police may have had, for instance, they would not have dreamed of the arrest of thousands in a single night, of mass executions, the victims standing by a pit, still in their evening clothes, the women in their city shoes. They would never have imagined that whole populations could be exiled, entire ethnic groups, a million Germans, half a million Chechens. The idea that the penal system could provide an economically significant labor force—again numbered in millions—would also have appeared absurd. By 1953, however, whole rooms were full of cardboard files listing the economic targets met. From the political point of view, dissension reemerged when Stalin died, but even then the Party's monopoly would face no serious challenge for another thirty years. "It was not only forbidden to criticize Stalin," a citizen of this era recollects, "it was perhaps even more forbidden to announce this very prohibition."[24]

Among the different precedents, too, there were other influences at work besides Russia's violent history. The traditions of Bolshevism itself also played their part. The people who eventually had most to lose, the Party activists and the elite themselves, unanimously failed to stop the process. At any stage, in 1919 and 1920, when the first political arrests began, in 1921, when factions in the Bolshevik Party itself were outlawed, in 1927, when Trotsky and his followers were banned and exiled, there might have been a greater protest, more debate. Even the most prominent of Lenin's former colleagues did not act. Instead, they used the increasingly powerful machinery of political exclusion to destroy their own enemies. They even used—or thought they used—the dull, the tireless, inarticulate Georgian, Stalin. "It was an experiment that cost each his life," Angelica Balabanoff wrote of the duel between Trotsky and Zinoviev. "Both died by the same arm. It was an arm which neither of them had refused to use against the others."[25] The Bolsheviks had never tolerated opposition in their ranks. Throughout the 1920s, and always with the blessing of the ones who stayed in power, the penalties for speaking out became successively crueler.

It was the same, in subtler ways, for Soviet intellectuals. The areas of permitted criticism shrank progressively, but there was always an apparent reason to keep silent. The revolution, for many of the Soviet Union's artists, was still a star worth following, individual difficulties were temporary, they were errors. "In our sort of life people had to shut their eyes to their surroundings," wrote Nadezhda Mandelstam. "To shut your eyes like this is not easy and requires a great effort . . . Soviet citizens have achieved a high degree of mental blindness, with devastating consequences for their whole psychological make-up."[26]

The path that led to the mass terror was not even. The first stage, from 1929 to 1932, was linked with the turbulent campaigns of mass collectivization and rapid industrialization. Arrest and scapegoating were desperate expedients, intended to suppress all possibility of armed resistance and to regain control of an economic and social catastrophe. Local officials had already learned to be circumspect in their complaints to Moscow, but no threats could protect some witnesses from their despair. There was near-anarchy in some provinces, and even in Moscow there were politicians, members of the elite circle, who could not keep their eyes closed firmly enough.

One such figure was the Moscow Communist M. N. Riutin. His criticisms were far too accurate for publication, but they represented what many of his colleagues in the provinces were secretly thinking. In 1930 and again in 1932, he issued warnings of disaster. He denounced the policy of rapid industrialization as "adventurism," and he described collectivization as a policy accompanied by "expropriation . . . by means of all kinds of extortions and forced requisitions." He also insisted, openly, that Stalin was personally responsible. "With the help of deception and slander, with the help of unbelievable pressures and terror," he declared in 1932, "Stalin has sifted out and removed from the leadership all the best, genuinely Bolshevik party cadres, has established . . . his personal dictatorship . . . and has embarked on a path of the most ungovernable adventurism and wild personal arbitrariness." The worst years of famine were still in the future, but Riutin's conclusion that the country faced "a mortally dangerous crisis" was unequivocal.[27]

Ideas like Riutin's would circulate in whispers among those who thought that the collapse of their civilization was imminent.[28] For a beleaguered leadership, however, even whispers were intolerable. The GPU made thousands of arrests, especially in the provinces, between 1930 and 1932. It would be several years, however, before the forced confessions and the shooting could begin inside the Party elite itself. The Politburo had not yet resolved to kill its own internal critics. Riutin was arrested and denounced, but for the time being Stalin's attempt to have him shot was outvoted by his colleagues.[29]

While the elite was spared (though former oppositionists, such as Zinoviev and Kamenev, were endlessly harassed, arrested, released, denounced), administrators in the provinces, and economic managers in the capitals, were already the targets for official investigation and attack. There were several high-profile trials during the years of revolution from above. The trials of the so-called Industrial Party (a group of engineers, academics, and other specialists accused of spying and terrorism) in 1930 and of the Mensheviks in 1931 (more spies, more plots) both followed the new charade of false legality, with the prosecutor at his polished desk and rows of broken men awaiting the inevitable in the dock. The angry crowds gathered outside, and some could be relied upon to call, not quite, perhaps, spontaneously, for the death penalty for traitors. The prosecutor duly carried out his revolutionary duty.[30]

Political vigilance was the province of the OGPU, the heirs of the Cheka, until 1936. The OGPU was an organization whose membership included some who still retained a shred or two of so-called proletarian morality. In the early 1930s, too, some party activists still deemed it worthwhile to write and complain of the GPU's excesses, which would not have been a wise move with its successor five years later. From December 1934, however, two things would happen that would change the bureaucratic processes of terror. The first was the proposal to supplant the OGPU, which Stalin now deemed to be too weak, by a new organization, the NKVD (People's Commissariat of Internal Affairs), under the leadership of Nikolai Yezhov. The second, which delayed this slightly, was the assassination, in Leningrad, of the popular Party secretary, Sergei Mironovich Kirov.

Kirov's murder, which may or may not have been Stalin's work, was followed by a furious campaign of reprisal, including mass arrests in Leningrad itself. It also provided the pretext for a shift in policy, the final approval of summary execution as a punishment for terrorism. This would apply even if the suspect were a former aide of Lenin's. Yezhov, a person whose vigilance and loyalty could not be questioned, at least as far as Stalin was concerned, was also given greater powers to investigate the former oppositionists. He claimed to have discovered a series of "counter-revolutionary blocs," Zinovievites and Trotskyites working in league with rightists, Bukharinites, white guardists, spies. By 1936, when Yezhov became People's Commissar for Internal Affairs, the case against Zinoviev and Kamenev was ready. A fresh round of arrests and interrogations was launched at the same time, and in the winter of 1936–1937 the NKVD itself was purged.[31]

The narrative thread begins to fray from 1936, the rationality to blur. There were so many contradictions that it was not always clear what purpose was at work. Stalin's personal authorship, including the fact of his signature on thousands of death warrants, is no longer a matter of doubt. Nor is that of Yezhov himself. The murder of almost all the most illustrious of the Leninist elite was part of a systematic policy, and from Stalin's point of view at least it represented the culmination of a long-held drive for undisputed personal supremacy. The arrest of "wreckers," "spies," "enemies" and "terrorists" in the provinces was sometimes connected with this, too, and sometimes grimly logical in terms of local economic and political circumstances. But it is also true that the details of the unfolding mass phenomenon were not always under anyone's control. Among the most plausible explanations for the chaos that accompanied the terror are social and administrative dislocation, smoldering personal enmities, the alarmingly rapid turnover of officials, and the conflicting short-term practical priorities of the different bureaucratic organs.[32]

But details that could look random—and genuinely, often, were unplanned—were not always without meaning. Some processes were very public—political show trials, for instance, the first of which, the trial of Kamenev and Zinoviev, was held in August 1936. Others took place under almost total cover, at night, the prisoners transported in closed vans. These vans—the infamous "black crows"—were sometimes camouflaged by painted signs that declared them to be carrying meat. Overall, however, the basic effect was consistent. That is to say, whatever plans the different perpetrators of repression may have had, whatever methods they adopted, the cumulative impact of their work, from the victim's point of view, was of a piece. It had a simple message. "You are dust" conveys it perfectly.

Historians in Britain and North America have recently pointed out that the purges of the 1930s affected a limited range of social groups.[33] "He's not a Party member and he's not a Jew, so why has he been arrested?" was a question commonly asked by Leningrad workers in the 1930s.[34] The purges played on the popular idea of "us" and "them," the high-ups, the elite, versus the mass.[35] Only members of the elite, it seemed, were really likely to be shot. The rest of us could get on with our lives, turning a blind eye, worrying about bread, scheming for an extra five square meters of living space. The great purge of 1937–1938, broadly speaking, confirmed this view. Its most conspicuous victims were political activists, most of them Bolsheviks, economic and civil administrators (by this time most of these were members of the Party also), members of the armed forces (again, the Party members suffered most), and, to a lesser extent, intellectuals of all kinds, religious believers, artists, writers, and poets.[36]

It was because of this class-consciousness that ordinary people sometimes shunned witch-hunting propaganda and avoided listening to the news. They had preoccupations of their own. Show trials might have seemed to be great public spectacles, reported endlessly in every newspaper, transmitted on loudspeakers in the streets, but if they were a case, as one historian put it, of "justice as theater," then parts of the audience for whom they were apparently intended took no notice.[37] "We clean the floor," a group of Leningrad workers answered when they were asked about the trial of the so-called anti-Soviet Trotskyite parallel center. "That does not concern us."[38] The point is that it did not matter. It did not matter that the ritual of the court was never part of ordinary life, that the venomous language of the prosecutor was unbelievable. The trials' messages and threats were clear enough to anyone who was likely to become a victim. Until that moment, in fact, not knowing was something of a luxury. If anything, the people's taste for dissociation made the shock of enforced knowledge worse.

Yudif Borisovna insists that she knew very little about the terror until her own father was arrested on 22 January 1937. If that is true, then even members of the elite could close their eyes and ears until the police forced them to see and listen. She would have known about the trial of Zinoviev and Kamenev, of course, and, as a Komsomol, she must in some way have accepted it. What she did not see was that the process was unlimited, that even "good" people like herself were vulnerable. "Some people will tell you now that they knew everything about it all along," she says. "They say that they knew all about Stalin, but actually I don't really believe them these days." Her father was living in Tula, in Moscow province, when he was arrested, and she was a third-year chemistry student in Moscow. There was not time for depressing, potentially subversive, rumor in her optimistic, busy, privileged life. "We knew nothing at all," she says. "We did not know that they were arresting people."

Stalin occasionally demanded that the details of execution should be reported after the fact, but this was not a revolution that built its scaffolds in the market squares. This time, the lack of information was not luxury, but torment. In 1937 and 1938 the families of executed prisoners were usually told that the accused had been sentenced to "ten years hard labour without right of correspondence." It was a cruel phrase that left survivors with their hopes, depriving them of a focus for their anger or their grief. The women gathered at the prison window, anxious for any news. They pleaded to have their parcels taken. In some places, they went to the timber yards to check each fresh delivery of logs, because sometimes a prisoner had carved an initial or a message in the bark before the wood was shipped.

The torment could go on for years. As the alleged ten years of someone's term came to an end, the mothers, wives or children would start laying plans. The widow of Isaac Babel, the writer, was told that he was still alive in 1947. She had his room prepared, and lovingly redecorated their flat. Years later, when he had not come home, in 1955, she was told that he had died, while serving his sentence, on 17 March 1941. But even this was an elaborate lie. He had, in fact, been shot in January 1940.[39]

It must have made the thought of execution worse to think, after a public career, that it was secret, futile. Execution soon acquired a formidable penumbra of myth, at least where its potential victims—the most important audience—were concerned. Secret killing was the obvious technique to use in a culture that permitted rumor to circulate but not to coalesce. It was more fitting for a regime whose basic message was that human life, without the state, was worthless. The threat of casual extinction, like the accompanying fear of torture, could penetrate a person's sense of integrity, of basic dignity, it could make almost anyone reach for a red banner, sign a confession, write a poem. Public executions, after all, retain a certain human drama, and there is always a possibility that the victim may make eye contact with members of the crowd, or even, while the crowd is watching, with the man who is about to kill him.[40] Even with a blindfold, the victim, while still living, is a man or woman. Clandestine shooting, with the prisoner in a cellar or a field, turns people into nothing, their lives not even worth a spectacle.

The fact that the average police recruit was thinking mainly of the job in hand just underlined the point. The executioners had no time to think about the symbolism of their actions. Like anyone else, they were obeying orders. An employee of the NKVD later told Lev Razgon what he remembered about working at a "special facility" in Siberia. The prisoners were held there for two or three days before being taken on the short journey to a waiting pit. "They'd climb out, huddle," he said. "We shot them, and if anyone was still moving, we would finish them off and get back into the trucks." It was hard work, you earned the vodka that they gave you later in the guardroom. "I slept well," he went on. "And during the day, I'd hike around, there are some beautiful spots there."[41]

When it came to formal executions (as opposed to the slower deaths that took place in the camps), the preferred technique was usually a bullet in the back of the neck. About half a million people are thought to have died this way during the 1930s.[42] It was industrial killing—quick, relatively bloodless, relatively clean—and the killer did not need to meet his victim's eyes. Other methods were also used on an experimental basis. One policeman, Isai D. Berg, gassed some of his prisoners to death in batches in the back of a specially adapted airtight van.[43] He then had them buried in the mass graves at Butovo, often in the trenches that other victims had already dug, where they already lay. It was a night's work, a trip out from the city center.

Burial sites, like execution methods, were secret yet not secret, hidden yet known. For Moscow's police, the most secure were at Butovo and Kommunarka, both several miles outside the city to the south. Kamenev and Zinoviev were buried at Kommunarka, and so, in all probability, was Bukharin. Leningrad's police created a similarly prestigious mass burial compound at Levashovo, about an hour's drive from the Finland Station.[44] Every other major city had a sinister new earthwork in its outskirts by the summer of 1937. These places were protected, ringed by high fences (and later by houses allocated to trusted members of the secret police). The sound of shooting was disguised, at least at Butovo, by a policy of using the site for genuine target practice during daylight hours. But public spaces were also taken over for police disposal. In Moscow these included the grounds of the Don and Novospasskii monasteries and the busy, much-frequented Kalitnikov and Vagan'kov cemeteries. In Leningrad, the Preobrazhenskoe cemetery, the site which also contained the victims of Bloody Sunday, was used again for mass burials, as was the Bogoslovskoe cemetery nearer to the city center.[45]

The process also involved people who were not trusted members of the security police. When prisoners themselves could not be used to dig the pits, the NKVD employed cheap laborers, many of whom received little payment other than the permit that they needed if they were to live legally in Moscow, Leningrad, or Kiev.[46] The staff of Moscow's new crematorium were also obliged to accept consignments from the city's major prisons through the night. The bodies arrived in batches, accompanied by stamped and duplicated forms that requested they be burned immediately. "They were such handsome men," recalled a crematorium worker. "Some of them were still warm. Some of them were not even dead when we put them into the furnace."[47] The practice was not secret, at least as far as women like her were concerned. The ashes were buried in two or three common pits in the cemetery grounds.

The people who cleaned floors and welded pipes could not rely entirely on the selectivity of the purges. When he described the grip of fear, the writer Lev Razgon insisted that "no-one, absolutely no-one, was safe." The threat of arbitrariness was integral to the system. There were also new categories of enemy to consider at almost any point. In 1939, following the Molotov-Ribbentrop Pact, there were the nationalists, former partisans, and local elites of the territories that the Soviet Union claimed and annexed, people in western Ukraine and eastern Poland. In 1941 there were panic-mongers and naturalized Germans. After the war almost anyone who had encountered foreign troops, especially if they had been American, was vulnerable. It was not always a matter of class or educational status. Nonetheless, the bias against people with any desire to think, especially if they were Communists, would never entirely disappear. Lev Kopelev, who was arrested at the front in 1945, was treated for his back injury by a prison doctor who jokingly described herself as a member of the SPI, "the society for the preservation of the intelligentsia."[48]

The justification that some people still believed, even in 1945, the year of final victory, was that enemies were waiting to overthrow the fragile gains of revolution. Even the future victims of repression understood this. Lev Kopelev was as frank about his attitude toward the purge as he had been when writing of the famine. "I never believed that Bukharin and Trotsky were Gestapo agents or that they wanted to kill Lenin," he wrote, "and I was sure that Stalin never believed it either. But I regarded the purge trials of 1937 and 1938 as an expression of some farsighted policy; I believed that, on balance, Stalin was right in deciding on these terrible measures in order to discredit all forms of political opposition once and for all. We were a besieged fortress; we had to be united, knowing neither vacillation nor doubt."[49]

Such was the atmosphere against which terror would evolve, the propaganda and the faith in which even the victims had been nourished. The very prisoners of the purge, reflecting in their cells, considered, often, that their fate was nothing more than they deserved. Osip Mandelstam described his state of mind in one of his final letters. He wrote after the last of a succession of arrests. They had freed him, briefly, months before, and he had agreed to say that the people who condemned him had been right. "I found historic sense in it all," he wrote. "For this, they beat me. I am treated like a dog. I am a shadow. I do not exist. I only have the right to die."[50]

Although they did not always know exactly what was going on, many of the purge's destined victims suspected in advance that the days of their freedom were numbered. The testimonies of survivors describe the conversations that went on, the plans that people laid. Their options, however, were limited. "They watched us all the time," said Ol'ga Ern, whose father had been arrested near Kharkov in 1937. "Put in my name when you write that. They know everything else about me. There's no point in hiding." One way of coping, which almost everyone tried, was to conform, to join the mass and praise the leader. Generally speaking, however, this would turn out not to be enough.

The only other obvious escape, and the one that thousands dreamed about, was suicide. Nadezhda Mandelstam described the methodical preparations that her husband made. "Nobody was so full of life and joy as M.," she wrote. Nonetheless, he had his shoes adapted so that he could keep a razor blade in the sole. At the time of his first release, days after they were reunited, he jumped through an upper-floor window in the vain hope of killing himself. "Many other people thought about it too," Nadezhda Mandelstam wrote. The real problem, as she added, was that "many people who were determined never to fall alive into the hands of the secret police were taken by surprise at the last moment."[51]

The other kinds of preparation people made included plans for immortality. It was not safe to write things down. Instead, with chilling fatalism, some people asked their wives to memorize their testaments and dreams. Nikolai Bukharin's young wife, Anna Larina, learned his last sermon to the Party and preserved it in her memory for fifty years.[52] Nadezhda Mandelstam saved many of her husband's poems in the same way. "There are many women like me who for years have spent sleepless nights repeating the words of their dead husbands over and over again," she wrote. "Until 1956 I could remember everything by heart—both prose and verse."[53]

At other times the only fitting mood was numb depression. "The fear rises in my throat," Lyubov Shaporina wrote in her diary in 1937, "when I hear how calmly people say it: he was shot, someone else was shot, shot, shot. I think that the real meaning of the word does not reach our consciousness."[54] Anna Akhmatova, whose son, Lev Gumilev, and partner, Nikolai Punin, were both arrested in 1935, called it "the torpor common to us all." Anna Larina, herself a prisoner by 1938, described the misery of waiting for her husband's death. "I had prepared myself for it already," she wrote. "The lifting of the pressure of waiting, and the knowledge that, at last, his suffering was over, even brought me some relief, but at the same time I was in a depressed state of mind. Everything around me changed, became an enormous, meaningless grey blur. And it was amazing to think that somewhere life went on in this world, and human happiness, earthly pleasures."[55] She had no time, that day, to pause and mourn. The warden of her prison had given her a particularly heavy cleaning job to finish.

The moment of arrest took people in various ways, and there were different conventions, among adult bystanders, for avoiding the discussion of it. Children often saw the process with the clearest eyes. Magdalena Alekseyevna was given the task of watching for the secret police. Her parents knew that someone would be coming for the grandfather, and they did not want to be seen checking the street whenever there was a knock on the front door. She took her duties without question. She even knew when the policeman's son, who went to school with her, was watching back.

Moscow children, especially those of privileged parents, coralled in special apartment blocks and marched to the exclusive schools, also became accustomed to the rituals of arrest. "In our building things were a bit special," one of them told me. "They arrested five or six people every night. That was because it was a housing development for executives, built in 1928. The children there were all about the same age. So we would go to the doorman every morning before school and he would tell us: today they took those people, today they took these."[56] There was a double problem for such children in these circumstances. For now their former friends and classmates were enemies. They might not see them again, they might not have the chance to nod good-bye.

And at the same time, they could not ask questions, for their parents were afraid. "I started to say it wasn't right," another person told me. "My parents told me that we did not talk about it."[57]

The adults suffered differently. "We had no time to say goodbye to each other," Nadezhda Mandelstam remembered. Her husband was arrested on their anniversary, the first of May. "We were interrupted when we tried to say goodbye."[58] Luisa Karlovna, whose father, an Old Bolshevik, was arrested in 1937, remembered that her mother had been absent at the time. She was, in fact, in hospital preparing for the birth of their third child. She lost the baby in her shock, and through her absence also nearly lost her other children, too. The two toddlers were taken away in a black car, and it would take her nearly eight months to find them. That, too, was part of the process. The strain of it all eventually told on the older woman's mind.[59]

Yudif Borisovna's father was shot soon after his arrest. His body was taken to the crematorium in the Don monastery and incinerated. The ashes were dumped in the common grave. His daughter, desperately anxious for news, and trusting, still, in the essential justice of the system, was told that he had been sentenced to ten years without right of correspondence. She herself spent nearly nine more months at liberty. Her mother disappeared on 1 August. Her own turn came on 1 September. They took her first to the Lyubyanka—in Moscow that was usual—and they threatened but did not torture her.

In her account, she only began to understand the meaning of it all after she was transferred to the Butyrki prison some days later. She shared a bare room there with a group of three hundred very well-informed and frightened women—including the wife of the former premier, Rykov, and the wives of commissars like Sulimov and Yakovlev. She met another familiar face in the back of the van that was transporting her from the Lyubyanka to Butyrki. Her companion that night, an opera singer ten years into her career, would become Yudif's "second mother." The two women also ended up in the same camp. "I visited her often when we were both back in Moscow," Yudif Borisovna said.

It was in her third prison, Taganskaya—"It doesn't exist any more"—that Yudif Borisovna encountered torture for herself, listening to the screams of fellow prisoners as they begged for death. But for that detail, her own account is relatively free of pain, although she dreamed of getting the bedbugs out of her scalp and longed to take a bath. She acknowledges that she was kept in what she calls "elite" conditions. For others, however, and especially for the men, it was a different story. The theater director, Vsevolod Meyerhold, a frail man of sixty-five at the time of his arrest in 1939, described his torture. "They sat me on a chair and beat my feet from above with considerable force," he wrote. "For the next few days, when those parts of my legs were covered with extensive internal hemorrhaging, they again beat the red-blue-and-yellow bruises with the strap and the pain was so intense that it felt as if boiling hot water was being poured on these sensitive areas. I howled and wept from the pain. They beat my back with the same rubber straps and punched my face, swinging their fists from a great height."[60] The photographs of other men show broken faces, bruises, missing teeth. It was a standard part of the routine.

The method worked. Most people signed the confessions that were required of them, the ones that were read in court or placed inside a convict's file when he or she was shot. Such documents were crucial to the general scheme, for though the police did not need a pretext for every execution, it mattered that there were thousands of confessions on the shelves, that a pantomime of legal process should take place. But the point of torture was not just to make a person sign. Its other function was to deepen the terror both inside and beyond the prison walls. It helped to destroy desire, the last threads of an independent mind—"they want kill the intellect itself," as Mandelstam perceived. Physical extinction—death—could follow at any time, occasionally after a delay of months. Meyerhold wrote about this, too. "Immediately after my arrest," he explained, "I was cast into the deepest depression by the obsessive thought: this is what I deserve! The government thought, so I began to convince myself, that the sentence I had received . . . was not sufficient . . . for my sins . . . and that I must undergo another punishment, that which the NKVD was carrying out now . . . I split into two individuals. The first started searching for the 'crimes' of the second, and when they could not be found, he began to invent them." Meyerhold was shot on 2 February 1940.[61]

Most people remember thinking that they were going to die. It was a common—and tormenting—reaction to arrest. "I thought about my father all the time," said Nadezhda Ivanovna. "I thought I'd be going to join him. I talked to him a lot in my head." Despite the precautions taken in the prisons, suicides were also frequent. "The amount of energy expended in prison to obtain a piece of crumpled tin which can be transformed into a knife to commit . . . suicide is incredible," wrote Shalamov.[62] "The bodies were piled up outside Butyrki like firewood," someone told me. "I wanted to kill myself," said another, "but they told me that only a real enemy of the people would do such a cowardly thing. Soviet people do not kill themselves." That idea—the trap of that collective myth—was enough to stop him, even in his prison. Two Moscow-based psychologists who had studied or worked in the Gulag system insisted to me that suicide and mental illness were rare in the prisons and camps. They were surprised—and modestly offended—when I cited evidence from these interviews. They myth of stoicism is not dead.

The assertion that there were no suicides is odd (and it is incorrect), but other conflicts between stories, especially when it comes to the Gulag itself, are inevitable. People's experiences were individual, they understood things differently, the regime varied over time, and not all camps were the same. "Everyone expected either execution or a sentence in a prison camp," a former subject of the NKVD's torture process wrote. "Most dreamed of sentence in a prison camp, as of deliverance."[63] "Razgon is right to say that the camps were the only place where you could feel free," said Yudif Borisovna, remembering her own exile, the people she had met, the things she learned. But that fragile sense of freedom, and even survival itself, was a lottery. "Help me," wrote Mandelstam from his prison. "I shall not survive if I am again sentenced to exile."[64]

The journey north and east was the first hurdle. Even the optimistic Yudif Borisovna remembered hers with a shudder. Only in the Soviet Union could such a surreal trainload have been assembled. There were six "politicals" in Yudif's car, including the opera singer and Yudif herself. There was a party of about fifty middle-aged former nuns. And there was another band of younger women, criminals—murderers, prostitutes, and thieves. "They were the very worst elements," Yudif Borisovna insisted. "They all had blood on their hands." It was dark and cold. There was almost nothing to eat, no water for days on end, no chance to breathe clean air. The nuns began to die. "It was horrible," she remembers. "You know why. Just because they were dead." Their corpses shared the carriage for hundreds of miles at a time. It was only when the train stopped—only a few times in three weeks—that the guards could open the doors and throw them out into the snow.

Yudif Borisovna has other memories of the journey, however, and not all of them are grim. She tells one particularly romantic tale, perhaps now something of a fable. She says that she made friends with the rough girls. Almost every former "political" describes his or her special relationship with the criminals, the Gulag aristocracy, in the same sort of way. It is a common fantasy, it seems, a hope that you, at least, were no longer a class enemy in the proletarian state, that you could become classless, lawless, free. In Yudif Borisovna's case, the key was to befriend the girls' appointed leader, which she did. And then, as she remembers it, she sat, the chemistry student, fluent German speaker, and won the rest of them by reciting tales from Pushkin. It is an unlikely sounding story, but it is not unique. "The only privileged political prisoner," Evgeniya Ginzburg, wrote, "was the one who could tell stories or give a verbal rendition of some adventurous novel."[65]

Ginzburg herself, who was exiled in 1939, had a different view of criminal women, colloquially known as the "apaches," in transit. "They were the cream of the criminal world," she wrote. "To this day I remain convinced that the proper place for such people is a psychiatric hospital, and not a prison or a camp. When I saw this half-naked, tattooed, ape-like hoarde invade the hold, I thought that it had been decided that we were to be killed off by mad women."[66] Accounts of the bullying, beating, and even murder of "politicals" by criminal gangs, male and female, abound. Organized groups of them ran protection rackets, extorted tithes from even meager rations, and imposed their primitive kind of justice among the ranks. They were especially brutal with informers. Indeed, the moral order they imposed has echoes of the czarist village, *samosud.* Even the technology of killing was the same. "They always killed them," said Nadezhda Ivanovna. "Informers, yes, they killed them." Lev Kopelev listened to an account of such a killing from the "village tough," Vasya. "We took this stool-pigeon by the arms and legs and swung him up—high, high. Then we brought him down on the floor, right on his ass. Again, again, and again. You couldn't see any marks on him. But the next day he was spitting blood. A week later he was dead. His kidneys were gone."[67]

Yudif Borisovna's narrative steers clear of murder. She preferred her forced labor, in fact, to the so-called freedom she experienced after her release, when she went looking for her mother, and found her, a stranger, depressed, uncomprehending, in the Kazakh town of Kustanai. In the camp, she said, "You could always do something." Still faithful to the Komsomol, she worked as an agitator, making speeches (she was reinstated in the Communist Party in 1956). "The agitation brigade was my real happiness," she remembers. Her extraordinary energy and her positive outlook were among the reasons for her survival. The regime of her exile killed thousands of women like her. "It is my father's good genes," she insists. "I still have my strong teeth." Her baby boy was born in 1942—the worst year in the prison regime, the time of the meanest rations and the highest mortality—but he was healthy and weighed 3.8 kilos. "How I did that even I don't know," she smiles. "There was absolutely nothing to eat."

It helped that the birth was attended by one of Moscow's most distinguished former professors of gynecology, now, like her, an exile. The camps sometimes sound more like universities or informal Party conferences than prisons.[68] "We had the best mathematicians to teach us," two other women told me. "They were very patient. I suppose we all had lots of time." Other people, even Communists, enjoyed the chanting and the prayers of exiled priests and nuns. "They invited us to their service for five voices at Easter," said Yudif Borisovna. "It was amazing! They knew every word, remembered everything, five hours, five voices. We really enjoyed listening to it."

It sounds almost jolly, sometimes, until you press the speakers for the details of their rations, their clothes, the health of the people sleeping next to them. The memories of elite "politicals," the descriptions of fulfilling conversations and unaccompanied chant, belie the reality, which was that large numbers—a majority—of the Gulag population were peasants (often former kulaks), criminals, and workers. They were the ones who did not write their memoirs, but their images can still be seen in the old pictures, and their individual biographies, the barest details, are being collected now, if they exist, by human-rights organizations in Russian cities.[69] Life in the camps, for everyone, was a matter of basic survival—heavy manual labor, subsistence rations (if you were lucky), and brutal social relations. Some of the details of mortality rates in the Gulag have been released from archives in the last few years. As ever, they speak for themselves. In 1941, before the privations of the war began, the death rate in the camps was about 30 per 1,000 (only a little higher than the national average). By 1942, when Yudif Borisovna's baby was born, that figure had increased to 250 per 1,000.[70]

"We could not always break the soil to bury them," Kuz'ma Gavrilovich remembered. "We would just cover them with ice." "They would lie in a pile by the fence until the thaw," said Boris Leonidovich. "Then someone would make a trench and they would all be thrown in together." "It was weird, really," said Kuz'ma Gavrilovich. It was not frightening, sickening, but "weird to know that someone else had gone and you were still there." The rule by which most prisoners lived was catch as catch can. "You can die today and I will die tomorrow," was the slogan by which everyone survived.

In the group of five, all except Yudif Borisovna admitted that they had considered killing themselves. The best way to commit suicide, and usually the quickest, was to attempt to escape. Almost everyone was shot immediately. Their corpses made an appalling spectacle. They were displayed, deliberately, where prisoners had to walk, lying unburied for days at a time, sometimes with a notice by their faces that reminded passersby that this was just another "dog's death for dogs." The few who not only planned their escapes but also managed to break out of the barbed wire were usually brought back later in much the same way. "Young people, nineteen-year-olds, sixteen-year-olds, they would decide that it was better to die than to be in the camp for long," Nadezhda

Ivanovna remembered. "Women, too. It was very common. They would say: I'm going to die anyway, and it's better to die outside the zone."

Sometimes an escapee was killed too far from the camp for the gang of guards to carry him back. Sometimes the local reindeer herders, who were paid a bounty for assisting the police, would catch someone, and they, too, had no desire to lift and lug a heavy, stinking body. The answer was to hack off the person's hands—everyone can talk about this, it seems self-evident to an ex-prisoner. The Yakuts, too, the reindeer herders, still remember what they did.[71] The hands, with their fingerprints, provided identification for the camp records. Shalamov's account of the "corpse" who "came back to the camp, pressing his bleeding wrists against his chest," was not a ghost story. "Fever devoured him," Shalamov wrote. "His padded coat, his trousers, his rubber boots were stained with black blood."[72] A hasty bullet in the cold had missed again. Shalamov's escapee was fed and bandaged and then shot.

Memories like these are related reluctantly, but without surprise. These things used to be evident, normal, part of life. It was also clear on every occasion that I talked to former prisoners, that my questions were intrusive, uncomfortable, and—ironically in view of the gender of many of the respondents—socially unacceptable in a woman. Former prisoners, no less than any others of their generation, dislike being forced to look too hard at the images that decent people could ignore, that Stalinism censored. "We thought you wanted to talk about repression," someone told me later (the Russian word, *repressiya,* is just as disembodied as the English version). "But all your questions were about death."

Psychoanalysts teach us that memories of trauma are often repressed. Former prisoners are skeptical about this—they are skeptical about psychoanalysis in general—and they deny that they are traumatized. Routine deaths, they said, were not a problem, and nor were hunger, cold, hard labor—the things that people learned to take as part of their existence. No interview, however long, can go much further than that, than the routine, the things that people choose to tell because they do not hurt. But sometimes someone would say something troubled, out of sequence, related in a different voice.

Sitting proudly in his dark coat and medals, bearded, upright, Boris Leonidovich looked like what he was, a veteran of many battles in the Great Patriotic War. He did not say a lot at the beginning, and there was a diffidence, too, when the rest of us were talking about hardship. He, after all, had seen so many atrocities at the front, on the way to Berlin, so many deaths. As a member of the artillery, he had also killed plenty of men himself: "I always considered it to be my sacred duty." But in the end he talked about his nightmares. "I dream about corpses sometimes," he said. "The criminals, they used to disembowel people. I dream about it often." Nadezhda Ivanovna interrupted him. They had all seen all those things. But he insisted. "They used to take someone who was alive. Alive. And disembowel them. It's not normal, is it?" Kuz'ma Gavrilovich chipped in with his own most vivid memory. "I had to cut a man down once after he'd hanged himself," he said. "Yes, you get used to death. But I cried when I cut him down. I cried. It hurt to think that this man had been alive, and I'd seen him the previous evening, and we'd chatted, and today here he was and he'd hanged himself."

"That's enough talking about death," Nadezhda Ivanovna said sharply, getting up, wrapping her cardigan tightly around her chest, pacing the room behind our chairs. "Death. Why can't we talk about something else?" The others were trying to answer the question of meaning. "Death in war is sacred," someone said, picking up an earlier theme. "It's natural, if you know what I mean. But death in the camps is, well . . . " Someone else repeated another phrase we'd heard before. "A dog's death for dogs." "It's shameful. Nothing." Aside from one or two intrusive memories, no one had thought about it much. Even those who were writing memoirs for the archives of the Memorial society had not spent time considering death. Others avoided the whole subject, everything. "I've lived in Moscow for forty years," said Kuz'ma Gavrilovich, "and still there aren't many of my friends who know I was a prisoner once." Until recently it was the rule: You did not mourn, you made your life, your memories were another world. You survived.

In the end, even for poets, the death that Stalin's purges brought was dull, prosaic. In December 1938, Yuri Moiseyenko walked into the delousing room in Svitlag, near Magadan. "We undressed, hung up our clothes on a peg, and then handed them over for heat treatment," he remembered. The Pacific storms were blowing, it was nearly New Year, and it was as cold inside the crowded hut as out. Everyone was shivering. The man next to him, whom people called "the poet," was Osip Mandelstam. "He was no more than a skeleton," Moiseyenko wrote.

"A smell of sulphur struck our noses," he went on. "Immediately it became stuffy, the sulphur drilled into our eyes until we cried . . . Osip Emil'evich took a few steps, turned away from the heat treatment room, raised his head proudly, and collapsed."[73] The corpse was tossed into the common grave. There was a wooden tag around its shin, a graphite scrawl: his number.

8

RUSSIA AT WAR

"You get used to seeing death," said Nina Pavlovna, a former partisan. "It loses its impact. It's a bit like eating red caviare every day. Eventually you don't even notice it."[1] Tat'yana Evgenyevna, a veteran of other kinds of fighting, disagreed. "You never quite get used to it." she insisted. "But you learn to live by different rules." Like most veterans of the Soviet Union's Great Patriotic War, she has an anecdote that helps her to make the point. It is an image from Leningrad under siege, from the terrible winter of 1941–1942. "I remember that a man died on the steps of our building," she begins. "It was quite early on, and he was one of the first. He seemed to have frozen to death." It often took days to clear the bodies in the starving city at that time. There was no one, often, with the strength to move them. "On the first day," she continues, "someone covered him with a newspaper. But after a few more days I noticed that the newspaper had been moved. Someone had made him sit up and put it into his hands as if he was going to read it. We laughed. We had grown so used to seeing him there."[2]

Most survivors of the Soviet Union's Great Patriotic War have their own stories of death, and all agree that it was something that you lived with, worked with, used to it or not. "I was walking along a street with my son," a woman from Belarus remembers. "There were dead bodies lying on both sides of the street. I was telling him about Little Red Riding Hood, and all around us there were dead bodies."[3] At the time, little boys like hers were not surprised by death. "Got my hat off a dead Rumanian," a ten-year-old told Alexander Werth, the war correspondent, in 1943. "And these boots? That's off the dead Fritz over there in the orchard." As Werth remarked, "Corpses had become part of his daily routine, and for him there were only good corpses and bad corpses."[4]

Although they were part of daily life in the Soviet Union for four years, the details of death and dying are not the first things people generally mention when they recall the war. Whatever it was really like for them, they usually begin with the set pieces—the German invasion of June 1941, the loss of Ukraine, the siege of Leningrad, the defense of Moscow. They will tell you about the capture and destruction of historic Russian cities—of Novgorod, for instance, where 201,000 civilians were slaughtered in a few weeks, and whose population, by 1943, had been reduced, through death and deportation, to 30 people.[5] They will always talk of Stalingrad, the city that held out through fire and siege, its few inhabitants trapped and starving, huddled in the basements and sewers, daily awaiting discovery and death. It was Stalin's refusal to cede that city, they will say, a refusal that cost a million Soviet lives, that would decide the war by the beginning of 1943. And then there are the later Soviet victories, the long march to Berlin. The people's war has a shape, its battles have an order, place and meaning. Years of talk have given them a pattern. The talking still goes on. "Stop us, or we'll be here all night," one group of veterans laughed. The Patriotic War, unlike some other tales of death and grieving, has always been a part of Soviet public memory.

There are good reasons for the war's place in the collective consciousness. The struggle against Nazism was the greatest test the Soviet people ever endured; perhaps the greatest in the whole history of Russia. The effort of will, the tenacity and stoicism that it demanded was beyond the range of previous experience, more terrible and more prolonged than anything most of the Soviet people, veterans of so many emergencies already, had ever seen. Paradoxically, too, the danger released a new sense of community, even of liberation, among ordinary people, and lit a spark of genius in some of the country's poets and writers. When the old people gather now, they may remember the words Ol'ga Berggol'ts, one of these poets, wrote of the siege of Leningrad, which she survived:

In filth, in gloom, in hunger, in sorrow,
When death trailed us like a shadow,
We used to be so happy
Inhaled such a tempestuous freedom
That our grandchildren would have envied us.[6]

Left to themselves, the veterans enjoy reminiscences of this kind. They also share a common language when they meet—nostalgia, reverence, escapism. Remembering, like the songs they like to sing, has form and cadence. It is calming. It helps them to forget. There are some notable conventions. By talking about plans and purposes the veterans overlook despair. Unless they are forced to dwell upon the ugly details, they will usually edit out the panic, the guilt, the noise, the boredom and stench. Most people have their chilling anecdote, their shapely horror story—it is useful, sometimes; certain audiences like to hear of blood and brains and shattered bone. But most prefer to keep to the accustomed formulas. Public war is kitsch, whatever private memories still linger. Even frontline doctors, the men and women whose task it was to return the walking wounded to the field, are keen to keep away from death. "We never talked about it," they insist. "We never told anyone they were going to die. You do not say that kind of thing."[7]

Some of these features of remembrance are not unique to Russia. The development of postwar myths was universal among the former combatant states of Western Europe after 1918, for instance.[8] But in Stalin's Soviet Union, the processes of commemoration and forgetting were more than usually distorting. It was an isolated world, where news and even talking were controlled, and so there were specific pressures to accept a single, public line. The distortions began during the war itself—although all nations waging total war use censorship—and they continued after it for nearly sixty years. The formal history was challenged, briefly, during Khruschev's thaw in the 1960s, but very little happened to fragment it until the years of glasnost.[9] The shared story of Patriotic War is still so real, to the survivors, that for years it has engulfed the witnessed images and documented facts.

The myths of war were not all shaped by Soviet leaders. Stalin was not eager to encourage popular remembrance. It was clear at once that the memory of fighting could be personally liberating, and that made it dangerous.[10] Later on, after the dictator's death, the massive structures of state-led commemoration coexisted with the people's own imaginings. The war was remembered as a time of freedom, a time when the threat of death brought every person fully to life. These days, when so much else has changed, the pensioners gather to remember a time of certainty, a time when their lives had meaning, when their contributions mattered. "There is a colossal difference between that time and now," one of them told me. "We knew our motherland, we knew Stalin, we knew where we were going."

The sacrifices that the people made to defeat fascism also subsumed the other, darker stories, the ones of uncommemorated loss. The war often redeemed the pain that preceded it. "The friendships that we made were so strong," said the dispossessed former kulak Anna Timofeyevna. New forms of collectivity took over from prewar communities; new memories and an urgent common purpose helped to crowd out some of the bleaker silences. Some victims of the purge were grateful. The war gave them a chance to make another life.[11] But others suffered from redoubled kinds of pressure. Labor norms in the Gulag increased from 1941, and rations were severely cut. The death rates peaked in 1942 and 1943.[12]

The war would also throw its shadow forward. The memory would justify a good deal of the superpatriotism of the late Soviet empire.[13] The mentality of "us" and "them", "our" sacrifice, "our" victory, helped shape the callousness of later Stalinism. The 1940s saw a revival of institutional anti-Semitism (despite the fact that it was the Soviet army that had been the first to come upon the horror of the Nazi death camps, at Miadanek, in July 1944[14]), a continuation of the policies of mass arrest and deportation. Cold War rearmament, which bled the Soviet economy nearly to death, was justified in terms of foreign danger, Soviet pride. Behind it all lay the sacred bodies of the fallen, the millions whose memory no one would dare betray.

"I never lost the feeling that this was a genuine People's War," Werth wrote. "The thought that this was *their* war was, in the main, as strong among the civilians as among the soldiers."[15] Werth was right. It was everyone's war, and everyone was liable not only to contribute but also to suffer. Almost no family escaped some form of loss. "In my year," remembered Grigorii Vasilyevich, a sculptor from southern Russia (he makes war memorials), "there were two classes of first years, and there were two more in the next village and one more in Gayevo. That makes four classes altogether, but we all knew each other. We kept in touch through all our years at school. So I know how many died in the war. Out of about a hundred of us, ninety-two definitely died at the front. And five or six were wounded, they came home as invalids. I'm the only one who is not injured in some way."[16]

Grigorii Vasilyevich was born in 1922. As he pointed out, boys of that generation were liable to be called for duty between 1939 and 1941. They were the first to go to Finland in 1939, and the first to die after the Germans invaded in the summer of 1941. At least four-fifths of them were dead by 1945. In European Russia, Ukraine, and the other western republics, the figure was higher. As many as 90 percent of the young men of Grigorii Vasilyevich's generation died before their twenty-fifth birthdays. Overall, more than four-fifths of the 34.5 million men and women who were mobilized during the Soviet Union's war had been killed, wounded, or captured by 1945.[17]

"They lied about the number of deaths," an army doctor told me. "They lied because there were so many unnecessary losses. They would put up a marker that said twenty or thirty bodies were buried in a new mound. But in fact there were two or three hundred in it."[18] The Soviet army was certainly profligate with life. Soldiers were often treated like livestock—the word crops up in almost any testimony. The results could be devastating. During one operation, in the Crimea, L. Z Mekhlis ordered that no trenches should be dug because they spoiled the "spirit of aggression."[19] In twelve days, 176,000 men were slaughtered. Even after 1942, when a more thoughtful approach to military strategy began to take precedence, the casual waste of human lives continued, the use of human decoys, frontal assaults on armored lines, vicious punishments of one's own men for alleged cowardice.

The spending of lives was accompanied, as ever, by the old tradition of denial. The lies began at once. Certain types of death, including most of those for which the NKVD was responsible, were not discussed at all. But even the global figures for Soviet losses were scaled down. Stalin himself gave the total as about 7 million. In a mood of openness, Khrushchev later inflated the figure to 20 million.[20] But current estimates for overall Soviet deaths, military and civilian, generally exceed 25 million. Between 8 million and 11 million of these were so-called battlefield losses.[21] The rest were the deaths of civilians.

The figures are still contentious: as Khrushchev once remarked, "No-one was keeping count." Since the 1980s, Russian historians have tried to calculate the human costs of the war in other ways. What they have done is to look at the Soviet Union's population in 1939 and ask how much it should have grown by 1945, under normal circumstances, if the birth and death rates of the prewar years had been maintained. Total war destroys families; its frontline victims are adults in the prime of their strength. Fewer children are conceived, and fewer of these are born alive. The Soviet "population deficit" in 1945, according to this reckoning, was well over 40 million human lives. Some say that it was nearer 50 million.[22] Loss on this scale was an economic catastrophe, it was a demographic disaster whose echoes are still perceptible in the post-Soviet population, but most of all it was a human tragedy. There were no precedents.

The veterans, naturally, talk of life. It is survival—courage, endurance, patriotism—that they gather to discuss. "We suffered so much," Tat'yana Evgenyevna said. "We were so glad when it was over. We did not count the costs." People like her remember many of the individual dead, but their talk does not linger on the sea of deaths, the piles of corpses and the crows. "Do not believe those who present the war in the trenches as casual rifle fire interspersed with cinema shows," wrote Aleksandr Mikhailov, a former frontline soldier, in 1987.[23] It was a remark guaranteed to cause offense among official veterans' groups. Whatever their private memories, their public language finds the details of real dying unaesthetic.

You can hear all this on any evening at the veterans' club, at any dacha where they meet and talk. The Russian soldier, it is said, defends the sacred soil of the motherland to his last drop of blood. He is not unafraid, but he is brave. He rushes at the enemy with the name of Stalin on his lips, and he dies with the memory of summer birch woods before his eyes, the image of his mother, or of a tearful girl, his Tanya, Masha, Olya, vowing to wait forever. "Most of them asked for their mothers," one of the nurses told me. "And we would promise to write to them." The echoes of traditional lament, of the old culture, are never far away in tales like this. "Remember, Alyosha, the roads of Smolensk . . . the endlessly falling rain," begins a popular song from 1941. The poet confesses to fear, but as he concludes:

Still I was proud of that which was dearest,
The Russian soil on which I'd been born,
That I have been destined to die in this land,
That it was a Russian mother who gave birth to us,
That seeing us off to battle, a Russian woman
Has embraced me three times in the old Russian way.[24]

The power of sentimental songs was something that the Communist Party recognized at once. In the teeth of the first and most devastating German advance, with the bombs already falling on Moscow, a directive from its agitation department called for free harmonicas to be distributed among the troops.[25]

There are thousands of old soldiers who will still relate their memories of war and death in almost perfect rhythm with the songs and marches of the Soviet state. In 1997, for instance, I had the pleasure of meeting Nikolai Viktorovich, a retired officer and one of the directors of the Society for Veterans of the Great Patriotic War in Moscow. To understand this man you must overlook his current setting—a dingy, cheaply furnished room in a converted flat—and you must disregard his own civilian clothes, the old fawn cardigan and the polyester trousers. Nikolai Viktorovich is a former Soviet officer, a Stalinist, and a patriot. You meet his eyes and see another world, the expression of a soldier who remembers different orders and stricter, more predictable social codes.

I have asked another former officer to conduct the interview—I wanted to see what difference it made to watch a conversation between fellow soldiers, fellow Russians, men—but Nikolai Viktorovich addresses all his most important answers directly to me. At least, he agrees to begin to answer on condition that I reveal my social origins (petty bourgeois—this is Marxism-Leninism) and the ethnic identity of both my parents (confusing). It seems that this information will affect the answers he will give. I wish, as the guarded words begin to flow, that I had lied and said my father was a welder. Nikolai Viktorovich is on the defensive, as if waiting for the trick question that he knows a class enemy and a foreigner will always ask.

We discuss the fighting and the dying, and we talk about the men that he has led, their qualities and strengths. "I suffered for every one of my men who died," he says. But grief is a weakness. "I did not give way to it." After an hour or so, my colleague asks him to consider what type of soldier he would pick if he had another deadly mission to carry out behind the enemy lines. The question is asked neutrally, without reference to any particular kind of category. But Nikolai Viktorovich's answer is emphatic: "Soviet soldiers—Russian men—know how to fight and how to die." Only the Finns, in his view, have anything like that kind of courage, that stoicism. If he ever had to assemble another army, if he could choose any kind of soldier from any time or place, he would choose Russians. In fact, he adds, he would prefer survivors of the Gulag. Discipline and endurance are desirable qualities in a soldier. He offers a thin smile. At least I am not French.

It is not difficult to find the documents—including letters written by ordinary Soviet civilians—that testify to the authenticity of Nikolai Viktorovich's kind of patriotism. "I should be proud to defend the Soviet land," a woman from Moscow wrote in a private letter of 1941. Thousands like her volunteered for military service at once. Their tears, as they packed into the workplace meetings, were as much for Russia as for themselves. NKVD officers noted a sharp rise in productivity in the factories.[26] Some of the patriotism was Communist rather than Russian. "I decided that I would prevent myself from being a coward," another woman said, "by dipping my Young Communist League membership card in the blood of a wounded man and buttoning it to my breast pocket."[27] Heroic stories, like that of the partisan Zoya Kosmodemyanskaya, who was tortured, mutilated, and hanged for her part in a minor act of local sabotage, inspired whole classes of teenage schoolchildren to sign up. "The Party taught us that there is nothing dearer than motherland," said one of these, a Belorussian woman who eventually served as a sergeant. She was weeping as she talked of it.[28]

You did not have to kill or die to share the feelings. A group of former medical personnel, seven people, echoed the same slogans when we talked about the war that they had witnessed. "Patriotism was our treasure of gold, the wealth of our beloved Motherland, our Russia," said a former nurse. "The people were extraordinary. There is nothing more to say. You will never see anything like it again." Frontline medicine, like combat itself, is remembered now in terms of courage, justice, the motherland, and Stalin. The doctors and orderlies I met had all seen many deaths, had almost died themselves, had written letters of condolence, and had received their own in turn, but what they talked about, at least while they were all together, was pride. As if to underline the point, some of them came along wearing their medals, rainbow colors inches deep across their chests. But something else was also clear. All had suffered materially in Russia's latest revolution; some were struggling on their pensions. The past was the only part of their lives that was still certain.

It would have been offensive, then, to remind them of the panic that they had forgotten. Moscow was not the citadel of patriotism that they remember in the autumn of 1941. The German army was advancing rapidly from Smolensk, and there were fears that the capital was about to fall. Preparations were made to evacuate the city (Lenin's corpse was among the first to leave, by special train). Many government departments left for Kuibyshev, on the Volga, in late September. As Ilya Ehrenburg, the war correspondent and propagandist, remembered, "The mood in Moscow was appalling." Some people even welcomed the idea of German rule. "In 1919–20 the people fought for freedom, for its rights," a works director wrote in 1941. "But today there is nothing to die for. Soviet power has driven the people to the limits of exasperation."[29] "The memory of Moscow was unbearable," Kostantin Simonov wrote later. "Like the face of a person you love distorted by fear."[30]

We know about the panic and the private letters because the NKVD read every piece of correspondence that the people sent from Moscow at the time.

The government had such little faith in its own citizens that it ordered mass arrests on the day of the German invasion in June 1941. Orders were also given to accelerate the execution of political prisoners.[31] The arrests and shootings would continue through the war. It was the NKVD, in fact, which established civilian discipline in Moscow in October 1941.

Looters were shot, as was anyone suspected of spreading panic, including many of those caught trying to flee the city. For good measure, orders were also given to shoot every tenth apartment building manager.[32] The genuine patriotism of millions of Soviet citizens was reinforced by terror. Successive orders to the troops, for instance, most of which remained unpublished until the 1980s, reminded them that cowardice was not a viable option. Soviet territory was to be defended to the last drop of blood, as Stalin said, and those who failed to hold their few square meters were liable to summary execution or to almost certain death in one of the so-called punishment battalions.[33]

"No-one wanted to die," the doctors agreed. But "they were all ready to die if they had to. We all were. War demands victims." I remembered Boris Leonidovich, the artillery man who came home to seven dismal years in the Gulag, who had regarded the deaths that he had witnessed at the front as "natural." "Iron discipline and a steady nerve are the conditions of our victory," declared *Pravda* on 30 July 1942. "Soviet soldiers! Not a step back!"[34] "We were not afraid," another doctor, Valentina Mikhailovna, told me later. "I do not remember crying. Our work was important." She had worked in a city hospital throughout the siege of Leningrad. She could not even remember the first death that she had witnessed.[35]

Heroism is easy to talk about. Brutality is more dangerous. Valentina Mikhailovna did not mention it. Her colleagues in Moscow even claimed that the war had made them into kinder people. "We have bigger hearts," a former nurse, who had served at the front from 1941, insisted. Army doctors with frontline experience, as one of them explained, "act from the soul, from the heart, from patriotism." The benefits last for the rest of their lives. "You won't hear us saying things like 'I can't, I don't want to'," another medical orderly said. There was no dissension from the view that the war had made them better people, more fully human, and certainly better doctors, better nurses, more able to sympathize and to care. Sixty years after the war, there are no grounds for telling them that they are deceived.

At the time, however, in 1943, there were people who were less certain about the virtue of this patriotic morality. Lev Kopelev, the activist who had worked with such determination through the famine of 1933, was openly alarmed. As he and his men advanced through Poland and toward the Prussian border, he began to consider the ways in which the Soviet army fought, and especially the effects of the lies that had sustained it. As he saw it, "Millions of people had been brutalised and corrupted by the war and by our propaganda—bellicose, jingoistic and false. I had believed such propaganda necessary on the eve of war, and all the more so for the war's duration. I still believed it, but I had also come to understand that from seeds like these came poisoned fruit."

Kopelev's anxieties centered around what he described as the "relativist morality" of the war: "Whatever helps us is good, whatever helps the enemy is bad." He was worried even by the daily realities of fighting, the prospect of a country peopled by "young fellows . . . straight from school" who had "learned nothing except how to shoot, dig trenches, crawl through barbed wire, rush the enemy and toss grenades." But he also knew that there was a deeper problem, not mere soldiering, and certainly not the heroic fighting of the songs and speeches, but routine and unreported cruelty. "Each new day," he wrote, brought the young troops "fresh evidence that the war they read about in the papers and heard about on their radios and in their political meetings was not the war they saw and experienced for themselves."[36] It was, he considered, an unwritten license for atrocity.

Kopelev's dedication to the Communist cause had dulled his ability to criticize the same kinds of euphemism and evasion in the 1930s. Military language was not new in Stalin's Russia in 1941. The evocation of emergency, of the motherland in danger, was one of Soviet Communism's favorite tactics. It had been honed and practiced in many areas of life since the Civil War. Dissociation has its uses. The Soviet army's ability to condone atrocity may well have helped it to win the Patriotic War, especially in the winter of 1942–1943. This was a real emergency, and there was more at stake, in the international struggle against fascism, than just the Soviet Union's security. But the culture of brutality and forgetting cost all of Eastern Europe dear, and no one paid a higher price for it than the Soviet people themselves.

Lies and cynicism, as ever, began with the leadership. In 1945 the Yugoslav Communist Milovan Djilas complained to Stalin about the rape of Yugoslav women by Soviet troops. "Imagine a man who has fought from Stalingrad to Belgrade," the dictator replied. "Over thousands of kilometres of his own devastated land, across the dead bodies of his comrades and dearest ones. How can such a man react normally? And what is so awful in his having fun with a woman after such horrors?"[37] Aleksandr Solzhenitsyn wrote that the rape and shooting of German women by Soviet troops was widely regarded as "almost a combat distinction." One of Kopelev's colleagues, an officer called Belyaev, felt much the same. "The Fritzes have plundered all over the world," he said. "That's why they've got so much. They burned down everything in our country, and now we're doing the same in theirs. We don't have to feel sorry for them."[38]

Thousands of Russian troops would have agreed. The desperate times had turned them into avenging killers, the conventions of civilian life forgotten. Even a foreigner like Werth had caught the mood by 1943. On his last day in Stalingrad he visited the ruins of the Red Army House. The scene in the yard behind it was appalling. No Western prisoners of war saw anything like the hunger or neglect. Horses' skeletons were rotting in piles beside a yellowed cesspool—"fortunately frozen solid"—and the ground was littered with the emaciated corpses of German prisoners of war. Some of the men, however, were still alive. One of them "had been crouching over another cesspool . . . Now, noticing us, he was hastily pulling up his pants, and then he slunk away into the door of a basement . . . As he passed, I caught a glimpse of the wretch's face—with its mixture of suffering and idiot-like incomprehension. For a moment I wished the whole of Germany were there to see it." There was, he wrote, a "rough but divine justice" in the scene.[39]

By 1944, however, when the war was all but won, Kopelev permitted himself to be disgusted by Soviet cruelty. He and his men reached the Prussian town of Neidenburg on a chilly evening, just as dusk was falling. They were not the first Soviet troops to arrive. "The place was in flames," Kopelev wrote. "Again, the work of our own men. On a side street, by a garden fence, lay a dead old woman. Her dress was ripped; a telephone receiver reposed between her scrawny thighs. They had apparently tried to ram it into her vagina . . . One of them explained that the dead woman was a spy." It was a common pretext—the flimsiest, the most incredible—for the mutilation, torture, and killing of the few civilians who had not fled. A little farther on, the men encountered another woman, this time alive, and wearing "a mangy boa and a hat wound around with some kind of shawl." She was the sort of person that does not escape, confused, elderly, unable to grasp what tragedy had overtaken her. She kept asking the Russians to help find her daughter. "She's probably crazy," was the general view.

An argument broke out between Kopelev and Belyaev. Belyaev wanted the woman to be shot. No order, however, was given. None was needed. "There's a commotion behind us," Kopelev wrote. "One of the soldiers gives the old woman a push. She collapses on a bank of snow; there is a shot. She gives a rabbity whimper; the soldier fires his carbine a second time, and a third. The black bundle in the snow is still. The soldier, a mere boy, bends down looking for something—her boa."[40]

Official propaganda actively encouraged the hatred that drove acts of cruelty like this. It was rooted in an incontestable reality, the fact of Nazi atrocities, the torture and killing of civilians, the repeated threat of annihilation. Hitler himself had decreed that Leningrad and Moscow were to be destroyed completely. Moscow, he said, should be razed and excavated. The site was to be turned into a massive lake. The Soviet response was sacred vengeance. "If you haven't killed a German in the course of a day," wrote Ilya Ehrenburg, "your day has been wasted . . . If you have killed one German, kill another: nothing gives us so much joy as German corpses. Your mother says to you: kill the German! Your children beg of you: kill the German! Your country groans and whispers: kill the German! Don't miss him! Don't let him escape! Kill!"[41]

Konstantin Simonov echoed the same words in his poem "Kill him!" It was published in *Pravda* in 1942. "If your home is dear to you where your Russian mother nursed you," it declares, "If your mother is dear to you, and you cannot bear the thought of the German slapping her wrinkled face . . . If you do not want her, whom for so long you did not dare even kiss, to be stretched out naked on the floor, so that amid hatred, cries and tears, three German curs should take what belongs to your manly love; If you do not want to give away all that you call your Country, Then kill a German, kill a German every time you see one."[42] Poems like this were not for the elite. Soldiers on their way to Berlin in 1944 remember pinning rhymes and mottoes to the sides of their tanks, traditional Russian lines adapted for the war. Hatred of "Fritz" was their main theme. If he was lucky, "Fritz" was "sausage."[43]

According to one former soldier, the ethnographer Pushkarev, it was hatred of the enemy, more than anything, that drove the Soviet army in the West. One of Kopelev's comrades reminded him of a poem by Shevchenko in which the hero cuts up his own children. "That's war, buddy," the soldier said. "First let's send Germany up in smoke, then we'll go back to writing good, theoretically correct books on humanism and internationalism. But now we must see to it that the soldiers will want to go on fighting. That's the main thing."[44] "If the Germans treated our prisoners well," a colonel told Werth in 1942, "it would soon be known. It's a horrible thing to say, but by ill-treating and starving our prisoners to death, the Germans are helping us."[45] Ninety-five percent of the German troops who had been taken prisoner at Stalingrad would die on Soviet soil. Four out of five Soviet prisoners of war would die in German hands. In both instances, some were executed (this was, of course, illegal by the standards of the distant, Western, world), some tortured, some merely left to starve.[46]

"We were fighting for our land, for our soil," the doctors said. They did not think about the social cost. But others thought the war had thrown a shadow over everyone's humanity. Far from finding that people "acted from the soul," as the doctors had insisted, the writer Vasili Grossman was troubled by the harshness of human relations by 1945. It was, he wrote, as though ordinary people "had made an agreement to refute the view that one can always be sure of finding kindness in the hearts of people with dirty hands."[47] The poet Joseph Brodsky had the same impression. He described the "primeval chaos" at a suburban station in Leningrad in 1945, and the desperation of the crowd as it "besieged" the train. "My eye caught sight of an old, bald, crippled man with a wooden leg," he wrote. "He was trying to get into car after car, but each time was pushed away by the people who were already hanging on the footboards. The train started and the old man hopped along. At one point he managed to grab a handle of one of the cars, and then I saw a woman in the doorway lift a kettle and pour boiling water straight on the old man's bald crown."[48]

The war itself explains most of this callousness. That was certainly what witnesses at the time, including Werth, said and wrote, and it remains the view of many former soldiers and partisans. "I still have in my ears the cry of a child as it was thrown into a well," a woman from Belarus recalled. "It was not a child's cry, and it was not a human cry, it was a cry from beyond the grave. After that, when you went on a mission, your whole spirit urged you to do only one thing: to kill them [the Germans] as soon as possible and as many as possible, destroy them in the cruellest way."[49] Behind each account of atrocity, however, there remains the larger question of its cause. Brutality on either side was not an accident of culture or geography. It was shaped, perhaps decisively, by politics. In Russia, as in Nazi Germany, the state pressed hard on people's lives. As Grossman put it, "The extreme violence of totalitarian systems proved able to paralyse the human spirit throughout whole continents."[50] There is no reason to assume that he was thinking only of the Nazi version.

A harder question, perhaps, concerns the role of the recent past, the lessons of experience. The people whom the Germans overran in June 1941 had just survived a decade of Stalinism, famine, mass arrest. A generation earlier, their parents had seen revolution, civil war, the pain of families divided and of neighborhoods in flames. There had been daily shootings, hangings, torture, hunger, fear. Ten years later, collectivization, dekulakization, and the famine had once again made life a desperate business; survival, often, a matter of grim competition. Immediately before the war began there had been further rumors of mass killings, the shooting of Polish officers in the Katyn forest, the torture and shooting of thousands of prisoners in the occupied territories of Galicia and the Baltic.

It is difficult to say in what ways killing and cruelty were judged by ordinary people (the leadership's views are fairly clear) in a society that hosted crimes like these, what new or old traditions fed the violence of the troops. Practices learned in the village, the traditions of *samosud,* were not forgotten in the countryside and in the camps, and they had not died in the memories of many workers, either. But more significantly, the people had a special view, a lesson drawn from their daily experience, of what it took to avoid death. They were not brutes, the children of some damaged, less than human breed. They were realists in their own world. At a time of emergency, Stalin's people learned, there were no boundaries except survival. Blockade survivors from Leningrad often talk of their mothers' life-saving experience, the lessons learned from earlier famines. Soldiers mention the village—the village of the 1930s—and talk grimly of the harshness of life. The allusions sound like ancient wisdom—"God is high and the czar is far"—but the specificities of these people's biographies suggest a darker, sharper link with hardship. A human being could learn to steal and lie, in other words, could learn to kill, despite his decency, despite his hopes, despite his poetry and the letters in the pocket of his soldier's coat.

The other lesson that the Soviets learned was stoicism. As Vasili Grossman wrote, in 1946, "The Stalingrad epic is a page written in fire and blood, and stamped with the staunchness of our troops, the courage of our workers, their unbounded patriotism."[51] The same images are invoked by almost every writer on the war.[52] Ideology played a part here, too. The image of the leader, Stalin, seems to have toughened many faltering hearts. But Communism was always weakest when it came to death. The people may have fought for the motherland and Stalin—some of them say they did—but they did not usually choose to die for socialism, for Marx, or for the abstract values of a political dream. Their thoughts turned to the land, to their families, to Russia in its mythic, spiritual guise. The war packed the churches. Millions returned to the open practice of religion.

The church, or parts of it, was quick to join the cause. "Our Orthodox Church has always shared the destiny of the people," Metropolitan Sergii of

Moscow declared in 1941. "For us, above all, it is right to recall Christ's commandment: greater love hath no man than this, that a man lay down his life for his friends."[53] There was a widespread (and mistaken) belief, behind the Soviet lines, that German rule would put a stop to Russian religious life. In fact, the occupying troops in Ukraine had won the hearts of many local people early on by opening the churches and permitting Christian worship.[54] Both leaderships, the German and the Soviet, recognized at once the value of restoring selected kinds of religious practice.

From the autumn of 1941, the Stalinist restrictions on the church's work were tacitly forgotten. The citizens of Moscow celebrated the first Easter of the war, in 1942, with a procession and public prayers. As they carried the icons through gaunt, deserted streets, believers wept in gratitude and relief. "Dear God," sighed one. "Our Stalin let us process all night in our Easter vigil. God grant him health."[55] The people were allowed to celebrate eternal life, and soon they would be helped to pray over their grief. In 1943, a curator in Leningrad's Museum of Atheism (the former Kazan' cathedral) sat down to draft a memorandum about consolation. His first lines were tactful. "Atheist materialism has made great progress in the ranks of the party," he noted. "But personal grief at the loss of relatives, and suffering in connection with the absence of information about loved ones and so forth are all giving rise to religious feelings."

He continued with a criticism of official social organizations—trade unions, workers' clubs, and all those voluntary groups. They were not doing enough, he wrote, to comfort the bereaved, their failings left the people with "feelings of isolation and loneliness" and these in turn "gave rise to religious feelings." As for the Communist Party's own propaganda clubs and Red Corners, these were "not working at all, if working is even the right word." When people mourned, he wrote, they went to the churches. Practices such as the draping of icons had never actually stopped—the people seemed to need them—even under socialism. The curator of the atheist museum recommended that more churches should be opened.[56] In fact, the Leningrad hierarchy, like that in Moscow, was already contributing a great deal to the war effort through its sermons, admonitions, and prayers.

The force of Orthodox religion, especially when it was linked to mystical notions of Russianness, is still clear when the people talk. Leningrad's Kazan' virgin, the city's most sacred icon, was what preserved the city, they will say, "My father was a political agitator [*politruk*]," a man from St. Petersburg said to me. "He was supposed to instruct the people and to maintain the ideological line. He was a bit of a fanatic in the 1930s. But I have seen the diary he kept during the blockade. It was a private diary, just for him. And all he writes is 'God save us, God save us', over and over again. I think he stopped believing in the Party during the war." The frontline doctors, too, would set their ideology aside when they talked of death itself. Many soldiers prayed when they were dying, and many apparent atheists, they said, demanded crosses at the end. "It is one thing to flirt with death," quoted one, "but another to die in fact." "Oh, yes," the staunch Nikolai Viktorovich conceded. "Most of the recruits had been baptised at one time or another. And it mattered to them in the end."

Religion left its mark on memory, too. The light of redemption, of sacrifice for a just cause, shines on the patriotic myth. Ehrenburg distinguished between Soviet and Nazi killing in these kinds of terms. "The Russian people have risen up in order to hurl back the invasion of death," he wrote at Easter 1942. "Each one of us loves life, his work, his family and his home . . . In dying for their country, our heroes die for a living life, and we must remember this now, when the earth is awakening under the April sun."[57] The doctors and the nurses, like the former soldiers, echoed this. "We never really said all that," one of them confided in me after the group interview. "We did not fight for Stalin. We fought for our families, for our city. They talk about the motherland and Stalin, but it's not real." The Russian earth itself, in fact, was holy. Suffering, they always say, brought people face to face with their basic nature, the things that always matter. Pain stripped away the vanity of city life; it reminded the Russian of his soul. Endurance, in the end, was always worth it.

The stories other people tell, and the songs that they still know and sing, return to this theme almost every time. Even death becomes unreal. "Wait for me, and I'll come back," begins Konstantin Simonov's famous poem, the one that every veteran knows:

It's hard for them to understand,
For those who did not wait,
That in the very heat of fire,
By waiting here for me,
It was you that saved me.
Only you and I will know
How I survived—
It's just that you knew how to wait
As no other person.[58]

Ilya Ehrenburg's collected war journalism is entitled *Russia at War,* and so is Alexander Werth's great history. Other writers have followed suit, adopting titles that evade the ugly terminologies of the old Soviet Union.[59] Despite their names, however, all these books describe a war whose character was partly ideological. Many people on both sides regarded it as a confrontation between Soviet Bolshevism and a Nazism based on fantasies of race. Communist Party activists, whatever their nationality, were singled out from the mass of prisoners of war and executed, in contravention of international law, by Nazi *einsatzgruppen*. At least half a million of them were shot in the first five months of the war.[60] Others were hanged in public in the ruined squares of towns like Kharkov, Kiev, and Orel. Influential Nazi generals ignored the "traditional" rules of "gentlemanlike warfare." As one of them scribbled on the margin of a note that licensed the atrocities, "This is an ideological war of extermination; I, therefore, approve and authorise the measures stipulated in this directive."[61]

The Great Patriotic War also involved the entire Soviet population. That is to say, it drew in almost all the Soviet Union's populations, and also many different faiths and factions, ideologies, and cultures. The particular fates of certain groups, the tales of disproportionate suffering, were long subsumed into the image of a common motherland. Support for Stalin was not universal, all agree, but nor were Orthodoxy, love for Russia. Some people—notably some representatives of non-Russian (and non-Jewish) ethnic groups in the western territories—greeted the Germans with relief, at least for a time. Later on, the anti-Soviet partisan struggles in the Baltic and Ukraine were among the bitterest episodes of the whole war. But what is more damaging, from the point of view of mythic Russian patriotism, is the fact that the majority of the Soviet Union's citizens joined in the greater struggle for their country with enthusiasm. The sacrifices that non-Russians made were lost in the universal story. Their disappearance was not entirely accidental.

The citizens of what is now Belarus, for instance, suffered heavier losses than their eastern neighbors. Mass graves outside some Belorussian towns suggest that many of the deaths—certainly some tens of thousands—predated the German invasion. But Belarus was in the front line. Its woods, marshes, and elegant towns were occupied by the Nazis from the summer of 1941. Shops, farms, and houses were plundered and torched. The republic's Jewish population was almost entirely destroyed. Those who had not managed to flee were burned alive, gassed, or shot, some in woods and fields near their homes, others in the infamous camps of East Prussia and Poland.

"I think one person in every four died in my area, perhaps even more," a Belorussian partisan explained. "The Germans destroyed whole villages completely. I mean, when the partisans were active especially. They just burned the houses to the ground. The wells were choked with bodies: everyone, old people and tiny children, and everyone, I saw it myself, with my own eyes . . . Seven or eight villages, just burned, in a single night . . . After the war, when you went to places like Gomel', it was obvious that there were fewer people about."[62] Another woman told me that she cannot bear to visit Minsk because the rebuilt streets still smell, to her, of rotting brick and burning meat.

The collapse of the Soviet empire has turned stories like these into foundation myths for the emerging nations. Ukrainian historians are compiling lists of the Ukrainian fallen, writers elsewhere collect fresh testimonies in Latvian, Polish, and the dialects of provincial Galicia.[63] The dead are being pressed to useful work again, and again, as always, the myths to which they must contribute are neither absolutely true nor false, merely alternatives. Some people fought for national liberation, others for their families, for personal survival, for any side or cause that might have won. Sometimes they fought for several things at once, or just because there was no other way of life. But millions of men and women were genuinely motivated, too, by Communism and internationalism—Soviet patriotism. Many of the Ukrainians and Belorussians who fought in the Soviet army were proud to do so, as were many of the Jews, the Uzbeks, Abkhazians, Kasakhs. People like this have lived to watch their own identities changed, shaped, and changed again as history moves under them, and as the living alter, so does the meaning of the dead.

Aleksei Grigor'evich lives in the Ukrainian city of Lviv (Lvov), the capital of a fanatical nationalism, the heartland of ethnic Ukrainian culture. His soldier's memories, however—and those of his friends—are of a Soviet war, a war fought side by side with Russians. "Even now we have a tradition," he says. "The first glass of vodka we drink standing, in silence, in memory of fallen comrades. In this city, there are only two others, one man from my division and one from my army—think about it, my *army*. But we still honour that tradition, for the dead . . . And we do remember them by name, our friends at least. Even now, when I'm getting so sclerotic that I can't seem to remember anything, I can remember those names."[64] His best friend, who was killed at the front, was an Ossetian from the North Caucasus. Aleksei Grigor'evich has visited the dead man's village. The family regard him as their own.

Beyond that Soviet patriotism, however, are all the problems of a multiple identity. It is not clear, at any moment, what meaning Aleksei Grigor'evich will choose to give to any death, what story he will fit to it. He is a Ukrainian by nationality, and Ukraine, like Belarus, has a new history of suffering (including that of genocidal famine), a history that has grown since independence. But Aleksei Grigor'evich is also a Jew, and once, too, he was a Soviet citizen. He is uncomfortable, for different reasons, with each version of himself, and often they compete.

The aspect of his conflicted life that most troubled me, coming from Britain, was not, perhaps, the one that haunted him (his friend's death was his most important memory, he said). No one who came from my world could now have told his story as he did. For Jewishness was not a source of bitter pride, of justifiable anger, sacred guilt, for Aleksei Grigor'evich. "There was absolutely none of that [distinction between different nationalities] in the war," he said. But then he started on a different tack. His greatest fear was not that he would die, although he was afraid that if he did his mother would be left alone. "It was that I would turn out to be a coward," he said. "And since I am a Jew I do not have the right to be a coward." His comrades reassured him. "You're one of the lads," they said. "You're not a bit like a Jew." His father died in the first weeks of the war. To this day he does not know how. "According to the documents, he went missing at the front," Aleksei Grigor'evich explains. "But the neighbours said after the war that they had seen him in occupied Kiev. So he would have ended up in Babi Yar. There are no other possibilities."

The Holocaust on Soviet soil was probably the most ominous of the silences at official ceremonies of commemoration. Even now, most people talk only of the general Soviet sacrifice. "So they killed Jews," a priest in Kiev said to me. "So what? We know that the Jews bear a lot of guilt. They killed a lot of Ukrainians, too." It took a word from Magdalena Alekseyevna, the bishop's granddaughter, to check him on the brink of what would soon have been a flood of chauvinistic cant. "They killed the Jews because they were Jews," she said. "Don't you see? Everyone else died for a reason. They were Communists or they were partisans or they were in the way for some reason. But they killed the Jews because they were Jews. It makes it different." The priest was hushed but not convinced. Magdalena Alekseyevna has the authority of a pious woman; she is a regular member of his congregation, but he will not be changing his opinion.

The priest's remarks seem more obscene when they are set in context. Kiev, where we were talking (and where he had spent his war), was the site of a notorious massacre of Jews. A ravine on the edge of the city, Babi Yar, became the grave for more than thirty-three thousand people in September 1941. "My grandmother went with the Germans," a survivor remembered. "She was so trusting. They just said: 'Come on, auntie.' They were even smiling."

It took two days, 29 and 30 September, to kill them all. The men who did the shooting worked in one-hour shifts, and they took the night off, locking the prisoners who still lived into empty garages to await the dawn. When they had finished, they covered the site with sand and rubble. Limbs and fingers poked through wherever the covering of dust and leaves was thinnest, and gases from the decaying flesh caused small explosions and strange lights. But it was only as the Germans began their retreat from Kiev that some prisoners of war were detailed to hide the evidence by burning the human remains, dynamiting the site, and burying the surviving bones.[65] Elsewhere in Ukraine and Belarus, Jews were forced to dig their own graves outside the cities where their families had lived and worked for generations. It is estimated that about 1.5 million of the Shoah's 6 million Jewish victims were citizens of the USSR.[66]

The local people knew what was happening. Few did much to prevent it. Some—the infamous local *polizei*—were willing to assist with the murders. Jewish veterans often insist that the Germans had very little to do in some parts of Ukraine. This angry prejudice is fueled by continuing racism. Survivors are wary of talking about the past.[67] Even the Ukrainians who helped them—Magdalena Alekseyevna is one—are careful what they say about the war.

The danger of racial violence is not the only thing that keeps survivors silent. Unlike the tales of Patriotic War, the story of the genocide has not been much rehearsed on former Soviet territory; it is an almost buried memory. Since glasnost, and since the film *Schindler's List,* some of the witnesses have tried to talk, and many have been asked to testify to interviewers working for organizations like the Spielberg Shoah Foundation. The social workers who support them shake their heads.[68] They tell me that the elderly have suffered since their interviews. They had to force their memories to live again, find words to meet the expectations of interviewers from abroad. Some could talk of nothing but the death camps after their interviews, I was told, and others suffered palpitations, heart attacks, nights of anxious sleeplessness, or bouts of depression. The stories that they tell are familiar to anyone in Western Europe, North America, or Israel. In the former Soviet Union, however, they are still discoveries, disorientating secrets, uncomfortable, frequently, for narrator and audience alike. They seem fantastic after years of silence, prejudice, and shame.

The people who agreed to talk to me were the ones who had escaped. They remembered running from the Germans, hiding in woods, joining the partisans. Others described how they had grown up in alien families, fostered as infants to Ukrainian parents as a way of saving their lives. Everyone had lost most of their friends and kin. Some could describe the killing; others never knew where their parents or siblings had died. Today they yearn to find more detail for their rediscovered pasts, to add some personal emblem to the stark facts, the lists of names.

Few will ever succeed. The fate of Ukraine's Jews provided the theme for one of the most moving war despatches that the writer Vasili Grossman sent home from the Soviet army's westward advance toward Berlin. "There is no house in Ukraine where there have not been tears in these two years," he wrote in 1943. "There is no house where there are not orphans and widows . . . But there are villages in Ukraine where you do not hear any complaints, where you see no tears, where peace and silence reign."

One of these villages was Kozara. That Easter, 750 people had been locked into their houses and burned there. No one had survived. "I thought about it," Grossman wrote. "And I decided that silence is more terrible than tears, worse than loud lamenting. And that is how it is for the Jews of Ukraine. Silence. Quiet. A people has been killed . . . This is not the death of soldiers in war. They had no weapons in their hands. It is the murder of a people, of houses, families, books, beliefs, the killing of root and branch. It is the death of memories, stories, the experience of trades and skills, the death of songs and poetry."[69]

Grossman himself would try to fill this silence by collecting stories of the Holocaust on Soviet soil and publishing them, with the help of Ilya Ehrenburg, in the *Black Book*. In 1946, however, every Russian-language copy of the book was collected and destroyed, as was the type from which the books were set. It would be years before the stories it contained were ever heard again in Russian homes. Reading them now, it is the yearning that is striking, the indignation, shock, and loss, but also the longing for a last message from the dead. "At the beginning of September this year I happened to be in the town of Kovel' looking for information about my mother and mother-in-law," a soldier called Gruntman wrote to Ehrenburg in 1944. Kovel', in western Ukraine, was in an area where Jews had lived for centuries, and it was also one of the first to be occupied by German troops in 1941. "I knew what had happened to them already," Gruntman wrote. "But all the same I wanted to find something that I could keep as a reminder of them, a photograph, perhaps, or something of the kind." What the soldier found instead would haunt him.

Most of the synagogues, he discovered, were gone, demolished. Only one, the largest one, survived. Reluctantly, he went inside. The building was designed to hold at least fifteen hundred people. It was empty. The altar had been taken out, the Torah burned, and the walls had been pitted by machine-gun bullets. The only witnesses to what had happened in the ruined hall were two stone lions.

Gruntman wanted to leave, but he was also curious to look more closely at the damaged plaster, to feel the pits and scars with his own hands. As his eyes grew better used to the dim light, he saw that the walls bore other marks, not just the bullets. There were pencil messages along the chunks of shattered plaster. "The building spoke," he wrote. "There was no blank space. It was the last words of the doomed. It was a people's farewell to life . . . I felt ashamed before those walls, as if they were saying or thinking of me: 'You left us and went away, you did not take us with you, you knew what would happen and you left us alone.' "

For Gruntman, the most important message was the single word *otomstite,* "take revenge." But most of the messages were desperate. "Know that they killed us all," someone had scrawled. "I am going to my death with my wife and children," wrote another; "Remember your sister," a third. Few of the people for whom these messages were written were still alive to read them. Families that were separated would often wait to die in different prisons, separate camps, but all under the same regime. "Liza Reizen, the wife of Leibish Reizen," began one pencil line. "A mother's dream of seeing her only daughter, Beba, again, who lives in Dubno, never came about. She went to her death in great distress." Dubno, another town in the same region, had seen a slaughter of its own.[70]

The old communities were almost wiped out, the people that survived in hiding or in exile. Without their families and social networks, refugees would soon rebuild their lives as misfits, making the best of what was left, joining the wider, Soviet, world, their story and their faith a burden to conceal. They would usually be treated as outsiders, lucky to be tolerated, wisest to conform. "We were so hungry that we started to eat grass," Irina Matveyevna, who had escaped from Kiev with her parents and brother, remembered. "But the local people moved us on. We were stealing their pasture."[71] The family had fled to the high plains of Uzbekistan. They could not even communicate with their temporary hosts, let alone overcome the locals' suspicion of outsiders.

The courage that had sustained the entire family through weeks of danger finally failed them when they came to settle. Both parents died within days. The two remaining children, Irina and her brother, were bundled into a hospital bed together. The next morning, Irina's brother was dead, lying beside her as if asleep. The little girl, the sole survivor, was made to work for her keep as soon as she could stand. Until that time, some of her food was paid for by the local woman who had kindly agreed to take and sell her mother's wedding ring.

There were many other stories, many exiles. Some were the work of Stalin's government, which decreed, at different points throughout the war, that entire ethnic groups—including the long-established community of Volga Germans, as well as the Chechens, Tartars, and Meskhetian Turks—were a danger to security and should be dispossessed, en masse, and shipped out to the east and north. The earliest deportations, involving Germans and Poles, were described as preemptive security measures. Later on, as the German army was retreating, citizens of the territories that it had occupied, including the Chechens and Crimean Tartars—entire nations—were accused of collaboration.[72] Either way, the total number of men, women, and children who would suffer deportation in the years of Patriotic War was not less than 2 million.[73] Their stories, their losses, separations, and the deaths of thousands of their people, were not the ones that shaped the public image of heroic struggle. The epics of Stalingrad, a city on the Volga, and of Leningrad, the empire's former capital, remain its paradigm stories.

Patriotism, in the last of Europe's multinational empires, was and remains a contentious and distorting passion. "The Azerbaijanis were the most afraid to die," said one of the medical orderlies. "And the Tadzhiks. The, er, Asiatics. Russians are the least afraid. It's our psychology." Now that the Soviet Union has gone, the idea of a Russian war has become the basis for a great deal of contemporary Russian self-understanding, a splinter on the brain of modern Russian personhood.

You can tell any number of alternative stories of the Patriotic War—all of them crucial to its meaning—but in the end there is no minimizing the reality of Russia's loss, the deaths of millions, the truth that lies behind the military myth. The people's grief was overwhelming. It is not easy, ever, to bury wartime dead. In a culture based on earth, bones, and belonging, the quest to lay the ghosts can take a lifetime. When he wanted to evoke a poetic landscape for the graves, Simonov talked, nostalgically, of "villages, villages, villages with churchyards."[74] Reality was nothing like the dream.

"In and around the Red October plant [at Stalingrad] fighting had gone on for weeks," wrote Werth. "Trenches ran through the factory yards and through the workshops themselves; and now at the bottom of the trenches there still lay frozen green Germans and frozen grey Russians and frozen fragments of human shapes; and there were helmets, Russian and German, lying among the debris, and now half-filled with snow."[75] "They lied about the numbers," I remember. They also lied about the manner of the deaths. "We always wrote and told their mothers they had died a hero's death," a nurse who wrote the letters told me. They often told the relatives about the grave as well, even when it was a shallow trench, an unmarked field, even if there had been nothing left to bury.

Vasili Grossman, a veteran of Stalingrad himself, imagined a mother's visit to her son's grave, one of the tens of thousands in the fields outside the town. "Lyudmila walked up to the small mound of earth," he wrote. "On a plywood board she read her son's name and rank . . . On either side, stretching right to the railings, were rows and rows of the same small grey mounds. There were no flowers on them, just a single wooden stem shooting straight up from the grave . . . There were hundreds of these boards. Their density and uniformity made them seem like a field of grain."[76]

This cheerless view was not the worst that mothers like Lyudmila could expect. Aleksei Grigor'evich was quick to modify it. When I asked him to describe wartime death and burial, he paused. "That," he said, "is a very, very painful question. During the fighting, of course, we didn't bury anyone. We just carried on . . . and our friends, they remained behind. There were special teams, they were called funeral teams, behind the front line . . . mostly old men, not fighting fit, as we said. They collected the bodies and buried them. They buried them in several ways. Usually in trenches. The antitank trenches that there often were. There weren't any cemeteries." He hesitated, breathing heavily, so I prompted him with a question about markers. Were there any signs—crosses, stars, or stones—to indicate these makeshift graves? "Dear God!" he replied. "We had enough trouble finding spaces to get the bodies in. They were just shoved into the earth, without coffins of course, and if we were lucky, in the very best case, we might find a bit of wood to put over the place as a reminder. The token might be a bit of plywood, perhaps with a red star—if we had any red paint, that is. Otherwise, it was a bit of plywood."

The ones who were not buried simply lay among the reeds and birch. There was no one left, perhaps, to do the digging. Even today, old battlefields yield piles of bones. Local people in some districts remember avoiding the gazes of unburied corpses in ruined suburbs and in woods. The first spring, the first thaw, after any battle was the grimmest. "In the spring the ice on the Volga began to break," one woman said. "And one day we saw an ice floe [sic] drifting downstream and on it two or three Germans and one Russian soldier. They had died gripping one another, got frozen into the flow, and the whole floe was splashed with blood."[77]

To see how the facts of dying have been weighted, boxed, and buried since the war, you have only to visit one of the great memorials of the post-Stalin era. The blockade cemetery outside St. Petersburg, Piskarevskoe, is typical. Presided over by a doughty Mother Russia with a stone garland in her arms, it is a geometrical masterpiece, a jigsaw of solid marble, reassuring symmetry, heavy on the earth. It suggests colossal sacrifice without evoking agony or disorder. In the 1970s it was used for parades and patriotic meetings. There are photographs of schoolboys in neat uniforms, of girls in white socks, their hair tied back in starched white bows. They carry banners, march and sing. It all looks hearty and uncomfortable; it could be a rally of the scouts and guides.

The main inscription at the site concludes with Ol'ga Berggol'ts's words, "No-one is forgotten, nothing is forgotten." This is not true, of course, but the story of forgetting is more complicated than a mere tale of censorship. There are innumerable written memoirs of the Leningrad blockade. At first, too, as every witness says, the Leningraders talked—endlessly, repetitively, obsessively.[78] But after a while, most of their stories, like their military decorations, would become objects for display. When some of Leningrad's defenders were issued with bronze medals in the summer of 1943 (embossed with portraits of Stalin, as well as tasteful flowers, slogans, and a crest), they were proud, and some were moved to tears, but the medals were not things for every day. "Many workers put their medals away because they were afraid that the bronze would darken," the official report of the award ceremony explained. "Some, who wanted to avoid this, covered the crest with cellophane." "My clothes are often dirty," said a factory worker called Ivanov, "and I do not want to spoil my medal. I will wear it only on special occasions."[79] You do not grime your stories by exposing them to certain kinds of daylight, either. They are for hoarding, after all, and you must tell them as you choose.

Ten times more people died in Leningrad during the blockade than were lost in the atomic bombing over Hiroshima.[80] At first they died during the bombardments. Later, during the siege, they also starved and froze. The Germans had encircled the city by the end of September 1941, and the siege would hold for nearly two more years. As the first winter of the blockade began, the authorities took stock of its human costs. "Mortality in the city on the grounds of hunger, the severe cold, and the lack of firewood rose sharply in December," ran their report. "According to incomplete figures for the Funeral Trust [it] reached at least 42,050, which represents a 247 percent increase upon November."[81] In fact, the precise number of deaths would soon become impossible to count. The piles of bodies grew jumbled, the limbs and faces broke and twisted, and parts of some would disappear into the hungry people's canvas bags.

Neither the hospitals nor the Funeral Trust could cope with the thousands of deaths. There were not enough coffins, not enough trucks, no petrol, and by the early winter there was no more space in the common graves that a provident local council had made ready the previous summer. Workers in the Funeral Trust (a department of the Soviet), put in as many hours as they could, but they, too, were dying. "They would drag a body to the grave with their last energy," a city report later said. "And then they would fall into the pit themselves." Anyone who could still walk that far would drag their relatives' bodies out to the cemetery themselves. Photographs from that first winter show figures shuffling through the snow, shadowy in the arctic light. Some pull sledges, others drag bundles wrapped in sheets and rags. Some of the bundles are firewood, others human dead. The informal processions of mourners "made a sad impression on the people," wrote a health official. "In the thick haze of the bitterest of frosts walked densely-muffled, silent, human figures . . . carrying their string bags and dragging behind them sledges and plywood boards bearing home-made coffins, boxes, or . . . bodies wrapped in sheets or blankets."[82]

The remains of the dead were a reproach to the living. "I was looking for a room in the city," one man wrote. So many buildings had been bombed that housing was a problem even after the evacuation and the first few thousand deaths. If your own rooms were destroyed, you went and searched the silent apartment blocks, pushing open any door that was not locked. This man, like many others, came upon a two-roomed flat and gently tried the latch. Inside he found the corpse of an adult man, frozen solid. On a chair beside him was a child of fourteen or so, also dead, while a smaller child, the baby, lay dead in a crib in the corner. In the second room, on the bed, lay the corpse of their mother. A girl, her last surviving child, was washing the body with a rough towel. This child, too, would die the following day.[83]

As the population dwindled, the number of unclaimed bodies would begin to grow. They piled up at the hospitals until there was no space inside to keep them.[84] After that, the doctors had to leave them in the yards, stacked up under the walls and by the gates. Health department statisticians, still diligently collecting their figures, observed that most of those who died had collapsed at work, or even in the streets.[85] In many cases, the corpses were simply bundled into doorways, or even left with the garbage, by local residents too exhausted to move them. Gruesome evidence of this came to light as a result of the evacuation of art treasures from the Hermitage. A group of packers sent down to the basement of the abandoned museum found more than a hundred bodies there. They were the corpses of museum employees who had died at work, left underground by fellow staff too pressed for time and space to move them further.[86]

The city's morgues were no less macabre. At the time, an official account described them as "sinister." The problem was that the Funeral Trust staff and volunteer brigades who cleared the streets each day did not have time for delicacy. Mortuary shelves were piled with "disfigured bodies," the report explained, and even with "parts of bodies, that is, severed heads, arms, and legs, shattered skulls, and the bodies of foetuses, of pregnant women, and of children of all ages." The public was not spared this grisly scene. They might begin their search for a missing child or partner in the hospitals, they might search the streets, the yards, the basements, the canals. But ultimately they always ended up in the line at the reception desk of a local mortuary, turning their caps in their hands, or fingering worn scarves, clutching anxious children, hoping, weeping. "From morning until the onset of darkness the morgues were full of people with desperate, bitter faces," said one report, "wandering and searching—parents for their dead children, children, for their dead parents, brothers for sisters, sisters for brothers, and everyone just for their friends."[87] The city authorities took black-and-white photographs of the mortuaries for their records. Today they look like medieval images of hell.[88]

Besieged Leningrad was a scene of stoicism, but it was also a hunting ground for crime. "Speculators" and "parasites" offered to arrange a burial in exchange for vodka, beer, or bread; they promised to obtain a coffin; they demanded advance payment in meat or ration cards. Some refused to move a body unless they were generously bribed.[89] Local criminals also offered to help convey the bodies to the cemeteries. They would pile several onto a cart, offload them quickly, cook the books. You got a ration of vodka for each corpse, and it was easy to inflate the numbers. No one really checked, not in the cold, the twilight, the dense fog. Vodka, like bread, was money, and money, also like bread, was life.

The city tried to curb this grisly crime by checking individual documents, by issuing each corpse with papers. But this created a new problem. The bureaucratic mania deterred some people from engaging with officialdom at all.

The relatives of the dead were "afraid that they did not have the right papers," and so they stopped taking bodies to the morgue or the cemetery for themselves. Their unwillingness simply added to the scores of fresh corpses "which were dumped anonymously into streets and stairwells."[90] The crisis was contained, in the end, when special blockade cemeteries (including Piskarevskoe) were designated in the suburbs. Eventually, too, an old brickworks was converted into an emergency crematorium.[91] Miraculously, there were no major epidemics in Leningrad through all the months of siege.

The hunger, however, was murderous. Inevitably, the most desperate measure was cannibalism. The official record does not evade it. "The cemeteries were poorly-guarded," it observed, and "bodies or parts of bodies, and especially those of children," began to disappear.[92] One woman was arrested on her way back from a graveyard with five children's bodies in a sack. Corpses left in hospital yards were butchered so often that guards had to be posted there as well as in the graveyards and the morgues. "I went to a bread store that was not far from my home," one survivor recalled. "I would walk past people lying dead in the street and then walk past these same bodies going home again and parts of their bodies would be missing. It was an hour or so sometimes and body parts would be taken."[93] "Even now," another survivor added, "I cannot buy meat pies from traders on the streets. I'm always afraid of what might be inside them." Every Leningrader shudders at the thought.

The predominant memory of the blockade today, however, is one of dour stoicism. "We had no sympathy for the people who just gave up," Lyudmila Eduardovna explained. "Everyone felt bad sometimes, but you kept going to work, it was the only way to keep your mind alive." After work, there were also concerts in the besieged city. "The people who stopped coming were the ones who died," Lyudmila Eduardovna said. "The people who complained. The ones who could only think about bread were usually the ones who stopped working, and then they died." She remembered the rehearsal of Shostakovich's Leningrad symphony. The Leningrad Philharmonic had been evacuated to Novosibirsk before the siege, and the only remaining ensemble, the Radio Orchestra, had been reduced, by hunger and cold, to a mere fourteen players. But its conductor, Karl Eliasberg, somehow scraped together enough reinforcements—including retired musicians and amateurs—to stage a performance of Shostakovich's new Seventh Symphony in August 1942. Another witness remembered that "people who no longer knew how to shed tears of sorrow and misery now cried from sheer joy."[94]

Stories like this are easy to tell. The city's solidarity remains impressive, and tears of joy are never shaming. But it would have been another thing entirely if the people in the tales had given way to grief or to despair. Some did, but their stories are not celebrated now. The memory of trauma—of minds and bodies frozen by their fear and by the horror that everyone was forced to see—has been almost entirely lost. Even some professional psychiatrists have forgotten that there were individuals who had scars that were not simply in their flesh. "I did have nightmares," one of the medical orderlies assured me. "But what is this post-dramatic [sic] stress?"

One of the most respected psychiatrists in St. Petersburg, a woman in her late forties, assured me that there was no evidence of post-traumatic stress after the blockade. Her older colleague, now retired, corrected her. "There was," she said. "But no one ever talks about it now. There were even suicides. And there were lots of other problems."[95] The documents support the latter view. They also show how memories of mutilating fear were easily suppressed. In 1948 a phenomenon called Leningrad hypertension was described by a group of doctors. It arose, they wrote, from "two factors: a prolonged and intensive nervous-psychological trauma and dietary deficiencies." Of these, it continued, "the nervous-psychological factor is of the first importance." It added (tellingly for residents of other frontline towns) that the most transparently neurotic symptoms—the ones that in another time would have been linked to shell shock—were more common among survivors of bombardment and artillery fire than among those who had merely starved.[96]

The problem was neglected and forgotten partly because there were so few resources to attend to the neurotic and the haunted. "Trauma?" a group of doctors laughed. "We would have been happy if there had been enough to eat." Vitamins, in fact, were the first drug that doctors looked for when they treated anxious or disturbed out-patients in the aftermath of war. Adequate or not, there was often there little else to hand. And there was hardly any expertise. Even military doctors had no training in the treatment of the shell-shocked, they explained, although some of their older colleagues drew on memories of the earlier war, of 1914, when they encountered inexplicable paralysis or panic. By the 1940s, the treatment of choice, at the front, was overwhelming chemical intervention. The idea was to return the patient to active service within days, and certainly within the prescribed maximum of three weeks.[97] The frontline neurological units that the czarist doctors had hoped for did not feature in the patriotic war. Stalin's medical theorists had never given much consideration to the individual soldier and his darkness.

Behind the lines, too, the hospitals were not inviting. They were run-down and cold, and, without staff—there was a labor shortage everywhere—they were usually filthy. There were almost no male orderlies to restrain the patients whose illness made them violent or aggressive. As a result, no one with a choice would stay, in-patients fled, and even people with head injuries refused the surgery they might have needed.[98] This was a society that stigmatized the deviant, the weakling, or the so-called coward—thousands of invalids would soon face exile in a drive to get them off the streets.[99] Referrals for hypertension, anxiety, and neurosis dropped dramatically after 1946. Even the amputees appeared less often at the hospitals. They knew there were few drugs to give them, anyway.

"Forgive me for my weakness," one of the nurses said when she found herself in tears in the middle of a recollection. She could not speak. But the same woman, half an hour later, was describing how she used to think about the dying. "One of the men came to that evening," she said, brisker now, and smiling. "All I can remember feeling was relief. Now I can get his surname for the form, I thought." She reached, in other words, for irony. Others glance at memory through the prism of the surreal. "Do you know what was on the first train, the very first that got through the blockade?" Lyudmila Eduardovna asked me. "Cats. A whole trainload of cats." She laughed. "There were all those rats, you see, and there was nothing left alive to kill them. There were no cats left by the end. And the rats were a real problem, especially if you think about the bodies. When that train came in we all went down to watch. And there were all these cats looking out of the windows. It was funny, really."

Lyudmila Eduardovna lost her husband in the war and nearly starved herself. She does not weep. Tat'yana Evgenyevna, too, sat upright, not recalling pain. "It helped that we were young," she said. "I would not want to do it now." But then, as always, I asked her about the first death she had witnessed. He was a sixteen-year-old boy, a teenager like her, someone she knew from school. He was a victim of the Finnish war, the winter war of 1939. Tat'yana Evgenyevna started to tell his story in her usual tone, but could not. We stopped the tape. There almost always is a point at which you have to stop. These tears, it is made clear, are not appropriate subjects for the record. They make demands, which will not do (this is a world in which demands are seldom met). They are shameful. They are private, secret, out of line. Uncontrollable grief, like mutilating trauma, is one of the things that Russians do not wish to find encoded in their memorials of concrete, bronze, and stone.

9

THE PANTHEON

Alexander Werth was in Moscow on 9 May 1945, the day the Soviet people celebrated their victory in Europe. It was, he wrote, "an unforgettable day . . . The spontaneous joy of the two or three million people who thronged the Red Square that evening—and the Moscow River embankments, and Gorki Street, all the way up to the Belorussian Station—was of a quality and a depth I had never yet seen in Moscow before." People walked the wide boulevards until dawn; they gathered under the windows of forbidding government buildings and laughed, sang, shouted, enjoying their city again, eager at the promise of a future. Young men were so happy, Werth remarked, "that they did not even have to get drunk." The Muscovites had "thrown all reserve and restraint to the winds. The fireworks display that evening was the most spectacular I have ever seen."[1]

May 9 is still among the most important anniversaries for the veterans of the war. The old people, in their seventies now, still meet in springtime parks and squares, sunning themselves under the tight buds of the lilac trees, they wear their medals, exchange tales, and watch the strange new generation pass, uncomprehending, in its Western clothes, its gaudy makeup, all its wealth. But back in 1945, the largest celebration took place on 24 June, when tens of thousands of soldiers and their officers marched through Red Square in steady and unseasonal rain. They carried the captured standards of their enemy, hundreds of Nazi banners, and they flung them, the spoils of such endurance, so much death, on to the steps of Lenin's Mausoleum, at Stalin's feet. This was the Red Army's day, but it was also the day of Stalin's great banquet, the day he began to make the war his own, when he uttered his famous, damning praise of the "little people," the "little screws and bolts," without whom his own great victory would never have been won.[2]

The contrast between the people's own remembrance and the choreographed ceremonies of official triumph was evident. In 1945 the euphoria of victory would soon be overshadowed by realities of loss, confusion, and continuing hardship. The official celebration in June was somber, as if the generals were out of step with many people's mood. Some people could not wait to see Stalin and the generals in triumph—"I have been waiting for four whole years," said one Muscovite—but others were less eager to turn out for the marching, or even to watch the military show, the white horses, and the glinting brass. "I cannot celebrate," a widow said. "My situation is really difficult. I have two children and no-one anywhere to help me. I have nothing to be cheerful about." "I won't be going to the demonstration," another person explained. "They killed my son. I would sooner go to a requiem."[3]

Even the soldiers, coming home that summer, hitching lifts on battered trucks or squeezing into stifling railway cars, knew that their memories were too complicated to gather into any single act of remembrance. The prospect of home was dreamlike; but nostalgia for the war, for comradeship, anticipated journeys, and the pleasures of talk, damp tobacco, and German schnapps still filled their real lives. Some were thinking of lost friends; others trying not to think of shameful killing, not battle, perhaps, but the knife in the dark, the stolen watch. It was all too recent, too alien, and too vivid to make sense. A fictional soldier ponders this, in a poem of 1946, as he folds his uniform, packing away the evidence of war. "But how can I part with the days of war?" he asks. "How can I ever be rid of them? A soldier's huge memory does not fit into a trunk."[4] Looking out of the car window on the journey home, the same man might have wondered, too, how his civilian neighbors would turn out, how anyone was ever going to make the life of which they had dreamed, month after dreary month, in 1942 and 1943.

The railway journey east from Berlin would have taken a returning soldier past the ruins of Prussia and Poland and through the blackened towns of Belarus. The route was perilous still—the retreating German army had blown up hundreds of bridges, ripped up track, and laid innumerable mines, some of which were boxed in wood to make them harder to detect. Both sides, at different times, had destroyed thousands of buildings of every kind—sheds, huts, and stores as well as factories and apartment blocks. Over seventeen hundred towns and more than seventy thousand villages had been laid to waste.[5] In most of the cities of the former occupied zone, fewer than half of the buildings were still habitable.[6] Kiev was a ruin, its most famous street, the Khreshchatyk, reduced to smoking rubble. Minsk, Gomel', and Pskov were piles of brick and ash. The suburbs of the hero city, Leningrad, had been demolished by retreating troops, their historic palaces smashed with hammers and pitted with bullets. The Germans had cut down three thousand ancient trees in the grounds of the Peterhof palace. Elsewhere, at Pushkin for example, where hostages and prisoners had been held in 1942, the local people could show visitors the troubled landscape of fresh graves.[7]

"There's nothing left of Stalingrad, not a thing," a soldier said to Alexander Werth. "If I had any say in the matter, I'd rebuild Stalingrad somewhere else: it would save a lot of trouble. And I'd leave this place as a museum."[8] Acres of the industrial port had been reduced to desolation, half-walls, half-chimneys, crazy sticks of steel that looped up out of concrete scree. The temptation not to clear and rebuild must have been strong. Ehrenburg, who visited the city of Leningrad in 1945, was another who thought that there was a case for keeping some of the ruins as perpetual memorials. He wanted to see the Peterhof and Pushkin palaces preserved as shells and rubble; dangerous, perhaps, but lyric testimony to an enemy's vandalism and brutality.[9]

The citizens of Leningrad, however, and especially the team that worked with its chief architect, N. V. Baranov, had plans to rebuild everything—the city and the magnificent palaces in its suburbs—before the siege was even lifted. The task ahead was daunting, but it was as much a part of Leningrad's recovery as the arrival of the first red-bannered trains. As Zhdanov, the city's Party boss, would put it, "Our task is not just reconstruction but the restoration of the city—not to restore it as it was, or simply to change its facade, but to create a city even more comfortable than it was."[10] In such an optimistic mood, it was as if the devastation were itself a gift, an opportunity to remake an entire world. The years 1944 and 1945 were the first in the modern period when the word *perestroika,* "restructuring," was heard in Soviet conversations.

The will may have been there, but the resources to implement the dream were scarce. "Traces of the terrible years were visible everywhere," Ehrenburg wrote. "Each house bore a wound or scar. There were still notices on walls here and there, warning of the danger of walking on this or that side of the street."

But it was not just the buildings that were lost. "Scanning the crowds," the writer added, "I was struck by the fact that so few of them were natives of Leningrad."[11] The human costs of the war had been so heavy that even a visitor, casually strolling in the fenced-off ruins, could miss the faces that were not there. Each person would find their own uncanny detail to remember. For Ehrenburg, the intellectual, it was the secondhand bookshops. They were, he noted, "stacked with rare books: the private libraries of Leningraders who had died of hunger."[12]

The Soviet world that would begin to grow amid this loss was a place of canvas bags and rucksacks, of railway tickets, strangers, need; an economy of barter. Twenty-five million people were on the move in the empire in 1945; not just returning soldiers but also former and future exiles, government officials, desperate peasants, partisans, criminals, and bandits. For all these millions, the war was far from over. In parts of Western Ukraine, for instance, anti-Soviet partisan activity would continue until the 1950s. Others found themselves under unwarranted state accusion and suspicion. Returning prisoners of war and whole deported populations, the slave labor of the eastern Reich, faced arrest and interrogation by their own people, and millions were exiled to Siberia in the wake of their own country's victory. The enforced exile of entire ethnic groups continued, too, the continued persecution of the Kalmyks, Germans, Balts, Tartars, the Chechens and Ingush.[13] But even for the Russians, even for triumphant troops on their way home, the victory was hollow. They faced, first, the pain of psychological adjustment, the strange new laws of peace, and then they faced old enemies again, first hunger, then poverty, hard labor, and repression.

Little enough was being produced. The output of the Soviet economy—the parts of it that functioned after years of ruin and abuse—was roughly cut in half by 1945. The emphasis on war production meant that even less of that than usual was available for civilian purposes, for transport, housing, heating, health.[14] Agricultural output was also low, even by the standards of the dismal 1930s, and the rural population, worse than decimated, was overwhelmingly composed of women, children, and the very old. "I was left with three sons," a widow told the Belorussian writer Svetlana Alexiyevich. "They were small boys, too young to look after each other. I carried sheaves of corn on my back and wood from the forest, potatoes, and hay . . . I pulled the plough myself and the harrow, too. In every other hut or so there was a widow or a soldier's wife. We were left without men. Without horses—they were taken for the army, too."

The ritual blessing of earth: a funeral ceremony at the Alexander Nevsky Monastery, St. Petersburg, 1914

Bourgeois death: lying-in-state of Major General Kulnev, St. Petersburg, 1909

Unorthodox grave ornaments: the monument to Airman Balabushkin, Volkovo Cemetery, St. Petersburg, 1913

Famine relief, 1891

The First World War: funeral service at a mass grave, 1915 or 1916. The site was intended to form the basis for a permanent memorial.

The victims of February 1917: onlookers at the "red" funeral, Petrograd, March 1917

Part of the procession at the "red" funeral

Red funeral, Petrograd, June 1919

Internment of revolutionary leaders in Mars Field, 1918

Holy relics: revolutionary officials open and examine the coffin of Alexander Nevsky in the presence of church leaders, 1922.

Bolshevik style: guard of honor by the coffin of S. M. Kirov, December 1934

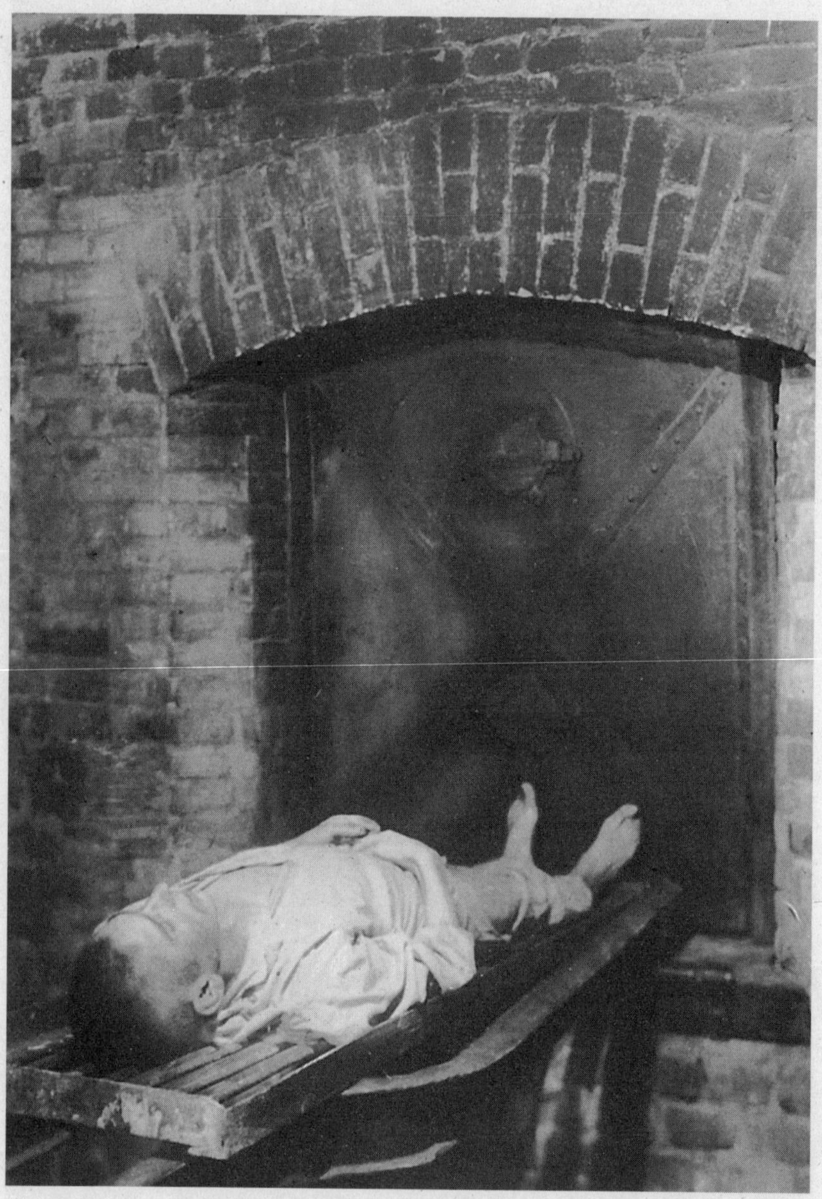

Scientific cremation: a corpse awaiting the furnace at the experimental bathhouse crematorium, Petrograd, 1920

The Siege of Leningrad: survival in 1942. The square in front of St. Isaac's Cathedral has been planted with cabbages, and a watchtower protects the crop.

The Siege of Leningrad: mourners transport their dead on sledges, 1942.

Collecting the dead and wounded from Vosstaniya Square after an artillery attack, Leningrad, October 1941

Corpses at a suburban cemetery during the blockade of Leningrad

Stalin's funeral: the line to view the corpse, Moscow, March 1953

Muscovites weep as the dictator's coffin is placed in the mausoleum in Red Square, March 1953.

Stalin's funeral: the official mourners. Malenkov is in the center of the picture; next to him are Chou-en-lai, Lavrenti Beria, and Nikita Khrushchev.

Commemoration: participants in the fourth All-Union meeting of Pioneers (the children's Communist organization) beneath the statue of Mother Russia at the Piskarevskoe Cemetery, Leningrad, 1960

Exhuming bones:
a Stalinist mass grave
near Voronezh, early 1990s

Religious commemoration: ceremony at Butovo, near Moscow, 1994

Official commemoration: statue at the entrance to the mass grave at Levashovo, October 1997

Private commemoration: a wooden marker after the ceremony in the forest at Sandormokh, October 1997

"After the war," the widow added, "to tell you the truth, the village women took the place of men and horses."[15] In fact, there were about 20 million more women than men in the postwar Soviet Union. In some country areas, women of working age outnumbered men by six to one.[16] A passport system tied them to the land. They could not go and seek a different life elsewhere, companionship, a new routine. Their shape and style, their peasant clothes, the coarseness of their manner and their skin would delight the Cold War satirists of the west. More seriously, H. Kent Geiger, the historian of the Soviet family, wrote of the "mother-centred family," the domineering character of the postwar matriarch. The power of these women, he observed, derived in part from inequality, since "many of the men who died prematurely were the most vigorous and courageous specimens."[17]

In fact, it was not kitchen tyranny but unremitting toil, thankless, changeless work, that shaped the babushkas of the 1970s. Nadezhda Mandelstam had her own view about the women of the Stalin era, and also about mortality among the strong. "At the beginning it was the women who were affected most [by the strain of revolution]," she wrote. "But in the long run they were tougher and the more likely to survive . . . The statistics keep talking about the rise in life expectancy [she was writing in the 1960s], but this must be due to the high proportion of women—we are certainly as tough as the devil!"[18]

Mandelstam's words ring true, but her invocation of the stoicism myth, the property of survivors, overlooks the evidence that some, the ones who could not testify, were crushed. "It was not so bad in the cities," the psychiatrist Valentina Karlovna told me. (Other city women, no younger than their seventies now, still giggle when you ask them what the world was like with so few men. "We shared, of course," they say.[19]) Valentina Karlovna worked in the Leningrad region, and saw women from both the suburbs and the countryside in the 1940s. "In the villages," she said, "they had a very, very difficult time. They stopped being women really. They stopped menstruating, of course, but it wasn't just the hard work or the hunger. It was because they weren't really female anymore. They said they didn't think about it—about sex, or even about their old lives. They just survived. They were not even like nuns. It was very, very hard."[20] Valentina Karlovna's remarks, which others echoed, are a depressing commentary to set beside that other postwar change, the institution of the hero-mother—the state's response to its own casual waste of lives. In the 1940s and 1950s, prizes were given for fecundity, and there were high taxes on childnessness and on divorce. Despite all this, as Alain Blum remarks in his demographic survey, there was no postwar baby boom in the Soviet Union.[21]

Everyone remembers the work, carrying pails of milk and potatoes, sweeping dirt, minding animals. While rural children helped on the struggling farms, the ones who found themselves back in the ruined towns worked with their mothers clearing debris, carrying bricks and rubble, passing buckets hand to hand along the lines of volunteers. That was how they restored the Khreshchatyk, Magdalena Alekseyevna remembered, and how Lyudmila Eduardovna watched them building new squares and theaters in Leningrad. There were so many women doing the hard work that people joked about "cosmetic repairs."[22] Lyudmila Eduardovna herself was working to finish her training. She had no time, she says, for grief. It was the same for Irina Matveyevna, who was already working after school as a part-time telephone operator in her distant new world.

Luisa Karlovna spent her free time at home. Her mother was too ill to go out, and the family earned the money to eat by sticking envelopes. As they sat together, they constantly talked of their father. His "ten years without right of correspondence" came to an end in 1947, and like thousands of others, they were waiting for him to come home. It would be years before they knew for certain that he was dead; that he had, in fact, been shot within hours of his arrest. Yudif Borisovna, freed from her prison camp in 1947, would face the same long wait, the same uncertainty. She and her mother were banned from returning to Moscow and spent their first few yeas of freedom in Kazakhstan. But as soon as she was able to visit the capital, the younger woman made the journey, taking her little son. Her only thought was to find her father, or at least to know where he had died. While Stalin lived the rumors were like whispers, but gradually the individual murmurs and the questions built into a chorus. By the 1950s, there was a real hunger for information, an assembly of voices, not yet in the foreground, not yet, perhaps, consistently audible, not quiet demanding justice (who would dare), but troubling and uneasy as they sought the pieces of the story that would free them from uncertainty and give them, too, the right to grieve.[23]

The deaths and disappearances affected Soviet children, too. Yudif Borisovna's son, like Luisa Karlovna and Irina Matveyevna, was typical of an entire extended generation, the children who grew up, for the most part, without fathers. Some mothers, like Yudif Borisovna herself, taught the children carefully, insisted on their reading, worried till they knew their sums and tables, but others, and especially the ones whose work kept them away from home, had no time to think about the children's minds. Many of the postwar generation were reared, as their own children would be, by their grandmothers, others knew almost no adults at all. It was a wild kind of childhood, inspired by stories of heroism but set in a real world of hunger and hard work. The children who had learned to steal the boots of frozen German dead now had to live amid adults whose usual mood was dour and preoccupied. "What games did we play?" A child of the 1940s, from Kiev province, thought for a moment. "We didn't play much at all," he said, reaching first for the familiar myth. "We had to grow up fast. We were the first generation after the war. No books, no radio. Not till the 1950s. I suppose we played football." But then he remembered something else. "Oh yes," he said. "That's it. We played 'the ravine of terror.' We used to throw grenades into this gully near the town, and wait to see which ones were live." It was a game that cost his best friend both his hands.[24]

Thousands of soldiers did come back, sometimes to their old homes, sometimes to something new, an unexpected family or none. They generally found the pace of civilian life unnerving. Everyone was finding the transition difficult. Recurrent nightmares were part of it.[25] "Even now," a former sniper told Alexiyevich in the 1980s, "we still have nightmares that we are at war, now running for shelter, now changing position. I wake up and find it hard to believe that I am still alive . . . And I don't want to recall it."[26] It was also difficult to shed the reflex of hatred, the search for hidden enemies. Many did not stop fighting even when the guns were silent. There were rumors that another war would soon begin. The police scribbled down whatever whispers they were able to pick up. "I have heard there is already a war in China and Greece," the people were saying. "America and England are involved in it. Sooner or later they will invade the Soviet Union." Others were certain that "the first columns of wounded have already been seen in Simferopol."[27] For a few months, the first of postwar life, imaginary wars like this were probably more attractive, and must certainly have seemed more natural, than the dreary burden of peace that people were about to shoulder.

"The soldiers had become grown-ups, you see," the son of one explained to me. "At first, when they got back, they would bang on the tables with their fists and demand that the administration got things done. They would yell about nonpayments for work and that kind of thing. But gradually even they were brought into line." When I asked where all the fire had gone, the speaker shrugged. "They told jokes," he said. "And they drank a lot. There was a lot of *samogon* [home-distilled vodka] in the villages in those days."[28] There was also crime, mostly theft, and in some places, banditry, terrorism, and bitter armed resistance against enforced Soviet rule. But the will to change the world would soon begin to break. "Some got married, others joined the Party," said another survivor. "We knew no other life."[29]

This bleak fatalism was an unexpected postscript to the optimism of 1943 and 1944. Alexander Werth described Moscow in 1944 as a place of "frivolity and escapism." The Russian people liked to think that life would soon be easier," he wrote, "and that Russia could 'relax' after the war." People started to hope that life would "become pleasant." The writer Vsevolod Vyshnevsky predicted that "there will be much coming and going, with a lot of contacts with the west."[30] Soldiers talked endlessly of the postwar world as they marched back from Berlin, and those who waited for them also had their dreams. Evacuees talked wistfully of home. They peopled it with the relatives that many of them would never see again. In Leningrad, and in the crowded cities of Central Asia to which so many had fled, there were tens of thousands whose imaginations could get little further than the thought of having enough to eat. Whatever the fantasy, however, life was going to be good—it had to be, after the price that they had paid.

Optimism like this turned bitter as the peace began to harden. "When we were in the army we often talked about what life was going to be like after the war," recalled the journalist Galin. "We did not always realise how great the destruction had been, or the scale of the work that we were going to have to do in order to heal the wounds the Germans had inflicted on us."[31] The nationalist writer Victor Astaf'ev added a piercing note of self-reproach. "The most painful thing," to him, "was the realisation that, because we were exhausted by the war, because of the strain of the postwar years, we were not going to be able to maintain the high level of moral development which we had achieved during the war, and which we had created for ourselves, in spite of the soullessness and obstructiveness of our own immoral and criminal leadership."[32]

The actions of this leadership indeed defy belief. A postwar mood which has been described as "spontaneous de-Stalinization" was vigorously crushed. Among the prominent victims were the war leaders themselves, including Marshal Zhukov, whose popularity was deemed to be a threat to Stalin's own. Remembrance ceremonies themselves were curbed, muted. Stalin required allegiance in the present, not a wistful service to the past.[33] The repression of former prisoners of war, minority ethnic groups, suspected dissidents, partisans, misfits, and excessively efficient local bosses was followed by two new campaigns, the targets of which were mainly intellectuals and Jews. "Of course I lost my job," said the former Communist and former soldier Semyen Pavlovich. "I was a Jew, and it was the 1940s. That's what they said at the time.

You are a Jew. It was enough in those days." While he had been away at the front, a patriotic volunteer, his whole family had been murdered by the Nazis. What he came home to was suspicion, prejudice, and a shattered career.[34]

War heroes were one kind of target, hero cities another. The people of Leningrad had put together a museum of their ordeal, "The Defense of Leningrad," which included documentary collections, photographs, and other memorials to the city's epic siege. It was closed in 1949. It would be another decade before a new museum was permitted, this time a bland and modest one, described by a blockade historian as "utterly inadequate."[35] The people's most distinguished poets would suffer, too. Anna Akhmatova was among the targets of the new inquisitorial mood, attacked, in 1946, despite her loyalty and the work that she had done to maintain popular morale. She was, wrote Andrei Zhdanov, "a nun or a whore, or rather, a nun and a whore, who combines harlotry with prayer. Akhmatova's poetry is utterly remote from the people."[36] The standing ovations were forgotten, at least officially, and some of the haunting poetry all but lost. The message to Leningrad's intelligentsia was clear. By 1948, most of them had at least one friend who was under an official cloud. A good many intellectuals prepared their suitcases again, and kept them ready, with a couple of changes of underwear and a toothbrush, for the night the black van parked outside.[37]

The backbone of the new society, its basic pool of support, would come from a group that might, despite Marxism-Leninism, be called the middle class. Postwar technicians, teachers, government inspectors, doctors, middle managers, and clerks would be the beneficiaries of what Vera Dunham has called the "Big Deal."[38] What Stalinism offered to these people, if they managed to avoid the camps, was a comfortable life, a genteel decency—hot water, sentimental poetry, and coordinated soft furnishings—in exchange for political passivity and dissociation. While the Big Deal held, while they were doing well and politics was other people's work, these people would have no objection to a little nicely balanced censorship. They did not mind when the streets were suddenly cleared of amputees; they did not argue about intellectual freedom or the ethics of forced labor. As Dunham explains, the regime appealed to this group's self-interests, working with its representatives as with a partner, "involving his prestige, involving his pride in his work, the satisfaction derived from his professionalism, and from his apolitical conformism."[39] The old antipathy between us and them, between the good, conformist citizen and the rest, the outsiders, the criminals and dissidents, was back in prominence again.

This aspect of the postwar mood drew heavily on hypocrisy. One of the few professions that saw a steady increase in salary in the 1940s was that of censor. The context for such censorship was set by fear, pervasive fear, like bad weather, never really lifting though it was not always noticed or remarked. But there was no shortage of accomplices for the work of postwar expurgation. Consider, for example, the problem of the nursery story. The Russian tradition is as rich as any, and its themes are typically lurid—cruelty, torture, mutilation, misogyny, and murder feature prominently, as does that universal archetype, the wicked stepmother. All this, by 1949, would come to seem deplorable. Fairy stories had become a threat to social cohesion. A group of folklorists—academic researchers, antiquarians, and case-hardened ethnographers—gathered in Moscow on a November afternoon and set about rewriting them.

It was ironic that a group of people whose lives had been devoted to the study of popular culture should talk about reshaping it. "What we need," one of them said, "is a folklore that will nurture a love for our motherland, a love of work, which will help to build a sense of manliness, resilience." Others agreed. Fables that described "successful immorality," such as Emelio the Fool and Ivan-Durak, and stories that featured "gratuitous or excessive cruelty," such as Vasilisa Prekrasnaya and the ever-popular Baba-Yaga, were listed for censorship. The suggestion that fate was preordained and could not be avoided (a very deeply held idea in Russian culture, and a lifeline for survivors of catastrophe) was described as "an ideological mistake." Someone did ask what kind of child would read the bland result of so much well-intentioned writing (there was an awkward silence in the room). But on one point even that person could agree. The evil stepmother would have to go.[40] With 26 million dead, too many children were already having to get used to the real thing.

A decade later, in 1960, another group of editors, this time the board of the respected journal *Znamya* [*the Banner*], met to discuss an offering from Vasili Grossman. The meeting began with a speech by its chairman, Kozhevnikov, who chose to set his men the task of helping Grossman with his "ideological crisis," a crisis which, they all agreed, had driven the author to commit "a deep political error." The error in question was a manuscript, the draft of the war novel *Life and Fate.* Anyone who has read this will know that it is one of the most brilliantly observed and searing accounts of the Second World War in any language, and certainly one of the best in Russian. But Kozhevnikov and his men were not keen to publish it. *Life and Fate* did not observe the niceties and conventions of the postwar patriotic novel.

"This is not a book about great deeds," a member of the board whined to his colleagues. "It is not about the historic victory of our troops at Stalingrad, the home front, or our fighting spirit . . . It is about unbridled cruelty, meanness, and duplicity. Even the most honorable characters have to dissemble, cheat and generally play 'an exhaustingly complex game' in order to avoid betrayal and repression." Grossman, they considered, ought to have known better. He was, after all, unlike the people who now judged his writing, a veteran of Stalingrad himself. The plump men in their suits disliked the way that he insisted on discussing cowardice and fear (they wanted heroism), they objected to the fact that he occasionally portrayed death, and none could credit his account of lust on the eve of battle.

Grossman never saw his great work in print. When he died, in 1964, he still believed that every copy of it had been destroyed. The editors of *Znamya* told him that his characters "lacked human warmth," that they were "devoid of human feelings: friendship, love, and care for children." They accused him of suggesting that "in our country, during the war as well as before it, a totalitarian system was established, anti-humanitarian and inimical to the human spirit, obliging the people to live in fear, to behave immorally towards each other, to betray each other, to lie, deceive, abandon wives and children." One wonders what they felt, the citizens of precisely such a world, as they condemned the book. It was "not historically objective," they concluded. "It is a great pity to have to say all this, but principles are principles."[41]

Hypocrisy is seldom an attractive habit, and it is tempting, with the arrogance of hindsight, simply to condemn it. But the postwar euphemisms and heroic myths did serve a purpose, easing some of the awkward pains of adaptation, grief, and guilt. Just as traditional laments evade the blood and bone, repetitively turning through the loops of sentiment until they take a formal, manageable shape, so kitsch war poetry and film created a consensual world, a fantasy of survival and endurance. It was a collective escape, a voluntary anesthetic, and the people who remember it believe that it worked.

Soviet survivors of the war do not remember trauma. They do not see themselves as victims but as heroes. Their buoyancy, it is true, depended on a steady concentration, collective encouragement, and a refusal to look closely at the murky details of their recent past. There had been casualties, the Leningrad doctors knew it, and although, as they explained, the ones whose "nervous systems were the weakest" had generally been the first to give up and to die, there still were many people (no one knows how many) whose lives were haunted by the images and sounds of war.[42] The state itself made some of these survivors disappear, exiling them, interning them in clinics for the long-term sick. But coercion, the pressure to keep going, to stay alive and make the world again, was something that neither state nor medical professionals monopolized.

The pressure came from several directions. The collective tradition was fundamental, and so was the habit of euphemism and silence. The enormous burden of work was also part of it—no one who talks about postwar life neglects to mention that there was no time for introspection. But the result was a society in which the secrets were innumerable—stories of hunger, theft, and cannibalism, memories of the disappeared, tales of wartime slaughter, the bullet in the comrade's back, of rape and butchery across civilian Prussia—while silence was the overwhelming rule. Some people say they always talked within the family. "Mother told us everything," said Luisa Karlovna. "We always talked about it," said another, younger, woman, the granddaughter of a Bolshevik intellectual. "We would sit in the kitchen in the evenings and remember." But not everyone had a family, and many did not have a kitchen, either.

Postwar Russia was a land of migrants. The 1940s and 1950s were years of urban expansion. Younger people had their papers stamped and moved to the industrial towns, many returning soldiers stayed on in the cities if they could. There was no family, for them, with whom to share the tales, and there was little private space for talk. The majority of city-based Russians now lived in communal apartments, *kommunal'ki.* These consisted of several rooms, in each of which might live a whole family—three generations—or else a group of ill-assorted strangers. Any facilities, including kitchens and lavatories, were shared between the whole group. The walls were thin. Some sounds—chatter, singing, radio, the imprecations of a sullen drunk—were so common that no one really noticed them. But hushed voices and tears, any authentic words, the confidences that make friendships and potentially make factions, these were another matter. The police were interested. Gossip always carried fast.

The effects of this silence varied. War veterans talk as if they scarcely noticed it, especially since the clamor of official or at least permitted remembrance drowned it out. But the victims of other kinds of loss have other tales, tales that it has only been possible—let alone advantageous—to tell since glasnost. At the time, most of them, like Anna Timofeyevna, chose to talk of the war as the most vivid moment in their lives, a celebration of collective effort. But some—like Anna Timofeyevna's mother—took a secret, lonely pride in what they saw as their special destiny. Their isolation, their sense of uniqueness, left them with little other means of understanding their own stories.

For everyone whose life the state had touched, the most effective strategy was to bury and ignore the past. There would be loneliness, but it was best endured. Anna Timofeyevna got on with her music. Other former kulaks, like Nina Antonovna, a pediatrician whom I met in St. Petersburg, made equally successful new careers. Their lives depended, now, on their ability to conceal the truth about their childhoods. Nina Antonovna married for a second time at the end of the 1940s (her first husband had been killed at the front). She told her new husband nothing.[43] Luisa Karlovna told me that when her brother had admitted on an application form that his father had been repressed, he had found that his path to university was blocked forever. She herself decided to dress up the truth when she answered official questions. "I always put that Father had died of a cerebral hemorrhage," she said.

Of course, it was not quite enough merely to hold your tongue. Ironically and sometimes cruelly, most people had to connive with the official story that life was getting better, happier, and more prosperous. "I know of no other country, where a man can breathe more freely," ran the popular song. Since they had to go on singing it, perhaps it was better if people did not look too closely for the secrets that their neighbors were keeping to themselves. For some, the endless repetition, like a mantra, worked. They started to believe the fable. They were the ones who took the high road, waving banners and saluting the Soviet achievement every May. But there were others, mostly the men, who took to drink. On average, households were spending as much as a fifth of their income on alcohol by the early 1960s. The poor, proportionately, spent more—perhaps as much as 40 percent.[44] State-produced vodka came in a foil-topped bottle. No one planned to keep some for another day.

Although they strained to sing the anthems, and although the monuments they built got larger as the years went by, the people all remember feeling guilt. Deaths for which they cannot atone haunt soldiers' memories. Aleksei Grigor'evich was in a field hospital behind the lines on the day his best friend was killed. The loss alone would have been bad enough, but the sense that he might have helped, even if all he had done had been to witness his friend's death, has weighed on him ever since. Another person smiled when I mentioned guilt. "Of course," she said. "It's in my genes, isn't it? In all our Russian genes." In one of his last lectures about the war, the historian and ex-soldier Mikhail Gefter described his own guilt by quoting a popular song. "I know," it begins, "that I am not to blame / For the fact that other people did not return from battle." But the doubt which, as Gefter put it, "tortures our memory" is "that I could, but did not, save them."[45]

Guilt like this was so widespread that, like grief and silence, it became as unremarkable as autumn rain. It was no less sharp for being so common. "I said I would talk about myself," a former dissident answered when I asked whether he had mourned for his aunt. She had been murdered by the Nazis, but there would be no *kaddish* for her. "I understand your question perfectly," the old man said. "But the most important thing for me is that I was arrested."[46]

Masha's family were also Jews. They were untypical because they were peasants. Unusually, therefore, they survived the Nazi occupation of Belarus by several months. But eventually, inevitably, someone betrayed them. They were forced to take to the woods. What happened next is unclear. Both parents were shot, the mother in full view of the daughter. But Masha is vague about her own survival, and she contradicts herself when she tries to describe her escape. It was impossible, as we talked, to clarify the details. If I asked a question that she did not like, Masha, a determined woman in her sixties, would change the subject. We talked about death and loss, but we also covered yoga, chocolate, and the price of new spectacles. Finally, we touched upon the issue of Jewish identity. "I know now," Masha told me, "that the Jews were responsible for killing Jesus Christ. And their religion says you must take an eye for an eye. That is why I am an Orthodox now." We shared another pot of tea, and I returned, gently, to the one person whose fate she had left unresolved in her account. "What happened to your brother?" I asked. For the first time in our three-hour conversation, she burst into tears. We did not speak of it again.[47]

In 1998 I was invited to hear the stories of a group of middle-aged men from the Kiev region. None of them had been in combat—they had been too young—but all were invalids of war. My host, Stepan Ustimovich, had been blinded at the age of seven, in 1951, in an accident. The hand he offered readily in greeting had no fingers. Another of the men who came to talk had no hands at all. Like thousands of other children they had been injured by the debris of the fighting. They had been playing in woods, perhaps; they had picked up a strange piece of metal in the dust; they had found a gun or a grenade. Ukraine is still a deadly place. In the first six months of 1997 alone, thirteen hundred unexploded bombs, shells, and mines were discovered in suburbs, woods, and fields. In any five-year period, Stepan Ustimovich told me, up to a quarter of a million Second World War explosives still turn up in Ukraine's soil.[48]

While Soviet propaganda bruited the themes of reconstruction, socialism, victory, and hard work, the injury and dying were still going on. As ever, there was little sympathy for victims, little public knowledge of the casualty rates.

"They said we wanted to avoid the army," one of Stepan Ustimovich's comrades told me. He was accused, a child not in his teens, of deliberate self-mutilation. "They punished us by trying to force us to live outside the city," Stepan Ustimovich said. His own story was especially poignant. His father, himself an invalid from the First World War, had decided to write to Stalin when the boy, his only child, was blinded. He was illiterate, so he had to get some help from an official of the local Soviet. The man and his son waited, and eventually an official letter arrived from Moscow that neither of them could read. They took it to the Soviet again. Stepan Ustimovich now believes that the letter offered them a thousand rubles to pay for his treatment. "But because father was an illiterate and all that," he says, "they . . . only gave him two hundred rubles." There was not enough money to pay for the operation that might have made him see. It was no good begging, no good spinning stories about need. Stepan Ustimovich learned to read braille. He now has two degrees in philosophy and has made a career in Ukraine as a journalist.

This story is not simply yet another tale of postwar callousness, an echo of the unkind mood that Grossman and Brodsky had observed in Leningrad in 1945. It was not merely that the people had grown used to corpses and to other people's tears. The second half of the 1940s was difficult because the hardship and, indeed, the hunger, did not stop. There was a continuing need to keep in mind the lessons of survival you had learned—a flexible approach to property, for instance, and a careful husbanding of food. The two years, 1946 and 1947, would see another famine.

Immediately after the war, collective farmers worked in exchange for food. The rations were always meager. "We get 200 grammes of bread for a work day [*trudoden'*]," wrote a peasant from the Ukrainian town of Kamenets-Podolsk in the spring of 1946. "We have been getting by without bread for ages now. We don't know what is going to happen, but we cannot go on like this for long." "A lot of people are hungry," wrote another. "There aren't even any potatoes, and people are going to the fields to work without food."[49] Stepan Ustimovich was three in 1947, but he remembers what the hunger meant. "At first we went without bread and ate potatoes," he told me. "Then we ate leaves. And then we ate the weeds."[50]

The spring came late in 1946. The ground was still frozen, in many places, well into May. But the lengthening days brought little hope. June and July were unusually hot and dry. The crop in the fields was thin, the wheat scorched and the potatoes so small, where they grew at all, that people began, in July, to talk of a real famine. "We don't want to starve to death," wrote a peasant from the Kiev region. "It is going to be like 1933." "It's still summer," another complained, "so what is it going to be like this winter? I survived the whole war, I'm still alive, but now it seems I am to die of hunger."[51]

Just after Christmas, a woman from the Ukrainian province of Poltava wrote to her husband, who was living two days' journey from his family, in Bryansk. "Please ask your bosses to give you some time off or at least to get some kind of document for me," she begged, "so that they will take the children at the orphanage. The children have already swollen up, and I don't know what's going to happen to them. My own arms have swollen . . . I cannot carry flour any more . . . Lena is especially swollen, but we are all ill. It's already worse at the markets than it was in 1933, everything is expensive. I beg you for the last time, find a way out for your own family . . . We are dying like dogs, cold, hungry and barefoot."[52]

It was to be a famine that affected the industrial north as well as the agricultural regions of the south and Ukraine. It would last for eighteen months and account for tens of thousands of lives. Although the state would play it down, denying reality once again, this famine was less brutal, in many respects, than that of 1933. The government's response to it was certainly less callous. The war, in fact, had made some local administrators more sensitive, respectful, perhaps, of the widows and fathers of men beside whom they had fought. Some collective farm chairmen kept back grain and other supplies during the requisition season in 1946, and though many were arrested, the punishment they faced was often more lenient than expected. There were even attempts to secure foreign aid for the starving through the United Nations, the Red Cross, and other charitable organizations.[53] But the 1947 famine was more than a mere postscript to the war. Death from starvation is always terrible, and the memory of 1933 was still fresh. Hunger inspired panic and despair. Once again, it seemed, the government was going to take its grain and butter from the villages while children swelled and died. The war had solved nothing.

By February 1947, the echoes of 1933 were everywhere: in the haunted faces of the children, in the despair of the mourners as they dragged the corpses to the pit, and always, when the last dogs and sparrows had been shot and skinned, in the unaccustomed silence. "We ate the animals," remembered one survivor, "we cut up the horses. When they were all eaten, we hunted gophers, hares and sparrows . . . In the spring of 1947, when the swans came back, we started to eat them, we boiled them with bran and grits."[54] The weakness followed, the dysentery and the first deaths. "A great many people are dying," a woman wrote that spring, "and now they take them to the cemeteries and leave them there. The local officials have made bigger graves, common graves, and they have started burying people in them all together."[55]

"Grandfather died in our house, although he was not old—only sixty," remembered one old man. "But there were families in the village where everyone died. The people were too weak to bury the bodies of their relatives, and sometimes the corpses would lie for days."[56] Stepan Ustimovich's mother died. "Most people survived it somehow," he told me. "They made porridge with husks and peelings; they ate cats, even. But mostly they got through. But Mother, well, she caught a cold, and there weren't any doctors. And then there were complications, and it got worse. I think it was February—I was three—February 1947. I remember the last days, how I was still sitting on her lap, and then I remember the funeral."[57] In some villages, mortality was a lot higher than Stepan Ustimovich remembers. The survivors left, just as their parents had done less than fifteen years before.[58]

Yet again, but this time in a land where scientists were working on a new atomic bomb, their hunger drove some people to cannibalism. On 19 February 1947, a bag containing human remains was discovered under a bridge near Kiev. The body was identified as that of a youth of sixteen or seventeen, but all that was left was his head, and "both his legs, from which all the meat had been cut with a sharp knife." Three weeks later, a woman was arrested for killing her seven-year-old daughter. She and the child's older sister had already eaten most of the corpse. At about the same time, it was discovered that another woman had killed, butchered, and salted her seventy-year-old husband.[59]

Beneath the euphemism and concealment, then, beyond the world of Stalin's middle class, there was a struggle going on about the basic means to live. You need no theory of long-term brutalization to explain the desperation in the villages in 1947. In public, certainly, there was a facade of decorous grief, mild envy of dead heroes, and good, solid stoicism. But the land of the censored nursery rhyme was also a place where little boys played football in the streets with the skulls of unburied soldiers. On summer nights, too, their fathers stamped on glowing cigarettes and crept out to the silent battlefields in search of necessary plunder. Even in the 1970s there were corpses with gold teeth. Their uniforms had rotted, but there might be metal crests and buttons to collect, and even, on a really good night, a handgun that would work if you could get it clean.[60]

It was a single death rather than a mass catastrophe that punctured the postwar public fantasy. "It was a cold wintry day," wrote Ehrenburg. "To keep myself occupied and ward off unhappy thoughts for a few hours I was working on a translation of Villon when suddenly Ivan Petrovich the caretaker came in: 'They've just announced on the radio that Stalin's ill, paralyzed. His life's in danger.' I remember my journey to Moscow. There was a lot of snow. Children were rolling in the snowdrifts. I tried to think out what would happen to us all now but was quite unable to. Like so many of my compatriots at that moment, I was in a state of shock."[61]

Everyone remembers the grief, the apprehension, and the public weeping. "What's going to happen now?" people asked, "isn't it terrible, how will we live?"[62] There were even rumors of impending civil war. But what distinguished Stalin's death from Lenin's was something else. Ehrenburg was walking home along Gorky Street the night after the funeral when, as he recalls, "I suddenly stopped. A simple thought had struck me: I did not know whether things would be worse or better, but they were going to be different."[63] The poet Boris Slutsky put it more gracefully: "The time for circuses is over," he told his friends. "A break for smoking has been granted to all those who were storming heaven."[64]

Stalin's health had been failing for some time. No one had dared to plan for his death, however. When he collapsed, on the night of 1 March 1953, the gang of politicians whose lives depended on him did now know how to react, and there are rumors that the paralyzed leader was left to die where he had fallen, on the carpet in his study. Some people think he was poisoned. Whatever the truth, it would be four days before the group of doctors at his dacha definitely pronounced him dead. Only then did the newspapers begin to break the story, informing their readers that Stalin had suffered a stroke, that his pulse was weak and rapid, and that his condition was deemed to be serious.[65] He had been dead for at least forty-eight hours before the truth was printed.

The first announcements were characteristically banal. "The immortal name of STALIN will always live in the hearts of the Soviet people," the official notice said.[66] The embalmers were already at work. Stalin's body, like Lenin's, would not be allowed to rot. His successors, however, were less enthusiastic about his political legacy. When Lenin died, the priority had been to prove that his burden would be shouldered by true heirs. No one was really going to take up Stalin's mantle in the same way. There was a wind of change in the air that March. The problem was to temper it, and at the same time to exploit but contain the nation's grief.

In every town and city in the land the crowds began to gather in the squares. At first, they were silent, listening to the radio news on crackling loudspeakers.

Men and women wept, their shock giving way to bereavement and confusion. The crowds became hysterical. Mass demonstrations would continue until the day of the funeral, and in several cities, including Moscow and Tbilisi, the capital of Stalin's own republic of Georgia, hundreds of people were crushed to death. "Anyone who says they did not cry when they heard about Stalin's death is lying," one woman insisted to me. "Everyone was in tears. We did not know what was going to happen next. We had never known anything different."

Stalin lay in state in the Hall of Columns for three days. A guard of honor stood over his corpse, and solemn music played, just as it had for Lenin, as the silent mourners filed past. Hundreds of thousands of people descended on Moscow in the space of a few hours. The chief mourners wore suits. Few peasants in felt boots got to Moscow in the 1950s, and the party's zealots had given up their leather jackets for broadcloth. The rest dressed for the cold, some of them in the furs—fox, dog, bear, or rabbit—that they had cobbled together for themselves in the lean years since the dictator came to power. The most incongruous figures in the crowd were the priests. Most of Moscow's hierarchy turned out for a solemn leave-taking, aware, no doubt, of the strategic importance of attending this dictator's wake. There were reserved places in the line, tickets and signed passes, for the elite. But the rest would wait, as always, in a line that stretched for miles, snaking around the icy streets like a dark scar.

The sight for which they waited would awe them all. The Hall of Columns was decked outside with a giant poster of the dead leader. Mountains of wreaths, most of them bound in scarlet, lay at the entrance, and there were more inside, by the catafalque. The Central Committee's own tribute said simply, TO THE LEADER AND TEACHER OF THE COMMUNIST PARTY AND THE SOVIET PEOPLE, J. V. STALIN. Others echoed older slogans: PROLETARIANS OF ALL COUNTRIES, UNITE! Branches of evergreens, red roses and lilies gleamed in the dim electric light. Everything appeared to be in order, though there were one or two visitors, connoisseurs, by now, of the iconography of the public corpse, who criticized the finer details. "My dear Central Committee," wrote a Muscovite visitor, "do not be angry, but in the name of all that is holy please rearrange Comrade Stalin's hands, or he'll look awful. It's not me who's noticed this, it's everyone. I have no idea who can have thought of doing it the way you have."[67] There is no evidence that this letter received a reply, and the details of Stalin's embalming remain secret. The corpse's hands hung impotently at its sides for as long as it shared the mausoleum with Lenin. What happened to them while it was being surreptitiously removed and buried a few years later is anyone's guess.

Stalin was buried, then, or rather, displayed under glass, with appropriate ceremony, on 9 March. Overnight, the name of Stalin, cut in marble, was added to Lenin's on the facade of the mausoleum on Red Square. Bands played Tchaikovsky, Beethoven, Chopin, and Grieg (the *Internationale,* with its call to universal revolution, had been downgraded during the war in deference to the Soviet Union's capitalist allies). The solemn procession, which included such unlikely mourners as Bulganin, Malenkov, and the odious police chief Beria, shuffled dutifully across the Moskva River from the Hall of Columns to the Kremlin. The coffin itself was conveyed on a horse-drawn carriage. Photographs of the cortege show a well-nourished but anxious-looking driver and a posse of prosperous-looking men in winter coats and warm hats, most of whom retain an air of inscrutable dignity. Beria, characteristically, frequently appears to be assessing the credentials of the photographer rather than concentrating on his country's loss. But no one in the official procession really betrays much emotion. To see that, you would have had to look back at the crowd, at the women in headscarves and shabby overcoats, the children sheltering beside them, and the scattering of tired-looking men, for once without cigarettes, all of them weeping or silent.

The country's new leaders, Malenkov, Beria, and Molotov in particular, mounted the podium and addressed the crowd, just as their predecessors had done in 1924. But there was something insincere about the speeches. Malenkov promised that the Communist Party would continue its historic work, but he said relatively little about Stalin himself. He stressed that the people should remain vigilant, and assured them that their material well-being was still in safe hands.[68] A similar announcement had accompanied the first bulletins about the leader's death a few days earlier.[69] Molotov was more visibly upset; Beria, whose speech promised to uphold the new constitution, decidedly cool. In private, indeed, he was already cursing the dictator's memory.[70] Not everyone gets the funeral they deserve, but the emotion on display at Stalin's was suitably hard to read, as well as justly cynical.

The leaders' speeches were inscrutable, but the outpourings of the Soviet people were surreal. There was a real panic in the air, uncertainty about the future, and uneasiness about the future of the past. The workers in a Moscow rubber factory, for example, agreed that it was "hard, inexpressibly hard" because "the person who gave happy lives to millions of people—the leader, the teacher, the friend of the workers, has gone, the greatest of the great men of all times and nations . . . Our party has been orphaned, the Soviet people has been orphaned, the working people of the whole world have been orphaned."[71] "I have no strength and no words in which to express the sorrow, pain, and the bitterness which have gripped our whole people and the whole of progressive humanity because of the passing of our dear, our greatly beloved leader, friend, teacher, father, and regimental commander," wrote another impassioned citizen. "Stalin is no more," began another, "we no longer have our beloved and great party leader, the friend and teacher of the whole of progressive humanity. His ardent heart has ceased to beat." Not to be outdone, Soviet youth produced declarations of its own. "The dear name of J. V. STALIN is among the first words which any infant in the Soviet land ever learns to pronounce," averred a representative of the Young Communist League. A group of schoolchildren vowed to honor the memory of the world's greatest ever human being by dedicating themselves, as he had ordered, to "learning, learning, learning."[72]

The most common outlet for the people's mourning was the workplace funeral meeting. These began on 6 March and were held in virtually every office, collective farm, and factory in the land. The nation's typewriters were busy every afternoon. "We, the workers and engineering technical staff of the Moscow gelatine factory . . . We, the workers, women workers, engineers, technical staff, and administrators of the Sosenskii concrete works . . . We, the collective farmers of the Stalin collective farm . . ." Each resolution had to end with a promise. "We resolve," a group of health administrators agreed, to "make it our task every day to improve our people's medical services, since we must care for people in the same way that Stalin himself used to care for them."[73] When the typist had wiped away his last tear, resolutions like this were checked, stamped, and immediately passed to the relevant office at Agitation and Propaganda. Reading them now, it is difficult to separate grief from hysteria. It is also impossible to test them for sincerity. "In these days the people wept in unison and were not ashamed to weep in public," one resolution explained. "But our ineffable love for the great STALIN has dried the tears in our very eyes."[74] To some extent, it was where you were that mattered. "Granny read the announcement in the paper," a woman from Kazakhstan told me. "She just said: Stalin's dead. And a good thing, too."[75]

The problem was that Stalin was a war hero. His efforts on behalf of the people had been untiring, they said. "Comrade Stalin gave up his whole life, and all his blood, drop by drop, in the service of the people," declared one factory director.[76] Commemorating such sacrifice was not going to be easy, but officials knew that they had at least to say something. The Soviet people had been deprived of authentic words for years. In desperation now they grasped for the usual lifeless substitutes. A steelworker told his comrades to "unite more closely around the Central Committee of the Communist Party . . . to follow the path which leads to Communism in our country by the route which was indicated and worked out by J. V. Stalin . . . The memory of the Great Stalin will live in the heart of every Soviet person, and that memory will not die over the centuries." Someone else told his audience to "guard the unity of the party, to educate communists to be active fighters for the implementation of the party's policies and resolutions, to educate communists and all working people in the spirit of political vigilance, in the spirit of uncompromising and resolute struggle against internal and external enemies."[77]

Expressions of individual grief also poured into the Party's files. In the weeks after the funeral, citizens wrote to the Central Committee and to their local Party leaders with their suggestions for the future. Though some of their letters contained advice about policy ("Comrade Malenkov, since you are now our beloved leader, we hope and trust that you will follow the right path"[78]), the majority offered proposals about commemoration. The most conservative proposed things like the mass planting of trees, the creation of new coins bearing Stalin's silhouette, the renaming of Red Square, and the permanent designation of a five-minute silence on the anniversary of his death. But a more nauseating set of correspondence related to the idea of a pantheon, something that would really put dead Soviet leaders on the map, a building grander than Shchusev's famous granite cube. "I am neither an architect nor a building engineer," begins one letter, "but my proposal comes straight from my heart and soul." The eccentric hyperbole that followed was also typical, as was the suggestion that a "fountain of tears" should play in perpetuity outside what would become the nation's grandest building.

The pantheon was not just a tomb. Nor was it merely a monument to Stalin, "the greatest of all great human beings." The writers who offered their advice all seem to have grasped that Stalin's death marked the end of the foundation period of Soviet Communism. This sense of ending, in fact, was often the real reason for their dismay. Many of them proposed, therefore, that the building should express the completion of a historical sequence. "The foundation of the pantheon should consist of a square of green-coloured mineral," begins one proposal, "which will represent primitive society, where people only used the things which could be gathered directly from nature." The next two levels, in black and gray granite, respectively represented slave society and feudalism, while capitalism was best commemorated in a red-veined gray marble. The ultimate level, however, "in dark red marble, will reflect the happy life in our country. This will culminate in the highest square of all, on which will stand the column I have drawn here for you."[79] Instead of prayers or masses, the solemn ceremony to be enacted at this building's heart was to take the form of daily lectures on Marx's theory of history and the era of Lenin-Stalin.[80]

Architecturally, the designs were unimaginative. Most of them followed the usual pseudo-classical prescriptions—columns, pediments, raised atria. As one person put it, the pantheon "should look like the Central Soviet Army Theatre, only on a larger scale." At least half the recommendations also advocated that a globe should be included in the design, usually on the grounds that Communism represented the future of all mankind. "I want you to build a globe of the whole world, a big one," wrote a peasant from the Leningrad region, "and I want there to be images of J. V. [Stalin] and of you, G. M. [Malenkov] on it so that this globe can show the great project of building Communism and the future heaven on earth."[81] Perhaps there was no need to stop at one planet. "The second section of my Pantheon is dedicated to the cosmos," wrote a Muscovite. "Here will be displayed the life and development of our universe, our solar system and our earth according to the principles of Marxist-Leninist dialectics."[82]

The pantheon was a cathedral, then, and like any other it was to be founded on bones. It was also a memorial to the eternal life that selected representatives of the Communist Party of the Soviet Union were destined to enjoy. "The whole world must see that Stalin lives and will live until the full realization of Communism," declares one letter. In another, cosmism reemerges in a proposal to reanimate the dead leader's brain and vital organs. But popular science had not conquered religion, and beliefs more ancient than Christianity also continued to inspire the zealots of dialectical materialism. Earth, for example, the central element in Russian funerary culture, was to be used in several of the pantheon projects. Some people suggested that visitors should bring a handful of their native soil to the site; others, that it should be built with colored sand and stone from each of the Union republics, "because J. V. Stalin is buried not only in Moscow but also everywhere in the earth of our land." A nostalgic Slavist from Ukraine even proposed that a traditional burial mound, or *kurgan,* should be raised in Red Square, and that the soil of every republic should be added to it for generations to come.

The pantheon was never built. Like the Palace of Soviets, whose site it was due to share, it remained a grandiloquent dream. Their letters are all that is left of the people's fantasy. They illustrate the confusion of the late Stalin era, the uncertainty about death and the afterlife, about religion, science, and atheism, that a generation of contradictory propaganda and inconsistent dogma had left behind. There is that fascination with science, that faith in Marxism, and that determination to build a proletarian state, world revolution—all things that inspired whole cohorts of young Soviets in the great age of socialist construction. But there is also fear, superstition, magic, and a desperate clinging to personalities and heroes, the legacy of an older world of czars and saints, the shadow of an absent god. The pantheon proposals are a scrapbook of unfinished plans and hopes, stills from the spiritual discourse of a generation whose universe has long since disappeared.

When their own turn came to die, the people's ceremonies would be drearily functional. It has been estimated that more than 60 percent of people wanted some from of religious ritual at their funerals in these years, but there were not enough priests to go round. Indeed, there were so few of them that most believers had to read the prayers for themselves. If they could not read, or if there was no text, they recited whatever they could remember. In the villages, it was the women who prayed, and the women, too, who threw themselves across the graves in eerie, timeless cycles of lament.[83]

City funerals were less anarchic, at least. But the people who attended them remember drab and empty ceremonies. Eternal life had been abolished for the masses, so the mourners could only really focus on their work. If they were lucky, there was an orchestra to play Communist anthems, or perhaps a relative with the self-possession to stand and read a poem—Konstantin Simonov's *Wait for Me* was still as popular as ever. For some, this Communist ritual, if it addressed their beliefs, was more than adequate. Some elderly people still ask for it. "Bury me with an orchestra," one old man said to his granddaughter, a friend, in 1998. "I do not want your prayers." But unbelievers—those who were not Communists—found the heart of the ceremony dull. It consisted of a recitation of the dead person's contribution; his work, his war record, his party activities.[84] Each colleague would add a sentence or two—the meetings were tediously repetitious—and then they would shuffle awkwardly past the coffin in a last farewell.

Only the earth retained its magic. There were people who kept cups of it at home to scatter on their graves. Some brought it from their villages, others stooped to gather a handful as they wept, bareheaded, beside a mound somewhere in Kursk, the Volga, or ravaged Belarus. Families without prayer were reunited in dust and clay. For some believers, the power of this ritual was so vivid that "funerals by correspondence" were instituted. A priest could bless a cup of earth and return it by post. Well over half—perhaps, in some places, as many as 80 percent—of rural funerals included earth like this by the late 1960s.[85] It was enough, in those days, that the prayers had been said at all.

"Even if we did not know where the bodies were we said the prayers," surviving believers told me. Though the church was shut, though it was now a museum or a pigsty, the bravest of them took their cakes to the cemetery wall on ancestors' Saturdays. The old rituals were comforting, and they preserved a sense of connectedness in a time of lies. It was a different story, however, for the millions who no longer believed in fables. The resurrection myth, for them, was dead, but few found their inspiration in its official substitute. And when you looked back on a life, however you looked back, the private memories would come back, too—spiky memories of emotion, quirkiness, courageous nonconformity, awkward words and images. They contrasted with the bland realities of agitprop. They surfaced unexpectedly, disconcertingly. They became the sudden confidences that might be exchanged between strangers in a railway carriage or on a fishing trip. They were jokes, graffiti, anecdotes, and even underground poems. It was as if the people simultaneously believed and mocked the official line. "We were afraid," they say. Whatever the crucial element was—fear, escapism, prudishness, gloom—it deprived an entire generation of the freedom to explore and test its collective truth.

"A Moscow garden looks dead in winter," Ehrenburg wrote as he tried to explain the thaw. "But in the tree trunks and in the roots invisible processes are going on in preparation for the spring flowering."[86] As a charmed representative of the Stalinist literary elite, he had good reason to insist that the spring had begun only after the dictator's death. In general, too, he was right. His own book *The Thaw,* which was published in 1954, was a landmark in the process. Nikita Khrushchev's famous secret speech to the Twentieth Congress of the Communist Party followed, in 1956, and in 1961 another Party Congress agreed to remove Stalin's body from the mausoleum and to bury it quietly in a simpler grave. The following year, 1962, saw the publication of Aleksandr Solzhenitsyn's classic account of life in the prison camps, *One Day in the Life of Ivan Denisovich.*

It was no accident that the thaw's most famous product should have been the work of an ex-prisoner, a "zek," as the politicals were called. The camps were one of the few reservoirs of brute reality to survive the war. Conditions were appalling. The inmates' lives were short and hard. But as Lev Razgon, the former prisoner, Communist, and historian, remarked, there was an air of freedom in the midst of all the squalor of the Gulag.[87] A paradox like that, the fact that a society might rely on the most wretched of its victims for its truth, bears out the comment that a St. Petersburg psychiatrist offered when I asked him about the impact of the mass releases of the 1950s. "You have to remember," he said, "that in those days the whole society was, well, not quite normal."[88]

The reception given to many of the liberated zeks was one of the tragedies of the Khrushchev years. Some were welcomed home, some settled, even if their health had suffered, even if the world seemed strange. Tens of thousands of others, however, would receive a bleak welcome when they returned to the streets and courtyards of their youth. Their families were uncomfortable with them. The contagion they were thought to bring was widely feared. "After Ivan had washed himself in their bathtub," calculates the fictional sister-in-law of a returner, "it would never be clean again, even with acid and lye."[89]

The prisoners' world lives on in the imaginations of ex-zeks. Their words and stories are a far cry from the prim accounts of Stalinism's middle class. Many of the zeks I met would quote the slogan, "You can die today and I will die tomorrow."[90] Prison songs and rhymes were known for their frankness, crudeness, and violence.[91] Former convicts still resent the euphemism of ordinary life. In Shalamov's short story "On Tick," a man is skinned alive for the sake of a hand-knitted sweater. "Read it," a former zek shouted at me. "Read it! You won't know anything until you do." He was a mild man, a carpenter, and we were both surprised to discover that he was shaking his fist in my face.

The ex-zeks do not talk of Stalin's death with reverence. The tone of their recollections on this subject, as on so many others, is blunt and frank. "We were at work," one woman remembered. "It was a very cold day, a really severe frost. And we were there with the politicals, and the repeat offenders, and the people who were having to serve time under god knows what article, you understand . . . I'm telling you, we were the real elite! So there we were, and it was forty degrees below, at least forty degrees, and there was snow, and everything was stone hard. Everything around was white, and suddenly some officers appeared and spoke to our guards and told them that father Stalin was dead, which meant such pain, such sorrow, such a loss—all those stupid adjectives. And we stood there and shouted 'Hurrah!' We started to sing, too, we sang lots of songs. I remember 'The Red Guelder Rose' in particular."[92]

Vasili Grossman, as usual, knew how to turn this joy into fiction. "Columns of prisoners marched out to work in deep darkness," he wrote. "The roar of the taiga drowned out the barking of the guard dogs. And then, in a moment, as if the northern lights had flashed the signal across their ranks, came the words: Stalin is dead! Tens of thousands of prisoners marching under guard passed the news along in whispers: 'He's croaked, he's croaked.' And this whisper of the thousands upon thousands roared like the wind. Black night hung over the arctic earth. But the ice in the Arctic Ocean had begun to break up and the ocean rumbled."[93]

In the ensuing years, tens of thousands of prisoners set off on the long train ride westward. "They were euphoric," the psychologist Aron Belkin told me. "They thought they would be able to do anything now. They were thinking of life, not death. They wanted their old lives back, their jobs, their families."[94] The problem was that they were traveling to a life they would not recognize, and they were witnesses to a world most people had tried hard to forget. Damage on such a massive scale is not repaired so fast. Neither side was ready for the encounter. There were moments of catharsis, to be sure, including the publication of works like Solzhenitsyn's. "We all read it," survivors of repression will say, and their gratitude and respect are evident. "Khrushchev made an enormous difference, and God bless him," said Lyudmila Eduardovna. But the living water that Ehrenburg described was still flowing under thick ice, and the spring would be long and cold.

The first thing many of the returners found was that they could not talk about their lives in exile. Grossman's fictional ex-prisoner, Ivan Grigorevich, realizes at once that he will not be able to confide in his brother. Earlier on, he had "pictured to himself how, reclining in an armchair and sipping a glass of wine, he would begin talking of the people who had gone into eternal darkness." But real life was not to be like that. "The fate of many of them seemed so poignantly sad," he reflects, as he studies the balding, soft-fleshed man across the room, "that to speak of them in even the most tender, quiet, kind words would have been like touching a heart torn open with a rough and insensitive hand. It was really quite impossible to speak of them at all."[95] It was the same for everyone I met. The revelation that the prisoners had glimpsed was just too vivid. The most honest of them knew this, just as they also knew that their own survival depended on oblivion. Like so many others, Lev Razgon survived his return to liberty by conforming. "I became two-faced," he said. "Inside I was still afraid. But on the outside I was just like everyone else."

A prisoner's stretch is a long time to wait, and for many of the relatives who remained at liberty the dream of reunion had died. The ex-zeks shouldered their packs as the trains drew into town and stepped down among alien crowds. Some people still whispered that they were enemies, spies, criminals.

Freedom, under Khrushchev, did not have to mean rehabilitation. "They said we would never have been arrested if we were not guilty," said Yudif Borisovna. "There goes one of the ones we didn't quite manage to shoot," her neighbors jeered when she took her son to school.[96] Among Stalin's many legacies, the habit of vigilance was one of the most enduring. "If you mention your father, you will end up working in some godforsaken cockroach hole," one woman was warned. But others did not need to be told. They could make a judgment like that for themselves.

The true Soviet way of coping with emotion was to keep working and salute the flag. "My mother was a great optimist," recalled the daughter of another murdered Bolshevik. "She was determined that her children should not make life difficult for themselves. She brought us up in the Soviet spirit. My brother died in 1943 with the name of Stalin on his lips . . . He was twenty one. My older brother, it is true, was spared. But all his life, till he drew his last breath, two years ago, he was a member of the Communist Party, and he went on all the demonstrations and thought that all that perestroika stuff was rubbish. They say my father left us in 1935. But I know nothing else about him."[97] It was not merely self-deceit. The people believed in their utopia. Yudif Borisovna joined the Party as soon as she could after her release. Lev Razgon, who spent his first years of freedom writing books for children, describes himself as a Communist to this day.

"Mother had told me that my father was killed in the war," remembered Nellie, the daughter of a former colonel. "Missing in action. That's what she said. I used to sleep with a photograph of him under my pillow. I read a book called *The Tale of a Real Man*—I don't know if you've read it, but the story goes that they all froze to death, it's a war story. And that's how I imagined my father's death . . . And then I grew up. I was eighteen when the letter came. When did Stalin die? Fifty-three? It must have been just after that." Nellie took the letter with her to school and opened it at her desk. She remembers her irritation that one of her friends was looking over her shoulder as she read. "It began, 'My dear little daughter'," she said. "It was from my father, of course. And it said that what had kept him alive all that time was his love for his daughter. The letter was about a father's love. But mother, well, I can't judge her. I'm afraid, she, well, she'd brought me up differently."

Nellie's mother was in hospital at the time. Her operation was due to take place in a couple of days. When her daughter told her about the letter she froze. "Yes," she said. "'It's from your father. He's been in prison. He's an enemy of the people." "I don't know what happened, I was doing exams, I think I was confused," Nellie continued. "And I was all there was left for mother. I wrote a letter back. It said something about refusing him. 'I do not want to know you'—that phrase was in it somewhere . . . I did not want to meet this man with no teeth and not a hair on his head."[98] She never did. Her father stayed on the train as it drew into Moscow. He made a new life in Lvov.

10

DEATH IN THE AGE OF "DEVELOPED SOCIALISM"

Former prisoners—like Nellie's father—returned to neighbors, families, or strangers who could not always hear, let alone understand, the things they had to say. Some people avoided the returners, others cast them out. The few who listened must have found the task heartbreaking, beyond the range of day-to-day imagination. The mere fact of the returners' existence was a reproach, a jarring note, perhaps a threat, the more distressing in a world that had tried so hard, and at such cost, to rearrange its past. But Soviet life was changing. It was already harder, two or three years after Stalin's death, to preserve the comfortable illusions. The prisoners' stories of injustice and abuse could not be overlooked for long.

By 1955 a distinctive generation of Soviet intellectuals, people who had reached adulthood in the last years of the war, the years of sharpest individual hope, and who had barely known the full weight of political terror, was reaching maturity. New men—former soldiers, but seldom former prisoners—were joining the editorial boards of influential journals, making decisions about local economic policy, replacing their grandparents (for many of their parents and their older siblings had been killed) in government, academic, and Party posts. These people would begin to ask new questions, they would challenge many silences, and some would try to count the costs of cronyism and dictatorship. Some of the children of the dispossessed, too, of former kulaks, for instance, or of Stalin's more obviously political victims, would also, in the wake of the dictator's death, begin to think again about their silence, passivity, and accommodation. The minority who had never let themselves forget would take their chance to make demands.[1]

The 1960s and 1970s were destined to be decades of submerged conflict, a struggle over Communism's future (though rarely a fight to overthrow it altogether). While Khrushchev ruled, and until his successor, Brezhnev, died in office in 1982, the formal organs of the state contained but could not crush it. Support for this containment came from some veterans of the war (the ones who still revered its leader), from conservative members of the technical intelligentsia (that Stalinist middle class with its prim stories and its job security), and from large parts of the bureaucracy, the military, the Party, and security police. Even Gorbachev, a generation later, would find that these opponents of reform, with their strong views about the meaning of the past, were difficult to subdue.

The new generation used two principal kinds of language. The first, familiar from the writings of the dissidents, was one of repentance, self-reproach, and justifiable anger. It was exemplified by Andrei Tvardovskii's banned poem of guilt and remembrance, an account of his own thoughts about his kulak father, *By Right of Memory.*[2] Writers, journalists, historians, and poets began to explore the Stalinist past. They generally avoided engaging with the question of totalitarian politics, confining themselves, as Khrushchev had done in his secret speech, to the issues of personal dictatorship and corruption, but their work was shocking, moving, and, for most, relentlessly informative. Not everyone approved. Even within the literary establishment, as the suppression of Grossman's *Life and Fate* had demonstrated, there were people who preferred security to truth. Brezhnev, too, succeeding Khrushchev after 1964, would find the questions and the anger threatening. The thaw that Ehrenburg had celebrated eventually went into reverse.

What even Brezhnev did not stop, however, was the rise and spread of the anti-Soviet joke. It is difficult to follow some of the oldest of these jokes to their roots. The antiregime humor of the Stalin era was filtered by the secret police, and they were not collecting it for laughs.[3] It was not part of printed, public, celebrated culture, either—the Stalinist regime did not invite burlesque. Nonetheless, there was a steady stream of underground sardonic criticism, antiestablishment humor to set beside the stock jokes about race and color, nagging wives and drunken husbands. Sharp details of this humor reemerged as the atmosphere of terror lifted. The camps, for instance, had produced a good deal of murderous irony. By the 1960s the middle class was repeating it in their kitchens. Antiestablishment entertainers were also testing it on stage, sometimes through monologue, sometimes in songs.[4] In private, too, the people explored darker themes. There were purge jokes, execution jokes (the victims often beg the executioner to shoot), corpse jokes, Stalin jokes—all of them told alongside the innumerable anecdotes about the other Soviet leaders.[5]

Humor was used, especially by the younger generation, to reduce the weight of the past, to explode the old taboos, to create a counterculture. Living politicians made easy targets—the confusion in a photographic caption between Khrushchev and a group of well-scrubbed pigs, for instance, was ruthlessly exploited, as was the fact of Brezhnev's obvious infirmity. But though it was apparently subversive, like the new writing that the censors nodded through, ironic humor did not usually undermine the Party leaders' world. It pointed out the rank absurdities and mocked the lies—and this was breath of life itself after the stifling years of fear—but even as the people laughed the system was endured. "We are all opposed," says the old joke, "but we all vote yes."

A continuing inspiration for the irony was the mismatch between the rhetoric of unity, progress, and improvement—the trite slogans of "developed socialism"—and the realities of social dislocation, hardship, dissidence, corruption, and sheer bad government. Loosed from the prison of dictatorship, the sirens of religion, memory, guilt, nationalism, profit, consumerism, and permissive morality seemed destined to distract upstanding Soviet citizens. Demands for openness, too, for a greater freedom to travel, more liberal government, and the relaxation of censorship, all threatened in the wake of Khrushchev's secret speech. The regime's answer was to maintain and even increase political control. Debate was muted, foreign broadcasts jammed. Leading dissidents of the 1970s were routinely harassed. Open protest brought the army out, with its tanks and bullets and tear gas. The humor of the Soviet 1960s and 1970s, then, is overwhelmingly the humor of the bondman. Whatever else it does, it always deprecates itself. "Is Communism a science?" the teacher asks his pupil. "No," replies the child. "For if it were, they would have tested it on dogs."

No one, it seems, took Communism seriously all the time. In what has since been called the Era of Stagnation, the 1970s, you would still live a double life, just as the first post revolutionary men and women had done in the

1920s. At the Party meeting, you talked a special language, heavy with abstractions and oxymorons—overfulfilment, really existing socialism—and at the end of the big speeches everyone would clap. But then, when you had left the public hall, loosened your tie, and poured the first of many rounds of vodka, you would start to joke. It was a privilege of power, in fact, to be the first in any group to denigrate the system and to show the sharpest wit. By the time the humorous possibilities were being explored in one room, however, the resolutions that had solemnly been passed an hour before would already have been typed and handed out for others to fulfill. The jokes are funny, the irony is seductive, the crimes and cruelties are Lilliputian ones in Stalinism's shadow, but the consequences of this newest form of dissociation were often dark and sometimes tragic.

The challenge was to rebrand Communism for an age of mass communication. The years of revolutionary zeal, and then the epic time of patriotic war, were followed by a blank, by ideological disillusionment. Some politicians plugged the holes with consumer goods; some, like Khrushchev, were keen to build new apartment blocks. There were new weapons programs, homemade blue jeans, sputniks, athletes, men and dogs in space. But if the Soviet empire were to have a meaning, its ideology had to be kept alive. Apathy was one of Communism's final enemies; competing, deeply held beliefs, another. Two of the most contentious issues of the time were history and faith. In each, the questions of memory and death were prominent. The war, the purges, the people's renewed search for truth, and the continuing evidence of religious belief still gave the Party's agitators anxious nights.

The 1960s and 1970s saw a feast of war commemoration—giant statues on the Volga and above the Dnipro Rivers, the creation of the complex at Piskarevskoe, the opening of the Tomb of the Unknown Soldier in Moscow.[6] The state was making its bid for memory. This patriotism, this sacred loss, was what it chose to keep alive. There was a generation—many millions—for whom the monuments had meaning, embodying a cherished image of the past. But the statues and the stones were raised in strange, restrictive times. It was also in the Brezhnev years that historians and veterans who wrote about the war were forbidden to refer to anything that had not already been published somewhere else. According to General Gorbatov, even the memoirs of protagonists were checked to make sure that they did not break new ground. "If the new text treated events or persons differently from memoirs of military leaders previously published," he explained, "the new evidence had to be . . . removed or corrected in accordance with the earlier publications."[7]

The memoirists could not refer to military blunders, wasted lives, or wartime political repression. They were also supposed to ignore genocide. The fate of Soviet Jews, exemplified by the massacre at Babi Yar, was subsumed into a larger story of collective loss. The victims of racist killing were nothing more than "Soviet citizens." Like many of the Soviet Union's secrets, however, this was one that would not simply die, although it suited many people to forget it. To speed the process of amnesia, and to close the route to popular, spontaneous, commemoration, the Party planned to develop the suburban site, the ravine of Babi Yar itself and the surrounding scrubland. There was a scheme to cover it with a dam and a sports stadium. It was abandoned in 1961. That March, after torrential rain, the floodgates of the dam had broken. "A wall of liquid mud thirty feet high poured from the mouth of Babi Yar," wrote a witness. "Whole crowds of people were swallowed up instantly in the wave of mud . . . The number of people who perished was never, of course, stated."[8]

The conflict over Babi Yar and its buried story continued, a proof that contests over memory, the war, and death could still cause worry, anger, insecurity. It was also in 1961 that the poet Yevgenii Yevtushenko published his meditation at the site, a poem of a hundred lines or so. "How vile these anti-semites," the Siberian wrote. "Without a qualm they pompously call themselves / 'The Union of the Russian People!' . . . The 'Internationale', let it thunder / when the last anti-semite on earth / is buried forever."[9] Khrushchev's spokesman on ideological issues, Leonid Ilyichev, was furious. "Is this a time to raise such a theme?" he ranted at the poet. "What's the matter with you? Babi Yar wasn't just Jews but Slavs."[10]

Yevtushenko was not the only one to feel the chill of Khrushchev's disapproval. The composer Dmitrii Shostakovich, whose Thirteenth Symphony was partly based on the dark poem, had difficulty getting his work staged, and the first performance, though rapturously received by the audience, was ignored by the critics. "Dmitrii Dmitrievich," a colleague of the composer blurted out. "Why did you choose this poem when there is no anti-semitism in the Soviet Union?"[11]

The applause that the controversial first movement of Shostakovich's work received at its rare performances would testify to the strength of support—at least among an elite circle of educated music lovers—for Yevtushenko's protest and for the composer's sympathetic response. The power of dissidence was like a current beneath the stagnant surface of late Communism. These were the years of the sell-out poetry reading, the packed recital, the man on stage with his guitar, the complex, subtle, allusive lyrics that everyone had learned by heart.[12] But dissidence, like religion, had its consistent devotees and its wavering fellow travelers. The former would turn out whenever they were free to come; they staged their protests, wrote their verse, and often suffered for their principles. The masses, alternately sympathetic or afraid, hostile, chauvinistic, or busy with their lives, were harder to reach. Neither the Party nor its critics could be sure of their support for long. Death worked to the advantage of both sides. Days of remembrance for the war turned into patriotic rallies. But at the same time, oddly, ironically, the deaths of antiestablishment figures provoked no lesser passion, gathered massive crowds.

People whose language had been abused mourned deeply for their poets. A whole generation still remembers the funeral of Boris Pasternak. The last months of his life had been particularly hard. Though he had won the Nobel Prize for his novel *Dr. Zhivago*, which was published abroad in 1958, the writer had been forced to refuse the honor and had also been condemned by the Soviet Writers' Union for his anti-Soviet portrayal of the civil war. The book was not published in Russia. Pasternak died in 1960, at the end of May. He was buried in the cemetery at Peredelkino, the enclave of country houses that was kept for Soviet writers and artists. No one had predicted that the crowds would be so great. The early summer woods were trampled by the pilgrims' boots, the lanes and stations overrun. The cemetery itself was packed. There was an echo of the old red funeral, of righteous protest, in the air. The foreign journalists could sense it. The secret policemen would later have it to report. People were talking openly, not just about one dead man's talent, but about the universal values of free speech, integrity, and art.

Other meetings followed. In May 1965 a memorial gathering was held to celebrate the work of Osip Mandelstam. The speakers included his widow, the writer Nadezhda Mandelstam, and also Il'ya Ehrenburg, Varlam Shalamov, and the film director Andrei Tarkovskii. A year later, when Anna Akhmatova died, a similarly distinguished crowd would stand in silence and remember the woman whose mission had been to "preserve Russian speech" and keep it "pure" and "free."[13] The speakers on that occasion included Lev Kopelev.[14]

Some poets would become cult heroes. When Vladimir Vysotsky, the nation's favorite actor and singer, died in July 1980, the public's grief overshadowed the Olympic Games, which were being held in Moscow at the same time. Some people said that nothing like it had been seen since Stalin's death in 1953. As Gerald Smith writes, "Vysotsky died on a Friday morning. As soon as the news began to spread, a crowd started to form near the Taganka Theater and continued to stand there until, on Monday, people without special invitations were allowed into the theater to pay their last respects to his body, which had been taken there on Saturday."[15] Vysotsky was buried in the Vagankovo cemetery. His grave, like Pasternak's, became a place of pilgrimage. If you visit it now, at any time of year, you will find that it is scattered with fresh flowers.

These funerals were exceptions, however, and the ritual was unique, each time reflecting something of the person who had died, designed and carried through by men and women used to words. The energy among the crowd, too, was fed by protest and solidarity. It was harder to be lyrical about a loyal member of the establishment, however distinguished he may have been. The funeral for Shostakovich, who died in August 1975, was stiff, cold, and soulless. The composer had specified in his will that no orchestra should play as he lay in state. No orchestra would have been available in Moscow anyway (it was the height of the summer touring season), but the lack of real music was an extra weight in an already heavy atmosphere.

The body was displayed in the Grand Hall of the Moscow Conservatoire. It was a state occasion. The press were there, as well as representatives of the government and artistic establishment. Policemen in plain clothes—many of them were said to be dressed as music scholars—patroled the crowd. Recordings of the composer's music played. There were the usual speeches. "First and foremost he was a Communist," repeated the official mourners. "All the speakers declared that they considered Shostakovich a genius," wrote his friend Mark Lubotsky. "These were approved statements." The ceremonial was approved as well. The mourners followed the coffin from the hall to the Novodevich'e cemetery, a prestigious burial site, far grander than the one that would be given to Vysotsky. "It was cold," Lubotsky wrote. "A military band was butchering its way through Chopin's Funeral March. We stood around a platform listening to more speeches . . . Hammers banged. They were nailing down the lid of the coffin. Then they moved. Then they stopped. The Soviet anthem was played. It was cold and it started to drizzle."[16]

The Party's insistence on words, a message, was the main problem. People did not always want or need the afterlife or God. Music, wordless but transcendent, was what they seemed to crave, certainly at secular funerals. But the agitators could not bear to leave them to their thoughts. There was a fight to win. Communism was losing ground. Traditional religion was making converts. Some forms of religious practice were even becoming fashionable. There were new groups, new sects, and some young people—for whatever reason—had taken to wearing crosses round their necks.[17] Established groups of believers also continued to meet, often in what were called house churches. "We used to have a table in the kitchen set up for a birthday party," Magdalena Alekseyevna told me. "Then, if a neighbor came to check what we were doing with all those visitors in the house, we could say that we were having a party. They didn't see that we were praying in the other room."[18]

In 1970 a young person told researchers that "religion gives a believer hope for something in life. Whether mythological or not, he believes in something, and without faith it is impossible to live."[19] Ironically, the state agreed, but the faith it wanted to encourage was a secular one. The result was a double-edged campaign. The 1960s saw a new round of church closures—the number of working churches shrank from around twenty thousand in 1961 to about sixty-five hundred in the 1970s[20]—and fresh repressions of clergy and of the activists who led the congregations. But there was also a renewed attempt to create new ritual, to replace the superstitious, antique faith with something secular and modern. The Party, not satisfied with irony and sullen acquiescence, demanded active, lively support. "What is needed," said a memorandum of 1960, "is a carefully worked-out and thought-through complex of measures to disseminate new Soviet traditions, customs, and practices; and also the revival and strengthening of some folk customs and practices, when they have been purged of religious overtones."[21]

The propaganda specialists designed a cycle of Soviet rituals. Traditional rites of passage—marriage, for instance, and the birth and naming of a child—were on the list, and so were new ceremonies to mark the first and last day at school, the acquisition of a passport, and the receipt of a person's first wage packet.[22] There were handbooks that told you how to do it. "We should hold our Day of Memory on the second or eighth of May," a Belorussian version suggests, "or even better, on the last Sunday in April or the first Sunday in May, since these are traditionally the days on which people go to the cemeteries to put their family graves in order."[23] The idea was to eclipse the so-called negative relics of tradition. Unlike many other new rites, the Day of Memory, a day for thinking of the war dead, rather than about the victory, was a success. Many veterans recall that it meant more to them than Victory Day, 9 May. More frequently, however, the extra public holidays were simply added to a calendar that went on as before. Sweets, cakes, and tins of peas turned up on special tables in the churches on Ancestors' Saturdays. Evergreens, palms, and willow branches decked the cemeteries at Trinity.[24]

Easter itself was always a thorn in the agitators' sides. The festival of eternal life was subjected to a multipronged assault, involving the harassment of believers and the artful exploitation of television schedules. The congregations for the midnight vigils and processions certainly thinned.[25] What everyone remembers, however, and what I witnessed for myself, was that the people ate their yeast cake when they had finished with Alla Pugacheva and Dinamo Kiev. The meaning of the feasting was the thing that varied. Even the believers did not all accept the entire fable anymore. Life after death, the researchers found, was something a majority of them doubted.[26] The struggle for belief was not a matter only for the Party and the church.

Individual funerals, however, were seldom mere charades. The ceremonial was intended, after all, to focus the emotions of the mourners, involve them in the death. A report of 1964 acknowledged that "our ritual for funerals, and for the commemoration of the dead, is absolutely undeveloped. In Moscow it is not rare to find non-believers who choose to bury their dead in a religious way because citizens' funerals are still not established. The funerals of ordinary workers and pensioners are quite often conducted along religious lines."[27] In rural areas the habit of observance was etched even more deeply. Researchers working in one central Russian village, Viriatino, found that in the five-year period of 1952 to 1956, only three nonreligious funerals had taken place there.[28]

The agitators saw religious funerals as a challenge. "The struggle between the old and the new takes place not only on the barricades," one of them wrote in 1970, "not only in the economic and political field, but also in the resting places of the dead."[29] The easy part of it would be the transformation of the earth, the creation of new cemeteries and the control of public monument design. The hard part, the nut that they would never manage to crack, was all that prayer, those words. The explanation that they favored for this, their excuse, was that religious rites answered some basic, inherited, human craving. Funerals, according to the ethnographer Tokarev were not mere "survivals of religious beliefs and rites." They arose instead from "universal human motives innate in man himself as a social creature."[30] Survivals of the cult, in other words, were testimonies to the weakness not of Communism, and not of the mechanisms of economic distribution, but of men (and, more specifically, of women).

The planners had acknowledged, then, that they could not defeat some of the habits of the past. They could, however, command the public space where rituals were enacted. Their mania for the grandiose combined conveniently with the demands of their politics. New cemeteries were built outside the major towns, some of them a good hour or more from the places where the people lived. You would think twice about a journey of that length, you might not make so many visits, the old customs would die naturally, and the whole thing was a blow for public health. The other details—the form filling, the demands for documents, the lines, the cost—were not intended to be cruel, though that is how they are remembered. Bureaucracies often just work that way.

Moscow's Khovanskoe, which opened in 1972, is the largest cemetery in Europe. It covers a staggering 206 hectares (more than 500 acres), which means that it is larger than many average-size English villages. If you visit it, you can see how the planners' dreams worked out. The landscape is bleak. No one could describe it as intimate. Getting there, especially without a car, is awkward, tiring, and slow. And when you do arrive, you have to find the grave. You set off round a maze of alleys and paths, walking carefully, for the site is marshy and liable to flooding. It is better, in fact, to go in winter, for at least the ground is solid then. You need a map. As you turn it over, following the lines and arrows, and as you walk, you will see thousands, many thousands, of monuments. You will also see the tables for the ritual food, the pictures of dead parents engraved into the stones, gilded words and dates, plastic flowers, real flowers, lengths of ribbon, bold red stars. Some of the graves have little roofs. The spirits would not want to shiver in the driving sleet.

The photographs in particular are strange. No one agrees about their meaning. They may be the last remnants of an icon culture, a victory for engraving science, or proof that the dead person's spirit really lives in this small house. In any case, the graves are hybrids, drawing from the old traditions (food and earth) and introducing elements of the new (the stars, the words, the plastic). While you are studying them, however, your friends will shudder at the rubbish and the dirt, the odd dead bird, graffiti, and discarded cigarettes. Khovanskoe, like its cousin, the slightly less extensive Nikolo-Arkhangel'skoe cemetery on the city's northern outskirts, is a place of burial that people use when they cannot afford the alternatives. The best that can be said is that the company is good. The politicians, and now the mafiosi, all have their grave plots in the city center.[31]

As long as there was earth and a grave, then, however distant and undignified, the old ways looked certain to linger. Cremation, on the other hand, seemed guaranteed to break religion's grip. They said it could be satisfying, an inspiration for the future, something beautiful. There had been problems in the past, but these could be forgotten now. It all depended on the crematorium itself.

Among the cities where the experiment was tried was Kiev. Ukraine's capital was the birthplace of Christianity among the Eastern Slavs, and in the 1960s it already had some impressive monuments to death. If you visit it now, for instance, you will probably be drawn to the Cathedral of Saint Sophia, which houses the tomb of Yaroslav the Wise. You will also be tempted to visit the Caves monastery, whose catacombs are full of desiccated saints. "Every civilization is really judged by the memorials it leaves behind," Vladimir Mel'nichenko, one of the architects of the Kiev crematorium, explained to me. "The Egyptians had their pyramids. What we wanted was to create something that would symbolize the meaning and value of life in our society."

Mel'nichenko is a serious man, even a dour one. He could not have intended irony. Nevertheless, the fate of his great project, which took thirteen years to realize, does say a lot about the world in which he used to live. The city council did not like its crematorium. The politicians thought it broke the rules of socialist realism, the ones that they, after a change of government, had recently redefined. The building and its grounds were deliberately defaced. Today the site itself is almost derelict.

The decision to begin to build the Kiev crematorium was taken in the 1960s. The budget was tight, 3 million rubles for the whole job, much of which was already committed to technical equipment such as the furnace and the refrigerated morgue. Most designers avoided tendering for the work. Two local artists, Vladimir Mel'nichenko and Ada Rybachuk, would have the project to themselves. "They were afraid," Rybachuk says of her colleagues. "They wanted nothing to do with death." She and Mel'nichenko, however, were devotees, fanatics. "Everything went well for us," they say. Everything. Even the first sketches look ambitious as they show them now. The engineers said the structure could not be built, but remarks like that are often the prelude to architectural triumph. The money ran out, too, but the last stages of the project—seven years of work—were completed with the help of unpaid volunteers. "People used to come and watch," Rybachuk told me. "They wanted to know what sort of bosses the building was for. They could not believe us when we said it was for everyone."

When Rybachuk and Mel'nichenko tell the story, eagerly unfolding their colored plans, it is their idealism that is most striking. They really wanted to create a new culture of death, "to give it back its artistic quality," as Rybachuk puts it. "Death had become something trivial," she explains. "Millions would be killed and there was nothing to say. We wanted to change all that, to make it beautiful, serious, to make it something to consider." The symbol that they chose to bear this message, back in the 1960s, bore more than a passing resemblance to the Sydney Opera House. A paper model, three intersecting arches, is passed around among the tea cups. The building it represents was made of concrete and set on an artificial hill in the heart of Kiev's prestigious Baikovo cemetery.[32] "It is not just a building," one of the artists explains. "We wanted to create a ceremonial complex. We took over the whole space. We wanted to describe the route through life, to explain that death is not the end. We told the authorities that. It was one of our disagreements with them."

Rybachuk and Mel'nichenko were criticized even by their friends. "They said we were trying to superimpose something new, to replace burial. They said that burial is the Slavic tradition. People did not want us to get involved with cremation." The artists, however, insisted—rightly—that a culture of burning had existed on the steppe in pre-Christian times. They were untiring in their research. They traveled to the Carpathian Mountains in search of supposedly authentic Slavic rites; they burrowed for old texts in Kiev's libraries. Their ultimate vision incorporated the spirits of landscape and urn burial. The heart of their ceremonial space, it is clear even from the model, was designed to open to the sky. The prototype urns are still on display in their kitchen, suspended on a rack above the cooker and rowed up along a wall behind the massive table.

Memories more recent than the introduction of Christianity haunted the plan to reintroduce cremation in their city. The artists wanted their construction to have all the right associations. As it was, the idea of burning, in Kiev, was bound to conjure images of the Holocaust and Babi Yar. "They always used German furnaces in the Soviet Union before the war," Vladimir Mel'nichenko explained. "Exactly the same technology as the Nazis used in the death camps. To do that was unthinkable in Kiev. You could not use a German furnace. We used an English one. Mason and Dawson. Even though it was more expensive." They also installed it underground. "The air had to be clean," Ada Rybachuk insisted. "And we didn't want to have anything that looked like a factory."

Rybachuk and Mel'nichenko became obsessed. They planned to combine the burial architectures of Mexico and ancient Rus'; they wanted stepped ziggurats and turf mounds, *kurgans* made entirely of the sacred Black Earth. Nearly every wall was to be decorated with concrete reliefs, huge figures in human form, brightly colored, vivid, and festive. A very extensive area of the cemetery was relandscaped, an artificial lake created. Meandering paths were designed and cut. "We wanted a source of living water in the hall," added Rybachuk. "Not a fountain of tears. No way. And no alleys of solemn lindens. None of that. Living water."

She banged the table with a teaspoon. "We brought the glass from Czechoslovakia. We found a place there that made it in exactly the right way." The glass is gone now, and so are the reliefs. The huge figures, some of them still incomplete, were tossed among the brambles. Some of them lie there still. The artists' bright colors were condemned. Most of the building's interior was painted black (to hide them) or left to fade to a dirty gray. The lake was drained. Now it is home to discarded bottles, old cardboard and dead leaves.

Mel'nichenko unfolded another well-thumbed plan, a map of the cemetery, and photographs of the building in each stage of its construction. He turned a saucer upside down and put the paper opera house–crematorium on top to give it height. It started to rain outside, and the room, with its large window open, suddenly filled with the smells of evening in a southern city—damp stone, burnt coffee, tobacco, chestnut leaves, the spring. The words and pictures seemed unreal, like relics of a distant past. The artists' good intentions, their idealism and their eagerness, began to jar. Idealism has no place in capitalist Kiev. The city, these days, has other needs, material ones, so many problems. Mel'nichenko eyed me sharply. He pushed the saucer nearer to an electric light. "This was north," he said. I nodded. It was a history seminar, and it had only just begun.

Aleksei Smirnov is a psychiatrist working in St. Petersburg. He was in the middle of his professional training when the Communist system collapsed. He has direct experience, in other words, of both the recent mental worlds, the Soviet and the Russian. Now trapped in a ruthlessly profit-oriented post-Communist economy, he tries not to resent the meagerness of his salary or the low status of his job. He is fond of irony, which he uses, deftly, as an antidote to pessimism. We met to discuss the work that he has done with war veterans, but he took the opportunity, after an hour or so, to talk more generally of life and death. "In your country, or at least, in America, I believe, there is this feeling that health is something valuable," he said, pausing to open the window on to a snow-covered courtyard. "If you don't smoke, if you don't drink, if you don't eat cholesterol or fat or sugar—you're a healthy person. Everyone will love you and you will earn lots of money. If you're psychologically healthy, too, that is. If you're not crazy, everyone will think you're a good person, and you will get on. If anything goes wrong, you take the organism to a specialist and get it put right. We don't have that attitude." He lit a cigarette and drew luxuriously on the smoke. He smiled. "I think this is called auto-aggressive behavior," he said.[33]

Aggression, or the study of it, is one of Dr. Smirnov's specialties. It is a corollary, he speculates, of some of Communism's other problems, a legacy of repressive politics, an answer to state violence. He talks of the persistent "prison camp mentality" among the healthy and the sick, of the profound mistrust of state and law that wrecks the chances of democracy. Like death, he thinks, aggression is something that most people prefer not to address. "There is something strange that we have," he explains. "Other societies have it, too. But with us it is taken to an absurd extreme. Dissociation. Everyone knows what is meant by the incongruity between a word and an action. In our society we have made this into something ridiculous. It is not an exception to the rule, it is the rule. To say one thing, and do another. That is the rule of life for the Soviet man. And you know what this is. It's schizophrenia. I mean this in the symbolic sense. There's a split going on . . . A man thinks that he's being governed by a bunch of monsters, but he'll still say: Long live our Party and government." Pausing between puffs he adds, "Oh, and I do mean Soviet. Soviet man. The type has not changed."

We could have talked all day about the contradictions and paradoxes of Soviet culture. What we did not mention was that this acceptance of Russian specificity, even if it is confined to psychiatry, produces a paradox in its turn. For though Smirnov is quick to insist that Russia is not "the West," and that its people have traditions of their own, he has devoted the first part of his professional life to a Western diagnostic concept. The subject of his doctoral thesis is Post-Traumatic Stress Disorder (PTSD). His work explores its incidence among the veterans of the Soviet Union's war in Afghanistan. It also asks about the consequences for their families.

Even in the United States of America, PTSD is a relatively recent addition to the canon of approved diagnoses of mental illness.[34] It is understood as a response to the witnessing of exceptional, usually violent, events—unnatural death (in combat, for example), natural disaster, fatal accident. It includes a range of symptoms, from paralysis and loss of speech, nightmares, and phobias to flashbacks so vivid that a sufferer can re-create an entire world, repeating the aggressive behavior that was appropriate to it, for instance, or crouching under a table to escape imagined bombs. In some Western societies, the diagnosis is crucial for compensation cases (the range of recognized "traumatic" stressors seems to be widening as a result). It is also regarded, by many international agencies, as an almost automatic consequence of war, a universal feature of victimhood.[35]

Although the Soviet Union was a violent place, the notion of trauma is not easy to apply to its people. PTSD is certainly not a diagnosis that they seek, and it is not a label that they wear with pride. To some extent, the fact that mental distress, far from leading to compensation, is stigmatized in post-Soviet Russia may explain their attitude. But there are other reasons, too. Pain, unquestionably, is universal, though individuals seem to tolerate it in different ways. But the cultural resources a society may develop for accommodating it will vary, and so will the other problems—unrelieved hunger, for instance, or widespread homelessness—beside which psychological insults must be endured. The individual mind is not the center of every human world. Words like collectivism and social effort crop up whenever former Soviet citizens attempt to explain why Stalin's Russia did not collapse under its burden of despair. To the extent that the people did not discuss some of the things that troubled them, the strategy carried costs of its own. For decades, however, there was no viable alternative.

The Afghan crisis was special because of its timing. The old diversions—flag waving and hard physical work—were losing their efficacy. Cynicism was widespread. Full employment, post war reconstruction, had given way to a world in which, as the joke goes, "We pretend to work and they pretend to pay us." There was not much community spirit to be found in Brezhnev's tower blocks. The Soviet Union, on the verge of final crisis, entered a war that no one really understood and few supported. In 1945 the veterans of the Patriotic War had warmed themselves in the enduring glow of moral victory. The Afghantsy, as the soldiers who fought in the mountains came to be called, would not be able to do the same. They would have to find new ways of thinking about wartime loss, and some, ironically, would turn to the West for help. Smirnov himself dismissed the range of home grown Soviet responses to death and trauma with a shrug. "We like to think that we have lessons to teach the world," he said. "But the only thing we can really teach you is how not to do it." Specialists like him, freed from old Soviet constraints, were quick to look abroad for inspiration. PTSD came to Russia fully formed, like Know-How economics and McDonald's fries. When the hospitals can afford to spend time on it (which in Russia these days is seldom), the diagnosis—and the treatment—sometimes help. But they also raise a lot of questions.

The Soviet army invaded Afghanistan in 1979. The resulting war was fought on a vaguely ideological pretext—the fragile Communist regime had appealed for Soviet support—but it was also meant to secure Moscow's position in a notoriously unstable region. There was, as ever, an element of racism involved in the mix as well. The Afghan insurgents were variously described as primitive barbarians, Muslim extremists, terrorists, smugglers of arms, missionaries of

Islam, and dealers in narcotic drugs. There were also fears that the United States would use Afghanistan's civil war to strengthen pro-Islamic movements in the adjacent areas of the USSR. But the Soviet intervention solved none of Brezhnev's problems. It inflamed the spirit of anti-Communist resistance, and even of holy war, inside Afghanistan itself, and it caused outrage everywhere else.[36] Economic and military observers agree that it was also a crucial factor in the Soviet system's ultimate collapse.

No one learned more than the men and women who fought in the war, the Afghantsy themselves. Another generation, though by no means everyone (national service was universal, but anyone with the right connections would try to buy their children out of the tour in Afghanistan), was about to lose its taste for euphemism. "Did we think about death beforehand?" a former soldier raised an eyebrow. "Of course not. Come on, we were children, kids. We were eighteen years old. Anything I know about death—or rather, about the value of life—I know from then. I knew nothing before, and nothing has changed my mind since. Those years, from eighteen to twenty, they are crowded years in any man's life. But especially in wartime." His friend laughed. "Perhaps we got to think more because we had all that time," he suggested. "After all, we didn't get any sleep."

"There's no mystery about death for people caught up in war," another Afghan veteran explained. "Killing means simply squeezing the trigger."[37] The idea came as a shock for many of the teenage recruits who joined the draft in the 1980s. For them, as for everyone else in the Soviet Union, heroism and combat were synonymous with the Great Patriotic War. Children were raised on their grandparents' stories. Veterans attended every school to tell new generations about their exploits.[38] These stories, and the perpetual crop of war films and novels, genuinely inspired a good many of the young men called up for national service under Brezhnev. "I wanted to do the things my grandfather always talked about," one Afghan war veteran explained. Others remembered a greater apprehensiveness, but it was mixed with curiosity. "The East, you know," said another former soldier. "I wasn't in the least thinking of the Great Patriotic War, not at all. This was different, and it was going to be exciting, fighting on the frontier, in a romantic place. I even had the chance not to go. It was a choice I made." "You never thought that they were going to kill you," his friend added. "Since childhood they drummed into us that our country was the best and our army was the strongest and all that stuff. And so they should. They should do that in every country."[39]

If the Afghantsy went to war to defend their country, however, they soon found that the only thing they could really fight for on the ground was their own and their friends' survival. The details of real guerrilla combat, they discovered, were among the things that had been left out of the heroic stories of World War Two. Everyone—soldiers, nurses, and auxiliary staff—remembers their shock. The Soviet state was not all-powerful, its allegedly righteous cause, in world historical Marxist-Leninist terms, was not an invincible shield, and the enemy, supposedly a foot soldier of medieval religious fanaticism, was neither inconsequential nor—it turned out—evil. "I have become an orientalist," said one of the Afghantsy. "I started to be interested in their religion while I was in Afghanistan. Now I would say that I am a bit of a Zen Buddhist and a bit of a Taoist or Shintoist, you know." Among his other interests, some of them learned during a visit to California, are nonviolence and the management of post-traumatic stress. He calls himself an intercultural facilitator.

Bleaker discoveries were also waiting in the foothills of the Hindu Kush. One of the first was that ground wars are savage. "There are men flying around in space," one survivor later remarked, "but down here we go on killing each other as we have done for a thousand years, with bullets, knives, and stones. In the villages," he added, "they killed our soldiers with pitchforks."[40] Like all guerrilla and partisan wars, this one was pitilessly cruel. It was not just a matter of land mines or sniper fire. At sunrise on any morning there might be bodies to bring home, the unlucky hostages of the Mujaheddin. Some had their eyes gouged out, others had stars or crescents carved into the skin on their backs or stomachs.[41] Soviet soldiers often went into battle wearing two identity tags, one for their bodies and one for their legs. They hoped that someone would be around to piece their corpse together and send it home. Perhaps they would. But even the hero's death would prove chimerical. "When a bullet hits a person you hear it," a soldier explained. "It's an unmistakable sound you never forget, like a wet slap. Your mate next to you falls face down in the sand . . . The first time it happens you react like in a dream . . . Within two or three weeks there's nothing left of you except your name. You've become someone else. This someone else isn't frightened of a corpse, but calmly (and a bit pissed off, too) wonders how he's going to drag it down the rocks and carry it for several kilometers in that heat."[42]

Their suffering alone might have done it, but it was isolation above all that forged the solidarity of most Afghantsy. Their sacrifice was marginalized and even ignored. "It was a small war," one of them told me. "There weren't many of us. So we stick together now. The people who fought in Chechnya will do just the same." The war was unpopular, and no one wanted to thank the men who had fought in it. "We never sent you there" is one of the phrases all Afghantsy repeat, spitting out the words with a bitterness that fifteen years of peace have not mellowed. Many of them experienced overt discrimination. Veterans of war were supposed to enjoy certain privileges in the Soviet Union. Bemedaled survivors of the Great Patriotic War could walk to the head of lines and even use different facilities in most public places. But Afghantsy seldom benefitted from the system. "I go to the window for war veterans," recalled one. "I hear someone say, 'Hey, you, boy! You're in the wrong line!' I clench my teeth and say nothing. Behind my back a voice says. 'I defended the motherland, but what has he done?' "[43]

The government played its part, predictably, by trying to conceal the war's human costs. It would be years before anyone knew how many troops had been deployed in Afghanistan, and the precise number of losses is still unknown. The zinc coffins were sent home for burial, but many were simply marked "Died," not "Killed in Action." "No one asked why these eighteen-year-olds were dying all of a sudden," someone commented. "We weren't allowed to tell the truth in the next of kin letters," remembered a nurse. "A boy might be blown up by a mine and there'd be nothing left except half a bucket of flesh, but we wrote that he'd died of food poisoning, or in a car accident, or he'd fallen down a ravine. It wasn't until the fatalities were in their thousands that they began to tell families the truth."[44] Generally speaking, the families had not known for certain that their son was in Afghanistan to start with. "I told mother in my letters that I was somewhere in Mongolia on exercises," said one man. "They didn't censor it, but I didn't want to let her know, all the same."[45] If he had died, she might never have known why.

It was often also forbidden to bury the bodies of Afghantsy in clearly demarcated war cemeteries. Their graves were scattered around in the hope that their numbers would have less impact, and the headstones seldom specified where or why death had occurred.[46] George Mosse, in his account of war and remembrance, described the innovation of separate war cemeteries—in Europe they were rare before 1914—as a stage in the elaboration of a patriotic myth. The sacred dead, it is made clear, are different from mere mortals.[47] Brezhnev's regime did not accord that honor to the conscripts who would die in Central Asia.

As usual, in fact, the Soviet government began this war without preparing much for death. There were not enough coffins. One survivor described how the dead "had sometimes to be dressed in ancient uniforms, even jodhpurs and so on from the last century; sometimes when there aren't even enough uniforms available, they are put into their coffins completely naked." When there was no body to send, they often put a bundle of old rags into the coffin, sealing it to be sure that the relatives would never know the truth. Corpses waiting to be shipped were put into primitive cold storage, "where they gave off a stench of rotting wild boar."[48] No one talks about ritual as they remember the dead. "If they had ceremonies when they buried them, well, they didn't ask me to come along," a veteran told me. And then he began to talk, as everybody does, about the cheap zinc coffins, the maggots, and the smell.

All this was bad enough, but for many veterans the story of Afghanistan did not end with their final demobilization. Large numbers—among Smirnov's respondents certainly a majority—were to find that images of the war would follow them into civilian life. All the men I talked to were certain that they had suffered from problems (not all of them used words like "stress") of one kind or another. The shadows took a long time to recede. Some of them remember thinking they would never recover their peace of mind. "One of the boys had dreams all the time," a group of veterans told me. "In the end he was afraid to sleep. He kept dreaming that they had machine guns, that they were coming for him, that he was going to be taken prisoner."

Others started to behave strangely, endangering themselves or the people whom they loved. They report throwing themselves to the ground in terror during holiday firework displays, or suffering panic attacks when they smelled the diesel at the local bus station. One of Smirnov's patients woke screaming from a nightmare of battle to find that the enemy he was smothering was his sleeping wife. Many of the worst affected turned to drink. "Virtually everyone" in Smirnov's survey used alcohol to relieve their tension when they first came home. Most continued to do so. A minority, but a large one—about one in five—eventually became alcoholics. Even those who, as one veteran put it to me, "had made their peace with spirits," occasionally found that a few drinks could send them whirling back to desert landscape and uncanny night. Heightened aggression, especially associated with drinking, is another near universal symptom of so-called Afghan syndrome. The words "We did not send you there" are enough, Smirnov observed, to provoke most men to rage.

Adapting to peace is not easy. Safety itself becomes a kind of shock. The men came home to city streets that they found eerily quiet. They could not understand the people's lack of fear. Some found that life without military orders and comrades was too complicated to bear. But for others, the two worlds, Afghanistan and St. Petersburg, were not distinct enough. "I kept dreaming that I was walking out of my flat," one man reported. "I got into the elevator, went down, and as I got out, and the doors closed behind my back, I found I was in Afghanistan, alone, unarmed." Another of Smirnov's patients, a man in his early twenties, retreated to his room when he got home. For months, he could tolerate no company but that of a former comrade. The two men spent hours sitting on his bed recalling the war. Their conversations did not help them to forget, or even to contain and shape their memories. The man began to fear that his personality was changing. His marriage collapsed in less than a year. He also became increasingly violent. He got help—which means that he was admitted to a Soviet mental hospital—only after he had attacked and nearly killed a fellow student on his technical course.

Behavior like this is identified in Smirnov's written work as part of the syndrome of PTSD. So, too, is the desire that many have to find new paths to danger. "They became so used to stress that they could not live without it," he explains. "That's why some of them have never stopped fighting." Some have volunteered as mercenaries in Yugoslavia's wars, others provide the muscle for the street gangs and mafia rings that run so much of Russia's banking and trade. Most resent the notion of psychiatric damage. They do not accept that a doctor in a hospital can cure so-called afflictions of the spirit. "The boys don't go to psychiatrists," Smirnov explains. "Okay, so they can't sleep or they are drinking or whatever. But they talk to each other. They don't see it as a problem that doctors can solve. The word got around that I was okay, but the ones with the real problems are still the ones who stay away." Stress is not, to most of these ex-soldiers, a medical condition.

A minority of the veterans, however, would eventually get help from an unexpected source. In the late 1980s, a group of American psychologists established a series of exchanges between Soviet veterans of Afghanistan and their American counterparts, a generation older, the men who had fought in Vietnam in the 1960s. The parallels between the two wars were obvious, and the inclusion of Soviet soldiers in the American rehabilitation programs seemed to help everyone. "We did not need interpreters," an exchange participant told me. "The boys understood each other straight away. There was no language problem. It was like a nonverbal understanding."[49]

A good deal of the therapy was nonverbal, too. One Californian exchange, for instance, included standard talking cures, but it also involved sweat huts, Native American chants and long retreats in wilderness.[50] Similar ideas are now being tried by a handful of people in Russia. Valerii Mikhailovskii, a psychologist by training, runs a trauma center in the suburban town of Zelenograd. He is idealistic, which is just as well, for he receives no public funds.

The center runs on a shoe-string. Nevertheless, and despite its obvious dilapidation, the place has a decidedly un-Soviet atmosphere. The day I visited it, the people with whom Mikhailovskii was working (there is no easy Russian word for "client," and he would himself reject the word "patient") were practicing tai chi. I was invited to participate in a group meeting, a self-help discussion, and a lengthy round of breathing exercises.[51] Back in St. Petersburg, in a state-run psychiatric hospital, Smirnov's approach is more orthodox. His work is in the careful tradition of the prerevolutionary psychiatrists who studied shell shock. Like them, he cites at least as much from British, American, and German publications as he does from the work of his own colleagues. His observations on treatment, too, are firmly aligned with mainstream American clinical practice.

The ex-servicemen who have tried these cures, and especially the ones who have been abroad, glow with the zeal of the born again. Some of the beneficiaries of the Californian exchange believe that a general recognition of PTSD would transform the lives of all veterans, and even that therapies might usefully be applied to the mass of Russia's population. One of them told me that he would like to see production-line clinics to treat the problem. "You know," he said, to the general approval of his friends, "something like those places that man Fyedorov has set-up to operate on people's eyes." This soldier regrets, and even resents, the dismissive attitude of the older veterans, the men and women who survived the Great Patriotic War. The older people's "psychological perception was entirely different," he explained. "Plus after the Second World War they didn't know, did they, what stress was, they didn't consider it. Even now most of the old men think it's some trendy new thing. It's the principle that says that if they hadn't discovered bacteria there wouldn't be any disease."

Views like this, however, are representative of a small minority. Smirnov is aware that his findings have been overlooked by many—though not all—of his professional colleagues.[52] Most of the Afghantsy that I met or read about are similarly unimpressed. Large numbers of survivors have succeeded in finding private ways of living with their pasts. "No one likes to go and see a psych," the men told me. "Nothing makes that easy. Just think about the history of our mental hospitals, for a start. It's not our way, is it?" Only the ones whose problems become disabling volunteer themselves for medical help.[53] Otherwise, Afghantsy stick together. When one of them dies, of violence, of alcohol poisoning, from the effects of drug abuse or malaria, his comrades generally help to pay for the funeral and the stone.[54]

These days, too, the men who still call themselves the boys do not talk much. "I get tired of answering the same questions," a former soldier told me. "If I visit a school they always ask the same things. Did I take drugs and did I kill anyone. Of course I killed people. I don't know how many. In the end you don't think about it any more."[55] Nearly half the respondents in Smirnov's study were reluctant to share their memories with people who had not been in the war, and almost a quarter preferred not to talk about it at all.[56] This reticence can be interpreted in various ways. As Smirnov explains, "the avoidance of the reexperience of trauma" is a standard feature of PTSD.

But perhaps the issue should be framed in a different way. No one could argue that there were no cases of trauma among Soviet veterans of war. Most soldiers, too, the ones who went through national service, tell stories of army initiation rites—you did not have to fight to get yourself abused, beaten, raped, burned, or drenched in human urine. Life in the Soviet army was brutal at the best of times. But trauma does not capture the whole tale. It is not just that the medicalization of Afghan syndrome in itself is controversial. There is also a wider issue in the background. State violence, political repression, and years of forgetting are also parts of the story. "I found it harder back here than in Afghanistan," the veterans often say.[57] Their anxiety is not necessarily a sign of illness. They might have been more unusual, in the circumstances, if they had not experienced that sense of isolation, or the anger, guilt, and even aggression that followed them back to their European Russian homes.

The list of problems is formidable. Prejudice is one. The society in which the Afghantsy have had to live denied the validity of their efforts, preferring to suppress their stories of real life and death. The Soviet government hid their comrades' bodies. It lied about the things that they had done. There was no public outcry in their support. There was little material compensation, either. The permanent invalids who survive have not been exiled from urban centers, that was a Stalinist trick, but they often have to beg for the money to pay for whatever it is that keeps them alive. Many of them work under the protection of able-bodied fellow veterans, and that is where the rumors start, the stories of mafia scams and bogus begging rackets. But many have no choice. You need someone to carry you to the deep platforms of the Moscow metro, which is where some of them sit and beg, if you have no legs. The way that people shun these men says more about civilian Russia and its insecurities than it does about their own behavior since the war. Neurotic responses and imagined threats, in other words, are not confined to former combatants. Nor are their other answers—alcoholism, for instance, and its associated criminality and violence.

Some of these ideas were formulated first by Vietnam veterans in the United States in the 1970s.[58] But the parallels between the two societies do not go very deep. The point about Soviet attitudes was—as Smirnov observed—that they depended so centrally upon dissociation. The Soviet state was seldom frank about death. Over the years, a pattern of evasion developed, including the censorship of basic information. Despair, even as a topic of psychiatric enquiry, was almost entirely taboo.[59] Suicide, too, was scarcely ever mentioned. Even the police did not have automatic access to the relevant statistics, some of which were never, in fact, kept.[60] While Soviet habits like this prevailed, it was not surprising that the Afghantsy should have learned to doubt which world was desert and which their unrecoverable home.

There was no reason to suppose, in the spring of 1986, that the habit of denial would be broken in Soviet Russia. It was convenient for too many people. The Khrushchev thaw had let some light play on the awkward past. A new generation, it was felt, might focus now on other things. There were so many other problems. The Soviet Union was noticeably lagging behind the United States—in labor productivity, scientific innovation, consumer goods production, food distribution, space and military technology. These issues were at the top of the reform agenda when Mikhail Gorbachev became the communist Party's First Secretary in 1985. Some people believe that the policy of glasnost that he introduced eighteen months later may have ruined at least one opportunity for state-led economic reform. Openness, it is argued, is not always the best policy when you want to close a factory and raise the price of bread.[61]

It was a nuclear catastrophe that forced Gorbachev's hand. The meltdown at the fourth Chernobyl nuclear reactor on the night of Friday 26 April 1986 is part of Europe's history. The cloud of radioactive particles it released could not remain an internal Soviet matter. It drifted across Poland. The beekeepers noticed that foraging bees were being stung to death as they returned to their own hives, though the Polish government, at this early stage, was less inclined to protest. Sweden was the next to register the cloud, and it was the Swedes who raised the first international questions about it. In the end, it blew westward, dropping radioactive caesium and strontium onto the Welsh uplands and the English Lakes, poisoning the forests of the Vosges. Inside the Soviet Union, meanwhile, the leadership of the Communist Party in Moscow were shocked to discover the layers of corruption, mismanagement, and misinformation within its own ranks. Chernobyl was the last catastrophe of the old order, and its consequences forced a reconsideration of every value for which that order stood.

The nuclear power station at Chernobyl is about sixty miles north of Kiev. For years, life around it went on in true Soviet style. The people who lived nearby knew there were risks, and even that there was mismanagement, but they preferred to get on with their fishing. The woods and the lake nearby were beautiful, and the land especially fertile. People suspected, in fact, that the fallout from the power station was one of the reasons for the extraordinary success of their vegetable plots.[62] When the experiment that led to the fire in the fourth reactor began that evening, most of them were packing for their dachas, cheerfully assembling sunhats, bottles, food, and newly purchased gardening tools. It was a public holiday, and it was also—by happy coincidence—the first weekend of spring, the moment when, suddenly, the wind turns warm and the countryside bursts into life. To be in the city on those days is almost intolerable, and it is impossible to stay indoors.

What happened next is no longer secret. A set of tests that had not been adequately prepared went out of control, a fire took hold, and the accident turned, in minutes, into a disaster that no one could contain. The staff at the plant that night, most of whom are now dead, did what they could to stop a meltdown. For weeks thereafter, volunteers and conscripts from the police, army, and fire services worked punishing and often lethal shifts to cool and seal the fuel rods, to clear the area of debris, and to build a concrete carcass for the ruined building. Posthumous testimonials to their courage festoon the walls of Kiev's Chernobyl museum. For the most part, by contrast, the government's response, meaning that of the Communist Party and its local ministries, was disgraceful.

It will never be possible to say exactly how many lives were wasted on this occasion as a result of the Soviet culture of denial. True, the people of Chernobyl, Pripyat', and the surrounding villages were evacuated in the course of the first weekend—there was nothing else to do with them. But the facts about the disaster were not made widely available. Even Moscow, possibly, was not sufficiently informed.[63] The officials on the spot and in Kiev gave away as few details as possible. If they could get away with it, indeed, their first response was to pack up the boots of their cars and make for somewhere else. The widow of an army officer who had been called to Chernobyl from a family party on the Saturday, and who had then worked on the cleanup for three months, told me that her granddaughter had gone to school as usual on the first day of the following week. "It was one of those elite schools," she said. "We had got her in there although we were not in those circles, you know what I mean. Well, she went to school after the holiday and there was no one left in her class. She was the only child there. The Party people had taken their kids away that weekend. We didn't know what it was about, but they did, and they got out straight away."[64]

If the civilian population as a whole had known about this, there would, of course, have been panic. But someone should have taken responsibility for basic public information. The people of Kiev did not know, as they marched in the streets for International Socialism and the first of May, that they would have been better off indoors with their windows shut. A man I talked to bowed his head as he remembered his teenage son. "He was an enthusiast; he believed in the Soviet thing," he said. "He insisted on going on the May Day March. He always did. No one told us that he should not have. He was an athlete. He probably breathed more of it than the rest of them."[65] Microscopic dust was not the only problem. A British student who flew home from Kiev in the middle of the crisis was found to have a piece of nuclear fuel attached to his shoe, and fragments of it were found embedded in the fabric of another tourist's trousers.[66]

The truth leaked out very slowly. Some of the rumors were contradictory. Because there had been so many lies, the people had no faith in information. Should they go outside or lock the doors? Should they stay in Kiev or make for Moscow? What was there left to eat or drink? Was the government still deceiving us or not? No one believed the government's strictures about "acceptable levels" of radiation. The "human robots" who shoveled the dust from the reactor's roof (many of whom were conscripts doing national service) were supposed to remain within a "maximum acceptable dose" each time they ran across the concrete, but most of them received far more, and they knew it. Kiev was supposed to be "safe," but its inhabitants still suspect its earth and dusty streets. On the other hand, there were many in the countryside who could not believe the government's story that their soil, air, and water had suddenly turned to poison. The ones who did not live within the exclusion zone began to creep back that summer, and by the autumn some of them were drying the first of the abundant mushrooms in the woods.

It is said that Gorbachev was shocked by the things he learned from Chernobyl. His government was also obliged to call in foreign specialists and to appeal for international aid. The disaster, the evidence of mismanagement, and the forced encounter with the west all spurred him on to a radical rethinking of reform.[67] One of the results would be the policy of glasnost, which began to burn its way through the first layers of historical fog in the summer of 1986. The leader's conversion to openness, however, would take years to alter Soviet mental habits and deeply held beliefs. No one trusted the state, its scientists had deceived the people, and the doctors, who could not cure the children of their strange cancers, seemed only to make things worse. Science and superstition clashed upon an epic stage. The people trusted neither state nor physics. They turned, in their emergency, to God and magic.

The escatalogical wisdom of the time was that Chernobyl was a disaster prefigured in the Book of Revelation. Fatalism, however, was not the only possible response. There were no village folk remedies for radiation poisoning, but this was a society that had lived by improvisation for decades. A story got about that vodka cleaned the organism of radioactive particles, and that a ration of the stuff was always given to the crews of Soviet nuclear submarines. The treatment was particularly effective, ran the tale, if red wine were consumed at the same time. It was probably no coincidence that the Chernobyl accident took place at the height of Gorbachev's campaign against alcoholism.[68] The lines for vodka (and for the sugar to make *samogon,* and even for certain brands of eau-de-cologne) were already long enough that spring. Now there was a minor panic among the intellectuals. A friend, who was seven months pregnant at the time, begged me to buy some vodka for her in a foreign currency shop. It was in vain that I told her about the wisdom of my own culture, which teaches that hard spirits are dangerous for an unborn child. How did I know, the family conference asked, that my British government was not weaving lies of its own?

The rumors are still circulating now. Some of them are true. The stories of a two-headed foal and human babies without faces sound like an apocalyptic nightmare. But if you visit the Chernobyl museum, the specimens are there, floating eerily in their yellow jars. There is nothing allegorical about an epidemic of childhood leukemia, about tumors of the lung, throat, and thyroid. What is truly remarkable, however, even if you remember all their history, is the resilience of Kiev's population, and especially of the evacuees, some of them sick or dying, who live in exile from their poisoned homes. An international team of psychologists and doctors, American and Ukrainian, has found that the families who live in the shadow of the accident generally do just that. They get on with their lives.[69]

Further away from the plant, however, the fear of apocalypse has released an anarchic riot of prejudice. Radioactive waste now features centrally in Russian urban myth. You can trip over it, they say, on any scrap heap, and everyone has heard of a mad old man who stockpiles it in a neighbor's basement. "Don't ever buy vegetables from the people with Ukrainian accents," a neighbor told me when I first set up in a Moscow flat. "And test everything. They are cunning, you know. They get people with Central Asian faces to sell the stuff so that we'll all think it's safe." Nothing that is not "ours," from our immediate family, is really "safe," to buy, eat, or use, unless it is definitely foreign, and preferably American, German, or Japanese. This uncritical faith in imports—technological gadgets no less than policy prescriptions—is something I find disconcerting. It is also frequently misplaced. The same neighbor gave me a house-warming present. It was a pocket Geiger counter, complete with Japanese instructions and spare batteries. It was probably the most expensive model you could buy in the local market in those days, and he was most insistent that I should use it. I felt guilty for months, because I never did. One afternoon a friend in Cambridge took it to his laboratory to give it a trial. It flashes impressively in three different colors, but it does not work.

11

A TIDE OF BONES

There was no ignoring Victory Day in the 1970s and early 1980s. The snow would usually have melted by early May, the mud would be receding, and the first dandelion leaves would have pushed through the concrete pavements in the suburban streets. In the city centers, meanwhile, there was action. It started a few days before the holiday, when the local team turned out to organize the flags. A battered truck would appear among the government buildings. It would be loaded with ropes and ladders. The blue-clad figures, men and women, would jump from the cab, and there would be discussion, irritation, effort, smoking. The banners were enormous, thousands of them, and when they were in place even the color of the light seemed to change under the cloud of scarlet cloth. Monumental posters also came out of store, some to be draped across the fronts of public buildings. There were twenty-foot portraits of Lenin and Marx, there were hammers and sickles, and there was always a supply of Brezhnevs, usually half-profiles, posed to show all the amazing medals that he had awarded to himself. Back in the corner shops, meanwhile, there would be a sudden run on hot-house carnations, vodka, and the chemical sponge cakes whose Russian name is *tort*.

The people did not have to go and march, in other words, but even if they planned to stay at home, and especially if they planned to get away, to take the dog, the family and all those bags, to get the train out to the country, few could avoid the holiday, the extra police, the cages channeling the crowds. "It was just another holiday," the children of the 1970s say these days. But at the time they would have spent a week or more on Victory at school, they would have colored in their drawings, flags and weapons, red and green, written short assignments, and answered the test questions. Their mothers, meanwhile, rushing back from work, would have been worrying about food and buses, the unavailability of shoe polish.

The bustle, light, and noise were intended to overwhelm a person's private images, their memories and apprehensions. But the spaces and the hours that lay beyond collective, civic reach were not mere darkness, silence. Even the keenest patriots had memories of their own. Their secrets were anarchic. Neither the church, whose full ceremonial was observed by very few, nor the state, with all its kitsch-invented custom, commanded the way that certain kinds of life were remembered, certain deaths were mourned. The vigor and variety of these private worlds were invisible for years. They surfaced and took shape at the end of the 1980s. The catalyst was the rediscovery of bones.

As soon as the existence of the first Stalinist mass graves was made a public fact the people began to come. They made their pilgrimages by bus, on foot, in someone's ancient car, squeezed in beside their grandchildren, and they left photographs, flowers, cellophane-covered copies of recently obtained official documents, candles, ribbons, tinsel, bread. There were no obvious conventions. At Levashovo, near St. Petersburg, a site where several thousand men and women were shot in 1937 alone, the pinewood is scattered with pictures, plastic flowers, and spent candles, but some people have simply made pyramids with the pine cones, and others, more officially, have beaten sheets of tin and hammered names and dates into them. In one part of the wood there is a group of artificial posts among the trees. Nailed to each is a metal image, a reindeer, commemorating Finnish dead.

The people say, today, that they always remembered, all through the 1970s, despite the pressures and distractions. It is hard to tell, in any instance, if this is really true. Some, a few, can show that they continued to ask questions. But for the rest, the secret memories would turn out to be elusive, slippery, easily lost because there was so little talk, no wider social meaning. The tokens that survived to be passed on were partial, ambiguous, sometimes even mutilated, like the photographs the people kept in their albums, the ones that had been defaced—literally, to prevent police reprisals in the event of search—with a black line across a person's eyes. Some, like Yudif Borisovna, still clung to legal papers—the notification of a death, for instance, or the answer to a formal enquiry. These bore official stamps, as if the past were done with (it would be a shock, for those who lived that long, to discover that the information they contained was faked). Many other relatives had nothing. Life had been lived and memory managed at different levels, people had newer tales of grief, of happiness, achievement. The talk and rediscovering of the 1980s created some new stories about the past. It did not merely resurrect the old ones.

The evidence of corporate rewriting, of attempts to claim the dead and give them a social role, is also there at Levashovo. There are several versions. The first, the work of a repentant state, is a clumsy monument in black stone. It stands opposite the entrance to the wood, and it is an ugly monster, like a robot or a giant vice, whose prey, draped passively across an anvil in its guts, is a seminaked human being, a male, as muscular as the heroes of socialist realism, but this time face down, dead. Survivors groups dislike it. Most, today, prefer the next version, which is a large Orthodox cross inside the wood, the first of several, fixed in a heap of stones and decorated with a photocopied icon of the Virgin and Child. The church has been working hard to reclaim Russian souls, including those of Communists; there will be priests at any ceremony here. If you do not like that memorial either, however, there is still the museum, home to a well-fed ginger cat. It is a hut, two rooms with an old stove, and if there is anyone to let you in, you can stand and warm yourself while studying selected documents, statistics, photographs, and plans.

Finally, you wander back into the wood. "We looked for you for fifty-two years," a message reads. "We will always remember you." Memorials, as everyone knows, assign a shape to memory, but as they do, precisely by their selectivity, they can also freeze it. There were some years—from 1986, when glasnost was first launched, until the early 1990s—when the rediscovery of the past was an active process in Russia, involving live emotion—anger, guilt, grief, sometimes remorse. Now there are memorials. What they mean—whether they testify to someone's truth (a triumph for survivors), to greater openness, to social fragmentation (these things are best forgotten), to piety, to a desire for memory or for its opposite—depends on who you are.

Unclaimed bones, of course, were nothing unusual in Soviet soil before the public campaign started. Reburials of a kind had been going on for decades. Most were treated as a matter of civic education and community service. Groups of teenage boys, calling themselves things like scout patrols, were encouraged to find and bury Soviet soldiers, some of the tens of thousands who lay rotting in the woods. "The most important thing for the young people to understand is that the bones were people," one of their leaders told an American visitor. "Only when we fully respect the dead will we respect the living."[1] At best, this was a classic piece of Soviet wishful thinking. There was also another team, after all, a secret one, or so they say, that worked to rebury—and conceal—some other types of corpse, including the victims of disasters such as the Armenian earthquake of 1988.[2] It was important to dispose of evidence, important not to count.

There was a casualness, even generations after the war, and after Stalin, about the bones and bits of uniform that children found. In Kolyma, recounts one visitor to the former Gulag, there were so many bones lying about "that in the summer children used human skulls to gather blueberries."[3] Elsewhere, local people had "always" known that a site was "theirs," meaning the property of the secret police. Such reputations clung to every kind of landscape, to mounds of tussocky grass, fenced-off corners of scrub or marsh, to regimented lines of spruce. There had been occasions, too, even in the years of stagnation, when the dead had forced themselves upon the living. The Communist Party could not command the weather. In 1979, for instance, a flood on the Ob River in Siberia washed up and beached a tide of corpses from a disused prison.[4] The bodies were quietly reburied.

The excavations that began in the late 1980s were different. They were angrier, more focused, and their motivation was political. The context was Gorbachev's limited policy of openness, but the people who led the hunt for evidence were no admirers of the Soviet government. The idea was to locate and even to identify the dead, to give them stories, names. As Aleksandr Mil'chakov, one of the most famous of the campaigners (and the one who found Yudif Borisovna's father's grave), explained to an American sociologist, the victims of Stalinism "couldn't really have vanished, their remains had to be somewhere."[5] When he found them, whether he found skulls or ash, he forced the KGB to admit, grudgingly, to some of the crimes its predecessors had concealed. The bones were disinterred as witnesses.

Mil'chakov was driven by a thirst for evidence, the journalist's ambition to find out. But others have continued the work of exhumation for years, and well after the fall of Communism, from a variety of motives. Yurii Dmitriev, who found the grave at Sandormokh, the site in Karelia where hundreds of the prisoners of Solovki were shot, is a restless, angry man. He has tried many kinds of life. He is a former engineer, former aspiring politician, the divorced father of the two children who sometimes help him with his unusual work. His mission, which he calls his "cross," is to exhume and rebury as many as possible of Stalins' victims in Karelia. He works for himself, and how he lives, who pays him, is not clear.

He talks a lot about the physical reality of dust and bone. His eyes are bright, his taut face always moving. It is essential to work without gloves, he says. You must feel through the earth for buried bone. Your hands will find it smoother, harder—warmer, even—but so desperately fragile. He no longer drinks, he tells me, but he keeps a bottle of vodka for the men who help him. They need it to kill their nerves. There was that time when one of them screamed, for instance. He had dug into sand, hunting for skulls, and had come upon a glass eye. It seemed to be watching him from the grave. As he tells the formulaic story, Dmitriev is looking for a reaction from me. I suspect that the tale is one of several that he keeps for the purpose. It is nearly midnight, and we are talking in a narrow hotel room. The Alsatian bitch that had lunged for my throat when I arrived an hour earlier now sleeps, occupying every inch of floor between us.

Sergei Alekseyev, by contrast, is a softly spoken, round-faced man, an academic, an archaeologist and ethnographer. We talked on a spring morning in a dusty room at the back of Moscow university's ethnographic museum. He has been involved in work at the grave site at Butovo, near Moscow, for several years, but the only bones to feature in our conversation were in the glass cases behind us: outmoded science, not memory. He and his associates decided long ago that Butovo's victims should lie in peace, however orderless their remains. Instead of digging, then, these volunteers, working in association with the Orthodox church, have built. Their wooden chapel stands on the edge of one of the long pits, and there are other monuments—a giant cross is one—scattered around the site. Alekseyev would point out, if you questioned this, that many of the dead were priests. He would also add, for he is a believer, that everyone who died at the site, whatever their belief on earth, is now a martyr, praying in the other light for us.

All the people who have dug and written about digging are interested in facts. The literalness of bone and bullet is shocking, but the shock is cathartic; truth of whatever sort is better than the Soviet regime's kitsch and lies. Among the facts that are now privileged, statistics are crucial. The numbers have been so contentious that it is tempting, now, to settle down beside the graves and count. Dmitriev wants to finger the bones themselves, but Alekseyev uses surveys. He and his friends have found a series of burial trenches at their site, each one of which is three meters wide and several kilometers in length. The pits run under apple trees, beneath an orchard that was planted in the 1960s and

1970s as deliberate camouflage. The documents state that 20,765 people were shot and buried at Butovo between August 1937 and October 1938, but the killing went on into the 1950s. It is on the basis of the ground survey that the team suggests that the total number of bodies may be as many as 100,000.[6]

Numbers are not the only reality that the excavations have exposed. In 1989 a group of volunteers discovered human remains in an abandoned military hospital. The bodies were those of the patients, and they had died together, each one of them shot with a single Soviet bullet.[7] Few testimonies to the brutality of Stalin's scorched earth policy of 1941 could have been more effective. Instead of evacuating the patients in the face of the Nazi advance, the Soviet army had murdered and then abandoned them. Atrocities like this had been the stuff of folk memory in many regions for decades, but the material evidence made them a part of everyone's reality. It made them—temporarily—impossible to ignore.

The idea that political purging was a limited or even rational process was also shattered. In 1989 and 1990, the front pages of popular newspapers and journals began to carry some unusual photographs. Young volunteers stood sweating in summer woodland. Beside them were fresh trenches and box upon box of femurs and vertebrae, sharp rib cages, and bits of pelvis. Used Soviet bullets were lined up on sacking for the camera, and there were always rows of skulls, hundreds of them at a time, fractured, blackened, anonymous, the ones in the front row chosen carefully so that each showed its single, jarring, neatly symmetrical hole.[8]

The forced encounter with historical reality was certainly painful. For the young people who did the physical work, the ones who, arguably, suffered least, the bones were history, albeit family history. But the questions they reawakened among the elderly were personal. The relatives of purge victims had their stories back at last. But the emergence of this buried history, at a time of continuing conflict, would guarantee them nothing. They needed more than glasnost. Most needed economic reparation, all craved a personal apology, some kind of recognition. For most, too, the search for their own grave, their father's ash, no longer an impossibility, would prove a lengthy and exhausting task.

Feuds opened between the different kinds of veteran, between the loyal Stalinist fighters who had starved and marched and narrowly escaped slaughter through three exhausting winters and the former prisoners who had spent the same years starving, freezing, and hacking rock. Everyone, suddenly, was talking about degrees of suffering. For the second and third generations, the people who had done the digging, the disputes, and even the stories themselves, would soon become unbearable. Eyewitness accounts of famine, war and murder, told by your own grandparents, told about your own village, are too accusing, too repetitively pleading, too intimate, even; you cannot enjoy your own life if you linger in their endless shadow. "Oh, those old people," a young historian sighed after we had talked. "They always want something. And I get so tired of the same old stories."

The survivors of Stalin's repressions now have their evidence and their earth. Few can hope to find a unique, personal grave, to touch and then rebury the remains of a man or woman whom they loved, but many can now stand, at last, in haunted forests and by granite stones, believing that they know the truth after a lifetime of official silence. They say their own deaths will be peaceful now. Many swear that they heard words of blessing as they stood and waited in the clearing in the trees, that they are now understood, forgiven. The value of that freedom is incalculable.

Beyond the circle of survivors and relatives, however, the dispute over facts and bones continues. The dead may whisper to their children, but they do not talk out loud. The work of interpretation falls to the living, to new generations. The motives that animated these campaigners have been far from simple, and the conclusions that they draw from their discoveries conflict. A process that remains a sacred rite of passage for the bereaved is part of an ongoing political struggle for their allies, while for the prurient and the ghoulish it is enjoyed as dark revenge. Some skeletons have been made to carry the banner of nationalist liberation, others, in an age when Orthodox Christianity has suddenly returned to fashion, have become martyrs in a religion that few, when living, had confessed. Mil'chakov was right. The bones are there. For those who see them as historical facts, however, the question of ownership remains unsolved.

The atmosphere was very different when the process of discovery began, in the mid-1980s. Back then, with an authoritarian state as adversary, the campaigners were optimistic, driven, apparently united. They marched to the internationally recognized music of human rights. Three generations worked together—the political radicals, the former dissidents, and the elderly survivors of Stalinist repression. Glasnost provided the context, but the popular coalition was far more ambitious than official policy allowed. It gathered, eventually, around one kind of organization. Memorial, which was the name of one of the original associations, began as a metropolitan gathering of intellectuals, none of whom was old enough to remember the Great Purge. But it soon expanded, and its activity attracted affiliation from like-minded groups across the USSR. Within six months of its foundation, by the early summer of 1988, it had collected forty-eight thousand signatures in support of its demands.[9]

The activists identified a number of immediate goals. In August 1987, Memorial's members dedicated themselves to "keeping alive the memory of the victims of repression."[10] To do this, they intended to campaign for the establishment of public memorials—the most conspicuous of which would stand in front of the headquarters of the secret police on Lyubyanka Square in Moscow—and also to develop a network of research centers to find out more about the repressions. They were committed to high-profile campaigning, to the collection of petitions and the writing of open letters, the publication of names and memoirs, and the initiation of the broadest possible debate.

Many of Memorial's leading activists were harassed and even arrested in the autumn and winter of 1987.[11] Their radicalism raised uncomfortable questions for a leadership that had not yet agreed to expose its past to scrutiny. Glasnost, at this stage, was little more than one of several possible strategies for the achievement of economic and social regeneration. Like Khrushchev's policy of de-Stalinization, it encouraged a form of public remorse, but only in limited quantities. There were no early plans for an open-ended policy of truth and reparation.

What Gorbachev's leadership wanted to achieve by all the talking was acceptance for the idea that pluralism and innovation were containable within the structure of single party rule. Accordingly, the Central Committee of the 1980s rehabilitated its own former members. One of the first to come back was Nikolai Bukharin, the Bolshevik theorist of the socialist market, murdered in 1938.[12] He became a posthumous celebrity in 1988, the face on the cover of all the best color magazines. Other "names" soon followed—Chayanov, Riutin, Rykov, Tomskii, and finally, scandalously, the renegade Trotsky himself.[13] For a time, the policy amounted to a kind of Kremlinology in reverse, a choreographed return of the rogues to the gallery. Selected files were reopened under the watchful supervision of the Institute of Marxism-Leninism, selected details calculatedly made public.

What was not envisaged was a wider debate about the political system that had made repression possible, nor any consideration of its ultimate scale and absurdity. For once, however, Soviet history took on a life of its own. Memorial played a part, though the brunt of the initiative was taken on an individual basis by film directors, novelists, journalists, poets, and even, occasionally, an amateur historian or two.[14] Within three years there was almost nothing sacred left to ransack. Even Lenin's immunity had gone.[15]

The reasons for glasnost's ultimate failure as a policy of containment are complex. The political revolution of the late 1980s owned more to economic problems than it did to history. The Soviet system was also undermined by a succession of environmental disasters, increasing levels of ethnic tension, a growing sense of inadequacy in the face of the West, and even by the simple fact that a new generation was coming of age, supplanting the old guard forever. But the pressure of decades of silence undoubtedly played a part. Among Memorial's founders, all of whom were young people between twenty-five and thirty-five in 1987, several, including the historian Arsenii Roginskii, had already suffered as a result of their curiosity or outspokenness.[16] Dmitrii Yurasov, who had started collecting of the names of the repressed when he was still a teenager, would lose a succession of archival jobs when his extracurricular interest in political murder was discovered.[17] But harassment could not prevent the questions and research for long.[18] Glasnost, with its prudishness and self-congratulation, was never going to be enough.

The weight of official suspicion was considerable at first, however, and Memorial was vulnerable as long as it remained a forum for young radicals. What saved it was the alliance that rapidly formed between its young initiators and some representatives of the dissident intellectual elite. Many of glasnost's greatest public figures chose to align themselves with the popular movement. Among them were human-rights campaigners such as Andrei Sakharov and a galaxy of poets, writers, and critics—Yevgenii Yevtushenko, Bulat Okudzhava, Anatolii Rybakov, Mikhail Shatrov. Memorial's council, elected by postal vote, also included the populist politician Boris Yeltsin, who at the time was still in opposition because of his earlier public quarrel with Gorbachev.[19] Yeltsin would remain a maverick, but the dissidents of the 1960s made the movement powerful. They were more than merely influential names. Many were also skillful publicists, political tacticians. "They taught us all a lot about what to do," a Memorial activist told me in 1997. Memorial became a force in current politics, an organization about future strategies, not just a campaign to reinstate the past.

The confident young activists would argue that even the frankest reckoning with history was not sufficient on its own. They were as determined as the elderly survivors to ensure that the story of totalitarian repression should not be censored again, as it had been in the Brezhnev years, and they were aware, too, that the last witnesses were beginning to die. Justice demanded that the dead should be remembered. But it was also crucial to ensure that there would never be a chance for re-Stalinization in Russia. It was time, as Yevtushenko had put it some years before, to remove Stalin from Stalin's heirs.

Memorial's work would stimulate the first public exploration within the Soviet Union of the full extent of all the killing that had taken place under Soviet rule. It also provoked the people to remember. This evocation of private memory may turn out to have been its most enduring achievement. In 1988 the broadsheet daily *Literaturnaya gazeta* appealed on Memorial's behalf for information. The letters began to come immediately. They were not literary masterpieces, the polished recollections of the famous. They were usually handwritten, on cheap paper, and they were the private stories of ordinary people in provincial towns, memoirs of the camps, accounts of arrest, of interrogation, of disappearance. Some of them were from former policemen or special troops, and these described the ways in which orders had been given and enforced. There were also appeals for help, the first of thousands. Everyone wanted information, details of the last days of lost parents, husbands, brothers, and sisters. The Memorial archive, which already included photographs, record cards, and the group's own correspondence, now swelled to accommodate the personal testimonies of thousands of survivors.[20]

The level of public interest in Stalinist repression was mirrored elsewhere in the press. In 1989, 1990, and 1991, several newspapers, including the popular evening daily *Vechernyaya Moskva*, carried regular features naming the dead and providing short biographies of them, sometimes accompanied by a photograph. The repressions, which had once seemed so remote, so much a matter for "them"—the Party, the poets, the elite—came home to ordinary people. The faces of train drivers, priests, teachers, farm laborers, and boilermakers stared back at modern Soviet readers. The men wore flat caps, self-conscious mustaches, lapel buttons in honor of forgotten agitational campaigns. The women were often neater, crisply bourgeois or defiantly revolutionary, confronting the camera with eyes that had seen too much of war and hunger already, though few were much older than forty. Some were police photographs, in profile and full face, taken at the moment of arrest. Others were studio shots, the portraits kept on file from happier times. The pictures were sometimes juxtaposed with copies of the official charge, which usually amounted to some violation of the infamous Article 58. As if to remind the reader of the lives and flesh that dry bone used to wear, the documents included poignant copies of the prisoners' fingerprints and signatures.

For column after column the faces stared, but worse was yet to come. Later on, the papers also began to publish photographs from the deeper sections of police files, the pictures that were taken to chart a prisoner's progress after questioning, sleeplessness, beatings, and torture. The written accounts of all this were never less than harrowing. Though Brezhnevite negligence and euphemism had robbed the word "repression" of its human force, no one could read these rediscovered stories of abuse with equanimity. Stalinism—the very word was an ideologized abstract—was detailed for the first time in individual narratives of nerve and muscle. These were not stories from distant prisons or arctic camps. Their location was usually a well-known street, a city center "big house," as the secret police headquarters in any town was called, and the faces of the more distinguished protagonists—Old Bolsheviks, artists, intellectuals, and poets—were familiar from everyone's school textbooks. Well-known photographs of these people were now set ruthlessly beside the unfamiliar ones, which showed the same people in their pain; unkempt, bruised, exhausted, and starved.[21]

For fifty years, in keeping with the Soviet strategy of dissociation, history had treated these men and women as if they had been alive one day and gone, "repressed," the next. The process of repression was now to be exposed. The papers told how their torturers had made them stand for days and nights, their arms outstretched, depriving them of sleep, of food, and water. Some had been drenched in water and then left to freeze, while others—the ailing Zinoviev, for instance—had been fed on salty gruel, kept close in cells that had no air, and offered only dust to ease their swelling tongues. Meyerhold, whose account of his own torture chronicles the beatings, had also been made to drink urine. Other prisoners had been forced to swallow the contents of spittoons.[22] There were beatings, broken bones, the burn marks of interrogators' cigarettes, electric shocks. The stories did not have to be sensational; the technology was not important. One old lady held the attention of an international television audience in 1990 as she described her sudden abduction, her fears for the children who were waiting for her at home, and her pain as men whose reasons she would never understand began, one by one, to break her teeth.

It is difficult to think about realities like these for long. Some people started to complain. Conservatives, naturally, disliked the revelations' accusatory tone, but even some survivors believed that the details of torture were distasteful and better kept from view.[23] On the other hand, and although Memorial's current staff includes some people who prefer to spare the old from this gratuitous pain, the cataloging of each story, once started, was an almost inescapable task. If one account was valid, if the ending of one life bore witness to the obscenity of an entire political system, then every story had to be collected. Repression was not the unique privilege of the elite, and the living who suffered directly from its consequences included some of the poorest and most neglected people in the country. In Akhmatova's phrase, the time had come to "remember each one of them by name." The words are inscribed around the memorial stone that commemorates the victims of repression in her adopted city of St. Petersburg.

The general level of interest in history has declined since Communism's collapse in 1991, but human-rights organizations like Memorial have continued to collect the pictures, names, and short biographies. Booklets with titles such as *Lists of the Shot, The Book of Memory,* and *How It Was* are still being published on cheap paper and in the largest editions that voluntary groups are able to afford. There are also occasional newspapers, such as *Fifty-Eight: Victims and Executioners,* that are circulated for free to keep the people writing and remembering. In addition to the names, the dates, and the pictures, these publications often contain snatches of memoir and details of local political history. The material is usually collected by unpaid researchers, their findings supplemented by anything they can collect from the relatives of the dead, or from local historians and journalists. Some of it has been recovered from the archives of the secret police and the courts. The books are not glossy, the research they contain is neither rigorous nor stylish, and the themes that they repeat are familiar to everyone these days. Nonetheless, the copies that are not given away to survivors and to visitors from abroad generally sell out in a few months. There are still tens of thousands of people in Russia with an urgent need to see their own histories in print.

Assembling testimonies was one of Memorial's projects, the other was its campaign to commemorate the dead in stone. Unlike the compilation of lists, the building of a monument requires a basic level of consensus. Public memorials, paid for by subscription and approved by the meetings of committees, are the products as well as the bearers of collective memory. If there is no agreed story, it is difficult to conceive of a form in which to embody the past. When Stalin died, the people's letters had poured in, recommending every kind of extravagance for his mausoleum. The letters expressed a range of ideas about death, certainly, but there was a unanimity about the leader himself. There had been more than enough propaganda, while Stalin lived, for everyone to understand his place in history. Finding a single image to represent the range of possible meanings that his victims' deaths might have was a very different matter.

As usual, the Communist Party's ideological leadership was ready with a series of banal proposals, some of which were principally intended to deprive Memorial of its moral high ground.[24] If glasnost had remained in bounds, it would, after all, have been easy enough to memorialize the famous "names." The all-purpose plinths in any Russian city could as easily carry a bust of Bukharin as of Dzerzhinskii. The problem was to find a representation for the others. There was no agreed story about the masses. Their fates had only just begun to feature in public discussion. The ordinary victims of Soviet repression, millions of men and women, had been missed and mourned in secret. There had been a Day of Remembrance for political prisoners, 30 October, since the 1970s, and from the 1980s it would gather support, but until glasnost it had been a minority affair, scarcely reported. When Memorial began its search for solid forms of commemoration, in other words, there was no large-scale collective memory, no national myth, for skillful architects to interpret. Remembrance was a public void, lacking both shape and script. Memorial's ambition, as the Soviet Union struggled to throw off its history of authoritarian rule, was that its ultimate form should be determined by the people, not the state.

The public responded with a bewildering range of suggestions for their monument. Some people wanted funereal images, the evocation of inconsolable private loss. Others wanted a grander reminder of totalitarianism as a system. These two extremes reflected the manner in which the dead had been remembered—in secret, as an empty space, or else as part of a dry, schematic public story. In this respect, even commemoration seemed to reflect the condition of the Soviet polity on the eve of its collapse. What was missing was a middle tier, the level of the community in mourning, the local organizations, the collectives of citizens accustomed to political give and take that political scientists refer to as civil society. Memorial was one of the first organizations to attempt to fill that space. It is one that is crucial for collective remembering, but it is difficult to create from scratch.[25] The activists wanted to find a new idiom, but the first proposals did not augur well. Labyrinths, towers, and barbed wire were one possibility, a simple grave or—for the Christians—a cross, another.[26] It was hopeless to expect agreement on this from people who had only just begun to learn to share their pasts in public.

Memorial's own policy on commemoration, formulated in the late 1980s, deliberately included every victim of the totalitarian system. In other words, it drew no firm distinction between the prisoner and the guard who shared his exile, the woman intimidated into handing information to the police, the exiled kulak and the defrocked priest. It was no accident that Memorial's best years, the years when the maintenance of this attitude seemed possible, should have coincided with a brief interlude of hope, at least among its intellectual supporters. The Soviet Union was falling apart, but the possibilities inherent in its collapse seemed promising. The open-ended phase of commemoration captured this mood, a unity founded upon unrealized dreams. By the same token, the gradual narrowing of possible futures, the cold realities of economic gloom, unemployment, and the grinding fear of violence, all served to define and lessen the public's generosity in the years that followed. A broad, inclusive movement began to fragment. The contests for primacy among survivors began.

The divisions over victimhood followed the fault lines of current political tension. The collapse of Communism in 1991 accelerated the process, but the first signs of it could have been observed earlier, in the USSR's non-Russian republics, where the historical issue of repression was quickly subsumed into movements for national liberation. In most of these emergent nation-states, the commemoration of the past became a matter of recalling martyrs, partisans, and freedom fighters.

The way that the story of Stalinism was retold in Lviv (Stalin's Lvov), the capital of Eastern Galicia, and the most nationalist enclave in Ukraine, was typical. In 1941 the Soviets had shot large numbers of the prisoners they had been holding in the city as they retreated in the face of the German advance. As the nationalist movement in Galicia gathered pace after 1985, these men and women, not all of whom were ethnic Ukrainians, were rediscovered, for public purposes, as victims of imperialist oppression. The massacre of Jews that had followed in 1941 and 1942, a Nazi operation involving more mass shootings and another common grave, has all but disappeared from the Ukrainian story. The site of the Jewish massacre is difficult to get to from the city center, and the guidebooks scarcely mention it.[27] The Christian Church, meanwhile, has reinvented its feud with Moscow. The Ukrainian Orthodox Church, based in Kiev, rejects Great Russian chauvinism, while the Graeco-Catholic Church ("Orthodox in form, Catholic in content") rejects the Orthodox as a whole, whoever they are.[28] The story of the past has changed, the priorities have been adjusted, and this year's group of winners mediates the latest process of commemoration.

In Russia itself, religion, not nationalism, became the means by which the search for memory would be curtailed. The church increasingly involved itself in the commemoration of Stalin's victims, and in some places, memorials based entirely on Orthodox imagery have come to dominate the landscape. The mass burial site at Butovo is a case in point, adopted by the Church and marked by a chapel, an elaborate cross, and a series of notices that emphasize the Christian aspects of martyrdom. When the site was dedicated, in 1991, it was the priesthood, fully vested and wreathed in holy incense, that led the ceremony.[29] It is the same at Levashovo, too, and there are similar calvaries at sites across the Gulag archipelago.

As an organization, Memorial has avoided identification with the church, but the survivors themselves often find it comforting. Part of the reason, as the church itself would stress, is that priests and believers were among the most conspicuous of Communism's opponents.[30] But piety is not reserved for the faithful. Religion, like nationalism, has emerged from the depths after seventy years of repression. It speaks the language of the underground—or rather, that is what it used to do, in the first years of glasnost. It also offers an alternative world view, as basic as nationalism, a view of Russianness, by which a people can perceive themselves to have historic meaning, despite the fact that Communism has gone. To that extent, it fills the vacuum left by vanishing totalitarianism, replacing one dogma, and one priesthood, with another.

The basic scheme, ironically, remains one of blood sacrifice. At one time, not long after they were shot, the dead of Sandormokh, Levashovo, and the other sites like them were ideological outlaws, the enemies of the proletariat, who died because they could not see the real future of history. Now they are martyrs. The universe within which their deaths make sense is still a place that demands tribute, a place where it is the unattainable future that everyone is waiting for. Death makes sense, in this old scheme, because there must always be some form of payment—the other word is still redemption—in exchange for better things to come. The dead are no longer people, individuals whose lives were brutally ended. They are the burnt offerings to a better life.

As James Young remarked. "Once we assign a monumental form to memory, we have to some degree divested ourselves of the obligation to remember."[31] Memorial, with its research teams and its archive, has tried hard to avoid this pitfall. But the monuments that it set in place during its best years now tend to be described as provisional. They do not make sufficient use of history for the current taste, they do not preach. Critics argue that they seem, now, to betray, by their simplicity, the very cause for which they were created.

Perhaps, however, an openness, a generous inclusivity, is the best response to set beside the writing and research. What is striking about the memorials is their minimalism. The stones that stand outside the Lyubyanka in Moscow and on Trinity Square in St. Petersburg are typical—plain, stark lumps of granite undecorated with faces or figures. Such pieces (they hardly qualify as sculptures) make no reference to religion and they do not refer to specific events. There is nothing in the history of Soviet state-sponsored violence that they preclude, and that has been their greatest value.

The collapse of Communism was swift and complete. Within five years, between 1987 and 1991, almost everything that had once been sacred in the Soviet system had been challenged, and many long-established structures had been swept away. Among the most spectacular acts of all was the Soviet Union's own dissolution in 1991. A cluster of new states succeeded it, some of them sheltering within Boris Yeltsin's new commonwealth, while others, such as the three Baltic states and Georgia, struck out entirely on their own.[32] It was a process largely welcomed by nationalists and democrats throughout the former Soviet territories, but inside Russia itself there were many who viewed the end of the empire with dismay. Die-hard Communists despaired among the ruins of their moral universe, and there were widespread predictions of civil war and economic catastrophe. Only the young, it seemed, could benefit from new opportunities. Older people, whether pensioners, industrial workers, or employees of an ossified and discredited state bureaucracy, faced acute stress. They were powerless, as they had often been, and they watched their real incomes fall, their prospects vanish.

Desperation, then, was the context for the feuds and tensions that developed between Stalinism's many heirs. The people involved had lived for decades in the shadow of state violence. The traditions of mistrust, competitiveness, and fear that it had fostered were never going to disappear overnight. Stalinism's history had been so complex, in terms of victimhood, guilt, responsibility, and collaboration, that it was always futile to dream of an easy miracle, an instant lightening of the burden of memory. Memorial's gradual slide from prominence could easily have been foreseen, as could the increasing disunity within its ranks after 1991, but the outcome in society as a whole might not have been so bitter if the people had been less apprehensive, less cynical, and less hungry. Even in Moscow, the canny citizens were stockpiling macaroni, salt, and matches by 1991. It was the present and immediate future that they really feared, but their anger found expression through much older, simpler tales—of ethnic or family oppression, unavenged betrayal, rape, fraud, and anti-Semitism.

Whatever else they needed, the pensioners would find that unity was at a premium. Soviet-style habits of silence persisted, the networks of self-protection that guaranteed survival in the past remained in place. So did the mentality that could not shed the last suspicion that arrest and imprisonment—when they happened to someone else—were usually justified. It was as if each group, each network, had to define itself in part by reference to someone it excluded, the "aliens" or "enemies." It looked like the old Stalinist mentality, and even the older peasant one, but it was a learned response to hardship, fear, and scarcity.

There was also a struggle going on to assert the meaning of lives that were ending. Self-deceptions, euphemisms, and private truths were as precious as old medals, and the challenge of new information could sometimes feel like injury. Even now, the elderly insist on the importance of their own witness, the heroic, the charmed or fateful secrets of their own endurance. "Don't listen to them," old people would say as I left a meeting of their life-long friends and neighbors. "I will tell you what it was really like." Group interviews, with few exceptions, remained anarchic choruses of monologue. Few really wanted time to listen, and very few were keen to change their minds. The break for tea and biscuits, designed to help them to relax, was just another opportunity to make the case: I know the truth, my life was important, my suffering is the proof of it. Listen first to me.

The largest single group of survivors remained the veterans of the Great Patriotic War. They continued to regard themselves as the ones with the deepest and most justifiable grievances. As victims with pension rights they would reasonably claim that their suffering called for special consideration. Their contribution to the collective good was certainly evident; they had defeated fascism. For years they had been accustomed to their privileges—a small income, extra food items, the right to avoid some of the longest lines. They also received help with medical care, and they needed it, for many had their physical scars, wounds, and disabilities whose treatment was no cheaper than that of the ex-prisoners with their hypertension or their pleurisy.

The assistance that the veterans received, then, was materially important—crucial, even—but it was also a sign of moral privilege, superiority. The people who survived the Great Patriotic War, the ones who had, at least notionally, been free enough to fight, had shared in the greatest victory of Soviet socialism, and they saw themselves as members of the strongest and most valued collective in history. It was a memory and a myth that shed some light on even the most dismal lives. It was also a status that the veterans guarded jealously, and to preserve it they would assert its exclusivity, disdaining newcomers like the young Afghantsy, and closing their ears to the pleas of noncombatant survivors like the invalids who talked to me in Kiev.

All this would change when the Soviet Union began to collapse at the end of the 1980s. The first signs, an increasing impatience with stories about the war, a growing materialism, a resentment of the elderly with their medals and their special passes, had been apparent for some time. The disintegration of reverence for the war can be traced back to the 1970s, when schoolchildren whose parents had been too young to have fought or died began to joke and fidget as the old men told their tales. Officially, however, nothing had changed. New war memorials went up every year, the parades were no less pompous, and the state continued to honor its veterans with plastic medals and extra sausage. The fortieth anniversary of the victory, however, in 1985, would be the last untroubled celebration. The years that followed saw increasing hardship, a shrinkage in the value of money and food parcels, more plastic and less meat.

A war veteran who was telling me about all this decided to illustrate his point by handing me the chocolates he had been given to mark the fiftieth anniversary of victory in 1995. "It's disgusting, isn't it?" he muttered. "They're not even good chocolates." He gestured at his tiny room, the shabby decorations, the single broken bookshelf, and the row of medicine bottles. "It would be better if they did something about all this. We fought and our comrades died. We were all ready to die. And look at this."[33] His economic problems were everyone's; he was not unique. But they represented a sharp loss, and they were felt more bitterly because the veterans' tale of sacrifice was also being questioned. The repressions, it turned out, were not to be the only aspect of the Stalin years that young campaigners sought to reassess. "Unfortunately," wrote a critic of the new openness, "some publicists have apparently forgotten about the pride, the achievement and the triumphs of our great Soviet people."[34]

The process of reappraisal began in 1988. After a tentative start, the Soviet Union's liberal newspapers began to carry war stories of an unfamiliar kind. The months to come would see accounts of the leadership's mistakes and malicious profligacy, evidence of continuing wartime repression, uncensored images of real death and maiming, and long-forgotten stories of alleged cowardice, of panic and retreat. Death itself was one of the first issues to be reassessed. The understatement and concealment involved in official estimates of wartime Soviet losses were exposed, some by demography, the rest by talking, counting archive files. By 1991 veterans heard that the number of war deaths was substantially higher than they had believed, some said as much as twice as high.[35] At the same time, the details of how some of the deaths had really happened began to see the light. Soviet troops had been massacred as they rode horses against German tanks; they had been forced to fight in open fields, sent to their deaths to prove their loyalty, shot by police from their own side. Even the sacred defense of Stalingrad came in for a new scrutiny.[36]

These were not forgotten stories, but like so many other aspects of Stalinism they were secrets, the property of dissidents, witnesses, survivors, and their families. Cowardice and wasted life were not part of the war's official myth. All the new history involved, most of the time, was a shift of emphasis, a focus on neglected aspects of the familiar tale. To the conservative ex-soldiers, however, the bitter stories and the criticism felt personal. They thumbed the pages of the latest journals, bought and passed around the memoirs, and it was not always history that they were reading, but rather a retrospective and impertinent readjustment of the value of their lives.

The reconsideration of the war has meant different things in the various parts of the former Soviet Union. The alternative stories are not subplots. Every survivor is dealing with the most dramatic and often the defining event of his or her life. It is not always true, either, especially outside Russia, that the process of reappraisal has caused the veterans to suffer. In some places, and especially in the republics of Ukraine and Belarus, as well as in the Baltic states of Latvia, Lithuania, and Estonia, the story of the war has been rewritten with an emphasis on Soviet ("imperial") atrocities and an answering national endurance.[37] The neglected history of the Soviet invasion of 1939 and the first months of repression has been resurrected.[38] In western Ukraine and the Baltic, the atrocities associated with this, including the murder of nationalist partisans, were widely remembered, but the discussion of them had been banned for half a century.[39] Nationalist historians in these areas could also emphasize that their republics saw the heaviest wartime losses. There have been graves to rediscover, bodies to rebury or honor, and new monuments, with national meanings, to commission. Reappraisal, at least from the point of view of the dominant nationalities in each case, has been part of a collective act of liberation.

It has been relatively easy, then, to rewrite the story of the war from within the borders of a newly independent nation-state. For ethnic groups without this luxury the process has been more painful and the questions of reparation and justice are harder to resolve. The nationalities whom Stalin exiled in the

1940s have not found it easy to return to their ancestral territories. The Crimean Tartars, for example, face lengthy legal battles to establish their right to the homes and small farms that were theirs until their enforced exile to Kazakhstan in 1943 to 1944. Few have succeeded. The present occupiers regard the land as their own. The Tartars who have made the journey home have often been condemned to poverty. The best glimpse they are likely to get of the comfortable houses their grandfathers built is usually from the outside of a high perimeter wall.[40]

The issue of the Holocaust, as ever, remains unique. Glasnost allowed for its reappraisal, and there have been conferences of historians, research projects, and a series of excellent publications, many of them partially funded from abroad.[41] There are also support groups, and the Israeli and American governments send aid to any Jewish survivors that they can find.[42] The process has not been smooth, however, and the idea that the Jewish people were singled out for annihilation is still resisted in Russia and elsewhere in the former Soviet Union.

It is also difficult to get Holocaust monuments built. A scandal attended the attempt to add one to the war memorial complex in the victory park at Pokhlonnaya Gora in Moscow. This complex, a large area, formerly a wood and civic gardens, was the last and greatest of the Brezhnev-era monuments, although it was not finished till the 1990s. The reference to the Jews looks like an afterthought. The locals like to quip that it was the style, rather than the subject, of the memorial that caused all the trouble, and indeed it is a fine piece of kitsch, featuring a line of increasingly thin and ghostlike stone figures, the last of whom appear to be falling backward off the plinth. On the other hand, the whole memorial complex, including the Orthodox Cathedral of Saint George the Victor, which sports a fairground angel on a separate gilded pole, is no less clumsy in conception. Clearly there was something else at stake. The duma, Russia's parliament, explained its opposition to a specifically Jewish monument in terms of the potential it might create for ethnic tension. Journalists at the time dismissed its bigoted resolution on the matter as "a posthumous victory for Hitler."[43]

There is a monument, now, at Babi Yar. That is to say, a monument now stands, at last, at the top of the ravine, on the true site of the massacre, and it is an appropriate image, a bronze menorah, a seven-branched candlestick, contrasting with the ugly piece of socialist realism that Brezhnev's sculptors finally set up a couple of miles away—a desperate concession—a sculpture that commemorated only Soviet, not Jewish, dead. By the time the menorah was built, however, in the 1990s, the problem that its sponsors faced in Kiev was not so much resistance as apathy. Alexander Shlayen, the Kiev-based film director who helped to organize and fund it, explained that Kiev's anti-Semites had found new targets for their rage. As Communism crumbled, they had started persecuting living Jews.[44]

If you visit the menorah, and even more if you look at the photographs that Shlayen has kept from the days of his campaign to get it built, some of which feature the likes of George Bush and Bill Clinton (the latter incongruously attired in a yarmulke), it is the contrast between American and former Soviet attitudes to the site of the first major massacre in the history of the Holocaust that is most striking. Babi Yar is not a place of pilgrimage for Ukrainians. Many of them do not even know how to find it.

None of these details would come as a surprise to Il'ya Altman, the current director of Moscow's Holocaust Foundation. The foundation itself is new, a product of the last years of glasnost. Its work, like Memorial's, consists of research, commemoration, and the provision of as much social support as it can muster to the dwindling number of Holocaust survivors who still live in Moscow. As part of its educational work, it runs a course of lectures for university students. Many of the students who attend are Jewish themselves. Nonetheless, as Altman can explain, their attitudes have been hard to influence. Even after ten lectures, a whole term, he found that the young people were reluctant to accept that the Holocaust was an act of targeted genocide. The story that the Nazis wanted to destroy the Soviet people in general still persists. Many of the students had not even remembered how many Soviet Jews had perished.[45] I was so surprised by this that I decided to ask some of my Moscow friends, all academics in their thirties, including two who happen to be Jewish, what they understood by the word Holocaust. I was met by blankness. "Genocide?" I tried. "Jews?" "Oh, that," they said at last, exchanging a glance that confirmed that I was being especially dim-witted that day. "That. We know all about it, of course. Didn't someone just make a film about it? What was it called? *Schindler's List.*"

While the story of the gas chambers and Polish camps survives, then, the history of the Holocaust on Soviet soil is likely to fade still further as the Jewish population continues to leave. Those who remain are reluctant to identify themselves by reference to a story and a memory that their neighbors do not honor. Few would willingly describe themselves as victims. There are sometimes even dangers in doing so, including a risk of discrimination and abuse. When the Israeli government first offered to assist Jewish pensioners in

Ukraine in the mid-1990s, the aid workers found it difficult to persuade people to accept the help. "They live in remote places, a lot of them," one of the organizers of the scheme explained. "The ones who could get out and go to Israel or the States or wherever did so a long time ago. So we're talking about old people, simple people, mostly, and they are very careful what they tell anyone. Especially now. We had to get the rabbis to explain it to them, and then, when they did, there were plenty of people out there." He added that the old people were correct to fear that the distribution of aid would inflame their neighbors' resentments. "We try to keep this under control," he said. "If we have medicine with a short shelf life, or something like that, we give it to whoever needs it. But it's tricky."[46]

The story of Ukraine's surviving Jews is one of many that suggests that certain kinds of victimhood, as ascriptions, are optional. It is not always beneficial, or even possible, to identify oneself as part of an injured group of survivors, to tell one's life in terms of collective damage. The reopening of the past in the former Soviet Union remains selective. One person's reparation, too, can often be another's shame. The overwhelming majority of war veterans, and especially the ethnic Russians, are not survivors of the Holocaust and did not witness it. Their grievances are smaller, but nonetheless they are bitter. For most of their lives, they have been official heroes. Now they are impoverished, marginal, and, if not dishonored, largely overlooked. At the same time, they have no inclination to regard themselves as victims. Because they still believe they saved the world from fascism—they, at least, and the sacred dead whose memory they will not see repudiated—it is humiliating, now, that they must apply for help. Their mere survival, after all, ought to be proof enough that these people are not weak, but strong.

Some veterans are so poor, however, that they have no option. It is important not to miss the crumbs and kopecks that a grudging state may offer. Money—depressingly small amounts of it—remains one of the things that is at stake in the rivalry between the various heirs of Stalin. The other, however, especially at a time when history appears to be so unpredictable, is still the issue of personal self-justification. Few old people, unlike the young, the new Russians, believe that material prosperity defines success. The society that shaped their values had always talked more grandly of sacrifice for the common good, the cause of the international proletariat, the motherland and Stalin. It was important to be a good comrade. Compensation, or at least the right to a living pension, is symbolic of their status and their rights. These rights, however, like war heroism or high output at the workbench, are defined competitively.

War veterans, then, are liable to talk of loss when they describe the past decade. The survivors of Stalin's repressions generally talk more positively, but only because their earlier position was so weak. The collapse and discrediting of Communism assisted many in their search for justice, finally bringing the possibility of documentary proof and even, following a decree by President Yeltsin in 1991, a specific compensatory pension.[47] Former kulaks were given the same kind of recognition as political prisoners and their families. But the pensions were small and the recognition that they represented felt grudging. Talking to me in her Moscow office, Valeriya Ottovna began to weep as she explained the essence of the last and meanest insult. "We have had to ask to be rehabilitated," she said. "As if we had ever done anything wrong. We have had to write and apply, another application—you know, 'I hereby request'—but they should be requesting us. They should have asked us for our forgiveness. Instead we have to ask them. We have had to write so many letters, and we always have to beg."

As Valeriya Ottovna explained, a good many people, including St. Petersburg Memorial's Venyamin Iofe and Moscow's Lev Razgon, have refused to apply. They do not regard themselves as criminals. The price they pay, which includes the withholding of formal "victim's" pension rights, is set against the benefit they derive from the maintenance of living anger. It is not reconciliation they demand, but justice. Their principles, however, are a luxury. "They won't beg," said Valeriya Ottovna. "But we old people, we need the pension. We had no choice, did we?"[48]

When it comes to money, the survivors of Stalin's political purges have a good case for special treatment. Valeriya Ottovna reminded me that very few of them would ever have been allowed to train professionally. They were barred from university courses, from institutes, and even from apprenticeships, and many spent years in exile, gratefully taking whatever work they could get. Their health was broken, precluding many types of manual work. Large numbers need expensive medicines. Many, including the former kulaks, had lost everything they possessed at the time of their exile, and those who managed to conceal a treasure of some kind—a watch, gold rings, a silver spoon—had usually to barter it away for basic food. Yudif Borisovna, the only daughter of Bolshevik grandee, now shares her single room with a lumpy pile of potatoes, her store for winter, piled under the window and covered with a blanket. People like her have been humiliated for most of their lives. It is a cruel new market system that is letting them die without a year of two of ease.

The trouble is that almost everyone over retirement age has suffered since the revolution of the 1980s and 1990s. The veterans and prisoners can do no more than join the line of millions. The value of everybody's pensions has collapsed, the clinics they all have to visit for their many ailments, the ailments of old age in any world, have no drugs left to dispense. They all worry about the violence on the streets, they are all concerned about the future of their grandchildren, none can afford the funeral or the grave plot that they want.

Many, including surprisingly large numbers of former victims—Yudif Borisovna is one—would add that the collapse of Communism itself has caused a moral crisis. Like many lifelong Communists, she tries to distinguish between the ideology in its utopian form and the corrupt and criminal abuse that ruined it in the Soviet case. But many of her contemporaries do not. It is a combination of economic and ideological despair that brings today's Stalinists onto the streets, to stand, as they do most days, outside the Gostinyi Dvor in St. Petersburg and heckle the shoppers and tourists, to march in their old coats and shabby boots with their red banners held high. The system that once inspired them has gone, and its replacements, including—as they see it—pornography, price inflation, and all-night disco music—seem tawdry by comparison. As they wait in the snow for the buses that take so long, these days, to come, they stare in bewilderment at posters advertising Nescafé, an unattainable holiday in Egypt, a new Mercedes car. Most old people cannot afford basic luxuries—a train fare, the video their grandson is demanding, decent winter boots—and the fact that there are Mexican soap operas to watch on television is hardly adequate compensation for the loss of an empire.

When everyone is suffering, it is hard for an outsider to discern a hierarchy of victimhood. To make matters more complicated still, a great many people suffered repeatedly; they can describe themselves as war veterans, victims of repression, the children of the repressed, and even as survivors of famine with equal facility. The case of Aleksandra Matveyevna, who wrote to Memorial in 1988, is typical. Her father was arrested on a collective farm in 1937 after a foolish conversation in which he mentioned the name of Trotsky. The family all thought him dead, but he reappeared in 1948, released from the Gulag, to tell his grown-up children some stories they would never forget. In the intervening years, however, their own lives, too, had changed. Their village had been occupied by the Germans from 1942, and their mother had been shot as a suspected partisan. Their house, like all the others, had been burned, and they had been left to starve.[49] Memorial's archive bulges with the letters that document this kind of history. Its strategy of commemoration seems fully justified. It tries not to encourage victims' feuds. The survivors of Stalin's rule can only unite, it would insist, if they can recognize that they share a common experience. Their lives have all been shaped by the same extraordinary, violent, corrupt, dishonoring, and abusive political system. Some of them see this. Many cannot.

The sadness of Stalinism's final legacy was brought home to me by the miserable story of a consignment of potato flakes. This coveted item of capitalist humanitarian aid was assigned, by a busy Moscow council, to the local war veterans' association. The veterans were told that the packets of white fluff were to be distributed among all the local pensioners, including the former victims of repression. "Dried potato is something we like, we old people," Yudif Borisovna explained. "You don't have to scrub it or peel it, and you don't need teeth to eat it, so we think it's a good thing. But we never saw any of it. They didn't share any of it with us. They said we were not on the list. We suffered, too. And we worked. But they do not recognize what we did in the war. Some of them still call us criminals."[50]

Stories like this are played out almost daily, though the role of the dehydrated potato is sometimes filled by theater tickets, subsidized canteen meals, or new galoshes. The cultural legacy of Stalinism persists alongside modern cash machines and internet cafes. The energy that might have worked for the collective effort of reconstruction is dissipated in a million feuds and personal crusades. Meanwhile, the state that made the laws to which the elderly appeal, that created their alliances and rivalries, has been dead and dishonored for a decade.

More poignant still are the cases of the political prisoners whose forced labor undoubtedly helped to win the war. A few years ago, Yeltsin's government finally agreed to recognize their contribution, and those who survived were given victory medals like any other veteran and former combatant. Yudif Borisovna showed me hers. It is a cheap, lightweight disc, a piece of Soviet kitsch. Yudif Borisovna has suffered all her life because of Soviet power. Her father was shot, her mother arrested, and she herself was imprisoned, interrogated, threatened, and exiled for years. But the medal that symbolized her contribution of Stalin's war, to the great collective effort of a people who spat at her in the street after her release, is one of her proudest possessions. She let me take away a copy of each of her father's death certificates, and also some photographs of the site of his grave, but there were tears in her eyes as she passed the medal across to me. She was tired. It had been a difficult conversation. But she was not crying from exhaustion, and it was not self-pity that moved her. The tears, she smiled, were those of final vindication.

Yeltsin's government was not entirely deaf to tales like this. The need for a solemn final act to end the past was widely recognized after 1991. Famously, the symbol that was chosen was another pile of bones. In this instance, and unlike most bones, they were identified, counted, and carefully tested for their DNA. There was even a last-minute hunt for a couple of missing vertebrae, now thought stolen, before the ceremony went ahead. The bones were those of Nicholas II, Russia's last czar, and of his family, shot with him in a cellar in the Urals town of Ekaterinburg, latterly Sverdlovsk.

Boris Yeltsin, who, as the Communist Party's first secretary in Sverdlovsk, had given the order to destroy the Ipatiev house some years before, the house where the last czar and his family spent the end of their lives and were murdered, was hoping now that the reburial of the royal relics would help to reconcile the factions in Russian society, to lay the ghosts of the past and unite the people around another martyr. "By committing the bodies of those who were unlawfully killed to the earth," he declared, "the current generation of Russian people is trying to atone for the sins of its ancestors."[51] *Sovetskaya Rossiya*, a newspaper whose very title might once have suggested a different political tack, was even more expansive. "As it holds the requiem service in every cathedral across the land today," it purred, "the Russian Orthodox Church, in the name of the whole people, is marking its repentance for the sins of unbelief and regicide that waited eighty years for their expiation.[52]

In fact, of course, the reburial, in July 1998, was just another stunt. Nicholas II was no more capable of enacting a miracle when he was dead than he had been while alive. Critics muttered that Yeltsin himself was making up for his vandalism at the Ipatiev house.[53] They noticed that the crowds in St. Petersburg's streets on the day of the funeral were distinctly thin. "But then," one writer commented, "Nicholas II was not exactly the most distinguished of autocrats."[54] Others pointed out that the repentance on offer was selective. "Ten years after glasnost our memories are still being controlled from above," wrote one journalist. The czar might be reburied, but the greater priority, the body of Vladimir Il'ich, was still inviolate in its mausoleum.[55]

In the end, the discordant voices were probably more clamorous than the hymns of the faithful. No other outcome was ever likely at a time when so many histories stood unresolved. Debts from the past cannot be paid so easily. As the ceremony's organizer in St. Petersburg, Governor Vladimir Yakovlev, might have observed, the event provided an irresistible focus for eccentric faddists. His postbag included endless requests for special passes from the slightly mad, as well as bogus claims to royal lineage and crazy testimonials to the late czar's sainthood. But it was also weighed down by protest. The criticisms came from every point on the political spectrum. On the right were the Communists and the war veterans. "Do not allow Nicholas the Bloodstained back into Leningrad," they wrote. "It was not for this that we defended our Soviet homeland!" As a last resort, they argued, at least it should be made clear that not a single German should attend the ceremony.[56] Among ex-zeks the criticisms were different. "You know," one of them said to me, "they want us to accept this. They want us to shut up now. And the only other thing we're going to get is a monument to the civil war. The civil war! That's history! What is the use of that to us?"[57]

12

LISTENING FOR THE DEAD

"I don't know why you don't just sit down and write it," a friend in Cambridge said to me at the start of the two years of my research project. "You must know already what you want to say. You don't have to go back to Russia, do you?" It was an interesting idea. It would have meant staying, intellectually as well as physically, within the English-speaking academic world. The questions that I asked would have been sanctioned by that world, and my answers would have addressed a familiar, powerful, and respected tradition, the one that talks of brutality, trauma, and memory, the one that will always begin and end in the shadow of the death camps. The Russian material I already had, much of it from archives and libraries, would have made an excellent case study of violent death and its consequences, and it would have added to the growing literature on Soviet, and especially Stalinist, mentalities at the same time. I had already given papers on the basis of it. I had even published one or two. If I had added a few empirical planks to an existing framework, I could have written a quicker book, and the process would have been a lot easier.

I did not take the advice. Instead I spent the greater part of those two years in another world. When I came back, I was seldom really present in England. Russian priorities, Russian conversations, and Russian ways of looking at things intruded all the time. It is one of the delights of oral history. The past talks back, debates, corrects. The effect is particularly strong in Russia, too, for the Soviet past—or rather, the survivors who discussed it with me—talks back in unusually forthright, confident language; it remembers a different set of values; perhaps—it is implied and sometimes frankly stated—a better one; and it faces a representative of the west with a mixture of warmth, suspicion, and didactic firmness. The legacy of lives spent in a closed world, and one that proclaimed its collective moral purpose to itself through every possible medium, still influences many of the things that people say. It colored the basic business of being a person, too, helped to define each individual response to grief, to loss.

The evidence that I collected is often contradictory—people can contradict themselves in a single breath—and many would say different things if I interviewed them a second time, or found someone to talk to them later in a different way. But there is a tone, a theme, a sense of self, that runs through all the talk, and it is difficult to render it in English, let alone to turn it into a conclusion. The problem is not merely about translation. It is about conveying the darkness of Russia's twentieth century, and the extraordinary suffering of its citizens, neither of which have equivalents in my own society's recent history, while simultaneously doing justice to the vitality of its people, their sense of their own rightness, and their dignity.

I tried to talk about these things during my visits home, to give the occasional paper or write draft chapters for debate, but I learned very quickly that the strangeness of it all was difficult to discuss in Cambridge or in London, at least while it was raw, at least until the rough, the unfamiliar, and the jarring edges had been smoothed away by time—until, in fact, I had begun a little to forget. The average seminar audience, so moved in the past by the broad idea, sat silent in those first few months, polite, as always, but almost without questions, until it was time for the sandwiches or the beer. It may have been my choice of language, too, that made things awkward. Research is meant to be cool-headed, scientific. No one expected me to tell this story without passion, but there were times when the sadness was the only vivid thing I could convey. Emotion, recounted, is hypnotic, and there is something numbing about other people's grief. It can disable formal intellectual criticism, unwarrantably stifle questions. A group of students, bolder than my colleagues, reminded me of this after a lecture on collectivization. "Shouldn't you be a little more detached?" the designated spokesman began. "We wonder if you aren't a little too identified with your material. Isn't history supposed to be objective?"

As I render my account for those two years, then, as I try to explain what it was that could only be learned by spending months at a time away from students, colleagues, and my desk, I am bound at last to lay my conclusions at the door of the intellectual world I left. I started with some hypotheses. Most of them have turned out to be misapprehensions. They concern the notions of individual trauma and brutalization; the work of testimony; the processes of cultural continuity, memory, and change; and the meaning of the dead. These are not negligible subjects. There are few societies that have not developed sets of attitudes toward them, unexamined, perhaps, but crucial to any response that might be made to fresh catastrophe. They are themes on which the English-speaking world has entire literatures. I would have written differently about them if I had stayed at home. In answer to my students, too, I would, I am sure, have been a good deal more detached.

The social effects of catastrophes like war and genocide are not exclusively subjects for historians. The literature about trauma in particular, and about the talking and silence that come after it, includes papers by psychoanalysts, psychiatrists, literary critics, and every kind of social scientist.[1] When it comes to the effects upon the victims, the most influential scholarship, in the English-speaking world, at least, tends to fall within a broadly psychoanalytic tradition. Its imagery is medical. It talks about wounds and healing; sees silence, often, as a sign of damage; talking, where it is structured and directed, as therapy; and testimony, though painful, as rebirth.[2]

Nina Tumarkin, who otherwise writes so brilliantly on death and memory, is one who has accepted these metaphors from medicine and applied them to the Soviet world. "It is fair to suggest," she says, "that for decades the populace of the Soviet Union was both individually and collectively suffering from post-traumatic stress syndrome."[3] If this is what I had expected to find in Russia, an entire society scarred by generations of violence; men, women, and children in need of healing, then I would have searched in vain. The people I talked to certainly described their suffering, and many of them relived it as they talked. Some of them revisited, in conversation, events that they had tried for years to keep in check, images and memories that made them weep and that were to keep them awake, they would ring and tell me, for many nights to come. "Don't tire yourself," a wife would scold her ex-zek husband as we settled down with our cups of tea and I picked and scrabbled at the cellophane wrapper on the latest blank cassette. "Yurii Nikolayevich never sleeps if he talks about those days," she would add, turning to me. "He will be taking his pills again tonight."

It was a familiar story, but it was not a tale of mental illness. It might have been more strange, in fact, if the retelling of a harrowing narrative had not called out an echo of distress. Most of the people I talked to knew that their memories were a source of pain to them, but it was a pain they had lived with through decades of eventful life. Other sorrows have been added, and other losses, too, including the loss of a familiar, purposeful world, their state, whatever joy or pain its passing may have caused them. Most of them have very effective ways, not always involving pills or vodka, of dealing with it all as well—the telephone call to a sister or grandchild, the walk in the park, the noisy talk and laughter round a long kitchen table.

It was typical of the people that I met that their concern could turn outward, in this case focusing on me. "These are not beautiful things," some of them would say. "It must be hard for you." And then there would be more tea, and people whose pensions hardly pay their heating bills would produce bread and cheese, would pitch the piebald cat onto my lap, or find an album of photographs to fill in the happier parts of whatever story it was that they had just been telling. Their generosity, as I look back, was often just as moving as the stories that they told. Some said that kindness was the basic lesson they had drawn from hardship, that life would have been meaningless without that warmth. These were the ones who talked of survival in terms of their neighbors and their friends, extended families, the sense of collective responsibility. Others, of course, were bitter or gloomy—people take life in different ways—but even they had memories of endurance. Whatever they had seen or lost—and in this respect, there was little to choose between war veterans, ex-zeks and the survivors of a famine—their accounts were tales of ultimate survival.

The language that they used to talk about their lives repeated the same themes often enough for certain issues to be obvious. It became clear, for instance, that the Russian history of victimhood was as closely linked to a specific culture, and especially to the country's recent political and social history, as it was to the supposedly more universal features of human psychology. It was also the product of a particular historical moment. Russia's was the last of the great empires to collapse. The imperial mentality survives. For the time being, in other words, Russia's older citizens do not appear to be suffering from a crisis of origin or identity; they do not need what Ian Buruma has called "the pseudo-religion of victimhood" to give their history a shape.[4] To speak as a former Soviet citizen and a Russian is to speak—securely, if one chooses—from a culture of endurance and heroism; it is to use the language of historical destiny, to talk (however ironically) of the audacity involved in leading the collective struggle for human liberation.

None of this negates the experience of suffering—Soviet triumphalism is often seen as scant compensation for lifetimes of uncertainty and hardship—but it frames the discussion of pain and bereavement in a specific way. "We did not have time for that," people would laugh when I talked about unfinished mourning. "Of course it was terrible. But we had to rebuild our town. We were carrying everything ourselves, there was no other way. We had defeated the fascists, and now we were building socialism, right there in Kiev."

These stories will probably change as the first generation of survivors dies. There is already a bitterness in some of the tales, a sense of futility, especially for those who see present-day change in terms of degeneration or betrayal. Pain can be transformed by history. It becomes a symbol, a passport, as well as a burden, for the people who claim to be its heirs. Russia may also continue to assimilate the Western language of trauma and healing. Psychoanalysis, they say, has already become fashionable among the rich. At the end of the 1990s, however, the dominant images were not those of individual distress but of pride. Even those whose stories spoke of anger or self-pity did not accept that they might need a cure. I never completed an interview, not one, without asking whether talk therapy, with a priest, a doctor, a friend, or a Party comrade, might not have helped. "Psychotherapy, you mean," laughed one respondent. "Dear girl, this isn't your England!"

Another strategy that was denied to almost all the Russian survivors was that of bearing witness.[5] There was no chance for people to testify in Soviet Russia, or not in Stalin's lifetime. The impulse to talk is strong in Russian culture. Blockade survivors from Leningrad talked—no one could stop them—in the first few years of food and warmth after the war. But their case was exceptional. The postwar famine was a different story, for instance, and even most war veterans lived with edited public histories. They could, with justice, congratulate each other on their supreme labor, and they could calm themselves with shared fables (not all recollection is traumatic; some talking stills the mind), but they were seldom encouraged to explore in company their uglier, more horrifying images and fears. Overall, the silence that was imposed—in public space, at least—was stifling. It often prevented the bereaved and the frightened from rehearsing their stories, from sharing them, from the comfort that comes from discovering a social framework for events that otherwise retain the quality of a guilty dream. The survivors' confusion persists; their private images remain too awkward, or so they fear, to fit a social history whose outlines even now remain unclear.

Confusion, however, is not the same as generalized psychological damage.

Russians really do seem to have lived with their histories of unspeakable loss by working, singing, and waving the red flag. Some laugh about it now, but almost everyone is nostalgic for a collectivism and common purpose that have been lost. Up to a point, totalitarianism worked. If healing is the metaphor that we must use, then Russia's model was not psychoanalysis—the individual, the unique biography—but cognitive psychotherapy. The theory goes that there are techniques for tricking the mind, any mind, into the cooperative, cheerful condition that currently corresponds to health. Look in the mirror for two minutes a day and smile, says a popular manual, *How to Be Happy*, published in England in 1996.[6] The Communist Party's agitation and propaganda department's recommendations were very much the same.[7] Much of today's nostalgia, and some of its chauvinism, yearns openly for that simplicity.

It would still be possible to make the case that "they," those Russians, really "need" a therapy they do not understand. "You probably didn't rip them open far enough, if you know what I mean," the representative of an international aid program suggested publicly to me.[8] The idea is as absurd as it is patronizing. Like missionaries setting off for darkest Africa, the therapists and counselors can cut their way into this most abused of societies. They will find what they are seeking because they always do.[9] What they will miss is everything that is specific about this story and its narrators, everything that they have learned and have to tell.

All this is not to say that no one ever uses languages of victimhood. Although the public role of victim is not yet chic, there are already circumstances in which it can be useful, even profitable. "It must have been so good for all those poor old things to have had the chance to talk to you," well-meaning people, often with a glass in their hands, have said to me since I came back. Experience has taught me not to be too frank in answer. Certainly, I can say, there were occasions when all of us felt better for a conversation, and sometimes people thanked me for the courtesy of listening. In truth, however, it was they who were doing me a favor. I wanted to hear stories, after all. I remain grateful to everyone who talked to me, for their courage, their patience, their humbling generosity. It would be foolish not to add that other motives sometimes crossed their minds. Some people, in fact, regarded the transaction in a business light.

Narratives of victimhood can be commodities for exchange. There was the man who talked for hours about the Leningrad blockade, for instance, forcing a plateful of biscuits into my hands as I listened. "I cannot let a crumb go to waste," he insisted. "That is what we are like, we survivors. Bread. Food. It is sacred." His memories, however, were definitely for sale. At the end of our conversation, he produced a picture book from France. "I want to go back again before I die," he said. "I wondered if you could help. There must be someone you know. About a ticket, I mean. It wouldn't be much money where you come from, would it? That's what they say. I only need the ticket. And a visa." "Stand up," a widow from Odessa ordered at the end of our quick, prefabricated survey of her war. "Turn round. You're not married, are you? My son needs a new start. He can do anything. But not here, not in Ukraine. I think you should meet him."

I do not wish to simplify the story. Some people—a small minority—have never learned to make their peace with images of death. Others find their memories more disturbing now, as they grow old. There is no doubt that talking, too, remains important for a majority of the rest, whether it is described as testimony, witness, or autobiography. The suppression of shared memory was an act of state violence, and the freedom that glasnost has brought is widely and justly celebrated. Visit Memorial or the Society of Veterans on any weekday and offer to listen. You will still be taking down the names and memories when the offices are due to close, and if you give your number to the people there your phone will not stop ringing. It is the prejudgment, the assumption that medical diagnoses will generally apply, that is mistaken. What accompanies it, too, is also violent; the implication being that all silences are potentially pathological, that privacy, like democracy and international peacekeeping, is a luxury that can healthily be enjoyed only after everything that was twisted is straight and every personal history aired. Ironically, it is quite possible to hold this view—that victims need to talk and heal—and simultaneously to believe that the time is not yet ripe for the public trial of individual perpetrators.[10]

The pathology of trauma extends, it is argued, to the second generation. Here again, there are grounds for caution. The psychiatrist Derek Summerfield has likened the notion to the doctrine of original sin. "Without more empirical evidence," he comments, "we do no justice to the uncounted millions of largely non-Western peoples who somehow reassemble their lives, to assume that they are intrinsically damaged human beings who cannot but hand this on to their children."[11] It was in search of such empirical evidence, the trace of second generation problems, that I gathered together a group of the grown-up children of purge victims and dekulakized peasants—one of several such groups interviewed for this project—in the spring of 1997. The meeting was instructive for us all. The woman who attended it, all in their sixties, had never thought of comparing their own experiences, their personal stories. They had regarded themselves as children of the repressed, victims, in a way, of the totalitarian system, but always—for the purposes of victimhood—as the bearers of their parents' standard, not as people with injuries of their own. They were surprised, then, to find they shared some kinds of memory. They enjoyed discovering that they all had a story of concealment. They also shared a corresponding tale of guilt. Beyond that, however, there was very little that they had in common except their lifelong hardship.

Some people offered me a social explanation when I asked them to consider second-generation trauma. It was another instance of Soviet collectivism. Partly by tradition, partly because of the pressures on housing space, and partly because of the deadly effects of war, there were few classic nuclear families in Soviet Russia. Children were not usually brought up by a single parent or parents. Grandparents typically played a central part—some of the people I met, including two of the women in that group, had been raised entirely by them—and then there were the pioneer camps, the school clubs, the Young Communists, the brigades. The opportunity for a parent's secret pain to be transmitted, by words or in long silences, was nearly always limited. The opportunities for children to nurse and discuss their fears and phobias, too, were curtailed by the ethos of the group.

I heard accounts of lives remade, of fragments gathered up and reassembled, many times, hundreds of times, in different settings and from people talking from a variety of motives. But none of the second-generation survivors whom I met—variously heirs of repression, civil war, and famine—reported intrusive nightmares, phobias, or nervous illness for themselves. To some extent, of course, this could be the effort of a taboo. Far from receiving compensation, people who have been diagnosed as mentally ill (including sufferers from depression) risk losing some of their civil rights, and even their driving licenses, in Russia.[12] But it is also clear that the Western illness, posttraumatic stress, is not a problem that is recognized, to any significant extent, by Russians of the second and later generations.

One of the respondents in the second-generation group that met that day in Moscow brought along her granddaughter, a child of four. Most of the time the little girl sat and drew, patiently ignoring us all. At one point, however, she demanded that I take her outside and watch her practicing the dance she had just learned. The two of us spilled out into the corridor of the third-floor offices of the Institute of Oriental Studies, a space that I had borrowed for the afternoon. She danced, she tolerantly instructed me, and we giggled, but always as quietly as we could. There was a tape still running on the other side of the door, a conversation about political murder and its consequences was being recorded. When she is old enough, her grandmother told me, the family will tell her everything. She wants to be an actress.

The generation whose conscious lives began in the mid-1980s, who have never known anything more repressive than glasnost, is now at school and college. They are not obsessed with the past, but many of them are surprisingly well informed, and certainly more so than their counterparts in Britain would be. I interviewed a class of eighteen students in St. Petersburg, surely future members of the elite, who could talk in detail about the First World War, the civil war, the Nazi-Soviet Pact of 1939, collectivization and political repression. They knew the history, the dissident poetry, the theories, and critiques. They also knew, which most of their grandparents did not, where to put Russia in an international league table of violence and political murder, talking in an informed way about South Africa ("very violent") and the United States ("they don't really have the same kind of problem"). "It is better now that we do not have to talk about the past all the time," one of them said. "Our problems are bad enough without all that." Most of them agreed. The past has become history; it is not, for these young adults, a source of rage. "I always feel sad for Babushka [grandmother] when she starts to talk about the war," one of them said. "She seems to have had such a tough life."[13]

A group whose education had been less thorough, teenagers from Karelia, agreed. This general knowledge of the past was very weak, but their own families were all-important. The war, for them, was Soviet Karelia's war, a war against the Finns. Babushka's stories were no less sad. Their hunger to know more, even from a foreigner, was keen. But the balance of their interest was reassuring, unremarkable. "What did happen at Sandormokh, then?" one of them asked me later on the bus. "What is going on there today?" We talked, but then a group began to gather on the three backseats. The conversation was eager, hopeful, certainly not gloomy. "What's it like in England? Do lots of you come here?"

Conversations like this were so straightforward, despite the subject matter and the setting, that it is hard to remember that these people are supposed, on some models of historical causation, to have been brutalized, to have a scant regard for human life, to resort too readily to violence. Perhaps the teenagers may be exempted, since they are now a third or even fourth generation, but the same cannot be said for the scores of older people that I met. Russia's history is often invoked in explanation of the violence of later events—Ivan the Terrible towers over Stalin, peasant brutality would blacken Lenin's revolution, the civil war fed the mentality of the purge. The generalization that violence brutalizes people is the exact opposite of the conclusion to be drawn from the Holocaust literature, most of which states that trauma makes victims, not torturers, of any who survive it. If the victimhood idea is too simple for Russia's longer, more ambiguous tale, then so is the story that war and political violence, as lived events, leave two generations of murderers in their wake.

Ironically, it is the survivors themselves who are the first to repeat the old line. "The revolution, the civil war, they left the people brutalized," Shlayen—among many others—insisted. "They were more violent, life was worth nothing to them. It has been like that for decades, a century. Russians have the mentality of the pogrom." "When you put it like that," I said, "your theory sounds like racism." "No, not at all," he replied, instantly discarding one generalization for another. "You must remember, Russian is also Sakharov, it's also Pasternak, Pushkin, Tolstoy, Dostoevsky." It is less spectacular to add that it is also Yudif Borisovna, Lyudmila Eduardovna, Valeriya Ottovna, Aleksei Grigor'evich, Venyamin Viktorovich, and all the others. Brutalization works, as a general theory, for as long as you do not try to apply it to anyone you actually know. But it is used so widely, and applied so often to Russia, that it still needs serious consideration. There are two main sets of assumptions at work behind the notion. The first is based on individual trauma; the second upon culture.

The psychological explanation derives from the finding that people apparently become accustomed to atmospheres of emergency. The Russian children who played games of death penalty in the 1910s had certainly learned something about violence, and so had the child survivors of the Patriotic War, the ones who played with handguns and grenades. There are studies from several recent civil wars—in Rwanda, in Angola, and elsewhere—that show how other generations of children have become used to violence in the same way, through endless exposure, and so have many adults. But what this means, in terms of their later choices and actions, is not easy to predict. The experience of catastrophe—the fear, uncertainty, physical pain, and stress—almost always changes people, and it can cast deep shadows over their later lives. But other things will change survivors, too, including poverty or wealth, homelessness or security, companionship or isolation.[14] The individual person also matters in this respect, his or her previous history and disposition, the support that each can take from family and friends.[15]

Criminality, ruthlessness, and even cruelty may be, from an objective point of view, the best ways to survive some kinds of crisis. Some people, those who are disposed to use these methods, will flourish through emergencies and wars.

Others will respond to the same problem in less violent ways, and they may also be the first to seek a quiet life, even a numbing one, when the emergency is over. Societies, like individuals, are changed by the violence they witness. Different people come to power after a long crisis, new kinds of voice begin to resonate with the public mood. Western Europe changed radically after the First World War. Elsewhere, too, taboos have been challenged, democratic processes interrupted, and networks of trust destroyed, but these are social processes. It is too simple to talk of universal patterns of psychological damage.

The cultural explanation traces continuities down through the decades, throwing up its hands (or washing them—what can we do, it is their fate, their way, not ours) at Russia's violent story. There is a thread of continuity, it would be futile to deny it, and much of it comes from the stories that the people tell themselves, the myth of the war (a myth that inspired many Afghantsy), the myth of endurance. Russians who disdain popular tales may read the same kinds of story in their extraordinary literature. "We are multitude and multitude and multitude," wrote Alexander Blok in 1918. "Come, fight! Yea, we are Scythians! . . . And flesh we love, its colour and its taste, Its deathly odour, heavy, raw."[16] Writing like this, when it gains wide acceptance, when it strikes a popular chord (the British tabloid press would be fortunate indeed if it could find its Ehrenburg or its Simonov), becomes an influence in its own right.

The point is that a cultural heritage is a resource, that it contains a range of different potential images. Russians may be Scythians, loving flesh, but they are also weeping mothers, kitsch, idealized family members, strong, clear-sighted and humane survivors. The hunt for continuities, when you consider this, can easily become a kind of game, a search for glib rhetorical links, but as a form of explanation it is seldom really serious. It is difficult not to see a brutal echo of the Great Patriotic War, for instance, of Stalingrad, in the 1999 bombing of the Chechen capital city, Grozny, the threat to raze it to the ground. The rhetoric was much the same, but the circumstances certainly were not. The bombing of Chechnya was a political choice, a set of calculations with alternatives, and it was based on real decisions about costs, about votes, about the likelihood of reprisals. Russian history was not the only context, either. Vladimir Putin's appalling strategy was predicted, in part, on the knowledge that his was not the first democracy to have dropped bombs on a civilian target in the 1990s.

The same kinds of observation also apply to other apparent traditions within the violence. The terrible mortality rates among Russian and Soviet troops in the two world wars, for instance, do share some common origins—

economic and transport difficulties, extreme weather, the fantasy that boundless Mother Russia will always bear more sons to send off to the front. One of the lessons that successive Russian governments have not forgotten is that mortality statistics can be massaged, corpses hidden. But military thinking has changed significantly over time. The arrogance of the czarist officer corps, with its honor codes and its casual demand for other men's sacrifice, may well have been an inspiration for the Stalinists in their clean boots, for the men, like Mekhlis, with whom the Soviet Union began its struggle against fascism, but by 1942 a different kind of general was taking the Soviet army's main decisions. It was a professional soldier, Vasilii Chuikov, who presided over the slaughter at Stalingrad, "learning all the time from German military habits."[17] The city was defended for strategic reasons, and if the fantasy of honor was invoked, it was for propaganda use.

The myth of a barbaric culture, the idea of the brutal peasant or the cruel Slav, also deflects attention from individual and collective choice and action. It elides the human misery of civil war, to say that "they" had grown accustomed to these things, it smoothes away the real tragedy of state violence, which forced so many people to collude, whether they became willing executioners or not. The point is not about blame—though there are some, a few, who took decisions, issued commands, and should be held accountable—it is about memory and darkness, the price the people paid. Whatever the justification for it, killing, unless you are a psychopath, is not a part of "normal" life. It is exceptional. Whether you were sickened, stimulated, frightened, or all these things at once, it is not something you forget. The idea of brutalized nations, of an inherited taste for evil, is either rhetoric or it is prejudice.

If this theory is to be sustained, if Soviet Russia's turbulence cannot be attributed to the personal brutalization of its citizens, then explanations will have to be sought in other places. There is no reason to dismiss the evidence that thousands of men and women were driven by hate, fear, rage, hunger, sadism, revenge, cowardice, and ideological dogma into killing, torturing, robbing, and imprisoning their neighbors. Certain things were learned, such as the best way to kill someone and leave no visible scar, the ease with which a group of men could be reduced to tears. But perhaps it is a fortunate society, in the modern world, that has not learned these things. There was also plenty of crime in Stalin's Russia, gratuitous cruelty, petty acts of vengeance or denial. There was no need, on many occasions, for the state somehow to force its soldiers and policemen to do their brutal work. Here again, however, the different kinds of impulse must not be confused. Famine produces panic of a specific kind. So does war. The rage that drives the soldier to throw a toddler into a well is different from the determination of the revolutionary commissar who hangs two hundred partisans, and different again from the disappointment of the same commissar, thirty years later, and now a grandfather, who wearily signs a warrant against the life of a man whose innocence he does not doubt because his career, his comfort, and his family depend on it.

To understand the scale of it all, however, it is neither the individual psyche nor some ill-defined national characteristic—a genetic freak—that should be the starting point. Ideological bigotry played a part—the certainty that one is right is always chilling—but so did three other things: the political framework (largely defined by the state); repeated emergency; and almost universal fear. In the first of these categories comes Russia's failure to establish a strong legal system as a counterweight to state power; an absence, at every level, of effective citizenship; a fierce but exclusive localism whose corollary was the mistrust of outsiders; and a tradition of autocracy that all too easily adapted itself for Stalinism. The second set of explanations needs no further discussion. The crises Russia faced in the twentieth century were of a kind that might have driven any human being to rob or kill, and even, had they but the skill, to murder, salt, and slowly eat their children or their husbands. Famine, war, civil war, and expropriation have been the subjects of every chapter of this book. Fear, too, has featured prominently. The perpetuation of closed circles, of "us" and "them," so damaging to social cohesion, was in large measure the result of it.

The responsibility for ensuring that Russia's citizens do not begin to starve again should be, in part, an international one. Nothing is more important than material security—food, heat, and drinking water. But the political legacies of an autocratic state and weak legal system are also real issues, and they have to be tackled from within. Political cultures cannot be imported and imposed, although some kinds of technical advice seem to be helpful. If there is going to be a move to counteract the legacies of the past, to build new patterns of trust, it has to be a choice that Russian people make. The first step might be a reconsideration of the relationship between the citizen and the state, an exploration of legality, openness (despite the recent abuse of that word), and accountability. That, rather than a series of individual trials, was the route the Russian government appeared to favor when it banned the Communist Party and rehabilitated its victims in 1991 and 1992.[18] But its motives were not really truth and reconciliation. Like the reburial of Nicholas II's bones, the idea was to crate up and inter the past, to save embarrassment, head off the witch-hunt, and keep a whole skin.

The decision to bury the past was not widely contested. The case was made that many of the guards, informers, and interrogators were victims in their turn, either literally (many were indeed arrested) or in terms of a system that left them with no option. It sounds humane, this explanation, but lurking beneath it is a widespread apprehensiveness. As a friend confided to me, "No one in my family was shot. No one was arrested. We didn't even lose anyone in the war. Grandfather was a good Communist—you know, he was there when they took the bells down from the church. So I don't know what they'd find if they looked at my family. I was a student when it all started coming out—glasnost and all the Memorial stuff. I remember I was away on an expedition with the others in the summer of '89. I used to be afraid because I didn't know what would be waiting for me when we all got back." It was after that conversation, some weeks later, that he discovered that his family's charmed life was not an accident. His grandfather indeed had a secret. He had been a sniper at the beginning of the war. His medals include one that praises him for shooting scores of his own neighbors during the Moscow panic of 1941. Thereafter he had worked, in various capacities, for the secret police.

Fear of discoveries of this kind is common but not universal. There are people who would like to see each profligate general, each executioner and torturer in court—Razgon is one—to answer charges of personal criminality. The merits of this line are clear. Russia's is a culture in which the idea of individual responsibility remains too vague. It is a society in which the law is still a cipher, where people do not believe, fundamentally, that legal or democratic processes can help them. It is still a place of "family circles," networks of influence and protection, catch-as-catch-can. It is too easy, when reviewing the violent past, to talk impersonally of "the system." The new enthusiasts for capitalism and international trade concessions, themselves the children of the old elite, discuss it with a most attractive urbanity. Influence accumulated under Soviet rule still matters—the old Communist Party is heavily represented in the new mafia—and secret policemen still live in their comfortable apartments, sharing their memories and their Scotch and congratulating themselves on a particularly gratifying kind of survivorship. The government may pension off the victims—if they apply on the appropriate form—but it has never canceled its obligations to its predecessor's faithful employees.

All this is not justice. It is the extremist form of political expediency, to say one thing and do another, to spare the torturers of the past, and leave their victims in a judicial limbo, in order to save an effort, and perhaps more violence, in the present. The alternative carries formidable costs. The current political and economic crisis is deep enough. At the same time, too, this is a society that has been torn apart too often, where legal inquisitions have a tainted pedigree. Digging out names, reopening old quarrels, it is a dangerous path to choose. The trouble is that the other choice is an abdication, another silence, yet more fear. Trials and sentences, of course, are tricky things, especially if they take place fifty years after the fact. But the identification of specific criminals, a few corrupt old men, need not be the only objective. It is the attempt to establish a framework of legality, the hope, that matters, especially—above all—if it is generated from within the society itself. To refuse to explore the possibility of reconciliation, moreover, to refuse to look without cynicism at the collective past, to fear that anger cannot be controlled, to deny the possibility that one's own society contains the embryo of its own regeneration—all these are gestures of despair, capitulation to the idea that a people marked by violence is destined always to repeat it.

The other route out of the past is education. Some of the schoolchildren I met talked about their desire to make a future—though their ideas about the means and ends were vague—in which the violence of Russia's past would not recur. Their openness, their eagerness, and their sense of responsibility already represent a triumph—for their teachers, their families, and themselves. There are no guarantees of a good life for any of them yet. No judicial enquiry will secure their futures if the economy continues to collapse, if censorship is further tightened, or if the violent interethnic competitions for resources are not stopped. But the desire to know is a first step. The culture that makes abuses possible cannot be washed away in a tide of dollars. Corruption cannot be destroyed by stealth.

Arthur Kleinman, a psychiatrist who has spent some years in China, describes the pitfalls hidden in any cross-cultural assumptions about death that we might make. "Because the cultural worlds in which people live are so dramatically different," he writes, "translation of terms for emotion involves much more than the identification of semantic equivalents. Describing how it feels to grieve or be melancholy in another society leads straightway into analysis of different ways of being a person in radically different worlds."[19] In Soviet Russia, the issue of "being a person" was complicated by the Bolshevik Revolution, by Communism, scientific atheism, a social revolution involving massive urbanization, and by the huge population losses that accompanied a century of war and political upheaval. Before I had interviewed the elderly, the funeral directors, the nuns and priests, the geriatric-ward sisters and the social workers, I might have assumed that Soviet cultural policy had largely been a success, at least on its own terms. By the end of the 1960s, it had, according to many secondary works, destroyed tradition and imposed a new set of truths and customs, even where death, the last and most intractable occasion for ritual, was concerned.[20]

I began my work with a certain skepticism on this score, however, and everything I have found has deepened it. I have also become more generally cautious. Surveys and statistics about belief do not really tell us very much, especially under conditions of political censorship; and death, of all things, is so personal, so secret, that the heart of any person's understanding will elude all but the most inspired of social scientists. When he had finished telling me about his work at Butovo, Sergei Alekseyev, the ethnographer, got talking about death. "Come and see what I have in here," he said, leading me past the cases of skulls into a darkened store. He handed me a sculpture of a woman and a man in a horse-drawn carriage, a troika, molded crudely out of clay and daubed with brightly colored paint. "That is death," he said. "An old lady made it for me a couple of years ago. Death as the carriage that takes the soul away. See the horses? And that is the guardian angel. That's what she believes in, what she sees. But you'd have to spend a few weeks up there to get them to do these for you. You have to live with them." You do. Even then, I suspect, the answers will depend on who you are and when you ask.

Most of the private images of death that were offered to me—in a society that still segregates the sexes quite rigidly—came from conversations in the kitchen, hours making pirozhki or playing with the children, drinking tea, sitting up late, out at the dacha, swatting gnats and watching an endless summer twilight magnificently turn to dawn. A man might listen differently, staring companionably at a televised game of ice hockey, or splitting a few beers and a foil-topped bottle of rough Armenian brandy. It is in these places, and after all these hours—by which time you will no longer really be a researcher, and the person who is talking to you will not be a respondent—that you will learn that death, in Russia after Communism, is still a bird, the extinction of a star, the flight of a winged and vulnerable soul, like a newborn child, a stroke from the scythe of fate. There are seas or a dark river to be crossed, by boat, perhaps, or in a carriage drawn by galloping horses, and on the other side—the words now will not vary—there waits that other light in which the soul must watch.

Somewhere in the conversation come the dead. This is not the moment to ask supplementaries or look for clarification. These images are fragile, fluttering, tender. There are some weights they will not bear. "Babushka is always here, I feel. But especially—no, don't laugh, we all know what you're always on about—if I go to the cemetery. I went the other day, you know, to ask her what to do." "Yes. Father died. But ever since I have felt stronger. It is because he is praying for me from a different place now. I know that's what he does. I pray for him here, and he is praying for me in the other light. It's probably awful to say it, but I feel closer to him now, really, than I did when he was alive." "I knew that father was watching. He was there, behind the door, and it was not a very nice sensation. That was when I was sure he was dead. Killed. Not somewhere off in the north." "I know it's odd, but I really did feel that she was leaving us on the third day. She was there—even the dog seemed to be looking for her. And then she was gone."[21]

The people who described these things might not, on another day, have passed an examination about nineteenth-century Russian attitudes to death or the finer points of Orthodox theology. The practices were changing before 1917, the meaning of the prayers was different for each new generation. Seventy years of Soviet Communism, and even more effectively, of urban life and secular culture, could not but change the ways that death was celebrated and remembered. Belief survives, especially among nonbelievers, at the level of metaphor, in the images we use to comfort ourselves at a bleak moment, or to picture, somehow, a process whose physical reality no mourner is encouraged to contemplate. Communism, through seventy years in power, undoubtedly added to the layers of disbelief. What it did not do was to destroy those basic metaphors.

It remains difficult to specify the things we can read off from it all. As Jacques Meunier memorably asked, "Is it possible, starting from a scrapyard, to reconstruct the Highway Code?"[22] In answer, it does seem clear that the way the dead live on, their presence as a source of comfort, the way their souls must leave, and the nature of the journey that everyone expects, eventually, to take—the judgment, hell, and heaven—all help to shape a moral landscape, individual understandings of the self. They do not give the whole answer, but without considering them we will not understand how another culture views the value and meaning of life, or the precise kinds of pain that are evoked, in another mental universe, by an unmarked grave, the prospect of a death in battle, or the discovery of a trench whose contents are crematorium ash.

"A lot of foreigners come here and ask stupid questions," Aleksei Levinson, one of the senior researchers at Moscow's Center for the Study of Public Opinion, told me. "What's different about you is that you ask stupid questions that we can't answer."[23] On another occasion, he put his skepticism differently. "I think what you will find is just a blank," he said. His remark was based on an unease, a sense, which other Russian intellectuals share, that theirs is a culture that has lost its knack for dignifying death. Nostalgia and embarrassment are awkward emotions, and questions about grief, in an academic setting, can easily provoke them both. Higher education, and literacy more generally, has played its part in closing off the paths leading to heaven and hell. For all that, however, and for all that Soviet citizens have claimed for decades, in questionnaires and surveys, that they do not believe in an afterlife, their children still go along to the graves to talk. People from every kind of social background pack into the trams with their evergreen branches and bags of fruit at Easter and at Trinity. They half believe, or choose to hope, that someone listens. There are some favored cemeteries where they even write their messages for the dead on the monuments, combining, like their grandparents once did, an ill-assorted selection of religious fantasies—belief in ghosts, belief in ancestral spirits, belief in the efficacy of graves, in consecrated ground. "Lord God!" one of the messages signed "Vladimir," reads. "Let my dreams come true."[24]

Funerals continue to reflect the collectivism of Russian and Soviet life. British corpses may travel to the grave or crematorium alone, in a separate hearse, pursued down suburban highways by a hierarchy of mourners in their limousines and private cars, but the Soviet and post-Soviet cortege moves in a single, rather battered-looking bus. The coffin is in the middle, the mourners sit around, some smoking, some studiedly obeying orders not to smoke, conversing in an absentminded way, the family, the friends, and colleagues, all of them in the same one space. The corpse is not excluded from it all. Your funeral is certainly an occasion that you plan and will attend, and the old Soviet decencies will have to be observed. "They still have their clothes set out," a social worker who cares for the elderly explained to me. "They are very proud of them. 'I want you to make sure I am buried in this,' they will say. They have it all. The shoes, the new shirt, the unworn suit. Some of them have trouble paying for it, but I know that it matters. I have to be sure the relatives know—if there are any—so that there aren't any mistakes."[25]

Among the bleaker legacies, for ritual, of Soviet power, the general impoverishment of death is one of the most notable. Large cemeteries are impersonal, the crematoria are grim, the language and the music have become, to a post-Communist audience, banal. It is the post-Soviet impoverishment of Russian citizens, however, that leaves the saddest impression. The cost of funerals has become a major worry for the urban poor. When granny dies, in her fifteenth-floor flat, the first problem is to get her to the morgue. The men who drive the mortuary vans demand substantial bribes, they do not come for days—twenty-four, thirty-six hours—they sometimes do not come at all. There was a minor scandal about this in 1997.[26] Some families solved the problem by bundling the body into the back of the Lada and driving it round to the morgue themselves (another bribe was often needed at this point). There were stories of despairing relatives who simply threw the corpse out of a window. Those high-rises are quite impersonal, and there are always bodies in Russia's winter snow.

My friend Dima works amid a clutter of specimen coffins and plaster angels in an office near the main gate of Vagankovskoe, the largest cemetery in central Moscow. He got the job at the labor exchange, but he finds that it suits him. Apart from anything else, he gets a lot of foreign visitors; journalists, mostly. They always ask him about the mafia funerals, the big and vulgar ones, the cost of which, he says, "can go to anything. Anything." I bought his glossy magazine, which carries soothing articles about embalming, and a specimen funeral contract, assuring to its signatory the very best of service at all times. For those who are anxious about etiquette, there are long sections about ritual food, advertisements for table decorations, and suggestions for the tasteful wording of an epitaph.[27]

We laughed about the manias of the new rich, but he was surprised to be asked about the others. The whole issue is a bit embarrassing; there's something wrong with a world in which the disposal of a body is a matter of finance. But he got the price list out in the end. "The poor count every ruble," he said. In 1997 a wreath of artificial flowers cost 450,000 rubles (real ones were a mere 250,000). The bus could be hired for 625,000. Perhaps these were optional extras, but the basic costs—110,000 to get the documents signed, 450,000 to have the body laid out, and never less than a couple of hundred thousand more to buy the cheapest coffin—were inescapable. The average total was seldom less than 2.5 million. It sounds like a fortune. Of course, inflation always adds those meaningless noughts. But they are not meaningless if your pension is 500,000 a month, and even less so if it has not been paid for half a year.

Soviet propaganda was most effective where it locked into older patterns of belief. The most influential, for the understanding of death, were the ones concerning redemption, martyrdom, sin, and punishment. Even before the Bolshevik Revolution, the heroes of the new order died as martyrs in its cause. Lenin's corpse, immortalized, embodied this sacrifice, as well as earthly sainthood and the newfound omnipotence of science. The men and women who died in battle on behalf of Soviet power—a modern version of the "good" dead—were martyrs, too, and their memory became as sacred as those of all the rest. By contrast, the scapegoats and the traitors, the enemies of the people, were not allowed their yard of consecrated soil. There is a feeling, still, of hierarchy, and it matters if your body rots in marsh or under gilded railings and a marble star.

Hierarchy is not the only feature of tradition for which the Russian people sometimes yearn these days. It is easy to forget that some of the old ways were cruel. The Bolsheviks were right to challenge obscurantism in the church, the oppression of women, and fatalism—the acceptance of poverty, disease, and grotesque inequality. Where thinking of this kind survives, the basic criterion of humanity toward the weak can still be overlooked. The core of the problem lies in the confrontation between religion—hieratic, stubborn, beautiful Orthodox Christianity—and science, "progress."

One of the best places to look for the effects of these related prejudices is in the world of medicine itself. The hospice movement, for instance, is relatively new in Russia. In Soviet times, cancer patients were seldom given pain relief, and if they could not heal, usually after radical surgery, they just went home and died. People still believe that cancer, like any illness, is God's judgment, that bad luck is infectious, and that all kinds of pain bear messages and must be consciously endured.[28] "Oh no," a psychologist who works with the dying replied when I asked about the relief of her own father's last agony. "He would not have wanted that. It is always important not to interfere, so that the spirit can find its way to wanting death."[29] There are also fears that the dying will enjoy an addiction to narcotics—"you never know where those things will end up"—and the whole bundle of prejudices is wrapped in a blanket of disapproval. They are not really worth the money. There are so many other things we have to do ("This is not your England"). "If you go there," a colleague—with a Ph.D.—declared when I said I was going to visit the new AIDS help center in Moscow, "you can go on your own. You just don't know, do you. They don't really know how you catch it, do they? Do you really have to go?"

A bastardized religion is used to justify some curious views about despair as well. Russian mental hospitals work hard to care, on limited budgets, for the acutely ill. They also provide shelter for some elderly patients whose symptoms are less serious, but whose families will not support them and whose vagueness, senility, or depression makes independent living difficult. In a society that regards such disabilities as signs of weakness and even of bad character, bad genes, a sinful soul, it is not surprising that the institution staff should put the able-bodied elderly to work.

One of the women I was fortunate to interview had just showed me her pride and joy, the fourth-floor lavatories, as clean as the ones in McDonald's. Now we sat together to talk. She wanted to explain how much she missed the people who had died beside her in the war, her brother, friends, a whole world gone. The psychiatrist, who insisted on sitting through our conversation, began to play with his tie. He kept trying to catch from me the conspiratorial look that is exchanged on these occasions, he expects, by beneficiaries of higher education like ourselves. He was about to become the only man with whom I lost my temper in two years of more or less professional good behavior. "Yes," his patient was saying. "I miss them and I do think about them all. I suppose it is because I miss them that I get depressed." The doctor interrupted her. "You do not get depressed," he said firmly. "No, you don't, do you? Remember, depression is a sin. It says so in the Bible."[30]

Since death is unknowable, the desire to make sense of it in terms of our own language is almost overwhelming. The deaths of strangers, Russians, foreigners, are viewed through lenses made in England, or wherever else, and it is to the viewer's culture that they speak. Part of my problem, when I came back to England, was the translation of terms, in Kleinman's sense, the problem of conveying, in English, ideas of death and of the self that had been learned and understood in Russian.

If coming home is difficult, however, journeys are exhausting. It was often tempting, in this long exploration of Russia's story, to close the window on the images, to barricade the door, to dream, in the heart of that continent of arid steppe, of cliffs and hills, a landscape in the rain. The urge to escape leads anyone who thinks for long about death to try to draw the story to a close. The dead—and especially the victims of state violence—are easier to face if they become statistics. More poignantly, they can be martyrs, departed souls who pray, on the other side, for the peace of living children. Whatever happens, they are gone. Their memory is something for the living to exchange. What we do with them is our business. Bury them, burn them, weave stories in their honor, but do not spend much time in company with real lives that have ended.

This process of forgetting is inescapable. The danger is that it may begin too soon. There is good reason to resist the Soviet mistake of treating the dead as instruments, the "repressed," the "fallen," numbers that can too easily be massaged and concealed. It is more painful to remember each of them by name, and of course in reality it is impossible even to attempt to do so, but the idea that lives can count as human costs remains repugnant. The third or fourth generation may consider them so, but the testimony of survivors, and the photographs they nail and stick to all those wooden crosses, insist that other views remain alive.

Bearing with the dead as people is one challenge; the other is to resist the many temptations to build shelters for yourself within their story. There are probably a thousand ways of doing this—it is a matter of personal taste—but I will mention only one. The clearest memory I have of it is from Medvezhegorsk, the second night we stayed, and the scene was a dreary bedroom in that crumbling, dank hotel. We were due to meet the Murmansk to St. Petersburg train as it passed through the town at two A.M., but there were hours to kill, and a group of us assembled, while the older people dozed or packed, to chew the fat. We were not an inspiring sight. The hotel had not been heated, and most of us had slept—or attempted to sleep—in the clothes we were still wearing (it was during the day that I removed my woolly hat). Our surroundings were no more glamorous. There were piles of papers on the floor and on all the chairs, so we were sitting on the twin beds. Our ashtrays were smoldering on bundles of unused publicity leaflets, mugs of tea and instant coffee, long congealed, balanced dangerously on the lid of an empty suitcase, and there was orange peel in the folds of a pillow beside a pair of unclaimed socks.

When I think about that evening, however, and also about the many afternoons that I have spent in the cramped offices of Memorial and of other organizations like it—always surrounded by papers, always filtering out someone else's noisy conversation, always generously supplied with tea—it is not the discomfort that I remember, but a paradoxical feeling of security. There is a part of me that will always regard those places as a kind of home. It is easy to see why. The informality, the openness, the human warmth, the sharing of a cause, even the sense of siege—any political activist will recognize these things. Then there is the companionship, the lively chat, the humor—none of them unimportant to someone whose working life is spent so much among the papers of the dead. But there is also something darker going on. When you are incorporated into the society of these people, you are tacitly exonerated from complicity with the murderers and bureaucrats whom they have worked to expose. You are one of "us." The gnawing question, what would I have done, would my courage have failed, would I have colluded, is answered, effortlessly. The nightmare is silent. You walk in at the end of the drama. You took no decisions, ran no risks, and still you get to share the flowers.

The illusion is seductive, and it is deadly. It creates a fantasy world where ethical choices appear simple, where good and evil have been exposed, and where, by doing very little, anyone can feel that they have joined the better side. Real life was not like that at any time. The issues were not simple—even Stalin's victims had a range of different views—the choices that were made were seldom clear or permanent, and to relate those complex, individual debates and fears to single issues from another world, to make them into icons for freedom, consumerist democracy, or loosely defined human rights is the most complacent kind of moral tourism.

"Ask them to try to understand," Valeriya Ottovna had said. I find that I cannot offer the right formula. The survivors, as I have probably said often enough, were engaging, generous, original, clever, unpredictable—in short, alive. But it was the dead that I had traveled to consider. Theirs is not a story that can be read for one's own redemption. These are not our martyrs. It is not one to use as evidence of our own triumphant ideological position. There is nothing in this tale of other people's suffering, courage, tenacity, and repeated disappointment that should be taken as an affirmation of a system that they never knew. Even the familiar comforts of another story of victimhood are not available, for Russians themselves reject it. Instead of turning my conclusion into something for the world I left, making it another case history in an ongoing debate, cross-referencing and filing it, like the names and numbers of the dead, I find that I am merely listening, waiting for the words that need no translation and are only heard in silence.

There have been many voices in this book. Whenever I needed to remember something specific, I would put down the typed transcript of an interview and switch on the tape recorder. The sounds would bring it all back, not just the talking, the precise tone of voice and the pauses, but also the chink of the teacups, the rattle of a tram in the street, the telephone ringing next door, and the birds—crows in winter, swifts in June—outside. As I write now, I am conscious of other kinds of voice, the ones that make up my own responses to death. Sir Thomas Browne is one, and all those desolate Central Europeans—a metaphor is never one's own—Rainer Maria Rilke, Walter Benjamin. However long I listen, however, and I realize that this is a thought too obvious to state, the voices that I really need to hear will never speak. Human beings are resourceful, and every culture has attractive ways of imagining a world in which the dead are really still alive. But whether we choose to believe in them or not, these other worlds do not belong to history. That leaves me with the silence. I cannot make it any clearer, and I do not think I have come home.

NOTES AND SOURCES

Interviews

The interviews I conducted were of three kinds: formal individual interviews, formal group interviews, and more spontaneous conversations, not all of which I could record. I planned individual and group interviews to involve four different kinds of respondents and four different kinds of locations. The categories of respondents were: survivors of the main catastrophes of twentieth-century Soviet history; the children of survivors; medical and other professionals responsible for the care of the dying and bereaved at the time (including doctors, nurses, priests, and Communist Party activists); and medical and other professionals responsible for the care of survivors today. The locations were Moscow, St. Petersburg, Kiev, and a provincial town (in fact, because of the difficulty of finding people with the right backgrounds, I talked to veterans from three provincial towns and two villages).

The schedule called for five individual interviews and one group meeting for each category in each location (a total of twenty-five respondents for each category). I found the respondents initially with the help of the Memorial Association, the Society for Veterans of the Great Patriotic War, the Russian Center for the Study of Public Opinion, the Holocaust Educational Society, and a network of other religious, medical, and social organizations in each of the main centers.

With the help of my research assistant, Elena Stroganova, and with the cooperation of more than a hundred respondents, I was able to complete this schedule. But a number of unplanned interviews were also added. I had forgotten, in the original scheme, to include the testimonies of people who had no experience of violent death and whose families had no memory of it, so these were added to the list deliberately. But most of the extra interviews were spontaneous, the results of a conversation on the train, a whispered exchange in a corridor at the archive, or even—in the case of one veteran gravedigger—an offer of a lift in the rain. I did not keep an exact tally of all of these, but I find that I have more than 150 different voices on record (on audio or videotape or described in written notes). Although I chose to focus on a small number of these when I began to write this book, its language and tone were influenced by them all. With few exceptions (such as public figures or people whose autobiographies have been published), I have changed the names of all the respondents to safeguard their privacy.

Introduction

1. See *Posev,* no. 5, 1997, pp. 35–37.
2. For other accounts of the ceremony, see *Ogonek,* no. 45 (4528), November 1997, pp. 8–9, and *Itogi,* No. 44 (77), November 1997, pp. 20–23.
3. The quotations from Custine and Bedell Smith come from Robert C. Tucker, "What Time Is It in Russia's History?," in Catherine Merridale and Chris Ward, eds., *Perestroika: The Historical Perspective,* Sevenoaks, 1991, p. 38.
4. For an example, see the cartoon of the Russian bear in the *Observer,* December 12, 1999.

Chapter 1: Another Light

1. "I Am Not One of Those Who Left the Land," trans. Stanley Kunitz and Max Hayward, in *Anna Akhmatova, Selected Poems,* London, 1974, p. 75.
2. Konstantin Simonov, "Remember, Alyosha," trans. Lyubov Yakovleva, in *Twentieth-Century Russian Poetry: Selected with an Introduction by Yevgenii Yevtushenko,* London, 1993, pp. 619–21.
3. Ol'ga Berggol'ts, "Conversation with a Neighbor," trans. David Weissbort, *Twentieth-Century Russian Poetry,* pp. 572–74.
4. "The Scythians," trans. Babette Deutsch, ibid., pp. 81–83.
5. Monakh Mitrofan, *Zagrobnaya zhizn': Kak zhivut nashi umershchie, kak budem zhit' i my po smerti. Po ucheniyu pravoslavnoi tserkvy,* St. Petersburg, 1897; reprinted Kiev, 1991.
6. *Obikhodnye pesnopedeniya panikhidi i otpevaniya,* Moscow, 1997, p. 17.
7. The Very Rev. D. Konstantinow, *Stations of the Cross: The Russian Orthodox Church, 1970–1980,* trans. S. I. Lee, London, Ontario, 1984, p. 123.
8. The synod's papers, available in the State Historical Archive (RGIA) in St. Petersburg, are full of evidence of these kinds of concerns.
9. *Sankt Peterburgskaya gazeta,* October 21, 1894.
10. See St. John of Damascus, *On the Divine Images: Three Apologies Against Those Who Attack the Divine Images,* trans. David Anderson, Crestwood, New Jersey, 1980; see also L. Danforth, *The Death Rituals of Rural Greece,* Princeton, 1982.
11. *Sankt Peterburgskaya gazeta,* October 21–30, 1894; *Argumenty i fakty,* 1998, No. 5.
12. *Sankt Peterburgskaya gazeta,* October 22, 1894.
13. Konstantin P. Pobedonostsev, *Reflections of a Russian Statesman,* trans. Robert Crozier Long, Ann Arbor, Mich., 1965, p. 139.
14. *Sankt Peterburgskaya gazeta,* October 27, 1894.
15. Leo Tolstoy, *War and Peace,* 1869, trans. Rosemary Edwards, London, 1982, pp. 1273, 1260–61.
16. Leo Tolstoy, *Anna Karenina,* 1877, trans. Louise and Aylmer Maude, Oxford, 1983, p. 788.
17. Extract from *Cancer Ward,* cited in Philippe Ariès, *L'homme devant la mort,* Paris, 1977, p. 23.
18. The journals *Etnograficheskoe obozrenie (Ethnographic Review)* and *Zhivaya starina (Living Antiquity)* were founded in 1889 and 1890; S. A. Tokarev, *Religioznye verovaniya vostochnoslavyanskikh narodov XIX-nachala XX vekov,* Moscow, 1957, p. 11.
19. K. V. Chistov, *Irina Andreevna Fedosova: Istoriko-kul'turnyi ocherk,* Petrozavodsk, 1988.
20. E. V. Barsov, *Prichitaniya severnogo kraya,* Vols. 1 and 2, Moscow, 1872.
21. Maxim Gorky, "On the Russian Peasantry," cited in Teodor Shanin, ed., *Peasants and Peasant Societies,* Harmondsworth, 1971, pp. 369–71.
22. Alexander Pasternak, *A Vanished Present: The Memoirs of Alexander Pasternak,* trans. Ann Pasternak Slater, Oxford, 1984, p. 101.
23. Mikhail Bulgakov, *A Country Doctor's Notebook,* trans. Michael Glenny, London, 1975, pp. 13–14.
24. Shanin, op. cit., p. 369.
25. See Richard Stites, *Revolutionary Dreams: Utopian Vision and Experimental Life in the Russian Revolution,* Oxford, 1989, pp. 14–19.
26. Rose Glickman, "Peasant Women and Their Work," in Ben Eklof and Stephen P. Frank, eds., *The World of the Russian Peasant,* London, 1990, pp. 48–49.
27. See S. G. Wheatcroft, "Agriculture," in R. W. Davies, ed., *From Tsarism to the New Economic Policy,* Houndmills, 1990, pp. 79–92.
28. Vera Shevzov, "Chapels and the Ecclesial World of the Pre-revolutionary Russian Peasants," *Slavic Review,* Vol. 55: 3, Fall 1996; Tenishev Archive, 7/2/1444, 1.

29. On sects, see Robert O. Crummey, *The Old Believers and the World of Anti-Christ: The Vyg Community and the Russian State,* Madison, 1970; Frederick Conybeare, *Russian Dissenters,* Cambridge, Mass., 1921; K. V. Chistov, *Russkie narodyne sotsialno-utopicheskie legendy, XVII–XIXvv.,* Moscow, 1967.
30. See Reginald E. Zelnik, ed., *A Radical Worker in Tsarist Russia: The Autobiography of Semen Ivanovich Kanatchikov,* Stanford, 1986, p. 34.
31. Wheatcroft, op. cit., p. 92.
32. I. S. Belliustin, *Description of the Parish Clergy in Rural Russia: The Memoir of a Nineteenth-Century Parish Priest,* 1858, trans. Gregory L. Freeze, Ithaca, N.Y., 1985, p. 26; Tenishev Archive, 7/2/1444, 1.
33. Zelnik, op. cit., p. 3.
34. Linda J. Ivanits, *Russian Folk Belief,* Armonk, 1989, p. 21.
35. This point is made in every source. See for example D. K. Zelenin, *Ocherki russkoi mifologii: Umershchie neestestvennoyu smert'yu i rusalki,* St. Petersburg, 1916; reprinted Moscow, 1995, pp. 39–73.
36. E. Y. Zalenskii, *Iz zapisok zemskogo vracha,* Pskov, 1908, pp. 45–46.
37. Tenishev Archive, 7/2/1305; Belliustin, op. cit., p. 26.
38. See RGIA, 796/183/4885, 1–10.
39. V. Smirnov, *Narodnye pokhorony i prichitaniya v Kostromskom krae,* Kostroma, 1920, p. 15.
40. Tenishev Archive, 7/1/29, 36; 7/2/1055, 8.
41. Some people also believed that soap that had been used for washing a corpse had magical qualities. Women sometimes kept it for washing their faces (it preserved their youth) or for hexing their men.
42. N. M. Borodin, *One Man and His Time,* London, 1955, p. 5.
43. Ivanits, op. cit., p. 59; M. M. Gromyko, "Dokhristyanskie verovaniya v bytu sibirskikh krest'yan XVIII–XIX vv," in *Iz istorii sem'i i byta sibirskogo krest'yanstva XVII–nachala XXvv, sbornik nauchnykh trudov,* various authors, Novosibirsk, 1975, p. 74.
44. Tenishev Archive, 7/2/1305, 1.19.
45. *Zhivaya starina,* 1994, no. 2, pp. 22–26. See also Tenishev Archive, 7/1/26, 1. 21.
46. Tenishev Archive, 7/1/67, 20 gives a systematic picture.
47. Tenishev Archive, 7/1/26, 2. This tradition may be descended from the ancient bear cults of Siberia. See James Forsyth, *A History of the Peoples of Siberia, 1581–1990,* Cambridge, 1992, pp. 15–16.
48. Smirnov, op. cit., p. 26.
49. Ivanits, op. cit., p. 6; W. F. Ryan, *The Bathhouse at Midnight: Magic in Russia,* Stroud, 1999, p. 46.
50. Russian State Archive of Literature and Art (RGALI), 361/1/4, ll. 118–9. See also Gail Kligman, *The Wedding of the Dead: Ritual, Poetics and Popular Culture in Transylvania,* Berkeley, 1988.
51. Barsov collected different kinds of lament to show how the formula might vary according to the dead person's status. The first example he reproduced was a widow's lament for her husband, which included a prayer to God and the archangels for help in the midst of bitterness, hard work, and solitude. Barsov, op. cit., Vol. 1, pp. 1–44.
52. Peter the Great attempted to ban lamenting, and the Church continued to inveigh against it into the twentieth century. On the eighteenth and nineteenth centuries, see Barsov, op. cit., Vol. 1, p. xi.
53. Tenishev Archive, 7/1/29, 31.
54. Barsov, op. cit., Vol. 1, p. xi.
55. Ibid., p. x.

56. "Stikh o strannike," recorded in 1996 as part of a collection of spiritual songs of death, *Kak po moryushku.*
57. Cited in Chris Ward, *Stalin's Russia,* London, 1993, p. 108.
58. See below, pp. 35–36.
59. Stephen P. Frank, "Popular Justice, Community and Culture, 1870–1900," in Ben Eklof and Stephen P. Frank, op. cit., pp. 146–49.
60. Felix J. Oinas, *Essays on Russian Folklore and Mythology,* Columbus, Ohio, 1984, p. 99; Smirnov, op. cit., p. 17; Tenishev Archive, 2/943, 8; Tokarev, op. cit., pp. 38–39.
61. Ivanits, op. cit., p. 48.
62. Archive of the Russian Center for the Preservation and Study of Documents of Contemporary History (RTsKhIDNI), 89/4/121, 9; this refers to an exhumation in 1924.
63. On vampires, see Paul Barber, *Vampires, Burial and Death: Folklore and Reality,* New Haven and London, 1988; Oinas, op. cit., pp. 111–23; Tokarev, op. cit., p. 40.
64. Mitrofan, op. cit., p. 49.
65. Several instances of this are discussed in RGALI, 2009/1/159.
66. Gorky was thinking particularly of the thirteenth-century classic *The Golden Legend,* a collection about the lives—and deaths—of the saints. See Victor Serge, *Memoirs of a Revolutionary 1901–1941,* trans. Peter Sedgwick, Oxford, 1963, p. 73.
67. Tenishev Archive, 7/2/1619.
68. Paul Thompson, *The Voice of the Past: Oral History,* Oxford, 1988, p. 7.
69. Tenishev Archive, 7/2/1444.
70. Contribution to a conference organized in Moscow by the author and hosted by the Macarthur Foundation, Dec. 1997.
71. T. A. Listova, "Pokhoronno-pominal'nye obychai i obryady russkikh smolenskoi, pskovskoi i kostromskoi oblastei, konets XIX–XXv.," in *Pokhoronno-pominal'nye obychai i obryady,* various authors, Moscow, 1993, p. 77; Ivanits, op. cit., p. 48; Tenishev Archive, 7/1/32, 11–12.
72. Ariès, op. cit., p. 440.
73. Tenishev Archive, 7/2/1398, 2–7.
74. Stories of individual "special" children feature in the interviews that I have used in later chapters of this book. Among them was Anna Timofeyevna's brother Valya, "a unique child, so talented, so special." See Chapter 6, pp. 155–63.
75. RGIA, 796/171/2594.
76. Richard Huntington and Peter Metcalf, *Celebrations of Death: The Anthropology of Mortuary Ritual,* Cambridge, 1979, p. 1.
77. See Keith Thomas, *Religion and the Decline of Magic,* London, 1971, pp. 721–22.

Chapter 2: A Culture of Death

1. See V. Shkol'nikov, F. Meslé, and J. Vallin, "La Crise sanitaire en Russie," parts i and ii, *Population,* 4–5, 1995, pp. 907–44 and 945–82; Julie DaVanzo and Gwendolyn Farnsworth, "Russia's Demographic 'Crisis,'" RAND Conference Proceedings, n.d.
2. Lincoln Chen, speaking at the Common Security Forum symposium, "The Human Security Crisis in Russia," Harvard University, Cambridge, Mass., April 1996. See also Michael Specter, "Russian Demography: A Case for Dostoyevsky," *International Herald Tribune,* June 9, 1997; Judith Shapiro, "The Russian Mortality Crisis and Its Causes," in Anders Aslund, ed., *Russian Economic Reform at Risk,* London, 1995, pp. 149–78.
3. Shkol'nikov et al., Annex 1 (Comparison of Changes in Life Expectancy, 1891–1993, figures for

Russia, France, Japan, and U.S.A.), *Moscow Times,* February 18, 1997, citing World Health Organization statistics.

4. Shkol'nikov et al., "La Crise sanitaire," p. 908.
5. Sub-Saharan Africa and Afghanistan, respectively. Figures from the United Nations' *Demographic Yearbook,* 47th edn., New York, 1997.
6. Robert Gildea, *Barricades and Borders: Europe, 1800–1914,* Oxford, 1987, p. 278.
7. S. A. Novosel'skii, *Smertnost' i prodol'zhitel'nost zhizni v Rossii,* Petrograd, 1916, p. 181; M. B. Mirskii, *Meditsina Rossii XVI–XIX vekov,* Moscow, 1996, p. 311.
8. The Pirogov Society, the professional body representing Russian doctors, debated a report on this problem in 1912; see F. D. Markuzon, "Sanitarnaya statistika v gorodakh predrevolyutsionnoi Rossii," in *Ocherki po istorii statistiki SSSR,* Moscow, 1995, p. 126.
9. RGIA, 1290/2/585 and 875.
10. Novosel'skii, op. cit., p. 186. There were about five million Jews in the Russian empire at the time of the 1897 census, and approximately two and a half times that number of Lutherans and Catholics.
11. Ibid., p. 185.
12. Interview, Moscow, March 1997.
13. The method is brilliantly applied by Alain Blum. See *Naître, vivre et mourir en URSS, 1917–1991,* Paris, 1994.
14. On the cheapening of human life, see Michael Specter, "Climb in Russia's Death Rate," *New York Times,* March 6, 1994. On continuity in general, see Tucker, "What Time Is It in Russia's History?"
15. Novosel'skii, op. cit., p. 179.
16. See Markuzon's commentary on Y. Gubner, *Statisticheskie issledovanie sanitarnogo sostoyaniya S Peterburga v 1870 g.,* St. Petersburg, 1872, in *Ocherki po istorii statistiki SSSR,* p. 130.
17. Pobedonostsev, *Reflections of a Russian Statesman,* p. 221.
18. On the zemstvos, see Orlando Figes, *A People's Tragedy,* London, 1996, p. 39; Christopher Read, *From Tsar to Soviets: The Russian People and Their Revolution, 1917–21,* London, 1996, p. 15; H. Seton-Watson, *The Decline of Imperial Russia, 1855–1914,* London, 1952, pp. 49–51; J. N. Westwood, *Endurance and Endeavour: Russian History, 1812–1992,* Oxford, 1993, pp. 85–86.
19. In 1915, for example, the Ministry of the Interior attempted to keep statistical information, crucial for the war effort, away from its own subdepartment of public health.
20. Westwood, op. cit., pp. 114–15.
21. RGIA, 565/6/21498; Novosel'skii, op. cit., p. 181.
22. The main new sites were the Preobrazhenskoe and Uspenskoe cemeteries. RGIA, 565/6/21498, sets out the new regulations.
23. Stephen White, *Russia Goes Dry: Alcohol, State and Society,* Cambridge, 1996, pp. 5–11.
24. Westwood, op. cit., p. 173.
25. S. G. Wheatcroft, "Agriculture," in R. W. Davies, ed., *From Tsarism to the New Economic Policy,* p. 87.
26. H. H. Fisher, *The Famine in Soviet Russia, 1919–1923,* New York, 1927, p. 476.
27. Tenishev Archive, 2/1053, 1. 1.
28. Nancy Mandelker Frieden, *Russian Physicians in an Era of Reform and Revolution, 1856–1905,* Princeton, 1981, pp. 135–53.
29. *Sotsial'naya gigiyena,* 1922, No. 1, p. 68.
30. Novosel'skii, op. cit., p. 98.
31. RGIA, 1290/2/373.

32. Figes, op. cit., pp. 157–62.
33. Barbara Alpern Engel, *Between the Fields and the City: Women, Work and Family in Russia, 1861–1914*, Cambridge, 1996, p. 35.
34. Westwood, op. cit., p. 180.
35. Mortality was highest in the tobacco industry and in the factories that processed toxic minerals; *Sotsial'naya gigiyena*, 1922, No. 1, p. 96.
36. Novosel'skii, op. cit., p. 159.
37. Markuzon, op. cit., p. 130.
38. Novosel'skii, op. cit., pp. 140–41.
39. Figures from UNDP *Human Development Report*, Oxford, 1996.
40. M. N. Gernet, *Detoubiistvo*, Moscow, 1911. Infanticide remained rare (peasant women who did not want another child were more likely to resort to abortion), but the cases that did occur were seldom reported to the police or other officials. Tenishev Archive, 2/943, 5.
41. Russian State Archive of the Economy (RGAE), 1562/329/103, 218; Blum, op. cit., p. 145.
42. Markuzon (p. 137) gives a terrifying figure of 962 per 1,000 for mortality in the children's home in Moscow between 1867 and 1871. Unfortunately, it is not clear what source he is citing.
43. Mikhail Bulgakov, *A Country Doctor's Notebook*, pp. 113–44.
44. E. Y. Zalenskii, *Iz zapisok zemskogo vracha.*
45. Frieden, op. cit., p. 17.
46. Zalenskii, op. cit., pp. 48–50, 108, 113, 138.
47. Ibid., pp. 142–49.
48. Frieden, op. cit., pp. 145–46.
49. Zalenskii, op. cit., p. 148.
50. Tenishev Archive, 2/1053; Frieden, op. cit., p. 148.
51. A range of written or spoken charms for keeping evil at bay is presented in Ryan, *The Bathhouse at Midnight*, pp. 184–95.
52. Zalenskii, op. cit., pp. 45–46.
53. Ibid., p. 138.
54. Frieden, op. cit., p. 149.
55. Zalenskii, op. cit., p. 108.
56. RGIA, 1319/1/50.
57. Its records are in RGIA, 1319/1/56.
58. *Birzhevye vedomosti*, May 23, 1907.
59. Figes, op. cit., p. 18.
60. O. G. Shavel'skii, *Vospominaniya poslednogo protpresvitra russkoi Armii i Flota*, Vol. 1, New York, 1954, p. 97. The memoirs were written in 1919–20.
61. Cited in Westwood, op. cit., p. 181.
62. Pasternak, *A Vanished Present*, pp. 88, 96.
63. John D. Klier and Shlomo Lambroza, eds., *Pogroms: Anti-Jewish Violence in Modern Russian History*, Cambridge, 1992, p. 216.
64. Richard Pipes, *The Russian Revolution, 1899–1919*, London, 1990, pp. 10–15.
65. W. Sablinsky, *The Road to Bloody Sunday: Father Gapon and the St. Petersburg Massacre of 1905*, Princeton, 1976, pp. 265–66. The lower figure is the more likely as the latter was used by Soviet propagandists eager to inflate the number of casualties to the maximum credible.
66. Ibid., p. 266.
67. Ibid.
68. Anna Geifman, *Thou Shalt Kill: Revolutionary Terrorism in Russia, 1894–1917*, Princeton, 1993, pp. 21, 251.

69. Public execution was ended in the Russian empire in 1881. Hangings were usually arranged in the yards of prisons, which is where a large number of the Bolsheviks' killings also took place after 1917.
70. M. M. Gernet, *Smertnaya kazn',* Moscow, 1913, pp. 53–58.
71. Gernet cites Illyudor's call, in 1904, for public hangings from an aspen tree on Red Square: op. cit., p. 30. See also V. Venozhinskii, *Smertnaya kazn' i terror,* St. Petersburg, 1908, p. 33.
72. Gernet, op. cit., p. 100.
73. According to a group of Russian academics (including Gernet), eighteen thousand people were condemned to death in England and Wales between 1810 and 1826. V. M. Ustinov, I. B. Novitskii, and M. N. Gernet, *Osnovniya ponyatiya russkogo gosudarstvennogo, grazhdanskogo i ugolovnogo pravo,* Moscow, 1910, pp. 261–62.
74. N. S. Tagantsev, *Smertnaya kazn',* St. Petersburg, 1913, p. 93.
75. Ibid., p. 94.
76. Gernet, *Smertnaya kazn',* pp. 146–47.
77. *Orenburgskaya gazeta,* November 18, 1908; RGIA, 733/199/122, 31.
78. RGIA, 733/199/124, 62 and 20.
79. RGIA, 733/199/360, 23.
80. RGIA, 733/199/124, 12.
81. Y. L. Liebovich, *Tysyacha sovremennykh samoubiistv,* Moscow, 1923, p. 3. Like Liebovich, the more progressive of Russian social scientists, even before the revolution, were already aware of Durkheim's work on suicide, published in 1897.
82. RGIA, 733/199/124, 42.
83. RGIA, 733/199/124, 10.
84. Cited in Figes, op. cit., p. 402.
85. My account is based on Edward H. Judge, *Easter in Kishinev: Anatomy of a Pogrom,* New York, 1992; and Klier and Lambroza, op. cit., Cambridge, 1992.
86. A photograph of the ceremony is in the St. Petersburg Archive of Cinema, Photography and Sound, ref. Gr 28078.
87. Information displayed at the museum of the mass grave at Levashovo, St. Petersburg region.
88. P. Sorokin, *Leaves from a Russian Diary,* London, 1925, p. 279.
89. Anna Akhmatova, *Selected Poems,* p. 71.

Chapter 3: The Palace of Freedom

1. R. Luxemburg, *The Russian Revolution,* Ann Arbor, 1961, p. 40.
2. "Marxism and Insurrection," September 1917; this translation in Robert C. Tucker, ed., *The Lenin Anthology,* New York, 1975, p. 410.
3. Accounts of the February revolution can be found in Figes, *A People's Tragedy,* pp. 307–53; and Robert Service, *A History of Twentieth-Century Russia,* London, 1997, pp. 32–41.
4. *Pravda,* April 9, 1917.
5. Ibid.
6. "April Theses," published in *Pravda,* April 7, 1917.
7. "Advice from an Onlooker," October 8, 1917, cited in Tucker, op. cit., p. 413.
8. Luxemburg, op. cit., pp. 34–39.
9. "To the Citizens of Russia," October, 25, 1917.
10. *Pravda,* December 26, 1917.
11. R. Service, *Lenin: A Political Life, Vol. 2: Worlds in Collision,* Houndmills, 1991, p. 273.
12. Luxemburg, *The Russian Revolution,* pp. 68–69 and 71.

13. The most important were in Germany, beginning in Kiel and Berlin, in Hungary, where a socialist regime was briefly organized under Bela Kun, and in Italy, where the phase of open political violence began and ended slightly later.
14. G. Hoare and G. Nowell Smith, eds., *Antonio Gramsci: Selections from the Prison Notebooks,* London, 1971, p. 238.
15. *New Statesman and Society,* November 10, 1989.
16. In reality, Bauman was a callous man, widely disliked by those who knew him. See Service, op. cit., p. 47.
17. *A Vanished Present,* pp. 116–17.
18. Stites, *Revolutionary Dreams,* especially pp. 13–36.
19. See for example, Neil Harding, *Lenin's Political Thought,* Vol. 1, Houndmills, 1983, pp. 72–77.
20. N. S. Polishchuk, "Obryad kak sotsial'noe yavlenie," *Sovetskaya etnografiya,* No. 6, 1991, pp. 34–35; *Istoricheskie kladbishcha Peterburga, spravochnik-putevoditel',* St. Petersburg, 1993, p. 49.
21. *Istoricheskie kladbishcha,* pp. 46–49.
22. See for example O. A. Trubnikova, "Istoriya nekropolya Novodevich'ego monastyraya," in *Moskovskii nekropol': Istoriya, arkheologiya, iskusstvo, okhrana,* Moscow, 1991, pp. 106–23.
23. St. Petersburg Archive of Cinema, Photography and Sound, D1900, G 14610.
24. Polishchuk, op. cit., p. 27.
25. Discussed in J. Bowker, *The Meanings of Death,* Cambridge, 1991, pp. 6–10.
26. Cited in *Pravda,* March 23, 1917.
27. The quotation is from the final section of Lenin's *Materialism and Empirio-criticism,* written in 1908.
28. See also below, pp. 73–75.
29. This point is made most frequently about Stalin, whose early intellectual formation included a spell in a religious seminary. See for example Robert H. McNeal, *Stalin: Man and Ruler,* Houndmills, 1988, pp. 8–9.
30. As Dmitrii Volkogonov puts it in his biography of Lenin, Soviet propaganda itself further downplayed the importance of individual emotion. *Lenin: Life and Legacy,* trans. Harold Shukman, London, 1994, pp. xxxii–iii.
31. Cited in Read, *From Tsar to Soviets,* p. 202.
32. The issue of prerevolutionary collectivism is discussed in Oleg Kharkordin, *The Collective and the Individual in Russia: A Study of Practice,* Berkeley and London, 1999, especially pp. 49–61.
33. Harding, op. cit., p. 11.
34. Robert Service, *Lenin: A Political Life, Vol. 1: The Strengths of Contradiction,* Houndmills, 1985, p. 22.
35. Larisa Vasil'eva, *Deti Kremlya,* Moscow, 1996, p. 25.
36. *Moskovskii Nekropol',* p. 14.
37. Vasil'eva, op. cit., p. 85.
38. He never visited his late wife's grave. See Robert C. Tucker, *Stalin in Power: The Revolution from Above, 1928–1941,* New York, 1990, p. 217; Roy Medvedev, *Let History Judge: The Origins and Consequences of Stalinism,* revised edn., New York, 1989, pp. 302–3; Vasil'eva, op. cit., p. 85.
39. *Time of Troubles: The Diary of Yurii Vladimirovich Got'e,* trans., ed. Terence Emmons, London, 1988, p. 232. See also V. E. Baranchenko, "Konchina i pokhorony P. A. Kropotkina," *Voprosy istorii,* No. 3, 1995, pp. 149–54.
40. For a discussion of workers' reading habits at this time see J. Brooks, *When Russia Learned to Read: Literacy and Popular Literature, 1861–1917,* Princeton, 1985; Stites, op. cit., pp. 24–36.
41. Zelnik, *A Radical Worker in Tsarist Russia,* p. 34.

42. A photograph showing a religious service in a factory in the Urals is reproduced in Victoria E. Bonnell ed., *The Russian Worker: Life and Labor under the Tsarist Regime,* Berkeley and London, 1983, p. 42.
43. M. M. Persits, *Ateizm russkogo rabochego, 1870–1905,* Moscow, 1965, p. 100.
44. Figes, op. cit., p. 65.
45. Zelnik, op. cit., p. 30.
46. Mark D. Steinberg, "Workers on the Cross: Religious Imagination in the Writings of Russian Workers, 1910–1924," *Russian Review,* Vol. 53, No. 2, April 1994, p. 222.
47. Ibid., p. 218; A. I. Klibanov, *Istoriya religioznogo sektanstva v Rossii,* Moscow, 1965, pp. 266–68.
48. Persits, op. cit., p. 106.
49. Ibid., p. 113.
50. Zelnik, op. cit., p. 32.
51. Polishchuk, op. cit., p. 28.
52. *Russkie pesni i romansy,* Moscow, 1989, pp. 490–91.
53. Steinberg, op. cit., p. 220.
54. *Rabochaya zhizn',* No. 2, 1918, p. 2. See also No. 9, 1917, p. 3, for a similar image.
55. Maria Carlson, "Fashionable Occultism," in Bernice Glatzer Rosenthal, ed., *The Occult in Russian and Soviet Culture,* Ithaca, N.Y. 1997, pp. 136–39.
56. *Ottuda,* No. 15, 1907, pp. 3–4.
57. *Ottuda,* No. 22, 1911, pp. 1–2.
58. Peter Wiles, "On Physical Immortality," *Survey,* Nos. 56–57, 1965, pp. 132–33. On cosmism more generally, see S. G. Semenova and A. G. Garcheva, eds., *Russkii kosmizm: antologiya filosofskoi mysli,* Moscow, 1993.
59. "Ancestors and Resurrectors," cited in Wiles, pp. 134–35.
60. See Chapter 5, pp. 150–53.
61. *Pravda,* March 23, 1917.
62. *Istoricheskie kladbishcha,* p. 49 (on Gorky's intervention and the choice of site); after 1918, when the capital moved to Moscow, the most prestigious burial site of all would be Red Square.
63. *Pravda,* March 23, 1917.
64. *Pravda,* March 25, 1917.
65. *Pravda,* March 23, 1917.
66. A. Abramov, *U Kremlevskoi steny,* Moscow, 1984, pp. 31–36.
67. See pp. 221–22 and 257–58.
68. People I have asked remember monuments in the western republics of the USSR, and notably Galicia, which was not incorporated into the Soviet Union until the Second World War, but no one can think of a monument on any national scale in Russia itself, and I have never seen one.
69. On suicide, see Y. L. Leibovich, *Tysyacha sovremennykh samoubiistv,* pp. 3–4. On patriotism, see Figes, op. cit., pp. 251–52.
70. A. S. Senin, "Armeiskoe dukhovenstvo rossii v pervuyu mirovuyu voinu," *Voprosy istorii,* No. 10, 1995, pp. 160–62.
71. S. G. Wheatcroft and R. W. Davies, "Population," in R. W. Davies, Mark Harrison, and S. G. Wheatcroft, eds., *The Economic Transformation of the Soviet Union, 1913–1945,* Cambridge, 1994, p. 62.
72. G. L. Mosse, *Fallen Soldiers: Reshaping the Memory of the World War,* Oxford, 1990, pp. 85–96.
73. *Olonetskaya nedelya,* No. 42, 1914, pp. 6–7.
74. See pp. 96 and 196–98.

75. K. Hodgson, *Written with the Bayonet: Soviet Russian Poetry of World War II,* Liverpool, 1996, pp. 20–24.
76. These letters are cited from hundreds kept in the State Archive of St. Petersburg (TsGASPb), 7384/9/268, May 1917.
77. M. N. Pokrovskii, the Marxist historian, wrote a collection of essays on the First World War (*Imperialisticheskaya voina: Sbornik statei, 1915–27,* Moscow, 1927); a more systematic bibliography of military and other works is provided by G. Khmelevskii, *Mirovaya imperialisticheskaya voina 1914–18gg., sistematicheskii ukazatel' kmizhnoi i stateinoi voenno-istoricheskoi literatury za 1914–35gg.*, Moscow, 1936.

Chapter 4: Transforming Fire

1. On pogroms, see State Archive of the Russian Federation (GARF), R-1244/2/11, 359 (letter from Jewish troops); more generally, see TsGASPb, 7384/9/245, which contains letters and documents relating to civil disorder. See also Figes, *A People's Tragedy,* p. 462.
2. Eduard M. Dune, *Notes of a Red Guard,* trans. and ed. Diane P. Koenker and S. A. Smith, Urbana and Chicago, 1993, p. 56.
3. Ibid., p. 57.
4. Got'e, *Time of Troubles,* pp. 28–29, 39–40.
5. Davies and Wheatcroft, "Population," in Davies et al., *The Economic Transformation of the Soviet Union,* pp. 62–64.
6. See pp. 141–45.
7. Borodin, *One Man and His Time,* p. 26.
8. Leon Trotsky, *My Life: An Attempt at Autobiography,* Harmondsworth, 1971, p. 411.
9. Service, *A History of Twentieth-Century Russia,* p. 88, gives a figure of three million; Davies and Wheatcroft, also citing F. Lorimer's 1946 classic *The Population of the Soviet Union,* give two million (Davies and Wheatcroft, op. cit., p. 63).
10. Got'e, op. cit., p. 70.
11. Dune, op. cit., p. 58.
12. Got'e, op. cit., p. 95.
13. The capital was moved from Petrograd to Moscow in March 1918, partly because of a threat from the White army of General Yudenich.
14. S. G. Wheatcroft, "Soviet statistics," in *Cahiers du monde russe,* Vol. 38, No. 4, 1997, p. 544.
15. Got'e, op. cit., p. 218.
16. Davies and Wheatcroft, op. cit., p. 62.
17. Hiroaki Kuromiya, *Freedom and Terror in the Donbass: A Ukrainian-Russian Borderland, 1870s–1990s,* Cambridge, 1998, p. 111.
18. Read, *From Tsar to Soviets,* p. 192.
19. Victor Serge, *Memoirs of a Revolutionary,* p. 115. See also Alan Ball, *Russia's Last Capitalists: The Nepmen, 1921–1929,* Berkeley, Los Angeles, and London, 1987, pp. 6–8.
20. Serge, op. cit., pp. 115–16.
21. Ibid., pp. 78–79.
22. See Peter Gatrell, *A Whole Empire Walking,* Bloomington, Ind., 1999.
23. Accounts of some of these journeys are collected in RGALI, 1712/1/600.
24. State Archive of the Moscow Region (GAMO), 4557/1/48, 11.
25. The local paper in Vologda described this situation well in 1922, see *Zhizn' goroda,* No. 2, April 1922, pp. 21–22, and No. 6, September 1922, pp. 5–6.
26. GARF, 482/4/31, 14; GARF 482/4/44, 138.

27. Service, op. cit., pp. 102–3; Read, op. cit., pp. 193–98.
28. Lev Razgon, interviewed by the author in Moscow, February 1997. Contemporary sources all talk of this desperation.
29. Accounts of this occur in many sources. For one collection, see RGALI, 2009/1/159. Photographic evidence (rows of bloated corpses) from the St. Petersburg Archive of Cinema, Photography and Sound, Gr 8645 and Gr 41614.
30. *Slovo,* IV, p. 79.
31. RTsKhIDNI, 364/2/1, 20.
32. In fact, the figure was just under two hundred thousand, as the editors of Dune's memoir point out.
33. Dune, op. cit., p. 124.
34. See L. D. Gerson, *The Secret Police in Lenin's Russia,* Philadelphia, 1976, pp. 77–80; Read, op. cit., pp. 206–8; Robert Conquest, *The Great Terror,* Harmondsworth, 1971, p. 310.
35. *Petrogradskaya pravda,* September 5, 1918.
36. Sorokin, pp. 232–33. See also Serge, op. cit., p. 99.
37. *Izvestiya Orenburgskogo voenno-revolyutsionnogo komiteta,* No. 23, November 1918.
38. Borodin, op. cit., p. 19.
39. Ibid., pp. 19–20.
40. Got'e, op. cit., p. 307.
41. GARF, 4390/12/40, 24.
42. Cited in Kuromiya, op. cit., p. 105.
43. Ibid., pp. 95–96.
44. Sorokin, op. cit., pp. 257–58. Victor Serge heard of similar atrocities from Maxim Gorky. Serge, op. cit., p. 73.
45. R. W. Davies, *Soviet History in the Yeltsin Era,* Houndmills, 1997, p. 130.
46. Trotsky, op. cit., p. 417.
47. Orlando Figes, *Peasant Russia: Civil War,* Oxford, 1989, pp. 312–20.
48. TsGASPb, 7384/9/268, 111. Other examples in the same vein appear elsewhere in the same document, which is a collection of soldiers' letters addressed to the Petrograd soviet in the last months of 1917.
49. Dune, op. cit., p. 125.
50. Trotsky, op. cit., pp. 417–18.
51. On the petitions from 1917, see GARF, R-1244/2/11; see also Ger P. Van den Berg, "The Soviet Union and the Death Penalty," *Soviet Studies,* 35, April 2, 1983, p. 155.
52. Trotsky, op. cit., p. 418.
53. RTsKhIDNI, 364/2/1, 20-44 (letters to *Pravda*).
54. Borodin, op. cit., p. 21.
55. *Russkaya pravoslavnaya tserkov' i kommunisticheskoe gosudarstvo, 1917–1941: dokumenty i fotomaterialy,* Moscow, 1996, p. 146.
56. See Chapter 5, pp. 117–19.
57. *Rabochaya zhizn',* No. 14, 1917, pp. 3–4.
58. L. A. and L. M. Vasilevskii, *Kniga o golode: Populyarnyi mediko-sanitarnyi ocherk,* Petrograd, 1922, pp. 174–75.
59. Remarks remembered in an interview by a group of psychiatrists who trained in the 1920s, Moscow, March 1997.
60. For one exposition of this commonly expressed view, see Ante Ciliga, *The Russian Enigma,* London, 1979, pp. 284–85.
61. Geifman, *Thou Shalt Kill,* pp. 253–54.

62. On banditry, see Figes, op. cit., pp. 340–53; on the treatment of corpses, see RGALI, 1712/1/600, 115.
63. See A. M. Selishchev, *Yazyk revolyutsionnoi epokhi,* Moscow, 1928.
64. Hunger and memory are discussed in Chapter 6. Survivors of the Leningrad blockade also report numbness, remembering that they no longer even thought about food when they were at their weakest.
65. Service, op. cit., p. 117.
66. The most important example in the interwar period was probably the "war scare" of 1927, which was used as a pretext for increasing the pace of industrialization and for the collectivization of agriculture.
67. The most controversial statement of this position has been J. A. Getty, *Origins of the Great Purges: The Soviet Communist Party Reconsidered, 1933–38,* Cambridge, 1985. A more recent, subtler, and better documented account is J. A. Getty and Oleg V. Naumov, *The Road to Terror: Stalin and the Self-Destruction of the Bolsheviks, 1932–39,* New Haven and London, 1999.
68. RTsKhIDNI, 5/1/2558, see also Catherine Merridale, "The Making of a Moderate Bolshevik: An Introduction to L. B. Kamenev's Political Biography," in Julian Cooper, Maureen Perrie, and E. A. Rees, eds., *Soviet History, 1917–53,* Houndmills, 1995, pp. 35–37.
69. J. L. Keep, "Lenin's Letters as an Historical Source," in B. W. Eissenstat, ed., *Lenin and Leninism: State, Law and Society,* Lexington, Ill., 1971, p. 260.
70. Interview, Moscow, February 14, 1997.
71. Mark D. Steinberg and Vladimir M. Khrustalev, *The Fall of the Romanovs: Political Dreams and Personal Struggles in a Time of Revolution,* New Haven and London, 1995, pp. 290–94.
72. Got'e, op. cit., p. 179.
73. Cited in Mikhail Agursky, *The Third Rome: National Bolshevism in the USSR,* Boulder, Col., 1987, pp. 258–59.
74. Got'e, op. cit., pp. 172–73.
75. V. Alexandrovich, "Sev," cited in Steinberg and Khrustalev, op. cit., p. 282.
76. *Rabochaya zhizn',* 1918, No. 7, p. 7.
77. Selishchev, op. cit., p. 89.
78. Ibid., p. 121–22.
79. *Rabochaya zhizn',* No. 18, 1917, p. 7, and No. 1, 1918, p. 2.
80. *Rabochaya zhizn',* No. 13, 1918, p. 3.
81. Archive Collection of the International Institute for Social History, Amsterdam, Balabanoff Archive, file 223.
82. GARF, 4537/1/831, 74–5 (report to Vserokompom).
83. Dune, op. cit., p. 230.
84. This story was one of those discussed by a group of women whose parents had been repressed in the 1930s. Interview, Moscow, March 7, 1997.
85. Borodin, op. cit., pp. 56–57.
86. GARF, 4347/1/94, 101.
87. GARF, 4347/1/94, 70.
88. The phenomenon was discussed in the pages of *Psikhiatricheskaya gazeta* from 1914 (see for example contributions by N. A. Yurman, No. 9, 1915, pp. 139–43, and V. V. Khoroshko, No. 1, 1916, p. 3). See also S. A. Preobrazhenskii, *Materialy k voprosu o dushevnykh zabolevaniyakh voinov i lits prichastnykh k voennym deistviyam,* Petrograd, 1917. A fuller discussion of this story is in Catherine Merridale, "The Collective Mind: Trauma and Shell-shock in Twentieth-Century Russia," *Journal of Contemporary History,* Vol. 35, No. 1, January 2000, pp. 39–56. The

general history of shell shock is presented in Allan Young, *The Harmony of Illusions: Inventing Post-Traumatic Stress Disorder,* Princeton, 1995, pp. 25–66.

89. For patriotic criticism of the new diagnosis, see *Olonetskaya nedelya,* No. 42, 1914, p. 6.
90. GARF, 4347 (catalogue summary of Vserokompom's role).
91. GARF, 4347/1/853, 11–16.
92. GARF, 4347/1/854, 3.
93. GARF, 4347/1/831, 75.
94. *Bol'shevik,* Nos. 21–22, 1925, pp. 61–74.
95. Aleksandr Etkind, *Eros nevozmozhnogo. Istoriya psikhoanaliza v. Rossii,* St. Petersburg, 1993, p. 281.
96. N. B. Lebina, "Tenevye storony zhizni sovetskogo goroda 20–30 godov," *Voprosy istorii,* No. 2, 1994, p. 36.
97. Etkind, op. cit., p. 222. See also *Izvestiya,* April 26, 1925, and M. N. Gernet, *Prestupnost' i samoubiistvo vo vremya voiny i posle nee,* Moscow, 1927, p. 11.
98. Y. L. Liebovich, *Tysyacha sovremennnykh samoubiistv,* pp. 2–7. See also Gernet, op. cit., Moscow, 1927, pp. 217–23.
99. Liebovich, op. cit., p. 4.
100. Ibid., p. 9.
101. *Partiinaya etika,* reprinted Moscow, 1989, p. 246.
102. Lebina, op. cit., p. 36.
103. Etkind, op. cit., p. 221.
104. Cited ibid., p. 253.
105. Ibid., p. 243.
106. Cited in David Joravsky, *Russian Psychology: A Critical History,* Oxford, 1989, p. 250.
107. Ibid., p. 259.
108. Interview with psychiatrist D. V. A. Ababkov, Bekhterev Institute, St. Petersburg, October 1997.
109. Interview with Dr. Aleksei P. Smirnov, St. Petersburg, October 1997.
110. Selishchev, op. cit., p. 132.
111. Cited ibid., p. 123.
112. Details of its extent during the war were given in *Psikhiatricheskaya gazeta,* No. 1, 1916, p. 6. On prohibition in these years, see White, *Russia Goes Dry,* pp. 17–19.
113. GARF, 4547/1/854, 3.
114. Religion is discussed more fully in the next chapter.
115. RGALI, 2950/1/126, 26.
116. RGALI, 2950/1/126, 5.
117. RGALI, 2950/1/126, 28–29.
118. RGALI, 2950/1/126, 1.
119. Some years later, it would be this ethnographer who argued against including frightening images in new Soviet editions of traditional children's stories. See Chapter 9, p. 250.
120. Y. Yakovlev, *Derevnya kak ona est',* Moscow, 1923, pp. 7–8.
121. Sorokin, op. cit., pp. 270–71.
122. Got'e, op. cit., p. 411.

Chapter 5: Common and Uncommon Graves

1. "Pis'mo komisariata yustitsii Soyuza kommun Severnoi oblasti—Presidiumu Petrosoveta o neobkhodimosti issledovaniya moshchei sv. Aleksandra Nevskogo," March, 24, 1919, cited in *Russkaya pravoslavnaya tserkov',* pp. 56–58.

2. RTsKhIDNI, 364/2/1, 154, relating to religious belief in Kaluga province in 1919.
3. Got'e, *Time of Troubles,* p. 139.
4. "Tsirkulyar VIII otdel Narkomata yustitsii—Vsem gubispolkomam i gubkompartam," April 1, 1921, in *Russkaya pravoslavnaya tserkov',* pp. 61–62.
5. *Russkaya pravoslavnaya tserkov',* pp. 57–58.
6. Got'e, op. cit., p. 258.
7. Ibid.
8. *Russkaya pravoslavnaya tserkov',* p. 105.
9. Y. Yakovlev, *Nasha Derevnya,* Moscow, 1924, pp. 131–32.
10. Got'e, op. cit., p. 104.
11. See Chapter 10, pp. 276–79; see also H. Kent Geiger, *The Family in Soviet Russia,* Cambridge, Mass., 1968, p. 148.
12. Sorokin, *Leaves from a Russian Diary,* p. 229.
13. Ibid., p. 230.
14. Got'e, op. cit., pp. 214–15.
15. Ibid., p. 448.
16. GARF, 482/4/31, 40.
17. GAMO, 4557/1/50, 2 (norm set in January 1919).
18. TsGASPb, 142/1/24, 1.
19. GAMO, 4557/1/48, 15.
20. GARF, 4390/12/40, 7.
21. TsGASPb, 7455/2/20, 3.
22. GAMO, 4557/1/54, 1.
23. GAMO, 4557/1/54, 2.
24. GAMO, 4557/1/48, 13–14.
25. GARF, 4390/12/40, 33.
26. GAMO, 4557/1/48, 14.
27. Ibid.
28. GARF, 4390/12/40, 17 (January 1919).
29. GARF, 4390/12/40, 17.
30. GAMO, 4557/1/48, 15.
31. GAMO, 4557/1/48, 11.
32. GAMO, 4557/1/48, /11–12.
33. GAMO, 4557/1/51, 5.
34. GAMO, 4557/1/51, 17–18.
35. TsGASPb, 1001/10, 77, 73.
36. TsGASPb, 1001/3/177, 1–2.
37. TsGASPb, 1001/10/77, 49–50.
38. TsGASPb, 1001/10/77, 47.
39. TsGASPb, 1001/10/77, 15–23.
40. TsGASPb, 1001/10/77, 6.
41. TsGASPb, 3199/20/5, 1.
42. GARF, 9531/1/16, 1.
43. *Moskovskii nekropol',* p. 50.
44. Ibid., p. 49.
45. St. Petersburg Archive of Literature and Art, p. 49. (GALIGSPb), 32/1/8, 16.
46. See *Kommunal'nyi rabotnik,* Nos. 13–14, 1924.
47. GARF, 5263/1/12, 226.

48. Cited in Konstantinow, *Stations of the Cross,* p. 45.
49. Stites, *Revolutionary Dreams,* p. 44.
50. *Russkaya pravoslavnaya tserkov',* p. 90.
51. Ibid., pp. 80–83.
52. Ibid., pp. 88–92.
53. Ibid., p. 69; GALIGSPb, 1001/9/46, 1; interview with Fr. Agapii, March 1997.
54. GARF, 5263/1/7, 71–72.
55. Mikhail Bulgakov, *The Master and Margarita,* trans. Michael Glenny, London, 1967, p. 16.
56. *Bezbozhnik u stanka,* No. 6, 1923, RTsKhIDNI, 364/2/1, 124 (which relates to religious observance among Communists).
57. Ilya Il'f and Yevgenii Petrov, *The Twelve Chairs* (1928), trans. John Richardson, London, 1965, p. 3.
58. Its constitution is kept in the Moscow City Archive, 2512/1/1.
59. *Bezbozhnik u stanka,* No. 3, 1923, p. 4.
60. Sarah Davies, *Popular Opinion in Stalin's Russia 1934–1941,* Cambridge, 1997, p. 81.
61. Konstantinow, op. cit., p. 8.
62. Geiger, *The Family in Soviet Russia,* pp. 124–25.
63. In fact there were five altogether, and all, as Shaporina says, were packed at Easter in the years 1938 and 1939. *Russkaya pravoslavnaya tserkov',* p. 321; Davies, op. cit., pp. 79–81.
64. Cited in Véronique Garros, Nataliya Korenevskaya, and Thomas Lakusen, eds., *Intimacy and Terror: Soviet Diaries of the 1930s,* New York, 1995, p. 368.
65. GARF, 5263/1/12, 7–8.
66. GARF, 5707/1/150, 31, cites the case of an antireligious agitator who kept icon lamps burning at home.
67. The story of postwar ritual is taken up in Chapter 9.
68. Interviews with Fr. Agapii (Moscow, February 1997) and Mother Leonida (St. Petersburg, October 1997).
69. Interview with Dr. Elena Ivanovna Volkova (Moscow, November 1997).
70. Garros, Korenevskaya, and Lakusen, op. cit., pp. 364–65.
71. RTsKhIDNI, 89/5/36, 7.
72. I. I. Shmal'gauzen, *Problemy smerti i bessmertiya,* Moscow and Leningrad, 1926, p. 91.
73. V. Rozhitsyn, *Sushchestvuet li zagrobnaya zhizn'?,* Kiev, 1923, p. 6.
74. RTsKhIDNI, 89/5/36, 3.
75. *Petrogradskaya pravda,* June 13, 1918, gives an example.
76. *Petrogradskaya pravda,* June 22–26, 1918.
77. *Petrogradskaya pravda,* October 10, 1918.
78. *Petrogradskaya pravda,* March 23/April 5, 1918.
79. *Petrogradskaya pravda,* April 4/17, 1918.
80. TsGASPb, 1000/3/75.
81. Got'e, op. cit., pp. 132, 232.
82. On Kamenev, see Merridale, "The Making of a Moderate Bolshevik." I am grateful to Mr. Oleg Danilov of the State Archive of the Russian Federation for further details about his work, including the reference to the dinner described here.
83. Valentinov, cited in Nina Tumarkin, *Lenin Lives!,* Cambridge, Mass., 1983, p. 141.
84. Tumarkin, op. cit., pp. 112–33.
85. RTsKhIDNI, 16/1/47, 17.
86. See Y. M. Lopukhin, *Bolezn', smert' i bal'zamirovanie V. I. Lenina,* Moscow, 1997.
87. RTsKhIDNI, 16/1/34, passim.

88. RTsKhIDNI, 16/1/112, 1–4.
89. Lopukhin, op. cit., p. 65.
90. Tumarkin, op. cit., p. 140.
91. Interview, February 14, 1997.
92. RTsKhIDNI, 16/1/20, 16.
93. RTsKhIDNI, 16/1/34, 1.
94. RTsKhIDNI, 16/1/20, 2.
95. RTsKhIDNI, 16/1/16, 119.
96. RTsKhIDNI, 16/1/28, 1–4.
97. RTsKhIDNI, 16/1/22, 1.
98. Lopukhin, op. cit., p. 65.
99. RTsKhIDNI, 16/1/102, 1.
100. Tumarkin, op. cit., pp. 157–58.
101. Ibid., p. 161.
102. RTsKhIDNI, 16/1/16, 45.
103. RTsKhIDNI, 16/1/352, 1–35.
104. RTsKhIDNI, 16/1/352, 65.
105. RTsKhIDNI, 16/1/91, 1.
106. RTsKhIDNI, 16/1/100, 12.
107. RTsKhIDNI, 16/1/112, 55.
108. RTsKhIDNI, 16/1/100, 16.
109. Tumarkin, op. cit., p. 181.
110. Ibid., pp. 179–80.
111. RTsKhIDNI, 16/1/21, 1; Lopukhin, op. cit., p. 67.
112. RTsKhIDNI, 16/1/105, 13.
113. Lopukhin, op. cit., p. 74.
114. Ibid.
115. Tumarkin, op. cit., p. 188.
116. Ibid., p. 194.
117. N. N. Stoyanov, *Arkhitektura mavzoleya Lenina,* Moscow, 1950.
118. Lopukhin, op. cit., p. 117.

Chapter 6: The Great Silence

1. *Plan,* December 10, 1936.
2. *Pravda,* January 2, 1937.
3. Kraval to Molotov, cited in *Sotsiologicheskie issledovaniya (SI),* vi, 1990, p. 9.
4. The whole story is discussed in more detail in Catherine Merridale, "The 1937 Census and the Limits of Stalinist Rule," *Historical Journal,* Vol. 39, No. 1, 1996, pp. 225–40.
5. William Krunskal, *Research and the Census,* 1984, cited by Nathan Keyfitz in his address to the opening of the Population Research Center, University of Groningen, 1991.
6. Kustolyan to Kraval, January 10, 1937, cited in *SI,* vii, 1990, p. 8.
7. Russian State Archive of the Economy (RGAE), 1562/329/152, 8–9.
8. For a discussion, see Davies and Wheatcroft, "Population," in Davies et al., *The Economic Transformation of the Soviet Union,* pp. 76–77; see also E. Andreyev, L. Darskii, and T. Kharkova, "Opyt otsenki chislennosti naseleniya SSSR, 1926–41," *Vestnik statistiki,* 7, 1990.
9. RGAE, 1562/329/107, 157.

10. Ibid.
11. Marco Carynnyk, L. Y. Luciuk, and B. S. Kovdan, eds., *The Foreign Office and the Famine: British Documents on Ukraine and the Great Famine of 1932–1933,* Kingston, Ontario, 1988, p. 290.
12. Ukrainian National Council in Canada report, September 15, 1933, Carynnyk et al., op. cit., p. 341.
13. James E. Mace and Leonid Heretz, eds., *Oral History Project of the Commission on the Ukrainian Famine,* Washington, D.C., 1990, p. 55.
14. See Mace and Heretz, op. cit., for recent translated examples. A thousand oral testimonies in Ukrainian are collected in L. B. Kovalenko and V. A. Manyak, eds., *33-i golod: Narodna kniga-memorial,* Kiev, 1991.
15. Some crossed into China; others fled to Siberia or European Russia. According to the data in the 1937 census, many of these assumed new ethnic identities, describing themselves, for example, as Russians or Uzbeks: RGAE, 1562/329/116, 149.
16. This discovery is questioned, in my opinion wrongly, by Luisa Passerini in her introduction to the special edition of the *International Yearbook of Oral History and Life Stories, Vol. 1: Memory and Totalitarianism,* Oxford, 1992, p. 14.
17. Interview, Moscow, February 1997.
18. Cited in Robert Conquest, *The Harvest of Sorrow,* Oxford, 1986, p. 256.
19. Sheila Fitzpatrick, *Stalin's Peasants,* Oxford, 1994, pp. 75–76; for Leningrad region, see Davies, *Popular Opinion in Stalin's Russia,* pp. 55–56.
20. V. V. Kondrashin, "Golod 1932–3 godov v derevnyakh Povolzh'ya," *Voprosy istorii,* vi, 1991, pp. 176–81.
21. Interview, Kiev, May 23, 1998.
22. The reports are in RGAE, fond 1562. See Merridale, op. cit.
23. May 23, 1933, cited in Carynnyk et al., op. cit., p. 262.
24. Cited in R. W. Davies, *Soviet History in the Gorbachev Revolution,* Houndmills, 1989, p. 52.
25. Cited in Mace and Heretz, op. cit., p. 62.
26. Cited in ibid.
27. Got'e, *Time of Troubles,* p. 327.
28. Fisher, *The Famine in Soviet Russia,* p. 49.
29. Sorokin, *Leaves from a Russian Diary,* p. 284.
30. Fisher, op. cit., p. 506.
31. Ibid., p. 15.
32. Ibid., pp. 556–57.
33. Ibid., pp. 96–98.
34. GARF, 482/4/247, 4; Fisher, op. cit., p. 108.
35. GARF, 482/4/247, 4; 482/4/336, 109.
36. Sorokin, op. cit., pp. 284–85.
37. Fisher, op. cit., p. 98.
38. This was the case in Orenburg, for example: Fisher, op. cit., p. 109.
39. Borodin, *One Man and His Time,* pp. 35–36.
40. Cited in Harding, *Lenin's Political Thought,* p. 19.
41. *Kommunal'nyi rabotnik,* Nos. 5–6, August–September 1921, p. 1.
42. Vasil'evskii, *Kniga o golode,* pp. 174–76.
43. Fisher, op. cit., p. 222.
44. RTsKhIDNI, 89/4/121, 3 (report to Yaroslavskii).

45. Ol'ga Litvinenko and James Riordan, *Memories of the Dispossessed,* Nottingham, 1998, pp. 54–55.
46. Ibid., pp. 66, 80.
47. Cited in R. W. Davies, *The Socialist Offensive: The Collectivization of Soviet Agriculture, 1929–30,* Houndmills, 1980, p. 233.
48. On dekulakization and kulaks in general, see Conquest, op. cit., pp. 117–43; Stefan Merl, "Socio-economic Differentiation of the Peasantry," in Davies, ed., *From Tsarism to the New Economic Policy,* pp. 47–65; Lynne Viola, "The Second Coming: Class Enemies in the Soviet Countryside, 1927–35," in J. Arch Getty and Roberta T. Manning, eds., *Stalinist Terror: New Perspectives,* Cambridge, 1993, pp. 65–98. See also *Neizvestnaya Rossiya: XX vek,* Moscow, Vol. 1, 1992, pp. 238–39.
49. *Pravda,* September 16, 1988, p. 3; Davies and Wheatcroft, op. cit., p. 68.
50. For one set of accounts, see V. Vasil'ev, "Krest'yanskie vosstaniya na Ukraine, 1929–30 gody," *Svobodnaya Mysl',* No. 9, 1992, p. 74.
51. Cited in Davies, *The Socialist Offensive,* p. 214.
52. Darya Khubova, Andrei Ivankiev, and Tonia Sharova, "After Glasnost: Oral History in the Soviet Union," in Passerini, op. cit., p. 70.
53. For an account, see Lynne Viola, *The Best Sons of the Fatherland: Workers in the Vanguard of Soviet Collectivization,* New York, 1987.
54. This was the explanation that Victor Kravchenko gave for his own actions in his memoir of collectivization, *I Chose Freedom,* London, 1947, pp. 114–15.
55. V. Vasil'ev, "Krest'yanskie vosstaniya na Ukraine 1929–30," in *Svobodnaya mysl',* 9, 1992, p. 73. See also Viola, "Second Coming," pp. 77–80.
56. Cited in Conquest, op. cit., p. 148.
57. Passerini, op. cit., p. 71.
58. Kravchenko, op. cit., p. 108.
59. Vasili Grossman, *Forever Flowing,* trans. Thomas P. Whitney, New York, 1986, p. 143.
60. Litvinenko and Riordan, op. cit., p. 36.
61. Fitzpatrick, op. cit., p. 57.
62. Interview, Kiev, May 23, 1998.
63. Passerini, op. cit., p. 74.
64. Merl, op. cit., p. 60.
65. Passerini, op. cit., p. 70.
66. Davies, op. cit., p. 257.
67. Litvinenko and Riordan, op. cit., p. 56.
68. Interview, Moscow, February 8, 1997.
69. Litvinenko and Riordan, op. cit., p. 41.
70. Cited in Conquest, op. cit., p. 138.
71. Aleksandr Solzhenitsyn, *The Gulag Archipelago, 1918–56,* trans. Thomas P. Whitney and Harry Willetts, London, 1999, p. 429.
72. Memorandum to Sir John Simon, September 27, 1993, Carynnyk et al., op. cit., p. 318.
73. Kovalenko and Manyak, op. cit., p. 253.
74. Ibid., p. 252.
75. *Second Interim Report of Meetings and Hearing Before the Commission on the Ukrainian Famine Held in 1987,* Washington, D.C., 1988, pp. 20–21.
76. Kovalenko and Manyak, op. cit., p. 253.
77. Conquest, op. cit., pp. 256–58.
78. Carynnyk et al., op. cit., p. 290.

79. The infamous law on socialist property, under which many thousands of peasants were sentenced to death or hard labor for gleaning or scavenging, was passed on August 7, 1932.
80. Cited in Conquest, op. cit., p. 233.
81. See Chapter 7, pp. 194–96.
82. *Byl'shovits'ka pravda,* December 26 and 29, 1932.
83. Vasil'ev, op. cit., p. 74.
84. On armed resistance, see Kuromiya, *Freedom and Terror in the Donbass,* pp. 189–90.
85. Ibid., p. 156.
86. Carynnyk et al., op. cit., p. 342.
87. RGAE, 1562/329/107, 157–58.
88. Conquest, op. cit., p. 142.
89. *Kolektivizatsiya i golod na Ukraini 1929–1933; sbirnik dokumentiv i materialiv,* Kiev, 1992, p. 642 (OGPU report dated December 29, 1933).
90. Fitzpatrick, op. cit., p. 80.
91. "Dry Rations," in Varlam Shalamov, *Kolyma Tales,* trans by John Glad, Harmondsworth, 1994, p. 43.
92. Interview, Moscow, February 1997.
93. Luisa Passerini, *Fascism in Popular Memory: The Cultural Experience of the Turin Working Class,* trans. Robert Lumley and Jude Bloomfield, Cambridge, 1987, p. 1.
94. Cited in Stephen Kotkin, "Terror, Rehabilitation and Historical Memory: An Interview with Dmitrii Iurasov," *Russian Review,* 51, April 1992, p. 262.

Chapter 7: Nights of Stone

1. Shalamov, *Kolyma Tales,* pp. 280–81.
2. The numerical estimates proposed by Robert Conquest (especially in his classic of 1968, *The Great Terror*) are generally agreed to be significantly higher than average and probably higher than the evidence supports. See Edwin Bacon, *The Gulag at War: Stalin's Forced Labour System in the Light of the Archives,* Houndmills, 1994, pp. 6–22; S. G. Wheatcroft, "More Light on the Scale of Repression and Excess Mortality in the Soviet Union in the 1930s," in Getty and Manning, *Stalinist Terror,* pp. 275–90.
3. Among the initiators of this line of thought were Lion Feuchtwanger and Romain Rolland, both of whom believed that, as Rolland put it, "the cause was bigger" than the details of its costs. See Medvedev, *Let History Judge,* pp. 475–76.
4. Bacon, op. cit., p. 10. A recent Russian estimate, based on a range of archival documents and recent research, gives the size of the Gulag population in 1940 as 3,350,000; A. K. Sokolov, *Lektsii po sovetskoi istorii,* Moscow, 1995, p. 272. For other recent estimates, see O. Khlevnyuk, "Prinuditel'nyi trud v ekonomike SSSR," *Svobodnaya mysl',* No. 14, 1992, pp. 73–84; and V. N. Zemskov, "Zaklyuchennye v 1930e gody," *Otechestvennaya istoriya,* No. 4, 1997, pp. 54–78.
5. V. N. Zemskov, "Arkhipelag Gulag: glazami pisatelya i statistika," *Argumenty i fakty,* No. 45, 1989.
6. Bacon, op. cit., p. 31; on Memorial, see Chapter 11.
7. Interview, Kiev, May 26, 1998.
8. This was the article of the penal code that covered almost all political crimes.
9. Shalamov, op. cit., p. 43.
10. I am grateful to Aleksei Levinson and to the staff at the Russian Center for the Study of Public Opinion for hosting this interview there on February 20, 1997.

11. See Chapter 11, pp. 318–21.
12. See Chapter 9, pp. 267–69.
13. Shalamov, op. cit., p. 506.
14. Anton Chekhov, *A Journey to Sakhalin,* trans. Brian Reeve, Cambridge, 1993. The seaboard region of the Amur River territory, acquired by the Russian empire in the 1840s, was developed from the 1850s.
15. Firsthand accounts can be found in Irina Reznikova, *Pravoslavie na Solovkakh,* St. Petersburg, 1998, pp. 37–81.
16. Bacon, op. cit., p. 45.
17. Cited in Kuromiya, *Freedom and Terror in the Donbass,* p. 184.
18. For a discussion of economic goals, see Bacon, op. cit., pp. 124–26.
19. Kathleen E. Smith, *Remembering Stalin's Victims: Popular Memory and the End of the USSR,* Ithaca, N.Y., and London, 1996, p. 24.
20. Kuromiya, op. cit., pp. 146–47.
21. Robert Conquest, *Kolyma: The Arctic Death Camps,* London and New York, 1978, pp. 44–54; Bacon, op. cit., pp. 53–60.
22. Bacon, op. cit., p. 126.
23. Boris Starkov, "Narkom Ezhov," in Getty and Manning, op. cit., p. 34.
24. Slavoj Zizek, *The Plague of Fantasies,* London, 1997, p. 28.
25. Balabanoff archive, file 216, p. 5.
26. Nadezhda Mandelstam, *Hope Against Hope: A Memoir,* trans. Max Hayward, New York, 1970, p. 58.
27. *Izvestiya tsentral'nogo komiteta KPSS,* No. 6, 1989, pp. 103–15.
28. Kuromiya, op. cit., p. 177; see also Kravchenko, *I Chose Freedom,* pp. 130–31.
29. A. Vaksberg, "Kak zhivoi s zhivymi," *Literaturnaya gazeta,* June 29, 1988, p. 13.
30. Medvedev, op. cit., pp. 263–72.
31. Starkov, op. cit., p. 30.
32. The best known statement of this view is J. Arch Getty, *Origins of the Great Purges.* Criticism immediately followed, a summary of which appears in Geoffrey Hosking's review of Getty and Naumov's more recent work, *The Road to Terror.* See also the *Times Literary Supplement (TLS),* January 28, 2000.
33. Robert Thurston, "Fear and Belief in the USSR's 'Great Terror': Response to Arrest, 1935–39," *Slavic Review,* Vol. 45, No. 2, 1986; Sheila Fitzpatrick, "The Impact of the Great Purges on Soviet Elites," in Getty and Manning, op. cit., pp. 247–60; Davies, *Popular Opinion in Stalin's Russia,* pp. 124–44.
34. Davies, op. cit., p. 132.
35. Ibid., p. 124.
36. Medvedev, op. cit., pp. 395–455; Roger R. Reese, "The Red Army and the Great Purges," in Getty and Manning, op. cit., pp. 213–14.
37. Tony Judt, "Justice as Theatre," *TLS,* January 18, 1991, pp. 5–6.
38. Davies, op. cit., p. 119.
39. Vitaly Shentalinsky, *Arrested Voices: Resurrecting the Disappeared Writers of the Soviet Regime,* trans. John Crowfoot, New York and London, 1996, pp. 70–71.
40. Richard Sennett, *Flesh and Stone: The Body and the City in Western Civilisation,* London, 1994, pp. 298–304.
41. Cited in Adam Hochschild, *The Unquiet Ghost: Russians Remember Stalin,* New York, 1994, p. 23.
42. Alec Nove, "Victims of Stalinism: How many?," in Getty and Manning, op. cit., pp. 265–74.
43. Timothy J. Colton, *Moscow: Governing the Socialist Metropolis,* Cambridge, Mass., 1995, p. 286.

44. Exhibitions at Butovo and Levashovo now list some of the better known victims who lie buried there.
45. Information from the permanent exhibition at the Levashovo museum.
46. Colton, op. cit., p. 286.
47. Interview, Moscow, February 14, 1997.
48. Lev Kopelev, *No Jail for Thought,* trans. Anthony Austin, London, 1977, p. 143.
49. Ibid., p. 92.
50. Cited in Shentalinsky, op. cit., p. 185.
51. Mandelstam, op. cit., pp. 56–59.
52. "Nezabyvaemoe," her account of her husband's last years and of her own arrest and exile, was serialized in *Znamya,* Nos. 10–12, 1988.
53. Mandelstam, op. cit., p. 276.
54. Garros et al., *Intimacy and Terror,* pp. 352–53.
55. Anna Larina, "Nezabyvaemoe," *Znamya,* 1988, No. 10, p. 145.
56. Interview, Moscow, March 7, 1997.
57. Interview, Moscow, February 13, 1997.
58. Mandelstam, op. cit., p. 362.
59. Interview, Moscow, March 7, 1997.
60. Cited in Shentalinsky, op. cit., p. 25.
61. Ibid., p. 53.
62. Shalamov, op. cit., p. 420.
63. Cited in Medvedev, op. cit., p. 493.
64. Shentalinsky, op. cit., p. 185.
65. Cited in Conquest, op. cit., p. 80.
66. Ibid., p. 30.
67. Kopelev, op. cit., pp. 151–52.
68. See also Conquest, op. cit., p. 91.
69. The proportion of camp inmates with higher education was greater than in the population as a whole, but it remained low. One Russian figure (from A. K. Sokolov) suggests that in 1939 it was as little as 2 percent and that only 7 percent of prisoners had been educated to secondary level. Sokolov, op. cit., p. 271.
70. Bacon, op. cit., pp. 148–49. See also accounts in the Memorial Archive, in particular Nikolai Ivanovich Popov's testimony (fond 1/3/4068) of mortality in wartime Magadan.
71. I am grateful to the anthropologist Piers Vitebsky for information about contemporary Yakutiya. See also Memorial Archive 1/3/4068 on the slaughter of escapees in this region.
72. "The Green Procurator," *Kolyma Tales,* pp. 378–79. In this story, the multilation had been carried out by Corporal Postnikov, "a man who hungered for murder."
73. Shentalinsky, op. cit., p. 196.

Chapter 8: Russia at War

1. Interview, Moscow, February 8, 1997.
2. Interview, Moscow, February 17, 1997.
3. Svetlana Alexiyevich, *War's Unwomanly Face,* Moscow, 1988, p. 227.
4. Alexander Werth, *Russia at War,* London, 1963, p. 520.
5. *Velikaya Otechestvennaya voina 1941–45,* Moscow, 1990, p. 187.
6. Ol'ga Berggol'ts, "February Diary," 1942, *Aprel':* 4, 1991, pp. 128–44; cited in Nina Tumarkin, *The Living and the Dead: The Rise and Fall of the Cult of World War II in Russia,* New York, 1994.

7. Interview with wartime medical workers, Moscow, March 1997.
8. Mosse, *Fallen Soldiers,* p. 85.
9. This issue is discussed by Mark von Hagen, "From Great Fatherland War to the Second World War: New Perspectives and Future Prospects," in Ian Kershaw and Moshe Lewin, eds., *Stalinism and Nazism: Dictatorships in Comparison,* Cambridge, 1997, pp. 237–50.
10. Von Hagen, op. cit., p. 246. Postwar society is discussed in Chapter 9.
11. See Yudif Borisovna's comments in Chapter 11, pp. 321–22.
12. Bacon, *The Gulag at War,* pp. 148–49.
13. V. N. Basilov, "K 50-letiyu pobedy nad germanskim fashizmom," *Etnograficheskoe obozreniye,* 1995, No. 2, pp. 3–21.
14. Werth, op. cit., p. 890.
15. Ibid., p. xvi.
16. Interview, Kiev, May 23, 1998.
17. R. Overy, *Russia's War,* London, 1997, p. 287.
18. Interview with veteran medical workers, Moscow, March 1997.
19. Basilov, p. 8; Werth, op. cit., pp. 388–89. Mekhlis was demoted immediately, although the reason for his disgrace was played down.
20. This bizarre bidding-up of statistics is documented in Tumarkin, *Living,* pp. 134–36. See also Michael Ellman and S. Maksudov, "Soviet Deaths in the Great Patriotic War: A Note" in *Europe-Asia Studies,* Vol. 46, No. 4, 1994, pp. 671–80.
21. John Erickson, "Soviet War Losses," in John Erickson and David Dilks, eds., *Barbarossa,* Edinburgh, 1994, pp. 257–77.
22. The Russian statistics are discussed in Erickson, op. cit. The main source for the higher figure is V. I. Kozlov, "O lyudskikh poteriyakh Sovetskogo Soyuza v Velikoi Otechestvennoi Voine 1941–45 godov," *Istoriya SSSR,* No. 2, 1989, pp. 132–38.
23. Davies, *Soviet History in the Gorbachev Revolution,* p. 107.
24. K. Simonov, "Remember, Alyosha . . . ," trans. Lyubov Yakovlevna, *Twentieth-Century Russian Poetry,* pp. 619–21.
25. RTsKhIDNI, 89/11/1, 9.
26. K. I. Bukov, M. Gorinov, and A. N. Ponomarev, *Moskva voennaya, memuary i arkhivnye dokumenty, 1941–1945,* Moscow, 1995, pp. 41–42.
27. Alexiyevich, op. cit., p. 107.
28. Ibid., p. 33.
29. Bukov et al., op. cit., p. 52.
30. Werth, op. cit., p. 238.
31. P. N. Knyshevskii, "Gosudarstvennyi komitet oborony i metody mobilizatsii trudovykh resursov," *Voprosy istorii,* No. 2, 1994, p. 55.
32. Overy, op. cit., p. 98.
33. Ibid., pp. 80, 158–60; Werth, op. cit., pp. 420–21.
34. Cited in Werth, op. cit., p. 418.
35. Interview, St. Petersburg, October 22, 1997.
36. Kopelev, *No Jail for Thought,* pp. 13–14.
37. Cited in Overy, op. cit., 261–62.
38. Kopelev, op. cit., p. 37.
39. Werth, op. cit., pp. 562–63.
40. Kopelev, op. cit., pp. 40–41.
41. Anatol Goldberg, *Ilya Ehrenburg,* New York and London, 1984, p. 197.
42. Werth, op. cit., p. 417.

43. L. N. Pushkarev, "Pis' mennaya forma bytovaniya frontovogo fol'klora," *Etnograficheskoe obozrenie,* No. 4, 1995, pp. 27–29.
44. Kopelev, op. cit., p. 53.
45. Werth, op. cit., p. 422.
46. Klaus-Jurgen Muller, "The Brutalization of Warfare: Nazi Crimes and the Wehrmacht," in Erickson and Dilks, op. cit., p. 230.
47. Vasili Grossman, *Life and Fate,* trans. Robert Chandler, London, 1995, p. 141.
48. Tumarkin, op. cit., p. 97.
49. Alexiyevich, op. cit., p. 194.
50. Grossman, op. cit., p. 141.
51. Vasíli Grossman, *The Years of War, 1941–45,* Moscow, 1946, p. 187.
52. On the Leningrad spirit, for instance, see Werth, op. cit., pp. 355–59.
53. William C. Fletcher, "The Soviet 'Bible Belt': World War II's Effects on Religion," in Susan J. Linz, ed., *The Impact of World War II on the Soviet Union,* Totowa, N.J., 1985, pp. 91–92.
54. Ibid., p. 91.
55. Bukov et al., p. 216.
56. GALI GSPb, 195/1/43, 2–3.
57. Ilya Ehrenburg, *Russia at War,* trans. Gerard Shelley, London, 1943, pp. 124–25.
58. *Twentieth-Century Russian Poetry,* pp. 624–25.
59. Richard Overy's recent book is similarly called *Russia's War.*
60. Muller, op. cit., p. 231.
61. Ibid., p. 232.
62. Interview, Moscow, February 4, 1997.
63. An example of a recent Ukraine-centered patriotic history of the war is I. T. Mukovs'kii and O. E. Lisenko, *Zvityaga i Zhertovnist': Ukraintsi na frontakh drugoi svitovoi viini,* Kiev, 1997.
64. Interview, Lviv, June 1998.
65. Interviews, Kiev, June 1998.
66. Information based on figures provided by Ilya Altman, director of the Moscow Center for Holocaust Studies and the Moscow Holocaust Library.
67. See below, p. 297.
68. Interviews with Ilya Altman, Moscow, November 1997 and Boris Mikhailovich Zabaiko, Kiev, May 24, 1998.
69. RGALI, 618/14/1355, 1–6, (draft of Grossman's article "Ukraina bez evreev" for *Krasnaya zvezda*).
70. I. Arad and others (compilers), *Neizvestnaya chernaya kniga,* Jerusalem and Moscow, 1993, pp. 150–53.
71. Interview, Kiev, May 27, 1998.
72. Vera Tolz, "New Information About the Deportation of Ethnic Groups in the USSR During World War 2," in John Garrard and Carol Garrard, eds., *World War 2 and the Soviet People,* New York, 1993, pp. 161–64.
73. The best available figures, broken down by ethnic group, were presented by V. N. Zemskov, "Spetsposelentsy (po dokumentatsii NKVD-MVD SSSR)," in *Sotsiologicheskie issledovaniya,* No. 11, 1990, pp. 3–17, especially p. 8.
74. "Remember, Alyosha," *Twentieth-Century Russian Poetry,* p. 620.
75. Werth, op. cit., p. 560.
76. Grossman, pp. 151–52.
77. Alexiyevich, op. cit., p. 86.
78. Ehrenburg, for instance, noted this. *Postwar Years, 1945–1954,* trans. Tatiana Shebunina and Yvonne Kapp. London, 1966, p. 11.

79. Reports to A. A. Zhdanov, dated June 19 and 24, 1943, cited in *Leningrad v osade: Sbornik dokumentov o geroicheskoi oborone Leningrada v gody velikoi otechestvennoi voiny, 1941–4,* St. Petersburg, 1995, pp. 482–86.
80. Edward Bubis and Blair A. Ruble, "The Impact of World War II on Leningrad," in Linz, op. cit., p. 189.
81. *Leningrad v osade,* p. 295.
82. Ibid., p. 324.
83. TsGASPb, 8557/6/1096, 15 (this is one of many such testimonies in the file).
84. The accumulation of corpses, month by month, is traced in TsGASPb, 9156/4/311.
85. *Leningrad v osade,* p. 297.
86. Ibid., p. 337.
87. Ibid., p. 321.
88. St. Petersburg Archive of Cinema, Photography and Sound, O-345701.
89. *Leningrad v osade,* p. 324.
90. Ibid., p. 328.
91. Ibid., pp. 316, 339–40.
92. Ibid., p. 329.
93. William Moskoff, *The Bread of Affliction: The Food Supply in the USSR During World War II,* Cambridge, 1990, p. 197.
94. Cited in Elizabeth Wilson, *Shostakovich: A Life Remembered,* London, 1994, p. 149.
95. Interview with Drs. Myagyer and Vyanchakova, October 20, 1997.
96. TsGASPb, 9156/4/321, 14–15. The principal signatory of the report was Prof. I. Y. Razdol'skii.
97. *Voennaya Psikhiatriya,* Leningrad, 1974, describes the regime for treatment as it was taught in the 1940s.
98. TsGASPb, 9156/4/491, 1; 9156/4/1516, 104; and elsewhere.
99. Tumarkin, op. cit., p. 98.

Chapter 9: The Pantheon

1. Werth, *Russia at War,* p. 969.
2. Ibid., pp. 1002; on the victory demonstration more generally, see Tumarkin, *The Living,* pp. 92–94.
3. Burkov et al., *Moskva voennaya,* pp. 706–8.
4. Y. Yakovlev, "Frontovaya shapka," cited in Vera S. Dunham, *In Stalin's Time: Middle-Class Values in Soviet Fiction,* Cambridge, 1976, p. 9.
5. Tumarkin, op. cit., pp. 96–97.
6. Sheila Fitzpatrick, "Postwar Soviet Society," in Linz, *The Impact of World War II on the Soviet Union,* p. 137.
7. TsGASPb, 8557/6/1096 (documents relating to atrocities committed by the German army of occupation in the Leningrad region, 1942–43); Ehrenburg, P. 13.
8. Werth, op. cit., p. 554.
9. Harrison E. Salisbury, *The Siege of Leningrad,* London, 1969, p. 574.
10. Ibid., p. 573.
11. Ehrenburg, op. cit., p. 11.
12. Ibid.
13. Tolz, "New Information," in Garrard and Garrard, *World War 2 and the Soviet People,* p. 166. "On 26 November 1948," she writes, "the Presidium of the USSR Supreme Soviet issued a de-

cree stating that all the deported peoples . . . were to remain under the special settlements regime for life."

14. Werth, op. cit., pp. 1004–5.
15. Alexiyevich, *War's Unwomanly Face,* p. 206.
16. Fitzpatrick, op. cit., p. 131.
17. Geiger, *The Family in Soviet Russia,* p. 235.
18. Mandelstam, *Hope Against Hope,* p. 307.
19. Medical workers interview, Moscow, March 1997; interview with former women prisoners, Lviv, June 1998.
20. Interview, St. Petersburg, October 20, 1997.
21. Blum, *Naître, Vivre et mourir en URSS,* pp. 75, 132.
22. Ehrenburg, op. cit., p. 11.
23. Smith, *Remembering Stalin's Victims,* pp. 133–34.
24. Interview, Kiev, May 24, 1998.
25. Mentioned by respondents at the medical workers' interview by Aleksei Grigor'evich and by other individual soldiers and civilians.
26. Alexiyevich, op. cit., p. 21.
27. E. Y. Zubkova, *Obshchestvo i reformy, 1945–1964,* Moscow, 1993, p. 43.
28. Interview, Kiev, May 1998. Zubkova, op. cit., pp. 22–23, cites similar testimonies.
29. Cited in Zubkova, op. cit., p. 27.
30. Werth, op. cit., pp. 941–42.
31. Zubkova, op. cit., p. 35.
32. Ibid., p. 16.
33. Lazar Lazarev, "Russian Literature and the War," in Garrard and Garrard, op. cit., pp. 30–31. On the abandonment of the "war theme" in poetry, see Hodgson, *Written with the Bayonet,* p. 260.
34. Interview, Moscow, April 4, 1997.
35. Cited in Werth, op. cit., pp. 358–59.
36. Introduction to Anna Akhmatova, *Selected Poems.*
37. Among them was the composer Dmitrii Shostakovich: Wilson, *Shostakovich,* p. 183.
38. Dunham, *In Stalin's Time,* pp. 4–5, 13–15.
39. Ibid., p. 17.
40. RGALI, 2950/1/156, 44–50.
41. RGALI, 618/18/18, 1–32.
42. For references to nervous weakness as a predictor of wartime mortality and for local statistics about postwar mental illness, see TsGASPb, 9156/4/491 (report from group of Leningrad psychiatric hospitals, 1946).
43. Interview, St. Petersburg, March 27, 1997.
44. White, *Russia Goes Dry,* p. 35.
45. Mikhail Gefter, "Zhizn' pamyatu," 1985 and 1994, reprinted in his book *Ekho kholokosta,* Moscow, 1995, pp. 104–5.
46. Interview, Moscow, February 13, 1997.
47. Interview, Moscow, March 14, 1997.
48. Citing from broadcast and published figures, May 25, 1998.
49. *Golod v Ikraini, 1946–1947: Dokumenty i materiali,* Kiev, 1996, p. 30.
50. Interview, May 28, 1998.
51. *Golod v Ukraini,* pp. 82–83.
52. Ibid., pp. 172–73.

53. Hiroaki Kuromiya, *Freedom and Terror in the Donbass,* p. 305.
54. *Golod v Ukraini,* p. 321.
55. Ibid., p. 179.
56. Ibid., p. 321.
57. Interview, May 28, 1998.
58. *Golod v Ukraini,* p. 321.
59. Ibid., pp. 208, 219.
60. Tumarkin, op. cit., p. 160. See also Andrei Voznesenskii's poem of 1984, "The Ditch."
61. Ehrenburg, *Postwar Years,* p. 300.
62. For examples, see Ehrenburg, op. cit., p. 308–9; Kuromiya, op. cit., pp. 323–24.
63. Ehrenburg, op. cit., p. 309.
64. Ibid., p. 243.
65. See for example *Literaturnaya gazeta,* March 5 and 7, 1953.
66. *Literaturnaya gazeta,* March 7, 1953.
67. Tsentr xhraneniye sovremennoi dokumentatsii (TsKhSD), fond 5, opis 16 (Agitation and Propaganda Department of the Central Committee), ed. khr. 594. It was an agreed condition that I did not cite precise references to these documents, the copying of which is forbidden, or to the material on Stalin's funeral in the Moscow archive (notes 71 ff.).
68. *Literaturnaya gazeta,* March 10, 1953.
69. *Literaturnaya gazeta,* March 7, 1953.
70. Service, *A History of Twentieth-Century Russia,* pp. 327–28.
71. TsKhSD, 5/16/594.
72. Tsentral'nyi Arkhiv Oblastnykh Dokumentov Moskvy (TsAODM), fond 4, MK i MGK KPSS, opis 83, ed. khr. 76 and 95.
73. TsAODM, 4/83/95.
74. Ibid.
75. Interview, Moscow, March 7, 1997.
76. TsAODM, 4/83/95.
77. Ibid.
78. TsKhSD, 5/16/594.
79. Ibid.
80. Ibid.
81. Ibid.
82. Ibid.
83. Geiger, op. cit., p. 134; a social worker from Zelenograd who works with a team caring for the elderly confirmed that many still remember this.
84. For an example, including transcripts of the major graveside speeches and letters of condolence, see the account of the 1967 funeral of Osipov, who worked at the Leningrad Museum of Atheism: GALISPb, 195/1/368.
85. J. Ellis, *The Russian Orthodox Church: A Contemporary History,* Bloomington, Ind., 1986, p. 180.
86. Ehrenburg, op. cit., p. 248.
87. Interview, Moscow, February 22, 1997.
88. Interview, St. Petersburg, October 23, 1997.
89. Grossman, *Forever Flowing,* p. 42.
90. The first time I heard it from a survivor was during an interview in Moscow on February 13, 1997.
91. See Gerald S. Smith, *Songs to Seven Strings, Russian Guitar Poetry and Soviet "Mass Song,"* Bloomington, 1984, p. 75.

92. Interview, Lviv, May 29, 1998.
93. Grossman, op. cit., p. 29.
94. Interview, Moscow, February 27, 1997.
95. Grossman, op. cit., p. 43.
96. Interview, February 14, 1997.
97. Interview, March 7, 1997.
98. Interview, March 7, 1997.

Chapter 10: Death in the Age of "Developed Socialism"

1. Smith, *Remembering Stalin's Victims,* pp. 25–34; Westwood, *Endurance and Endeavour,* pp. 414–16.
2. The poem was completed in 1969 but would not be published (in both *Znamya* and *Novyi Mir*) until 1987; *Novyi Mir,* No. 3, 1987, pp. 162–205.
3. Davies, *Popular Opinion in Stalin's Russia,* pp. 10–11.
4. Gerald Smith, *Songs to Seven Strings,* pp. 80–86.
5. Some of these are collected in the joke book of Nikulin, the comedian (*Anekdoty ot Nikulina,* Moscow, 1997). I collected others by talking to folklorists (not the most efficient means—again, their priorities are different) and by prompting two of the groups of war and prison camp veterans.
6. Michael Ignatieff, "Soviet War Memorials," *History Workshop Journal,* 17, Spring 1984, pp. 157–63.
7. Gorbatov's comments appeared in *Ogonek* in 1988. Cited in Davies, *Soviet History in the Gorbachev Revolution,* p. 101.
8. Tumarkin, *The Living and the Dead,* pp. 121–22.
9. *Twentieth-Century Russian Poetry,* pp. 806–7.
10. Cited in Wilson, *Shostakovich,* p. 356.
11. Ibid., p. 358.
12. See Gerald Smith, op. cit., and especially his discussion of the work of Galich, Okudzhava, and Vysotsky.
13. From "Courage," Akhmatova, *Selected Poems,* p. 125.
14. The text of his speech was reproduced in the samizdat journal *Granii,* No. 63, 1967, pp. 111–13. For Mandelstam's memorial meeting, see *Samizdat,* Vol. 5.
15. Gerald Smith, op. cit., p. 175.
16. Cited in Wilson, op. cit., pp. 472–76.
17. Konstantinow, *Stations of the Cross,* pp. 106–7.
18. See also Ellis, *The Russian Orthodox Church,* p. 31.
19. *Voprosy nauchnogo ateizma,* 1970, cited in Konstantinow, op. cit., p. 101.
20. Ellis, op. cit., pp. 14–16. It is difficult to assess the totals because the official figures conflict with those given to the World Council of Churches. Ellis estimates that there was approximately one church for every 7,700 believers, but again the figure for believers is uncertain.
21. GALISPb, 195/1/196, 12.
22. See V. K. Bondarchuk's introduction to *Novye grazhdanskie obryady i ritualy,* Minsk, 1978, p. 6; GALISPb, 195/1/196, 12.
23. L. I. Min'ko and A. V. Selezneva, "Den' pamyati," in *Novye grazhdanskie obryady,* pp. 72–89.
24. Interviews, Kiev, June 1998; Don Monastery, Moscow, March 1997; Zelenograd, March 1997.
25. Ellis, op. cit., pp. 14–18.
26. A. I. Kvardakov, *Religioznye perezhitki i soznanii v bytu sel'skogo naseleniya i puti ikh preodoleniya,* Novosibirsk, 1969, p. 6.

27. GAMO, 1782/1/224, 13–14.
28. Geiger, *The Family in Soviet Russia,* p. 148.
29. Cited in Christel Lane, *The Rites of Rulers,* Cambridge, 1981, p. 83.
30. Cited in Stephen P. and Ethel Dunn, *The Peasants of Central Russia,* New York and London, 1967, p. 104.
31. The Moscow funeral company Ritual-Service produced a catalogue in 1997 that gave the details of each of the Moscow cemeteries, including their size, location, and most famous dead.
32. The details here were given by the artists themselves (interviewed in Kiev, May 19, 1998). The story was well known to other artists in the city, and the journalists regard it as a cause célèbre. Aspects of their design were described in *Dekorativnoe iskusstvo,* No. 8, 1975.
33. Interview, October 23, 1997.
34. It was introduced to the *Diagnostic Statistical Manual of Mental Disorders (DSM)* in 1980. For a commentary on the process of its creation, see Allan Young, *The Harmony of Illusions.*
35. "Trauma" is regarded in these circles as a universal human response, independent of culture, language, or history. The classic statement of this view, cited in Smirnov's own work, is M. J. Horowitz, *Stress Response Syndromes,* New York, 1976.
36. The war in Afghanistan helped to destroy détente; see Caroline Kennedy-Pipe, *Russia and the World, 1917–1991,* Cambridge, 1998, pp. 176–78.
37. Interview, Zelenograd, February 10, 1997; Svetlana Alexiyevich, *Zinky Boys: Soviet Voices from a Forgotten War,* London, 1992, p. 16.
38. Tumarkin, op. cit., pp. 153–55.
39. Interview, Zelenograd, February 10, 1997.
40. Alexiyevich, op. cit., p. 20.
41. Ibid., p. 22.
42. Ibid., p. 16.
43. Ibid., p. 57.
44. Ibid., 23–4.
45. Interview, Zelenograd, February 10, 1997.
46. Alexiyevich, op. cit., p. 87.
47. Mosse, *Fallen Soldiers,* p. 192.
48. Alexiyevich, op. cit., p. 7.
49. Interview, Zelenograd, February 10, 1997.
50. See also Benjamin Colodzin, *How to Survive Trauma,* New York, 1993. This book, which is based on the work of the Olympia Institute, describes the exchange in detail.
51. Interview and visit, February 21, 1997.
52. His unpublished thesis, from which he has generously allowed me to cite, refers to the proceedings of the Twelfth Congress of Russian Psychiatrists (Moscow, 1995), where papers on PTSD were debated, and to numerous published studies of the Armenian earthquake of 1988—one of the first catastrophes to involve direct collaboration on the spot between western psychiatrists and their Soviet counterparts. See for example *Psikhicheskie rasstroistva u postradavshikh vo vremya zemletryaseniya v Armenii,* various authors, Moscow, 1989.
53. Smirnov, unpublished thesis, pp. 130–31.
54. Interview, Zelenograd, February 10, 1997.
55. Ibid.
56. Smirnov, op. cit., p. 73.
57. Ibid., p. 106.
58. See for example B. Drummond Ayres Jr., "The Vietnam Veteran: Silent, Perplexed, Unnoticed," in *The Vietnam Veteran in Contemporary Society: Collected Materials,* Washington D.C., 1972;

Charles R. Figley, ed., *Stress Disorders Among Vietnam Veterans: Theory, Research and Treatment,* New York, 1978; Paul Starr, *The Discarded Army: Veterans after Vietnam,* New York, 1973.

59. Interview with Drs. Vyanchakova and Myager, St. Petersburg, October 20, 1997.
60. Interview with Aleksandr Solomonovich Mikhlin, the jurist and police colonel who monitored the collection of suicide statistics in the 1960s, Moscow, March 1, 1997. See also A. G. Ambrumova, S. V. Borodin, and A. S. Mikhlin, *Preduprezhdenie samoubiistv,* Moscow, 1980, pp. 76–81.
61. Gorbachev himself appeared to endorse this view in his memoirs, published in 1995. "We were not so simple," he wrote, "as not to recognise that no significant transformations could be carried out without a firm grip on the reins of power and without an ability to overcome the inevitable opposition to the proposed reforms": Mikhail Gorbachev, *Memoirs,* London, 1996, p. 408.
62. Interview, Kiev, May 20, 1998.
63. Service, *Twentieth-Century Russia,* p. 445.
64. Interview, Kiev, May 20, 1998.
65. Interview, Kiev, May 21, 1998.
66. Anna Reid, *Borderland: A Journey Through the History of Ukraine,* London, 1997, p. 199.
67. Service, op. cit., p. 445.
68. White, *Russia Goes Dry,* pp. 57–81. The Temperance Society explicitly campaigned against the rumor that alcohol protected against radiation.
69. Joint U.S.-Ukrainian project conference on psychological consequences of Chernobyl, Kiev, May 21, 1998.

Chapter 11: A Tide of Bones

1. Tumarkin, *The Living and the Dead,* p. 13.
2. Interview with Yurii Dmitriev, Medvezhegorsk, October 26, 1997.
3. Hochschild, *The Unquiet Ghost,* p. xxiv.
4. Nanci Adler, *Victims of Soviet Terror: The Story of the Memorial Movement,* Westport, 1993, p. 93.
5. Smith, *Remembering Stalin's Victims,* p. 163.
6. Sergei Alekseyev and K. G. Kaleda, *Poligon "Butovo": Istoricheskaya spravka,* Moscow, 1997.
7. Tumarkin, op. cit., p. 15.
8. Photographs of the exhumations are kept in the photographic archive of the memorial organization. For examples, see M2, Nos. 55, 64, and 92 (from Donetsk, 1989), and M2, Nos. 111, 113, and 119 (Voronezh, 1990–93).
9. Kotkin, "Terror, Rehabilitation and Historical Memory," p. 239.
10. Adler, op, cit., p. 51.
11. Ibid., p. 60; Rosalind Marsh, *History and Literature in Contemporary Russia,* Basingstoke and London, 1995, p. 44.
12. A laudatory article about Bukharin was published in *Pravda,* October 9, 1988, p. 3.
13. See for example *Vozvrashchennye imena* (Returned Names), Moscow, 1989, which lists and briefly describes the lives of each of these public figures.
14. Among the most prominent protagonists were the filmmakers Tengiz Abuladze and Elem Klimov (the latter was elected to the chairmanship of the Union of Cinematographers in 1986). The historical works of writers such as Anatolii Rybakov, the novelist, and Mikhail Shatrov, the playwright, were also published in the 1980s, although they had originally been written in the 1960s during Khrushchev's thaw.
15. The first public attack on Lenin came from a philosopher with close links to the party's own

Central Committee, Aleksandr Tsipko. Tsipko's extended essay on the sources of Stalinism appeared in *Nauka i zhizn',* Nos. 11, 1988 (pp. 45–55) and 12, 1989 (pp. 40–48), Nos. 1 (pp. 46–56) and 2 (pp. 53–61).

16. Roginskii served four years in a labor camp for trying to find out more about his father: Adler, op. cit., p. 1.
17. Kotkin, op. cit., passim.
18. Marsh, op. cit., p. 14.
19. Smith, op. cit., pp. 91–92.
20. Most of the memoirs and letters are in fond 1, which is available for general consultation.
21. Some of these photographs, including pictures of Vsevolod Meyerhold, are reproduced in Vitalii Shentalinsky, *Arrested Voices,* passim.
22. R. W. Davies, *Soviet History in the Gorbachev Revolution,* p. 169; Shentalinsky, op. cit., pp. 25–26, 175, 185–86, and passim.
23. The most famous conservative statement took the form of a letter from a chemistry teacher called Nina Andreeva entitled "I Cannot Give Up My Principles," *Sovetskaya Rossiya,* March 13, 1988. Reactions to the discussion of torture from former prisoners and their families are collected in the Moscow-based archives of memorial; Irina Reznikova, of St. Petersburg Memorial, discussed her organization's view about revealing the details of torture to relatives with me in St. Petersburg in March 1997.
24. On the party's bid for the moral high ground, see Smith, op. cit., p. 162. The statue at Levashovo was an example of its taste.
25. Jay Winter and Emmanuel Sivan, eds., *War and Remembrance in the Twentieth Century,* Cambridge, 1999, pp. 27–29.
26. Smith, op. cit., pp. 154–59.
27. Interview with Rudol'f Mirskii, Lviv, June 3, 1998. It was with difficulty that I obtained permission to interview a group of local survivors at the Lviv synagogue in May 1998. Regular members of the congregation described continuing discrimination and the vandalization of Jewish public buildings in the area.
28. These remarks are based on conversations with Bishop Augustin of Lviv (June 1, 1998) and with two priests from Graeco-Catholic churches in the city (June 2 and 3, 1998).
29. The photographic record is in the Memorial Archive, C18.130.
30. A list of the best known religious figures who were buried at the Butovo site is appended to Alekseyev and Kaleda, op. cit.
31. *Critical Inquiry,* 18, No. 2, 1982, p. 273.
32. Service, *Twentieth-Century Russia,* p. 506.
33. Interview, Moscow, March 1996.
34. Vera Tkachenko, cited in Davies, op. cit., p. 113.
35. See Chapter 8, pp. 215–16.
36. Davies, op. cit., pp. 103–8.
37. Mukovs'kii and Lisenko, *Zvityaga i Zhertovnist';* interview with historians Petro Panteleimonovich Panchenko and Roman Gnatovich Vishnevskii, Kiev, June 5, 1998.
38. On Latvia, see Vieda Skultans, *The Testimony of Lives: Narrative and Memory in Post-Soviet Latvia,* London, 1998.
39. On the Katyn' massacre, details of which were released by Boris Yeltsin after communism was discredited in 1991, see Davies, *Soviet History in the Yeltsin Era,* p. 45.
40. See Tolz, "New Information," p. 173; Neal Ascherson, *Black Sea: The Birthplace of Civilisation and Barbarism,* London, 1995, p. 33.

41. The first conference of the Moscow Holocaust Center was held in 1991. Its current director, Il'ya Altman, the successor to Mikhail Gefter, also edits the occasional series *Biblioteka Kholokosta.*
42. Interview with Boris Mikhailovich Zabaiko, Kiev, May 24, 1998.
43. Davies, op. cit., p. 74. See also Nina Tumarkin, "Story of a War Memorial," in Garrard and Garrard, *World War 2 and the Soviet People,* pp. 125–46.
44. Interview, Kiev, May 20, 1998.
45. Il'ya Altman, interview, Moscow, February 12, 1997.
46. B. M. Zabaiko, interview, Kiev, May 24, 1998.
47. Smith, op. cit., p. 200–21.
48. Interview, Moscow, November 19, 1997.
49. Memorial Archive, fond 1/3/4088.
50. Interview, Moscow, February 14, 1997.
51. Cited in *Moskovskaya pravda,* July 17, 1998.
52. *Sovetskaya Rossiya,* July 18, 1998.
53. *Nezavisimaya gazeta,* July 17, 1998.
54. *Trud,* July 17, 1998.
55. *Itogi,* July 15, 1998, p. 13.
56. Ibid., p. 15.
57. Interview, December 9, 1997.

Chapter 12: Listening for the Dead

1. The debate can be tracked, for example, in Shoshana Felman and Dori Laub, M.D., *Testimony: Crises of Witnessing in Literature, Psychoanalysis and History,* London, 1992; Barbara Heimannsberg and Christoph J. Schmidt, eds., *The Collective Silence: German Identity and the Legacy of Shame,* San Francisco, 1993; Alexander and Margarete Mitscherlich, *The Inability to Mourn: Principles of Collective Behavior,* New York, 1975; Rubie S. Watson, ed., *Memory, History and Opposition Under State Socialism,* Santa Fe, Calif., 1994.
2. See Dori Laub, "Bearing Witness," in Felman and Laub, op. cit., pp. 57–74; Nandine Fresco, "La Diaspora des cendres," *Nouvelle revue de psychoanalyse,* 24, 1981, pp. 206–20.
3. Tumarkin, *The Living and the Dead,* p. 224.
4. Ian Buruma, "The Joys and Perils of Victimhood," *New York Review of Books,* Vol. 46, No. 6, April 8, 1999, pp. 4–9.
5. On the psychological importance of testimony, see Elie Wiesel, "Why I Write," in Alvin Rosenfeld and Irvin Greenberg, eds., *Confronting the Holocaust,* Ind., 1978.
6. Brian Edwards and Wendy Sturgess, *How to Be Happy,* London, 1996.
7. For graphic evidence, see *Agitatsiya za shchast'e (Agitation for Happiness),* the catalogue of an exhibition of Stalinist paintings on this theme, Bremen, 1994.
8. The comment was made by a participant at a conference that I organized in Cambridge in July 1998 to discuss the issue of trauma as a cultural construct.
9. See Allan Young, *The Harmony of Illusions,* p. 107.
10. The vogue for psychoanalysis in Chile, for example, had no obvious effect on the proposed extradition and trial of General Pinochet in 1999–2000.
11. Derek Summerfield, "The Psychological Legacy of War and Atrocity: The Question of Long-Term and Transgenerational Effects and the Need for a Broad View," *Journal of Nervous and Mental Disease,* Vol. 184, No. 1, 1996, p. 376.
12. I am grateful to another psychiatrist, Ian Collins, for reminding me of this.

13. Interview, Akademiya gosudarstvennyi sluzhby, St. Petersburg, October 14, 1997.
14. This argument holds true of child survivors of abuse in less turbulent societies. See Cathy Spatz Widom, "PTSD in Abused Children Grown Up," *American Journal of Psychiatry,* 156:8, August 1999, pp. 1223–29.
15. Smirnov's research emphasizes this point. He would also insist that, though some Afghantsy became addicted to their stress, his own clinical data in fact produced far more examples of the opposite response, a numbness and withdrawal and a fear of unexpected stimuli.
16. "The Scythians," *Twentieth-Century Russian Poetry,* p. 81.
17. Overy, *Russia's War,* p. 172.
18. Smith, *Remembering Stalin's Victims,* pp. 200–209.
19. Arthur Kleinman, *Social Origins of Distress and Disease: Depression, Neurasthenia and Pain in Modern China,* Cambridge, Mass., 1986, p. 44.
20. This is the view of most of the Russian ethnographers who have worked on the subject, including I. A. Kremleva; see her "Pokhoronnoprominal'nye obryady u russkikh: traditsii i sovremennost'," Kremleva et al., eds., in *Pokoronno-pominal'nye obychai i obryady,* Moscow, 1993.
21. Conversations in Moscow and Moscow province, April–December 1997.
22. Cited in Nigel Barley, *Dancing on the Grave: Encounters with Death,* London, 1995, p. 83.
23. Conversation, February 3, 1997.
24. "Zapiski na tot svet," *Stolitsa,* No. 18, October 13, 1997.
25. Interview, Zelenograd, 10 Feb 1997.
26. "Pokoiniki i moshenniki," *Argumenty i fakty,* No. 5, 1997.
27. *Ritual Proshchaniya,* No. 1, Moscow, 1997.
28. A survivor of arrest and exile, now living in Lviv, was among several who described the cancer from which one of her former neighbors now suffers as a punishment for passing information to the secret police.
29. Interview, Moscow, March 4, 1997.
30. Moscow, March 3, 1997.

BIBLIOGRAPHY

Archives

GALISPb	St. Petersburg Archive of Literature and Art
GAMO	State Archive of the Moscow Region
GARF	State Archive of the Russian Federation
	Memorial Association Archive
RGAE	Russian State Archive of the Economy
RGALI	Russian State Archive of Literature and Art
RGIA	Russian State Historical Archive
RTsKhIDNI	Russian Center for the Preservation and Study of Documents of Contemporary History
	Russian State Archive of Cinema, Photography and Sound
	St. Petersburg Archive of Cinema, Photography and Sound
	Tenishev Archive of the Museum of Ethnography, St. Petersburg
TsAODM	Central Archive of the Moscow Region
TsGASPb	State Archive of St. Petersburg
TsKhSD	Center for the Preservation of Contemporary Documents

Newspapers and Periodicals

Argumenty i fakty
Bezbozhnik u stanka
Birzhevye vedomosti
Bol'shevik
Etnograficheskoe obozrenie (later also Sovetskaya etnografiya)
Itogi
Kommunal'nyi rabotnik
Kostromskii listok
Novyi mir
Ogonek
Olonetskaya nedelya
Orenburgskaya gazeta
Otechestvennaya istoriya
Ottuda
Plan
Posev
Pravda (variously also Petrogradskaya pravda, etc.)

Psikhiatricheskaya gazeta
Rabochaya zhizn'
Rossiiskii etnograf
Russian Review
Samizdat
Sankt Peterburgskaya gazeta
Slovo
Sotsial'naya gigiyena
Sotsiologischeskie issledovaniya
Soviet Studies
Svobodnaya mysl'
Trud
Vestnik statistiki
Voprosy istorii
Zhivaya starina
Znamya

Published Books and Scholarly Articles

Abramov, A., *U Kremlevskoi steny,* Moscow, 1984.

Adler, Nanci, *Victims of Soviet Terror: The Story of the Memorial Movement,* Westport, 1993.

Afanas'ev, Y. N., ed., *Golod 1932–1933 godov,* Moscow, 1995.

Agursky, Mikhail, *The Third Rome: National Bolshevism in the USSR,* Boulder, Col., 1987.

Akhmatova, Anna, *Selected Poems,* trans. Stanley Kunitz and Max Hayward, London, 1974, reprinted 1989.

Alekseyev, Sergei, and Kaleda, K. G., *Poligon "Butovo": Istoricheskaya spravka,* Moscow, 1997.

Alexiou, M., *The Ritual Lament in Greek Tradition,* Cambridge, 1974.

Alexiyevich, Svetlana, *War's Unwomanly Face,* Moscow, 1988.

———, *Zinky Boys: Soviet Voices from a Forgotten War,* London, 1992.

Ambrumova, A. G., Borodin, S. V., and Mikhlin, A. S., *Preduprezhdenie samoubiistv,* Moscow, 1980.

Anatol'ev, P., *Devyatoe yanvarya 1905–1925: Khrestomatiya dlya agitatorov,* Khar'kov, 1925.

Andreyev, E., Darskii, L., and Kharkova, T., "Opyt otsenki chislennosti naseleniya SSSR, 1926–41," *Vestnik statistiki,* 7, 1990.

Arad, I., et al., eds., *Neizvestnaya chernaya kniga: svidetel'stva ochevidtsev o katastrofe sovetskikh evreev, 1941–1944,* Jerusalem and Moscow, 1993.

Argun, A. M., "Zhertvy 9/22 yanvarya 1905 goda (vospominaniya)," *Krasnaya letopis,* 33, 6, 1929.

Ariès, Philippe, *L'Homme devant la mort,* Paris, 1977.

Ascherson, Neal, *Black Sea: The Birthplace of Civilisation and Barbarism,* London, 1995.

Aslund, Anders, ed., *Russian Economic Reform at Risk,* London 1995.

Azbeleva, S. N., *Narodnaya proza,* Moscow, 1992.

Babichenko, D. L., *Pisateli i tsenzory: sovetskaya literatura 1940kh godov pod politicheskim kontrolem TsK,* Moscow, 1994.

Bacon, Edwin, *The Gulag at War: Stalin's Forced Labour System in the Light of the Archives,* Houndmills, 1994.

Baddeley, A., *The Psychology of Memory,* London, 1976.

———, *Your Memory: A User's Manual,* London, 1992.

Ball, Alan, *Russia's Last Capitalists: The Nepmen, 1921–1929,* Berkeley, Los Angeles and London, 1987.

Barber, Paul, *Vampires, Burial and Death: Folklore and Reality,* New Haven and London, 1988.

Barley, Nigel, *Dancing on the Grave: Encounters with Death,* London, 1995.

Barsov, E. V., *Prichitaniya severnogo kraya. Chast' I: plachi pokhoronnye, nadgrobnye i nadmogil'nye,* Moscow, 1872.

Bastide, R., "Memoire collective et sociologie du bricolage," *Année sociologique,* 21, 1970.

Belliustin, I. S., *Description of the Parish Clergy in Rural Russia: The Memoir of a Nineteenth-Century Parish Priest,* 1858; trans. with an interpretative essay by Gregory L. Freeze, Ithaca, N.Y., 1985.

Benjamin, W., *Illuminations,* London, 1970.

Berg, G. P. van den, "The Soviet Union and the Death Penalty," *Soviet Studies,* 35, 2, April 1983.

Bergman, J., "The Image of Jesus Christ in the Russian Revolutionary Movement: The Case of Russian Marxism," *International Review of Social History,* 35, 1990.

Bloch, M., and Parry, J., eds., *Death and the Regeneration of Life,* Cambridge, 1982.

Blum, Alain, *Naître, vivre et mourir en URSS, 1917–1991,* Paris, 1994.

Bohdan, V. A., *Avoiding Extinction: Children of the Kulak,* New York, 1992.

Bonch-Bruevich, V. D., *Vospominaniya o Lenine,* Moscow, 1969.

Bondarenko, V. K., et al., eds., *Novye grazhdanskie obryady i ritualy,* Minsk, 1978.

Bonnell, Victoria E., *Roots of Rebellion: Workers' Politics and Organization in St. Petersburg and Moscow, 1900–1914,* Berkeley, 1983.

———, *The Russian Worker: Life and Labor Under the Tsarist Regime,* Berkeley, Calif., and London, 1983.

Borodin, N. M., *One Man and His Time,* London, 1955.

Bowker, J., *The Meanings of Death,* Cambridge, 1991.

Boyarskii, A. Y., *Kurs demografii,* Moscow, 1985.

Brooks, J., *When Russia Learned to Read: Literacy and Popular Literature, 1861–1917,* Princeton, 1985.

Bruce, S., ed., *Religion and Modernization: Sociologists and Historians Debate the Secularization Thesis,* Oxford, 1992.

Bukov, K. I., Gorinov, M., and Ponomarev, A. N., compilers, *Moskva voennaya: memuary i arkhivnye dokumenty, 1941–45,* Moscow, 1995.

Bulgakov, Mikhail, *The Master and Margarita,* trans. Michael Glenny, London, 1967.

———, *A Country Doctor's Notebook,* trans. Michael Glenny, London, 1975.

Buruma, Ian, "The Joys and Perils of Victimhood," *New York Review of Books.* Vol. 46, No. 6, April 1999.

Bushnell, J., *Mutiny Amid Repression: Russian Soldiers and the Revolution of 1905–6,* Bloomington, 1985.

Butler, T., ed., *Memory, History, Culture and the Mind,* Oxford, 1989.

Carynnyk, Marco, Luciuk, L. Y., and Kordan, B. S., *The Foreign Office and the Famine: British Documents on Ukraine and the Great Famine of 1932–1933,* Kingston, Ontario, 1988.

Chase, W. J., *Workers, Society and the Soviet State: Labor and Life in Moscow, 1918–1929,* Urbana, 1987.

Chekhov, Anton, *A Journey to Sakhalin,* trans. Brian Reeve, Cambridge, 1993.

Chistov, K. V., *Prichitaniya: Biblioteka poeta osnovana M. Gor'kim,* Leningrad, 1960.

———, *Russkie narodnye sotsialno-utopicheskie legendy, XVII–XIX vv.,* Moscow, 1967.

———, *Kul'tura i byt gornyakov i metallurgov Nizhnego Tagila, 1917–1970,* Moscow, 1974.

———, *Irina Andreevna Fedosova: Istoriko-kul'turnyi ocherk,* Petrozavodsk, 1988.

Chornobil'ska tragediya: Dokumenti i materiali, Kiev, 1996.

Ciliga, Ante, *The Russian Enigma,* London, 1979.

Cohen, J. E., "Childhood Mortality, Family Size and Birth Order in Pre-Industrial Europe," *Demography,* 12, 1, 1975.

Cohen, S., *Bukharin and the Bolshevik Revolution,* Oxford, 1980.

Colodzin, Benjamin, *How to Survive Trauma,* New York, 1993.

Colton, Timothy J., *Moscow: Governing the Socialist Metropolis,* Cambridge, Mass., 1995.

Connerton, P., *How Societies Remember,* Cambridge, 1989.

Conquest, Robert, *The Great Terror,* Houndmills, 1968; reprinted Harmondsworth, 1971.

———, *Kolyma: The Arctic Death Camps,* New York and London, 1978.

———, *The Harvest of Sorrow,* Oxford, 1986.

Conybeare, Frederick, *Russian Dissenters,* Cambridge, Mass., 1921.

Cooper, Julian, Perrie, Maureen, and Rees, E. A., eds., *Soviet History, 1917–53,* Houndmills, 1995.

Crummey, Robert O., *The Old Believers and the World of Anti-Christ: The Vyg Community and the Russian State,* Madison, 1970.

Curtiss, J. S., *Church and State in Russia: The Last Years of the Empire, 1900–1917,* New York, 1940.

———, *The Russian Church and the Soviet State,* Boston, 1953.

Dal', V., *O poveriyakh, sueveriyakh i predrassudkakh russkogo naroda,* St. Petersburg, 1880.

Damascus, St. John of, *On the Divine Images: Three Apologies Against Those Who Attack the Divine Images,* trans. David Anderson, Crestwood, N.J., 1980.

Danforth, L., *The Death Rituals of Rural Greece,* Princeton, 1982.

Davies, N., *A Long Walk to Church: A Contemporary History of Russian Orthodoxy,* Boulder, Colo., 1995.

Davies, R. W., *The Socialist Offensive: The Collectivization of Soviet Agriculture, 1929–30,* Houndmills, 1980.

———, *Soviet History in the Gorbachev Revolution,* Houndmills, 1989.

———, ed., *From Tsarism to the New Economic Policy,* Houndmills, 1990.

———, *Soviet History in the Yeltsin Era,* Houndmills, 1997.

———, Harrison, Mark, and Wheatcroft, S. G., eds., *The Economic Transformation of the Soviet Union, 1913–1945,* Cambridge, 1994.

Davies, Sarah, *Popular Opinion in Stalin's Russia, 1934–1941,* Cambridge, 1997.

Davydov, A., *Nauchnoe dokazatel'stvo nashego lichnogo bessmertiya,* Moscow, 1914.

Day, P. D., ed., *The Liturgical Dictionary of Eastern Christianity,* Collegeville, 1993.

Drozdov, V. N., Beridze, M. Z., and Razin, P. S., *Meditsinskie, sotsial'no-psikhologicheskie, filosofskie i religioznye aspekty smerti cheloveka,* Kirov, 1992.

Dune, Edward M., *Notes of a Red Guard,* trans. and ed. Diane P. Koenker and S. A. Smith, Urbana and Chicago, 1993.

Dunham, Vera S., *In Stalin's Time: Middle-Class Values in Soviet Fiction,* Cambridge, 1976.

Dunn, Stephen P. and Ethel, *The Peasants of Central Russia,* New York and London, 1967.

Dyadkin, I. G., *Unnatural Deaths in the USSR, 1928–1954,* New Brunswick, 1983

Eberstadt, N., "Health and Mortality in Eastern Europe," *Communist Economics,* Vol. 2, No. 3, 1990.

Edwards, Brian, and Sturgess, Wendy, *How to Be Happy,* London, 1996.

Ehrenburg, Ilya, *Russia at War,* trans. Gerard Shelley, London, 1943.

———, *Postwar Years, 1945–1954,* trans. Tatiana Shebumina and Yvonne Kapp, London, 1966.

———, and Grossman, Vasili, eds., *The Black Book,* New York, 1981.

Eissenstat, B. W., ed., *Lenin and Leninism: State, Law and Society,* Lexington, Ill., 1971.

Eklof, Ben, and Frank, Stephen P., eds., *The World of the Russian Peasant,* London, 1990.

Eksteins, M., *Rites of Spring: The Great War and the Birth of the Modern Age,* Boston, 1989.

Ellis, James, *The Russian Orthodox Church: A Contemporary History,* Indiana, 1986.

Ellman, Michael, and Maksudov, S., "Soviet Deaths in the Great Patriotic War: A Note," *Europe-Asia Studies,* Vol. 46, No. 4, 1994.

Engel, Barbara Alpern, *Between the Fields and the City: Women, Work and the Family in Russia, 1861–1914,* Cambridge, 1996.

Erickson, John, and Dilks, David, eds., *Barbarossa,* Edinburgh, 1994.

Etkind, Aleksandr, *Eros nevozmozhnogo: Istoriya psikhoanaliza v Rossii,* St. Petersburg, 1993.

Fedotov, G. P., *The Russian Religious Mind,* Cambridge, Mass., 1946.

Felman, Shoshana, and Laub, Dori, M.D., *Testimony: Crises of Witnessing in Literature, Psychoanalysis and History,* London, 1992.

Figes, Orlando, *Peasant Russia: Civil War,* Oxford, 1989.

———, *A People's Tragedy,* London, 1996.

Fireside, H., *Icon and Swastika: The Russian Orthodox Church Under Nazi and Soviet Control,* Cambridge, Mass., 1971.

Fisher, H. H., *The Famine in Soviet Russia, 1919–1923,* New York, 1927.

Fitzpatrick, Sheila, *Stalin's Peasants,* Oxford, 1994.

Fletcher, William C., *The Russian Orthodox Church Underground, 1917–1970,* Cambridge, 1971.

———, "The Soviet 'Bible Belt': World War II's Effects on Religion," in Linz, ed., *The Impact of World War II on the Soviet Union,* 1985.

Forsyth, James, *A History of the Peoples of Siberia, 1581–1990,* Cambridge, 1992.

Frank, S. P., and Steinberg, M.D., eds., *Cultures in Flux,* Princeton, 1994.

Freeze, G. L., *The Parish Clergy in Nineteenty-Century Russia,* Princeton, 1983.

Fresco, Nandine, "La Diaspora des cendres," *Nouvelle revue de psychoanalyse,* 24, 1981.

Frieden, Nancy Mandelker, *Russian Physicians in an Era of Reform and Revolution, 1856–1905,* Princeton, 1981.

Friedlander, S., *When Memory Comes,* New York, 1979.

Fussell, P., *The Great War and Modern Memory,* Oxford, 1979.

Garrard, John, and Garrard, Carol, eds., *World War 2 and the Soviet People,* New York, 1993.

Garros, Véronique, Korenevskaya, Nataliya, and Lakusen, Thomas, eds., *Intimacy and Terror: Soviet Diaries of the 1930s,* New York, 1995.

Gatrell, Peter, *A Whole Empire Walking,* Bloomington, Ind., 1999.

Gefter, Mikhail, *Ekho kholokosta,* Moscow, 1995.

Geifman, Anna. *Thou Shalt Kill: Revolutionary Terrorism in Russia, 1894–1917,* Princeton, 1993.

Geiger, H. Kent, *The Family in Soviet Russia,* Cambridge, Mass., 1968.

Geldern, J. von., *Bolshevik Festivals,1917–1920,* Berkeley, Calif., and London, 1993.

Gernet, M. N., *Detoubiistvo,* Moscow, 1911.

———, *Smertnaya kazn',* Moscow, 1913.

———, *Prestupnost' i samoubiistvo vo vremya voiny i posle nee,* Moscow, 1927.

Gerson, L. D., *The Secret Police in Lenin's Russia,* Philadelphia, 1976.

Getty, J. Arch, *Origins of the Great Purges: The Soviet Communist Party Reconsidered, 1933–1938,* Cambridge, 1985.

———, and Manning, Roberta T., *Stalinist Terror: New Perspectives,* Cambridge, 1993.

———, and Naumov, Oleg V., *The Road to Terror: Stalin and the Self-Destruction of the Bolsheviks, 1932–1939,* New Haven and London, 1999.

Gildea, Robert, *Barricades and Borders: Europe, 1800–1914.* Oxford, 1987.

Glatzer Rosenthal, Bernice, ed., *The Occult in Russian and Soviet Culture,* Ithaca, N.Y., 1997.

Goldberg, Anatol, *Ilya Ehrenburg,* New York and London, 1984.

Goldman, W. Z., *Women, the State and Revolution: Soviet Family Policy and Social Life, 1917–36,* Cambridge, 1993.

Golod v Ukraini 1946–1947: Dokumenti i materiali, Kiev, 1996.

Gorbachev, Mikhail, *Memoirs,* London, 1996.

Gorer, G. and Richman, J., *The People of Great Russia: A Psychological Study,* London, 1949.

Gorer, G., *Death, Grief and Mourning,* New York, 1965.

Got'e, I. V., *Time of Troubles: The Diary of Yurii Vladimirovich Got'e,* trans. and ed. Terence Emmons, London, 1988.

Graham, L. R., *Science in Russia and the Soviet Union,* Cambridge, 1993.

Gromyko, M. M., "Dokhrisyanskie verovaniya v bytu sibirskikh krest'yan XVIII-XIX vv," in *Iz istorii sem'i i bytu sibirskogo krest'yanstva XVII–nachala XX vv.*

Gross, J. T., *Revolution from Abroad: The Soviet Conquest of Poland's Western Ukraine and Western Belorussia,* Princeton, 1988.

Grossman, Vasili, *Life and Fate,* trans. Robert Chandler, London, 1995.

———, *Forever Flowing,* trans. Thomas P. Whitney, New York, 1986.

———, *The Years of War, 1941–45,* Moscow, 1946.

Harding, Neil, *Lenin's Political Thought,* Houndmills, 1983.

Hartman, G. E., ed., *Holocaust Remembrance: The Shapes of Memory,* Oxford, 1994.

Heimannsberg, Barbara, and Schmidt, Christoph J., eds., *The Collective Silence: German Identity and the Legacy of Shame,* San Francisco, 1993.

Hoare, G., and Nowell Smith, G., eds., *Antonio Gransci: Selections from the Prison Notebooks,* London, 1971.

Hochschild, Adam, *The Unquiet Ghost: Russians Remember Stalin,* New York, 1994.

Hodgson, K., *Written with the Bayonet: Soviet Russian Poetry of World War II,* Liverpool, 1996.

Horowitz, M. J., *Stress Response Syndromes,* New York, 1976.

Huntington, Richard, and Metcalf, Peter, *Celebrations of Death: The Anthropology of Mortuary Ritual,* Cambridge, 1979.

Il'f, Ilya, and Petrov, Yevgenii, *The Twelve Chairs,* trans. John Richardson, New York, 1961, reprinted London, 1965.

Il'in, N. A., *Nauka i religiya o zhizni i smerti,* Moscow, 1956.

Iofe, B., "Bol'shoi terror i imperskaya politika SSSR: Po sledam bol'shogo solovetskogo rasstrela 1937 goda," *Posev,* 5, 1997.

Isakov, S. K., *1905 god v satire i karikature,* Leningrad, 1928.

Istoricheskie kladbishcha Peterburga, spravochnik-putevoditel', St. Petersburg, 1993.

Istoriya russkoi pravoslavnoi tserkvy, 1917–1990, Moscow, 1994.

Ivanits, Linda J., *Russian Folk Belief,* Armonk, 1989.

Iz istorii sem'i i byta sibirskogo krest'yanstva XVII-nachala XXvv, sbornik nauchnykh trudov, various authors, Novosibirsk, 1975.

Joravsky, David, *Russian Psychology: A Critical History,* Oxford, 1989.

Judge, Edward H., *Easter in Kishinev: Anatomy of a Pogrom,* New York, 1992.

Kennedy-Pipe, Caroline, *Russia and the World, 1917–1991,* London, 1998.

Kershaw, Ian, and Lewin, Moshe, eds., *Stalinism and Nazism: Dictatorships in Comparison,* Cambridge, 1997.

Kharkordin, Oleg, *The Collective and the Individual in Russia: A Study of Practice,* Berkeley, Calif., and London, 1999.

Khatskevich, A. F., *Soldat velikikh boev: Zhizn' i deyatel'nost' F. E. Dzerzhinskogo,* Minsk, 1987.

Khmelevskii, G., *Mirovaya imperialisticheskaya voina 1914–1918gg. sistem-aticheskii ukazatel' knizhnoi i stateinoi voenno-istoricheskoi literatury za 1914–1935 gg.,* Moscow, 1936.

Khubova, D., Ivankiev, A., and Sharova, T., "*After Glasnost: Oral History in the Soviet Union,*" in Passerini, ed., *International Yearbook of Oral History.*

———, "Chernye doski: Tabula raza golod 1932–1933 godov v ustnykh svidetel'stvakh," in Afanas'ev, ed., *Golod 1932–1933 godov.*

Kingston-Mann, E., and Mixter, T., *Peasant Economy, Culture, and Politics of European Russia, 1800–1921,* Princeton, 1991.

Kleinman, Arthur, *Social Origins of Distress and Disease: Depression, Neurasthenia and Pain in Modern China,* Cambridge, Mass., 1986.

Klibanov, A. I., *Istoriya religioznogo sektantstva v Rossii,* Moscow, 1965.

Klier, John D., and Lambroza, Shlomo, eds., *Pogroms: Anti-Jewish Violence in Modern Russian History,* Cambridge, 1992.

Kligman, Gail, *The Wedding of the Dead: Ritual, Poetics and Popular Culture in Translyvania,* Berkeley, Calif., 1988.

Kolektivizatsiya i golod na Ukraini 1929–1933: sbirnik dokumentiv i materialiv, Kiev, 1992.

Kompanets, S. E., *Nadgrobnye pamyatniki XVI-pervoi poloviny XIX vv,* Moscow, 1990.

Kondrashin, V. V., "Golod 1932–3 v derevnyakh Povolzh'ya," *Voprosy istorii,* 6, 1991.

Koni, A. F., *Samoubiistvo v zakone i zhizni,* Moscow, 1923.

Konstantinow, Very Rev. D., *Stations of the Cross: The Russian Orthodox Church, 1970–1980,* trans. S. I. Lee, London, Ontario, 1984.

Kopelev, Lev, *No Jail for Thought,* trans. Anthony Austin, London, 1977.

Kotkin, Stephen, "Terror, Rehabilitation and Historical Memory: An Interview with Dmitrii Iurasov," *Russian Review,* 51, April 1992.

Kovalenko, L. B., and Manyak, V. A., eds., *33-i golod: Narodna kniga-memorial,* Kiev, 1991.

Kozlov, V. I., "O lyudskikh poteriyakh Sovetskogo Soyuza v Velikoi Otechestvennoi voine 1941–45 godov," *Istoriya SSSR,* No. 2, 1989.

Kozulin, A., *Psychology in Utopia,* Cambridge, Mass., 1984.

Kravchenko, Victor, *I Chose Freedom,* London, 1947.

Kremleva, I. A., et al., eds., *Pokhoronno-pominal'nye obychai i obryadi,* Moscow, 1993.

Kselman, T. A., *Death and the Afterlife in Modern France,* Princeton, 1993.

Kuromiya, Hiroaki, *Freedom and Terror in the Donbass: A Ukrainian-Russian Borderland, 1870–1990s,* Cambridge, 1998.

Kushner, P. I., ed., *Selo Viriatino v proshlom i nastoyashchem,* Moscow, 1958.

———, "O nekotorykh protsessakh proizkhodyashchikh v sovremennnoi kolkhoznoi seme," *Sovetskaya etnografiya,* 3, 1956.

Kvardakov, A. I., *Religioznye perezhitki v soznanii i bytu sel'skogo naseleniya i puti ikh preodoleniya,* Novosibirsk, 1969.

Lane, Christel, *The Rites of Rulers: Ritual in Industrial Society—The Soviet Case,* Cambridge, 1981.

Laub, D., and Auerhahn, N., "Annihilation and Restoration: Post-Traumatic Memory as a Pathway and Obstacle to Recovery," *International Review of Psychoanalysis,* 2, 1984.

Lebina, N. B., "Tenevye storony zhizni sovetskogo goroda 20–30 godov," *Voprosy istorii,* No. 2, 1994.

Leibovich, Y. L., *Tysyacha sovremennnykh samoubiistv,* Moscow, 1923.

Leningrad v osade: Sbornik dokumentov o geroicheskoi oborone Leningrada v gody velikoi otechestvennoi voiny 1941–4, St. Petersburg, 1995.

Lewytzkyj, B., *Politics and Society in Soviet Ukraine, 1953–80,* Edmonton, 1984.

Linz, Susan J., ed., *The Impact of World War II on the Soviet Union,* Totowa, 1985.

Lisovskii, M., ed., *Devyatoe yanvar'ya v klubakh: sbornik materialov,* Moscow and Leningrad, 1925.

Listova, T. A., "Pokhoronno-pominal'nye obychai i obryady russkikh smolenskoi, pskovskoi i kostromskoi oblastei, konets XIX–XXvv," in Kremleva et al., eds., *Pokhoronno-pominal'nye obychai i obryady.*

Litvinenko, Olga, and Riordan, James, *Memories of the Dispossessed,* Nottingham, 1998.

Loftus, E., *Eyewitness Testimony,* Cambridge, Mass., 1979.

Lopukhin, Y. M., *Bolezn', smert' i bal'zamirovaniya V. I. Lenina,* Moscow, 1997.

Lotman, Y. M., and Uspenskii, B. A., "Rol' dual'nykh modelei v dinamike Russkoi kul'tury," *Trudy po Russkoi i Slavyanskoi filologii,* 28, 1977.

Lukov, G. D., *Psikhologiya: Ocherki po voprosam obucheniyu i vospitaniyu sovetskikh voinov,* Moscow, 1960.

Luxemburg, R., *The Russian Revolution,* Ann Arbor, Mich., 1961.

———, *Leninism or Marxism?,* Ann Arbor, Mich., 1961.

Mace, James E. and Heretz, Leonid, eds., *Oral History Project of the Commission on the Ukrainian Famine,* Washington, D.C., 1990.

McNeal, Robert H., *Stalin: Man and Ruler,* Houndmills, 1988.

Mandelstam, Nadezhda, *Hope Against Hope: A Memoir,* trans. Max Haywardy, New York, 1970.

Markuzon, F. D., "Sanitarnaya statistika v gorodakh predrevolyutsionnoi Rossii," *Ocherki po istorii statistiki SSSR,* Moscow, 1955.

Marsh, Rosalind, *History and Literature in Contemporary Russia,* Basingstoke and London, 1995.

Masing-Delic, I., *Abolishing Death: A Salvation Myth of Russian Twentieth-Century Literature,* Stanford, Calif., 1992.

Medvedev, Roy, *Let History Judge: The Origins and Consequences of Stalinism,* revised ed., New York, 1989.

Merridale, Catherine, "The Making of a Moderate Bolshevik: An Introduction to L. B. Kamenev's Political Biography," in Cooper, Julian, et al., *Soviet History, 1917–53.*

———, "The 1937 Census and the Limits of Stalinist Rule," *Historical Journal,* Vol. 39, No. 1, 1996.

———, "The Collective Mind: Trauma and Shell-Shock in Twentieth-Century Russia," *Journal of Contemporary History,* 35, No. 1, January 2000.

———, and Ward, Chris, *Perestroika: The Historical Perspective,* Sevenoaks, 1991.

Miller, F., *Folklore for Stalin: Russian Folklore and Pseudofolklore of the Stalin Era,* Armonk, 1990.

Mir detstva i traditsionnaya kul'tura, Moscow, 1996.

Mirskii, M. B., *Meditsina Rossii XVI–XIX vekov,* Moscow, 1996.

Mitrofan, Monakh, *Zagrobnaya zhizn': Kak zhivut nashi umershie, kak budem zhit' i my po smerti. Po ucheniem pravoslavnoi tserkvy,* St. Petersburg, 1897; reprinted Kiev, 1991.

Mitscherlich, Alexander and Margarete, *The Inability to Mourn: Principles of Collective Behavior,* New York, 1975.

Moskoff, William, *The Bread of Affliction: The Food Supply in the USSR During World War II,* Cambridge, 1990.

Moskovskii nekropol': istoriya, arkheologiya, iskusstvo, okhrana, Moscow, 1991.

Mosse, G. L., *Fallen Soldiers: Reshaping the Memory of the World War,* Oxford, 1990.

Mukovs'kii, I. T., and Lisenko, O. E., *Zvityaga i Zhertovnist': Ukraintsi na frontakh drugoi svitovoi viini,* Kiev, 1997.

Muller, Klaus-Jurgen, "The Brutalisation of Warfare: Nazi Crimes and the Wehrmacht," in Erickson and Dilks, eds., *Barbarossa.*

Nachinkin, N., "Materialy etnograficheskogo biuro V. N. Tenisheva," *Sovetskaya etnografiya,* 1, 1955.

Neuberger, J., *Hooliganism, Crime, Culture and Power in St. Petersburg, 1900–1914,* Berkeley, Calif, 1993.

Nikiforov, N., *Protiv starogo byta,* Moscow and Leningrad, n.d.

Nikulin, *Anekdoty ot Nikulina,* Moscow, 1997.

Novosel'skii, S. A., *Smertnost' i prodol'zhitel'nost zhizni v Rossii,* Petrograd, 1916.

Obikhodnye pesnopedeniya panikhidi i otpevaniya, Moscow, 1997.

Ocherki po istorii statistiki SSSR, Moscow, 1955.

Oinas, Felix J., *Essays on Russian Folklore and Mythology,* Columbus, Ohio, 1984.

Overy, R., *Russia's War,* London, 1997.

Owen, S., *Remembrance: The Experience of the Past in Classical Chinese Literature,* Cambridge, Mass., 1986.

Passerini, Luisa, *Fascism and Popular Memory: The Cultural Experience of the Turin Working Class,* trans. Robert Lumley and Jude Bloomfield, Cambridge, 1987.

———, ed., *International Yearbook of Oral History and Life Stories, Vol. 1: Memory and Totalitarianism,* Oxford, 1992.

Pasternak, Alexander, *A Vanished Present: The Memoirs of Alexander Pasternak,* trans. Ann Pasternak Slater, Oxford, 1984.

Persits, M. M., *Ateizm russkogo rabochego, 1870–1905,* Moscow, 1965.

Pesennik, Moscow, 1950.

Petrovskii, B. V., "Krizis otechestvennoi meditsiny," *Vestnik Rossiiskoi Akademii Meditsinskikh Nauk,* 12, 1995.

Pipes, Richard, *The Russian Revolution, 1899–1919,* London, 1990.

Pobedonostsev, Konstantin P., *Reflections of a Russian Statesman,* trans. Robert Crozier Long, Ann Arbor, Mich., 1965.

Pokrovskii, M. N., *Ocherki po istorii russkoi kul'tury,* Moscow, 1925.

———, *Imperialisticheskaya voina: Sbornik statei, 1915–1927,* Moscow, 1927.

Polishchuk, N. S., "Obryad kak sotsial'noe yavlenie," *Sovetskaya etnografiya,* 6, 1991.

Popov, V. E., *Psikhologicheskaya reabilitatsiya voenno-sluzhashchikh posle ekstremal'nykh vozdeistvii (na materiale zemletryaseniya Leninakane, mezhdunatsional'nogo konflikta v Fergane i boevykh deistvii v Afganistane),* Moscow, 1992.

Porter, C., and Jones, M., *Moscow in World War II,* London, 1987.

Preobrazhenskii, S. A., *Materialy k voprosu o dushevnykh zabolevaniyakh voinov i lits prichastnykh k voennym deistviyam,* Petrograd, 1917.

Psikhiatricheskie rasstroistva u postradavshikh vo vremya zemletryaseniya v Armenii, various authors, Moscow, 1989.

Psikhologicheskaya nauka v Rossii XX stoletiya, Moscow, 1997.

Pushkarev, L. N., *Moi pervyi boi v ryadakh 3-i Moskovskoi Kommunisticheskoi divizii v gody voiny. Stat'i i ocherki,* Moscow, 1985.

———, "Pis'mennaya forma bytovaniya frontovogo fol'klora," *Etnograficheskoe obozrenie,* No. 4, 1995.

Rapoport, Y., *The Doctors' Plot: Stalin's Last Crime,* London, 1991.

Read, Christopher, *From Tsar to Soviets: The Russian People and Their Revolution, 1917–21,* London, 1996.

Reid, Anna, *Borderland: A Journey Through the History of Ukraine,* London, 1997.

Reznikova, Irina, *Pravoslavie na Solovkakh,* St. Petersburg, 1994.

Ritual proshchaniya, No. 1, Moscow, 1997.

Robbins, R. D., *Famine in Russia, 1891–1892,* New York, 1975.

Rosenfeld, Alvin, and Greenberg, Irving, eds., *Confronting the Holocaust,* Bloomington, Ind., 1978.

Rosenthal, B. G., ed., *The Occult in Modern Russian and Soviet Culture,* Ithaca, N.Y., 1997.

Roslof, E. E., "The Heresy of 'Bolshevik' Christianity: Orthodox Rejection of Religious Reform During NEP," *Slavic Review,* 55, 3, 1996.

Rozhitsyn, V., *Sushchestvuet li zagrobnaya zhizn'?,* Kiev, 1923.

Rudnev, V. A., *Sovetskie prazdniki, obryady, ritualy,* Leningrad, 1979.

———, *Obryady narodnye i obryady tserkovnye,* Leningrad, 1982.

Russkaya pravoslavnaya tserkov' i kommunisticheskoe gosudarstvo 1917–1941: dokumenty i fotomaterialy, Moscow, 1996.

Russkie pesny i romansy, Moscow, 1989.

Ryan, W. F., *The Bathhouse at Midnight: Magic in Russia,* Stroud, 1999.

Rybakov, V. A., *Yazychestvo drevnykh slavyan,* Moscow, 1981.

Sablinsky, W., *The Road to Bloody Sunday: Father Gapon and the St. Petersburg Massacre of 1905,* Princeton, 1976.

Saitov, V. I., and Modzalevskii, B. L., *Moskovskii nekropol'*, 3 vols., Moscow, 1907–8.

Saladin, A. T., *Ocherki istorii Moskovskikh kladbishch*, Moscow, 1997.

Salisbury, Harrison E., *The Seige of Leningrad*, London, 1969.

Samoubiistvo v SSSR 1922–1925, Moscow, 1927.

Selishchev, A. M., *Yazyk revolyutsionnoi epokhi*, Moscow, 1928.

Semenova, S. G., *Tainy tsarstviya nebesnogo*, Moscow, 1994.

———, and Garcheva, A. G., eds., *Russkii kosmizm: antologiya filosofskoiu mysli*, Moscow, 1993.

Sennett, Richard, *Flesh and Stone: The Body and the City in Western Civilisation*, London, 1994.

Serge, Victor, *Memoirs of a Revolutionary, 1901–1941*, Oxford, 1963.

Service, Robert, *Lenin: A Political Life, Vol. 1: The Strengths of Contradiction*, Houndmills, 1985.

———, *Lenin: A Political Life, Vol. 2: Worlds in Collusion*, Houndmills, 1991.

———, *A History of Twentieth-Century Russia*, London, 1997.

Seton-Watson, H., *The Decline of Imperial Russia, 1855–1914*, London, 1952.

Shalamov, Varlam, *Kolyma Tales*, trans. John Glad, Harmondsworth, 1994.

Shanin, Teodor, ed., *Peasants and Peasant Societies*, Harmondsworth, 1971.

Shavel'skii, O. G., *Vospominaniya poslednogo protpresvitra Russkoi Armii i Flota*, Vol. 1, New York, 1954.

Shentalinsky, Vitaly, *Arrested Voices: Resurrecting the Disappeared Writers of the Soviet Regime*, trans. John Crowfoot, New York and London, 1996.

Shepeleva, E. V., *Osobennosti diagnostiki i prognozirovaniya istericheskikh rasstroistv u voennosluzhashchikh. Aftoreferat dissertatsii na soiskanie uchenoi stepeni kandidata meditsinskikh nauk*, St. Petersburg, 1995.

Shevsov, Vera, "Chapels and the Ecclesial World of the Pre-revolutionary Russian Peasants," *Slavic Review*, Vol. 55: 3, Fall 1996.

Shkol'nikov, V., Meslé, F. and Vallin, J., "La Crise sanitaire en Russie: I. Tendances récentes de l'espérance de vie et des causes de décès de 1970 à 1993," *Population*, 4–5, 1995.

Shmal'gauzen, I. I., *Problemy smerti i bessmertiya*, Moscow and Leningrad, 1926.

Skultans, Vieda, *The Testimony of Lives: Narrative and Memory in Post-Soviet Latvia*, London, 1998.

Smidovich, S., *Byt i molodezh*, Moscow, 1926.

Smirnov, V., *Narodnye pokhorony i prichitaniya v Kostromsom krae*, Kostroma, 1920.

Smith, Gerald S., *Songs to Seven Strings: Russian Guitar Poetry and Soviet "Mass Song,"* Bloomington, Ind., 1984.

Smith, Kathleen E., *Remembering Stalin's Victims: Popular Memory and the End of the USSR*, Ithaca, N.Y., and London, 1996.

Sokolov, A. K., *Lektsii po sovetskoi istorii, 1917–1940*, Moscow, 1995.

Solzhenitsyn, Aleksandr, *The Gulag Archipelago, 1918–1956*, trans. Thomas P. Whitney and Harry Willetts, London, 1999.

Sorokin, P., *Leaves from a Russian Diary*, London, 1925.

"Statistique demographique et sociale: Russie-URSS," *Cahiers du monde russe*, 38, 4, 1997.

Steinberg, Mark D., "Workers on the Cross: Religious Imagination in the Writings of Russian Workers, 1910–1924," *Russian Review*, 53, 2, April 1994.

———, and Khrustalev, Valdimir M., *The Fall of the Romanovs: Political Dreams and Personal Struggles in a Time of Revolution*, New Haven and London, 1995.

Stites, Richard, *Revolutionary Dreams: Utopian Vision and Experimental Life in the Russian Revolution*, Oxford, 1989.

Stoyanov, N. N., *Arkhitektura mavzoleya Lenina*, Moscow, 1950.

Summerfield, Derek, "The Psychological Legacy of War and Atrocity: The Question of Long-Term and Transgenerational Effects and the Need for a Broad View," *Journal of Nervous and Mental Disease*, Vol. 184, No. 1, 1996.

———, "A Critique of Seven Assumptions Behind Psychological Trauma Programmes in War-Affected Areas," *Social Science and Medicine,* 48, 1999.

Tagantsev, N. S., *Smertnaya kazn': Sbornik statei,* St. Petersburg, 1913.

Thomas, Keith, *Religion and the Decline of Magic,* London, 1971.

Thompson, Paul, *The Voice of the Past: Oral History,* 2nd ed., Oxford, 1988.

Thurston, R. W., "The Soviet Family During the Great Terror, 1935–41," *Soviet Studies,* 43, 3, 1991.

Tokarev, S. A., *Religioznye verovaniya vostochnoslavyanskikh narodov, XIX-nachala XX vekov,* Moscow and Leningrad, 1957.

Tolstoy, Leo, *War and Peace,* trans. Rosemary Edwards, London, 1982.

———, *Anna Karenina,* trans. Louise and Aylmer Maude, Oxford, 1983.

Tolz, Vera, "New Information About the Deportation of Ethnic Groups in the USSR During World War 2," in Garrard and Garrard, eds., *World War 2 and the Soviet People.*

Trotsky, Leon, *My Life: An Attempt at Autobiography,* Harmondsworth, 1971.

Tucker, Robert C., ed., *The Lenin Anthology,* New York, 1975.

———, *Stalin in Power: The Revolution from Above, 1928–1941,* New York, 1990.

———, "What Time Is It in Russia's History?," in Merridale and Ward, eds., *Perestroika: The Historical Perspective.*

Tumarkin, Nina, *Lenin Lives!,* Cambridge, Mass., 1983.

———, *The Living and the Dead: The Rise and Fall of the Cult of World War II in Russia,* New York, 1994.

———, "Story of a War Memorial," in Garrard and Garrard, eds., *World War 2 and the Soviet People.*

Twentieth-Century Russian Poetry, selected with an introduction by Yevgenii Yevtushenko, London, 1993.

Ustinov, V. M., Novitskii, I. B., and Gernet, M. N., *Osnovniya ponyatiya Russkogo gosudarstvennogo, grazhdanskogo i ugolovnogo pravo,* Moscow, 1910.

Vasil'ev, V., "Krest'yanskie vosstaniya na Ukraine 1929–30 gody," *Svobodnaya mysl',* 9, 1992.

Vasil'eva, Larisa, *Deti Kremlya,* Moscow, 1996.

Vasil'evskii, L. A. and L. M., *Kniga o golode: Populyarnyi mediko-sanitarnyi ocherk,* Petrograd, 1922.

Vasil'evskii, L. M., *Bor'ba so starost'yu i smert'yu v istorii,* Moscow, 1924.

Veletskaya, N. N., *Yazycheskaya simvolika slavyanskikh arkhaicheskikh ritualov,* Moscow, 1978.

Velikaya otechestvannaya voina 1941–45: Sobytiya, lyudi, dokumenty, Moscow, 1990.

Velikii perelom glazami sovremennikov: Iz pisem v "Pravdu" o kollektivizatsii, Moscow, 1990.

Venozhinskii, V., *Smertnaya kazn' i terror,* St. Petersburg, 1908.

Veselovskii, A. A., *Dokumenty po etnografii Vologodskoi gubernii,* Vologda, 1923–24.

Vinogradov, G. S., *Materialy dlya narodnogo kalendarya russkogo starozhitel'skogo naseleniya Sibiri,* Irkutsk, 1918.

Viola, Lynne, *The Best Sons of the Fatherland: Workers in the Vanguard of Soviet Collectivization,* New York, 1987.

Voennaya Psikhiatriya: Uchebnik dlya slushatelei akademii i voennomeditsinskikh fakul'tetov meditsinskikh institutov, Leningrad, 1974.

Volkogonov, Dmitrii, *Lenin: Life and Legacy,* trans. Harold Shukman, London, 1994.

Vovelle, M., *Idéologies et mentalités,* Paris, 1982.

———, *La Mort et l'occident de 1300 à nos jours,* Paris, 1983.

Vozvrashchennye imena, Vols. 1 and 2, Moscow, 1989.

Vyltsan, M. A., "Deportatsiya narodov v gody velikoi otechestvennoi voiny," *Etnograficheskoe obozrenie,* 3, 1995.

Ward, Chris, *Stalin's Russia,* London, 1993.

Watson, Rubie S., ed., *Memory, History and Opposition Under State Socialism,* Santa Fe, Calif., 1994.

Werth, Alexander, *Russia at War,* London, 1963.

Westwood, J. N., *Endurance and Endeavour: Russian History, 1812–1992,* 4th ed., Oxford, 1993.

White, Stephen, *Russia Goes Dry: Alcohol, State and Society,* Cambridge, 1996.

Widom, C. S., "PTSD in Abused Children Grown Up," *American Journal of Psychiatry,* 156, 8, 1999.

Wiles, Peter, "On Physical Immortality," *Survey,* 56 and 57, 1965.

Wilson, Elizabeth, *Shostakovich: A Life Remembered,* London, 1994.

Winter, Jay, and Sivan, Emmanuel, eds., *War and Remembrance in the Twentieth Century,* Cambridge, 1999.

Worobec, C. D., "Death Ritual Among Russian and Ukrainian Peasants," in Frank and Steinberg, eds., *Cultures in Flux.*

Yakovlev, Y., *Derevnya kak ona est',* Moscow, 1923.

———, *Nasha Derevnya,* Moscow, 1924.

Young, Allan, *The Harmony of Illusions: Inventing Post-Traumatic Stress Disorder,* Princeton, 1995.

Young, J., "The Counter-Monument: Memory Against Itself in Germany Today," *Critical Inquiry,* 18, 2, 1992.

———, *The Texture of Memory: Holocaust Memorials and Meaning in Europe, Israel, and America,* New Haven, 1993.

Zalenskii, E. Y., *Iz zapisok zemskogo vracha,* Pskov, 1908.

Zbarskii, B. I., *Mavzolei Lenina,* Moscow, 1946.

Zbarsky, I., and Hutchinson, S., *Lenin's Embalmers,* London, 1998.

Zelenin, D. K., *Ocherki russkoi mifologii: Umershchie neestestvennoyu smert'yu i rusalki,* St. Petersburg, 1916, reprinted Moscow, 1995.

———, *Drenvnerusskii yazycheskii kul't "zalozhnikh" pokoinikov,* Petrograd, 1917.

———, *Vostochnoslavyanskaya etnografiya,* Moscow, 1926, reprinted 1991.

———, *Izbrannye trudy. Ocherki Russkoi mifologii I: Umershchie neestestvennoyu smert'yu i rusalki,* Moscow, 1995.

Zelnik, Reginald, ed., *A Radical Worker in Tsarist Russia: The Autobiography of Semen Ivanovich Kanatchikov,* Stanford, 1986.

Zemskov, V. N., "Spetsposelentsy (po dokumentatsii NKVD-MVD SSSR)," *Sotsiologicheskie issledovaniya,* No. 11, 1990.

———, "Zaklyuchennye v 1930e gody," *Otechestvennaya istoriya,* No. 4, 1997.

Zima, V. F., "Golod v Rossii 1946–47 gg.," *Otechestvennaya istoriya,* No. 1, 1993.

Zizek, Slavoj, *The Plague of Fantasies,* London, 1997.

Zubkova, Elena Y., *Obshchestvo i reformy, 1945–1964,* Moscow, 1993.

INDEX

PHOTO CREDITS

Photos on pages 1–14 of the photo insert: Courtesy of the St. Petersburg Archive of Cinema, Photography, and Sound

Photos on page 15 of the photo insert: Courtesy of the Memorial Association, Moscow

Photos on page 16 of the photo insert: Courtesy of Catherine Merridale